P9-DBT-037

America

A CONCISE HISTORY

bedfordstmartins.com/henrettaconcise

FREE Online Study Guide

GET INSTANT FEEDBACK ON YOUR PROGRESS WITH

- Chapter self-tests
- Key terms review
- Map quizzes
- Timeline activities
- Note-taking outlines

FREE History Research and Writing Help

REFINE YOUR RESEARCH SKILLS AND FIND PLENTY OF GOOD SOURCES WITH

- Suggested references for each chapter compiled by the textbook authors
- A database of useful images, maps, documents, and more at *Make History*
- A guide to online sources for history
- Help with writing history papers
- A tool for building a bibliography
- Tips on avoiding plagiarism

FIFTH EDITION

America

A Concise History

VOLUME 2: SINCE 1865

James A. Henretta
University of Maryland

Rebecca Edwards
Vassar College

Robert O. Self
Brown University

Bedford / St. Martin's
Boston • New York

For Bedford / St. Martin's
Publisher for History: Mary Dougherty
Executive Editor for History: William J. Lombardo
Director of Development for History: Jane Knetzger
Developmental Editor: Danielle Slevens
Senior Production Editor: Deborah Baker
Production Supervisor: Andrew Ensor
Senior Marketing Manager for U.S. History: Amy Whitaker
Associate Editor: Robin Soule
Copyeditor: Janet Renard
Indexer: Leoni McVey
Photo Researcher: Pembroke Herbert and Sandi Rygiel/Picture Research Consultants & Archives
Permissions Manager: Kalina K. Ingham
Senior Art Director: Anna Palchik
Text Designer: Joan O'Connor
Cover Designer: Billy Boardman
Cover Photo: Washington, D.C., 1963. Demonstrators sing in protest in front of the Washington Monument. Photographer: Hiroji Kubota. Magnum Photos — New York.
Cartography: Mapping Specialists Limited
Composition: Jouve
Printing and Binding: RR Donnelley and Sons

President: Joan E. Feinberg
Editorial Director: Denise B. Wydra
Director of Marketing: Karen R. Soeltz
Direction of Production: Susan W. Brown
Associate Director, Editorial Production: Elise S. Kaiser
Managing Editor: Elizabeth M. Schaaf

Library of Congress Catalog Card Number: 2010929002

Manufactured in the United States of America.

2   3   4   5   6   16   15   14   13   12

For information, write: Bedford / St. Martin's, 75 Arlington Street, Boston, MA 02116 (617-399-4000)

ISBN: 978–0–312–64327–0 (Combined edition)
ISBN: 978–0–312–64328–7 (Vol. 1)
ISBN: 978–0–312–64329–4 (Vol. 2)
ISBN: 978-1-4576-2907-5 (High School)

Preface

How can history teachers reach their students? How do we help them engage the past — not as a rote list of names and dates but as the fascinating, conflicted prelude to their lives today? Helping instructors meet this challenge has long been the mission of *America: A Concise History*. The book's brevity makes it more affordable and more easily complemented by outside readings, but it also facilitates the development of students' sense of the big ideas and broad eras that make American history meaningful. Indeed, our aim has been to produce a concise narrative not simply by omitting extraneous detail but by employing a strong interpretive framework and big-picture analysis that helps students recognize the importance of major developments. We are proud that our book has become one of the most frequently adopted U.S. history surveys, and we attribute its success to the way that our big-picture analysis orients students and gives them a solid foundation for engaging with lectures and with primary documents, monographs, and other readings. This latest edition builds on the explanatory power of the narrative that has long been a hallmark of the book.

The changes in this edition begin with the author team. All three of us — James Henretta, who has guided the book from the start, and new authors Rebecca Edwards and Robert Self — have spent our careers working to integrate "top-down" narratives of politics and economic affairs with "bottom-up" narratives of lived experience. Using the findings of the new social history and details of the experiences of ordinary people, James Henretta has in his work offered new ways of looking at the lives of early Americans, both free and enslaved. Rebecca Edwards has used insights from women's and gender history to reinterpret nineteenth-century electoral politics. Robert Self has explored the relationship between urban and suburban politics, social movements, and the state. In *America: A Concise History*, we bring those perspectives to bear on the full sweep of America's past. Our goal is to help students achieve a richer understanding of politics, diplomacy, war, economics, intellectual and cultural life, and gender, class, and race relations, by exploring how developments in all these areas were interconnected.

The core of a textbook is its narrative, and we have endeavored to make ours clear, concise, accessible, and lively. In it, we focus not only on the marvelous diversity of peoples who came to call themselves Americans, but also on the institutions that have forged a common national identity. Without losing our central focus on U.S. history, we call attention to connections with the histories of Canada, Latin America, Europe, Africa, and Asia. Meanwhile, we confront political problems of global scope, ranging from financial crises and oil spills to terrorist attacks. As it has since its inception, *America: A Concise History* helps students understand the world in which we live, by drawing links between events in the United States and those elsewhere.

New Parts and New Scholarship

One of the greatest strengths of *America: A Concise History* is its part structure, which helps students to understand the key forces and major developments that shaped each era. A four-page Part Opener begins each part, using analysis, images, and a detailed timeline to orient students to the major themes of the era and the ways in which those themes were manifest in society, culture, politics, and the economy. By organizing U.S. history into seven distinct periods, rather than just thirty-one successive chapters, we provide a strong interpretive framework and highlight the book's big-picture analysis. This, we believe, is the key to making events and developments meaningful and memorable.

While retaining a seven-part framework, the latest edition significantly reshapes it, offering instructors a bold reconceptualization of U.S. history that reflects the latest, most exciting scholarship in the field. Throughout the book, we have given increased attention to political culture and political economy, using this analysis to help students understand how society, culture, politics, and the economy informed one another. A sharpened continental perspective, in this edition, is based on expanded coverage of Native American history, environmental history, and the trans-Mississippi West. Religion receives new attention throughout the text, particularly in the late nineteenth and twentieth centuries. Enhanced coverage of gender, ethnicity, and race includes greater emphasis on gay and lesbian history, Asian and Latino immigration, and the Civil Rights Movement, the last of which now has a complete chapter of its own.

Part 1, "The Creation of American Society," focuses on the period 1450–1763. This part explores the impact of men and women of European origin on Native American cultures, and the creation of new kinds of social, political, economic, and cultural life in the English mainland colonies. **Part 2, "The New Republic"** — spanning the years 1763–1820 — explores the evolving values and institutions of the colonial social order and the fundamental changes Americans made in their economic, religious, and cultural practices. **Part 3, "Overlapping Revolutions,"** now focuses on the period 1820–1850 and the political, economic, and social and cultural revolutions that shaped it: the creation of a democratic polity, the shift from a predominantly agricultural to a booming industrial economy, and the advent of the Second Great Awakening, as well as a host of social reforms and a complex intellectual culture.

Three fields of scholarship contribute many of the additions to Parts 1–3. New research on Native Americans informs and deepens our treatment of Bacon's Rebellion in Virginia in the 1670s, the interaction between Lewis and Clark and the Mandans of the Upper Missouri River Valley in the 1800s, and the character of the buffalo-hunting peoples of the Great Plains between 1820 and 1870. New findings in African American history likewise enhance our discussion of the transition to slavery in Virginia, the repercussions of the Haitian Revolution, and many other aspects of the black experience. Finally, using new scholarship on the building of early modern empires, we have sharpened our analysis of Britain's purposeful pursuit of trade and imperial power between 1650 and 1750.

Part 4, "Creating and Preserving a Continental Nation" — now covering the period from 1846 to 1877 — traces the rise of America's continental empire. It places the shattering events of the Civil War in the context of other wars that textbooks too often underemphasize: the Mexican American War, and the final conquest of North

America's native peoples. Part 4 treats these as three interrelated conflicts, showing how all of them contributed to confirmation of the nation's modern borders and to the consolidation of federal authority. This analysis helps students situate North-South sectionalism and the Civil War in broad contexts, and to compare the end of slavery and the emergence of the modern American nation with similar projects in other countries. Part 4 also provides expanded coverage of the California Gold Rush and development of the Pacific coast; Native American history during and after the Civil War; and Reconstruction as it was experienced by ordinary Southerners, both black and white.

The reorganization of Part 4 also offers instructors expanded options as they decide where to draw the dividing line between the first and second halves of the U.S. survey. The entirety of Part 4 — including not only the chapter on Reconstruction (Chapter 15) but also a substantially revised chapter on post–Civil War diplomacy, economic development, and the trans-Mississippi West (Chapter 16) — is included in Volume 1 of *America: A Concise History*. First-half instructors can thus either choose the Civil War or Reconstruction as the end point for their classes, or they can include Chapter 16 and invite students to explore additional long-term consequences of Union victory, with special attention to the West. As Volume 2 begins with Chapter 15, those teaching the second half of the survey can, likewise, choose the chapter and context in which they wish to begin their course.

Part 5, "Bold Experiments in an Era of Industrialization," now covers the years between 1877 and 1929 as a single, unified era. In doing so, it offers a streamlined and innovative treatment of the decades when the United States became a global industrial power. Reflecting recent scholarship, we locate the origins of modern America in the post-Reconstruction years, rather than after 1900. Revising older views of Progressivism as primarily an elite and middle-class, urban phenomenon, we also emphasize the significant roles played by rural and working-class Americans in demanding stronger government to combat the ills of industrialization. Women's political activism in the post–Civil War decades also receives new emphasis. This approach allows students to get a more inclusive and coherent picture of state-building from the era of Reconstruction to the New Deal.

Part 5 also gives more attention to topics that all students will enjoy, such as the rise of high school and college education and the emergence of college and professional sports. In keeping with the urgent economic issues that confront the United States today, such as "The Great Recession" that began in 2008, a reorganized chapter on the 1920s connects the "boom" of that decade more clearly to the "bust" of the Great Depression that followed. And the United States' military and diplomatic involvement in World War I, formerly covered in a distinct chapter, is now folded into broader treatment of America's rise to global diplomatic power. The result is a clearer, more compelling analysis of the ways in which Americans both contributed to and critiqued imperialism, extending through the catastrophic legacies of the Great War. As an added benefit of Part 5's new integrated narrative, a chapter has also been trimmed from this section, enabling instructors to move ahead briskly and devote more attention to later events.

Part 6, "The Modern State and the Age of Liberalism," has been reconceptualized to include the period between the start of the Great Depression in 1929 and the economic turmoil that began in 1973. This broader canvas places the New Deal, World

War II, and the 1960s into a single interpretation of the growth, flowering, and retreat of political liberalism. Students can view the depression-era welfare state and the rights-based politics of the 1960s as part of a continuum in twentieth-century American politics. Taking the narrative into the early 1970s brings the women's movement, the later antiwar movement, and the Chicano and Native American movements into this structure, rather than arbitrarily breaking apart those histories at 1968.

In Part 6, we have devoted an entire chapter to the Civil Rights Movement, which covers the full period between World War II and the early 1970s — what many historians have called the "long Civil Rights Movement." We have also expanded our coverage of women, gay and lesbian communities, suburbanization, and the rise of the Sunbelt. Finally, a major theme of Part 6 remains the emergence of the United States as a major force in global geopolitics during and after World War II. A largely reluctant international power outside of the western hemisphere before 1941, the United States came to project its military power and economic might into the far corners of the globe during and after the Second World War. We have retained the traditional focus on the Cold War at home and abroad, while revising themes and topics to reflect new scholarly interpretations. Our aim is for students to see the close connections between developments at home and abroad in this turbulent era.

In **Part 7, "Global Capitalism and the End of the American Century,"** we have sought a delicate balance between the historian's scholarly distance and the immediacy of recent events. For instance, we treat globalization as a unique force reshaping American society and its economy, but we stress that global economic networks have always been intimately linked to national history. Students will find that our approach to the recent past helps them connect developments in their own lives with deeper, more long-term historical patterns. American involvement in the Middle East, the nation's increasing racial and ethnic diversity, and the role of digital technology, to name just three examples, have each been contextualized in terms of developments across much of the twentieth century.

Part 7 includes a new emphasis on how ordinary Americans experienced and tried to make sense of the sexual revolution, economic malaise, and changing family structure in the 1970s. This includes treatment of religious fundamentalism and the extraordinary growth of evangelical churches in recent decades. Of special interest in Part 7 is our enhanced treatment of domestic political events in the era after 1973, a year of profound domestic and international shifts. Drawing from recent work in gender and sexuality studies, the history of race, women's history, and political economy, we offer a synthetic treatment of the complex movement known as the New Right. And while it is still too early to offer definitive historical interpretations of Barack Obama's presidency, we encourage students to assess the significance of these events with the knowledge they've gained from Part 7 as a whole.

Primary-Source Features and Study Aids

To offer further entry points into this appealing narrative, each chapter provides aids to student comprehension and study. A **thematic introduction** and **epigraph** orient readers to the central themes of each chapter. At the end of each chapter, we use a

timeline to remind students of important events and reiterate the themes in an **analytic summary**. We append **focus questions** to the major sections of each chapter. Where students are likely to stumble over a key concept, we boldface it in the text wherever it is first mentioned and provide a **glossary** that defines each term. Brief end-of-chapter essays entitled **"For Further Exploration"** direct students to resources for additional reading, and a **full bibliography** is available online at **bedfordstmartins .com/henrettaconcise**.

America: A Concise History has long emphasized primary sources. In addition to weaving lively quotations throughout the narrative, we offer students engaging excerpts from historical documents — letters, diaries, autobiographies, public testimony, and even poems and novels. These documents allow students to experience the past through the words and perspectives of those who lived it and, equally important, to gain skill in interpreting historical evidence. Each chapter contains two primary-source features: **American Voices** helps students to understand how important events and phenomena were viewed domestically, while **Voices from Abroad** uses commentary from foreign observers — and occasionally from Americans who traveled overseas — to situate U.S. history in its global context. Many instructors rely on these rich and varied features — as well as the book's free documents reader, *Documents for America's History* — to introduce beginning students to primary-source analysis.

For the fifth edition, we have revised one-third of the primary-source features, choosing topics that will engage students' interest and sharpen their understanding of the past. "American Voices," for example, now includes selections that compare two women's thoughts on the challenges of early-nineteenth-century married life; a Cherokee perspective on Indian removal; and a debate between Phyllis Schlafly and one of her feminist opponents. In Voices from Abroad, we have incorporated more non-European documents for a truly global perspective. In Chapter 27, students can read an Ethiopian journalist's account of American race relations. New Asian voices are present in the account of a Chinese woman sold into sexual slavery in nineteenth-century San Francisco; the demand of merchant Norman Assing (Yuan Sheng) for equal treatment of Chinese migrants in California in 1852, a Japanese Buddhist's 1893 assessment of Christian missions in his country; Monica Itoi Sone's description of her family's internment during World War II; and the account of a Chinese woman working in the American garment industry in the 1990s. In keeping with the growing economic strength of East Asia in the twentieth century, we have included the perspectives of a Japanese commentator on the American economy in Chapter 30.

As in past editions, a strong **visual program** engages students' attention. The fifth edition features over 150 paintings, cartoons, illustrations, photographs, and charts, most of them in full color and many new to this edition. We also provide informative captions that set the illustrations in context. Keenly aware that many students lack geographic literacy, we have included dozens of **maps** and cross-referenced them in the narrative text; map captions help students interpret what they see.

In addition to providing instructors with a rich, flexible teaching tool, we believe that this edition will appeal to your students. Whatever their backgrounds, interests, and concerns may be, *America: A Concise History* will help students link the complex events of U.S. history to their experiences today, in ways that increase their understanding of the world around them and provoke critical engagement with the American past.

Acknowledgments

In this fifth edition of *America*, we have revised the full-length and concise texts together for the first time, with the goal of using the concise narrative for both books. We are grateful to the following scholars and teachers who reported on their experiences with the text or reviewed chapters of the manuscript-in-revision. Their comments often challenged us to rethink or justify our interpretations and always provided a check on accuracy down to the smallest detail.

Paul C. Anderson, Clemson University
Alexis Antracoli, Saint Francis University
Charles Pete Banner-Haley, Colgate University
Heather Barry, Saint Joseph's College
Ken Bridges, South Arkansas Community College
Jennifer Brooks, Auburn University
Jared S. Burkholder, Augustana College
Laurie Chin, California State University–Long Beach
Stephen Cresswell, West Virginia Wesleyan College
Paul Doucette, Frederica Academy
Elisa Guernsey, Monroe Community College
Dixie Haggard, Valdosta State University
Michael Harkins, William Rainey Harper College
Andrew Johns, Brigham and Young University
David Johnson, University of South Florida
Jon Timothy Kelly, West Valley College
Jeff Kleiman, University of Wisconsin–Marshfield
Rebecca Kosary, Texas Lutheran University
Derek Maxfield, Capital Community College
Ryan McMillen, Santa Monica College
Michelle Morgan, University of Wisconsin–Whitewater
Scott Newman, Loyola University Chicago
Robert Owens, Wichita State University
Ronnie Peacock, Community College of Aurora
Donald Rogers, Central Connecticut State University
Mary Ellen Rowe, University of Central Missouri
Matthew Schaffer, Florence Darlington Technical College
Lois Scozzari, Holyoke Community College
Aaron Shapiro, Auburn University
David Sicilia, University of Maryland–College Park
John Simpson, Pierce College
E. Timothy Smith, Barry University
Nikki Taylor, University of Cincinnati
Jennifer Terry, American River College
Ruth Terry, Johnson County Community College and Lee's Summit Community
   Christian Schools
David Thompson, Illinois Central College

Russell Tremayne, College of Southern Idaho
Jere Vincent, New Hampshire Community Technical College–Stratham
Cheryl Waite, Community College of Aurora
Eddie Weller, San Jacinto College
Jennifer Williams, Firelands College

As the authors of *America: A Concise History*, we know better than anyone else how much this book is the work of other hands and minds. We are grateful to departing author David Brody, who extended a welcoming hand and wise guidance to his successors. We are indebted to Mary Dougherty, William J. Lombardo, and Jane Knetzger, who oversaw this edition, and Danielle Slevens, who asked the right questions, suggested a multitude of improvements, and expertly guided the manuscript to completion. As usual, Joan E. Feinberg generously provided the resources we needed to produce an outstanding volume. Deborah Baker did a masterful job consulting with the authors. Karen Melton Soeltz and Jenna Bookin Barry in the marketing department understood how to communicate our vision to teachers; they and the members of the sales force did wonderful work in helping this edition reach the classroom. We also thank the rest of our editorial and production team for their dedicated efforts: Robin Soule; Janet Renard, who copyedited the manuscript; Pembroke Herbert and Sandi Rygiel at Picture Research Consultants and Archives; and Kalina Ingham and Diane Kraut. Finally, we want to express our appreciation for the invaluable assistance of Rebecca Henretta, who redesigned many of the charts and graphs; Michelle Cantos and Mark Seidl, for invaluable research aid; and Linglan Edwards and Hiraku Shimoda, for assistance with translations. Many thanks to all of you for your contributions to this new edition of *America: A Concise History*.

Versions and Supplements

Adopters of *America: A Concise History* and their students have access to abundant extra resources, including documents, presentation and testing materials, the acclaimed Bedford Series in History and Culture volumes, and much, much more. See below for more information, visit the book's catalog site at **bedfordstmartins.com/henrettaconcise/ catalog**, or contact your local Bedford/St. Martin's sales representative.

Get the Right Version for Your Class

To accommodate different course lengths and course budgets, *America: A Concise History* is available in several different versions and e-book formats, which are available at a substantial discount.

- Combined Volume (Chapters 1–31) — available in paperback and e-book formats
- Volume 1: To 1877 (Chapters 1–16) — available in paperback and e-book formats
- Volume 2: Since 1865 (Chapters 15–31) — available in paperback and e-book formats

The online, interactive **Bedford e-Book** can be examined or purchased at a discount at **bedfordstmartins.com/ebooks**. Your students can also purchase *America: A Concise History* in other popular e-book formats for computers, tablets, and e-readers.

Online Extras for Students

The book's companion site at **bedfordstmartins.com/henrettaconcise** gives students a way to read, write, and study, and to find and access quizzes and activities, study aids, and history research and writing help.

FREE Online Study Guide. Available at the companion site, this popular resource provides students with quizzes and activities for each chapter, including multiple-choice self-tests that focus on important concepts; flashcards that test students' knowledge of key terms; timeline activities that emphasize causal relationships; and map quizzes intended to strengthen students' geography skills. Instructors can monitor students' progress through an online Quiz Gradebook or receive e-mail updates.

FREE Research, Writing, and Antiplagiarism Advice. Available at the companion site, Bedford's **History Research and Writing Help** includes the textbook authors'

Suggested References organized by chapter; **History Research and Reference Sources**, with links to history-related databases, indexes, and journals; **More Sources and How to Format a History Paper**, with clear advice on how to integrate primary and secondary sources into research papers and how to cite and format sources correctly; **Build a Bibliography**, a simple Web-based tool known as the Bedford Bibliographer that generates bibliographies in four commonly used documentation styles; and **Tips on Avoiding Plagiarism**, an online tutorial that reviews the consequences of plagiarism and features exercises to help students practice integrating sources and recognize acceptable summaries.

Resources for Instructors

Bedford/St. Martin's has developed a wide range of teaching resources for this book and for this course. They range from lecture and presentation materials and assessment tools to course management options. Most can be downloaded or ordered at **bedfordstmartins.com/henrettaconcise/catalog**.

HistoryClass for America: A Concise History. HistoryClass, a Bedford/St. Martin's Online Course Space, puts the online resources available with this textbook in one convenient and completely customizable course space. There you and your students can access an interactive e-book and primary sources reader; maps, images, documents, and links; chapter review quizzes; interactive multimedia exercises; and research and writing help. In HistoryClass you can get all our premium content and tools and assign, rearrange, and mix them with your own resources. For more information, visit **yourhistoryclass.com**.

Bedford Coursepack for Blackboard, WebCT, Desire2Learn, Angel, Sakai, or Moodle. We have free content to help you integrate our rich content into your course management system. Registered instructors can download coursepacks with no hassle and no strings attached. Content includes our most popular free resources and book-specific content for *America: A Concise History*. Visit **bedfordstmartins.com/coursepacks** to see a demo, find your version, or download your coursepack.

Instructor's Resource Manual. The instructor's manual offers both experienced and first-time instructors tools for preparing for lectures and running discussions. It includes chapter review material, teaching strategies, and a guide to chapter-specific supplements available for the text.

Guide to Changing Editions. Designed to facilitate an instructor's transition from the previous edition of *America: A Concise History* to the current edition, this guide presents an overview of major changes as well as of changes in each chapter.

Computerized Test Bank. The test bank includes a mix of fresh, carefully crafted multiple-choice, matching, short-answer, and essay questions for each chapter. The questions appear in Microsoft Word format and in easy-to-use test bank software that allows instructors to easily add, edit, re-sequence, and print questions and answers. Instructors can also export questions into a variety of formats, including WebCT and Blackboard.

PowerPoint Maps, Images, Lecture Outlines, and i>clicker Content. Look good and save time with *The Bedford Lecture Kit.* These presentation materials are downloadable individually by clicking on the Instructor Resources tab at **bedfordstmartins.com/ henrettaconcise/catalog** and are also available on *The Bedford Lecture Kit* Instructor's Resource CD-ROM. They include ready-made and fully customizable PowerPoint multimedia presentations built around lecture outlines with embedded maps, figures, and selected images from the textbook and with detailed instructor notes on key points. Also available are maps and selected images in JPEG and PowerPoint formats; content for i>clicker, a classroom response system, in Microsoft Word and PowerPoint formats; and outline maps in PDF format for quizzing or handing out. All files are suitable for copying onto transparency acetates.

Make History — **Free Documents, Maps, Images, and Web Sites.** *Make History* combines the best Web resources with hundreds of maps and images, to make it simple to find the source material you need. Browse the collection of thousands of resources by course or by topic, date, and type. Each item has been carefully chosen and helpfully annotated to make it easy to find exactly what you need. Available at **bedfordstmartins .com/makehistory**.

America in Motion: Video Clips for U.S. History. Set history in motion with *America in Motion,* an instructor DVD containing dozens of short digital movie files of events in twentieth-century American history. From the wreckage of the battleship *Maine,* to FDR's fireside chats, to Oliver North testifying before Congress, *America in Motion* engages students with dynamic scenes from key events and challenges them to think critically. All files are classroom-ready, edited for brevity, and easily integrated with PowerPoint or other presentation software for electronic lectures or assignments. An accompanying guide provides each clip's historical context, ideas for use, and suggested questions.

Videos and Multimedia. A wide assortment of videos and multimedia CD-ROMs on various topics in U.S. history is available to qualified adopters through your Bedford/ St. Martin's sales representative.

Package and Save Your Students Money

For information on free packages and discounts up to 50%, visit **bedfordstmartins.com/ henrettaconcise/catalog**, or contact your local Bedford/St. Martin's sales representative.

Bedford e-Book. The e-book for this title, described above, can be packaged with the print text at a discount.

Documents for America's History, **Seventh Edition.** Edited by Melvin Yazawa, University of New Mexico (Vol. 1), and Kevin Fernlund, University of Missouri, St. Louis

(Vol. 2), this primary-source reader offers a chorus of voices from the past to enrich the study of U.S. history. Both celebrated figures and ordinary people, from Frederick Douglass to mill workers, demonstrate the diversity of America's history while putting a human face on historical experience. Brief introductions set each document in context, while questions for analysis help link the individual source to larger themes. Available free when packaged with the print text.

E-Documents for America's History, **Seventh Edition.** The reader is also available as an e-book. When packaged with the print or electronic version of the textbook, it is available for free.

The Bedford Series in History and Culture. More than one hundred and fifty titles in this highly praised series combine first-rate scholarship, historical narrative, and important primary documents for undergraduate courses. Each book is brief, inexpensive, and focused on a specific topic or period. For a complete list of titles, visit **bedfordstmartins .com/history/series**. Package discounts are available.

Rand McNally Atlas of American History. This collection of more than eighty full-color maps illustrates key events and eras from early exploration, settlement, expansion, and immigration to U.S. involvement in wars abroad and on U.S. soil. Introductory pages for each section include a brief overview, timelines, graphs, and photographs to quickly establish a historical context. Available for $3.00 when packaged with the print text.

Maps in Context: A Workbook for American History. Written by historical cartography expert Gerald A. Danzer (University of Illinois at Chicago), this skill-building workbook helps students comprehend essential connections between geographic literacy and historical understanding. Organized to correspond to the typical U.S. history survey course, *Maps in Context* presents a wealth of map-centered projects and convenient pop quizzes that give students hands-on experience working with maps. Available free when packaged with the print text.

The Bedford Glossary for U.S. History. This handy supplement for the survey course gives students historically contextualized definitions for hundreds of terms — from *abolitionism* to *zoot suit* — that they will encounter in lectures, reading, and exams. Available free when packaged with the print text.

U.S. History Matters: A Student Guide to World History Online. This resource, written by Alan Gevinson, Kelly Schrum, and the late Roy Rosenzweig (all of George Mason University), provides an illustrated and annotated guide to 250 of the most useful Web sites for student research in U.S. history as well as advice on evaluating and using Internet sources. This essential guide is based on the acclaimed "History Matters" Web site developed by the American Social History Project and the Center for History and New Media. Available free when packaged with the print text.

Trade Books. Titles published by sister companies Hill & Wang; Farrar, Straus and Giroux; Henry Holt and Company; St. Martin's Press; Picador; and Palgrave Macmillan are available at a 50% discount when packaged with Bedford/St. Martin's textbooks. For more information, visit **bedfordstmartins.com/tradeup**.

A Pocket Guide to Writing in History, **Seventh Edition.** This portable and affordable reference tool by Mary Lynn Rampolla provides reading, writing, and research advice useful to students in all history courses. Concise yet comprehensive advice on approaching typical history assignments, developing critical reading skills, writing effective history papers, conducting research, using and documenting sources, and avoiding plagiarism — enhanced with practical tips and examples throughout — have made this slim reference a best-seller. Package discounts are available.

A Student's Guide to History, **Eleventh Edition.** This complete guide to success in any history course provides the practical help students need to be effective. In addition to introducing students to the nature of the discipline, author Jules Benjamin teaches a wide range of skills from preparing for exams to approaching common writing assignments, and explains the research and documentation process with plentiful examples. Package discounts are available.

Going to the Source: The Bedford Reader in American History, **Third Edition.** Developed by Victoria Bissell Brown and Timothy J. Shannon, this reader's strong pedagogical framework helps students learn how to ask fruitful questions in order to evaluate documents effectively and develop critical reading skills. The reader's wide variety of chapter topics that complement the survey course and its rich diversity of sources — from personal letters to political cartoons — provoke students' interest as it teaches them the skills they need to successfully interrogate historical sources. Package discounts are available.

America Firsthand, **Ninth Edition.** With its distinctive focus on ordinary people, this primary documents reader, by Anthony Marcus, John M. Giggie, and David Burner, offers a remarkable range of perspectives on America's history from those who lived it. Popular Points of View sections expose students to different perspectives on a specific event or topic, and Visual Portfolios invite analysis of the visual record. Package discounts are available.

Brief Contents

Contents

CHAPTER 18 | The Victorians Meet the Modern, 1880–1917   *538*

CHAPTER 19 | "Civilization's Inferno": The Rise and Reform of Industrial Cities, 1880–1917   *568*

PART 6
The Modern State and the Age of Liberalism, 1929–1973   690

CHAPTER 23 | The Great Depression and the New Deal, 1929–1939   694

PART 7
Global Capitalism and the End of the American Century, 1973–2011 *878*

Maps

America

A Concise History

VOLUME 2: SINCE 1865

Reconstruction

1865–1877

> I felt like a bird out of a cage. Amen. Amen. Amen. I could hardly ask to feel better than I did on that day.
>
> —Houston H. Holloway, a former slave recalling his emancipation in 1865

In 1869, Wyoming Territory did something few Americans could have imagined before the Civil War: It gave women full voting rights. A few local women's rights advocates supported the measure, but one legislator endorsed it in a spirit of revenge. "Damn it," he said, "if you are going to let the niggers and pigtails [Chinese] vote, we will ring in the women, too." A decade later, similar arguments surfaced in California. "We give negroes, and Chinamen, and everything else, a right to vote," pointed out one delegate to a state constitutional convention. Another challenged him: "Are you going over to that doctrine of the universal brotherhood of man?" He answered, "In regard to women, I am."

In other spheres, as well, "universal brotherhood" was a subject of intense debate. Congress overhauled the Naturalization Act of 1790, which had limited citizenship to immigrants who were "free white persons." The most radical congressmen argued that racial barriers to citizenship should be dropped entirely. But their proposal foundered, largely because of opposition to Chinese immigration. One U.S. senator warned that Chinese American citizenship would put "an end to republican government" on the Pacific coast. In the end, Congress offered citizenship rights to people of African descent, but not to those from Asia.

As these debates suggest, the Civil War opened enormous questions about citizenship and nationhood. Americans engaged in intense, often violent struggles over the postwar order. Slavery was finished — that much was certain — and the South had been forcibly reattached to the Union. But how should the United States reincorporate former rebels into the political system? Could it also define a secure place for four million former slaves? What about immigrants from many parts of the world? And if the United States was no longer a "white man's country," might citizenship extend to women as well as to black men?

Reconstruction is often thought of as something that happened in the South. But events there were part of a much broader transformation. Far beyond the ex-Confederacy, the United States embarked on an ambitious process of nation building.

Chapter 16 will explore events in the West. There, the United States knit together a continental empire; military conflict with Native Americans entered its final phase, and the arrival of Asian immigrants raised new issues of citizenship and trade. In Chapter 15, we will focus on events in Washington, D.C., and in the former Confederacy, where freed slaves, former slave owners, and other southerners found their worlds turned upside down.

The Struggle for National Reconstruction

The U.S. Constitution does not address the question of how to restore rebellious states. After the Civil War, the nation had to determine whether the Confederate states, upon seceding, had legally left the Union. If so, then their reentry required action by Congress. If not — if even during secession they had retained their constitutional status — then restoring these states might be an administrative matter, best left to the president. Lack of clarity on this fundamental question made for explosive politics. In the early years of Reconstruction, the president and Congress struggled over who was in charge. Only by winning this fight did Republicans in Congress open the way for the sweeping achievements of radical Reconstruction.

Presidential Approaches: From Lincoln to Johnson

As wartime president, Lincoln had offered amnesty to all but high-ranking Confederates. When 10 percent of a rebellious state's voters had taken an oath of loyalty, he proposed, the state would be restored to the Union, provided that it approved the Thirteenth Amendment abolishing slavery (see Chapter 14). But Confederate states rejected Lincoln's Ten Percent Plan, and Congress proposed a tougher substitute. The Wade-Davis Bill, passed on July 2, 1864, required an oath of allegiance to the Union by a majority of each state's adult white men, new governments formed only by those who had never taken up arms against the North, and permanent disenfranchisement of Confederate leaders. Lincoln used a **pocket veto** to kill the Wade-Davis Bill; that is, he left it unsigned when Congress adjourned, while initiating talks with congressional leaders aimed at a compromise.

We will never know what would have happened had Lincoln lived. His assassination in April 1865 plunged the nation into political uncertainty and fueled Unionist fury against the South. As a special train bore Lincoln's flag-draped coffin slowly home to Illinois, tens of thousands of Americans lined the railroad tracks to pay respects. Grieving northerners blamed all Confederates for the acts of southern sympathizer John Wilkes Booth and his accomplices in the assassination. At the same time, Lincoln's death left the presidency in the hands of a man utterly lacking in Lincoln's moral sense and political judgment, Vice President Andrew Johnson.

Johnson was a self-styled "common man" from the hills of eastern Tennessee. Trained as a tailor, he built a career on the support of farmers and laborers. Loyal to the Union, Johnson refused to leave the U.S. Senate when Tennessee seceded. After federal forces captured Nashville in 1862, Lincoln appointed Johnson as Tennessee's military governor. In the election of 1864, placing this War Democrat on the Republican ticket had seemed a smart move, designed to promote unity and court southern Unionists. But after Lincoln's death, Johnson's presidency wreaked political havoc. Johnson, who was not even a Republican, often seemed to view ex-Confederates as his friends and abolitionists as his enemies.

In May 1865, with Congress out of session for months to come, Johnson advanced his own version of Reconstruction. He offered amnesty to all southerners who swore allegiance to the United States, except for the highest-ranking Confederates. Johnson appointed provisional governors for the southern states and required only that they revoke secession, repudiate Confederate debts, and ratify the Thirteenth Amendment. Within months, all the former Confederate states had met Johnson's terms and created functioning elected governments.

Many northerners were disgusted with Johnson. "The rebels have gotten back all their rights and have all been pardoned," wrote one angry Union army veteran in Missouri. He called Johnson "a traitor to the loyal people of the Union." Meanwhile, despite military defeat (see Voices from Abroad, p. 449), southerners' new legislatures moved to restore slavery in all but name. They enacted laws, known as **Black Codes**, designed to force former slaves back to plantation labor. The codes, for example, imposed severe penalties on blacks who did not hold full-year labor contracts and set up procedures for taking black children away from their parents and apprenticing them to former slave owners. Johnson, moreover, talked tough but then forgave ex-Confederate leaders easily when they appealed for pardons. Emboldened by Johnson's indulgence, ex-Confederates began to filter back into the halls of power. When Georgians elected Alexander Stephens, former vice president of the Confederacy, to represent them in Congress, many outraged Republicans saw this as the last straw.

Congress versus the President

Under the Constitution, Congress is "the judge of the Elections, Returns and Qualifications of its own Members" (Article 1, Section 5). Using this power, Republican majorities in both houses refused to admit southern delegations when Congress convened in December 1865, effectively blocking Johnson's program. Hoping to mollify Congress, some southern states dropped the most objectionable provisions from the Black Codes. But at the same time, antiblack violence erupted in various parts of the South. A Nashville newspaper reported that white gangs were "riding about whipping, maiming and killing all negroes who do not obey the orders of their former masters."

Congressional Republicans concluded that the South planned to circumvent the Thirteenth Amendment. The federal government had to intervene. Back in March 1865, Congress had established the Freedmen's Bureau to aid former slaves. Now, in early 1866, Congress voted to extend the bureau, gave it direct funding for the first time, and authorized its agents to investigate mistreatment of blacks. Even more extraordinary was a civil rights bill that declared formerly enslaved people to be citizens and granted them equal protection and rights of contract, with full access to the courts.

These bills provoked bitter conflict with Johnson, who vetoed them both. Johnson's racism, hitherto publicly muted, now blazed forth: "This is a country for white men, and by God, as long as I am president, it shall be a government for white men." Galvanized, Republicans in Congress gathered two-thirds majorities and overrode both vetoes, passing the Civil Rights Act in April 1866 and the Freedmen's Bureau law four months

The Devastated South   DAVID MACRAE

In this excerpt from *The Americans at Home* (1870), an account of his tour of the United States, the Scottish clergyman David Macrae describes the war-stricken South as he found it in 1867–1868, at a time when the crisis over Reconstruction was boiling over.

I was struck with a remark made by a Southern gentleman in answer to the assertion that Jefferson Davis [the president of the Confederacy] had culpably continued the war for six months after all hope had been abandoned.

"Sir," he said, "Mr. Davis knew the temper of the South as well as any man in it. He knew if there was to be anything worth calling peace, the South must win; or, if she couldn't win, she wanted to be whipped — well whipped — thoroughly whipped."

The further south I went, the oftener these remarks came back upon me. Evidence was everywhere that the South had maintained the desperate conflict until she was utterly exhausted. . . . Almost every man I met at the South, especially in North Carolina, Georgia, and Virginia, seemed to have been in the army; and it was painful to find many who had returned were mutilated, maimed, or broken in health by exposure. When I remarked this to a young Confederate officer in North Carolina, and said I was glad to see that he had escaped unhurt, he . . . pulled up one leg of his trousers, and showed me that he had an iron rod there to strengthen his limb, and enable him to walk without limping, half of his foot being off. He showed me on the other leg a deep scar made by a fragment of a shell; and these were two of but seven wounds which had left their marks upon his body. When he heard me speak of relics, he said, "Try to find a North Carolina gentleman without a Yankee mark on him."

Nearly three years had passed when I traveled through the country, and yet we have seen what traces the war had left in such cities as Richmond, Petersburg, and Columbia. The same spectacle met me at Charleston. Churches and houses had been battered down by heavy shot and shell hurled into the city from Federal batteries at a distance of five miles. . . . Over the country districts the prostration was equally marked. Along the track of Sherman's army especially, the devastation was fearful — farms laid waste, fences burned, bridges destroyed, houses left in ruins, plantations in many cases turned into wilderness again.

The people had shared in the general wreck, and looked poverty-stricken, careworn, and dejected. Ladies who before the war had lived in affluence, with black servants round them to attend to their every wish, were . . . so utterly destitute that they did not know when they finished one meal where they were to find the next. . . . Men who had held commanding positions . . . were filling humble situations — struggling, many of them, to earn a bare subsistence. . . . I remember dining with three cultured Southern gentlemen . . . all living together in a plain little wooden house, such as they would formerly have provided for their servants. Two of them were engaged in a railway office, the third was seeking a situation, frequently, in his vain search, passing the large blinded house where he had lived in luxurious ease before the war.

SOURCE: Allan Nevins, ed., *America through British Eyes* (Gloucester, MA: Peter Smith, 1968), 345–347.

Memphis Riot, 1866

Whites in postwar Memphis, as in much of the South, bitterly resented the presence in their city of former black soldiers mustered out of service with the U.S. Army. On April 30, 1866, when some black veterans — no longer protected by their uniforms — celebrated the end of their Army service by drinking, violence broke out. For three days, whites burned black neighborhoods, churches, and schools; raped several African American women; and killed dozens of black residents. Two whites also died in the rioting, which hardened Northern public opinion and prompted calls for stronger measures to put down ex-Confederate resistance. This tinted illustration is based on a lithograph that appeared in *Harper's Weekly*. Harper's Weekly/ Picture Research Consultants & Archives.

later. Their resolve was reinforced by continued violence in the South, which culminated in three days of rioting in Memphis, Tennessee, that left forty-six blacks dead and hundreds of African American homes, churches, and schools burned.

Radical Republicans and the Fourteenth Amendment Anxious to protect freedpeople and reassert Republican power in the South, Congress moved to ensure black civil rights. In what became the Fourteenth Amendment to the Constitution, they declared that "all persons born or naturalized in the United States" were citizens. No state could abridge "the privileges or immunities of citizens of the United States"; deprive "any person of life, liberty, or property, without due process of law"; or deny anyone "equal protection of the laws." Johnson was right on one thing: Republicans were tending toward "centralization." In a stunning increase in federal power, the Fourteenth Amendment declared that when people's essential rights were at stake, national citizenship henceforth took precedence over citizenship in a state.

Johnson urged the states not to ratify the amendment, but public opinion had swung against him. In August 1866, Johnson embarked on a disastrous speaking tour, during which he made matters worse by shouting at hecklers and insulting hostile crowds. In the 1866 congressional elections, voters inflicted humiliation on Johnson by giving Republicans a three-to-one majority in Congress.

Power had shifted to the so-called Radical Republicans, who sought sweeping trans-formations in the defeated South. The Radicals' leader in the Senate was Charles Sumner of Massachusetts, the fiery abolitionist who in 1856 had been nearly beaten to death by South Carolina congressman Preston Brooks. Radicals in the House followed Thaddeus Stevens of Pennsylvania, a passionate advocate of freedpeople's political and economic rights. With such men at the fore, and with congressional Republicans now numerous and united enough to override Johnson's vetoes on many questions, Republicans pro-ceeded to remake Reconstruction.

Radical Reconstruction

The Reconstruction Act of 1867, enacted in March, divided the conquered South into five military districts, each under the command of a U.S. general (Map 15.1). To reenter the Union, each former Confederate state had to grant the vote to freedmen and deny it to leading ex-Confederates. Each military commander was required to register all eli-gible adult males, black as well as white; supervise new state constitutional conventions;

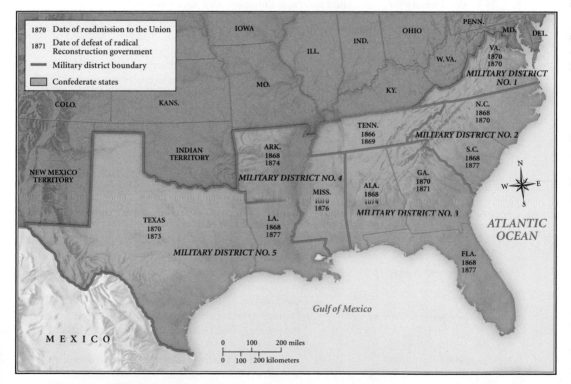

MAP 15.1 Reconstruction

The federal government organized the Confederate states into five military districts during radical Recon-struction. For the states shown in this map, the first date indicates when that state was readmitted to the Union; the second date shows when Radical Republicans lost control of the state government. All the ex-Confederate states rejoined the Union between 1868 and 1870, but the periods of radical rule varied widely. Republicans lasted only a few months in Virginia; they held on until the end of Reconstruction in Louisiana, Florida, and South Carolina.

and ensure that new constitutions guaranteed black **suffrage**. Congress would readmit a state to the Union once these conditions were met and the new state legislature ratified the Fourteenth Amendment. Johnson vetoed the Reconstruction Act, but Congress overrode his veto (Table 15.1).

The Impeachment of Andrew Johnson Johnson fought back. In August 1867, after Congress adjourned, he "suspended" Secretary of War Edwin M. Stanton, a Radical, and replaced him with Union general Ulysses S. Grant, believing Grant would be a good soldier and follow orders. Johnson, however, had misjudged Grant, who publicly objected to the president's machinations. When the Senate reconvened in the fall, it overruled Stanton's suspension. Grant, now an open enemy of Johnson, resigned so that Stanton could resume his place as secretary of war. On February 21, 1868, Johnson formally dismissed Stanton. The feisty secretary of war responded by barricading himself in his office, precipitating a crisis.

TABLE 15.1 Primary Reconstruction Laws and Constitutional Amendments	
Law (Date of Congressional Passage)	**Key Provisions**
Thirteenth Amendment (December 1865*)	Prohibited slavery
Civil Rights Act of 1866 (April 1866)	Defined citizenship rights of freedmen
	Authorized federal authorities to bring suit against those who violated those rights
Fourteenth Amendment (June 1866†)	Established national citizenship for persons born or naturalized in the United States
	Prohibited the states from depriving citizens of their civil rights or equal protection under the law
	Reduced state representation in House of Representatives by the percentage of adult male citizens denied the vote
Reconstruction Act of 1867 (March 1867)	Divided the South into five military districts, each under the command of a Union general
	Established requirements for readmission of ex-Confederate states to the Union
Tenure of Office Act (March 1867)	Required Senate consent for removal of any federal official whose appointment had required Senate confirmation
Fifteenth Amendment (February 1869‡)	Forbade states to deny citizens the right to vote on the grounds of race, color, or "previous condition of servitude"
Ku Klux Klan Act (April 1871)	Authorized the president to use federal prosecutions and military force to suppress conspiracies to deprive citizens of the right to vote and enjoy the equal protection of the law

*Ratified by three-fourths of all states in December 1865.
†Ratified by three-fourths of all states in July 1868.
‡Ratified by three-fourths of all states in March 1870.

Three days later, for the first time in U.S. history, legislators in the House of Representatives introduced articles of **impeachment** against the president, employing their constitutional power to charge high federal officials with "Treason, Bribery, or other high Crimes and Misdemeanors." The House serves, in effect, as the prosecutor in such cases, and the Senate serves as the court. The Republican majority brought eleven counts of misconduct against Johnson, most relating to infringement of the powers of Congress. After an eleven-week trial in the Senate, thirty-five senators voted for conviction — one vote short of the two-thirds majority required. Seven Republicans voted for acquittal along with twelve Democrats. The dissenting Republicans felt that removing a president for defying Congress was too damaging to the constitutional system of checks and balances. But despite the president's acquittal, Congress had shown its power. For the brief months remaining in his term, Johnson was largely irrelevant to Reconstruction policy.

The Election of 1868 and the Fifteenth Amendment The impeachment controversy made Grant, already the Union's greatest war hero, a Republican idol as well, and he easily won the party's presidential nomination in 1868. Although he supported radical Reconstruction, Grant also urged reconciliation between the sections. His Democratic opponent, Horatio Seymour, a former governor of New York, almost declined the nomination because he understood that Democrats could not yet overcome the stain of disloyalty. Grant won by an overwhelming margin, receiving 214 out of 294 electoral votes. Republicans retained two-thirds majorities in both houses of Congress.

In February 1869, in the wake of this smashing victory, Republicans produced the last Reconstruction amendment, the Fifteenth. It protected male citizens' right to vote irrespective of race, color, or "previous condition of servitude." Despite Radical Republicans' protests, the amendment left room for a **poll tax** (a tax paid for the privilege of voting) and literacy requirements, both necessary concessions to northern and western states that already relied on such provisions to keep immigrants and the "unworthy" poor from the polls. Congress required the four states remaining under federal control to ratify it as a condition for being readmitted to the Union. A year later, the Fifteenth Amendment became part of the Constitution.

Passage of the Fifteenth Amendment, despite its limitations, was an astonishing feat. Elsewhere in the Western Hemisphere, lawmakers had left emancipated slaves in a condition of semicitizenship, with no voting rights. But, like almost all Americans, congressional Republicans had extraordinary faith in the power of the ballot. African American leaders agreed. "The colored people of these Southern states have cast their lot with the Government," declared a delegate to Arkansas's constitutional convention, "and with the great Republican Party. . . . The ballot is our only means of protection." After the amendment was ratified, hundreds of thousands of African Americans flocked to the polls across the South, in an atmosphere of collective pride and celebration.

Woman Suffrage Denied

Northern women had played key roles in the antislavery movement and Union victory. Women's rights leaders, who had campaigned for women's voting rights since the Seneca Falls convention of 1848, fervently hoped that Reconstruction would bring votes

OUT IN THE COLD.

"Out in the Cold"

Though many women, including African American activists in the South, went to the polls in the early 1870s to test whether the new Fourteenth Amendment had given them the vote, federal courts subsequently rejected women's voting rights. Only the Wyoming and Utah territories fully enfranchised women. At the same time, revised naturalization laws allowed immigrant men of African descent — though not of Asian descent — to become citizens. With its crude Irish, African, and Chinese racial caricatures, this 1884 cartoon from the humor magazine *The Judge* echoes the arguments of some white suffragists that though men of races stereotyped as inferior had been enfranchised, white women were not. The woman knocking on the door is also a caricature, with her harsh appearance and masculine style of dress. Library of Congress.

for women as well as for black men. As Elizabeth Cady Stanton put it, women could "avail ourselves of the strong arm and the blue uniform of the black soldier to walk in by his side." The addition of a single word in the Fifteenth Amendment would have done it: The protected categories for voting could have read "race, color, *sex*, or previous condition of servitude." But that word proved impossible to obtain. For the authors of Reconstruction, enfranchising black men had clear benefits. It punished ex-Confederates and ensured Republican support in the South. But a substantial majority of northern voters — all men, of course — opposed women's enfranchisement. Even Radicals feared that this "side issue" would defeat the Fourteenth Amendment and overburden the party's program.

At the May 1869 convention of the Equal Rights Association, black abolitionist and women's rights advocate Frederick Douglass pleaded for white women to understand the plight in which former slaves found themselves, and to allow black male suffrage to take priority. "When women, because they are women, are hunted down, . . . dragged from their homes and hung upon lamp posts, . . . then they will have an urgency to obtain the ballot equal to our own." Some women's rights leaders joined Douglass in backing the Fifteenth Amendment, even without the word *sex*. But most white women in the audience rebelled. One African American woman remarked that they "all go for sex, letting race occupy a minor position." In her despair, Elizabeth Cady Stanton lashed out against "Patrick and Sambo and Hans and Ung Tung," maligning uneducated freedmen and immigrants who could vote while educated white women could not. Douglass's resolution in support of the Fifteenth Amendment failed, and the convention broke up in bitterness.

At this searing moment, a rift opened in the women's movement. The majority, led by Lucy Stone and Julia Ward Howe, reconciled themselves to disappointment. Organized into the American Woman Suffrage Association, they remained loyal to the Republican Party in hopes that once Reconstruction had been settled, it would be women's turn. A group led by Elizabeth Cady Stanton and Susan B. Anthony struck out in a new direction. They saw that the moment of radical innovation had passed and woman suffrage was unlikely in the near future. Stanton declared that woman "must not put her trust in man." The new organization that she headed, the National Woman Suffrage Association (NWSA), focused exclusively on women's rights and took up the battle for a federal suffrage amendment.

In 1873, NWSA members decided to test the limits of the new constitutional amendments. Suffragists all over the United States, including some African American women in the South, tried to register and vote. Most were turned away. In Rochester, New York, Susan B. Anthony cast a straight Republican ballot and was arrested afterward in her home, by a polite and rather embarrassed U.S. marshal. In one of a series of ensuing lawsuits, suffrage advocate Virginia Minor of Missouri argued that the registrar who rejected her had violated her rights under the Fourteenth Amendment. In *Minor v. Happersett* (1875), the Supreme Court dashed suffragists' hopes. It ruled that suffrage rights were not inherent in citizenship; women were citizens, but state legislatures could deny women the ballot if they wished.

Despite these defeats, radical Reconstruction created the conditions for a high-profile, nationwide movement for women's voting rights. Amid debates over the Fourteenth and Fifteenth Amendments, some Americans argued for the measure as part of a bold expansion of democracy. Others saw white women's votes as a possible counterweight to the votes of African American or Chinese men (while opponents pointed out that black and immigrant women would likely be enfranchised, too). When Wyoming Territory gave women the vote in 1869, its governor received telegrams of congratulation from as far away as Europe. Afterward, contrary to antisuffragist warnings, female voters in Wyoming did not appear to neglect their homes, abandon their children, or otherwise "unsex" themselves. In fact, suffragists argued that women's presence helped make Wyoming politics less corrupt and more respectable. The goal of votes for women could no longer be dismissed as the absurd notion of a tiny minority. It became a serious issue for national debate.

▶ How did Lincoln and Johnson each approach Reconstruction?

▶ What did the supporters of radical Reconstruction do to advance their vision for the postwar South?

The Meaning of Freedom

While political leaders in Washington struggled over Reconstruction, emancipated slaves acted on their own ideas about freedom (see American Voices, p. 456). Freedom meant many things — the end of punishment by the lash; the ability to move around; the reunion of families; and the opportunity to build schools and churches, and publish and read newspapers. Topmost among freedmen's demands was the right to vote. To achieve

Relishing Freedom   JOURDON ANDERSON

Folklorists have recorded the sly ways that slaves found, even in bondage, for "puttin' down" their masters. But only in freedom — and beyond reach in a northern state at that — could Anderson's sarcasm be expressed so openly, with the jest that his family might consider returning if they first received the wages due them, calculated to the dollar, for all those years in slavery. Anderson's letter, although probably written or edited by a white friend in Dayton, surely is faithful to what the ex-slave wanted to say.

Dayton, Ohio
August 7, 1865.
To My Old Master, Colonel P. H. Anderson,
Big Spring, Tennessee.
Sir:

I got your letter, and was glad to find that you had not forgotten Jourdon. . . . I thought the Yankees would have hung you long before this, for harboring Rebs they found at your house. I suppose they never heard about your going to Colonel Martin's house to kill the union soldier that was left by his company in their stable. Although you shot at me twice before I left you, I did not want to hear of your being hurt, and am glad you are still living. It would do me good to go back to the dear old home again, and see Miss Mary and Miss Martha and Allen, Esther, Green, and Lee. Give my love to them all, and tell them I hope we will meet in the better world, if not in this. . . .

I want to know particularly what the good chance is you propose to give me. I am doing tolerably well here. I get twenty-five dollars a month, with victuals and clothing; have a comfortable home for Mandy, — the folks call her Mrs. Anderson, — and the children — Milly, Jane, and Grundy — go to school and are learning well. . . . We are kindly treated. Sometimes we overhear others saying, "Them colored people were slaves" down in Tennessee. The children feel hurt when they hear such remarks; but I tell them it was no disgrace in Tennessee to belong to Colonel Anderson. Many darkeys would

have been proud, as I used to be, to call you master. . . .

Mandy says she would be afraid to go back without some proof that you were disposed to treat us justly and kindly; and we have concluded to test your sincerity by asking you to send us our wages for the time we served you. . . . I served you faithfully for thirty-two years, and Mandy twenty years. At twenty-five dollars a month for me and two dollars a week for Mandy, our earnings would amount to eleven thousand six hundred and eighty dollars. Add to this the interest for the time our wages have been kept back, and deduct what you paid for our clothing, and three doctor's visits to me, and pulling a tooth for Mandy, and the balance will show what we are in justice entitled to. . . .

In answering this letter, please state if there would be any safety for my Milly and Jane, who are now grown up, and both good-looking girls. . . . I would rather stay here and starve — and die, if it come to that — than have my girls brought to shame by the violence and wickedness of their young masters. . . .

Say howdy to George Carter, and thank him for taking the pistol from you when you were shooting at me.

From your old servant,
Jourdon Anderson

SOURCE: Stanley I. Kutler, ed., *Looking for America: The People's History*, 2nd ed., 2 vols. (New York: W. W. Norton, 1979), 2: 4–6, 24–27.

a true measure of freedom, former slaves had to overcome both the hostility of former Confederates and the ambivalence of many Unionist allies.

The Quest for Land

One of freedmen's most pressing goals was landownership. In the chaotic final months of war, freedmen had seized control of plantations where they could. In Georgia and South Carolina, General William Tecumseh Sherman had reserved large coastal tracts for liberated slaves and settled them on 40-acre plots. Sherman simply did not want to be bothered with refugees as his army crossed the region, but the freedmen assumed that Sherman's order meant that the land was theirs. After the war, resettlement became the responsibility of the Freedmen's Bureau. Thousands of rural blacks hoped for land distributions. "I have gone through the country," reported a black spokesman in South Carolina, "and on every side I was besieged with questions: How are we to get home-steads, to get lands?"

Johnson's amnesty plan, enabling pardoned Confederates to recover property seized during the war, blasted freedmen's hopes. In October 1865, Johnson ordered General Oliver O. Howard, head of the Freedmen's Bureau, to restore plantations on the Sea Islands off the South Carolina coast to their white owners. Dispossessed blacks protested: "Why do you take away our lands? You take them from us who have always been true, always true to the Government! You give them to our all-time enemies! That is not right!" Former slaves resisted efforts to evict them. Led by black Union veterans, they fought pitched battles with plantation owners and bands of ex-Confederate soldiers. But white landowners, sometimes aided by federal troops, generally prevailed.

Freed Slaves and Northerners: Conflicting Goals | The problem of land was broader than Johnson's policies or even ex-Confederate resistance. A profound gap lay between the goals of freed slaves and those of Republicans in Washington. The economic revolution of the antebellum period had transformed New England and the Mid-Atlantic states. Most congressional leaders believed, following in the tradition of antebellum Whigs, that once slavery was dead, the same kind of economic development would revolutionize the South. Republicans sought to restore cotton as the country's leading export. They envisioned former slaves as wageworkers on cash-crop plantations, not as independent farmers. Only a handful of radicals, like Thaddeus Stevens, argued that freed slaves had already *earned* a right to the land, through what Lincoln once referred to as "four hundred years of unrequited toil." Stevens proposed that large southern plantations be treated as "forfeited estates of the enemy" and broken up into small farms for the former slaves.

Today, most historians of Reconstruction agree with Stevens: Policymakers did not go far enough to ensure freedpeople's economic welfare. Left without land, former slaves were rendered poor and vulnerable. At the time, however, men like Stevens had few allies. Though often accused of harshness toward the defeated Confederacy, most Republicans — even Radicals — recoiled at the idea of confiscating private land. They could not imagine "giving" land to former slaves. The same congressmen, of course, had no difficulty giving homesteaders land on the frontier that had been taken from Indians. But Republicans were deeply reluctant to confiscate white-owned plantations. Some southern Republican state governments did try, without much success, to use tax policy

Wage Labor of Former Slaves

This photograph, taken in South Carolina shortly after the Civil War, shows former slaves leaving the cotton fields. Many freedpeople were organized into work crews probably not that different from earlier slave gangs, although they now labored for wages. Freedmen resisted such working conditions and sought greater freedom from constant threats and oversight. © Collection of the New-York Historical Society.

to break up large landholdings and get them into the hands of poorer whites and blacks. In 1869, South Carolina established a land commission to buy property and resell it on easy terms to the landless; about 14,000 black families acquired farms through the program. But such initiatives were the exception, not the rule.

Wage Labor and Sharecroppping | Freedmen and freedwomen wanted as much independence of work and life as they could achieve. Obtaining no land, however, most began with few options but to work for former slave owners. Serious conflict ensued. Landowners wanted to retain the old **gang-labor system**, with wages replacing the food, clothing, and shelter that slaves had once received. Southern planters — who had recently scorned the North for the cruelties of the wage-labor system — now embraced waged work with apparent satisfaction. Maliciously comparing freedpeople to free-roaming pigs, landowners told them to "root, hog, or die." Former slaves found themselves with rock-bottom wages, especially in agriculture; it was a shock to find that Emancipation and a "free labor" system did not prevent a hardworking family from nearly starving. African American workers used a variety of tactics to fight back. Some left the fields and traveled long distances to seek work on the railroads or in turpentine and lumber camps. Others organized to bargain for fairer wages. Not only black farmworkers but also factory workers and laundrywomen went on strike.

At the same time, a major conflict raged between employers and freedpeople over the labor of women. In slavery, African American women's bodies had been the sexual property of white men. Protecting black women from such abuse, as much as possible, was a crucial priority for freedpeople. When planters demanded that black women go back into the fields, African Americans resisted resolutely. "I seen on some plantations," one freedman recounted, "where the white men would . . . tell colored men that their wives and children could not live on their places unless they work in the fields. The colored men [answered that] whenever they wanted their wives to work they would tell them themselves."

There was a profound irony in this man's definition of freedom: It designated a wife's labor as her husband's property. In that, of course, freedpeople were adapting to white norms. Some black women asserted their independence and headed their own households — though in a society utterly disrupted by war, this was often a matter of necessity rather than choice. For many freedwomen and freedmen, the opportunity for a stable family life was one of the greatest achievements of emancipation. Many enthusiastically accepted the northern ideal of **domesticity**. Missionaries, teachers, and editors of black newspapers urged men to work diligently and support their families, and women (though many worked for wages) to devote themselves to motherhood and the home. Like their northern allies, many southern African Americans believed domesticity was the key to civilization and progress.

Even in rural areas, former slaves refused to work under the conditions of slavery. There would be no gang work, they vowed: no overseers, no whippings, no regulation of their private lives. All across the South, planters who needed labor were forced to yield to what one planter termed "the inveterate prejudices of the freedmen, who desire to be masters of their own time." In a few areas, waged work became the norm — for example, on the giant sugar plantations of Louisiana financed by northern capital. But cotton planters lacked the money to pay wages, and sometimes, in lieu of a straight wage, they offered a share of the crop. Freedmen, in turn, paid their rent in shares of the harvest.

Thus sprang up the distinctive laboring system of cotton agriculture known as **sharecropping**, in which freedmen worked as renters, exchanging their labor for the use of land, house, implements, and sometimes seed and fertilizer. Sharecroppers typically turned over half of their crops to the landlord (Map 15.2). In a credit-starved agricultural region that grew crops for a world economy, sharecropping was an effective strategy, through which laborers and landowners shared risks and returns. But it was a very unequal relationship, given sharecroppers' dire economic circumstances. Starting out penniless, they had no way of making it through the first growing season without borrowing for food and supplies.

Country storekeepers stepped in. Bankrolled by northern suppliers, they furnished the sharecropper with provisions and took as collateral a **lien** on the crop, effectively assuming ownership of the cropper's share and leaving him only the proceeds that remained after his debts had been paid. Once indebted at one store, sharecroppers could no longer shop around. They became easy targets for exorbitant prices, unfair interest

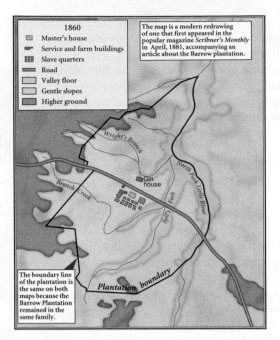
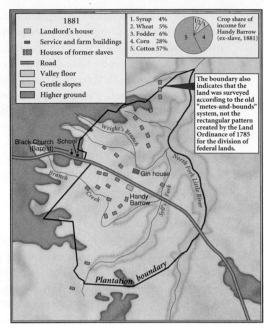

MAP 15.2 The Barrow Plantation, 1860 and 1881

This map is a modern redrawing of one that first appeared in the popular magazine *Scribner's Monthly* in April 1881, accompanying an article about the Barrow plantation. The boundary line is the same on both maps because the plantation remained in the same family. Comparing the 1860 map of this central Georgia plantation with the 1881 map reveals the impact of sharecropping on patterns of black residence. In 1860, the slave quarters were clustered near the planter's house. In contrast, by 1881 the sharecroppers were scattered across the plantation's 2,000 acres, having built cabins on the ridges between the low-lying streams. The surname Barrow was common among the sharecropping families, which means almost certainly that they had been slaves who, years after emancipation, still had not moved on. For sharecroppers, freedom meant not only their individual lots and cabins but also the school and church shown on the map.

rates, and crooked bookkeeping. As cotton prices declined during the 1870s, more and more sharecroppers failed to settle accounts and fell into permanent debt. If the merchant was also the landowner or conspired with the landowner, the debt became a pretext for forced labor, or **peonage**, though when things became hopeless, sharecroppers sometimes managed to pull up stakes and move on.

Sharecropping — a product of the struggles of Reconstruction — endured in part because it was a good fit for cotton agriculture. Cotton, unlike sugarcane, could be raised efficiently by small farmers (provided they had the lash of indebtedness always on their backs). We can see this in the experience of other countries that became major producers in response to the global cotton famine set off by the Civil War. In India, Egypt, Brazil, and West Africa, variants of the sharecropping system emerged. Most striking was the adoption everywhere of crop-lien laws, at the behest of international merchants and bankers who put up the capital. Indian and Egyptian villagers got the advances they needed to shift from subsistence agriculture to cotton but at the price of being placed, as in America, permanently under the thumb of furnishing merchants. American planters resisted sharecropping at first because they started at a different place: not traditional, subsistence economies that had to be converted to cotton but a proven plantation system over which they had been absolute masters.

For freedmen, sharecropping was not the worst choice, in a world where former masters threatened to impose labor conditions that were close to slavery. But for southern agriculture, the costs were devastating. With farms leased on a year-to-year basis, neither tenant nor owner had much incentive to improve the property. The crop-lien system rested on expensive interest payments — money that might otherwise have gone into agricultural improvements. And sharecropping committed the South inflexibly to cotton, which as a market crop generated the cash required by landlords and furnishing merchants. The result was a stagnant farm economy that blighted the South's future. As Republican governments tried to remake the South, they faced not only the challenges of wartime destruction and widespread poverty but also the failure of their hopes that free labor would create a modern, prosperous South, built in the image of the industrializing North. Instead, a rural economy emerged that remained mired in widespread poverty and based on an uneasy compromise between landowners and laborers.

Republican Governments in the South

Between 1868 and 1871, all the former Confederate states met congressional stipulations and rejoined the Union. Protected by federal troops, Republican administrations in these states retained power for periods ranging from a few months in Virginia to nine years in South Carolina, Louisiana, and Florida. These governments remain some of the most misunderstood institutions in all U.S. history. Ex-Confederates never accepted their legitimacy. Many contemporaries agreed, focusing particularly on the role of African American Republicans who began to serve in public office. "It is strange, abnormal, and unfit," declared one British visitor to Louisiana, "that a *negro* Legislature should deal . . . with the gravest commercial and financial interests."

During much of the twentieth century, historians echoed such critics, condemning Reconstruction leaders as ignorant and corrupt. These historians shared, at root, the racist assumptions of the British observer: Blacks were simply unfit to legislate. (In the early twentieth century, U.S. historians lived in a country that once again elected, year after year, an all-white Congress; the prospect of a nonwhite president was completely unthinkable.) In fact, Reconstruction governments were ambitious. They were hated, in part, because they undertook impressive reforms in public education, family law, social services, commerce, and transportation. Like their northern allies, southern Republicans admired the economic and social transformations that had occurred in the North before the Civil War, and during Reconstruction they worked energetically to import them.

The southern Republican Party included former Whigs, a few former Democrats, black and white newcomers from the North, and southern African Americans. From the start its leaders faced the dilemma of racial prejudice. In the upcountry, white Unionists were eager to join the party. But in most areas the Republicans also needed African

Outside the Freedmen's Bureau Office, Beaufort, South Carolina This photograph, taken in the 1870s, shows how offices of the Freedmen's Bureau became hubs of activity in southern cities and towns. Southerners, both black and white, gathered at the offices to sign contracts, resolve labor disputes, obtain official advice — even get married and mediate family conflicts. Bureau officials, whose numbers were pitifully small in comparison with the scope and number of their duties, had limited resources to address postwar devastation and the arrival of "free labor." Nonetheless, in the power vacuum of the ex-Confederacy, many bureau officials played a central role in restoring order and upholding justice. Miriam and Ira D. Wallach Division of Art, Prints and Photographs, The New York Public Library. Astor, Lenox and Tilden Foundations.

American voters, who constituted a majority of registered voters in Alabama, Florida, South Carolina, and Mississippi.

For a brief moment in the late 1860s, black and white Republicans joined forces through the Union League, a secret fraternal order. Formed in border states and northern cities during the Civil War, the Union League became a powerful political club that spread through the former Confederacy. Functioning as a grassroots wing of Radical Republicanism, league members pressured Congress to uphold justice to freedmen. After blacks won voting rights, the Union League organized meetings at churches and schoolhouses to instruct freedmen on political issues and voting procedures. League clubs also held parades and military drills, giving a public face to the new political order.

The Freedmen's Bureau also supported grassroots Reconstruction efforts. Though some bureau officials were hostile to freedmen and sympathized with planters' interests, most were dedicated, often idealistic men who tried valiantly to reconcile opposing interests. Bureau men kept a sharp eye out for unfair labor contracts and often forced landowners to bargain with workers and tenants. Bureau leaders advised freedmen on economic matters; provided direct payments to desperate families, especially women and children; and helped establish freedpeople's schools. In cooperation with northern aid societies, the bureau played a key role in founding African American colleges and universities such as Fisk, Tougaloo, and the Hampton Institute. These institutions, in turn, focused first on training teachers. By 1869, there were more than three thousand teachers instructing freedpeople in the South. More than half were themselves black.

Freedmen's School, Petersburg, Virginia, 1870s
A Union veteran, returning to Virginia in the 1870s to photograph battlefields, captured this image of an African American teacher and her students at a freedmen's school. Note the difficult conditions in which they study: Many are barefoot, and there are gaps in the walls and floor of the school building. Nonetheless, the students have a few books. Despite poverty and relentless hostility from many whites, freedpeople across the South were determined to get a basic education for themselves and their children. William L. Clements Library, University of Michigan.

Ex-Confederates viewed the Union League, Freedmen's Bureau, and Republican Party as illegitimate forces in southern affairs, and they bitterly resented the political education of freedpeople. They referred to southern whites who supported Reconstruction as **scalawags** — an ancient Scots-Irish term for worthless animals — and they denounced northern whites as **carpetbaggers**, self-seeking interlopers who carried all their property in cheap suitcases called carpetbags. Such labels glossed over the actual diversity of white Republicans. Many new arrivals from the North, while motivated by personal profit, also brought capital and skills. Interspersed with ambitious schemers were idealists hoping to advance the cause of freedmen's rights. The so-called scalawags were even more varied. Some were former slave owners; others were ex-Whigs or even ex-Democrats drawn to Republicanism as the best way to attract northern capital. But most hailed from the backcountry and wanted to rid the South of its slaveholding aristocracy. They had generally fought against, or at least refused to support, the Confederacy, believing that slavery had victimized whites as well as blacks.

Southern Democrats' contempt for black leaders, whom they regarded as ignorant field hands, was just as misguided as their stereotypes about white Republicans. The first African American leaders in the South came from the ranks of antebellum free blacks. They were joined by northern blacks who moved south to support Reconstruction. Many were Union veterans; some were employees of the Freedmen's Bureau and northern missionary societies. Others had escaped from slavery and were returning home. One of these ex-slaves was Blanche K. Bruce, who had been tutored on a Virginia plantation by his white father. During the war, Bruce escaped and established a school for freedmen in Missouri. In 1869, he moved to Mississippi and became active in politics; in 1874, he became Mississippi's second black U.S. senator.

During radical Reconstruction, African American speakers, some financed by the Republican Party, fanned out into the old plantation districts and recruited former slaves to participate in politics. Still, few of the new leaders were field hands; most had been preachers or artisans. Literacy helped freedman Thomas Allen, a Baptist minister and shoemaker, win election to the Georgia legislature. "In my county," Allen recalled, "the colored people came to me for instructions, and I gave them the best instructions I could. I took the *New York Tribune* and other papers, and in that way I found out a great deal, and I told them whatever I thought was right." Though never proportionate to their numbers in the population, blacks became officeholders across the South. In South Carolina, African Americans constituted a majority in the lower house of the legislature in 1868. Over the course of Reconstruction, twenty African Americans served in state administrations as governor, lieutenant governor, secretary of state, or lesser offices. More than six hundred served as state legislators and sixteen as congressmen.

Southern Republicans had big plans. Their Reconstruction governments eliminated property qualifications for the vote and abolished the Black Codes that hemmed in freedpeople. Their new state constitutions expanded the rights of married women, enabling them to hold property and wages independent of their husbands' — "a wonderful reform," one white woman in Georgia wrote, for "the cause of Women's Rights." Like their counterparts in the North, southern Republicans also believed in using government to foster economic growth. They sought to diversify the economy beyond cotton agriculture, and they poured money into railroads and other building projects to expand the region's shattered economy.

In myriad ways, Republicans brought southern state and city governments up to date. They outlawed corporal punishments such as whipping and branding. They established more humane penitentiaries as well as hospitals and asylums for orphans and the disabled. South Carolina offered free public health services, while Alabama provided free legal representation for defendants who could not pay. Some municipal governments paved the streets and installed streetlights. Petersburg, Virginia, established a board of health that offered free medical care during the smallpox epidemic of 1873. Nashville, Tennessee, created soup kitchens for the poor.

Most impressive of all were achievements in public education, where the South had lagged woefully. Republicans viewed education as the foundation of a true democratic order. By 1875, over half of black children were attending school in Mississippi, Florida, and South Carolina. African Americans of all ages rushed to the newly established schools, even when they had to pay tuition. They understood why slaveholders had criminalized slave literacy: The practice of freedom rested on the ability to read newspapers, labor contracts, history books, and the Bible. A school official in Virginia reported that freedpeople were "*crazy* to learn." One Louisiana man explained why he was sending his children to school, even though he needed their help in the field. It was "better than leaving them a fortune; because if you left them even five hundred dollars, some man having more education than they had would come along and cheat them out of it all." Meanwhile, thousands of white children, particularly girls and the sons of poor farmers and laborers, also benefited from the new public education system. Young white women's graduation from high school, an unheard of occurrence before the Civil War, became accepted and even celebrated in southern cities and towns.

Building Black Communities

In slavery days, African Americans had built networks of religious worship and mutual aid to sustain one another, but these operated largely underground. After emancipation, southern blacks could engage in open community building. In doing so, they cooperated with northern missionaries and teachers who came to help in the great work of freedom. "Ignorant though they may be, on account of long years of oppression, they exhibit a desire to hear and to learn, that I never imagined," reported African American minister Reverend James Lynch, who had traveled from Maryland to the Deep South. "Every word you say while preaching, they drink down and respond to, with an earnestness that sets your heart all on fire."

Independent churches quickly became central institutions of black life, as blacks across the South left white-dominated congregations, where they had sat in segregated balconies, and built churches of their own. These churches joined their counterparts in the North to become national denominations, including, most prominently, the National Baptist Convention and the African Methodist Episcopal Church. Everywhere, black churches served not only as sites of worship but also as schools, social centers, and meeting halls. Black ministers were community leaders and often political spokesmen as well. As Charles H. Pearce, a Methodist minister in Florida, declared, "A man in this State cannot do his whole duty as a minister except he looks out for the political interests of his people." Calling forth the special destiny of formerly enslaved southerners as the new "Children of Israel," black ministers provided a powerful religious underpinning for the politics of their congregations.

The flowering of southern black churches, schools, newspapers, and civic groups was one of the most enduring initiatives of the Reconstruction era. Dedicated teachers and charity leaders embarked on a project of "race uplift" that never ceased thereafter, while black entrepreneurs were proud to build businesses that served their own communities. The issue of **desegregation** — sharing public facilities with whites — was a trickier one. Some black leaders pressed for desegregated public facilities, but they were keenly aware of the backlash this was likely to provoke. Many freedpeople made it clear that they preferred their children to attend all-black schools, especially if they had encountered hostile or condescending white teachers. Others had pragmatic concerns. Asked whether she wanted her boys to attend an integrated school, one woman in New Orleans said no: "I don't want my children to be pounded by dem white boys. I don't send them to school to fight, I send them to learn."

At the national level, congressmen wrestled with similar issues as they debated an ambitious civil rights bill championed by Radical Republican senator Charles Sumner. Sumner first introduced his bill in 1870, seeking to enforce, among other things, equal access to schools, public transportation, hotels, and churches. Through a series of defeats and delays, the bill remained on Capitol Hill for five years. Opponents charged that shared use of public spaces would lead to race mixing and intermarriage. Some sympathetic Republicans feared a backlash, while others questioned whether, because of the First Amendment, the federal government had the right to regulate churches. On his deathbed in 1874, Sumner exhorted a visitor to remember the civil rights bill: "Don't let it fail." In the end, the Senate removed Sumner's provision for integrated churches, and the House removed the clause requiring integrated schools. But to honor the great Massachusetts abolitionist, Congress passed the Civil Rights Act of 1875. The law required "full and equal" access to jury service and to transportation and public accommodations, irrespective of race. It was the last such act for almost a hundred years — until the Civil Rights Act of 1964.

> ▶ In what ways did the freedmen's goal of landownership clash with the goals of northern Republicans and of southerners? What were the results of that clash?
>
> ▶ How did black communities develop during Reconstruction? Based on their collective activities, what priorities did they appear to have had in the wake of emancipation?

The Undoing of Reconstruction

Sumner's death marked the waning of radical Reconstruction. Leaders of that movement had accomplished more than anyone dreamed a few years earlier. But a chasm had opened between the goals of freedmen, who wanted autonomy, and policymakers, whose first priorities were to reincorporate ex-Confederates into the nation and build a powerful national economy. Meanwhile, the North was flooded with one-sided, often racist reports such as James M. Pike's *The Prostrate State* (1873), which described South Carolina in the grip of "black barbarism." Events of the 1870s deepened the northern public's disillusionment. Scandals rocked the Grant administration, and a sudden economic depression placed severe restraints on both private investment and public spending. At the same time, northern resolve was worn down by ex-Confederates' continued refusal to accept Reconstruction. Only full-scale military intervention could reverse the situation in the South, and by the mid-1870s the North had no political willpower to renew the occupation. Besieged by economic hardship and ex-Confederate resistance, Reconstruction faltered.

The Republican Unraveling

Republicans who banked on economic growth to underpin their ambitious programs found their hopes dashed by a severe depression that began in 1873. This global downturn affected much of Europe and even touched other parts of the world. In the United States, the initial panic was triggered by the bankruptcy of the Northern Pacific Railroad, backed by leading financier Jay Cooke. Cooke's supervision of Union finances during the Civil War had made him a national hero; his downfall was a shock, and since Cooke was so well connected in Washington, it raised suspicions that Republican financial manipulation had caused the depression. Grant's officials deepened public resentment toward their party when they rejected pleas to increase the money supply and provide relief from debt and unemployment.

The impact of the depression varied in different parts of the United States. But many farmers found themselves in a terrible plight as crop prices plunged, while industrial workers faced layoffs and sharp reductions in pay. Within a year, 50 percent of American iron manufacturing had stopped. By 1877, half the nation's railroad companies had filed for bankruptcy. Rail construction halted. With hundreds of thousands thrown out of work, people took to the road. Wandering "tramps," who camped beside railroad tracks and knocked on doors to beg for work and food, became a source of fear and anxiety for prosperous Americans.

In addition to discrediting Republicans, the depression directly undercut their policies, most dramatically in the South. The ex-Confederacy was still recovering from the ravages of war, and the region's new economic and social order, negotiated in the wake of emancipation, remained fragile. The ambitious policies of southern Republicans — for education, public health, and grants to railroad builders — cost a great deal of money. Federal support, offered through programs like the Freedmen's Bureau, had begun to fade even before 1873. Republicans had banked on major infusions of northern and foreign investment capital into the South; for the most part, these failed to materialize. Investors who had sunk money into Confederate bonds, only to have those repudiated, were especially wary. The South's economy grew more slowly than Republicans had hoped, and when the depression hit, growth screeched to a halt. State debts mounted rapidly, and as crushing interest on bonds fell due, public credit collapsed.

Not only had Republican officials failed to anticipate a severe depression; during the era of generous spending, considerable funds had been wasted or ended up in the pockets of public officials. Corruption was common in an era of railroad building and ambitious public contracts, and some notorious cases in the South rivaled the scandals that would soon be uncovered in Washington, D.C. Two swindlers in North Carolina, one of them a former Union general, were found to have distributed more than $200,000 in bribes and loans to legislators to gain millions in state funds for rail construction. Instead of building railroads, they used the money to travel to Europe and speculate in stocks and bonds. Not only Republicans were on the take. "You are mistaken," wrote one Democrat to a northern friend, "if you suppose that all the evils . . . result from the carpetbaggers and negroes. The Democrats are leagued with them when anything is proposed that promises to pay." Bipartisan or not, such corruption severely damaged the cause of Reconstruction.

One of the depression's most tragic results was the failure of the Freedman's Savings and Trust Company. This private bank, founded in 1865, had worked closely with the Freedmen's Bureau and Union army across the South. Former slaves associated it with the party of Lincoln, and thousands responded to northerners' call for thrift and savings by bringing their small deposits to the nearest branch. Not only African American farmers and entrepreneurs but also churches and charitable groups opened accounts at the bank. But in the early 1870s, the bank's directors sank their money into risky loans and speculative investments. In June 1874, the bank failed.

Some Republicans believed that, because the bank had been so closely associated with the U.S. Army and other federal agencies, Congress had a duty to step in. Even a southern Democratic representative argued that the government was "morally bound to see to it that not a dollar is lost." But in the end, Congress refused to compensate the sixty-one thousand depositors; about half recovered small amounts — averaging $18.51 — but the other half received nothing. Abandonment of the bank signaled that the party of Reconstruction was losing its moral leadership.

The Disillusioned Liberals | As a result of both the depression and a backlash against the activist government of the postwar years, a revolt took shape inside the Republican Party. It was led by influential intellectuals, journalists, and businessmen who were **classical liberals** — believers in free trade, smaller government, and limited voting rights. Unable to block Grant's renomination in 1872, these dissidents broke away and formed a new party under the name Liberal Republican. Their candidate was Horace Greeley, longtime publisher of the *New York Tribune* and veteran reformer and abolitionist. The Democrats, still in disarray, also nominated Greeley, notwithstanding his editorial diatribes against them. A poor campaigner, Greeley was assailed so bitterly that, as he said, "I hardly knew whether I was running for the Presidency or the penitentiary."

Grant won reelection overwhelmingly, capturing 56 percent of the popular vote and every electoral vote. Yet the Liberal Republicans had managed to shift the terms of political debate. The agenda they had advanced — civil service reform, smaller government, restricted voting rights, and reconciliation with the South — resonated with Democrats, who were working to reclaim their status as a legitimate national party. Democrats had long been the party of limited government, and the rise of Liberal Republicanism provided an opportunity to revive that message. Liberalism thus crossed party lines, uniting disillusioned Republicans with Democrats who denounced government activism, especially social welfare programs. E. L. Godkin of *The Nation* and other classical liberal editors played key roles in turning northern public opinion against Reconstruction. With unabashed elitism, liberals claimed freedmen were unfit to vote. They denounced universal suffrage, which "can only mean in plain English the government of ignorance and vice."

The second Grant administration gave the liberals plenty of ammunition for their anticorruption guns. The most notorious scandal involved Crédit Mobilier, a sham corporation set up by shareholders in the Union Pacific Railroad to secure government grants at an enormous profit. Organizers of the scheme protected it from federal investigation by providing gifts of Crédit Mobilier stock to powerful members of Congress. Another major scandal involved the Whiskey Ring, a network of liquor distillers and treasury agents who defrauded the government of millions of dollars of excise taxes on whiskey. The ringleader was a Grant appointee, and Grant's private secretary, Orville Babcock, had a hand in the thievery. The others went to prison, but Grant stood by Babcock, possibly perjuring himself to save his secretary from jail. The stench of scandal permeated the White House.

Counterrevolution in the South

While northerners became preoccupied with scandals and the shock of economic depression, ex-Confederates seized the initiative in the South. Most believed (as northern liberals had also begun to argue) that southern Reconstruction governments were illegitimate "regimes." Led by the planters, ex-Confederates staged a massive counterrevolution designed to take back the South.

Insofar as they could win at the ballot box, southern Democrats took that route. They got ex-Confederate voting rights restored and campaigned against "negro rule." But when violence was necessary, southern Democrats used it. Present-day Americans, witnessing violence and political instability in other countries, seldom remember that our own history includes the overthrow of elected governments by paramilitary groups. But this is exactly how Reconstruction ended in many parts of the South. Ex-Confederates organized to terrorize Republicans, especially in districts with large proportions of black voters. Black political leaders were shot, hanged, beaten to death, and in one case even beheaded. Many Republicans, both black and white, went into hiding or fled for their lives. Southern Democrats called this violent process "Redemption."

No one looms larger in this bloody story than Nathan Bedford Forrest, a decorated Confederate general. Born in poverty in 1821, Forrest had scrambled in the booming cotton economy to become a big-time slave trader and Mississippi plantation owner. A fiery champion of secession, Forrest had formed a Tennessee Confederate cavalry regiment, fought bravely at the battle of Shiloh, and won fame as a daring raider. On April 12, 1864, his troopers perpetrated one of the war's worst atrocities, the slaughter of black Union troops at Fort Pillow, Tennessee. Forrest's troops refused to take prisoners, instead shooting down black soldiers as they tried to surrender.

Nathan Bedford Forrest in Uniform, c. 1865
Before he became Grand Wizard of the Ku Klux Klan, Forrest had been a celebrated cavalry general in the Confederate army. This photograph shows him in uniform before he was mustered out. Library of Congress.

Forrest's determination to uphold white supremacy emerged again after the war's end, altering the course of Reconstruction. William G. Brownlow, elected as Tennessee's Republican governor in 1865, was a tough man, a former prisoner of the Confederates who was not shy about calling his enemies to account. Ex-Confederates struck back with a campaign of terror, targeting especially Brownlow's black supporters. Amid the mayhem, some ex-Confederates formed the first Ku Klux Klan group in late 1865 or early 1866. As it proliferated across the state, the Klan turned to Forrest, who had been trying, unsuccessfully, to rebuild his prewar fortunes. Late in 1866, at a secret meeting in Nashville, Forrest donned the robes of Grand Wizard. His activities are mostly cloaked in mystery, but there is no mistake about his goals: The Klan would strike blows against the despised Republican government of Tennessee.

In many towns, the Klan became virtually identical to the Democratic Party. In fact, Klan members — including Forrest — dominated Tennessee's delegation to the

Democratic national convention of 1868. At home, the Klan unleashed a murderous campaign of terror, and though Governor Brownlow responded resolutely, in the end the Republicans cracked. By March 1869, Brownlow retreated to the U.S. Senate. The Klan spread in the meantime to other states, where its members burned freedmen's schools, beat teachers, murdered and threatened Republican politicians, and attacked Republican gatherings. By 1870, Democrats had seized power in Georgia and North Carolina and were making headway across the South.

In responding to the Klan between 1869 and 1871, the federal government showed it could still exert power effectively in the South. Determined to end Klan violence, Congress held extensive hearings and passed laws designed to put down the Klan and enforce freedmen's rights under the Fourteenth and Fifteenth Amendments. These so-called Enforcement Laws authorized federal prosecutions, military intervention, and martial law to suppress terrorist activities. The Grant administration made full use of these new powers. In South Carolina, where the Klan became deeply entrenched, U.S. troops occupied nine counties, made hundreds of arrests, and drove as many as 2,000 Klansmen from the state.

This assault on the Klan, while raising the spirits of southern Republicans, also revealed how dependent they were on Washington. The potency of the anti-Klan legislation, a Mississippi Republican wrote, "derived alone from its source" in the federal government. "No such law could be enforced by state authority, the local power being too weak." But northern Republicans were growing disillusioned with Reconstruction, and in the South, prosecuting Klansmen was an uphill battle against all-white juries and unsympathetic federal judges. After 1872, prosecutions began to drop off. In the meantime, Texas fell to the Democrats in 1873 and Alabama and Arkansas in 1874.

As the increasingly divided Republicans debated how to respond, voters in the congressional election of 1874 handed the ruling party one of the most stunning defeats of the entire nineteenth century. Responding particularly to the severe depression that gripped the nation, they defeated almost half of the party's 199 representatives in the House. Democrats, who had held 88 seats, now commanded an overwhelming majority of 182. "The election is not merely a victory but a revolution," exulted one Democratic newspaper in New York.

After 1874, with Democrats in firm control of the House, Republicans who tried to shore up their southern wing had limited options. Bowing to election results, the Grant administration began to reject southern Republicans' appeals for aid. Events in Mississippi showed the results. As state elections neared in 1875, paramilitary groups such as the Red Shirts operated openly. Mississippi's Republican governor, Adelbert Ames, a Union veteran from Maine, appealed to the president for federal troops, but Grant refused. "The whole public are tired out with these annual autumnal outbreaks in the South," complained one Grant official, who went on to tell southern Republicans that they were responsible for their own fate. As Mississippi Republicans faced a rising tide of brutal murders, Governor Ames — realizing that nothing could result but further bloodshed — urged his allies to give up the fight. Brandishing guns and stuffing ballot boxes, Democratic "Redeemers" swept the 1875 elections and took control of Mississippi. Thus, by 1876, Reconstruction was largely over. Republican governments, backed by token U.S. military units, remained in only three southern states: Louisiana, South Carolina, and Florida. Elsewhere, former Confederates and their allies were back in power.

The Supreme Court Rejection of Equal Rights | Northern Democrats and so-called Redeemers in the South played decisive roles in ending Reconstruction. But even though, for the moment, Democrats had won control of the House and ex-Confederates had seized power in southern states, new landmark constitutional amendments and federal laws remained in force. If the Supreme Court had left these intact, subsequent generations of civil rights advocates could have used the federal courts to combat discrimination and violence. Instead, the court closed off this avenue for the pursuit of justice and equal rights, just as it had dashed the hopes of women's rights advocates.

As early as 1873, in a group of decisions known collectively as the *Slaughterhouse Cases*, the Court began to undercut the power of the Fourteenth Amendment. In these cases and a related ruling, *U.S. v. Cruikshank* (1876), the justices argued that the Fourteenth Amendment offered only a few, rather trivial federal protections to citizens (such as access to navigable waterways). In *Cruikshank* — a case that emerged from the massacre of African American farmers by ex-Confederates in Colfax, Louisiana, which was followed by a Democratic political coup — the Court ruled that voting rights remained a state prerogative unless the state *itself* violated those rights. So long as the civil rights of former slaves were being violated by individuals or private groups (including the Klan), that was a state responsibility and beyond federal jurisdiction. Therefore, the Fourteenth Amendment did not protect citizens from armed vigilantes, even if those vigilantes seized political power. The Court thus gutted the Fourteenth Amendment. In the *Civil Rights Cases* (1883), the justices also struck down the Civil Rights Act of 1875. The impact of these decisions endured for decades.

The Political Crisis of 1877

After the grim election results of 1874, Republicans faced an uphill battle in the presidential election of 1876. Abandoning Grant, they nominated Rutherford B. Hayes, a former Union general who was untainted by corruption and — even more important — was governor of the key swing state of Ohio. Hayes's Democratic opponent was New York governor Samuel J. Tilden, a Wall Street lawyer with a reform reputation. Tilden favored **home rule** for the South, but so, more discreetly, did Hayes. With enforcement on the wane, Reconstruction did not figure prominently in the campaign, and little was said about the states still ruled by Reconstruction governments: Florida, South Carolina, and Louisiana.

Once returns started coming in on election night, however, those three states began to loom very large. Tilden led in the popular vote and seemed headed for victory until sleepless politicians at Republican headquarters realized that the electoral vote stood at 184 to 165, with the 20 votes from Florida, South Carolina, and Louisiana still uncertain. If Hayes took those votes, he would win by a margin of 1. Republicans still controlled the election process in the three states; citing Democratic fraud and intimidation, they certified Republican victories. The "Redeemer" Democrats who had seized the states sent in their own electoral votes, for Tilden. When Congress met in early 1877, it confronted two sets of electoral votes from those states.

The Constitution does not provide for such a contingency. All it says is that the president of the Senate (in 1877, a Republican) opens the electoral certificates before the House (Democratic) and the Senate (Republican) and that "the Votes shall then be counted" (Article 2, Section 1). Suspense gripped the country. There was talk of inside deals, of a new election, even of a violent coup. Finally, Congress appointed an electoral commission to settle the question. The commission included seven Republicans, seven Democrats, and, as the deciding member, David Davis, a Supreme Court justice not known to have fixed party loyalties. Davis, however, disqualified himself by accepting an Illinois seat in the Senate. He was replaced by Republican justice Joseph P. Bradley, and by a vote of 8 to 7, on party lines, the commission awarded the disputed votes to Hayes.

In the House of Representatives, outraged Democrats vowed to stall the final count of electoral votes so as to prevent Hayes's inauguration on March 4. But in the end, they went along — partly because Tilden himself urged that they do so. Hayes had publicly indicated his desire to offer substantial patronage to the South, including federal funds for education, internal improvements, and economic growth. He promised "a complete change of men and policy" — naively hoping, at the same time, that he could count on support from old-line southern Whigs and protect black voting rights. Hayes was inaugurated on schedule. He expressed hope in his inaugural address that the federal government could protect "the interests of both races carefully and equally." But, setting aside the U.S. troops who were serving on border duty in Texas, only 3,000 Union soldiers remained in the South. As soon as the new president ordered them back to their barracks, the last Republican administrations in the South fell. Reconstruction had ended.

Lasting Legacies

In the short run, the fall of the last state Republican governments had little impact on the lives of most southerners. Much of the violent work of "Redemption" had already been done. What mattered was the broad political trend: the long, slow decline of Radical Republican power from the early 1870s through the mid-1880s, and the corresponding rise of ex-Confederate power in the South and Democrats on the national stage. It was obvious to most Americans that so-called Redeemers in the South had assumed power through violence. But many — including prominent classical liberals who shaped public opinion — believed that ex-Confederates had overthrown corrupt, illegitimate governments and that the end justified the means. Those who deplored the results had little political traction. The only remaining question was how far the revolution would be rolled back. In 1884, when Democrats elected their first post–Civil War president, Grover Cleveland, many freedpeople feared that he would seek to repeal the Thirteenth Amendment and reinstate slavery.

But the South never went back to the antebellum status quo. Sharecropping, for all its flaws and injustices, was not slavery. Freedmen and freedwomen managed to resist gang labor and work on their own terms. They had established their right to marry, read and write, worship as they pleased, and travel in search of a better life — rights that were not easily revoked. Across the South, black farmers overcame great odds to buy and work their own land. African American businessmen built thriving enterprises. Parents sacrificed to send their children to school, and a few proudly watched their sons and daughters graduate from college. Black religious and charitable leaders sustained networks of mutual aid. At the grassroots level, Reconstruction never entirely ended.

Reconstruction had also shaken, if not entirely overturned, the legal and political framework that had, since the founding of the United States, made it a white man's country. This was a stunning achievement, and though hostile courts and violent resistance undercut it, no one ever repealed the Thirteenth, Fourteenth, and Fifteenth Amendments. They remained in the Constitution, an enduring statement of belief in equality, even if equality in practice was as yet unfulfilled. It was on this constitutional framework that the civil rights movement of the twentieth century would be built (Chapter 26). Meanwhile, legal cases brought by Asian immigrants, Mexicans in the Southwest, and American-born women would show that the Fourteenth and Fifteenth Amendments had transformed the nature of American citizenship.

In fact, the new federal powers asserted in Reconstruction — what Andrew Johnson disparaged as "centralization" — were in some ways more potent in the West than in the South. Republicans boldly carried their nation-building project into the West, to consolidate a continental empire. U.S. policymakers and businessmen also developed networks of trade and finance that stretched overseas. Before 1865, Americans had often worried about European interference in their domestic affairs. After the Civil War, Americans seldom brooded over such matters. Instead, the United States proudly began to describe itself as Britain's leading rival, not only in championing Emancipation and other marks of "advancing civilization" but also as a naval and commercial power around the world. Though the cause of freedom did not always advance, the federal powers that had secured emancipation would find new outlets in the postwar era.

▶ What factors undermined Republican control of the federal government during the 1870s?

▶ What economic, social, and political legacies persisted after the end of Reconstruction?

SUMMARY

Postwar Republicans confronted two great tasks: restoring the rebellious states to the Union and defining the role of emancipated slaves. After Lincoln's assassination, his successor, Andrew Johnson, hostile to Congress, unilaterally offered the South easy terms for reentering the Union. Exploiting this opportunity, southerners adopted oppressive Black Codes and welcomed ex-Confederates back into power. Congress impeached Johnson, and though failing to convict him, seized the initiative. They placed the South under military rule. In this second, or radical, phase of Reconstruction, Republican state governments tried to transform the South's economic and social institutions. Congress passed innovative civil rights acts and funded new agencies like the Freedmen's Bureau. The Fourteenth Amendment defined U.S. citizenship and asserted that states could no longer limit or supersede it. The Fifteenth Amendment gave full voting rights to formerly enslaved men. Debate over this amendment precipitated a split among women's rights advocates, since women did not win inclusion.

Freedmen found that their goals conflicted with those of Republican leaders, who counted on cotton to fuel economic growth. Like Southern landowners, they envisioned former slaves as wageworkers, while freedmen wanted their own land. Sharecropping, which satisfied no one completely, emerged as a compromise suited to the needs of the cotton market and an impoverished, credit-starved region.

Nothing could reconcile ex-Confederates to Republican government, and they staged a violent counterrevolution in the name of white supremacy and "Redemption."

Meanwhile, struck by a massive economic depression, Northern voters handed Republicans a crushing defeat in the election of 1874. By 1876, Reconstruction was dead. Rutherford B. Hayes's extremely narrow victory in the presidential election of that year, decided by a federal commission, resulted in the withdrawal of the last Union troops from the South. A series of Supreme Court decisions also undermined the Fourteenth Amendment and civil rights laws, setting up legal parameters through which, over the long term, disenfranchisement and segregation would flourish. Nonetheless, grassroots community-building among African Americans continued in the South, even after national Reconstruction faded.

For additional primary sources from this period, see *Documents for America's History*, Seventh Edition.

For Web sites, images, and documents related to topics and places in this chapter, visit *Make History* at **bedfordstmartins.com/henrettaconcise**.

For Further Exploration

The best modern book on Reconstruction is Eric Foner's major synthesis, *Reconstruction: America's Unfinished Revolution, 1863–1877* (1988). Foner's *Nothing But Freedom* (1983) helpfully places Reconstruction in a comparative context. See also Michael Perman, *Emancipation and Reconstruction*, 2nd ed. (2003). *Black Reconstruction in America* (1935), by African American activist and scholar W. E. B. Du Bois, deserves attention as the first book on Reconstruction that stressed the role of blacks in their own emancipation. On freedmen's experiences, see Leon F. Litwack, *Been in the Storm So Long: The Aftermath of Slavery* (1979). More recent studies include Julie Saville, *The Work of Reconstruction: From Slave to Wage Laborer in South Carolina, 1860–1870* (1994). In *Gendered Strife and Confusion* (1997), Laura F. Edwards explores the impact of ordinary women and men on Reconstruction. For recent views of the Freedmen's Bureau, see Paul A. Cimbala and Randall M. Miller, eds., *The Freedmen's Bureau and Reconstruction* (1999). For national politics, see (in addition to Foner) *The Reconstruction Presidents* (1998), by Brooks D. Simpson. On Americans' fading support for Reconstruction at the national level, see Heather Cox Richardson, *The Death of Reconstruction* (1991), and David W. Blight's sweeping *Race and Reunion* (1991). The site for the PBS documentary *Reconstruction: The Second Civil War* (**www.pbs.org/wgbh/amex/reconstruction/index.html**) features many helpful primary documents and images.

Test Your Knowledge

For practice quizzes, activities, and other study tools, visit the Online Study Guide at **bedfordstmartins.com/henrettaconcise**.

TIMELINE

1864	▶ Wade-Davis Bill passed by Congress but killed by Lincoln's pocket veto
1865	▶ Freedmen's Bureau established
	▶ Lincoln assassinated; Andrew Johnson succeeds him as president
	▶ Johnson implements Lincoln's restoration plan
1866	▶ Civil Rights Act passes over Johnson's veto
	▶ Republican gains in congressional elections
1867	▶ Reconstruction Act
1868	▶ Impeachment crisis
	▶ Fourteenth Amendment ratified
	▶ Ulysses S. Grant elected president
1870	▶ Ku Klux Klan at peak of power
	▶ Fifteenth Amendment ratified
1872	▶ Grant reelected
1873	▶ Panic of 1873 ushers in severe economic depression of 1873–1877
1874	▶ Sweeping Democratic gains in congressional election
1875	▶ Whiskey Ring scandal undermines Grant administration
	▶ *Minor v. Happersett* Supreme Court rules that Fourteenth Amendment does not extend voting rights to women
1877	▶ Rutherford B. Hayes becomes president
	▶ Reconstruction ends

See, vast trackless spaces,
As in a dream they
change, they swiftly fill,
Countless masses debouch
upon them. . . .

—Walt Whitman,
"Starting from Paumanok"

On May 10, 1869, people across the United States poured into the streets for a giant party. In Chicago and other large cities, the racket was incredible. Cannons boomed, church bells rang, train whistles shrilled. New York fired a hundred-gun salute at City Hall. Congregations sang anthems, while the less religious gathered in saloons to celebrate with whiskey. In Philadelphia, joyful throngs at the statehouse reminded one observer of the day, four years earlier, when news had arrived of Lee's surrender. The festivities were triggered by a long-awaited telegraph message: Executives of the Union Pacific and Central Pacific Railroads had driven a golden spike at Promontory Point, Utah, linking up their lines. An unbroken track now stretched from the Atlantic to the Pacific. A journey across the United States, which until recently had taken several months, could now be made in less than a week.

The transcontinental railroad meant economic growth. When they heard the news, San Francisco residents got right to business: After firing a cannon salute, they loaded a shipment of Japanese tea onto a train bound for St. Louis, marking California's first overland delivery to the East. In the coming decades, trade and tourism in areas west of the Mississippi River fueled tremendous economic development. San Francisco, which in 1860 had handled $7.4 million in imports, increased that figure to $49 million by 1890. The new railroad would, as one speaker predicted in 1869, "populate our vast territory" and make America "the highway of nations."

The railroad was a political as well as an economic triumph for the Union. The Republicans who emerged victorious from the Civil War saw themselves as heirs to the American System envisioned by Henry Clay and other antebellum Whigs. They believed that government intervention in the economy was the key to nation building. Unlike the Whigs, whose plans had been stalled by Democratic opposition, Republicans enjoyed a decade of unparalleled power in Washington. They used that power vigorously: Federal spending per person, which skyrocketed during the Civil War, afterward remained well above earlier levels. Republicans argued that industrialization and economic integration

The Great West

In the wake of the Civil War, Americans looked westward. Republicans implemented an array of policies to foster economic development and the making of continental fortunes in the "Great West." Ranchers, farmers, and lumbermen cast hungry eyes on the remaining lands held by Native Americans. Steamboats and railroads, both visible in the background of this image, became celebrated as symbols of the expanding reach of U.S. economic might. This 1881 promotional poster illustrates the bountiful natural resources to be found out west, as well as the land available for ranching, farming, and commerce. The men in the lower left corner are surveying land for sale. Library of Congress.

were the best guarantors of lasting peace. As a New York minister declared, the transcontinental railroad would "preserve the Union of these states."

The minister was wrong on one point, however. He claimed the railroad was a peaceful achievement, in contrast to battlefield victories that had brought "desolation, devastation, misery, and woe." In fact, creating a continental empire caused plenty of woe. Incorporating the areas west of the Mississippi into the national economy required the conquest of native peoples and the establishment of friendly conditions for international investors — often at great domestic cost. Conquering the West helped make the United States into a major industrial power, yet it also deepened America's rivalry with the imperial powers of Europe and created new patterns of investment and exploitation in Latin America and Asia.

The Republican Vision

Reshaping the former Confederacy was only one part of Republicans' plan for a reconstructed nation. They remembered the era after Andrew Jackson's destruction of the Second National Bank as a period of economic chaos, when the United States had become vulnerable to international creditors and market fluctuations. Land speculation on the frontier had provoked dizzying cycles of boom and bust. Failure to fund a transcontinental railroad had left different regions of the country disconnected. This, Republicans believed, had helped trigger the Civil War, and they were determined to take economic policy in a new direction.

Even as the war still raged, the Republican-dominated Congress made vigorous use of federal power, launching the transcontinental rail project, developing a new national banking system, and passing the Homestead Act. Congress also raised the **protective tariff** on a range of manufactured goods, from textiles to steel, and on some agricultural products, like wool and sugar. At federal customhouses in each port, foreign manufacturers who brought merchandise into the United States had to pay import fees. These tariff revenues gave U.S. manufacturers, who did not pay the fees, a competitive advantage in America's giant domestic market.

The massive economic depression that began in 1873 set limits on Republicans' ambitious economic program, just as it hindered their Reconstruction policies in the South. But key policies endured. Tariffs, the national banking system, and public subsidies to railroads, in particular, continued to shape the economy. Though some historians argue that the late nineteenth century was an era of unrestrained capitalism, in which government sat passively by, the industrial United States was actually the product of a massive public-private partnership, in which government played a critical role. Secretary of State William Seward, already looking abroad for markets and raw materials, provided a blueprint for international trade, resource exploitation, and investment for a century to come.

Integrating the National Economy

Railroad development in the United States began well before the Civil War, with the first locomotives arriving from Britain in the early 1830s. Unlike canals or roads, railroads offered the promise of year-round, all-weather service. Locomotives could run in the dark and never needed to rest, except to take on coal and water. Steam engines carried them over steep mountains and rocky gorges, where pack animals could find no fodder and canals could never reach. West of the Mississippi, railroads opened vast regions for conquest, farming, trade, and tourism. Railroads "do wonders — they work miracles," declared one booster. Looking back later, a transcontinental railroad executive was only half joking when he said, "[T]he West is purely a railroad enterprise."

Railroads could be run by the government or financed by private investors. Unlike most European countries, the United States chose the private approach, but the federal government provided essential incentives in the form of loans, subsidies, and land grants. States and localities also lured railroads with offers of financial aid, mainly by buying railroad bonds. Without this aid, the rail network would have grown much more slowly and would most likely have concentrated in urban regions. With it, railroads enjoyed an enormous boom. By 1900, virtually no corner of the country lacked rail service (Map 16.1).

Railroad companies transformed American capitalism. They adopted a legal form of organization, the corporation, that enabled them to raise private capital in prodigious amounts. In earlier decades, state legislatures had chartered corporations for specific public purposes, binding these creations to government goals and oversight. But over the course of the nineteenth century, legislatures gradually began to allow any business to become a corporation by simply applying for a state charter. Among the first corporations to become large interstate enterprises, private railroads were much freer than earlier corporations to do as they pleased, and after the Civil War they received lavish grants

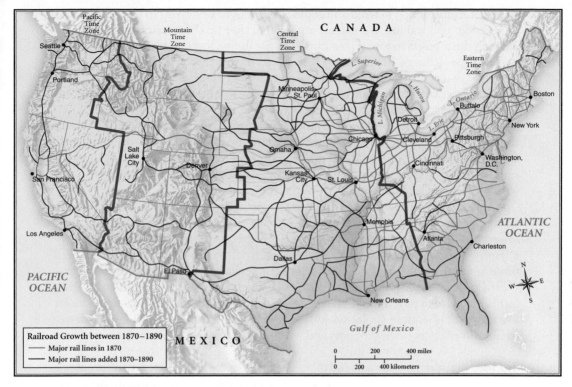

MAP 16.1 The Expansion of the Railroad System, 1870–1890

In 1860, the nation had 30,000 miles of rail track; by 1890, it had 167,000 miles. The tremendous burst of construction during the last twenty years of that period essentially completed the nation's rail network, although there would be additional expansion for the next two decades. The main areas of growth were in the South and in the lands west of the Mississippi. Time zones—introduced by the railroad companies in 1883—are marked by the gray lines.

of public resources with few strings attached. In this, their position was not unlike that of American banks in late 2008, after the big federal bailout: Even critics acknowledged that public aid to these giant companies was good for the economy, but they observed that it also lent government support to fabulous accumulations of private wealth.

Protective Tariffs and Economic Growth Along with the transformative power of railroads, the Republicans' protective tariffs helped build other U.S. industries, including textile and steel manufacturing in the Northeast and Midwest and (through a tariff on imported wool) sheep ranching in the West. Tariffs also funded government itself. In an era when the United States did not levy income taxes on corporations or individuals, tariffs provided the largest share of revenue for the treasury. The Civil War had left the Union with a staggering debt of $2.8 billion. Tariff income — which totaled $2.1 billion during the 1880s alone — erased that debt in two decades and then generated huge surpluses. These paid for a generous Union veterans' pension program, America's first steel battleships, and other federal projects.

As Reconstruction faltered and southern Democrats returned to Congress, tariffs came under political fire. Democrats argued that they taxed American consumers by denying them access to low-priced imported goods and forcing them to pay subsidies to U.S. manufacturers. Republicans claimed, conversely, that tariffs benefited ordinary workers because they created jobs, blocked low-wage foreign competition, and safeguarded America from the kind of industrial poverty that had arisen in Europe. According to this argument, tariffs helped American men earn enough to support their families; wives could devote themselves to homemaking, and children could go to school, not the factory. Republican campaign pamphlets described lurid conditions in "free trade" England, where women labored in mines and iron forges. For protectionist Republicans, then, high tariffs were akin to the abolition of slavery: They protected the most vulnerable workers and made the economy more just.

In fierce political debates over the tariff, which peaked in the 1880s, both sides were partly right. Protective tariffs did play a powerful role in economic growth. Along with other policies that promoted development, they helped transform the United States from a largely agricultural country into a world industrial power. Eventually, though, even protectionist Republicans had to admit that Democrats had a point: Tariffs had not prevented poverty in the United States. U.S. companies accumulated many benefits from tariffs but failed to pass most of these along to workers, who often toiled long hours for low wages. Furthermore, protective tariffs helped foster **trusts**, corporations that dominated whole sectors of the economy and wielded monopoly or near-monopoly power.

The Role of Courts | The rise of railroads and other giant corporations prompted many proposals for government regulation of these monster enterprises. But in this aspect of their economic policies, most historians agree, Republicans did not make government powerful enough. State legislatures did pass hundreds of regulatory laws after the Civil War, but with the federal government asserting new powers, interstate companies challenged such laws in federal courts. In *Munn v. Illinois* (1877), the U.S. Supreme Court acknowledged that states did have the right to regulate those businesses that served important public purposes, such as railroads and grain elevators. However, the justices feared that too many state and local regulations and impediments to business would fragment the national marketplace. Starting in the 1870s, they interpreted the "due process" clause of the new Fourteenth Amendment — which dictated that no state could "deprive any person of life, liberty, or property, without due process of law" — as shielding corporations from excessive regulation. Ironically, the Court refused to use that same amendment to protect freedpeople in the South.

In the Southwest, as well, federal courts promoted economic development at the expense of racial justice. Though the United States had taken control of New Mexico and Arizona after the Mexican War (1846–1848), economic change occurred slowly. In the 1870s, much land remained in the hands of Mexican farmers and ranchers. Many lived as *peónes*, under long-standing agreements with *patrónes*, or landowners, who held large tracts originally granted by the Spanish crown. But the post–Civil War years brought railroads and an influx of land-hungry Anglos. New Mexico's governor reported indignantly that Mexican shepherds were often "asked" to leave their ranges "by a cowboy or cattle herder with a brace of pistols at his belt and a Winchester in his hands."

Existing land claims were so complex that Congress eventually set up a special court to rule on land titles. Between 1891 and 1904, the court invalidated most traditional land claims, including those of *ejidos*, or village commons, in New Mexico. Mexican Americans lost about 64 percent of the contested lands on which the court ruled. In addition, much land was sold or appropriated through legal machinations like those of a notorious group of politicians and lawyers known as the Santa Fe Ring. The result was the displacement of thousands of Mexican American villagers and farmers.

Silver and Gold | In an era of nation building, U.S. and European policymakers sought new ways to rationalize economic markets. At a series of conferences, for example, industrializing nations tried to develop an international system of standard measurements and even a unified currency. Though this vision failed as each nation succumbed to self-interest, governments did increasingly agree that, for "scientific" reasons, money should be based on gold, which was thought to have an intrinsic worth above other metals. Great Britain had long been on the **gold standard**, meaning that paper notes from the Bank of England could be backed by gold held in the bank's vaults. During the 1870s and 1880s, the United States, Germany, France, Norway, and other countries also converted to gold.

Before they made the shift, these nations had been on a bimetallic standard: They issued both gold and silver coins, with the respective weights fixed at a relative value. The United States switched to the gold standard in part because treasury officials and financiers were watching developments out west. Geologists accurately predicted the discovery of immense lodes of silver, such as the Comstock Lode found at Virginia City, Nevada, without comparable new gold strikes. A massive influx of silver would clearly upset the long-standing ratio. Thus, with a law that became infamous to later critics as "the Crime of 1873," Congress chose gold. It directed the U.S. Treasury to cease minting silver dollars, and over a six-year period, to retire the **greenbacks** (paper dollars) that had been issued during the Civil War and replace them with notes from an expanded system of national banks. After this process was complete, in 1879, the treasury exchanged such notes for gold on request. (Advocates of bimetallism did achieve one small victory: The Bland-Allison Act of 1878 required the U.S. Mint to coin a modest amount of silver.)

By putting the United States on the gold standard, Republican policymakers sharply limited the nation's money supply, to the level of available gold. The amount of money circulating in the United States had been $30.35 per person in 1865; by 1880, it fell to only $19.36 per person. Today, few economists would sanction such a plan, especially for an economy growing at breakneck speed. They would recommend, instead, increasing money supplies to keep pace with development. But at the time, policymakers were reacting to the antebellum years of rampant speculation and the keenly felt hardships of inflation during the Civil War. The United States, as a developing country, also needed to attract investment capital from Britain, Belgium, and other European nations that were on the gold standard. Making it easy to exchange U.S. bonds and currency for gold encouraged European investors to bring their capital to the United States.

Republican policies fostered exuberant growth and a breathtakingly rapid integration of the economy. Railroads and telegraphs tied the nation together. U.S. manufacturers amassed staggering amounts of capital and built corporations of national and even global scope. To a large extent, the courts rejected federal regulation of these new enterprises. In 1900, census officials reported that "the mainland of the United States is the largest area in the civilized world . . . unrestricted by customs, excises, or national prejudice." With its immense, integrated marketplace of workers, consumers, raw materials, and finished products, the United States was poised to become a mighty industrial power.

The New Union and the World

The United States emerged from the Civil War with new leverage in its negotiation with European countries, especially Great Britain, whose navy dominated the high seas. Britain, which had permitted Confederate raiding vessels such as the CSS *Alabama* to be built in its shipyards, agreed afterward to submit to arbitration and pay the United States $15.5 million in damages. In the flush of victory, many Americans expected more British or Spanish territories to fall easily into the Union's lap. Senator Charles Sumner initially proposed, in fact, that Britain settle the *Alabama* claims by handing over Canada.

Such grand dreams were a logical extension of pre–Civil War conquests, especially in the Mexican War. With the East now linked to San Francisco by rail, merchants and manufacturers cast their eyes across the Pacific, hungry for trade with Asia. Americans had already established a dominant presence in the Hawaiian Islands, where U.S. whalers and merchant ships stopped for food and repairs. With the advent of steam-powered vessels, both the U.S. Navy and private shippers wanted more refueling points in the Caribbean and Pacific.

Even before the Civil War, these commercial aims had prompted the U.S. government to force Japan to open trade. For two centuries, after unpleasant encounters with Portuguese traders in the 1600s, Japanese leaders had adhered to a policy of strict isolation. Americans, who wanted refueling stations in Japan, argued that international trade would extend what one missionary called "commerce, knowledge, and Christianity, with their multiplied blessings." Whether or not Japan wanted these blessings was irrelevant. In 1854, Commodore Matthew Perry succeeded in getting Japanese officials to sign a treaty at Kanagawa, allowing U.S. ships to refuel at two ports. By 1858, America and Japan had commenced trade, and a U.S. consul took up residence in the Japanese capital, Edo (now known as Tokyo).

Union victory paved the way not only for increased trade with Japan and other parts of Asia but also for economic expansion in Latin America. While the United States was preoccupied with its internal war, France had deposed Mexico's government and installed an emperor. On May 5, 1867, Mexico overthrew the French invaders and executed Emperor Maximilian, events that have been celebrated ever since on Cinco de Mayo. Mexico — the part, that is, that the United States had not annexed in 1848 — regained independence. But without European backing, Mexico lay open to the economic designs of its increasingly powerful northern neighbor.

U.S. policymakers developed a new model for asserting power in Latin America and Asia, not by direct conquest of land and people but through international trade. The architect of this vision was William Seward, secretary of state from 1861 to 1869, under Lincoln and Johnson. A New Yorker of grandiose ambition and ego, Seward had been Lincoln's main rival for the presidential nomination in 1860. He believed, like many contemporaries, that Asia would soon become "the chief theatre of [world] events" and that trade there was key to America's prosperity. Seward urged the Senate to purchase

An American Merchant Ship in Yokohama Harbor, 1861
After the United States forcibly "opened" Japan to foreign trade in 1854, American and European ships and visitors became a familiar sight in the port of Yokohama. In these 1861 prints (which are two panels of a five-panel series), artist Hashimoto Sadahide meticulously details the activity on and around a merchant ship in Yokohama Harbor. On the left goods are carried onto the ship; on the right, two women dressed in Western style watch the arrival of another boat. In the background a steamship flies the French flag.
Library of Congress.

sites in both the Pacific and the Caribbean for naval bases and refueling stations. When Japan changed policy and tried to close its ports to foreign trade, Seward dispatched U.S. Navy vessels to join those of Britain, France, and the Netherlands. They reopened trade by force. At the same time, Seward urged annexation of Hawaii. He predicted that the United States would one day claim the Philippines and build a canal across the isthmus of Panama.

Seward's short-term achievements were modest. During his term of office, Congress was preoccupied with the Civil War and Reconstruction. After Lee's surrender, Americans had little enthusiasm for further military exploits. Seward achieved only two significant victories. In 1868, he secured congressional approval for the Burlingame Treaty with China, which guaranteed the rights of U.S. missionaries in China and set official terms for the emigration of Chinese laborers, some of whom were already clearing farmland and building railroads across the West. In the same year, Seward negotiated the purchase of Alaska from Russia. After the Senate approved the deal, Seward waxed poetic about his long-term dream:

> Our nation with united interests blest
> Not now content to poise, shall sway the rest;
> Abroad our empire shall no limits know,
> But like the sea in endless circles flow.

▶ What factors helped advance the integration of the national economy after the Civil War?

▶ How did the post–Civil War nation's economic goals shape its foreign policy? What role did William Seward play in advancing that policy?

Many Americans scoffed at the purchase of Alaska, a frigid arctic tract that the secretary of state's critics nicknamed "Seward's Icebox." But Seward mapped out a path that his Republican successors would follow thirty years later in an aggressive bid for global power. In the meantime, the United States laid foundations for its military and economic ascendance closer to home, through final conquest of the American West.

Incorporating the West

In the national economy they hoped to build, Republicans made a place for farms as well as factories. They sought to attract families to the West through the Homestead Act, which gave free public plots of 160 acres each to applicants who occupied and improved them. Lincoln administration officials not only promoted the Homestead Act in America but also advertised it in Europe, hoping to attract immigrants to serve in the Union Army and then settle the Great Plains. As early as 1860, Republicans hailed the future of "Uncle Sam's Farm" in popular lyrics written by the abolitionist Hutchinson Family Singers:

> A welcome, warm and hearty, do we give the sons of toil,
> To come west and settle and labor on Free Soil;
> We've room enough and land enough, they needn't feel alarmed —
> Oh! Come to the land of Freedom and vote yourself a farm.

Republicans hoped that hardworking families would cross the Mississippi River, claim homesteads, and help build up a continental empire — especially in the interior West, which was inhabited by Indian peoples but remained "empty" on U.S. government survey maps. They were eager to send miners and ranchers on the same mission.

Implementing this plan required innovative federal policies. In 1862, Congress created the federal Department of Agriculture to conduct research and distribute experimental seeds and advice to farmers. That same year, through the Morrill Act, Congress set aside 140 million acres of federal land to be sold by the states, to raise money for public universities; the goal, in part, was to foster technical expertise and scientific research. After the Civil War, Congress funded several geological surveys, dispatching U.S. Army officers, scientists, artists, and photographers west to map unknown terrain and catalog natural resources. In 1879, Congress consolidated these efforts into an influential new bureau in the Department of the Interior, the U.S. Geological Survey (USGS).

To a large extent, these policies succeeded in incorporating lands west of the Mississippi. European investors sank millions into mines and cattle operations. Railroads soon crisscrossed the West, and homesteaders and their families filed land claims by the thousands. The United States began to fully exploit its continental empire for minerals, lumber, and other raw materials that European nations obtained through overseas conquest. But in many parts of the West, dreams of unlimited growth outran reality. The Great Plains, in particular, proved resistant to conquest. After prospering in the 1870s, ranchers and farmers faced devastating blizzards and drought in the following decade. Republicans' bold initiatives proved insufficient to meet the challenges of life on the plains.

Cattlemen and Miners

As late as the Civil War years, great bison herds roamed the western grasslands. But overhunting and the introduction of European animal afflictions, like the bacterial disease brucellosis, were already decimating the herds. In the 1870s, hide hunters finished them off so thoroughly that, at one point, fewer than a hundred of the animals remained in U.S. territory. Hunters hidden downwind of a herd, under the right conditions, could kill

Cowboys on the Open Range
Cowboys were really farmhands on horseback, with the skills to work on the range. An ethnically diverse group, including blacks and Hispanics, they earned $25 a month, plus meals and a bed in the bunkhouse, in return for long hours of grueling, lonesome work. Cowboys were part of the system of open-range ranching, in which cattle (branded with their owners' mark) from different ranches grazed together. At roundups, cowboys separated the cattle by owner and branded the calves. Library of Congress.

four or five dozen bison at a time without moving from the spot. One Montana hunter told a visitor that he had killed sixty-three of the animals in less than an hour. Hunters took the hides but left the meat to rot, an act of vast wastefulness that shocked native peoples. An early conservationist called it "butchery [of the] most cruel kind."

Where bison had grazed, ranchers envisioned cow country. South Texas provided an early model for their ambitious plans. By the end of the Civil War, about five million head of longhorn cattle grazed on Anglo ranches there. In 1865, the Missouri Pacific Railroad reached Sedalia, Missouri, far enough west to be accessible as the Confederacy surrendered and Texas reentered the Union. A longhorn worth $3 in Texas might command $40 at Sedalia. With this incentive, Texas ranchers inaugurated the Long Drive, hiring cowboys to herd cattle hundreds of miles north to the new rail lines, which soon extended into Kansas. At Abilene and Dodge City, Kansas, ranchers sold their longhorns, and trail-weary cowboys crowded into saloons. These cattle towns captured the nation's imagination as symbols of the "Wild West." The reality was much less exciting. Cowboys, many of them African American and Hispanic, were actually farmhands on horseback who worked long, harsh hours for low pay.

News of easy money traveled fast. North of Texas, where land remained in the public domain, the grass was free and the rush was on. Open lands drew investors and adventurers eager for a taste of the West. By the early 1880s, as many as 7.5 million cattle were destroying the native grasses and trampling water holes on the plains, creating the conditions for a long-term ecological catastrophe. A cycle of good weather only postponed disaster, which arrived in 1886: record blizzards and bitter cold. An awful scene of rotting carcasses greeted cowhands as they rode onto the range in the spring. Further damaged by a severe drought the following summer, the cattle boom collapsed.

Thanks to new strategies, however, cattle ranching survived and became part of the integrated national economy. Ranchers had abandoned the Long Drive as railroads reached Texas in the 1870s. Meanwhile, northern cattlemen began to fence small areas of land and plant hay. Stockyards appeared beside the rapidly extending railroad tracks. Ranchers brought cattle there for sale, and trains took the gathered animals to giant slaughterhouses in Chicago and other midwestern centers, which turned them into cheap beef for customers back east. Hispanic shepherds from New Mexico also brought sheep to feed on the mesquite and prickly pear that supplanted native grasses. Sheep raising, previously scorned by ranchers as unmanly and threatening to cattle, became a major enterprise in the sparser high country of the Sierras and Rockies.

In these same years, extraction of mineral wealth became the basis for development in the Far West (Map 16.2). In the late 1850s, as easy pickings in the California gold rush diminished, prospectors had spread across the West in hopes of striking it rich elsewhere. They had found gold at many sites, including Nevada, the Colorado Rockies, and in South Dakota's Black Hills. As news of each gold strike spread, a wild remote area turned almost overnight into a mob scene of prospectors, traders, prostitutes, and saloon keepers (see Voices from Abroad, p. 488). At community meetings, prospectors would make their own laws, often using them as an instrument for excluding or discriminating against Mexicans, Chinese, and blacks.

At some sites, miners found other metals, including the copper, lead, and zinc that eastern industries demanded. The silver from Nevada's immense Comstock Lode, discovered in 1859, built the boomtown of Virginia City, which soon acquired fancy hotels, a Shakespearean theater, and even its own stock exchange. In 1870, a hundred saloons

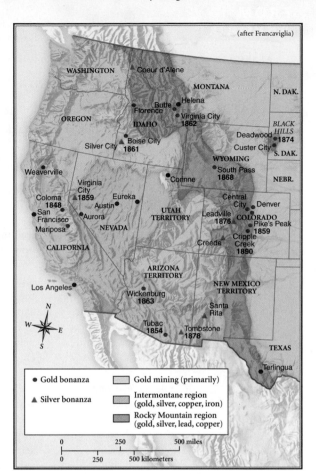

MAP 16.2 The Mining Frontier, 1848–1890

The Far West was America's gold country because of its geological history. Veins of gold and silver form when molten material from the earth's core is forced up into fissures caused by the tectonic movements that create mountain ranges, such as the ones that dominate the far western landscape. It was these veins, the product of mountain-forming activity many thousands of years earlier, that prospectors began to discover after 1848 and furiously exploit. Although widely dispersed across the Far West, the lodes that they found followed the mountain ranges bisecting the region and bypassing the great plateaus not shaped by the ancient tectonic activity.

operated in Virginia City, brothels lined D Street, and men outnumbered women two to one. In the 1880s, however, as the Comstock Lode played out, Virginia City suffered the fate of many mining camps: It became a ghost town. What remained was a ravaged landscape with mountains of debris, poisoned water sources, and surrounding lands stripped of timber. The insatiable demands of mining triggered the growth of smelting, lumbering, and other industries at many far-flung sites. Comstock, one critic remarked, was "the tomb of the forests of the Sierra." At the same time, booming California created a market for timber and produce from the Pacific Northwest. By the 1880s, Portland and Seattle blossomed into populous and important commercial centers.

Homesteaders

Before farmers would settle the western plains, they had to be persuaded that crops would grow there. Powerful interests worked hard to overcome the popular idea that the grassland was the **Great American Desert**. Railroads, eager to sell land the government had granted them, advertised aggressively. Land speculators, transatlantic steamship lines, and western states and territories joined the campaign. "Why emigrate to

A Western Boom Town
BARON JOSEPH ALEXANDER VON HÜBNER

During a leisurely trip around the world in 1871, Baron von Hübner, a distinguished Austrian diplomat, traveled across the United States, taking advantage of the newly completed transcontinental railroad to see the Wild West. After observing Mormon life in Salt Lake City, he went northward to Corinne, Utah, near the junction where the Central Pacific and Union Pacific railroads met. The baron might have arrived with romantic notions of the Wild West popular among Europeans of his class. That was not, however, how he departed.

Corinne has only existed for four years. Sprung out of the earth as if by enchantment, this town now contains upwards of 2,000 inhabitants, and every day increases in importance. It is a victualing center for the advanced posts of the [miners] in Idaho and Montana. A coach runs twice a week to Virginia City and to Helena, 350 and 500 miles to the north. Despite the serious dangers and the terrible fatigue of the journeys, these diligences are always full of passengers. Various articles of consumption and dry goods of all sorts are sent in wagons. The "high road" is but a rough track in the soil left by the wheels of the previous vehicles.

The streets of Corinne are full of white men armed to the teeth, miserable looking Indians dressed in the ragged shirts and trousers furnished by the federal government, and yellow Chinese with a business-like air and hard, intelligent faces. No town in the Far West gave me so good an idea as this little place of what is meant by "border life," the struggle between civilization and savage men and things. . . .

All commercial business centers in Main Street. The houses on both sides are nothing but boarded huts. I have seen some with only canvas partitions. . . . The lanes alongside of the huts, which are generally the resort of Chinese women of bad character,

lead into the desert, which begins at the doors of the last houses. . . .

To have on your conscience a number of man-slaughters committed in full day, under the eyes of your fellow citizens; to have escaped the reach of justice by craft, audacity, or bribery; to have earned a reputation for being "sharp," that is, for knowing how to cheat all the world without being caught — those are the attributes of the true rowdy in the Far West. . . . Endowed as they often are with really fine qualities — courage, energy, and intellectual and physical strength — they might in another sphere and with the moral sense which they now lack, have become valuable members of society. But such as they are, these adventurers have a reason for being, a providential mission to fulfill. The qualities needed to struggle with and conquer savage nature have naturally their corresponding defects. Look back, and you will see the cradles of all civilization surrounded with giants of Herculean strength ready to run every risk and to shrink from neither danger nor crime to attain their ends. It is only by the peculiar temper of the time and place that we can distinguish them from the back-woodsman and rowdy of the United States.

SOURCE: Oscar Handlin, ed., *This Was America* (Cambridge, MA: Harvard University Press, 1949), 313–315.

The Shores Family, Custer County, Nebraska, 1887
Whether the Shores family came west as Exodusters, we do not know. But in 1887, when this photograph was taken, they were well settled on their Nebraska farm, although still living in sod houses. The matriarch and patriarch of the family, Rachel and Jerry Shores (an ex-slave), are third and second from the right.
Nebraska State Historical Society.

Kansas?" asked a testimonial in *Western Trail*, the Rock Island Railroad's gazette. "Because it is the garden spot of the world. Because it will grow anything that any other country will grow, and with less work."

Newcomers found the soil beneath the native prairie grasses deep and fertile. Steel plows enabled them to break through the tough roots, while barbed wire provided cheap, effective fencing against roaming cattle. European immigrants brought strains of hard-kernel wheat that tolerated the extreme temperatures of the plains. As if to confirm the promoters' optimism, a wet cycle occurred between 1878 and 1886, shifting the zone of greater rainfall toward the Rockies. Americans decided that "rain follows the plow." Some attributed the increased rain to soil cultivation and tree planting. Others credited God. As one settler on the southern plains remarked, "The Lord just knowed we needed more land an' He's gone and changed the climate."

The motivation for most settlers, American or European, was to better themselves economically. Union veterans, who received favorable terms in staking homestead claims, played a major role in settling Kansas and other plains states. When a severe depression hit northern Europe in the 1870s, Norwegians and Swedes joined German emigrants in large numbers. At the peak of "American fever" in 1882, more than 105,000 Scandinavians left for the United States. Swedish and Norwegian became the primary languages in parts of Minnesota and the Dakotas.

For African Americans, the plains could represent a promised land of freedom. In 1879, some black communities chose to leave the South in a quest to escape poverty and white vengeance. Some six thousand blacks walked out of Mississippi and Louisiana, most carrying little but the clothes on their backs and faith in God. They called themselves **Exodusters**, participants in a great exodus to the prairie. The 1880 census reported 40,000 blacks in Kansas, by far the largest African American concentration in the West aside from Texas, where the expanding cotton frontier attracted hundreds of thousands of black migrants.

For all newcomers, taming the plains differed from "pioneering" in antebellum Iowa or Oregon. Dealers sold big new machines to help with plowing and harvesting. Western wheat traveled by rail to giant grain elevators, and it traded immediately on world markets. Hoping that frontier land values would appreciate rapidly, many farmers planned to profit from selling acreage as much as (or more than) from selling their crops. In boom times, many rushed into debt to acquire more land and better equipment. All these enthusiasms — for cash crops, land speculation, borrowed money, and new technology — bore witness to the conviction that farming was, as one agricultural journal remarked, a business "like all other business."

Women in the West | Those who came west to mine ore, to harvest lumber, or to tend cattle were overwhelmingly male, but homesteaders most often arrived as families. Women and children played critical roles in running farms. For this reason, farmers held a special place in Republicans' vision of a transformed nation. According to the ideal of domesticity, which had spread widely in the North before the Civil War, it was a man's devotion to his wife and children that caused him to work hard, be thrifty, and contribute to national progress. Meanwhile, women's commitment to the home, motherhood, and female Christian charity were considered crucial to the improvement of American civilization. Respectable settlers did not, of course, include in this vision of domesticity the thousands of prostitutes who worked in western mining camps and cattle towns.

Domesticity precipitated a political clash with a distinctive religious group that had already conquered part of the West: Mormons, or members of the Church of Jesus Christ of Latter-day Saints (LDS). Most Americans at the time were deeply hostile to Mormonism, especially the LDS practice of plural marriage — sanctioned by church founder Joseph Smith — through which some Mormon husbands married more than one wife. Mormons had their own view of women's role. In 1870, the Utah legislature granted full voting rights to women. This measure increased LDS power — since most Utah women were Mormons, and many men in mining camps were not — and recognized the central role of women in Mormon life. Amid the upheaval of Reconstruction, **polygamy** and women's voting rights became intertwined political controversies.

Utah was not the only place in the West where women found new rights and opportunities. As noted in Chapter 15, legislators in Wyoming Territory were the first to grant women full voting rights, in 1869. Western women also ran for public office and held government posts more often than in other regions of the country. Kansas women took the lead: Starting with Argonia in 1887, six towns elected women as mayors, and Oskaloosa boasted the nation's first all-female city council. Such work was part of a broader pattern of women's employment outside the home. Female lawyers, doctors, and entrepreneurs — even single female ranchers and homesteaders — were not uncommon in the West. A shortage of skilled labor and women's frontier self-reliance may have contributed to this marked trend.

Yet the vast majority of rural women endured considerable frontier hardship. This was especially true of those who bore and raised children on homesteads. For many, life on the plains was monotonous and isolated, especially when prosperity proved elusive. "Such an air of desolation," wrote a woman when she moved to the grasslands of Nebraska. Another, in Texas, spoke of "such a lonely country." In his novel *Giants in the Earth*, O. E. Rolvaag dramatically portrayed the fear and isolation of late-nineteenth-century Norwegian immigrant women on the Dakota prairie, far from the coastal fishing villages of their childhoods. Farmers' advocates soon warned that many farm wives on the plains were ending up in insane asylums. Though the claim was exaggerated, it circulated widely, suggesting that it resonated with homesteaders' personal experiences.

Debt and Aridity

Homesteading men suffered alongside women and children. In the late nineteenth century, due to technological innovation and the global expansion of export agriculture, farm products glutted world markets. The result was a long, precipitous drop in crop prices. Wheat, cotton, and corn farmers were especially vulnerable. In some years during the 1880s, the price of corn fell so low that Iowa farmers found it more cost-effective to keep their harvest and burn it in their stoves for winter heat than to sell it.

Farmers faced another problem: They were individual businessmen in a marketplace that rewarded **economies of scale**. Thus, they faced serious disadvantages in negotiating with the railroads and merchant companies that transported and sold their products, as well as bankers and equipment dealers who supplied them with machinery and loans. Many understood their dilemma all too keenly, and in the 1880s farmers in the West and South would build one of the most powerful protest movements in the history of American politics.

In the meantime, farmers on the Great Plains faced the additional challenge of a hostile environment. In the grasslands, a cloud of grasshoppers could descend and destroy a crop in a day; a prairie fire or hailstorm could do the job in an hour. In spring, homesteaders could face sudden, terrifying tornados; their winter experiences added the word *blizzard* to the American vocabulary in the 1870s. On the plains, also, farmers did not find what forested land had always provided — ample water and lumber for both fuel and construction. Newly arrived families often cut dugouts into hillsides and then, after a season or two, erected houses made of turf cut from the ground.

Over the long term, homesteaders discovered that the western grasslands did not receive enough rain to grow wheat and other grains. Despite the belief that "rain followed the plow," the cycle of rainfall shifted from wet to dry. "A wind hot as an oven's fury," reported the budding novelist Stephen Crane from Nebraska, "[f]rom day to day . . . raged like a pestilence," destroying the crops and leaving "farmers helpless, with no weapon against this terrible and inscrutable wrath of nature." By the late 1880s, some recently settled lands emptied as homesteaders fled in defeat — 50,000 of them from the Dakotas alone. It had become obvious that farming in the arid West required methods other than those used east of the Mississippi.

Clearly, 160-acre homesteads were the wrong size: Farmers needed either small, intensively irrigated plots or immense tracts that could support capital-intensive farming. The latter approach included dry farming, which involved deep planting to bring subsoil moisture to the roots and quick harrowing after rainfalls to turn over a dry mulch that slowed evaporation. Dry farming developed most fully on huge corporate farms in the Red River Valley of North Dakota. But even family farms, the norm elsewhere, could not survive on less than 300 acres of grain crops plus machinery for plowing, planting, and harvesting. Crop prices were too low, and the climate too unpredictable, to allow farmers to get by on less.

In this struggle, settlers regarded themselves as nature's potential conquerors, striving, as one pioneer remarked, "to get the land subdued and the wilde nature out of it." Much about its "wilde nature" was, of course, hidden to these strangers to the plains. They did not know that destroying biodiversity, which was what farming the plains really meant, opened pathways for exotic, destructive pests and weeds, and that plowing under the native bunch grasses rendered the soil vulnerable to erosion. By the turn of the twentieth century, about half the nation's cattle and sheep, one-third of its cereal crops, and nearly three-fifths of its wheat came from the Great Plains. But it was not a sustainable achievement. In the twentieth century, this renowned breadbasket was revealed to be, in the words of one historian, "the largest, longest-run agricultural and environmental miscalculation in American history."

John Wesley Powell, a one-armed veteran of the battle of Shiloh, predicted this catastrophe from an early date. Powell, employed by the new U.S. Geological Survey, led celebrated expeditions in the West. During one of these, he and his survey team navigated the rapids of the Colorado River in wooden boats through the Grand Canyon. In his *Report on the Lands of the Arid Regions of the United States* (1878), Powell told Congress bluntly that individual 160-acre homesteads would not work in dry regions. Impressed with the success of Mormon irrigation projects in Utah, Powell urged the United States to follow that model. He proposed that the government develop the West's water resources, building dams and canals and organizing landowners into local districts that would operate these democratically. Doubting that rugged individualism would succeed in the West, Powell proposed massive cooperation under government control.

Unfortunately, after heated debate, Congress rejected Powell's plan. His critics accused him of playing into the hands of large ranching corporations; boosters and would-be farmers were not yet willing to give up the dream of small homesteads dotted across the plains. But Powell turned out to be right. Though environmental historians do not always agree with Powell's proposed solution, they point to his *Report on Arid Lands* as a cogent critique of what went wrong on the Great Plains. By 1900, Americans would begin to agree with Powell that the federal government should not sell off this public land but instead hold and manage much of it in trust for the American people. At the same time, federal funding eventually paid for the dams and canal systems that supported intensive agriculture in many parts of the West.

Yellowstone | Though it took decades for Americans to accept irrigation and cooperative farming, the conquest of the West precipitated other innovations. So rapid and thorough was the West's incorporation into the national marketplace that some officials began to fear rampant overdevelopment. Amid the heady initiatives of Reconstruction, Congress therefore began to preserve sites of unusual natural splendor. As early as 1864, Congress gave 10 square miles of the Yosemite Valley to California for "public use, resort, and recreation." (In 1890, Yosemite reverted to federal control.) Praising the austere beauty of western landscapes, leading writers urged the United States to create more preserves. Congress responded in 1872 by setting aside 2 million acres of Wyoming's Yellowstone Valley "as a public park or pleasuring ground for the benefit and enjoyment of the people."

Tourism was at least as important a motive for Yellowstone's creation as dawning environmental consciousness. Here, again, railroads played a central role. Jay Cooke, owner of the Northern Pacific Railroad, lobbied Congress vigorously to get Yellowstone established. Luxury Pullman cars soon ushered visitors to Yellowstone's grand hotel, operated by the railroad itself. Thus, tourism became a booming enterprise in parts of the West at the same moment that farming, ranching, and mining did. Yellowstone and Yosemite became symbols of national pride, grander than Europe's castles. Busy urban Americans — especially members of the elite — began to find a refuge in the solitude of the natural parks. The national preserves of the West, as one senator put it, became a "great breathing-place for the national lungs."

The creation of Yellowstone National Park was fraught with complications. No one knew exactly what a "national park" was or how to operate it. The U.S. Army was dispatched to take charge of Yellowstone; only in the 1890s and early 1900s, when Congress established many more parks in the West, did consistent management policies emerge. In the meantime, soldiers spent much of their time evicting native peoples who hunted in the Yellowstone Valley. Congress's stipulation that the government keep the park in a "natural condition" required removing any Indians who might spoil its "natural" qualities. Yet, though native hunting was prohibited, wealthy eastern sportsmen quickly came out to hunt the big-game animals that had sustained Indian peoples like the Crows.

The creation of Yellowstone was an early, important step toward a public ethic of preservation and respect for land and wildlife. At the same time, the eviction of Indians from the park showed how creating small preserves of "uninhabited wilderness" was part of the process of conquest itself. Nothing demonstrated this more dramatically than what took place in Yellowstone in 1877. That year, the federal government forcibly removed the Nez Perce tribe from their ancestral lands in Idaho. Under the leadership of young Chief Joseph, the Nez Perce tried to flee to Canada. After a journey of 1,100 miles, they were forced to surrender just short of the border. On the way, five bands fled across Yellowstone; as Nez Perce warrior Yellow Wolf remembered, they "knew that country well." For thirteen days, Nez Perce men raided the valley for supplies, waylaying several groups of tourists. The following summer, just east of the park border, U.S. troops defeated a desperate group of Bannock Indians who, facing starvation on an assigned reservation, had fled to Yellowstone.

Both conflicts made headlines across the country. Americans, proud of their nation's new "pleasuring ground" at Yellowstone, were startled to find that the park was still a site of native resistance. Throughout the postwar decades, such conflicts reminded Americans that they were not, in fact, "settling" empty territory in the West. They were *unsettling* it from native peoples who already lived there. The drive toward settlement often trumped environmentalism. In 1874, for example, Congress tried to

▶ What environmental conditions did the homesteaders confront on the Great Plains? How did they respond to those conditions, and what were the consequences of that response?

▶ What prompted the U.S. government to set aside natural reserves such as Yellowstone? What were the results of that policy?

enact America's first wildlife protection bill, seeking to prohibit the killing of female bison by non-Indians. President Grant vetoed the bill. Treaties the United States had signed in 1867 and 1868 promised various Plains Indian tribes that they could live free and hunt as long as bison ranged "in such numbers as to justify the chase." Grant and the army knew that killing bison would cripple Indian resistance. To complete the work of conquest, the great herds of bison had to vanish from the plains.

A Harvest of Blood: Native Peoples Dispossessed

Before the Civil War, Congress reserved the Great Plains for nomadic peoples. After all, they did not believe the western prairie could be farmed. But in the era of railroads, steel plows, and Union victory, Americans suddenly had the power and desire to incorporate the whole plains. The U.S. Army fought against not only the loosely federated Sioux—who had become the major power on the grasslands—but also many other peoples who had agreed to live on reservations but found conditions so desperate that they fled in protest. These "reservation wars," caused largely by inconsistencies in federal policy, were messy and bitter. Faced with contradictory policies, failed military campaigns, a series of army atrocities, and egregious corruption in the Indian Bureau, Americans began to heed reformers who called for a new, more humane policy—one that would destroy native ways of life but "save" Indians themselves.

The Civil War and Indians on the Plains

In August 1862, the attention of most Unionists and Confederates was riveted on General George McClellan's failed campaign on the Chesapeake Bay peninsula. But in Minnesota, the Dakota Sioux were increasingly restive. In 1858, they had agreed to settle on a strip of land reserved for them by the government, in exchange for receiving regular payments and supplies. But Indian agents, contractors, and even Minnesota's territorial governor pocketed most of the funds meant for the Dakotas. When the Dakotas protested that their children were starving, state officials dismissed their appeals. Corruption was so egregious that one leading Minnesota clergyman, Episcopal bishop Henry Whipple, wrote an urgent appeal to President James Buchanan. "A nation which sows robbery," he warned, "will reap a harvest of blood."

Whipple's prediction proved correct: In the summer of 1862, a decade of anger boiled over. In a surprise attack, Dakota warriors fanned out through the Minnesota countryside, killing settlers and burning farms. They planned to sweep eastward to St. Paul but were repulsed at Fort Ridgely and the town of New Ulm. In the end, more than four hundred whites lay dead and thousands had fled. Panicked officials telegraphed for aid, spreading hysteria from Wisconsin to Colorado.

Enclosed Dakota Camp at Fort Snelling, Minnesota, 1862
During the trial of Dakota warriors involved in the 1862 rebellion, and through the harsh Minnesota winter that followed, more than a thousand members of the tribe were imprisoned inside an enormous enclosure on Pike Island, across from Fort Snelling, near St. Paul. A measles epidemic broke out in the crowded Dakota camp and dozens died, especially children. Though U.S. soldiers were often unfriendly toward their captives, local sentiment was even more hostile, and troops regularly marched through the camp, in part to protect the Dakota from vigilante violence. In 1863, all members of the tribe were forcibly removed from the state. In November 1862, photographer Benjamin Franklin Upton captured this image of Dakota tents within the Pike Island enclosure. Minnesota Historical Society.

Minnesotans' fierce response to the Dakota uprising set the stage for further conflict. A hastily appointed military court, bent on revenge, sentenced 307 Dakotas to death, making it clear that Indians who rebelled would be treated as criminals rather than captured warriors. Abraham Lincoln, who insisted on reviewing the trial records, commuted most of the sentences but authorized the deaths of 38 Dakota men. They were hanged just after Christmas 1862 in the largest mass execution in U.S. history. Two months later, Congress canceled all treaties with the Dakotas, revoked their annuities, and expelled them from Minnesota. Faced with these cruel conditions, scattered bands fled farther west to join nonreservation allies.

As this rebellion showed, the Civil War had created two dangerous conditions in the West. First, with the Union Army fighting the Confederacy, western whites felt especially vulnerable to Indian attacks. Second, fearful westerners found that when they chose to, they could fight Indians with minimal federal oversight. In the wake of the Dakota uprising, worried Coloradans favored a military campaign against the Cheyennes — allies of the Sioux — even though the Cheyennes had shown little evidence of hostility. Colorado militia leader John M. Chivington, an aspiring politician, determined to quell public anxiety and make his own career.

In May 1864, Chivington's militia attacked a Cheyenne encampment, shooting down a chief who had made peace terms with the United States. After witnessing this murder, Cheyenne chief Black Kettle surrendered his own band to federal agents, who instructed them to camp in the area of Sand Creek, in eastern Colorado, until a treaty could be signed. On November 29, 1864, Chivington's Colorado militia attacked this camp while most of the warriors were out hunting. They hunted down and killed more than a hundred women, children, and even infants, following an officer's orders to leave none alive. The militia rode back for a celebration in Denver, where they hung Cheyenne scalps (and women's genitals) from the rafters of the Apollo Theater.

The northern plains exploded in conflict. Infuriated by the Sand Creek massacre, Cheyennes carried war pipes to the Arapahos and Sioux, who attacked and burned settlements along the South Platte River. Ordered to subdue these peoples, the U.S. Army failed miserably: Officers were not even able to locate the enemy, who traveled rapidly in small bands and knew the country well. This humiliation was compounded in December 1866 when 1,500 Sioux warriors executed a perfect ambush, luring Captain William Fetterman and 80 soldiers from a Wyoming fort and wiping them out. With this victory the Sioux succeeded in closing the Bozeman Trail, a private road under army protection that had served as the main route into Montana.

General William Tecumseh Sherman, who had taken command of the army in the West, swore to defeat the Plains Indians, "even to their extermination." But the Union hero who had helped defeat the Confederacy met his match on the plains. Another year of fighting proved expensive, exhausting, and inconclusive. In 1868, the Sioux, led by the Oglala band under Chief Red Cloud, told a peace commission they would not sign any treaty unless the United States pledged to abandon all its forts along the Bozeman Trail. The commission agreed. Red Cloud had won.

In the wake of these events, eastern public opinion turned against the Indian wars, which seemed at best ineffective and costly, and at worst brutal. Congress held hearings on the slaughter at Sand Creek. Though Chivington, now a civilian, was never prosecuted, the massacre became an infamous example of western vigilantism. By the time Ulysses Grant entered the White House in 1869, the congressional leaders orchestrating radical Reconstruction in the South also began to seek solutions to the "Indian problem" out West.

Grant's Peace Policy

When he entered the White House, Ulysses S. Grant inherited an Indian policy in disarray. Federal incompetence was highlighted by yet another mass killing of friendly Indians in January 1870, this time on the Marias River in Montana, by an army detachment that shot and burned to death 173 Piegan (Blackfoot) women and children. Having run out of other promising options, Grant developed a peace policy for the West, based on recommendations from Christian reformers. He put reformers themselves in charge. These men and women, including many former abolitionists, had created such organizations as the Indian Rights Association and the Women's National Indian Association. They rejected the racism of many westerners and soldiers like General Philip Sheridan, who once declared, "The only good Indians I ever saw were dead."

Reformers argued that native peoples had the innate capacity to become equal with whites. They believed, however, that Indians could achieve that goal only if they were Christianized and educated in white ways. Reformers thus aimed to destroy native languages, cultures, and religions. As one put it, they would "kill the Indian and save the man." Despite their humane intentions, peace advocates' condescension was obvious. They ignored dissenters like Dr. Thomas Bland of the National Indian Defense Association, who suggested that instead of an "Indian problem" there might be a "white problem" — the refusal to permit Indians to live according to their own traditional ways. To most nineteenth-century Americans, such a notion was shocking and uncivilized.

Indian Boarding Schools Reformers focused their greatest energy on educating the next generation. Realizing that **assimilation**, or adoption of white ways, was difficult when children lived at home, agents and missionaries worked hard to enroll children in off-reservation schools. The most famous of these, Pennsylvania's Carlisle School, was founded in 1879. Native families were exhorted, bullied, and bribed into sending their children to such schools, where Indian children were required to speak only English and missionaries forced them to take up white ways (see American Voices, p. 498). The Lakota boy Plenty Kill, who became one of Carlisle's first students at age eleven and received the new name Luther, remembered his loneliness and terror

Indian School
This photograph was taken at the Riverside Indian School in Anadarko, Oklahoma Territory. The pupils have been shorn of their braids and clothed in Mother Hubbard dresses and shirts and trousers — one step on the journey into the mainstream of white American society. Children as young as five were separated from their families and sent to Indian schools that taught them new skills while pressuring them to abandon traditional Indian ways. University of Oklahoma, Western History Collections.

AMERICAN VOICES

Becoming White   ZITKALA-ŠA (GERTRUDE SIMMONS BONNIN)

Zitkala-Ša, known later as the author Gertrude Simmons Bonnin, recalled in 1900 her painful transformation from Sioux child to pupil at a Quaker mission school in Indiana.

The first day . . . a paleface woman, with white hair, came up after us. We were placed in a line of girls who were marching into the dining room. These were Indian girls, in stiff shoes and closely clinging dresses. The small girls wore sleeved aprons and shingled hair. As I walked noiselessly in my soft mocassins, I felt like sinking into the floor, for my blanket had been stripped from my shoulders. . . . Late in the morning, my friend Judewin gave me a terrible warning. Judewin knew a few words of English; and she had overheard the paleface woman talk about cutting our long, heavy hair. Our mothers had taught us that only unskilled warriors who were captured had their hair shingled by the enemy. Among our people, short hair was worn by mourners, and shingled hair by cowards! . . . In spite of myself, I was carried downstairs and tied fast in a chair. I cried aloud, shaking my head all the while until I felt the cold blades of the scissors against my neck, and heard them gnaw off one of my thick black braids. Then I lost my spirit. . . .

Now, as I look back upon the recent past, I see it from a distance, as a whole. I remember how, from morning till evening, many specimens of civilized peoples visited the Indian school. The city folks with canes and eyeglass, the countrymen with sunburned cheeks and clumsy feet. . . . Both sorts of these Christian palefaces were alike astounded at seeing the children of savage warriors so docile and industrious.

As answers to their shallow inquiries they received the students' sample work to look upon. Examining the neatly figured pages, and gazing upon the Indian girls and boys bending over their books, the white visitors walked out of the schoolhouse well-satisfied: they were educating the children of the red man! . . .

In this fashion many have passed idly through the Indian schools during the last decade, afterward to boast of their charity to the North American Indian. But few there are who have paused to question whether real life or long lasting death lies beneath this semblance of civilization.

SOURCE: Linda K. Kerber and Jane Sherron De Hart-Mathews, eds., *Women's America: Refocusing the Past*, 2nd ed. (New York: Oxford University Press, 1987), 254–257.

upon arrival: "The big boys would sing brave songs, and that would start the girls to crying. . . . The girls' quarters were about a hundred and fifty yards from ours, so we could hear them." After having his hair cut short, Plenty Kill felt a profound change in his identity. "None of us slept well that night," he recalled. "I felt that I was no more Indian, but would be an imitation of a white man."

Even in the first flush of reform zeal, Grant's peace policy faced daunting hurdles. Most Indian peoples had been yanked off their traditional lands and assigned to barren ground that would have defeated the most enterprising farmer. Poverty and dislocation made Indians especially vulnerable to the ravages of infectious diseases like measles and scarlet fever. In the meantime, Quaker, Presbyterian, and Methodist reformers fought nasty turf battles among themselves and with Catholic missionaries. Also, despite the efforts of reformers, agents and traders continued to skim off money and supplies from the people they were supposed to protect. Rutherford B. Hayes's administration (1877–1881) undertook housecleaning at the Bureau of Indian Affairs, but corruption lingered.

From the Indian point of view, reformers often became just another interest group in a crowded field of whites who sent hopelessly mixed messages. Individual army officers, agents, and missionaries ranged from sympathetic to utterly ruthless. Many times, after chiefs thought they had reached a face-to-face agreement, they found it denied or drastically altered by Congress or the Bureau of Indian Affairs. The Nez Perce chief Joseph observed, "[T]he white people have too many chiefs. They do not understand each other. They do not all talk alike. . . . I cannot understand why so many chiefs are allowed to talk so many different ways, and promise so many different things." A Kiowa chief agreed: "We make but few contracts, and them we remember well. The whites make so many they are liable to forget them. The white chief seems not to be able to govern his braves."

Native peoples were nonetheless forced to accommodate, as independent tribal governance and treaty making came to an end. Back in the 1830s, the U.S. Supreme Court had declared Indians no longer sovereign but rather "domestic dependent nations." On a practical basis, however, officers in the field and the Senate in Washington had continued to negotiate treaties as late as 1869. In 1871, the House of Representatives, long jealous of Senate privileges, passed a bill to abolish all treaty making with Indians. The Senate agreed, provided that existing treaties remained in force. It was one more step in a long, torturous erosion of native rights. Eventually, the U.S. Supreme Court ruled in *Lone Wolf v. Hitchcock* (1903) that Congress could make whatever Indian policies it chose, ignoring all existing treaties. That same year, in *Ex Parte Crow Dog*, the Court ruled that no Indian was a citizen unless Congress designated him so. Indians were henceforth wards of the government. These rulings remained in force until the New Deal of the 1930s.

Breaking Up Tribal Lands | While the United States exerted increasing legal power over native peoples, reformers made another effort to assimilate them through the Dawes Severalty Act, passed in 1887. This law had long been the dream of Senator Henry L. Dawes of Massachusetts, a leader of the Indian Rights' Association. Dawes saw the reservation system as an ugly relic of the past. He hoped to break up tribal landholding and give Indians **severalty** (individual ownership of land) by dividing reservations into homesteads, just like those of white farmers in the West. Supporters of the plan believed that ownership of private property would encourage Indians to adopt white ways. It would lead, Dawes wrote, to "a personal sense of independence." Property ownership, echoed another reformer, would make the Indian man "intelligently selfish, . . . with a *pocket that aches to be filled with dollars!*"

The Dawes Act was a disaster. It played into the hands of whites who coveted Indian land: They quickly urged that all reservation lands not needed for allotments be sold to non-Indians. Further, the Bureau of Indian Affairs (BIA) implemented the law carelessly, to the shock of Dawes and other sponsors. In Indian Territory, a government commission seized more than 15 million "surplus" acres from native tribes by 1894. This opened the way for whites to convert the last federal territory set aside for native peoples into the state of Oklahoma. Before the Dawes Act, American Indians had held more than

155 million acres of land across the United States; by 1900, this had dropped to 77 million acres. By the time of the Indian Reorganization Act of 1934, native peoples had also lost 66 percent of their individually allotted lands through fraud, BIA mismanagement, and pressure to sell to whites.

The End of Armed Resistance

Despite the glaring flaws that soon became apparent, Americans by the mid-1870s believed they had solved the "Indian problem" in the lands west of the Mississippi. In the Southwest, such formidable peoples as the Kiowas and Comanches had been forced onto designated reservations. The Navajo (or Diné) people, exiled under horrific conditions during the Civil War, were permitted to reoccupy their traditional homeland and abandoned further military resistance. An outbreak among California's Modoc people in 1873 — again, humiliating to the army — had at last been subdued. Only Sitting Bull, a leader of the powerful Lakota Sioux on the northern plains, openly refused to go to a reservation. He often crossed into Canada, where he told reporters that "the life of white men is slavery. . . . I have seen nothing that a white man has, houses or railways or clothing or food, that is as good as the right to move in open country and live in our own fashion."

Sitting Bull and Custer In 1874, the Lakotas faced a direct provocation. General George Armstrong Custer, a brash self-promoter who had graduated last in his class at West Point, led an expedition into South Dakota's Black Hills and loudly proclaimed the discovery of gold. Amid the severe depression that began in 1873, prospectors rushed in. The United States, reneging on its 1868 treaty, pressured Sioux leaders to sell the Black Hills, but the chiefs said no. Ignoring this answer, the government demanded in 1876 that all Sioux gather at the federal agencies. The policy backfired: Not only did Sitting Bull and others refuse to report, but other Sioux, Cheyennes, and Arapahos slipped away from reservations to join Sitting Bull.

Amid the nation's centennial celebration in July 1876, Americans received awful news. On June 25–26, General Custer had led 210 men of the Seventh Cavalry in an ill-considered assault on Sitting Bull's camp beside the Little Big Horn River in Montana. In defense, the Sioux and their allies had killed the attackers to the last man. The story of Custer's "last stand" quickly served to justify American conquest. Long after Americans forgot the massacres of Cheyenne women and children at Sand Creek and Piegan people on the Marias River, prints of the Battle of Little Big Horn hung in barrooms across the country. William F. "Buffalo Bill" Cody, in his traveling Wild West performances, enacted a revenge killing of the Cheyenne warrior Yellow Hand, in a tableau that Cody called "first scalp for Custer." Notwithstanding that the tableau featured a white man scalping a Cheyenne, Cody depicted this as a triumph for civilization in the West.

Little Big Horn was the last major military victory of Plains Indians against the U.S. Army. Pursued relentlessly after Custer's defeat, Sioux warriors watched their children starve through a bitter winter. Slowly, families trickled into the agencies, accommodating themselves to life on reservations that the U.S. government fragmented and drastically reduced in size. The next year the Nez Perce, fleeing desperately for the Canadian border, also surrendered. The last holdout was in the Southwest: Chiricahua Apache leader Geronimo. Like many others, Geronimo had accepted reservation life

Little Plume and Yellow Kidney

Photographer Edward S. Curtis took this photograph of Piegan (Blackfeet) warrior Little Plume and his son Yellow Kidney. Curtis's extensive collection of photographs of Native Americans remains a valuable resource for historians. Curtis, however, altered his images for publication to make his native subjects seem more "authentic": Even though Indians made widespread use of nonnative furniture, clothes, and other consumer goods (even Singer sewing machines), Curtis removed those from the frame. He also retouched photographs to remove items such as belts and watches. Note the circular "shadow" here, against the lodge wall, near Little Plume's right arm: The original photograph included a clock. Library of Congress.

but then took up arms out of sheer desperation. Recalling the desolate land the tribe had been allotted, one Apache said, "[T]here was nothing but cactus, rattlesnakes, heat, rocks, and insects. . . . Many, many of our people died of starvation." The army recruited other Apaches to track Geronimo into the hills; in September 1886, he surrendered for the last time. The Chiracahua Apaches never returned to their homeland. The United States had completed its military conquest of the West.

Strategies of Survival

Even though the warpath closed, many native peoples continued secretly to practice traditional customs. Away from the disapproving eyes of agents, missionaries, and teachers, they passed on their languages, oral histories, and traditional arts and medicine from each generation to the next. Frustrated missionaries often concluded that little could be accomplished on the reservations because bonds of kinship and custom were so strong. Yet they had difficulty enrolling students in off-reservation boarding schools because so many parents hated to relinquish their children. Thus, most Indian schools ended up on or near reservations, and white teachers were forced to accept their pupils' continued participation in the rhythms of reservation life.

Selectively, at least, most native peoples accepted some white ways. Many parents urged their sons and daughters to study hard at white-run schools, learn English, and develop skills to help them succeed in the new world that confronted them. Some of these children grew up to be writers and artists who interpreted native experiences for national audiences. Others took up law and medicine. While enrolled at the Carlisle School in Pennsylvania, the son of a Quechan chief from Arizona wrote to the agent on his family's reservation. He warned, in fluent English, that he knew about the agent's thievery and would write to Washington to expose him if he did not stop.

In practice, most native people relied upon both tradition and innovation as they sought the best path forward. One of the most famous examples was a Dakota boy named Ohiyesa, who grew up to become Dr. Charles Eastman. Posted to the Pine Ridge Reservation in South Dakota, Eastman practiced medicine side by side with traditional healers, whom he respected. While assimilating to European American culture, Eastman wrote many popular books under his Dakota name, Ohiyesa. He remembered that when he left for boarding school, his father said, "We have now entered upon this life, and there is no going back. . . . Remember, my boy, it is the same as if I sent you on your first war-path. I shall expect you to conquer."

Nothing exemplified this syncretism better than the Ghost Dance movement of the late 1880s, which fostered the hope that native peoples could, through sacred dances, resurrect the bison and create a great storm that would drive whites back across the Atlantic. The Ghost Dance drew on significant Christian elements as well as native ones. As it spread from reservation to reservation — from Paiutes to Arapahos to Sioux — native peoples across the West began to develop new forms of pan-Indian identity and cooperation.

Unfortunately, the outcome of the Ghost Dance movement bore witness to the lethal exertion of authority by misunderstanding whites. When a group of Lakota Sioux Ghost Dancers left their South Dakota reservation after police there killed Sitting Bull in December 1890, they were pursued by the U.S. Seventh Cavalry, in the fear that further spread of the Ghost Dance would provoke war. On December 29, at Wounded Knee Creek, the army caught up with the fleeing Indians and killed more than 150 Lakota men, women, and children. Like so many others — such as Sand Creek and the killing of Piegan on the Marias River — this massacre could have been avoided if U.S. officials had had a clearer understanding of native viewpoints, and had pursued a fairer and more consistent course of action. The deaths at Wounded Knee stand as a final indictment against decades of relentless U.S. expansion, chaotic and conflicting policies, and bloody mistakes.

Less than two months after the Wounded Knee massacre, General William T. Sherman died in New York. As the nation marked his passing with pomp and speech-making, commentators noted that Sherman's career had paralleled the rise of the United States. Sherman's first military exploits had been against Seminoles in Florida; later, during the Mexican War (1846–1848), the army sent him west to help claim California. After a stint in civilian life, Sherman returned to the military when the Civil War broke out, warning a friend in Virginia that northerners were "not going to let this country be destroyed." Before war's end, Sherman's name was infamous throughout the South. It was appropriate that this general who helped subdue the South was then sent west to defeat the Sioux and Cheyennes, until he declared that "the Indian question has become one of sentiment and charity, but not of war."

When Sherman had graduated from West Point in 1840, the United States counted twenty-six states, none of them west of Missouri. At his death in 1891, the nation boasted forty-four states, in settled territory stretching to the Pacific coast. The United States now rivaled Britain and Germany as an industrial giant, and its dynamic economy was drawing immigrants from Asia, Latin America, and Eastern and Southern Europe to join those from Africa and Western Europe. Over the span of Sherman's career, the United States had become a major player on the world stage. It had done so, in part, through the kind of fierce military conquest that Sherman himself made famous, as well as through bold expansions of federal power. Because of the conflicts and decisions made in Sherman's lifetime, the children and grandchildren of Civil War heroes inherited a vast empire. In the coming decades, it would be up to them to determine how to use the nation's new power at home and abroad.

▶ How did the Civil War affect relations between the Sioux and their allies, white settlers, and the U.S. government?

▶ What effect did Grant's peace policy and subsequent U.S. Indian policy have on native peoples? What survival strategies did conquered native peoples develop?

SUMMARY

Between 1861 and 1877, the United States completed its conquest of the continent. After the Civil War, the expansion of railroads fostered the integration of the national economy. Republicans in the federal government promoted this integration by erecting protective tariffs, while federal courts made rulings that facilitated economic growth and strengthened corporations. To attract foreign investment, Republican policymakers placed the nation on the gold standard. These policymakers also pursued a vigorous foreign policy, acquiring Alaska and asserting U.S. power indirectly through control of international trade in Latin America and Asia.

An important result of economic integration was the incorporation of the Great Plains. Cattlemen built an industry linked to the integrated economy, though in the process nearly driving the native bison to extinction. Homesteaders confronted harsh environmental conditions as they converted the grasslands for agriculture. Republicans championed homesteader families as representatives of domesticity, an ideal opposed to Mormon plural marriage in Utah. Homesteading accelerated the rapid, often violent, transformation of the western environment. Perceiving this transformation, the federal government began setting aside natural preserves such as Yellowstone, often clashing with Native Americans who wished to hunt on the land.

Such conflict over land ultimately led to the conquest of Native Americans. During the Civil War, white settlers clashed with the Sioux and their allies. Grant's peace policy sought to end this conflict by forcing Native Americans to assimilate western practices. Native American armed resistance continued through the 1870s and 1880s, ending with

Geronimo's surrender in 1886. Thereafter, Native Americans survived, though not without further conflict, by either secretly continuing their traditions or selectively adopting white ways. Due in part to the determined military conquest of this period, the United States claimed for itself a major role on the world stage.

For additional primary sources from this period, see *Documents for America's History*, Seventh Edition.

For Web sites, images, and documents related to topics and places in this chapter, visit *Make History* at **bedfordstmartins.com/henrettaconcise**.

For Further Exploration

On the subject of the economic consolidation of the West, see William Cronon's *Nature's Metropolis* (1991). John Stover's *American Railroads*, 2nd ed. (1997), is a good overview. On Republican policies, see Richard Bensel, *The Political Economy of American Industrialization, 1877–1900* (2000); on tariff debates, Joanne Reitano, *The Tariff Question in the Gilded Age* (1994); on monetary policy, Walter T. K. Nugent, *The Money Question During Reconstruction* (1967). On foreign policy after the Civil War, see the relevant sections of Walter LaFeber, *The American Search for Opportunity* (1993). Thomas Bender explores U.S. nation building in *A Nation Among Nations* (2006).

On the West, see Patricia Nelson Limerick's *The Legacy of Conquest* (1987), Richard White's *"It's Your Misfortune and None of My Own"* (1991), and Andrew Isenberg, *The Destruction of the Bison* (2000). On farming, see Frieda Knobloch, *The Culture of Wilderness* (1996); on women, see Susan Armitage and Elizabeth Jameson, eds., *The Women's West* (1987), and Sarah Barringer Gordon, *The Mormon Question* (2002). María Montoya explores Mexican displacement in *Translating Property* (2002). On the Indian wars, see Robert Utley, *The Indian Frontier of the American West* (1984), and Mark David Spence, *Dispossessing the Wilderness* (1999). Assimilation policies are covered in Frederick Hoxie, *A Final Promise* (1984), and David Wallace Adams, *Education for Extinction* (1995). Good sites are **www.americanwest.com** and **www.pbs.org/nationalparks**.

Test Your Knowledge

For practice quizzes, activities, and other study tools, visit the Online Study Guide at **bedfordstmartins.com/henrettaconcise**.

TIMELINE

1854	► United States "opens" Japan to trade
1859	► Comstock silver lode discovered in Nevada
1862	► Homestead Act
	► Dakota Sioux uprising in Minnesota
1864	► Sand Creek massacre of Cheyenne in Colorado
	► Yosemite Valley reserved as public park
1865	► Long Drive of Texas longhorns begins
1866	► Sioux under Red Cloud succeed in closing Bozeman Trail in Montana
1868	► Treaty confirms Sioux rights to Powder River hunting grounds
	► Burlingame Treaty with China
1869	► Transcontinental railroad completed
1870	► Utah gives full voting rights to women
	► Wyoming gives full voting rights to women
1875	► John Wesley Powell publishes *Report on Arid Lands*
	► Sioux ordered to vacate Powder River hunting grounds; war breaks out
1876	► Battle of the Little Big Horn
1877	► San Francisco anti-Chinese riots
	► *Munn v. Illinois* Supreme Court decision
1879	► Exoduster migration to Kansas
	► United States placed fully on gold standard
1886	► Dry cycle begins on the Great Plains
1887	► Dawes Severalty Act
1890	► Massacre of Indians at Wounded Knee, South Dakota

5
PART

Bold Experiments in an Era of Industrialization

1877–1929

Visiting the United States in 1905, British visitor James Bryce remarked on its "prodigious material development." He wrote that "rural districts are being studded with villages, the villages are growing into cities, the cities are stretching out long arms of suburbs." Bryce was witnessing America's birth as a global industrial power. In 1866 the nation was overwhelmingly rural and dependent on foreign capital as it recovered from a crippling civil war. By 1929, industrialization had introduced new ways of working and living. The United States also began to assert itself on the world stage, claiming overseas territories and playing a decisive role in World War I.

Industrialization required political innovation. As former president Theodore Roosevelt declared in 1910, American citizens needed to "effectively control the mighty commercial forces which they have called into being." Workers, farmers, and urban progressives worked to clean up politics, regulate corporations, and fight poverty. In their creative responses to the problems of a new industrial age, such reformers gave their name to the Progressive Era.

ECONOMY The post–Civil War economy grew rapidly, a trend intensified by industrial production during World War I. Millions of immigrants arrived from around the globe; though millions found places in the economy, Asians faced legal exclusion, and restrictions on overall numbers of immigrants were enacted in the 1920s. Giant corporations developed national and even global networks of production, marketing, and finance. Their complex structures opened new career opportunities for middle-class managers, salesmen, and women office workers. Traditional craftsmen, however, found themselves displaced, while factory workers and miners endured harsh conditions, low pay, and cycles of unemployment. Farmers also suffered from falling crop prices, caused by expanding world production.

POLITICS AND LAW The fierce struggles of post-Reconstruction politics centered on the scope of government power. In the 1880s, Republicans increasingly became champions of business. Though

Republican Theodore Roosevelt championed key reforms during his presidency (1901–1909), much reform energy passed to other parties. The Greenback-Labor, People's (or Populist), and Progressive parties all proposed expanding government powers in response to industrialization and concentrated wealth. While none won national power, these parties shaped the course of reform. Democrats, who had long called for limited government, began in the 1890s to advocate stronger government intervention to fight poverty and restrain big business. The party had little opportunity to enact national programs during the Republican-dominated years of 1894–1910 and the prosperous, complacent decade of the 1920s. But in between, during the presidency of Democrat Woodrow Wilson (1913–1921), the party enacted an impressive slate of reforms. By 1929, when the Great Depression hit, Democrats were poised to enact the New Deal.

REFORM An array of reformers, loosely known as progressives, responded to the problems caused by industrialization. More radical proposals tended to come from mass-based coalitions of workers and farmers; pressure from such groups combined with the efforts of middle-class and urban reformers to generate new policies. Reformers sought to enhance democracy, rein in the power of corporations, uphold labor rights, and promote public health and safety. Progressives ran up against formidable political obstacles, especially from the Supreme Court. Nonetheless, by 1920, national, state, and local governments enacted a range of landmark laws, representing the early emergence of the modern state.

CULTURE While the nineteenth-century values of thrift, piety, and domesticity never entirely faded, they faced serious challenges in the era of industrialization. Women asserted more independent roles within the family and in public life. The secular pleasures of consumer culture encouraged Americans to spend money and have fun. Americans cheered for professional sports teams, and by the 1920s flocked to the movies and purchased millions of automobiles. As early as the 1880s, literary realism marked a break with Victorian culture as one element of the modernism that led to such innovations as jazz music and abstract art.

FOREIGN RELATIONS Policymakers of the post–Civil War era focused on overseas trade. Victorious against Spain in the War of 1898, the United States claimed overseas colonies and asserted control over the Caribbean basin. Though President Woodrow Wilson attempted to maintain neutrality at the start of World War I, trade ties helped draw America into the conflict on the Allied side. Wilson sought to influence the peace, but Allied leaders ignored his proposals and the U.S. Senate rejected the treaty altogether. At war's end, though America exerted tremendous clout in global affairs, its role on the world stage remained uncertain.

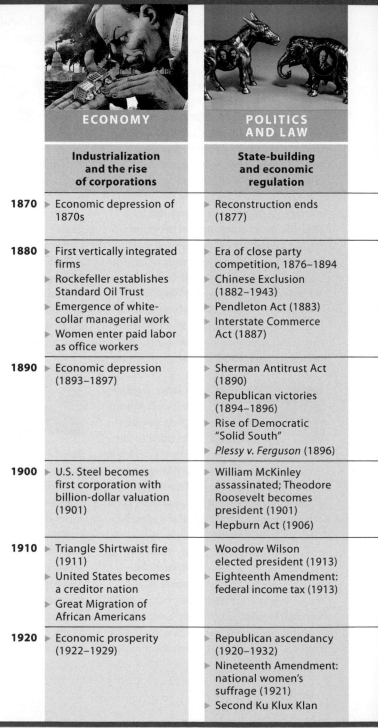

ECONOMY	POLITICS AND LAW
Industrialization and the rise of corporations	**State-building and economic regulation**

	ECONOMY	POLITICS AND LAW
1870	▸ Economic depression of 1870s	▸ Reconstruction ends (1877)
1880	▸ First vertically integrated firms ▸ Rockefeller establishes Standard Oil Trust ▸ Emergence of white-collar managerial work ▸ Women enter paid labor as office workers	▸ Era of close party competition, 1876–1894 ▸ Chinese Exclusion (1882–1943) ▸ Pendleton Act (1883) ▸ Interstate Commerce Act (1887)
1890	▸ Economic depression (1893–1897)	▸ Sherman Antitrust Act (1890) ▸ Republican victories (1894–1896) ▸ Rise of Democratic "Solid South" ▸ *Plessy v. Ferguson* (1896)
1900	▸ U.S. Steel becomes first corporation with billion-dollar valuation (1901)	▸ William McKinley assassinated; Theodore Roosevelt becomes president (1901) ▸ Hepburn Act (1906)
1910	▸ Triangle Shirtwaist fire (1911) ▸ United States becomes a creditor nation ▸ Great Migration of African Americans	▸ Woodrow Wilson elected president (1913) ▸ Eighteenth Amendment: federal income tax (1913)
1920	▸ Economic prosperity (1922–1929)	▸ Republican ascendancy (1920–1932) ▸ Nineteenth Amendment: national women's suffrage (1921) ▸ Second Ku Klux Klan

REFORM	CULTURE	FOREIGN RELATIONS
Labor, reform, and protest movements	**Immigration and urbanization: origins of modern mass culture**	**An emerging world power**
▶ Great Railroad Strike of 1877	▶ National League launches professional baseball (1876)	▶ Treaty brings Hawaii within U.S. orbit
▶ Woman's Christian Temperance Union (WCTU) becomes largest women's reform movement ▶ Knights of Labor at peak (mid-1880s) ▶ Hull House (1889)	▶ William Dean Howells calls for realism in literature (1881)	
▶ People's Party (1890) ▶ Sierra Club (1892) ▶ Coxey's Army (1894) ▶ Consumers' League (1899)	▶ William Randolph Hearst pioneers "yellow journalism" ▶ Disenfranchisement and Jim Crow in the South ▶ Rise of Social Gospel	▶ War of 1898 ▶ Hawaii annexed (1898) ▶ Philippine-American War (1899–1902)
▶ Growth of American Federation of Labor (AFL) ▶ American Socialist Party (1901) ▶ NAACP (1909)	▶ Popularity of ragtime music ▶ First World Series in baseball (1903)	▶ Platt Amendment (1902) ▶ Roosevelt corollary to Monroe Doctrine (1904) ▶ Panama Canal begun (1904)
▶ Women's suffrage movement grows	▶ Armory Show (1913) ▶ Anti-German nativism during World War I ▶ "Red Scare" (1919)	▶ Wilson intervenes in Mexico (1914) ▶ United States enters World War I (1917) ▶ Wilson's Fourteen Points (1918)
▶ Prohibition (1921–1933)	▶ Rise of Hollywood ▶ Harlem Renaissance ▶ Emergence of jazz	▶ Treaty of Versailles rejected by U.S. Senate (1920)

509

The Busy Hive: Industrial America at Work

1877–1911

> An almost total revolution has taken place, and is yet in progress, in every branch and in every relation of the world's industrial and commercial system.
>
> —David A. Wells, *Recent Economic Changes* (1899)

For millions of his contemporaries, the life of Andrew Carnegie exemplified American success. Arriving from Scotland as a poor twelve-year-old in 1848, Carnegie found work as an errand boy for the Pennsylvania Railroad and rapidly scaled the managerial ladder. In 1865, he struck out on his own as an iron manufacturer, selling to his network of friends in the railroad business, and he soon built a massive steel mill outside Pittsburgh. Its centerpiece was a state-of-the-art Bessemer converter, which broke a bottleneck in the process of the refining of iron into steel. With Carnegie showing the way, steel soon became a major U.S. industry, reaching an annual production of 10 million metric tons by 1900 — almost as much as the *combined* output of the world's other top producers, Germany (6.6 million tons) and Great Britain (4.8 million tons).

Americans hailed Carnegie as a genius, eagerly absorbing his ideas about the economic upheavals he was helping to cause. In his popular 1887 essay, "Wealth," Carnegie acknowledged that industrialization increased the gap between rich and poor. But that, he said, was progress. Industrialization brought cheap products to the masses; even if the benefits were unequal, everyone's standard of living rose. "The poor enjoy what the rich could not before afford," Carnegie wrote. "What were the luxuries have become the necessaries of life."

At the time Carnegie was writing that essay, skilled workers at his mill in Homestead, Pennsylvania, might have agreed with many of his views. Most earned good wages and lived comfortably. They had a strong union, and Carnegie had affirmed workers' right to organize. But by 1892, Carnegie — confident that new machinery gave him the upper hand — decided that collective bargaining was too expensive. The steel magnate withdrew to his estate in Scotland, leaving his partner, Henry Clay Frick, in command. A former coal magnate and veteran of labor wars in the coal fields, Frick was well qualified to do the dirty work. He announced that after July 1, 1892, members of the Amalgamated Association of Iron and Steel Workers would be locked out of the Homestead mill. If they wanted to return to work, they would have to abandon the union and sign new individual contracts. Frick had fortified the mill and prepared to bring in replacement workers if needed. The battle was on.

At dawn on July 6, barges chugged up the Monongahela River, bringing dozens of armed guards from the Pinkerton Detective Agency, hired to take possession of the steelworks. Some of the locked-out workers opened fire, beginning a gunfight that left seven workers and three Pinkertons dead. Frick appealed to Pennsylvania's governor, who called out the state militia. Labor leaders and town officials were arrested on charges of riot and murder. Most of the locked-out workers lost their jobs. The union was dead.

By the time of the bloody clash at Homestead, industrialization had transformed the United States. More and more Americans worked not as self-employed farmers or artisans, but as employees of large corporations whose operations spanned national and even global markets. Conditions of work had changed for people of all economic classes and backgrounds. The stream of immigration into the United States had become a torrent, creating a new American working class that was strikingly diverse. In many places, as at Homestead, these dramatic changes provoked working people to protest — not only through strikes, but also through new movements for political reform.

Business Gets Bigger

In the late 1800s, the industrialization of Europe and the United States revolutionized the world economy. It brought large-scale commercial agriculture to many parts of the globe, consolidating land in fewer hands and uprooting traditional farmers. It prompted millions of migrants — including both skilled workers and displaced peasants — to travel across continents and oceans in search of jobs. Industrialization also created a production glut. Because of the immense scale of production, prices fell worldwide, not only for crops and raw materials but also for manufactured goods.

Falling prices normally signal low demand for goods and services, and thus stagnation. In England, a mature industrial power, the late nineteenth century did bring economic decline. But in the United States, industrial production expanded. Between 1877 and 1900, Americans' average real income increased from $388 to $573 per capita. In this sense, Andrew Carnegie was right: Industrialization raised the average standard of living. Technological and business efficiencies allowed American firms to grow, invest in new equipment, and earn profits even as prices for their products fell. Growth depended, in turn, on America's large and rapidly growing population, its expansion into the West, and its integrated national marketplace.

Republican economic policies, such as high protective tariffs and subsidies for transcontinental railroads, played a key role in promoting growth. But while they created jobs, such policies also fostered the rise of giant corporations, which in many industries crowded out or swallowed up small competitors. Though small-scale manufacturers and merchants survived in many fields, large corporations became the dominant form of business. These big companies quickly expanded overseas. As early as 1868, the Singer Manufacturing Company established a factory in Scotland to produce sewing machines.

Rockefeller's Standard Oil became a multinational player. By World War I, such brands as Ford and General Electric had become familiar around the world.

The Rise of the Corporation

The United States became an industrial power by tapping North America's vast natural resources, including minerals, lumber, and coal, particularly in the newly developed West. Industries that had once depended on waterpower began to use prodigious amounts of coal. Steam engines replaced human and animal labor, and kerosene replaced whale oil and wood. By 1900, America's factories and urban homes were converting to electric power. Dependence on fossil fuels (oil, coal, natural gas), which powered machines of unprecedented speed and strength, transformed both the economy and the country's natural and built environments.

Vertical Integration | The use of fossil fuels was a starting point for a broader array of innovations. After Chicago's Union Stock Yards opened in 1865, middlemen shipped cows by rail from the Great Plains to Chicago and from there to eastern cities, where slaughter took place in local butchertowns. Such a system — a national livestock market with local processing — could have lasted, as it did in Europe. But Gustavus Swift, a shrewd Chicago cattle dealer, saw that local slaughterhouses lacked the scale to utilize waste by-products and cut labor costs. He realized that, through new slaughtering practices, he could reduce production expenses. Further, he understood that if he could keep beef fresh in transit, he could centralize processing in Chicago and cut beef prices below what local butchers could offer.

Building on his insights, Swift pioneered **vertical integration**, a business model in which one company controlled all aspects of production from raw materials to finished goods. Once his engineers designed a cooling system, Swift invested in a fleet of refrigerator cars and constructed a packing plant near Chicago's stockyards. In cities that received his chilled meat, Swift built branch houses and fleets of delivery wagons. He constructed factories to make fertilizer and chemicals from the by-products of slaughter, and he developed marketing strategies for those products as well. Several other Chicago pork packers followed Swift's lead. By 1900, five firms, all vertically integrated, produced nearly 90 percent of the meat shipped in interstate commerce (Map 17.1).

Big packers also invented new sales tactics. For example, Swift & Company periodically slashed prices in certain markets to below production costs, driving independent distributors to the wall. With profits from sales elsewhere, a large firm like Swift could survive temporary losses in one locality until competitors went under. Afterward, Swift could raise prices again. This technique, known as **predatory pricing**, helped give a few firms unprecedented market control.

Standard Oil and the Rise of the Trusts | No one used ruthless business tactics more skillfully than the king of petroleum products, John D. Rockefeller of Standard Oil. Inventors in the 1850s had figured out how to extract kerosene, a clean-burning fuel that was excellent for domestic heating and lighting, from crude oil. Then an enormous supply of oil was located at Titusville, Pennsylvania, just as the Civil War severely disrupted the whaling industry and forced whale-oil customers to

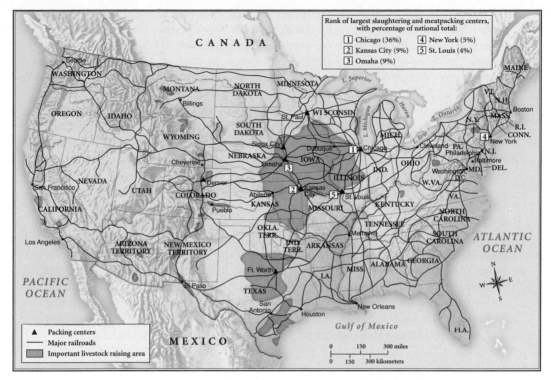

MAP 17.1 The Dressed Meat Industry, 1900

A map of the meatpacking industry clearly shows how transportation, supply, and demand combined to foster the growth of the American industrial economy. The main centers of beef production in 1900 — Chicago, Omaha, Kansas City, and St. Louis — were rail hubs with connections westward to the cattle regions and eastward to cities hungry for cheap supplies of meat. Vertically integrated enterprises sprang from these elements, linked by an efficient and comprehensive railroad network.

look for an alternative lighting source. Overnight, a forest of oil wells sprang up around Titusville. Connected to the Pennsylvania oil fields by rail in 1863, Cleveland, Ohio, became a great refining center. At that time, John D. Rockefeller was an up-and-coming Cleveland grain dealer, prospering due to the Civil War (during which he, like Carnegie and most other budding tycoons of that generation, hired a substitute to fight on his behalf). Rockefeller had strong nerves, a sharp eye for able partners, and a genius for finance. He went into the kerosene business and borrowed heavily to expand capacity. Within a few years, his firm — Standard Oil of Ohio — was Cleveland's leading refiner.

Like Carnegie and Swift, Rockefeller succeeded through vertical integration: to control production and sales all the way from the oil well to the kerosene lamp, he took a big stake in the oil fields, added pipelines, and developed a vast distribution network. Rockefeller allied with railroad executives who, like him, hated the boom-and-bust cycles in the oil market. What they wanted was predictable, high-volume traffic. The railroads offered Rockefeller secret rebates that gave him a leg up on competitors.

Rockefeller also pioneered a strategy that became known as **horizontal integration**. Like Swift, he pressured competitors through predatory pricing, but when he had driven them to failure, he invited rivals to merge their companies into his conglomerate. Most accepted the offer, often because they had no choice. Through such mergers, Standard Oil had wrested control of 95 percent of the nation's oil refining capacity by the 1880s. In 1882, Rockefeller's lawyers created a new legal form, the trust. In a trust, business owners assigned a small group of associates — the board of trustees — to hold stock from all the combined firms, managing them as a single entity. Rockefeller was soon investing in Mexican oil fields and competing in world markets against Russian and Middle Eastern oil producers. Other companies followed his lead, creating trusts to sell such products as linseed oil, sugar, and salt.

Distressed by the development of near monopolies, reformers began to denounce "the trusts," a term that in popular usage referred to any large corporation that seemed to wield excessive power. Some states outlawed trusts as a legal form. But in an effort to attract corporate headquarters to its state, New Jersey broke ranks in 1889, passing a law that permitted the creation of holding companies and other corporate combinations. Despite reformers' efforts, a huge wave of mergers in the 1890s further concentrated corporate power. By 1900, America's largest one hundred companies controlled a third of the nation's productive capacity. Such familiar firms as DuPont, Eastman Kodak, and Singer had assumed dominant places in their respective industries. The immense power of these corporations would henceforth be a recurring political concern.

A National Consumer Culture

In addition to vertical and horizontal integration, corporations innovated in other ways. Companies such as Bell Telephone and Westinghouse set up research laboratories. Steelmakers invested in chemistry and materials science to make their products cheaper, better, and stronger. Americans, introduced to awe-inspiring technological wonders, celebrated inventors as heroes. The most famous, Thomas Edison, operated an independent laboratory rather than working for a corporation. Edison, like many of the era's businessmen, was a shrewd entrepreneur who focused on commercial success. He and his colleagues helped introduce such lucrative products as the incandescent lightbulb, the phonograph, and moving pictures.

In retailing, the lure of a mass market brought comparable advances. New rail lines whisked Florida oranges and other fresh produce to the shelves of grocery stores. Retailers such as the F. W. Woolworth Company and the Great Atlantic and Pacific Tea Company (A&P) opened chains of stores that soon stretched nationwide. The department store, which sold many different products in separate "departments," was pioneered by John Wanamaker in Philadelphia and soon became an urban fixture, displacing many small retail shops. Department stores introduced large display windows, elaborate Christmas decorations, lavish newspaper advertisements, and other methods of dangling temptation in front of shoppers' eyes.

While department stores became fixtures in the city, retailers did not neglect the vast market of rural customers. At county fairs and agricultural expositions, farm families could examine the latest washing machines and kerosene lamps, or meet a promoter dressed as Quaker Oats' symbolic Quaker. Even more influential were huge mail-order

Kellogg's Toasted Corn Flakes
Like crackers, sugar, and other nonperishable foods, cereal was traditionally sold in bulk from barrels. In the 1880s, the Quaker Oats Company hit on the idea of selling oatmeal in boxes of standard size and weight. A further innovation by manufacturers was to process cereal so that it could be consumed right from the box (with milk) for breakfast. Lo and behold: Kellogg's Corn Flakes! This is one of Kellogg's earliest advertisements. Picture Research Consultants & Archives.

enterprises built by such retailers as Montgomery Ward and Sears. Rural families from Vermont to California pored over these companies' annual catalogs, making wish lists of tools, clothes, furniture, and toys. At first, mail-order companies had to coax wary customers to buy products they could not see or touch. Sears and its competitors offered money-back guarantees and simple instructions. "Don't be afraid to make a mistake," the Sears catalog counseled. "Tell us what you want, in your own way." By 1900, America counted more than twelve hundred mail-order companies, some of which produced specialized catalogs of bicycles, baby gear, or women's fashions.

The active attempt to shape consumer demand became, in itself, a new field of enterprise. The 1880s and 1890s brought a boom in colorful trade cards, small business cards that companies circulated to potential customers. By the turn of the century, magazine ads made use of vivid color images and lavish artwork. "It is hard to get mental activity with cold type; *you feel a picture,*" wrote one advertiser. Outdoors, advertisements appeared everywhere. In New York's Madison Square, the Heinz Company installed a 45-foot pickle made of green electric lights. Tourists had difficulty admiring Niagara Falls because billboards obscured the view.

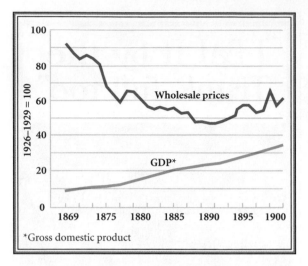

FIGURE 17.1 Business Activity and Wholesale Prices, 1869–1900 This graph shows the key feature of the performance of the late-nineteenth-century economy: While output was booming, wholesale prices were, on the whole, falling. Thus, while workers often struggled with falling wages — especially during decades of severe economic crisis — consumer products also became cheaper to buy.

Thus modern advertising was born. By 1900, companies were spending more than $90 million a year ($2.3 billion in today's money) to promote their wares in newspapers and magazines, as the press itself became a mass-market industry. Rather than charging subscribers the cost of production, newspapers and magazines began to cover their costs by selling ads. This allowed them to offer cheap subscriptions, which built a mass readership, which in turn attracted more advertisers. In 1903, the *Ladies' Home Journal* became the first magazine with a million subscribers. Along with articles on home decoration and family life, its pages encouraged Americans to bathe with Pears soap and use Western Electric vacuum cleaners.

Many Americans could not afford such luxuries. But the late nineteenth century was an era of price deflation (Figure 17.1) and, while wages suffered during periods of economic depression, consumer goods did become more affordable. By the early twentieth century, the proliferation of consumer goods had begun to reshape Americans' expectations and goals. For some, long hours on the job were worth it if payday brought the possibility of shopping for new clothes or putting favorite treats on the table. When asked to reflect on the difference between the Old Country and America, a railroadman who had emigrated from the Netherlands spoke of food: "In the good old USA we have two or three kinds of meat every day." A visiting German sociologist suggested that material abundance — or at least the *promise* of it — blunted the attractiveness of socialism and other radical political doctrines. In America, he suggested, protests against the new capitalist order would, like little storm-tossed boats, wreck on the "reefs of roast beef and apple pie."

The Corporate Workplace

Before the Civil War, most American boys had hoped to become farmers, small-business owners, or independent craft workers. Afterward, more and more Americans (both male and female) became accustomed to working for someone else. This change affected not only wage earners but also managers, salespeople, and engineers. Because they wore white shirts with starched collars, those who held professional positions within a corporation became known as **white-collar workers,** a term that differentiated them from **blue-collar workers** on the shop floor. For both managers and laborers, however, the shift from independent to corporate work had wide-ranging consequences. Blue-collar workers, for example, were more likely to join a labor union if they did not view the company that hired them as a temporary way station on the path to self-employment.

The Managerial Revolution | As their trunk lines stretched westward, railroad companies faced a management crisis. As Erie Railroad executive Daniel C. McCallum observed, a railroad superintendent on a 50-mile line could personally attend to every detail. But supervising a 500-mile line was an impossible task; trains ran late, communications failed, and crashes were frequent. Between the 1850s and the 1880s, railroad executives gradually invented the systems they needed to solve these problems. They distinguished top corporate managers from those responsible for day-to-day operations. They departmentalized operations by function (purchasing, machinery, freight traffic, passenger traffic) and established clear lines of communication. They perfected cost accounting, which allowed managers to assess performance in various operating units. Cost accounting allowed an industrialist like Andrew Carnegie to keep careful track of expenses and revenues, and thus to follow, on a sweeping scale, his Scottish mother's advice: "Take care of the pennies, and the pounds will take care of themselves."

With few exceptions, the vertically integrated corporations of the post–Civil War years drew on the railroad model. The headquarters of major corporations began to house executives and an array of departments handling specific activities such as purchasing, accounting, and auditing. These departments were supervised by "middle managers," something not seen before in American industry. Though managers of operating units functioned much like earlier factory owners, middle managers took on entirely new tasks, directing the flow of goods, labor, and information throughout the enterprise. Middle managers were key innovators, counterparts to the engineers in research laboratories who, in the same decades, worked to reduce costs and improve efficiency.

Company Salesmen | As early as the 1870s, the "drummer," or traveling salesman, became a familiar site on city streets and in remote country stores. Riding the rail networks from town to town, drummers introduced merchants to new products, offered incentives, and suggested sales displays. They built nationwide distribution networks for such popular consumer items as cigarettes and Coca-Cola. By the late 1880s, the leading manufacturer of cash registers produced a sales script for its employees, who presented their product as an aid to local merchants hoping to increase profits. "After you have made your proposition clear," the script directed salesmen, "take for granted that he will buy. Say to him, 'Now, Mr. Blank, what color shall I make it?' . . . Take out the order blank, fill it out, and handing him your pen say, 'Just sign here where I have made the cross.'"

With such companies in the vanguard, sales became systematized. Managers set individual sales quotas — one company awarded silver and gold crosses to its top salesmen, while those who sold too little were singled out for remedial training or dismissal.

Business leaders eagerly embraced the ideas of business psychologist Walter Dill Scott, who published *The Psychology of Advertising* in 1908. Scott's principles — which included selling to customers based on their presumed "instinct of escape" and "instinct of combat" — were soon taught at Harvard Business School.

Women in the Corporate Workplace | Beneath the ranks of managers, another class of employees emerged: female office workers. Before the Civil War, most clerks at small firms had been young men who expected to rise through the ranks. In a large corporation, secretarial work became a dead-end job, and employers began to assign it to women. By the turn of the twentieth century, 77 percent of all stenographers and typists were female; by 1920, women held half of all low-level office jobs.

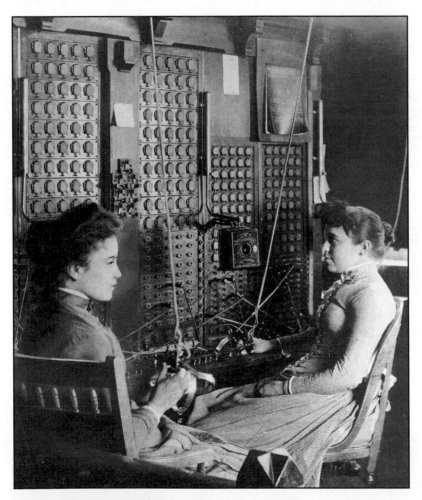

Telephone Operators, 1888

Like other women office workers, these switchboard operators enjoyed relatively high pay and comfortable working conditions — especially in the early years of the telephone industry, before operators' work routines speeded up. These young women worked for the Central Union Telephone Company in Canton, Ohio. Ohio Historical Society.

In the retail field, department stores hired increasing numbers of saleswomen to interact directly with customers. Though many women viewed sales jobs as far better than factory labor or domestic service, the work was poorly paid and grueling. "Our business was first to dust and condense the stock, and then to stand ready for customers," wrote an investigator who worked undercover at Chicago department stores. "We all served in the double capacity of floorwalkers and clerks, and our business was to see that no one escaped without making a purchase." When customers arrived, she continued, "there was one mad rush of clerks with a quickly spoken, 'What would you like, madam?'" Employees had to use aggressive sales tactics to earn the small commissions that made up their weekly pay.

For white working-class women, clerking and office work represented new opportunities. In an era before day care, married women most often worked at home, where they could tend children while also taking in laundry, boarders, or **piecework** (sewing or other assembly projects that were paid on a per-item basis). Unmarried daughters could leave the home for domestic service or factory work, but clerking and secretarial work were cleaner and better paid. Telegraph operators told one reporter that they felt they held "a social position not inferior to that of a teacher or governess." In 1900, more than 4 million women worked for wages. About a third worked in domestic service; another third in industry; and the rest in office work, teaching, nursing, or sales. As new opportunities arose, the percentage of wage-earning women in domestic service dropped dramatically, a trend that continued in the twentieth century.

On the Shop Floor

Despite the managerial revolution at the top, skilled craft workers — almost all of them men — retained considerable autonomy in many industries. A coal miner, for example, was not an hourly wageworker but essentially an independent contractor, paid by the amount of coal he produced. He provided his own tools, worked at his own pace, and knocked off early when he chose. The same was true for puddlers and rollers in iron works; molders in stove making; and machinists, glass blowers, and skilled workers in many other industries. Such workers abided by the stint, a self-imposed limit on how much they would produce each day. This informal system of restricting output infuriated efficiency-minded engineers, but to the workers it signified personal dignity, manly pride, and brotherhood with fellow employees. One shop in Lowell, Massachusetts, posted regulations requiring all employees to be at their posts by the time of the opening bell and to remain, with the shop door locked, until the closing bell. A machinist promptly packed his tools, declaring that he had not "been brought up under such a system of slavery."

Skilled workers — craftsmen, inside contractors, and foremen — enjoyed a high degree of autonomy. But those who paid helpers from their own pocket could also exploit them. Subcontracting arose, in part, to enable manufacturers to distance themselves from the consequences of shady labor practices. In Pittsburgh steel mills, foremen were known as "pushers," notorious for driving their gangs mercilessly. On the other hand, industrial labor operated on a human scale, through personal relationships that could be close and enduring. Striking craft workers would commonly receive the support of helpers and laborers, and labor gangs would sometimes walk out on behalf of a popular foreman.

As technology advanced, however, workers increasingly lost the proud independence characteristic of craft work. The most important cause of this was the de-skilling of labor under a new system of mechanized manufacturing that industrialist Henry Ford would soon call **mass production**. Over the course of the nineteenth and early twentieth centuries, everything from typewriters to automobiles came to be assembled from standardized parts. The machine tools that cut, drilled, and ground the metal parts were originally operated by skilled workers, but the machines soon could operate without human oversight. A machinist protested in 1883 that the sewing machine industry was so "subdivided" that "one man may make just a particular part of a machine and may not know anything whatever about another part of the same machine." Such a worker, noted an observer, "cannot be master of a craft, but only master of a fragment."

Employers, who originally favored automatic machinery because it increased output, quickly found that it also helped them control workers and cut labor costs. With mass production, corporations needed fewer skilled workers. They could pay unskilled workers less and replace them easily. Blue-collar workers — those who labored with their hands — therefore had little freedom to negotiate with their employers, and their working conditions deteriorated markedly as mass production took hold.

By the early twentieth century, managers had come to believe that they could further reduce costs by getting employees to work harder and more efficiently. The pioneer in industrial efficiency was Frederick W. Taylor, an expert on metal-cutting methods who dubbed his strategy **scientific management**. To get maximum output from the individual worker, Taylor suggested two basic reforms. First, eliminate the brain work from manual labor: Hire experts to develop "rules, laws, and formulae" for the shop floor. Second, withdraw workers' authority and require that they "do what they are told promptly and without asking questions or making suggestions." Decision making would lie in the hands of "management alone." In its most extreme form, scientific management called for engineers to time each task with a stopwatch; companies would then pay workers more if they met the stopwatch standard. Taylor assumed that workers cared only about money and that they would respond automatically to the lure of higher earnings.

Scientific management was not, in practice, a great success. Implementing it proved to be expensive, and workers stubbornly resisted the stopwatch method. One union leader declared, "This system is wrong, because we want our heads left on us." Far from solving the labor problem, scientific management created new conflicts. Corporate managers, however, adopted many bits and pieces of Taylor's system, and they enthusiastically adopted his idea that brain work should be the job of "management alone." Taylor's disciples went on to create the fields of personnel work and industrial psychology, whose practitioners purported to know how to extract more and better labor from workers. Over time, in comparison with their counterparts in other countries, American corporations created a particularly wide gap between the perspectives and experiences of white-collar managers and those of the blue-collar workforce.

As production was de-skilled, the ranks of factory workers came to include more and more women and children, who were almost always unskilled and lower paid. Men often resented women's presence in factories. By the early twentieth century, male labor unions also became outspoken leaders in the fight against child labor. In 1900, one of every five children under the age of sixteen worked outside the home. Child labor was most widespread in the South, where a low-wage industrial sector emerged

Child Labor

For many working-class families, children's wages — even though they were low — made up an essential part of the household income. These boys worked the night shift in a glass factory in Indiana. Lewis Hine, an investigative photographer for the National Child Labor Committee, took their picture at midnight, as part of a campaign to educate more prosperous Americans about the widespread employment of child labor, as well as the harsh conditions in which many children worked. Library of Congress.

after Reconstruction (Map 17.2). Textile mills sprouted in the Carolinas and Georgia, recruiting workers from surrounding farms.

Also at the bottom of the pay scale were most African American workers. Corporations and industrial manufacturers widely discriminated on the basis of race, and such racial prejudice was hardly limited to the South. In the decades after the Civil War, African American women who moved to northern cities found that they were largely excluded from office work and other new employment options; instead, they remained heavily concentrated in domestic service, with more than half employed as cooks or servants. African American men confronted the same exclusion. America's booming vertically integrated corporations turned away black men from all but the most menial jobs. In 1890, almost a third of African American men worked in personal service. Employers in the North and West recruited, instead, a different kind of low-wage labor: newly arrived immigrants.

▶ What factors led to the rise of the corporation after 1865? What means did corporate leaders use to expand their control of markets?

▶ What new patterns of work developed in the corporate and industrial workplaces? What were the consequences of these patterns for men and women?

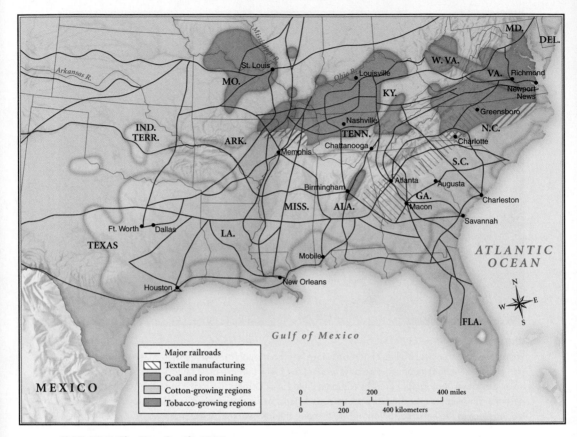

MAP 17.2 The New South, 1900

The economy of the Old South focused on raising staple crops, especially cotton and tobacco. In the New South, staple agriculture continued to dominate, but there was marked industrial development as well. Industrial regions evolved, producing textiles, coal, and iron. By 1900 the South's industrial pattern was well defined, though the region still served—like the West—as a major producer of raw materials for the industrial core region that stretched from New England to Chicago.

Immigrants, East and West

Across the globe, industrialization set people in motion. Farmers' children migrated to cities. Craftsmen entered factories. The lure of jobs, along with cheap steam transportation, pulled opportunity seekers to the United States from across the Atlantic and Pacific and over the Canadian and Mexican borders. Between the Civil War and World War I, 25 million immigrants entered the United States. They began to make the American working class truly global: Joining it were not only people of African and Western European descent but also Southern and Eastern Europeans, Mexicans, and Asians. In 1900, census takers found that more than 75 percent of all residents of San Francisco and New York City had at least one parent who was foreign-born.

For the new industrial order, immigrants made an ideal labor supply. They took the worst jobs at low pay; during economic downturns, many left the labor market and returned to their home countries, reducing the shock of unemployment within the United States. But many native-born Americans viewed immigrants with hostility, through the lens of racial, ethnic, and religious prejudices. They also feared that immigrants would compete for jobs and erode wages. For immigrants themselves, America was a new world — by turns disorienting, liberating, and disappointing.

Newcomers from Europe

Mass migration from Western Europe had started in the 1840s, when more than 1 million Irish fled a terrible famine. In the following decades, as European populations grew rapidly and agriculture became commercialized, peasant economies suffered, first in Germany and Scandinavia, and then across Austria-Hungary, Russia, Italy, and the Balkans. This upheaval displaced millions of rural people. Some went to Europe's mines and factories; others headed for South America. Millions more sailed for the United States.

"America was known to foreigners," remembered one Jewish woman from Lithuania, "as the land where you'd get rich. . . . There's gold on the sidewalk! All you have to do is pick it up." But the reality was much harsher. Even in the age of steam, the voyage to America was grueling. For ten to twenty days, passengers in steerage class crowded below-decks, eating terrible food and struggling with seasickness. An investigative reformer who traveled with immigrants from Naples asked, "How can a steerage passenger remember that he is a human being when he must first pick the worms from his food . . . and eat in his stuffy, stinking bunk?" After 1892, European immigrants were routed through the enormous receiving station at New York's Ellis Island.

Some immigrants were skilled, seasoned workers. Many Welshmen, for example, arrived in the United States as experienced tin-plate makers; Germans came as machinists and carpenters, and Scandinavians as sailors. But industrialization required, most of all, increasing amounts of unskilled labor. As poor farmers from Italy, Greece, and Eastern Europe arrived in the United States, heavy, low-paid labor became their domain. One investigator trying to get a job in the steel mills was told that blast furnace jobs were for "Hunkies," a derogatory term for Hungarians that was applied indiscriminately to Poles, Slovaks, and other ethnic Slavs. Visiting Pittsburgh to observe the plight of his countrymen who had emigrated, Hungarian count Vay de Vaya und Luskod testified that the work was, in fact, brutally hard (see Voices from Abroad, p. 524).

In an era of cheap, increasingly rapid travel by railroad and steamship, many immigrants came as "sojourners": They expected to work and save for a few years and then head home. More than 800,000 French Canadians moved to New England to find jobs in the textile mills. For $10, they could get a rail ticket from Montreal to Fall River, Massachusetts; with adults earning about $1 a day, and children working a full sixty-hour week for nearly $2, families hoped to scrape together enough savings to return to Quebec and buy a farm. Thousands of men came alone, especially from Ireland, Italy, and Greece. Many single Irishwomen also immigrated. Circumstances often changed their plans. Some would-be sojourners ended up staying a lifetime, while many immigrants

*All the nations and people I had hitherto passed throu[gh]
resembled our own in their manners, customs and langua[ge]*

Pittsburgh Inferno COUNT VAY DE VAYA UND LUSKOD

Count Vay de Vaya und Luskod, a Hungarian nobleman and high functionary in the Catholic Church, crossed the United States several times between 1903 and 1906 en route to his post as the Vatican's representative to Asia. In a book about his travels, he expresses his distress at the plight of his countrymen laboring in the mills of the Pittsburgh steel district.

The bells are tolling for a funeral. The modest train of mourners is just setting out for the little churchyard on the hill. Everything is shrouded in gloom, even the coffin lying upon the bier and the people who stand on each side in threadbare clothes and with heads bent. Such is my sad reception at the Hungarian workingmen's colony at McKeesport. Everyone who has been in the United States has heard of this famous town, and of Pittsburgh, its close neighbor. . . .

Fourteen-thousand tall chimneys are silhouetted against the sky . . . discharg[ing] their burning sparks and smok[ing] incessantly. The realms of Vulcan could not be more somber or filthy than this valley of the Monongahela. On every hand are burning fires and spurting flames. Nothing is visible save the forging of iron and the smelting of metal. . . .

And this fearful place affects us very closely, for thousands of immigrants wander here from year to year. Here they fondly seek the realization of their cherished hopes, and here they suffer till they are swallowed up by the inferno. He whom we are now burying is the latest victim. Yesterday he was in full vigor and at work at the foundry, toiling, struggling, hoping—a chain broke, and he was killed. . . .

This is scarcely work for mankind. Americans will hardly take anything of the sort; only [the immigrant] rendered desperate by circumstances . . . and thus he is at the mercy of the tyrannous Trust, which gathers him into its clutches and transforms him into a regular slave.

This is one of the saddest features of the Hungarian emigration. In making a tour of these prisons, wherever the heat is most insupportable, the flames most scorching, the smoke and soot most choking, there we are certain to find compatriots bent and wasted with toil. Their thin, wrinkled, wan faces seem to show that in America the newcomers are of no use except to help fill the moneybags of the insatiable millionaires. . . . In this realm of Mammon and Moloch everything has a value—except human life. . . . Why? Because human life is a commodity the supply of which exceeds the demand. There are always fresh recruits to supply the place of those who have fallen in battle; and the steamships are constantly arriving at the neighboring ports, discharging their living human cargo still further to swell the phalanx of the instruments of cupidity.

SOURCE: Oscar Handlin, ed., *This Was America* (Cambridge, MA: Harvard University Press, 1949), 407–410.

who had expected to settle permanently found themselves forced out of the country by a workplace accident or a sudden economic depression. One historian has estimated that one-third of immigrants to the United States in this era returned home.

Along with Italians and Greeks, Eastern European Jews were among the most numerous arrivals. The first American Jews, who numbered around 50,000 in 1880, were mostly of German-Jewish descent. In the next four decades, more than 3 million poverty-stricken Jews arrived from Russia, Ukraine, Poland, and other parts of Eastern Europe, transforming the Jewish presence in the United States. Like other immigrants, Eastern European Jews sought economic opportunity, but they also came to escape religious repression. These problems were especially acute after Russian officials made Jews scapegoats following the assassination of Czar Alexander II in 1881. Fleeing violence, Jews fled through German ports to the United States. Many were young people and men in skilled occupations, including tailors.

Wherever they came from, immigrants took a considerable gamble when they traveled to the United States. Some prospered. Others, by toiling for many years in harsh conditions, succeeded in securing a better life for their children and grandchildren. Still others met with economic catastrophe, injury, or early death. One Polish man who came with his parents in 1908 summed up his life over the next thirty years as "a mere struggle for bread." He added: "Sometimes I think life isn't worth a damn for a man like me. I get little money. . . . Look at my wife and kids — undernourished, seldom have a square meal." But an Orthodox Russian Jewish woman told an interviewer that she "thanked God for America," where she had married, raised three children, and made a good life for herself. She "liked everything about this country, especially its leniency toward the Jews."

Asian Americans and Exclusion

Compared with European immigrants, newcomers from Asia in the late nineteenth century faced harsher treatment from Americans. The first Chinese immigrants had arrived in the United States in the 1840s, during the California gold rush. After the Civil War, the Burlingame Treaty between the United States and China opened the way for increasing numbers to emigrate (see American Voices, p. 526). Fleeing poverty and upheaval in southern China, they, like European immigrants, filled low-wage jobs in the American labor market. But the Chinese confronted far more intense hostility in the form of abysmal pay and threats from coworkers, leading many men to withdraw to the only niches open to them: running restaurants and laundries. Nonetheless, some managed to build profitable businesses and farms. During the depression of the 1870s, hostility in the form of a rising tide of outrage against "Asiatics" was especially extreme in the Pacific coast states, where the majority of Chinese immigrants lived. "The Chinese must go!" railed Dennis Kearney, leader of the California Working Men's Party, who referred to Asians as "almond-eyed lepers." Incited by Kearney, a mob burned San Francisco's Chinatown and beat up residents in July 1877.

Facing intense political pressure, lawmakers shut out Chinese immigrants. In 1882, Congress passed the Chinese Exclusion Act, which specifically barred Chinese laborers from entering the United States. Each decade thereafter, Congress renewed the law and tightened its provisions; it was not repealed until 1943. Exclusion laws barred entry of

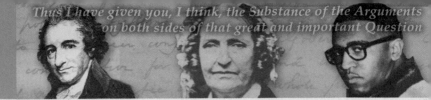

Thus I have given you, I think, the Substance of the Arguments on both sides of that great and important Question

Sold into Sexual Slavery   SUEY HIN

In 1899 Helen Grey, a reporter for the *San Francisco Call*, published a remarkable interview with Suey Hin, a Chinese woman sold into sexual slavery in the United States. Many such girls, who began work as young as age ten, died of abuse before they finished serving their illegal contracts. Suey Hin survived.

I was born in Shantung, where the flowers are more beautiful and the birds sing more sweetly than in any other place. But my people were poor. There was not enough for all our stomachs. Two baby girls had been left exposed — that is, to die, you know. They were born after me and my father said often, "She is too many."

Once there was an old woman came to our house and . . . talked to my father and mother. She put a piece of gold money in my hand and told me to give it to my father. . . . That night the old woman carried me away, and I kicked and screamed . . . I remember the ship, and I remember playing with other little girls. We were brought to San Francisco, and there were five or ten of us and we all lived with a woman on Ross alley. Every little while some one would come and see us, and as we grew older the girls were sold.

[When I was twelve] it was my turn. . . . I was a slave for ten years. There was a man who loved me, but he was a poor washman, and he worked eight years and saved all, all the time. I saved all I could get, too, but it took eight years before we had saved $3000. Then we bought me from my owner and we were married.

Then, ah, it's all of my life I like to think about. It wasn't but two next years, three years. My husband got sick and didn't get any better, and then he died. I didn't have any-thing but just myself, and I had to live. . . . So I got a little house [i.e., she went back to prostitution]. . . .

Pretty soon I went back to China, but I did not go to my own village. No, my parents would not want to see me. I went to Hong-kong and I bought three girls. Two of them are dead. . . . I went back to China again. I wanted to see my village . . . but I didn't let anybody know I was there. I went to the place where they put the babies to die. There was a baby there. A little bit of a brown baby, and she didn't look much good anyway. But I wanted some one from my own village, and so I took the baby, and she is Ah Lung. . . . She's not a slave you know. She's a good girl, just the same as white girls. She comes from Shantung, so I say she shall never be like the others. Slave girls most all die soon. It's bad, yes. . . .

That trip I brought home four girls besides Ah Lung. You see it was not hard to smuggle the girls into this country then. You can't do it so easy now. . . . [Last year] I brought back six girls. One girl I sold to Loo Wing. All the other girls are here now. I will not make them bad any more. . . . I suppose they get married. Only they must marry Christians. I Christian now. . . . I used to work hard for the devil, him you call, Satan, but now I work harder for Jesus.

S O U R C E : Judy Yung, *Unbound Voices: A Documentary History of Chinese Women in San Francisco* (Berkeley: University of California Press, 1999), 144–153.

Chinese Workers in a Salmon Cannery, c. 1900

Shut out of many fields of employment by racial discrimination, many Chinese immigrants founded their own restaurants, laundries, and other small businesses. Others, like these cannery workers in Astoria, Oregon, took on some of the most grueling and lowest-paid work in the American economy. Job segregation reinforced, in turn, racial prejudice. Visiting British author Rudyard Kipling, touring canneries along the Columbia River, described Chinese workers in the plants as "blood-besmeared yellow devils." These workers, refuting Kipling's slur, appear clean and respectable. Notice the man in an apron, on the left, who wears his traditional queue, or braided pigtail, tucked into his straw hat. Oregon Historical Society.

almost all Chinese women, forcing husbands and wives to spend many years apart when men took jobs in the United States. Some immigrants made vigorous use of the courts to protect their rights. In a series of cases brought by Chinese and later Japanese immigrants, the U.S. Supreme Court ruled that all persons born in the United States had citizenship rights that could not be revoked, even if their parents had been born abroad.

Nonetheless, well into the twentieth century, Chinese immigrants (as opposed to native-born Chinese Americans) could not apply for citizenship. By the turn of the twentieth century, Japanese and Korean immigrants had also begun to arrive; by 1909, there were 40,000 Japanese immigrants working in agriculture, 10,000 on railroads, and 4,000 in canneries. A few Japanese managed to become U.S. citizens, but in 1906 the U.S. attorney general ruled that they, like other Asians, were barred. In the meantime, Chinese exclusion did not halt violence and discrimination against those who had found a place in the United States. Most labor unions steadfastly refused to allow Chinese workers to join. During the depression of the 1890s, angry unemployed whites attacked Chinese farmworkers in California. In what many Chinese later remembered as "the driving out," they were rounded up, forced onto railcars, and sent out of the state.

The Chinese Exclusion Act created the legal foundations on which exclusionary immigration policies would be built after the 1920s. To enforce the law, Congress and the courts gave sweeping new powers to immigration officials, transforming the Chinese into America's first illegal immigrants. Drawn, like others, by the promise of jobs in America's expanding economy, Chinese men stowed away on ships and walked across the borders. Disguising themselves as Mexicans — who at that time could freely enter the United States — some perished in the desert as they tried to reach California.

Other would-be immigrants, known as "paper sons," relied on Chinese residents in the United States, who generated documents falsely claiming the newcomers as American-born children. (One federal judge commented in 1901: "If the story told in the courts were true, every Chinese woman who was in the United States twenty-five years ago must have had at least 500 children.") "Paper sons" memorized pages of information about their supposed relatives and hometowns. The San Francisco earthquake of 1906 helped their cause by destroying all of the port's records. "That was a big chance for a lot of Chinese," remembered one Chinese American. "They forged themselves certificates saying they could go back to China and bring back four or five sons, just like that!" Such ingenuity and persistence ensured that, despite the harsh policies of Chinese exclusion, the flow of Asian immigrants never entirely ceased.

▶ What factors typically shaped the experience of immigrants in the United States? How did these differ among different ethnic and racial groups?

▶ What impact did Americans' response to Asian newcomers have on immigration policies?

Labor Gets Organized

In the American political system, labor has always been weak. Industrial workers have tended to cluster in cities, near factories and jobs. But in comparison with voters in small towns and rural areas, those in urban areas have been underrepresented in state legislatures, the U.S. Senate, and the electoral college. This problem became acute in the era of industrialization, and it has lingered. Today, for example, the twenty-two U.S. senators elected from Alaska, Idaho, Iowa, Maine, Mississippi, Montana, New Mexico, North Dakota, Vermont, West Virginia, and Wyoming represent a smaller number of people, *combined*, than the two U.S. senators who represent California.

Faced with this obstacle, labor advocates could adopt one of two strategies. First, they could try to make political alliances with sympathetic rural voters who shared their problems. Second, they could reject politics and create narrowly focused **trade unions** to negotiate directly with employers. In general, labor advocates emphasized the first strategy between the 1870s and the early 1890s, and the latter in the early twentieth century. Across this era, while industrialization made America increasingly rich and powerful, it also brought large-scale conflict between labor and capital.

The Emergence of a Labor Movement

The problem of industrial labor entered Americans' consciousness dramatically with the Great Railroad Strike of 1877. Protesting steep wage cuts during the depression that had begun in 1873, thousands of railroad workers walked off the job. Their strike paralyzed the U.S. transportation network, bringing rail travel and commerce to a halt. Thousands of people poured into the streets of Buffalo, Pittsburgh, and Chicago to join the rail workers and protest the economic injustice wreaked by the railroads — as well as the fires caused by stray sparks from locomotives, and the injuries and deaths on train tracks in urban neighborhoods. When Pennsylvania's governor sent in the state militia to break the railroad workers' strike, Pittsburgh crowds reacted by burning railroad property and overturning locomotives. Similar clashes between police and protesters occurred in other cities across the country, from Galveston, Texas, to San Francisco, California.

The 1877 strike left more than fifty people dead and caused $40 million worth of damage, primarily to property owned by the railroads. "It seemed as if the whole social and political structure was on the very brink of ruin," wrote one journalist. For their role in the strike, many railroad workers were fired and **blacklisted**: Railroad companies circulated their names on a "do not hire" list to prevent them from getting any work in the industry. In the wake of the strike, the U.S. government also created the National Guard, not to protect Americans against foreign invasion, but to enforce order at home. National Guard armories — fortresses designed to withstand assault by future strikers and rioters — became part of the urban landscape.

In the post–Civil War decades, many rural people believed they faced the same enemies as industrial workers. In the new economy, they found themselves at the mercy of large corporations, from equipment dealers that sold them harvesters and plows, to railroads and grain elevators that shipped and stored their products. Though farmers appeared to have more independence than corporate employees, many felt increasingly caught up in a web of middlemen who chipped away at their profits, with international forces robbing them of decision-making power.

Farmers denounced not only corporations, but also the previous two decades of government policy. During the Civil War and Reconstruction, Republicans had passed an array of laws to foster economic development in the West. But those policies seemed wrongheaded to many farmers, especially those in the South and West. Farmers' advocates argued that high tariffs forced rural families to pay too much for basic necessities while failing to protect America's great export crops, cotton and wheat. At the same time, they charged, Republican financial policies benefited banks, not ordinary borrowers. The effect on interest rates was sharply regional. Despite expansion of the national bank system, most national banks lay in the Northeast, where loans were relatively easy to get. Farmers also blamed railroad companies, which had built their lines with the support of government land grants and subsidies but charged unequal rates that privileged big eastern manufacturers. From the farmers' point of view, public money had been used to build giant railroad companies that turned around and exploited ordinary people.

The most prominent rural protest group of the early postwar decades was the National Grange of the Patrons of Husbandry, founded in 1867. Like workingmen, Grange farmers sought to counter the new power of corporate middlemen through cooperation and mutual aid. Local Grange halls brought farm families together for recreation and conversation. The Grange set up its own banks, insurance companies, and grain elevators, and, in Iowa, even a manufacturing plant for farm implements. Many Grange members also advocated political action, building independent local parties that ran on anticorporate platforms.

In the wake of the 1870s depression, Grangers, labor advocates, and local workingmen's parties forged a national political movement: the Greenback-Labor Party. In the South, Greenbackers protested the fading of Reconstruction, opposed convict labor, and urged that every man's vote be protected. Across the country, Greenbackers advocated laws to regulate corporations and enforce an eight-hour limit on the workday. They called for the federal government to print more greenback dollars and increase the amount of money in circulation; this, they argued, would stimulate the economy, create jobs, and help borrowers by allowing them to pay off debts in dollars that, over time, slowly decreased in value. Overall, Greenbackers subscribed to the ideal of **producerism**. They dismissed middlemen, bankers, lawyers, and investors as idlers who lived off the sweat of those who labored with their hands.

The Greenback movement radicalized thousands of farmers, miners, and industrial workers. In Alabama's coal-mining regions, black and white miners worked together in the party. Texas boasted seventy African American Greenback clubs. In 1878, Greenback-Labor candidates won more than a million votes and the party elected fifteen congressmen: seven from the Northeast, five from the Midwest, and three from the South. Greenback pressure helped trigger a wave of economic regulatory actions, known in the Midwest, especially, as Granger laws. By the early 1880s, twenty-nine states had created railroad commissions to supervise railroad rates and policies; others formed commissions to regulate insurance and utility companies. Such early regulatory efforts were not always effective, but they were important starting points for reform. While short-lived, the Greenback movement created the foundation for subsequent farmer-labor movements and more sustained, vigorous efforts to regulate big business.

The Knights of Labor

The most important union of the late nineteenth century, the Knights of Labor, was founded in 1869 as a secret society of garment workers in Philadelphia. In 1878, when the Greenback movement was reaching its height, Knights from Ohio, Pennsylvania, Michigan, and other states served as delegates to Greenback-Labor conventions. Like the Grangers, the Knights believed that ordinary people needed control over the enterprises in which they worked. They proposed to set up factories and shops owned by employees, transforming America into what they called "the cooperative commonwealth." In keeping with this broad-based vision, the order practiced open membership, irrespective of race, gender, or field of employment (though, like other labor groups, the Knights excluded Chinese workers). The Knights had a strong political bent. They believed that only political action could bring about many of their goals, such as government regulation of corporations and mandatory arbitration of strikes. The Knights also

The Knights of Labor

The caption on this union card — "By Industry we Thrive" — expresses the core principle of the Knights of Labor that everything of value is the product of honest labor. The two figures are ideal representations of that "producerist" belief — handsome workers, respectably attired, doing productive labor. A picture of the Grand Master Workman, Terence V. Powderly, hangs on the wall, benignly watching them. Picture Research Consultants & Archives.

advocated personal responsibility and self-discipline, including temperance. Their leader, Terence Powderly, warned that the abuse of liquor robbed as many workers of their wages as did greedy employers.

Growing rapidly in the 1880s, the Knights became a sprawling, decentralized organization. The union included not only skilled craftsmen such as carpenters and ironworkers but also German beer brewers in Omaha, textile workers in Rhode Island, domestic workers in Georgia, and tenant farmers in Arkansas. Urban Knights organized workingmen's parties to advocate a host of reforms, ranging from an eight-hour workday to cheaper streetcar fares and better garbage collection. One of the Knights' key innovations was hiring a full-time women's organizer, Leonora Barry. An Irish American widow who was forced into factory work after her husband's death, Barry became a labor advocate out of horror at the conditions she found on the job.

The pattern of the Knights' growth showed the grassroots nature of labor activism in the 1880s. Increases in membership were often prompted by "wildcat strikes" — those that workers started spontaneously, without consulting union leaders. Powderly urged local Knights to avoid strikes, which he saw as costly and risky. But the organization's greatest successes resulted from grassroots strikes. In 1885, thousands of workers on the Southwest Railroad walked off the job to protest wage cuts; afterward, they telegraphed the Knights and asked to be admitted as members. The strike enhanced the Knights' reputation among workers and built membership to 750,000. By the following year, local assemblies had sprung up in every state and almost every county in the United States.

Just as the Knights reached a pinnacle of influence, an episode of violence brought them down. In May 1886, a protest at the McCormick reaper works in Chicago led to a clash with police that left four strikers dead. (Three unions, including a Knights of Labor assembly, had struck against the plant, but the Knights had reached an agreement and returned to work. Only the machinists' union remained on strike when the incident occurred.) Chicago was a hotbed of **anarchism** — the revolutionary advocacy of a stateless society. Local anarchists, many of them German immigrants, called a protest meeting the next day, May 4, 1886, at Haymarket Square. When police tried to disperse the crowd, someone threw a bomb that killed several policemen. The officers responded with gunfire. In the trial that followed, eight anarchists were found guilty of murder and criminal conspiracy. All were convicted, not on any definitive evidence that they threw the bomb (the bomber's or bombers' identity still remains unknown) but because they had given antigovernment speeches. Four of the eight anarchists were executed by hanging, one committed suicide, and the others received long prison sentences.

The Haymarket violence caused profound damage to the American labor movement. Seizing on anti-union hysteria set off by the incident, employers went on the offensive against the Knights. They broke strikes violently and forced workers to sign contracts in which they pledged not to join labor organizations. The Knights of Labor never recovered. In the view of the press and many prosperous Americans, the Knights were tainted by their supposed links with anarchism. Novelist and literary critic William Dean Howells, one of a handful of famous Americans who publicly opposed the hanging of the Haymarket anarchists, found that when he spoke out in defense of labor, former friends in Boston shunned him, even refusing to speak when he met them on the street.

Farmers and Workers: The Cooperative Alliance

Despite the aftermath of the Haymarket incident, the Knights' cooperative vision did not entirely fade. A new rural movement, the Farmers' Alliance, arose to take up many of the issues that Grangers and Greenbackers had earlier sought to address. Founded in Texas during the depression of the 1870s, the Farmers' Alliance spread across the Plains states and the South, becoming by the late 1880s the largest farmer-based movement in American history. The harsh conditions farmers were enduring — including drought in the West and plunging global prices for corn, cotton, and wheat — intensified the movement's appeal. Traveling Farmers' Alliance lecturers exhorted farmers to "stand as a great conservative body against the encroachments of monopolies and . . . the growing corruption of wealth and power."

Alliance leaders pinned their initial hopes on cooperative stores and exchanges that would circumvent middlemen. **Cooperatives (co-ops)** gathered farmers' orders and bought in bulk at wholesale prices, passing the savings on to farmers. Alliance cooperatives suffered from chronic underfunding and lack of credit. They also faced hostility

Industrial Violence: A Dynamited Mine, 1894

Strikes in the western mining regions pitted ruthless owners, bent on control of their property and work-force, against fiercely independent miners who knew how to use dynamite. Some of the bloodiest conflicts occurred in Colorado mining towns, where the Western Federation of Miners (WFM) had strong support and a series of Republican governors sent state militia to back the mine owners. Violence broke out repeat-edly between the early 1890s and the 1910s. At Victor, Colorado, in May 1894, as dozens of armed sheriffs' deputies closed in on angry WFM members occupying the Strong Mine in protest, the miners blew up the mine's shaft house and boiler. Showered with debris, the deputies boarded the next train out of town. Because Colorado then had a Populist governor, Davis Waite, who sympathized with the miners and ordered the deputies to disband, this strike was one of the few in which owners and miners reached a peaceful settlement — a temporary victory for the union. Library of Congress.

from the merchants and lenders they tried to circumvent. But they achieved notable victories in the late 1880s. The Dakota Farmers' Alliance, for example, offered members cheap hail insurance and low prices on machinery and farm supplies. The Texas Farmers' Alliance established a huge cooperative enterprise to market cotton and provide farmers with cheap loans.

When cotton prices fell further in 1891, however, the Texas exchange failed. The Texas Farmers' Alliance then proposed a federal price-support system for farm products, modeled on the national banking system. Under this plan, the federal government would hold crops in public warehouses and issue loans on their value until they could be profitably sold. When the Democratic Party — still wary of big-government schemes — declared the idea too radical, the Texas Farmers' Alliance joined the alliances of Kansas, Nebraska, South Dakota, and elsewhere to create a new political party.

Expanding on the earlier work of the Grange, and carrying it into the South and West, the Farmers' Alliance cooperated with the Knights of Labor, using rural reform-ers' substantial political clout on behalf of urban workers who shared their political vision. By this time, the farmer-labor coalition had made a considerable impact on state politics. But state laws and commissions were proving ineffective against corporations of national and even global scope. It was difficult for a state like Minnesota, for example, to enforce new laws against a railroad company whose lines might stretch from Chicago to Seattle and whose corporate headquarters might be in New York. Militant farmers and labor advocates began to demand federal action.

In 1887, Congress sent President Grover Cleveland two groundbreaking bills that he signed into law. The Hatch Act provided federal funding for agricultural research and education, directly meeting farmers' demands for government aid to agriculture. The landmark Interstate Commerce Act counteracted a Supreme Court decision of the previous year, *Wabash v. Illinois*, that had struck down states' authority to regulate railroads. The act created the Interstate Commerce Commission (ICC), charged with investigating interstate shipping; forcing railroads to make their rates public; and, when necessary, suing in court to force companies to reduce "unjust or unreasonable" rates.

Though creation of the ICC was a direct response to pressure from farmer-labor constituents, its final form represented a compromise. The most radical rural representatives, like Texas congressman John Reagan, wanted Congress to establish a direct set of regulations under which railroads must operate. If a railroad did not comply, any citizen could take the company to court; and if the new rules triggered bankruptcy, the railroad could convert to public ownership. But getting such a plan through Congress proved impossible. Lawmakers more sympathetic to business called instead for an expert commission to oversee the railroad industry. In a pattern that was repeated frequently over the next few decades, the "commission" model proved more acceptable to the majority of congressmen, but probably less effective in practice than the original plan would have been.

The ICC faced formidable challenges. Though the new law forbade railroads from reaching secret rate-setting agreements, evidence was very difficult to gather; secret "pooling" continued. At the same time, a hostile Supreme Court eroded the commission's powers. In a series of sixteen decisions over the two decades after the ICC was created, the Court sided with railroads fifteen times. The justices delivered a particularly hard blow in 1897, when they ruled that the ICC had no power to interfere with shipping rates. Nonetheless, creation of the ICC was a major achievement. In the early twentieth century, Congress would strengthen the commission's powers and the ICC would become one of the most powerful federal agencies charged with overseeing private business.

Another Path: The American Federation of Labor

While the Knights of Labor exerted political pressure, some workers pursued a different strategy. In the 1870s, printers, molders, ironworkers, bricklayers, and about thirty other groups of skilled workers organized nationwide trade unions. These "brotherhoods" focused in narrow, specific ways on the everyday needs of workers in skilled occupations. Trade unions sought a **closed shop** — with all jobs reserved for union members — that kept out lower-wage workers. Union rules specified the terms of work, sometimes in minute detail. Some unions emphasized mutual aid. Because operating trains was a high-risk occupation, for example, railroad brotherhoods pooled their contributions in funds that provided accident and death benefits. Above all, trade unionism defended craft workers' traditional rights and asserted their role as active decision-makers in the workplace, not just cogs in a management-run machine.

For a while, in the 1880s, many trade unionists joined the Knights of Labor coalition. But the catastrophe of Haymarket persuaded them to leave the order and create the separate American Federation of Labor (AFL). The man who led them out of the Knights was Samuel Gompers, a Dutch-Jewish cigar maker whose family had emigrated to New York in 1863. Gompers headed the new AFL until 1924. He believed that the Knights relied too much on electoral politics, where victories were likely to be limited and fleeting, and he did not share their sweeping critique of **capitalism**. The AFL, made up of relatively skilled and well-paid workers, was less interested in challenging the corporate order than in winning a larger profit share for skilled workers.

Having gone to work at age ten, Gompers always contended that what he missed at school he more than made up for in the shop, where cigar makers paid one of their members to read to them while they worked. As a young worker-intellectual, Gompers gravitated to New York's radical circles, where he participated in lively debates about the best strategy for workingmen to pursue. Partly out of these debates, and partly from his own experience in the Cigar Makers Union, Gompers hammered out a doctrine that he called "pure-and-simple unionism." *Pure* referred to membership: strictly limited to workers, organized by craft and occupation, with no reliance on outside advisors or allies. *Simple* referred to goals: only those that immediately benefited workers — better wages, hours, and working conditions. Pure-and-simple unionists distrusted politics. Their aim was collective bargaining with employers.

On one level, pure-and-simple unionism worked. The AFL was small at first, but between 1897 and 1904, its membership rose from 447,000 to more than 2 million. In the early twentieth century, it became the nation's leading voice for workers, lasting far longer than movements like the Knights of Labor. The AFL's strategy — personified by Gompers, who became the union's towering leader — was especially well suited to an era when Congress and the courts were hostile to labor. By the 1910s the political climate would become more responsive; at that later moment, Gompers would soften his anti-political stance and AFL leaders joined the battle for new laws to protect workers.

What Gompers gave up most crucially, in the meantime, was the inclusiveness of the Knights of Labor. Compared with the Knights, the AFL was far less welcoming to women and blacks, and it was limited mostly to skilled craftsmen. There was little room in the AFL for department-store clerks and other service workers, much less the farmworkers and domestic servants whom the Knights of Labor had organized. Despite the AFL's great success among skilled craftsmen, the narrowness of its base was a flaw that would come back to haunt the labor movement later on. Gompers made a crucial choice when he limited the AFL's scope because the impact of industrialization reached far beyond skilled workers — and even beyond the workplace, immigrants, and the political sphere. Industrialization was, in these decades, transforming the whole of American society and culture.

▶ What factors prompted the emergence of the labor movement? In what ways did farmers and industrial workers cooperate?

▶ Which of the national labor organizations that formed after 1865 do you think was most successful? In what ways, and why?

SUMMARY

The end of the Civil War ushered in the era of American big business. Exploiting the continent's vast resources, vertically integrated corporations emerged as the dominant business form and giant companies built near monopolies in some sectors of the economy. Corporations devised new modes of production, distribution, and marketing, extending their reach through the department store, the mail-order catalog, and the new advertising industry. These developments laid the groundwork for mass consumer culture.

Rapid industrialization drew immigrants from around the world. Until the 1920s, most European and Latin American immigrants were welcome to enter the United States, though they often endured harsh conditions after they arrived. Asian immigrants, by contrast, met with severe discrimination. The Chinese Exclusion Act blocked all Chinese laborers from coming to the United States; it was later extended to other Asians, and it built the legal framework for broader forms of exclusion later on.

Nationwide movements for workers' rights arose in response to industrialization. During the 1870s and 1880s, coalitions of workers and farmers, notably the Knights of Labor and the Farmers' Alliance, organized to seek political solutions to what they saw as large corporations' exploitation of working people. Pressure from such movements led to the first major attempts to regulate corporations, such as the federal Interstate Commerce Act. Radical protest movements were weakened, however, after public condemnation of anarchist violence in 1886 at Chicago's Haymarket Square — even though the Knights and Farmers' Alliance were obviously not responsible. Meanwhile, trade unions pursued a pure-and-simple approach to organization and negotiation, organizing skilled workers to negotiate directly with employers. Such unions became the most popular form of labor organizing in the early twentieth century.

For additional primary sources from this period, see *Documents for America's History*, Seventh Edition.

For Web sites, images, and documents related to topics and places in this chapter, visit *Make History* at **bedfordstmartins.com/henrettaconcise.**

For Further Exploration

Important works on industrialization include Walter Licht, *Industrializing America* (1995); Mira Wilkins, *The Emergence of Multinational Enterprise* (1970); and Alfred Chandler, *The Visible Hand* (1977). On managers and salesmen, see Olivier Zunz, *Making America Corporate* (1990), and Walter Friedman, *Birth of a Salesman* (2004). On changing views of wage work, see Lawrence Glickman, *A Living Wage* (1997); on women, see Susan Porter Benson, *Counter Cultures* (1986), and Angel Kwolek-Folland, *Engendering Business* (1994). Biographies include Joseph Frazier Wall, *Andrew Carnegie* (1970), and, on John D. Rockefeller, Ron Chernow, *Titan* (1998).

TIMELINE

1863	▶ Cleveland, Ohio, becomes nation's petroleum refining center	**1882**	▶ Congress passes Chinese Exclusion Act
1865	▶ Chicago's Union Stock Yard opens	**1886**	▶ McCormick reaper works strike
1867	▶ National Grange of the Patrons of Husbandry founded		▶ Haymarket Square violence
			▶ American Federation of Labor (AFL) founded
1869	▶ Knights of Labor founded	**1887**	▶ Interstate Commerce Act
		1900	▶ America's one hundred largest companies control one-third of national productive capacity
1875	▶ John Wanamaker opens nation's first department store in Philadelphia		
1877	▶ San Francisco mob attacks Chinatown; Great Railroad Strike		

On immigration, see Roger Daniels, *Coming to America* (1990); Walter T. K. Nugent, *Crossings* (1992); Mark Wyman, *Round-Trip to America* (1993); Ronald Takaki, *Strangers from a Different Shore* (1989); and Erika Lee, *At America's Gates* (2003). On 1877, see David Stowell, ed., *The Great Strikes of 1877* (2008). Studies of labor include David Montgomery, *The Fall of the House of Labor* (1987) and *Citizen Worker* (1993); Leon Fink, *Workingmen's Democracy* (1983); David Brody, *Steelworkers in America* (1960); and Paul Krause, *The Battle for Homestead* (1992). On the role of farmers and labor in state-building, see Elizabeth Sanders, *Roots of Reform* (1999). On Gompers, see Harold Livesay, *Samuel Gompers and Organized Labor in America* (1978), and the treasure trove at the Gompers Papers site, **www.history.umd.edu/Gompers**. Also see *Who Built America?* (second edition; 2008) by the American Social History Project.

Test Your Knowledge

For practice quizzes, activities, and other study tools, visit the Online Study Guide at **bedfordstmartins.com/henrettaconcise**.

The evolution of brains . . . has unsettled the standard of civilization and the relations of the sexes.

—Lucinda Chandler, Illinois temperance and women's rights advocate, 1891

In 1876, a popular biography of presidential candidate Rutherford B. Hayes told American boys and girls why he had achieved success. As a child, Hayes had always obeyed his loving mother. He "shunned the coarse and rude boys upon the street." At school, he "did not splinter his desk with his penknife, nor throw paper balls or apple-cores. . . . He was a model boy." Hayes grew up to marry a refined and educated woman, Lucy Ware Webb. She devoted herself to her children, while Rutherford, in turn, appreciated his wife's moral guidance. The two were faithful churchgoers; one of their favorite pastimes was gathering the family to sing hymns.

Hayes's biography summed up the ideal of domesticity that prevailed during the Victorian era (that is, the time of Queen Victoria's rule in Great Britain, 1837–1901, when English mores and culture profoundly influenced the United States). Domesticity called for masculine restraint and female moral influence. But industrialization was transforming domesticity, as Americans confronted modern conditions of life. While Hayes served as president, authors of children's books were already undermining older views. Boys and girls were snapping up flamboyant dime novels with titles like *Buffalo Bill's Death-Deal*. From playgrounds to summer camps, children's vigorous physical exercise became a national priority. By 1905, one of the most popular children's books was Ralph Henry Barbour's *The Crimson Sweater*, the story of a schoolboy who proves himself through rugged feats in football and hockey. The story's sassy heroine, Harriet, insists on the nickname "Harry" and sneaks out at night for adventures with the boys.

The shift in children's literature was a marker of America's changing culture. More and more, women sought to exert their influence outside the home, through involvement in politics, reform movements, and civic life. Women also expanded their place in the public sphere through their increasing presence as wage-earners. At the same time, the ideal of restrained Christian manhood gave way to aggressive calls for masculine fitness and self-assertion, exemplified in the rising popularity of athletics. An ethos of duty, self-restraint, and moral uplift gave way to new expectations of leisure and fun.

In the same decades, stunning scientific discoveries — from dinosaur fossils to distant galaxies — challenged nineteenth-century beliefs about humans' place in the universe. Faced with such wonders as electricity and medical vaccines, Americans celebrated technological solutions to human problems. But while scientific ways of thinking gained tremendous popularity, religion hardly faded. In fact, the diversity of religious practice grew — not only because immigrants brought new faiths from abroad, but also because religious innovators, confronted with the problems caused by industrialization, developed such creative ideas and institutions as the Social Gospel and the Salvation Army.

In these decades, Americans found themselves living in a **modern** society — one in which their grandparents' beliefs, assumptions, and ways of life no longer seemed to apply. Living in an increasingly market-driven economic order, many Americans championed the freedom of each individual to choose his or her path. At the same time, they expressed anxiety and distress over the attendant risks and upheavals. In the decades between the end of the Civil War and the start of World War I, industrialization transformed family life, education, leisure, religion, and the arts. During this era of dynamic change, Americans reshaped — without necessarily discarding — older attachments and beliefs.

Women, Men, and the Solitude of Self

Appearing before Congress in 1892, women's rights advocate Elizabeth Cady Stanton described what she called the "solitude of self." Stanton rejected the claim that women had no need for equal rights because they enjoyed the protection of male kin. "The talk of sheltering woman from the fierce storms of life is the sheerest mockery," she declared. "They beat on her from every point of the compass, just as they do on man, and with more fatal results, for he has been trained to protect himself." Stanton's arguments suited an era when women were taking up reform work and paid employment outside the home. Meanwhile, in a market-driven economy men faced increasing pressure to strive for success in "the battle of life."

Changes in Family Life

The average American family — especially among the middle class — decreased in size in the post–Civil War decades. A long decline in the birthrate, which began in the late eighteenth century, continued in this era. In 1800, white women who survived to menopause had borne an average of 7.0 children; by 1900, the average was 3.6. On the farm and in many working-class families, children were assets on the family balance sheet: at a young age, they went to work in the fields or factory. But in an industrial society, parents who had fewer sons and daughters could concentrate their resources, educating and preparing each child for success in the new economy. Family limitation was one of the keys to upward mobility.

Several factors limited childbearing. Americans married at older ages, and many mothers tried — as they had for decades — to space pregnancies more widely by nursing young children for several years, which suppressed fertility. By the late nineteenth century, couples also used a range of other contraceptive methods, such as condoms and diaphragms, though they rarely wrote about them. Their reluctance to do so was understandable, since contraceptives were deeply stigmatized. In 1873, Anthony Comstock, the crusading secretary of the New York Society for the Suppression of Vice, secured a federal law that banned obscene materials from the U.S. mail. The Comstock Act prohibited circulation of almost any information about sex and birth control. It appears, however, that Comstock had limited success in preventing the spread of contraceptives.

As they grew to adulthood, rural young people faced new dilemmas and choices. Traditionally, daughters had provided essential labor for spinning and weaving cloth, but industrialization had relocated those tasks from the household to the factory. "Fewer women than men are needed on the farm," reported one investigator. "One woman, ordinarily, does the work of the family." Finding themselves without a useful role in the household, many farm daughters sought paid employment. In an age of declining rural prosperity, many sons also left the farm and — like immigrants arriving from other countries — set aside part of their pay to help the folks at home. Explaining why she moved to Chicago, an African American woman from Louisiana declared, "A child with any respect about herself or hisself wouldn't like to see their mother and father work so hard and earn nothing. I feel it my duty to help."

The Rise of High School

For young people who hoped to secure respectable and lucrative jobs, the watchword was *education*. A high school education was particularly valuable for boys from affluent families who hoped to enter professional or managerial work. Daughters attended in even larger numbers than their brothers. Parents of the Civil War generation, who had witnessed the plight of thousands of war widows and orphans, encouraged daughters to educate themselves for teaching or office work, so they could find employment before marriage and would have skills to fall back on, "just in case." Both urban reformers and rural groups such as the Farmers' Alliance pushed for better public schools and for technical and business education. By 1900, 71 percent of Americans between the ages of five and eighteen attended school. That figure rose even further in the early twentieth century, as public officials adopted and enforced laws requiring school attendance.

Most high schools were coeducational. The curriculum included literature and composition, history and geography, biology and mathematics, and a mix of ancient and modern languages. Boys and girls engaged in friendly — and sometimes not-so-friendly — rivalry when girls captured an outsize share of academic prizes. In 1884, a high school newspaper in Concord, New Hampshire, published this poem from a disgruntled boy who caricatured his female classmates:

> We know many tongues of living and dead,
> In science and fiction we're very well read,
> But we cannot cook meat and cannot make bread
> And we've wished many times that we were all dead.

A female student promptly shot back a poem of her own, denouncing male students' smoking habit:

But if boys will smoke cigarettes
Although the smoke may choke them,
One consolation still remains —
They kill the boys that smoke them.

Almost every high school featured athletics, and girls found a place there, too. Recruited first as cheerleaders for high school boys' teams, they soon established field hockey and other teams of their own.

College Men and Women

Through most of the nineteenth century, the rate of Americans who attended college had hovered around 2 percent. Driven partly by the expansion of public universities, the rate began to rise steadily in the 1880s, reaching 8 percent by 1920. Much larger numbers attended the rapidly growing network of business and technical schools. "GET A PLACE IN THE WORLD," advertised one Minneapolis business college in 1907, "where your talents can be used to the best advantage." Typically, the school offered both day and night classes in subjects such as bookkeeping, typewriting, and shorthand.

The needs of the changing economy also influenced the curriculum at more traditional institutions. State universities emphasized agricultural and technical training. They fed the growing professional workforce with graduates trained in fields such as engineering. Many private colleges distanced themselves from such practical pursuits; their administrators argued that students who aimed to be leaders in business, politics, and society needed a broad-based knowledge of history and culture. They modernized their course offerings, emphasizing languages such as French and German, for example, rather than Latin and Greek. Harvard College, under dynamic president Charles W. Eliot from 1869 to 1909, pioneered the liberal arts. Students at the all-male college chose from a range of electives, as Eliot called for classes that developed each young man's "individual reality and creative power."

African American Education | In the South, one of the most famous educational projects was Booker T. Washington's Tuskegee Institute, founded in 1881. Washington, born in slavery, not only taught but exemplified the goal of self-help, and his autobiography, *Up from Slavery*, became an immediate bestseller in 1901. Because of the deep poverty in which most southern African Americans lived, Washington concluded that "book education" for most "would be almost a waste of time." He focused instead on industrial education. Students, he argued, would "be sure of knowing how to make a living after they had left us." Tuskegee sent many female graduates into teaching and nursing; men more often entered the industrial trades or farmed by the latest scientific methods.

Washington became the most prominent black leader of his generation. His style of leadership, based on avoiding confrontation with whites and cultivating patronage and private influence, was well suited to the difficult era after Reconstruction. Washington believed that money was color-blind: Whites, he argued, would respect economic success. Washington represented the hopes of millions of African Americans who expected

Booker T. Washington
In an age of severe racial oppression, Booker T. Washington emerged as the leading public voice of African Americans. He was remarkable both for his effectiveness in speaking to white Americans and for his deep understanding of the aspirations of blacks. Born a slave, Washington had plenty of firsthand experience with racism. But having befriended several whites in his youth, he also believed that African Americans could appeal to whites of good will — and maneuver around those who were hostile — in the struggle for equality. He hoped, most of all, that economic achievement would erase white prejudice. Brown Brothers.

that education, hard work, and respectability would erase white prejudice. That optimism proved ill-founded. As a tide of disfranchisement, segregation, and lynching rolled in during the 1890s, educated and prosperous blacks became targets of white anger. Washington soon came under fire from a younger generation of race leaders, who argued that he accommodated too much to white racism. Nonetheless, Tuskegee endured as an educational beacon.

Higher Education for Women In the Northeast and South, women most often attended single-sex institutions or teacher-training colleges where the student body was overwhelmingly female. For students from affluent families, private colleges offered an education equivalent to men's. Vassar College started the trend when it opened in 1861; Smith, Wellesley, and others soon followed. Some doctors warned that these institutions were dangerous: Intensive brain work, they said, would unsex young women and drain energy from their ovaries, leading them to bear weak children later in life. In response to such critics, Vassar implemented a strict regimen of regular exercise, nutritious meals, naps, and curfews to ensure that students stayed healthy. But as thousands of women earned degrees and suffered no apparent harm, fears faded. Single-sex higher education for women spread from private to public institutions, especially in the South, where the Mississippi State College for Women (1885) led the way.

Coeducation was more prevalent in the Midwest and West, where state universities opened their doors to female students after the Civil War. Women were also admitted to most of the southern African American colleges founded during Reconstruction. By 1910, 58 percent of America's 1,083 colleges and universities were coeducational. While women at single-sex institutions forged strong bonds with one another, women also gained many benefits from learning with men. When male students were friendly, they forged comfortable working relationships; when men were hostile, women learned coping skills that served them well when they later took up reform work or paid employment. One doctor who studied at the University of Iowa remembered later that he and his friends mercilessly harassed the first women who entered the medical school. But when the women showed they were good students, the men's attitudes changed to "wholesome respect."

Whether or not they got a college education, more and more women recognized, in the words of Elizabeth Cady Stanton, their "solitude of self." The rapidly changing economy offered both opportunities and dangers; it rewarded mobility and individual risk-taking. In such a world, women could not always count on the protection or support of fathers, husbands, and sons. Women who needed to support themselves could choose from dozens of guidebooks such as *What Girls Can Do* (1880) and *How to Make Money Although a Woman* (1895). Members of the Association for the Advancement of Women, founded in 1873, argued that women's paid employment was a positive good.

Today, many economists argue that education and high-quality jobs for women are keys to poverty reduction in the developing world. In the United States, that process also led to broader gains in women's political rights. As women began to earn advanced degrees, gain footholds in respectable and professional employments, and live independently, it became harder to argue that women were "dependents" who did not need to vote.

Masculinity and the Rise of Sports

In the decades after the Civil War, gender expectations also changed for middle-class men. Traditionally, the mark of a successful American man was his economic independence: He was his own boss. But by the late nineteenth century, more and more men worked in salaried positions or for wages. Increasing numbers also did brain work in an office, rather than using their muscles outdoors. Anxieties arose that the American male was becoming, as one magazine editor warned, "weak, effeminate, decaying." How could men assert their independence in the modern world? How could they develop toughness and physical strength? One answer was athletics. Before the Civil War, there were no distinctively American games except for Native American lacrosse. The most popular team sport was cricket. Over the next six decades sports became a fundamental part of American manhood.

The YMCA and "Muscular Christianity" | One of the first promoters of physical fitness was the Young Men's Christian Association (YMCA). Adapted from Britain and introduced to Boston in 1851, the YMCA combined vigorous activities for young men with an evangelizing appeal. In cities and towns across America, the YMCA built gymnasiums and athletic facilities where men could exercise their bodies and make themselves "clean and strong."

Begun as a Protestant effort to promote "muscular Christianity" for white-collar workers, the YMCA also developed a substantial industrial program between 1900 and 1917. Railroad managers and other corporate titans hoped that YMCAs would head off labor unrest, fostering a loyal and contented workforce. Business leaders also relied on sports to foster physical and mental discipline, and to help men adjust their bodies to the demands of the clock and stopwatch, enhancing performance on the job. Sports fostered men's competitive spirit, they believed; serving on employer-sponsored teams could instill a sense of teamwork and company pride.

But working-class men and boys had their own ideas about sports and leisure. YMCAs quickly became a site of negotiation. Could workingmen come to the "Y" to play billiards or cards? Could they smoke? At first YMCA leaders said no, but to attract working-class men, they had to make concessions. At the same time, the institution became a site for athletic innovation. YMCA instructors, searching for wintertime fitness activities in the 1890s, invented the new games of basketball and volleyball.

The YMCA sought to provide some of the amenities of elite athletic clubs that also flourished after the Civil War. Exclusive country clubs, which appeared in many affluent neighborhoods, combined facilities for tennis, golf, and swimming with a dining room and calendar of social events. By the turn of the century — perhaps because women were rapidly encroaching on their athletic turf — elite men took up even more aggressive physical sports, including boxing, weightlifting, and martial arts. Theodore Roosevelt became one of the first American devotees of jujitsu; during his presidency, from 1901 to 1909, he designated a judo room in the White House and hired an expert Japanese instructor. Roosevelt also famously wrestled and boxed, urging other American men to join him in pursuing the "strenuous life."

America's Game | In the summer of 1907, famous lawyer Clarence Darrow sweated in a Boise courtroom, defending three leaders of the Western Federation of Miners against charges that they had assassinated Idaho's ex-governor. The atmosphere was tense; when Darrow won acquittals on all counts, the outcome was a sensation. But the seriousness of the trial did not prevent the judge, jury, and lawyers on both sides from adjourning to the local baseball diamond. "Never has life held for me," Darrow once remarked, "anything quite so entrancing as baseball." He and other lawyers cheered as they watched a local telephone company employee, Walter Johnson, pitch a series of spectacular shutouts in the Idaho State League. Johnson, promptly signed by the Washington Senators, went on to become one of the game's legendary pitchers.

In the post–Civil War years, no other sport in America was as successful as baseball. As early as the late 1700s, Americans had begun to play various stick and ball games, some of which came to be called "base ball." More formal rules developed in the 1840s and 1850s, and baseball's popularity spread in military camps during the Civil War. Afterward, the idea that baseball "received its baptism in the bloody days of our Nation's direst danger," as one promoter put it, became part of the game's mythology.

Big-time professional baseball arose after the war, with the launching of the National League in 1876. The league quickly built more than a dozen teams in the large cities of the Northeast and Midwest, from the Brooklyn Trolley Dodgers to the Cleveland Spiders. Team owners were profit-minded businessmen who shaped the sport to please fans. Wooden grandstands gave way to the concrete and steel stadiums of the early twentieth century, such as Fenway Park in Boston and Forbes Field in Pittsburgh. By 1900, boys collected lithographed cards of their favorite players, and the baseball cap came into fashion. In 1903, two years after the creation of the American League, the Boston Americans defeated the Pittsburgh Pirates in the first World Series.

American men not only rooted for professional baseball teams; they got out on the diamond to play. Until the 1870s, most amateur players were clerks and white-collar

Football Practice, Chilocco Indian School, 1911
Football became widely popular, spreading from Ivy League schools and state universities to schools like this one, built on Cherokee land in Oklahoma. The uniforms of this team, typical of the day, show very limited padding and protection — a factor that contributed to high rates of injury and even death on the field. As they practiced in 1911, these Chilocco students had an inspiring model to look up to: In the same year Jim Thorpe, a fellow Oklahoman and a member of the Sac and Fox tribes, was winning national fame by leading the all-Indian team at Pennsylvania's Carlisle School to victory against Harvard. Thorpe, one of the finest athletes of his generation, went on to win gold medals in the pentathlon and decathlon at the 1912 Olympics in Stockholm, Sweden. National Archives.

workers who had the leisure time to play and the income to buy their own uniforms. Business frowned on baseball and other sports as a waste of time, especially for working-class men. But after the Civil War, employers came to see baseball, like other athletic pursuits, as healthy and uplifting. It provided fresh air and exercise, kept workers out of saloons, and promoted discipline and teamwork. Company teams became a widespread institution. The best players, wearing uniforms emblazoned with their companies' names, competed on paid work time during the ball season. Baseball thus set a pattern for how other American sports developed. Begun among independent craftsmen, it was taken up by elite men anxious to prove their strength and fitness. Well-to-do Americans then decided such sports could benefit wage-earning men.

Rise of the Negro Leagues Baseball was a site of negotiations over race as well as class. In the 1880s and 1890s, managers hired a few African American players into the major leagues. As late as 1901, the manager of the Baltimore Orioles succeeded in hiring Charlie Grant, a light-skinned black player from Cincinnati, by renaming him Charlie Tokohoma and claiming he was Cherokee. But as the manager's subterfuge suggested, black players were increasingly barred. A Toledo team with a black player received a threatening note before one game in Richmond, Virginia: If the "negro catcher" played, the writer warned, he would be lynched. Toledo put a substitute on the field, and at the end of the season the club terminated the black player's contract.

Shut out of white leagues, black players and fans turned instead to segregated professional teams. These emerged as early as Reconstruction, showcasing both athletic talent and race pride. Louisiana's top team, the New Orleans Pinchbacks, pointedly named themselves after the state's black Reconstruction governor. By the early 1900s, such teams organized into separate Negro Leagues. Though their players endured erratic pay and rundown ball fields, the popular leagues thrived until the desegregation of baseball after World War II. In an era of stark discrimination, they showcased the manhood and talent of black men. "I liked the way their uniform fit, the way they wore their cap," wrote an admiring fan of the Newark Eagles. "They showed a style in almost everything they did." Looking back on his career for Chicago's American Giants and other clubs, player-manager John Henry "Pop" Lloyd remarked, "I had a chance to prove the ability of our race in this sport. . . . We have given the Negro a greater opportunity now to be accepted into the major leagues with other Americans."

American | The most controversial sport was football, which began at elite Ivy League
Football | colleges during the 1880s. The great powerhouse was the Yale team, whose
| legendary coach Walter Camp went on to become a watch manufacturer.
Between 1883 and 1891, under Camp's direction, Yale scored 4,660 points while its opponents scored 92. Camp emphasized drill and precision, drawing on the emerging ideals of scientific management, which taught humans to move with machinelike efficiency. Coaches like Camp argued that football offered perfect training for the competitive world of business. The game was violent: The deaths of six players in the 1908 college season provoked a public outcry. Eventually, new rules protected quarterbacks and required coaches to remove injured players from the game. But such measures were adopted grudgingly, with supporters arguing that they ruined football as a site of manly combat.

Like baseball and the YMCA, football soon attracted business sponsorship. The first professional teams emerged around the turn of the twentieth century in western Pennsylvania's steel towns. Executives of Carnegie Steel organized teams in Homestead and Braddock, and the first league appeared during the anthracite coal strike of 1902. Most early professional teams arose in the industrial heartland. The Green Bay Packers were sponsored by the Indian-Acme Packing Company; the future Chicago Bears, first known as the Decatur Staleys, were funded by a maker of laundry starch. Like baseball, football initially encouraged men to develop their own strength and skills, but its professional form encouraged most men to buy in as spectators and fans.

The Great Outdoors

As the rise of sports suggests, Americans began to look back on Victorian life as stuffy and claustrophobic, and they revolted by heading outdoors. A craze for bicycling swept the country; in 1890, at the height of the mania, U.S. manufacturers sold an astonishing ten million bikes. Women were not far behind men in taking up athletics. By the 1890s even elite women — long confined to corsets and heavy, elaborate clothes that restricted their movement — donned lighter clothes and took up sports like archery and golf. Artist Charles Gibson became famous for his portraits of the "Gibson Girl," an elite beauty whom he often depicted playing on the tennis court or swimming at the beach. Commentators hailed the "New Woman" for her athleticism and public spirit.

Those with leisure time used the rail networks to get outdoors and closer to nature. For people of modest means, this most often meant Sunday afternoon by the lake. By the turn of the century, camping had become a recognized form of fun. As early as 1904, Coronado Beach in California was offering tent rentals for $3 a week. By the 1910s, campgrounds and cottages in many parts of the country catered to a working-class clientele. In an industrial and increasingly urban society, the outdoors became a site of leisure and renewal rather than danger and hard work. One journalist, looking at urban life from the vantage point of a vacation in the West, wrote, "How stupid it all seems: the mad eagerness of money-making men, the sham pleasures of conventional society." In the wilderness, he went on, "your blood clarifies; your brain becomes active. You get a new view of life."

Preservation | As Americans went searching for such renewal, national and state governments set aside more public lands for preservation and recreation. The United States substantially expanded its park system and, during Theodore Roosevelt's presidency, extended the reach of national forests, now overseen by the U.S. Forest Service. By 1916, President Woodrow Wilson provided consistent administrative oversight of the national parks, signing an act creating the National Park Service (Map 18.1). A year later the system numbered thirteen parks — including Maine's Acadia, the first that lay east of the Mississippi River. National parks became increasingly popular places to hike, camp, and contemplate natural beauty.

Further preservation was carried out after 1906 through the Lacey Act, which allowed the U.S. president, without congressional approval, to set aside "objects of historic and scientific interest" as national monuments. Two years later, Theodore Roosevelt used these powers to preserve 800,000 acres at Arizona's Grand Canyon. The Lacey Act proved to be a mixed blessing for conservation. Monuments received weaker protection than did national parks, and many fell under the authority of the U.S. Forest Service, which permitted logging and grazing. Thus, while many areas were preserved under the Lacey Act, business interests lobbied after 1906 to have coveted lands designated as "monuments" rather than "parks" so that businesses could more easily exploit resources. Nonetheless, more and more Americans called for preservation of the last remnants of unexploited land.

John Muir, who fell in love with the Yosemite Valley in 1869, was one of the first famous voices of this environmental movement. Muir, an imaginative inventor who grew up on a Wisconsin farm, was a keen observer of nature. Raised in a stern Scots Presbyterian family, he knew much of the Bible by heart and developed a deeply spiritual relationship with the natural world. His contemporary Mary Austin, whose book *Land of Little Rain* (1905) celebrated the austere beauty of the California desert, called him "a devout man." In cooperation with his editor at *Century* magazine, Muir founded the Sierra Club in 1892. Similar to the Appalachian Mountain Club, founded in Boston in 1876, the Sierra Club dedicated itself to preserving and enjoying mountain regions.

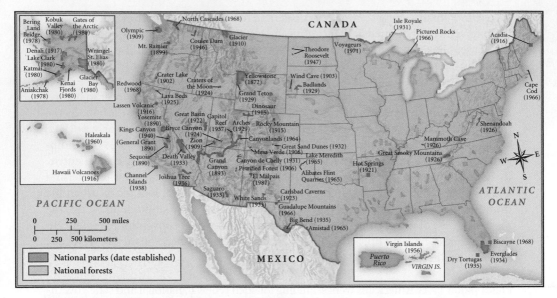

MAP 18.1 National Parks and Forests, 1872–1980

Yellowstone, the first national park in the United States, dates from 1872. In 1893, the federal government began to intervene to protect national forests. Without Theodore Roosevelt, however, the national forest program might have languished; during his presidency he added 125 million acres to the forest system, plus six national parks in addition to several that had already been created during the 1890s. America's national forest and park systems remain one of the most visible and beloved legacies of federal policy innovation in the decades between the Civil War and World War I.

Environmentalists worked not only to preserve land but also to protect wildlife. Soon after the Civil War, Congress created preserves on the Alaskan coast to protect sea lions and fur seals. By the turn of the twentieth century, local Audubon Societies began to advocate broader protections for wild birds, especially herons and egrets that were being slaughtered by the thousands for their plumes. Women played prominent roles in the movement, lobbying to protect wild birds and organizing campaigns to persuade women to avoid hats with plume decorations. In 1903, President Theodore Roosevelt created the first National Wildlife Refuge at Pelican Island, Florida. By the end of his term as president, Roosevelt had signed fifty-one executive orders creating wildlife refuges in twenty territories and states.

Many states also passed game laws to protect wildlife and regulate hunting and fishing, redefining these as recreational rather than subsistence activities. Such laws were often selectively enforced in ways that reflected prevailing racial biases. In New Mexico, for example, where Anglos and Hispanics were terrified by the prospect of Indians armed with guns, the territory's first fish and game warden argued that his job was to "protect the game and fish and see that Indians in particular are kept off the range."

In all parts of the country, new game laws triggered controversy over the uses of wildlife. In the South, conservationists got many game laws passed in the early twentieth century, but not until the late 1910s and 1920s did judges and juries begin taking them seriously. Results were mixed. Shifting from year-round subsistence hunting to a recreational hunting season brought hardship to many poor rural families who depended on game meat for food. At the same time, most Americans came to agree that regulation was beneficial: It suppressed such popular practices as the hunting of songbirds and the use of dynamite to kill fish in lakes and ponds. Looking back on the era before game laws, one Alabama hunter remembered that "the slaughter was terrific." While making it more difficult for rural people to support themselves by the bounty of the land, regulation prevented further extinctions like that of the passenger pigeon, which vanished around 1900.

► What new educational opportunities arose for young Americans in the late nineteenth century? How did those change the experiences and expectations of young men and women? Of African Americans, in particular?

► What role did sports play in the redefinition of masculine identities? How did sports reflect the racial and economic divisions of the era?

Women in the Public Sphere

In the early nineteenth century, many public spaces — from city streets and election polls to saloons and circus shows — remained the domains of men. A woman who ventured into such places without a chaperone risked damaging her reputation. But industrialization transformed public space. To attract an eager public, purveyors of consumer culture invited women and families to linger in department stores and enjoy new public amusements. Gradually, women of all classes and backgrounds began to claim their right to public space. At the same time, middle-class women sought in other ways to expand their place beyond the household, by building reform movements and taking political action. "Women's place is Home," journalist Rheta Childe Dorr wrote, but then added, "Home is the community. The city full of people is the Family. . . . Badly do the Home and Family need their mother."

Negotiating Public Space

No one promoted commercial domesticity more successfully than showman P. T. Barnum (1810–1891), who used the country's expanding rail network to develop his famous traveling circus. Barnum condemned earlier circus managers who had opened their tents to "the rowdy element." Proclaiming that his most important audience was children, Barnum set out to make his show a family entertainment for audiences of all classes and races (though in the South, black audiences sat in segregated seats or attended separate shows). He promised parents that his show would teach children about courage and promote the benefits of exercise. To make the show comfortable for women, Barnum's circus featured female performers and emphasized their respectability and refinement. Barnum's managers claimed, for example, that Isabella Butler, who in the early 1900s drove her miniature car in an act called the "Dip of Death," was a student at Vassar.

Finding Americans eager for excursions, railroad companies made their cars comfortable for families. Boston's South Terminal Station boasted of its modern amenities, including "almost everything that the traveler needs down to cradles in which the baby may be soothed." An 1882 tourist guide promised readers that they could live on the Pacific Railroad "with as much true enjoyment as the home drawing room." Its "neat and clean" cars would become "your home. Here you sit and read, play your games, indulge in social conversation." Railcars manufactured by the famous Pullman Company of Chicago set a national standard for taste and elegance. Fitted with rich carpets, upholstery, and woodwork, Pullman's Palace cars and sleeping cars influenced trends in home decor.

The best accommodations, of course, were in first-class cars, whose opulence marked passengers' wealth as well as their desire for domesticity. Part of the appeal of consumer culture, however, was that less affluent Americans could indulge their tastes in new ways. One train conductor noticed, after years of working on the railroads, that the luxuries of a Pullman car were enjoyed most by passengers of modest means. It was grocers' wives, he observed, who were most likely to "sweep . . . into a parlor car as if the very carpet ought to feel highly honored by their tread." First-class and "ladies' cars" also became sites of struggle for African American rights. Before the Supreme Court sanctioned segregation in 1896, blacks often succeeded in securing seats. One African American clubwoman noted, however, "There are few ordeals more nerve-wracking than the one which confronts a colored woman when she tries to secure a Pullman reservation in the South and even in some parts of the North." At the turn of the century, the exclusion of blacks from first-class cars became one of the most public and painful marks of racism.

The purveyors of modern consumer culture designed one popular site specifically for women: the department store. In earlier generations, men had largely controlled the family pocketbook; women's task was to labor at home to produce their families' food and clothing. By the late nineteenth century, especially in towns and cities, women became the chief family shoppers. Department stores attracted middle-class women by offering tearooms, children's play areas, and other welcoming features. Such tactics succeeded so well that New York's department store district became known as Ladies' Mile. Boston department store magnate William Filene called the department store an "Adamless Eden."

From Female Moral Authority to Feminism

Changing expectations about the use of public space reflected a broader expansion of women's public activities, from patriotic work to many types of reform. Starting in the 1880s, women's clubs sprang up in cities and towns across the United States. So many had been formed by 1890 that their leaders created a nationwide umbrella organization, the General Federation of Women's Clubs. Moving from educational and literary topics into reform, women's clubs began to study such problems as pollution, unsafe working conditions, and urban poverty. Such groups frequently justified their work through the ideology of **maternalism**; they appealed to what they saw as women's special talents as mothers, Christians, and moral guides. Maternalism was an intermediate step between domesticity and modern arguments for gender equality. It came in many forms. In dozens of organizations, women undertook "municipal housekeeping" in order to help other women, promote national patriotism, and engage in "race uplift." By the 1890s, humorist Josh Billings looked at all this public activity and joked, "Wimmin is everywhere."

The Woman's Christian Temperance Union | One of the first places women sought to reform was the saloon. The Woman's Christian Temperance Union (WCTU) was founded in 1874 and spread rapidly after 1879, when the charismatic Frances Willard became its leader. It became the leading U.S. organization advocating prohibition of liquor. The WCTU, more than any other group of the late nineteenth century, launched women into public reform. Willard knew how to frame political demands in the language of feminine self-sacrifice. She advised her followers: "Womanliness first; afterward, what you will." WCTU members vividly described the plight of hungry, abused wives and children whose husbands and fathers suffered in the grip of alcoholism. Willard's motto was "Home Protection," and though it placed all the blame on alcohol rather than other factors, the WCTU became the first national organization to identify and combat domestic violence.

The prohibitionist movement drew together reformers from many backgrounds. Middle-class city dwellers worried about the link between alcoholism and crime, especially in the growing immigrant wards. They saw a ban on drinking as beneficial to society. Rural citizens equated liquor with big-city sins such as prostitution, political corruption, and public disorder. Methodists, Baptists, Mormons, and members of other denominations condemned drinking for religious reasons. Immigrants passionately disagreed, however: Germans and Irish Catholics enjoyed their Sunday beer and saw no harm in it. Saloons were a centerpiece of working-class leisure and community life, offering free lunches, public toilets, and a place to sit and share neighborhood news. For many immigrants, prohibition was an attack on their ethnic cultures.

The WCTU did not focus solely on prohibition. Investigating alcohol abuse, Willard increasingly confronted a host of related problems. "Do Everything," she urged WCTU members. Across the United States, WCTU chapters founded soup kitchens and free libraries. They introduced a German educational innovation, the kindergarten. They investigated prison conditions. Addressing workers' issues — while Knights of Labor leaders simultaneously endorsed temperance — Willard advocated laws establishing an eight-hour workday and abolishing child labor.

Willard was one of the first mainstream American reformers to call for women's suffrage, lending considerable support to the small, independent women's rights movement that had emerged during Reconstruction. However, Willard avoided any talk of "rights" and spoke instead of "prayerful, persistent pleas for the opportunity of duty." Controversially, Willard threw the WCTU's influence behind a new political party, the Prohibition Party, which exercised considerable clout in the 1880s. Women worked in the party as stump speakers, convention delegates, and even candidates for local office.

The WCTU and Prohibition Party met formidable obstacles. Liquor was big business, and powerful interests mobilized to block Prohibition Party candidates and antiliquor legislation. In many parts of the country — particularly the growing cities — prohibition simply did not gain majority support. Willard, discouraged by the movement's failure to obtain a national prohibition law, retired to England, where she died in 1898. But the legacy of her work was powerful. After 1900, groups like the Anti-Saloon League took up the banner, and after World War I they finally won a constitutional amendment prohibiting "the manufacture, sale, or transportation of intoxicating liquors." In the meantime, the WCTU had taught women how to lobby, raise money, and even run for office. Willard wrote that "perhaps the most significant outcome" of the movement she led was women's "knowledge of their own power."

The movement for women's voting rights benefited from the influx of **temperance** support. Though it had split into two rival organizations during Reconstruction, the movement reunited in 1890 in the National American Woman Suffrage Association. Soon afterward, suffragists won two victories in the West: Colorado in 1893 and Idaho in 1896. In the following decade, movement leaders were discouraged by many state-level

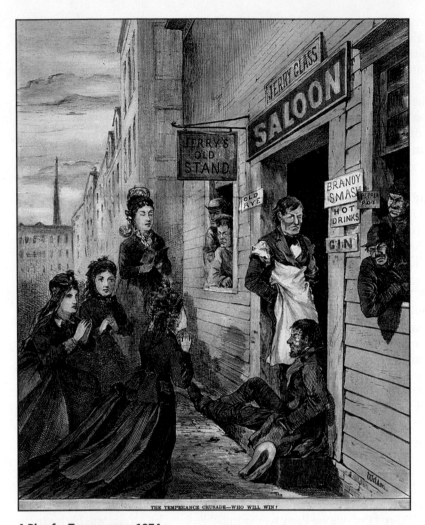

A Plea for Temperance, 1874

The origins of the Woman's Christian Temperance Union lay in spontaneous prayer meetings held by women outside local saloons, where they appealed for men to stop drinking and liquor sellers to destroy their product. A string of such meetings in Ohio won national attention, as in this image from a popular magazine, the *Daily Graphic*. "Who Will Win?" asked the artist. The answers varied. A few saloon owners, struck with remorse over the damage caused by alcohol abuse, smashed their beer kegs and poured their liquor into the gutters. Far more refused, but in the 1880s, temperance women succeeded in building the largest grassroots movement of their day to create support for outlawing liquor sales. The Granger Collection, New York.

defeats and by the continued refusal of Congress to take up a constitutional amendment for women's voting rights. But the movement picked up momentum again in 1911 (Map 18.2). By 1913, the majority of women living west of the Mississippi River had the vote. In many other states and localities, women had secured voting rights in municipal elections, in school elections, or on liquor licensing questions.

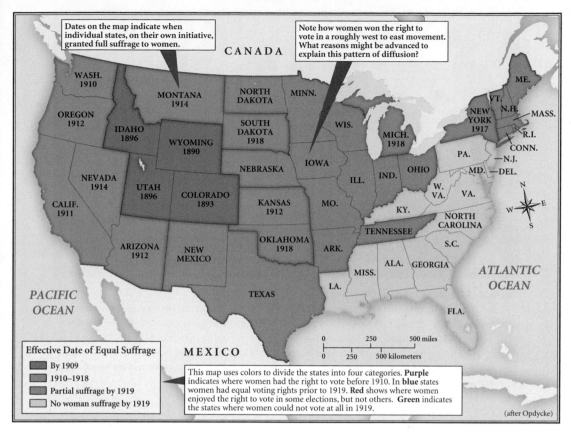

Dates on the map indicate when individual states, on their own initiative, granted full suffrage to women.

Note how women won the right to vote in a roughly west to east movement. What reasons might be advanced to explain this pattern of diffusion?

Effective Date of Equal Suffrage
- By 1909
- 1910–1918
- Partial suffrage by 1919
- No woman suffrage by 1919

This map uses colors to divide the states into four categories. **Purple** indicates where women had the right to vote before 1910. In **blue** states women had equal voting rights prior to 1919. **Red** shows where women enjoyed the right to vote in some elections, but not others. **Green** indicates the states where women could not vote at all in 1919.

(after Opdycke)

MAP 18.2 Woman Suffrage, 1890–1919

By 1909, after more than sixty years of agitation, only four lightly populated western states had granted women full voting rights. A number of other states offered partial suffrage, limited to voting for school boards and such issues as taxes and local referenda on whether or not to permit the sale of liquor licenses (the so-called "local option"). Between 1910 and 1918, as the effort shifted to the struggle for a constitutional amendment, eleven states joined the list granting full suffrage. The West remained the most progressive region in granting women's voting rights; the most stubborn resistance lay in the ex-Confederacy.

Women, Race, and Patriotism | Like temperance work, patriotic activism became women's special province in the post–Civil War decades. Members of the Daughters of the American Revolution (DAR), founded in 1890, devoted themselves to celebrating the memory of Revolutionary War heroes. Significantly, the DAR excluded African American women, even those who could prove they had descended from soldiers who had fought for U.S. independence. Equally influential was the United Daughters of the Confederacy (UDC), founded in 1894 to celebrate the memory of the South's "lost cause." The UDC's elite southern members played a central role in shaping Americans' memory of the Civil War by building monuments, distributing Confederate flags, and donating portraits of Robert E. Lee to southern schools. Starting in Georgia in 1896, the UDC also undertook a national campaign to edit U.S. history textbooks.

Christian Missions in Japan, 1909

Through this colorful postcard, Protestant missionaries in Japan demonstrate their success in winning converts (at least a few) and their adaptation of missionary strategies to meet local needs and expectations. Here, outside their headquarters, they demonstrate "preaching by means of banners." The large characters on the vertical banner proclaim the "Association of Christian Gospel Evangelists." The horizontal banner is a Japanese translation of Matthew 11:28, "Come unto me, all ye who labor and are heavy laden, and I will give you rest." © Bettmann/Corbis.

They ensured that such books portrayed the formation of the Confederacy as a noble effort, Reconstruction as a terrible mistake, and former slaves as unfit for citizenship. In the early twentieth century, such work played an important role in maintaining support for segregation and disfranchisement.

African American women did not sit idle in the face of this challenge. By 1896 they created the National Association of Colored Women, a network of local women's clubs that focused their attention on community support. Black club women arranged for the care of orphans, founded homes for the elderly, worked for temperance, and undertook public health campaigns. Such women shared with white women an abiding faith in domesticity — and a determination to carry it into the public sphere. Black journalist Victoria Earle Matthews hailed the American home as "the foundation upon which nationality rests, the pride of the citizen, and the glory of the Republic." African American women used the language of domesticity and respectability to seek white women's cooperation in their work.

The largest African American women's group arose within the National Baptist Church (NBC), which by 1906 represented 2.4 million churchgoers. Founded in 1900, the Women's Convention of the NBC promoted and funded night schools, health clinics, kindergartens, day care centers, and outreach programs for men and women in prison.

Paralleling the work of white reformers, one convention leader called for women to focus on education for children and youth, and "to extend the number of occupations for women."

Adella Hunt Logan, born in Alabama, exemplified how such work could lead women to demand political rights. Educated at Atlanta University, Logan became a club woman, a teacher at Tuskegee Institute, and an advocate of woman suffrage. "If white American women, with all their mutual and acquired advantage, need the ballot," she declared, "how much more do Black Americans, male and female, need the strong defense of a vote to help secure them their right to life, liberty, and the pursuit of happiness?"

Feminism | Despite divisions of race and ethnicity, many women recognized that they shared problems across lines of economic class. Some created new organizations to call attention to the plight of poorly paid female wage-earners and to agitate for better working conditions. The most famous example was the National Trade Union League, founded in New York in 1903. Financed by wealthy supporters, the league trained working-class leaders like Rose Schneiderman, who became a union organizer among garment workers. Although often frustrated by the patronizing ways of their well-to-do sponsors, trade-union women identified their cause with the broader struggle for women's rights. When New York State held suffrage referenda in 1915 and 1917, strong support came from Jewish and Italian precincts where many unionized garment workers lived.

By the early twentieth century, the most radical women took a public stance against women's "separate sphere." A famous site of sexual rebellion was New York's Greenwich Village, where radical intellectuals, including many gays and lesbians, created a vibrant community by the 1910s. Among their many other political activities, women in Greenwich Village founded the Heterodoxy Club (1912), open to any woman who pledged not to be "orthodox in her opinions." The club brought together intellectuals, journalists, and labor organizers. Almost all supported women's voting rights, but they had a more ambitious view of what was needed for women's liberation. Such women began to use the term **feminism** to describe their movement. They articulated broad goals for women's personal development. "I wanted to belong to the human race, not to a ladies' aid society," wrote one divorced journalist who joined Heterodoxy. As women entered the public sphere, feminists argued, they should not just fulfill Victorian expectations of self-sacrifice for others; they should work on their own behalf. Feminist thinker Charlotte Perkins Gilman imagined a transformation in women's private and public lives: "Here she comes, running, out of prison and off the pedestal; chains off, crown off, halo off, just a live woman."

Domesticity and Missions

While few American women fully shared the ideas of the Heterodoxy Club, hundreds of thousands engaged in more widely accepted forms of public activism, through their churches and religious groups. Some sponsored Christian missions in the American West, which eastern women regarded as uncivilized and in need of uplift. The Women's

National Indian Association, for example, funded missionary work on reservations, arguing that women had a special duty to promote "civilized home life" among Indians. In San Francisco, elite and middle-class white women built a rescue home for Chinese women who had been sold into sexual slavery. The project not only was racially condescending but also generated fierce opposition from white residents who hated Chinese immigration. The home nonetheless fulfilled its mission: It served many Chinese women who managed to reach its doors, escape from prostitution, and in some cases marry and start their own families.

Nowhere was the rhetoric of domesticity more powerful than in the movement for overseas missions, which grew from a modest start in the pre–Civil War period to a peak in the early twentieth century. By 1915, American religious organizations sponsored more than nine thousand overseas missionaries; these workers were supported at home by missionary society volunteers, including more than three million women. The largest number of American Protestant missionaries served in Asia, with smaller numbers posted to Africa and the Middle East. Most saw American-style domesticity as a central part of Christian evangelism. In particular, they sought to uplift foreign women who could, one missionary journal exhorted, "by the grace of God [be] nourished and cultivated into true Christian womanhood."

To accomplish this goal, missionary societies emphasized the importance of sending married couples into the field. Remarkably, by the turn of the century, many unmarried women also went overseas as missionary administrators, teachers, doctors, and nurses (though almost never as ministers). "To American woman, more than to any other on earth," declared one Christian reformer, "is committed the exalted privilege of extending over the world those blessed influences, that are to renovate degraded man."

As this woman's words suggest, missionaries who worked to foster Christianity and domesticity often showed considerable condescension toward their "poor heathen sisters." Potential converts often bristled at missionary assumptions (see Voices from Abroad, p. 557). In many places missionaries won converts, in part by offering medical care and promoting scientific progress and women's education. Some missionaries came to love and respect the people among whom they served. But others became deeply frustrated. One Presbyterian in Syria, who found Muslims uninterested in his gospel message, bitterly denounced all Muslims as "corrupt and immoral" and Muslim women in particular as "profane, slanderous, and capricious." By imposing their views on "heathen races" and criticizing those who did not agree with them, Christian missionaries sometimes ended up justifying and supporting Western imperialism.

▶ What political reform goals did women pursue in this era? Whose interests did these various movements serve? In your view, which of these projects was most beneficial, and to whom?

▶ How did Protestant missionaries define their goals abroad? What were some of the consequences of their work?

All the nations and people I had hitherto passed through resembled our own in their manners, customs and language

VOICES FROM ABROAD

A Japanese View of American Christianity   KINZO HIRAI

In 1893, during the World's Columbian Exposition, a World's Parliament of Religions met in Chicago. Representatives of many prominent religions discussed similarities and differences among their faiths. Though English-speaking Protestants dominated the program, several representatives from Asia spoke. One was Kinzo Hirai, a lay Buddhist delegate from Japan. Hirai set out to explain persistent opposition to Christianity in his country. At the time Hirai spoke, Japan's leaders had undertaken a program of rapid modernization.

I do not understand why the Christian lands have ignored the rights and advantages of forty million souls of Japan for forty years since the stipulations of the [1854 Treaty of Kanagawa]. One of the excuses offered by foreign nations is that our country is not yet civilized. Is it the principle of civilized law that the rights of and profits of the so-called uncivilized, or the weaker, should be sacrificed? As I understand it, the spirit and necessity of law is to protect the rights and profits of the weaker against the aggression of the stronger. . . . The claim is made that the Japanese are idolaters and heathen. . . . [A]dmitting for the sake of argument that we are idolaters and heathen, is it Christian morality to trample upon the rights and advantages of a non-Christian nation? . . .

You send your missionaries to Japan and they advise us to be moral and believe Christianity. We like to be moral, we know that Christianity is good; and we are very thankful for this kindness. But at the same time our people are rather perplexed and very much in doubt of about their advice. . . .

When legal cases are always decided by the foreign authorities in Japan unfavorably to us; when some years ago a Japanese was not allowed to enter a university on the Pacific coast of America because of his being of a different race; when a few months ago the school board in San Francisco enacted a regulation that no Japanese should be allowed to enter the public school there; when last year the Japanese were driven out in wholesale from one of the territories of the United States; when our business men in San Francisco were compelled by some union not to employ Japanese assistants and laborers, but the Americans; . . . when there are many who go in procession hoisting lanterns marked "Japs must go;" when the Japanese in the Hawaiian Islands were deprived of their suffrage; when we see some western people in Japan who erect before the entrance to their houses a special post upon which is the notice, "No Japanese is allowed to enter here" — just like a board upon which is written, "No dogs allowed"; when we are in such a situation, notwithstanding the kindness of the western nations from one point of view, who send their missionaries to us, that we unintelligent heathens are embarrassed and hesitate to swallow the sweet and warm liquid of the heaven of Christianity, will not be unreasonable.

SOURCE: *The World's Parliament of Religions*, ed. John Henry Barrows (Chicago: Parliament Publishing, 1893), 444–450.

Science and Faith

As the activities of missionaries showed, the United States continued to be a deeply religious nation. However, the late nineteenth century brought increasing public attention to another kind of belief: faith in science. Before the Civil War, most Americans had believed the world was about six thousand years old. No one knew what lay beyond the solar system. By 1900, however, paleontologists had traced the rise and fall of the dinosaurs, and many scientists — as well as ordinary Americans — accepted the theory of evolution. By the 1910s, astronomers had identified distant galaxies and scientists could measure the speed of light.

It is hardly surprising, amid these staggering achievements, that "fact worship" became a central feature of American intellectual life. Researchers in many fields became converts to scientific methods, arguing that one could rely only on hard facts and observable phenomena. In their enthusiasm, some economists and sociologsts rejected all reform efforts as romantic and sentimental. American fiction writers and artists kept a more humane emphasis, but they made use of similar methods — close observation and attention to real-life experience — to create works of literary and artistic realism. Other Americans sought to reconcile scientific discoveries with their religious faith, setting the stage for intellectual and political conflicts over Darwinism and evolution.

Darwinism and Its Critics

Evolution — the idea that species are not fixed, but ever changing — was not a simple idea on which all scientists agreed in the late nineteenth century. The idea was widely associated with British naturalist Charles Darwin and his immensely influential book *On the Origin of Species* (1859), which proposed the theory of **natural selection**. In nature, Darwin argued, all creatures struggle to survive. When individual members of a species are born with random genetic mutations that better fit them for their particular environment — for example, camouflage coloring for a bird or butterfly — these survival characteristics, since they are genetically transmissible, become dominant in future generations.

Darwin himself disapproved of the word *evolution* (which does not appear in his book) because it implied upward progression. In his view, natural selection was blind: environments changed randomly, and so did plants' and animals' adaptations. But other people were less scrupulous than Darwin about drawing sweeping conclusions from his work. British philosopher Herbert Spencer spun out an elaborate theory of how human society had advanced through competition and "survival of the fittest." **Social Darwinism**, as Spencer's idea became known, found its American champion in William Graham Sumner, a sociology professor at Yale. Competition, said Sumner, is a law of nature that "can no more be done away with than gravitation." Who were the fittest? "Millionaires," Sumner declared; their success showed they were "naturally selected." Sumner argued that industrialists "live in luxury, but the bargain is a good one for society."

Even in the heyday of Social Darwinism, Sumner's views were controversial (see American Voices, p. 559). Many scientists accepted evolutionary ideas but rejected Darwin's theory of natural selection. They followed a line of thinking laid out by French biologist Jean Baptiste Lamarck, who argued, unlike Darwin, that individual animals or plants could acquire transmittable traits within a single lifetime. A rhinoceros that

Social Darwinism   THEODORE DREISER

Many nineteenth-century Americans came to believe that human society advanced through fierce competition — an idea that reflected the cutthroat world of American business. In *The Financier* (1912), novelist Theodore Dreiser traces the rise of Frank Cowperwood, a character loosely based on that of real-life financier and streetcar magnate Charles Yerkes. Here, Dreiser suggests how one future businessman came to replace his mother's Christian faith with a belief in "survival of the fittest."

[Frank] could not figure out how this thing he had come into — this life — was organized. How did all these people get into the world? What were they doing here? Who started things, anyhow? His mother told him the story of Adam and Eve, but he didn't believe it. . . .

One day he saw a squid and a lobster put in [a] tank, and in connection with them was witness to a tragedy which stayed with him all his life and cleared things up considerably intellectually. The lobster, it appeared from the talk of the idle bystanders, was offered no food, as the squid was considered his rightful prey. He lay at the bottom of the clear glass tank . . . apparently seeing nothing — you could not tell in which way his beady, black buttons of eyes were looking — but apparently they were never off the body of the squid. The latter, pale and waxy in texture, looking very much like pork fat or jade, moved about in torpedo fashion; but his movements were apparently never out of the eyes of his enemy, for by degrees small portions of his body began to disappear, snapped off by the relentless claws of his pursuer. . . .

[One day] only a portion of the squid remained. . . . The boy stayed as long as he could, the bitter struggle fascinating him. Now, maybe, or in an hour or a day, the squid might die, slain by the lobster, and the lob-

ster would eat him. He looked again at the greenish-copperish engine of destruction in the corner and wondered when this would be. . . . He returned that night, and lo! the expected had happened. There was a little crowd around the tank. The lobster was in the corner. Before him was the squid cut in two and partially devoured. . . .

The incident made a great impression on him. It answered in a rough way that riddle which had been annoying him so much in the past: "How is life organized?" Things lived on each other — that was it. Lobsters lived on squids and other things. What lived on lobsters? Men, of course! . . . And what lived on men? he asked himself. Was it other men? Wild animals lived on men. And there were Indians and cannibals. And some men were killed by storms and accidents. He wasn't so sure about men living on men; but men did kill each other. . . .

[Frank] was already pondering on what he should be in this world, and how he should get along. From seeing his father count money, he was sure that he would like banking; and Third Street, where his father's office was, seemed to him the cleanest, most fascinating street in the world.

SOURCE: Theodore Dreiser, *The Financier* (New York: Harper and Brothers, 1912), 10–15.

fought fiercely, in Lamarck's view, could build up a stronger horn; its offspring would then be born with that trait. If Lamarck's ideas were true, then "evolution" had a very different meaning for humans: People who acquired education or good habits could pass these on genetically to their children. Other thinkers rejected the whole notion of applying evolutionary ideas to the realm of society and government. They pointed out that Lamarck's and Darwin's theories applied to finch and tortoise species, over thousands of years, and not to human relationships. Social Darwinism, they argued, was simply an excuse for the worst excesses of industrialization. By the early twentieth century, American intellectuals were in full revolt against Sumner and his allies.

Meanwhile, though, the most dubious applications of evolutionary ideas were codified into new reproductive laws. Some Americans embraced **eugenics**, a so-called science of human breeding. Eugenicists argued that mentally deficient people should be prevented from reproducing. They proposed sterilizing those deemed "unfit," especially residents of state asylums for the insane or mentally disabled. In early twentieth-century America, almost half of the states enacted eugenics laws. By the time belief in eugenics subsided in the 1930s, about twenty thousand people had been sterilized, with California and Virginia taking the lead. Eugenicists also had a broader impact on public policy. Because they associated mental unfitness with "lower races" — including people of African, Asian, and Native American descent — their arguments bolstered segregation and racial discrimination. By warning that immigrants from Eastern and Southern Europe would dilute white Americans' racial purity, eugenicists helped win passage of immigration restriction in the 1920s.

Realism in the Arts

Inspired by the quest for facts, American authors rebelled against the nineteenth century's most important artistic movement — romanticism — and what they saw as its unfortunate product, Victorian sentimentality. Instead, they took up literary **realism**. In the 1880s, William Dean Howells, one of the country's leading editors and novelists, began to call for writers "to picture the daily life in the most exact terms possible." Howells put his ideas into practice in novels such as *The Rise of Silas Lapham* (1885). By the 1890s, a younger generation of writers took up the call. Theodore Dreiser dismissed "professional optimists" who always arrived "at a happy ending." Stephen Crane's *Maggie: A Girl of the Streets* (1893), privately printed because no publisher would touch it, described the seduction, abandonment, and death of a slum girl. In *Main-Travelled Roads* (1891), a collection of stories based on his family's struggle to farm in Iowa and South Dakota, writer Hamlin Garland turned the same unsparing eye on the hardships of rural life.

Some authors believed that realism did not go far enough to overturn Victorian morality. Jack London spent his teenage years as a factory worker, sailor, and tramp. In stories such as "The Law of Life" (1901) and "To Build a Fire" (1908), London dramatized what he saw as the harsh reality of an uncaring universe. American society, he remarked, was "a jungle wherein wild beasts eat and are eaten." Similarly, Stephen Crane said that his fiction tried to capture "a world full of fists." London and Crane helped create literary **naturalism**. They suggested that human beings were not so much rational agents and shapers of their own destinies, but blind victims of forces beyond their control — including their own subconscious impulses and desires.

John French Sloan, *A Woman's Work*, 1912
The subject of this painting—a woman hanging out laundry behind a city apartment building—is typical of the subjects chosen by American artist John Sloan (1871–1951). Sloan and a group of his allies became famous as realists; critics derided them as the "Ash Can School" because they did not paint rural landscapes, still lifes, or other conventional subjects considered worthy subject matter for a painting. Sloan, though, warned against seeing his paintings as simple representations of reality, even if he described his work as based on "a creative impulse derived out of a consciousness of life." "'Looks like' is not the test of a good painting," he wrote: "Even the scientist is interested in effects only as phenomena from which to deduce order in life." Cleveland Museum of Art. Gift of Amelia Elizabeth White.

America's most famous fiction writer, Samuel Langhorne Clemens, who took the pen name of Mark Twain, came to take an equally bleak view. Though he achieved success with such lighthearted books as *The Innocents Abroad* (1869) and *The Adventures of Tom Sawyer* (1876), Clemens created controversy with his satirical *Adventures of Huckleberry Finn* (1884) — especially in its indictment of slavery and racism. Soon afterward, Clemens was devastated by the loss of his wife and two daughters, as well as by failed investments and bankruptcy. Starting with his novel *A Connecticut Yankee in King Arthur's Court* (1889), which ends with a bloody, technology-driven slaughter of Arthur's knights, Mark Twain became one of the bitterest voices criticizing America's idea of progress. He became an outspoken critic of imperialism and foreign missions, and he parodied the biblical story of Adam and Eve in his hilarious *Letters from the Earth* (1908). *The Mysterious Stranger*, published posthumously in 1916, denounced Christianity itself as a hypocritical delusion. Like his friend the industrialist Andrew Carnegie, Samuel Langhorne Clemens "got rid of theology."

By the time Clemens died in 1910, realist and naturalist writers had laid the groundwork for literary **modernism**. Modernists rejected traditional canons of literary taste. They tended to be religious skeptics or atheists. Questioning the whole idea of progress and order, they focused their attention on the subconscious and "primitive" mind. Above all, they sought to overturn convention and tradition; the poet Ezra Pound exhorted, "Make it new!" Modernism became the first great literary and artistic movement of the twentieth century — one that remains influential, even today.

In the visual arts, technological changes helped introduce a new aesthetic. By 1900, some photographers argued that the rise of photography made painting obsolete. But painters invented their own form of realism. The Nebraska-born artist Robert Henri became fascinated with life in the burgeoning eastern cities. "The backs of tenement houses are living documents," he declared, and he set out to put them on canvas. Henri and his followers, notably John Sloan, called themselves the New York Realists. Critics derided them as the "Ash Can School," because they chose subjects that were not uplifting or conventionally beautiful.

In 1913, New York Realists participated in one of the most controversial events in American art history, the Armory Show. Housed in an enormous National Guard building in New York, the Armory Show introduced America to modern art. Some painters whose work appeared at the show were experimenting with such styles as cubism, characterized by abstract, geometric forms. Along with works by Henri and Sloan, organizers featured paintings by European rebels such as Marcel Duchamp and Pablo Picasso. America's academic art world was shocked. One critic called cubism "the total destruction of the art of painting." The *New York Times* denounced the Armory Show paintings as "revolting in their inhumanity." But the exhibition went on to Boston and Chicago, and more than 250,000 people crowded to see it. The Armory Show transformed American art. It was another marker of the shift from Romanticism to various forms of realism, and then to modernism in its starkest forms.

A striking feature of both realism and modernism, as they developed, was that many of the movement's leading writers and artists were men. They denounced nineteenth-century culture as hopelessly feminized and ridiculed popular sentimental novels, especially those written for women. In making their work strong and modern, these men also wanted to make it masculine. Stephen Crane called for "virility" in literature. Jack London described himself as a "man's man" who was "lustfully roving and conquering by sheer superiority and strength." The artist Robert Henri urged his students to be "fighters"; he banned small brushes because they were "too feminine." In their own ways, these writers and artists contributed to a broad movement to masculinize American culture.

Religion: Diversity and Innovation

By the turn of the twentieth century, new scientific, literary, and artistic ideas posed a significant challenge to religious faith. Some Americans argued that science would sweep away religion altogether. "The old superstitions which connected unusual sickness with the wrath of offended Deity," decreed one Michigan doctor, "have faded in the light of science." Nonetheless, American religious practice remained vibrant. Protestants developed creative new responses to the challenges of industrialization, while millions of newcomers built their own institutions for worship and religious education. In fact, this very trend horrified some Protestants. By 1920, almost two million children attended Catholic elementary schools instead of public schools, and Catholic dioceses across the country operated more than fifteen hundred high schools. The era of mass immigration and the rise of great cities was marked by both religious innovation and tensions among people of different faiths.

Immigrant Faiths Arriving in the United States in large numbers, and facing the dominant assumptions and beliefs of Protestants, Catholics and Jews wrestled with many similar questions. To what degree should they adapt their faith to American society? Should children attend religious or public schools? What happened if they married outside the faith? Should the education of clergy be changed? Among Catholic leaders, Bishop John Ireland of St. Paul, Minnesota, felt that "the principles of the Church are in harmony with the interests of the Republic." But traditionalists, led by Archbishop Michael A. Corrigan of New York, denied the possibility of such harmony and sought to insulate the church from the pluralistic American environment. Many pointed to the same threats that frightened Protestants: On the one hand, industrial poverty and overwork kept working-class people away from worship services; on the other hand, new consumer pleasures offered somewhere else to go. Like Protestants, many Catholics and Jews succumbed to these new conditions and fell away from religious practice.

Those immigrant Catholics who remained faithful to the church were anxious to preserve what they had known in Europe, and they generally supported the church's traditional wing. But they also wanted religious life to express their ethnic identities. Italians, Poles, and other newly arrived Catholics wanted separate parishes where they could celebrate their customs, speak their languages, and establish their own parochial schools. When they became numerous enough, they also demanded their own bishops. The Catholic hierarchy, dominated by Irishmen, felt that the integrity of the church itself was at stake. The demand for ethnic parishes implied local control of church property. With some strain, the Catholic Church managed to satisfy the diverse needs of the immigrant faithful. It met the demand for representation, for example, by appointing immigrant priests as auxiliary bishops within existing dioceses.

In the late nineteenth century, many prosperous native-born American Jews embraced Reform Judaism, abandoning such religious practices as keeping a kosher kitchen and conducting services in Hebrew. But this was not the way of Yiddish-speaking Jews from Eastern Europe, who arrived in large numbers after the 1880s. Generally much poorer and also eager to preserve their own traditions, they founded Orthodox synagogues, often in vacant stores, and practiced Judaism as they had at home. But in the American city, even in a predominantly Jewish neighborhood, it proved difficult to recreate the world they had left behind. In the villages of Eastern Europe, Judaism had been an entire way of life, one not easily replicated in a large American city. Many Jews eagerly purchased a new suit or ready-made dress to mark their arrival in the New World. "The very clothes I wore and the very food I ate had a fatal effect on my religious habits," confessed the hero of Abraham Cahan's novel *The Rise of David Levinsky* (1917). "If you . . . attempt to bend your religion to the spirit of your surroundings, it breaks. It falls to pieces." Levinsky shaved off his beard and plunged into the Manhattan clothing business. Orthodox Judaism survived the transition to America, but it often did so by reducing its claims on the lives of the faithful.

Protestant Innovations | Like Catholics and Jews, Protestants found their religious beliefs challenged by modern ideas and ways of life. Some Protestant thinkers found ways to reconcile Christianity with Darwin's theory of natural selection and other scientific principles. But it was hard to ignore the fact that millions of American wageworkers were now Catholics or Jews — or, in the case of Chinese, even Buddhists and Confucians. Overall, in 1916, Protestants still constituted a majority (almost 60 percent) of Americans affiliated with a religious body. But they faced formidable rivals for political and cultural leadership, notably the Roman Catholic Church. The number of practicing Catholics in 1916 — 15.7 million — was greater than the number of Baptists, Methodists, and Presbyterians combined.

While some Protestants enlisted in foreign missions, others responded by evangelizing among the unchurched and indifferent. They provided reading rooms, day nurseries, vocational classes, and other services; they funded YMCAs and YWCAs. This movement to renew religious faith through dedication to public welfare and social justice became known as the **Social Gospel**. Its goals were epitomized by Charles Sheldon's novel *In His Steps* (1896), which told the story of a congregation whose members resolved to live by Christ's precepts for one year. "If the church members were all doing as Jesus would do," Sheldon asked, "could it remain true that armies of men would walk the streets for jobs, and hundreds of them curse the church, and thousands of them find in the saloon their best friend?" The characters in the book reform their small city after taking their pledge.

The Salvation Army, which arrived from Great Britain in 1879, spread a message of repentance among the urban poor, offering assistance programs that ranged from soup kitchens to shelters for former prostitutes. When all else failed, the down-and-outers of American cities knew they could count on the Salvation Army, whose bell ringers and bands became a familiar sight on city streets. The group used the latest business slang in urging its Christian soldiers, like traveling salesmen, to "hustle." Its leaders borrowed up-to-date marketing techniques. They advertised, and in the early twentieth century they issued stock in a profit-based company that sold used clothing, books, and domestic items to support the organization's work.

The Salvation Army succeeded, in part, because it managed to bridge an emerging divide between Social Gospel reformers and Protestants who were taking a different theological path. Disturbed by what they saw as rising secularism and abandonment of belief, conservative ministers and their allies held an annual series of Bible Conferences at Niagara Falls between 1876 and 1897. The resulting "Niagara Creed" reaffirmed the literal truth of the Bible and the certainty of damnation for those not born again in Christ. By the 1910s, a network of churches and Bible institutes emerged from these conferences. These Protestants called their movement **fundamentalism**, based on their belief in the fundamental truth of the Bible and its central place in Christian faith.

Fundamentalists and their allies made particularly effective use of revival meetings. Unlike Social Gospel advocates, revivalists said little about poverty or earthly justice, focusing not on the matters of the world, but on redemption. The pioneer modern evangelist was Dwight L. Moody, a former Chicago shoe salesman and YMCA official who won fame in the 1870s. Eternal life could be had for the asking, Moody promised. His listeners needed only "to come forward and take, TAKE!" Moody's successor, Billy Sunday, helped bring evangelism into the modern era. More often than his predecessors, Sunday took political stances that were grounded in his Protestant beliefs. Condemning the "booze traffic" was his greatest cause. Sunday also denounced unrestricted immigration and labor radicalism. "If I had my way with these ornery wild-eyed Socialists," he once threatened, "I would stand them up before a firing squad." Sunday supported some progressive reform causes; he opposed child labor, for example, and advocated voting rights for women. But in other ways, his views anticipated the nativism and antiradicalism that would dominate American politics after World War I.

Billy Sunday found his own way to break free of the influences of the Victorian era, and to participate in the project of "masculinizing" American culture. Not only was he a powerful, commanding presence on the stage, but before his conversion experience he had been a hard-drinking outfielder for the Chicago White Stockings. To advertise his revivals, Sunday sometimes organized local businessmen into baseball teams, then put on his own uniform and played on both sides. Through such feats, and the fiery sermons that followed, Sunday offered a model of spiritual inspiration, manly strength, and political engagement. His revivals were in many ways thoroughly modern productions: Advertised in a sophisticated way, they provided mass entertainment and the chance to see a pro baseball player. The celebrity of Billy Sunday showed that, in the wake of industrialization, Americans were adapting to new social and cultural expectations. At the same time, though, the immense popularity of Sunday's revivals showed that older beliefs and values would endure in new forms.

▶ What were some of the ways in which Social Darwinism, or the idea of "survival of the fittest," shaped American thought in this era?

▶ In what ways did realism and naturalism in the arts break with older traditions?

SUMMARY

The period between the 1880s and 1920s created the foundations for modern American culture. While middle-class families sought to preserve the Victorian domestic ideal, a variety of factors were transforming family life. Families had fewer children, and a substantial majority of young people achieved more education than their parents had obtained. The luckiest attended high school, and even college, in increasing numbers.

These changes brought new opportunities, particularly for women who devoted themselves to reform. The Woman's Christian Temperance Union primarily sought the prohibition of liquor, but it also addressed an array of such issues as domestic violence, poverty, and children's education. Members of women's clubs pursued a variety of social and economic reforms, while other women organized for race uplift and patriotic work. Gradually, the Victorian ideal of female moral superiority gave way to modern claims for women's equal rights. Foreign missions, in the meantime, spread the Christian gospel from the United States to other parts of the world, with mixed results for those receiving the message.

New intellectual currents, including Darwinism and its applications and pragmatism, challenged Victorian certainties. In the arts, realist and naturalist writers rejected both romanticism and Victorian domesticity. Many Americans were shocked by the results, including Theodore Dreiser's scandalous novel *Sister Carrie*, Mark Twain's rejection of Christian faith, and the boldly modernist paintings displayed at New York's Armory Show. Science and modernism did not, however, displace religion. Newly arrived Catholics and Jews, as well as old-line Protestants, adapted their faith to the conditions of modern life.

For additional primary sources from this period, see *Documents for America's History*, Seventh Edition.

For Web sites, images, and documents related to topics and places in this chapter, visit *Make History* at **bedfordstmartins.com/henrettaconcise.**

For Further Exploration

On family life and education see Andrea Tone, *Devices and Desires* (2001); Jane Hunter, *How Young Ladies Became Girls* (2003); Joseph F. Kett, *Rites of Passage* (1977); Kim Townsend, *Manhood at Harvard* (1996); and Barbara M. Solomon, *In the Company of Educated Women* (1985). Cindy Aron traces the rise of vacations in *Working at Play* (1999). On athletics see Thomas Winter, *Making Men, Making Class* (2002); Clifford Putney, *Muscular Christianity* (2001); and Neil Lanctot, *Negro League Baseball* (2004). Stephen Fox covers environmentalism in *The American Conservation Movement* (1985). See also Mark David Spence, *Dispossessing the Wilderness* (1999), and Karl Jacoby, *Crimes Against Nature* (2001).

On domesticity and the railroad see Barbara Young Welke, *Recasting American Liberty* (2001), and Amy Richter, *Home on the Rails* (2005). On women's public work see Ruth Bordin, *Woman and Temperance* (1981); Evelyn Brooks Higginbotham, *Righteous Discontent* (1993); Sharon Wood, *The Freedom of the Streets* (2005); Peggy Pascoe, *Relations of Rescue* (1990); Glenda Gilmore, *Gender and Jim Crow* (1996); Francesca Morgan,

TIMELINE

1872	▶ First national park established at Yellowstone	**1892**	▶ Elizabeth Cady Stanton delivers "solitude of self" speech to Congress
1873	▶ Association for the Advancement of Women founded		▶ John Muir founds Sierra Club
1874	▶ Woman's Christian Temperance Union founded	**1893**	▶ World's Parliament of Religions meets in Chicago
1876	▶ Baseball's National League founded	**1896**	▶ National Association of Colored Women founded
	▶ Appalachian Mountain Club founded		▶ Charles Sheldon publishes *In His Steps*
1879	▶ Salvation Army established in the United States	**1903**	▶ First World Series
			▶ First National Wildlife Refuge established at Pelican Island, Florida
1881	▶ Tuskegee Institute founded	**1906**	▶ Lacey Act passed
1885	▶ Mississippi State College for Women founded	**1913**	▶ Armory Show of modern art held in New York City
1890	▶ National American Woman Suffrage Organization and Daughters of the American Revolution founded	**1916**	▶ National Park Service created

Women and Patriotism in Jim Crow America (2005); and Karen L. Cox, *Dixie's Daughters* (2003). On missions see Patricia Hill, *The World Their Household* (1985).

On culture see Alan Trachtenberg, *The Incorporation of America* (1983); David Shi, *Facing Facts* (1994); and Richard Hofstadter, *Social Darwinism in American Thought* (1944). For religion, see Patrick W. Carey, *The Roman Catholics in America* (1996); Jonathan Sarna, *American Judaism* (2004); and on the Salvation Army, Diane Winston, *Red-Hot and Righteous* (1999).

Test Your Knowledge

For practice quizzes, activities, and other study tools, visit the Online Study Guide at **bedfordstmartins.com/henrettaconcise**.

"Civilization's Inferno": The Rise and Reform of Industrial Cities

1880–1917

These vast aggregations of humanity, where he who seeks isolation may find it more truly than in a desert; where wealth and poverty touch and jostle; where one revels and another starves within a few feet of each other — they are the centers and types of our civilization.

—Henry George, 1883

Clarence Darrow, a successful lawyer from Ashtabula, Ohio, felt isolated and overwhelmed when he moved to Chicago in the 1880s. "There is no place so lonely to a young man as a great city where he has no intimates or companions," Darrow later wrote. "When I walked along the street I scanned every face I met to see if I could not perchance discover someone from Ohio." Instead he saw "a solid, surging sea of human units, each intent upon hurrying by." At one point, Darrow felt "gloom amounting almost to despair. If it had been possible I would have gone back to Ohio; but I didn't want to borrow the money, and I dreaded to confess defeat."

In the era of industrialization, more and more Americans had experiences like Darrow's. In 1860, the United States was a rural country: Less than 20 percent of Americans lived in an urban location, defined by census takers as a place with more than 2,500 inhabitants. By 1910, more Americans lived in cities (42.1 million) than had lived in the *entire* United States on the eve of the Civil War (31.4 million). Most striking was the growth of giant urban centers. In 1860, only three cities — New York, Brooklyn (then considered separate from New York), and Philadelphia — had populations over 250,000. By 1910, nineteen cities fit that definition. The largest, New York, had almost 5 million inhabitants. Though the Northeast remained by far the most urbanized region, cities in the industrial Midwest and the West were beginning to catch up. Even the predominantly rural South boasted of such thriving cities as Atlanta and Birmingham.

Cities became the locus for vibrant economic and cultural experimentation. Here skyscrapers rose and immigrant neighborhoods grew. Here emerged new sites of working-class leisure and pleasure like the dance hall and the amusement park, along with a thriving intellectual world of artists, writers, and critics. As journalist Frederic C. Howe de-

Mulberry Street, New York City, c. 1900
The influx of immigrants — especially Southern and Eastern Europeans — in the late nineteenth century created densely populated ghettos in the heart of New York City and other major American cities. This view is of Mulberry Street in New York's "Little Italy," a thoroughfare famous for its pushcarts, street peddlers, and bustling traffic. The inhabitants are mostly Italians; some of them, noticing the photographer preparing his camera, have gathered to be in the picture. Library of Congress.

clared in 1905, "Man has entered on an urban age." Americans had long feared cities as centers of vice and sin, where saloons and brothels flourished and hucksters fleeced unwitting newcomers. Industrialization added more perceived dangers: slums, pollution, disease, and corrupt political machines. In particular, cities were places where the extravagantly wealthy bumped up against the homeless and destitute. As one African American observer put it, the city was "Civilization's Inferno." As a consequence of their urgent problems, industrial cities became important sites of political innovation and reform.

The New Metropolis

Mark Twain, arriving in New York in 1867, remarked that it was "too large. . . . You cannot accomplish anything in the way of business, you cannot even pay a friendly call without devoting a whole day to it. . . . [The] distances are too great." At that time, technologies like the steam engine and streetcar were already starting to allow engineers and planners to reorganize big cities like New York. Over the next fifty years, such cities developed a new geography. Their specialized districts included not only areas for finance, manufacturing, wholesaling, and warehousing but also immigrant neighborhoods, affluent suburbs, shopping districts, and business-oriented downtowns. It was an exciting and bewildering new world.

The Shape of the Industrial City

Before the Civil War, cities served the needs of commerce and finance, not industry. Early manufacturing sprang up mostly in the countryside, where mill owners could draw waterpower from streams, find plentiful fuel and raw materials, and recruit workers from farms and villages. The nation's largest cities were seaports, and most urban areas were places where merchants and traders bought and sold goods for distribution into the interior or to world markets.

As industrialization developed, cities became sites for manufacturing as well as finance and trade. Steam engines played a central role in this change: With them, mill operators no longer had to depend on less reliable water-driven power. Quick to make use of new railroad links, iron makers gravitated to Pittsburgh because of its access to coal and ore fields. Chicago, midway between western livestock suppliers and eastern markets, became a great meatpacking center. Steam power also vastly increased the scale of industry. In some places, a plant that employed thousands of workers instantly created a small city, in the form of a company town like Aliquippa, Pennsylvania, which belonged body and soul to the Jones and Laughlin Steel Company. Older commercial cities also became more industrial. Warehouse districts could readily convert to small-scale manufacturing; a distribution network was right at hand. In addition, port cities that served as immigrant gateways offered abundant cheap labor, an essential element in the industrial economy.

Mass Transit and the Suburb | New technologies helped residents and visitors negotiate the large distances of the industrial city. Steam-driven cable cars appeared in the 1870s. By 1887, engineer Frank Sprague designed an electric trolley system for Richmond, Virginia. It used electricity from a central generating plant, fed to the trolleys through overhead power lines, which each trolley touched with a long pole mounted on the top of its roof. The trolley quickly became the primary mode of transportation in most American cities. Congestion and frequent accidents, however, led to demands that trolley lines be moved off streets. The "el" — the elevated railroad, built as early as 1879 in New York City — became a safer alternative. Chicago developed elevated transit most fully. Other urban planners built down, not up. Boston opened a short underground line in 1897; by 1904, completion of a subway running the length of Manhattan demonstrated the full potential of high-speed underground trains.

Even before the Civil War, the arrival of railroads led to the growth of **suburbs**, outlying residential districts for the well-to-do. The high cost of transportation effectively segregated these affluent districts, and most working-class residents remained near the city center, where they could walk to work. In the late nineteenth century this trend accelerated. Businessmen and professionals built homes on large, beautifully landscaped lots in outlying towns such as Riverside, Illinois, and Tuxedo Park, New York. In the suburbs, affluent wives and children enjoyed refuge from the pollution and perceived dangers of the city. As men traveled daily from home to work and back, they became commuters, a word widely recognized by the early 1900s.

Los Angeles entrepreneur Henry Huntington, nephew of a wealthy Southern Pacific Railroad magnate, expanded the suburban ideal as he pitched the benefits of southern California sunshine. Huntington invested his family fortune in Los Angeles real estate and transportation. Along his trolley lines, he subdivided property into lots and built rows of bungalows, planting the tidy yards with lush trees and tropical fruits. Middle-class buyers flocked to purchase Huntington's houses. One new resident exclaimed, "I have apparently found a Paradise on Earth." Anticipating twentieth-century Americans' love for single-family homes in the suburbs, Huntington had invented southern California sprawl.

The rise of the suburb was abetted by another invention, Alexander Graham Bell's telephone (1876). Originally intended for business use on local exchanges, telephones were eagerly adopted by residential customers. By the 1890s, switchboards in most major cities and towns allowed suburban wives and urban businessmen to stay in touch during the workday. In 1893, two-thirds of the nation's telephones belonged to businesses; over the next fifteen years, residential users expanded by a factor of ten. Overall, by 1907, the nation had more than three million telephone customers.

Skyscrapers | By the 1880s, the invention of steel girders, durable plate glass, and passenger elevators began to revolutionize downtown building methods. Architects invented the skyscraper, a building that was supported by its steel skeleton while its walls bore little weight, serving instead as curtains to enclose the structure. The skyscraper was an expensive form of construction, but it enabled downtown landowners to leverage the cost of a small plot of land. By investing in a skyscraper, a landlord could collect rent for ten or even twenty floors of space. Large corporations also favored skyscrapers as symbols of business prowess and centralized corporate authority.

The first skyscraper built on the new design principles was William Le Baron Jenney's ten-story Home Insurance Building (1885) in Chicago. Although unremarkable in appearance — it looked just like other downtown buildings — Jenney's steel-girder building inspired the creativity of American architects. A Chicago school sprang up, dedicated to the design of buildings whose form expressed, rather than masked, their structure and function. The presiding genius of this school was architect Louis Sullivan, who developed a "vertical aesthetic" of set-back windows and strong columns that not only gave skyscrapers a "proud and soaring" presence but also offered plenty of natural light for workers inside. Chicago pioneered skyscraper construction, but New York, with its unrelenting demand for prime downtown space, took the lead by the late 1890s. The fifty-five-story Woolworth Building, completed in 1913, marked the beginning of the modern Manhattan skyline.

The Electric City | For ordinary citizens, one of the most dramatic urban amenities was electric light. Gaslight, produced from coal gas, had been employed for residential light since the early nineteenth century, but gas lamps were too dim to brighten streets and public spaces. In the 1870s, as generating technology became commercially viable, the first use of electricity was for better urban lighting. Charles F. Brush's electric arc lamps, installed in Wanamaker's department store in Philadelphia in 1878, created a sensation with their brilliant illumination. Electric streetlights soon replaced gaslights on city streets across the country. Electric lighting also entered the American home, thanks to Thomas Edison's invention of a serviceable incandescent bulb in 1879.

Before it had a significant effect on industry, electricity gave the city its modern tempo. It lifted elevators, illuminated department store windows, and powered street-cars and subway trains. Most of all, it turned night into day. Electric streetlights made residents feel safer; as one magazine put it in 1912, "A light is as good as a policeman." Electricity also made nightlife more appealing. One journalist described Broadway in 1894 as a place where "all the shop fronts are lighted, and the entrances to the theaters blaze out on the sidewalk like open fireplaces." At the end of a long working day, city dwellers flocked to this free entertainment. Nothing, declared an observer, matched the "festive panorama" of Broadway "when the lights are on."

Newcomers and Neighborhoods

The explosive growth of America's urban population made cities a world of newcomers, including millions of immigrants from overseas. Most numerous in Boston were the Irish; in Minneapolis, Swedes; in other northern cities, Germans. Arriving in the metropolis, immigrants confronted many difficulties. One Polish man, who had lost the address of his American cousins, felt utterly alone upon his arrival at Ellis Island. Then he heard someone speaking in Polish. "From sheer joy," he recalled, "tears welled up in my eyes to hear my native tongue." He was relieved to get help from a kindly Polish American couple. Such experiences suggest why most immigrants moved in well-defined networks, relying on relatives and friends to become oriented and find jobs. A high degree of ethnic clustering resulted, even within a single factory. At the Jones and Laughlin steelworks in Pittsburgh, for example, the carpentry shop was German, the hammer shop Polish, and the blooming mill Serbian. "My people . . . stick together," observed the son of an immigrant couple from Ukraine. "They attend their own churches." But, he added, "we who are born in this country . . . are different from those born in the old country. We feel this country is our home."

Patterns of settlement varied by ethnic group. Many Italians, recruited by padroni, or labor bosses, found work in northeastern and Mid-Atlantic cities. Their urban concentration was especially marked after the 1880s, as more and more immigrants — especially men — arrived from southern Italy. The attraction of America was obvious to one young man, who had grown up as the third of nine children in a poor southern Italian farm family. "I had never gotten any wages of any kind before," he reported after settling with his uncle in Newark, New Jersey. "The work here was just as hard as that on the farm; but I didn't mind it much because I would receive what seemed to me like a lot." A substantial number of Italians settled on the Pacific coast. Amadeo Peter Giannini, who started off as a produce merchant in San Francisco, soon turned to banking. After the San Francisco earthquake in 1906, his Banca d'Italia was the first financial institution to reopen in the Bay area. Expanding steadily across the West, it eventually became Bank of America.

Like Giannini's bank, institutions of many kinds sprang up to serve ethnic urban communities. Immigrants throughout America avidly read the newspaper *Il Progresso Italo-Americano* and the Yiddish-language *Jewish Daily Forward*, both published in New York. Bohemians gathered in singing societies, while New York Jews patronized a lively Yiddish theater. By 1903, Italians in Chicago had sixty-six mutual aid societies, mostly comprised of people from particular provinces or towns. These societies collected dues from members and paid support in case of death or disability on the job. Mutual benefit societies also functioned as fraternal and political clubs. "We are strangers in a strange country," explained one member of a Chinese *tong*, or communal order, in Chicago. "We must have an organization (*tong*) to control our country fellows and develop our friendship."

Sharply defined ethnic neighborhoods — such as San Francisco's Chinatown, Italian North Beach, and Jewish Hayes Valley — grew up in every major city, driven both by discrimination and by immigrants' desire to stick together (Map 19.1). In addition to patterns of ethnic and racial segregation, the residential districts of almost all industrial cities were divided along lines of economic class. In Los Angeles, Mexican neighborhoods around the central plaza became ethnically diverse, incorporating Italians and Jews. Later, as the plaza became a site for business and tourism, immigrants were pushed into working-class neighborhoods like Belvedere and Boyle Heights, which sprang up to the east. Though ethnically diverse, East Los Angeles was resolutely working-class, while middle-class white neighborhoods grew up predominantly in West Los Angeles.

Along with immigrants, African Americans also sought urban opportunities. At the turn of the twentieth century, 90 percent of American blacks still lived in the South, but increasing numbers moved to urban areas such as Baton Rouge, Jacksonville, Montgomery, and Charleston, all of whose populations were more than 50 percent African American. Blacks also settled in northern cities, albeit not in the numbers that would arrive during the Great Migration of World War I. Though African Americans constituted only 2 percent of New York City's population in 1910, they already numbered more than 90,000. These newcomers to the city confronted conditions that were even worse than those for foreign-born immigrants. Relentlessly turned away from manufacturing jobs, most black men and women took up work in the service sector, becoming porters, laundrywomen, and domestic servants.

Blacks faced another urban danger: the race riot, an attack by white mobs triggered by street altercations or rumors of crime. One of the most virulent episodes occurred in Atlanta, Georgia, in 1906. This set of events, which came to be known as the Atlanta race riot, was fueled by a nasty political campaign that generated sensational false charges of "negro crime." Roaming bands of white men attacked black Atlantans, even invading middle-class black neighborhoods and in one case lynching two barbers after seizing them in their shop. The rioters killed at least twenty-four blacks and wounded more than a hundred. The disease of race hatred was not limited to the South. Race riots similar to the one in Atlanta broke out in New York City's Tenderloin district in 1900; in Evansville, Indiana, in 1903; and in Springfield, Illinois, in 1908. By that year, one journalist observed, "in every important Northern city, a distinct race-problem already exists which must, in a few years, assume serious proportions."

Whether they arrived from the rural South or from Europe, Mexico, or Asia, working-class city residents needed cheap housing near their jobs (Map 19.2). They faced

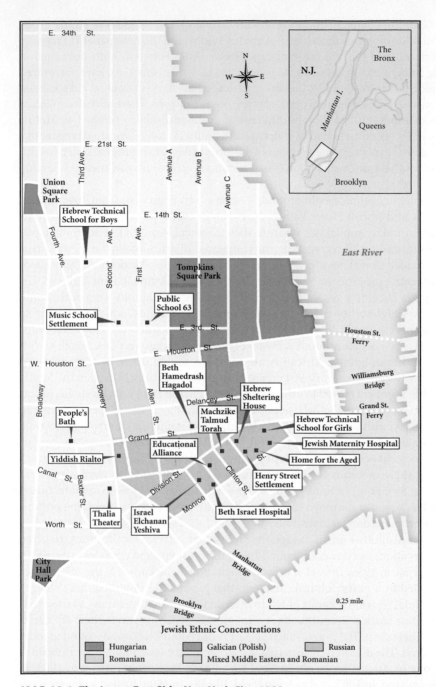

MAP 19.1 The Lower East Side, New York City, 1900

As this map shows, the Jewish immigrants dominating Manhattan's Lower East Side preferred to live in neighborhoods populated by those from their home regions of Eastern Europe. Their sense of a common identity made for a remarkable flowering of educational, cultural, and social institutions on the Jewish East Side. Ethnic neighborhoods became a feature of almost every American city.

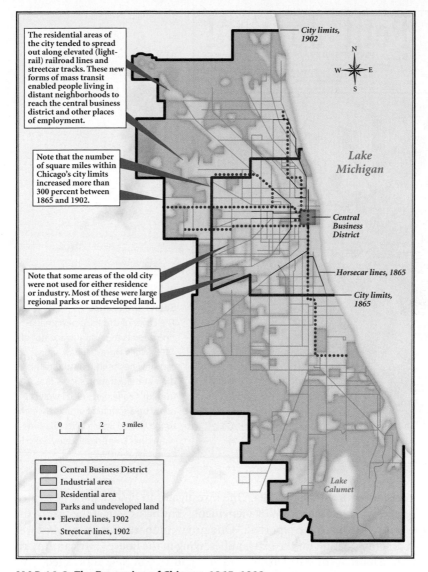

The residential areas of the city tended to spread out along elevated (light-rail) railroad lines and streetcar tracks. These new forms of mass transit enabled people living in distant neighborhoods to reach the central business district and other places of employment.

Note that the number of square miles within Chicago's city limits increased more than 300 percent between 1865 and 1902.

Note that some areas of the old city were not used for either residence or industry. Most of these were large regional parks or undeveloped land.

City limits, 1902

Lake Michigan

Central Business District

Horsecar lines, 1865

City limits, 1865

Lake Calumet

0   1   2   3 miles

■ Central Business District
□ Industrial area
□ Residential area
■ Parks and undeveloped land
•••• Elevated lines, 1902
— Streetcar lines, 1902

MAP 19.2 The Expansion of Chicago, 1865–1902

In 1865, Chicagoans depended on horsecar lines to get around town. By 1900, the city limits had expanded enormously and so had the streetcar service, which was by then electrified. Elevated trains eased the congestion on downtown streets. Ongoing extension of the streetcar lines, some beyond the city limits, ensured that suburban development would continue as well.

grim choices. As urban land values climbed, speculators tore down older houses that had been vacated by middle-class families moving to the suburbs. In their place, they erected five- or six-story tenements, buildings that housed twenty or more families in cramped, airless apartments. In tenements, disease was rampant and infant mortality horrific. In New York's Eleventh Ward, an average of 986 persons occupied each acre,

**The Atlanta Race Riot —
Seen from France**

The cover of this Paris newsmagazine depicts the Atlanta race riot of 1906. While the artist had almost certainly never visited Atlanta, his dramatic illustration shows that, from this early date, racial violence could be a source of embarrassment to the United States in its relations with other countries. Picture Research Consultants & Archives.

a density exceeded only in Bombay, India. One investigator in Philadelphia described twenty-six people living in nine rooms of a tenement. "The bathroom at the rear of the house was used as a kitchen," she reported. "One privy compartment in the yard was the sole toilet accommodation for the five families living in the house." African Americans often suffered most. A study of Albany, Syracuse, and Troy in New York noted, "The colored people are relegated to the least healthful buildings."

Denouncing these conditions, some reformers called for model tenements financed by public-spirited citizens willing to accept a limited return on their investment. When private philanthropy failed to make a dent, cities turned to housing codes. The most advanced was New York's Tenement House Law of 1901, which required interior courts, indoor toilets, and fire safeguards for new structures. The law, however, had no effect on 44,000 tenements already built in Manhattan and the Bronx. Reformers were thwarted by the economic facts of urban development. Industrial workers could not afford transportation to their low-wage jobs and had to live nearby; commercial development pushed up land values. Only high-density, cheaply built housing earned landlords a significant profit.

City Cultures

Despite their many dangers and problems, industrial cities could also be exciting places to live — places where people could challenge older mores. In the nineteenth century, the nation's white, Protestant middle class had set the cultural standard; immigrants and the poor were expected to follow their cues, working toward "uplift" and respectability. But in the cities, by the turn of the twentieth century, new mass-based entertainments emerged among the working classes, especially among working-class youth. These entertainments spread in reverse of prevailing expectations, *from* the working class *to* the middle class (much to the distress of many middle-class parents). At the same time, the great cities proved stimulating centers for intellectual life, featuring diverse institutions from museums and opera houses to newsmagazines.

Urban Amusements | One enticing attraction for city dwellers was **vaudeville**, which arose in the 1880s and 1890s. Vaudeville theaters invited customers to walk in anytime and watch a continuous sequence of musical acts, skits, juggling, magic shows, and other entertainment. First popular among the working class, vaudeville quickly broadened its appeal to include middle-class audiences. By the early 1900s, vaudeville faced growing competition from early movie theaters, or nickelodeons, which offered audiences the chance to see short films for a nickel entry fee. One reporter described the audience at a typical movie theater as "workingmen," "mothers of bawling infants," and "newsboys, bootblacks, and smudgy urchins." By the 1910s, even working girls who refrained from less respectable amusements might indulge in a movie once or twice a week.

Even more spectacular were the great amusement parks that appeared around 1900, most famously at New York's Coney Island (see Voices from Abroad, p. 578). These parks had their origins in World's Fairs, whose free educational exhibits proved less popular than their paid entertainment areas. Fairgoers flocked to ride giant Ferris wheels, take camel rides through "a street in Cairo," and watch exotic Middle Eastern dances. Entrepreneurs found that such attractions were big business. Between 1895 and 1904, they installed them permanently at a group of rival amusement parks near Coney Island's popular beaches. The parks offered millions a chance to come over by ferry, escape the hot city, and enjoy roller coasters, "shoot-the-chute" lagoon plunges, and "hootchy-kootchy" dance shows. Amusement parks soon offered similar fun at sites near Chicago, Kansas City, and other large cities. By the summer of 1903, Philadelphia's Willow Grove Park counted three million visitors annually; so did two amusement parks outside of Los Angeles.

Ragtime | Popular music also became a booming business in the industrial city. By the 1890s, Tin Pan Alley, the nickname for New York City's song-publishing district, produced such national hit tunes as "A Bicycle Built for Two" and "My Wild Irish Rose." The most famous sold more than a million copies of sheet music, as well as audio recordings on newly invented phonograph cylinders. To find out what would sell, publishers had musicians play their compositions at New York's working-class beer gardens, saloons, and dance halls. One publishing agent, who visited "sixty joints a week" to test new songs, declared later that "the best songs came from the gutter."

Coney Island, 1881   JOSÉ MARTÍ

José Martí, a Cuban patriot and revolutionary, was a journalist by profession. In exile from 1880 to 1895, he spent most of his time in New York City, reporting to his Latin American readers on the customs of the Yankees. Martí took special — one might say perverse — pleasure in observing Americans at play.

From all parts of the United States, legions of intrepid ladies and Sunday-best farmers arrive to admire the splendid sights, the unexampled wealth, the dizzying variety, the herculean surge, the striking appearance of Coney Island, the now famous island, four years ago an abandoned sand bank, that today is a spacious amusement area providing relaxation and recreation for hundreds of thousands of New Yorkers who throng to its pleasant beaches every day. . . .

Other nations — ourselves among them — live devoured by a sublime demon within that drives us to the tireless pursuit of an ideal of love or glory. . . . Not so with these tranquil souls, stimulated only by a desire for gain. One scans those shimmering beaches . . . one views the throngs seated in comfortable chairs along the seashore, filling their lungs with the fresh, invigorating air. But it is said that those from our lands who remain here long are overcome with melancholy . . . because this great nation is void of spirit.

But what coming and going! What torrents of money! What facilities for every pleasure! What absolute absence of any outward sadness or poverty! Everything in the open air: the animated groups, the immense dining rooms, the peculiar courtship of North Americans, which is virtually devoid of the elements that compose the shy, tender, elevated love in our lands, the theatre, the photographers' booth, the bathhouses! Some weigh themselves, for North Americans are greatly elated, or really concerned, if they find they have gained or lost a pound. . . .

This spending, this uproar, these crowds, the activity of this amazing ant hill never slackens from June to October, from morning 'til night. . . . Then, like a monster that vomits its contents into the hungry maw of another monster, that colossal crowd, that straining, crushing mass, forces its way onto the trains, which speed across wastes, groaning under their burden, until they surrender it to the tremendous steamers, enlivened by the sound of harps and violins, convey it to the piers, and debouch the weary merrymakers into the thousand trolleys that pursue the thousand tracks that spread through slumbering New York like veins of steel.

SOURCE: Juan de Onís, trans., *The America of José Martí: Selected Writings* (New York: Noonday Press, 1954), 103–110.

African American musicians brought a syncopated beat that, by the 1890s, began to work its way into mainstream hits like "A Hot Time in the Old Town Tonight." Black performers soon became stars in their own right with the rise of ragtime music. Ragtime was apparently named for its "ragged rhythm," which combined a steady beat in the bass (played with the left hand on the piano) and syncopated, off-beat rhythms in the treble (played with the right). Ragtime became wildly popular among audiences of all classes and races who heard, in its infectious rhythms, something exciting and modern — a decisive break with Victorian hymns and parlor songs.

For the master of the genre, composer Scott Joplin, ragtime was serious music. Joplin, the son of former slaves, grew up along the Texas-Arkansas border and took piano lessons as a boy from a German teacher. He and other traveling performers first introduced ragtime to national audiences at the Chicago World's Fair in 1893. Seeking to elevate African American music and secure a broad national audience, Joplin warned pianists, "It is never right to play 'Ragtime' fast." But his instructions were widely ignored. Young Americans embraced ragtime as dance music — and thus a way to embrace one another.

Ragtime ushered in an urban dance craze. By 1910, New York alone had more than five hundred dance halls. In Kansas City, shocked moral reformers counted 16,500 dancers on the floor on a Saturday night; Chicago had 86,000. Some young Polish and Slovak women chose restaurant jobs rather than domestic service so that they would have the free time to visit dance halls, one investigator reported, "several nights a week." New dances like the Bunny Hug and Grizzly Bear were overtly sexual: They called for close body contact and plenty of hip movement. In fact, many of these dances originated in brothels. Despite widespread denunciations, dance mania soon spread from the urban working classes to rural and middle-class youth.

By the 1910s, black music was achieving a central place in American popular culture. African American trumpet player and bandleader W. C. Handy, born in Alabama, electrified national audiences by performing music drawn from the cotton fields of the Mississippi Delta. This music became known as the blues. The blues featured banjo or guitar and a rasping vocal style, with instrument and voice following each other in a "call and response" drawn from traditional African American folk music. In its themes, blues music spoke of hard work and heartbreak, as in Handy's popular hit "St. Louis Blues" (1914):

> Got de St. Louis Blues jes blue as ah can be,
> Dat man got a heart lak a rock cast in the sea,
> Or else he wouldn't gone so far from me.

Though it first emerged in the rural South, blues music won fame in the city. It spoke to the emotional lives of young people who were far from home, experiencing dislocation, loneliness, and bitter disappointment along with the thrills of urban life. Like Coney Island amusements, ragtime and blues helped forge new collective experiences in a world of strangers.

Like other mass commercial amusements, ragtime dance music lacked educational or "uplifting" content; its purpose was sheer pleasure. It spread quickly and had a profound influence on twentieth-century American culture. By the time Handy published "St. Louis Blues," composer Irving Berlin, a Russian Jewish immigrant, was introducing altered ragtime pieces into musical theater — versions that eventually transferred to radio and the movies. The new music often featured sexual innuendo, as in the title of Berlin's hit song "If You Don't Want My Peaches (You'd Better Stop Shaking My Tree)." The popularity of such music showed that a modern youth culture was arriving on the scene. Its enduring features included "crossover" music that originated in the black working class — ragtime and jazz at first, rock and hip-hop in later decades — and a commercial music industry that brazenly appropriated such black musical styles.

Sex and the City | In the city, many young people found parental oversight weaker than it had been in previous generations. Amusement parks and dance halls helped foster the new custom of "dating," which like many other cultural innovations emerged first among the working class. Gradually, it became more acceptable for a young man to escort a young woman out on the town for commercial entertainments rather than spending the evening at home under a chaperone's watchful eye. For young people, dating opened a new world of pleasure, sexual adventure, and danger. Young women sometimes headed to dance halls alone to "pick up" men; the term *gold digger* came into use to describe a woman who wanted a man's money more than the man himself.

But it was young women, not men, who proved most vulnerable in the new system of dating. Having less money to spend than men did, because they earned half or less of men's wages, working-class girls relied on the "treat." Some tried to maintain strict standards of respectability, keenly aware that their prospects for marriage depended — much more than young men's did — on a virtuous reputation. But others became so-called charity girls, eager for a good time. Such young women, one investigator reported, "offer themselves to strangers, not for money, but for presents, attention and pleasure, and, most important, a yielding to sex desire." For some women, sexual favors could look like a matter of practical necessity. "If I did not have a man," declared one waitress, "I could not get along on my wages." In the anonymous city, there was not always a clear line between working-class treats and casual prostitution.

Dating and casual sex were hallmarks of an urban world in which large numbers of residents were young and single. Seeking jobs, greater personal freedom, or both, young unmarried women moved to urban areas in large numbers. The 1900 census found that more than 30 percent of women in St. Paul and Minneapolis, Minnesota, lived as boarders and lodgers, not in family units; the percentage topped 20 percent in Detroit, Philadelphia, and Boston. Single men also found opportunities in the city. One historian has labeled the late nineteenth century the Age of the Bachelor, a time when being an unattached male lost its social stigma. With its boardinghouses, restaurants, and abundant personal services, the city afforded bachelors all the comforts of home and, on top of that, an array of men's clubs, saloons, and sporting events.

In addition to informal and casual heterosexual relationships, many industrial cities developed robust gay subcultures. A gay world flourished in New York, for example, including an array of drinking and meeting places, as well as underground gay clubs and drag balls. Middle-class men, both straight and gay, frequented such venues for entertainment or to find companionship. One medical student remembered being taken to a ball at which he was startled to find five hundred gay and lesbian couples "waltzing to the music of a good band." By the 1910s, the word *queer* had come into use as slang for *homosexual.* Though episodes of harassment were frequent, and reformers like Anthony Comstock issued regular denunciations of "degeneracy," arrests were few. Gay sex shows and saloons were lucrative for those who ran them (and for police, who took bribes to look the other way, just as they did for brothels). The exuberant gay urban subculture offered a dramatic challenge to Victorian ideals.

Urban High Culture   For elites, the rise of great cities offered an opportunity to build museums, libraries, and other cultural institutions that could flourish only in major metropolitan centers. Millionaires patronized the arts partly to advance themselves socially but also out of a sense of civic duty and national pride. As early as the 1870s, symphony orchestras emerged in Boston and New York. National tours by leading orchestras planted the seeds for orchestral societies in many other cities. Composers and conductors embraced new musical forms. By the 1890s, the Metropolitan Opera drew enthusiastic crowds to hear the work of Richard Wagner. In 1907, the Met shocked audiences by presenting Richard Strauss's musically innovative and sexually scandalous opera *Salome*.

As the ferment of urban life overturned older cultural norms, some artists began to question the whole concept of "high culture." American composers began looking to folk music for inspiration. Edward McDowell, for example, called on American artists to free themselves from "the restraint that an almost unlimited deference to European thought and prejudice has imposed upon us." He called for "manly" music that represented Americans' "undaunted tenacity of spirit." Seeking authenticity, McDowell incorporated Native American musical themes into works like his *Indian Suite* (1896).

Art museums and natural history museums also emerged as prominent new institutions in this era. The nation's first major art museum, the Corcoran Gallery of Art, opened in Washington, D.C., in 1869, while New York's Metropolitan Museum of Art settled into its permanent home in 1880. In the same decades, public libraries grew from modest collections into major urban institutions. The greatest library benefactor was steel magnate Andrew Carnegie, who announced in 1881 that he would build a library in any town or city that was prepared to maintain it. By 1907, Carnegie had spent more than $32.7 million to establish about a thousand libraries throughout the United States.

Investigative Journalism   Patrons of Carnegie's libraries could read not only books but also an increasing array of mass-market newspapers. Joseph Pulitzer, owner of the *St. Louis Post-Dispatch* and, after 1883, the *New York Journal*, led the way in building his sales base with sensational investigations, human-interest stories, and targeted sections covering sports, fashion, and high society. By the 1890s, Pulitzer faced a vigorous challenge from William Randolph Hearst, who transformed himself from the pampered son of a California silver king into one of the nation's leading news barons. Starting with the *San Francisco Examiner* and then adding the *New York World*, Hearst went toe-to-toe with Pulitzer as advertising increased, newsstand prices dropped, and newspaper circulation escalated rapidly (Table 19.1).

TABLE 19.1	Newspaper Circulation, 1870–1909		
Year	Total Circulation	Year	Total Circulation
1870	2,602,000	1900	15,102,000
1880	3,566,000	1909	24,212,000
1890	8,387,000		

Source: *Historical Statistics of the United States*, 2 vols. (Washington, DC: U.S. Bureau of the Census, 1975), 2: 810.

Who Said Muck Rake?

A popular biographer in the 1890s, Ida Tarbell turned her journalistic talents to investigative journalism, or muckraking. The first installment of what would become her book *The History of the Standard Oil Company* appeared in *McClure's Magazine* in November 1902. The serial was a bombshell, with its exposure of the ruthless machinations used by John D. Rockefeller in building up his fabulous petroleum fortune. In this cartoon, Tarbell appears as a respectable lady — but note her threatening muck rake and, further in the background, a cowering President Theodore Roosevelt. That Roosevelt was paying attention, the cartoon suggests, is apparent in the headline of the newspaper she is reading. Drake Oil Well Museum.

The arrival of Sunday color comics, such as F. G. Outcault's *The Yellow Kid* (1894), lent their name to *yellow journalism*, a derogatory term used for mass-market newspapers. Disapproving commentators disliked these papers for their flagrant reliance on murders, scandals, sob stories, and anything that might arouse what Hearst's editor called "the gee-whiz emotion." Hearst's and Pulitzer's sensational coverage was often irresponsible, and in the late 1890s their papers helped whip up a nationwide frenzy for the United

States to go to war against Spain. But Hearst and Pulitzer also exposed many scandals and injustices. They believed their papers should challenge the powerful by speaking for, and to, ordinary Americans.

Some of Hearst's and Pulitzer's best reporters played a role in the emerging field of investigative journalism. As early as the 1870s and 1880s, news reporters and independent investigators drew attention to corrupt city governments, the abuse of power by large corporations, and threats to public health. Researcher Helen Campbell reported on tenement conditions in such exposés as *Prisoners of Poverty* (1887). Making innovative use of the invention of flash photography, Danish-born journalist Jacob Riis included photographs of tenement interiors in his famous book *How the Other Half Lives*. Riis had a profound influence on Theodore Roosevelt when the future president served as New York City's police commissioner. Roosevelt asked Riis to give him tours around the city, to help him better understand the problems of poverty, disease, and crime.

By 1900, new magazines such as *Collier's* and *McClure's* introduced middle-class readers to the work of such reporters as Ida Tarbell, who exposed the machinations of John D. Rockefeller, and David Graham Phillips, whose "Treason of the Senate," published in *Cosmopolitan* in 1906, documented the deference of U.S. senators — especially Republicans — to wealthy corporate interests. Such journalists usually lived and worked in big cities, where their magazines were published. President Roosevelt dismissed them as **muckrakers** who focused too much on the negative side of American life. But their influence was profound. They inspired thousands of readers to get involved in reform movements and tackle the problems caused by industrialization.

▶ What economic and technological factors shaped the development of cities and urban life after 1860?

▶ What conditions of life did immigrants and other newcomers face in cities during this period? How did urban popular culture challenge prevailing traditions and values?

Governing the Great City

One of the most famous muckraking journalists was Lincoln Steffens, whose book *The Shame of the Cities* (1904), first published serially in *McClure's*, denounced the corruption afflicting America's urban governments. Steffens used dramatic language to expose "swindling" politicians. He described, for example, how the mayor of Minneapolis turned his city over to "outlaws." In St. Louis, "bribery was a joke," while Pittsburgh's Democratic Party operated a private company that handled almost all the city's street-paving projects, at a hefty profit. Historians now believe that Steffens and other middle-class crusaders took a rather extreme view of urban politics; the reality was more complex. But charges of corruption could hardly be denied. As industrial cities grew with breathtaking speed, they posed a serious problem of governance.

Urban Machines

In the United States, cities relied largely on private developers to build streetcar lines and provide urgently needed water, gas, and electricity. This preference for business solutions gave birth to what one urban historian calls the "private city" — a place shaped by individuals, all pursuing their own goals and bent on making money. The lure of profit, Americans believed, spurred great innovations — trolley cars, electric lighting, skyscrapers — and drove urban real estate development. Investment opportunities looked so tempting, in fact, that new cities sprang up almost overnight from the ruins of a catastrophic Chicago fire in 1871 and a major San Francisco earthquake in 1906. Real estate interests were often instrumental in pushing streetcar lines outward from the central districts. When contractors sought city business, or saloonkeepers needed licenses, they turned to the **political machine**.

Machines were party organizations — like New York's infamous Tammany Society, referred to more often by the name of its meeting place, Tammany Hall — that remained in office, year after year, on the strength of their political clout and popularity among urban voters. To middle-class Americans, machines were corrupt, in part, because they relied on the support of recent immigrants. To serve these grassroots constituents, machines recruited layers of functionaries — precinct captains, ward bosses, aldermen — whose main job was to be accessible and, as best they could, serve the needs of the party faithful. The machine acted as a rough-and-ready social service agency, providing jobs for the jobless or a helping hand for a bereaved family. Tammany ward boss George Washington Plunkitt, for example, reported that he arranged housing for families after their apartments burned, "fix[ing] them up until they get things runnin' again. It's philanthropy, but it's politics, too — mighty good politics." Plunkitt was an Irishman, and so were most Tammany Hall leaders. But by the 1890s, Plunkitt's Fifteenth District was filling up with Italians and Russian Jews. On a given day (as recorded in his diary) he might attend an Italian funeral in the afternoon and a Jewish wedding in the evening.

The favors dispensed by men like Plunkitt came via a system of boss control that was, as Lincoln Steffens charged, corrupt. Though rural, state, and national politics were hardly immune to such problems, cities offered the most flagrant opportunities for bribes and kickbacks. The level of corruption, as Plunkitt put it, rose "accordin' to the opportunities." When politicians made contracts for city services, some of the money ended up in their pockets. In the 1860s, William Marcy Tweed, known commonly as Boss Tweed, had made Tammany Hall a byword for corruption, until he was brought down in 1871 by flagrant overpricing in the contracts for a lavish city courthouse. Thereafter, machine corruption became more surreptitious. Plunkitt declared that he had no need for outright bribes. He favored what he called "honest graft," the easy profits that came to savvy insiders. Plunkitt made most of his money building wharves on Manhattan's waterfront.

Middle-class reformers condemned immigrants for supporting machines. But urban voters believed that few middle-class Americans cared about the plight of poor city folk like themselves. Machines were hardly perfect, but immigrants could rely on them for jobs, emergency aid, and the only public services they could hope to obtain. Astute commentators saw that bosses dominated city government because they provided what was needed, with no moralistic lectures. As one put it, machines offered "neighborly kindness instead of annual political sermons."

Despite breakneck urban development and widespread corruption, machine-style governments achieved notable successes. They built extensive public parks and markets; paved streets; and supplied streetcars, clean water, gaslight, and sewage removal. As early as 1866, at the moment when Boss Tweed was divvying up tax money with his cronies, the very same Tammany Hall machine helped oversee a triumph of public health. When the arrival of a German ship with infected passengers threatened to spread cholera, political leaders sprang into action, keenly aware that a similar outbreak in 1849 had killed more than five thousand New Yorkers. This time, by appointing an expert board of health with the authority to clean streets, disinfect buildings, and impose quarantines, the city soon brought the epidemic under control.

In the following decades, city governance improved impressively. Though by no means free of corruption, municipal agencies became far better organized and more expansive in the functions they undertook. Nowhere in the world were there more massive public projects — aqueducts, sewage systems, bridges, and spacious parks — than in American cities. The nature of this achievement can be grasped by comparing Chicago, Illinois, with Berlin, the capital of Germany, in 1900. At that time, Chicago's waterworks pumped 500 million gallons of water a day, providing 139 gallons per resident; Berliners had to make do with 18 gallons each. Flush toilets, a rarity in Berlin, could be found in 60 percent of Chicago homes. Chicago lit its streets with electricity, while Berlin still relied mostly on gaslight. Chicago had twice as many parks as the German capital, and it had just completed an ambitious sanitation project that reversed the course of the Chicago River, carrying sewage into Lake Michigan, away from city residents.

Chicago's achievement was especially remarkable because American municipal governments labored under severe political constraints. Judges did grant cities some authority: In 1897, the State Supreme Court ruled that New York City was entirely within its rights to operate a municipally owned subway. The use of private land was also subject to whatever regulations the city might impose. But, starting with an 1868 ruling in Iowa, the American legal system largely classified the city as a "corporate entity" subject to state control. In contrast to state governments, cities had only a limited police power, which they could use, for example, to stop crime, but not to pass more ambitious measures for public welfare. States, not cities, also held most taxation power and received most public revenues. Machines and their private allies flourished, in part, because cities were starved for legitimate cash.

As cities continued to expand, the limits of machine government became increasingly clear. In addition to the problem of corruption, even the hardest-working ward boss could help individuals only on a local level, in limited ways. A city like New York might manage to ward off cholera. But Tammany Hall could not achieve systemic solutions to poverty, pollution, and unemployment, all of which were direct consequences of industrialization. Money talked; powerful economic interests warped city government. Working-class voters — even those who saw no alternative to the machine — knew that the cleanest sidewalks, newest electric lights, and most convenient trolley lines served affluent neighborhoods and suburbs, where citizens had the most clout. Hilda Satt, a Polish immigrant who moved into a poor Chicago neighborhood in 1893, recalled garbage-strewn streets and filthy backyard privies. "The streets were paved with wooden blocks," she later wrote, "and after a heavy rainfall the blocks would become loose and float about in the street." She remembered that on one such occasion, local pranksters posted a sign saying "The Mayor and the Aldermen are Invited to Swim Here."

The Limits of Machine Government

Even a casual observer could see that American cities were finding it difficult to cope with extremely rapid growth, and that some urban politicians (like their counterparts elsewhere) preferred personal gain to public welfare. The results were dramatically evident during the depression of the 1890s, when the working-class unemployment rate reached a staggering 25 percent in some cities. Homelessness and hunger were rampant. To make matters worse, most cities had abolished the early-nineteenth-century system of "outdoor relief," which provided public support for the indigent. Arguing that this promoted laziness among the poor, middle-class reformers insisted on private, not public, charity. Even cities that did continue to provide outdoor relief in the 1890s were overwhelmed by the magnitude of the crisis. Flooded with "tramps," police stations were forced to end the long-standing practice of allowing homeless individuals to sleep inside.

The crisis of the 1890s radicalized many urban voters, who proved none too loyal to the machines when better alternatives arose. Cleveland, Ohio, for example, experienced eighty-three labor strikes between 1893 and 1898; much frustration centered on the private businesses that provided urban services such as streetcar transportation. The city's Central Labor Union, dissatisfied with Democrats' failure to address its concerns, worked with middle-class allies to build a thriving local branch of the People's Party. Their demands for stronger government measures, especially to curb corporate power, culminated in citywide protests in 1899, during a strike against the hated streetcar company. That year, more than eight thousand workers participated in the city's annual Labor Day parade. As they passed the mayor's reviewing stand, each band fell silent, and the unions furled their flags in a solemn protest against the mayor's failure to support their cause.

To recapture support from working-class Clevelanders, Democrats made a dramatic change in 1901, nominating Tom Johnson for mayor. Johnson, a reform-minded businessman, advocated municipal ownership of utilities and a tax system in which "monopoly and privilege" bore the main burdens. (Johnson once thanked Cleveland's city appraisers for raising taxes on his own mansion.) Johnson's comfortable victory transformed Democrats into Cleveland's chief reform party. While the new mayor did not fulfill the whole agenda of the Central Labor Union and its allies, he became an advocate of publicly owned utilities, and one of the nation's most famous and innovative reformers.

Like Johnson, other reform mayors began to oust machines and launch ambitious programs. Some modeled their municipal governments on those of Glasgow, Scotland; Düsseldorf, Germany; and other European cities on the cutting edge of innovation. In Boston, Mayor Josiah Quincy built public baths, gyms, swimming pools, and playgrounds and provided free public concerts. Like other mayors, he battled streetcar companies to bring down fares. The scope of such projects varied. In 1912, San Francisco managed to open one short municipally owned streetcar line to compete with private companies. Milwaukee, Wisconsin, on the other hand, elected Socialists who experimented with a sweeping array of measures, including publicly subsidized medical care and housing.

Republican Hazen Pingree, mayor of Detroit from 1890 to 1897, was a particularly notable reformer who worked for better streets and public transportation. During the 1890s, Pingree opened a network of vacant city-owned lots as community vegetable gardens. "Pingree's Potato Patches" helped feed thousands of Detroit's working people during the harsh depression years. By 1901, a coalition of reformers who campaigned against New York's Tammany Hall began to borrow ideas from Pingree and other mayors. In the wealthier wards of New York, they promised to reduce crime and save taxpayer dollars. In working-class neighborhoods, they promised to provide affordable housing and municipal ownership of gas and electricity. They defeated Tammany's candidates, and though they did not fulfill all of their promises, they did provide more funding for overcrowded public schools.

Reformers also experimented with new ways of organizing municipal government itself. After a devastating hurricane killed an estimated 6,000 people in Galveston, Texas, in 1900, and destroyed much of the city, rebuilders adopted a commission system that became a nationwide model for efficient government. Leaders of the National Munici-pal League advised cities to elect small councils and hire professional city managers who would direct operations like a corporate executive. The league had great difficulty persuading politicians to adopt its business-oriented model; it won its greatest vic-tories in young, small cities like Phoenix, Arizona, where the professional classes held political power. Other cities chose, instead, to enhance democratic participation. As part of the "Oregon System," which called for direct voting on key political ques-tions, Portland voters participated in 129 munici-pal referendum votes between 1905 and 1913.

▶ What role did political machines play in city government? Do you think they served the goals of representative democracy? Why, or why not?

▶ What factors limited the effec-tiveness of machine govern-ment? How did reformers try to address these limits? To what extent did they succeed?

Cities as Crucibles of Reform

As experiments in city government showed, the challenges that arose in the industrial city presented rich opportunities for experimentation and reform. Thus it is not surpris-ing that progressivism (see Chapter 20) — an overlapping set of movements to combat the ills of industrialization — had a powerful urban basis. In the slums and tenements of the giant metropolis, grassroots reformers invented new forms of civic participation that soon shaped national politics.

Public Health

One of the most urgent problems of the big city was disease. In the late nineteenth cen-tury, scientists in Europe came to understand the role of germs and bacteria. Though researchers could not yet cure epidemic diseases, they could recommend effective mea-sures for prevention. Following up on New York City's victory against cholera in 1866, city and state officials began to champion more public health projects. With a major clean-water initiative for its industrial cities in the late nineteenth century, Massachusetts demonstrated that it could largely eliminate typhoid fever. Memphis, Tennessee, after a horrific yellow fever epidemic in 1878 that killed perhaps 12 percent of the population, invested in state-of-the-art sewage and drainage. Though the new system did not elimi-nate yellow fever, it unexpectedly cut death rates from typhoid and cholera, as well as in-fant deaths from waterborne disease. Other cities followed suit. By 1913, a nationwide survey of 198 cities found that they were spending an average of $1.28 per resident for public health measures.

The public health movement became one of the era's most visible and influential reforms. In cities, the impact of pollution was more obvious than it was in rural areas.

Hull House Playground, Chicago, 1906
When this postcard was made, the City of Chicago's Small Parks Commission had just taken over manage-ment of the playground from settlement workers at Hull House, who had created it. In a pattern repeated in many cities, social settlements introduced new institutions and ideas — such as safe places for urban children to play — and inspired municipal authorities to assume responsibility and control. Private Collection.

Children played on piles of garbage, breathed toxic air, and consumed poisoned food, milk, and water. Infant mortality rates were shocking. In the early 1900s, a baby born to a Slavic woman in an American city had a one-in-three chance of dying in infancy. Outraged, urban reformers mobilized to demand safe water and better garbage collec-tion. Hygiene reformers taught hand-washing and other techniques to fight the spread of tuberculosis.

Rising fears of unsafe food and drugs also led to government action to improve food and drug safety. At the end of the Civil War, federal and state governments provided no regulation of food or medical products. In 1904, a riveting series of articles in *Collier's* exposed many popular pharmaceutical products as "undiluted frauds." Two years later, journalist Upton Sinclair published his novel *The Jungle*, an exposé of labor exploitation in Chicago meatpacking plants. What caught the nation's attention was not Sinclair's ac-count of workers' plight, but his descriptions of rotten meat and filthy packing conditions. With constituents up in arms, Congress passed the Pure Food and Drug Act and created the Food and Drug Administration (1906) to oversee compliance with the new law.

Reformers worked in other ways to make cities healthier and more beautiful to live in. Many municipalities adopted smoke-abatement laws, though they had limited success with enforcement until the post–World War I adoption of natural gas, which burned cleaner than coal. Recreation also received attention. Even before the Civil War, urban planners had established sanctuaries, like New York's Central Park, where city people could stroll, rest, and contemplate natural landscapes. By the turn of the twentieth century, the "City Beautiful" movement arose to advocate more and better urban park spaces. Though most parks still featured flower gardens and tree-lined paths, they also made room for skating rinks, tennis courts, baseball fields, and swimming pools. Many included play areas with swing sets and seesaws, promoted by the National Playground Association as a way to keep urban children safe and healthy.

Campaigns against Urban Prostitution

Distressed by the commercialization of sex in American cities, reformers also launched a nationwide campaign against prostitution. They warned, in dramatic language, of the perils of "white slavery," alleging (in spite of considerable evidence to the contrary) that young white women were being kidnapped and forced into prostitution. In *The City's Perils* (1910), author Leona Prall Groetzinger wrote that young women arrived in the city "burning with high hope and filled with great resolves, but the remorseless city takes them, grinds them, crushes them, and at last deposits them in unknown graves."

Practical investigators found a more complex reality: Women entered prostitution as a result of many factors, including low-wage jobs, economic desperation, abandonment, and often sexual and domestic abuse. Some workingwomen — even working-class housewives — undertook occasional, casual prostitution to make ends meet. Women who bore a child out of wedlock were often shunned by their families and forced into prostitution. For decades, female reformers had tried to "rescue" such women and retrain them for more respectable employment. Results were, at best, mixed. Efforts to curb demand — that is, to focus on arresting and punishing men who employed prostitutes — proved unpopular with voters.

Nonetheless, with public concern mounting over "white slavery" and the payoffs that machine bosses exacted from brothel keepers, many cities appointed vice commissions in the early 1900s. A wave of brothel closings crested between 1909 and 1912, as police shut down red-light districts in cities nationwide. Meanwhile, Congress passed the Mann Act (1910) to prohibit the transportation of prostitutes across state lines.

The crusade against prostitution accomplished its main goal — closing brothels — but in the long term it worsened the conditions under which many prostitutes worked. Though conditions in some brothels were horrific, sex workers who catered to wealthy clients made high wages and were relatively protected by madams, many of whom set strict rules for clients and provided medical care for their workers. In the wake of brothel closings, such women lost control of the prostitution trade. Instead, almost all sex workers became "streetwalkers" or "call girls," more vulnerable to violence and often earning lower wages than they had in earlier years.

The Movement for Social Settlements

The most celebrated urban reform institution of the industrial era, and one of the most effective, emerged out of Christian urban missions, educational and social welfare centers that were founded in the 1870s and 1880s. Some of these, like the Hampton Institute, sprang up to aid former slaves in Southern cities during Reconstruction; others, like

Grace Baptist Temple and Samaritan Hospital in Philadelphia, served northern working-class and immigrant populations. To meet the needs of urban residents, missions offered such services as employment counseling, medical clinics, day care, and sometimes an athletic facility in cooperation with the Young Men's Christian Association (YMCA).

At the same time, other reformers were focusing on the plight of urban working-class women, tackling such problems as low wages and lack of day care for working mothers. Some groups created cooperative exchanges through which women could support themselves by selling needlework and crafts. In the 1880s, heiress Grace Dodge founded a network of working girls' clubs in New York City that featured housekeeping and self-improvement classes. In Davenport, Iowa, professional women and dozens of female clerks and wageworkers joined together to create the Working Women's Lend a Hand Club. The club rented a comfortable suite in the downtown business district where its members could rest, change clothes, or share lunch.

Such projects soon evolved into a far more ambitious project: the **social settlement**. The most famous of these was Hull House on Chicago's West Side, founded in 1889 by Jane Addams and her close companion Ellen Gates Starr. The project was an idea they had borrowed not only from American missions but also from Toynbee Hall, a London settlement they had visited while touring Europe. The dilapidated mansion they called Hull House, flanked by saloons in a neighborhood of mainly Italian immigrants, served as a community center and a spark plug for neighborhood betterment and political reform.

Jane Addams, a daughter of the middle class, first expected that Hull House would offer art classes and "cultural uplift" to the poor. But Addams's views quickly changed as she got to know her new neighbors and struggled to keep Hull House open during the depression of the 1890s. Addams's views were also reshaped by her conversations with fellow Hull House worker Florence Kelley, who had studied in Europe and returned to the United States as a committed socialist. Dr. Alice Hamilton, who opened a pediatric clinic at Hull House, wrote that Addams "looked upon Hull House as a bridge between the classes. . . . She always held that this bridge was as much of a help to the well-to-do as to the poor." Settlements offered idealistic young people "a place where they could live as neighbors and give as much as they could of what they had."

Addams and her colleagues came to believe that immigrants already *knew* what they needed. What they lacked were the resources to fulfill those needs, as well as a strong political voice. These, settlement workers tried to provide. Hull House was typical in offering a bathhouse, a playground, a kindergarten, and a day care center. Hamilton soon investigated lead poisoning and other health threats at local factories. Addams, meanwhile, encouraged local women to inspect the neighborhood and bring back a list of dangers to health and safety. Together, they prepared a complaint to city council. The women, Addams wrote, had shown "both civic enterprise and moral conviction" in carrying out the project themselves, with her aid.

In the early twentieth century, social settlements sprang up all over the United States. They engaged in an array of public activities and took many forms. Some attached themselves to preexisting missions and African American colleges. Others were founded by energetic graduates of Smith, Vassar, and other women's colleges. The St. Elizabeth Center in St. Louis was run by Catholics; Boston's Hebrew Industrial School was Jewish. Whatever their origins, social settlements sought to serve poor urban neighborhoods.

"FRIENDS" MEETING EMIGRANT GIRL AT THE DOCK
"The girl was met at New York by two 'friends' who took her in charge. These 'friends' were two of the most brutal of all the white slave traders who are in the traffic."
—U. S. Dist. Attorney Edwin W. Sims.
Foreign girls are more helplessly at the mercy of white slave hunters than girls at home. Every year thousands of girls arriving in America from Italy, Sweden, Germany, etc., are never heard of again.

The Crusade against "White Slavery"

With the growth of large cities, prostitution was a major cause of concern in the Progressive Era. Though the number of prostitutes per capita in the United States was probably declining by 1900, the presence of red-light districts was obvious; thousands of young women (as well as a smaller number of young men) were exploited in the sex trade. This image appeared in *The Great War on White Slavery*, published by the American Purity Foundation in 1911. It illustrates how immigrant women could be ensnared in the sex trade by alleged "friends" who offered them work. Reformers' denunciations of "white slavery" show an overt racial bias: While antiprostitution campaigners reported on the exploitation of Asian and African American women, the victimization of white women received the greatest emphasis and most effectively grabbed the attention of prosperous, middle-class Americans. From *The Great War on White Slavery*, by Clifford G. Roe, 1911. Courtesy Vassar College Special Collections.

In the words of Jane Addams, they were "an experimental effort to aid in the solution of the social and industrial problems which are engendered by the modern condition of life in a great city."

Social settlements used their resources and influence in many ways. They opened libraries and gymnasiums for working men and women. They operated employment bureaus, penny savings banks, and cooperative kitchens where tired families could purchase a meal at the end of the day. (Addams humbly closed her Hull House kitchen when she found that her bland New England cooking had little appeal for Italians, who were accustomed to spicier food. Her coworker, Alice Hamilton, became a convert to the health benefits of garlic.) In cities across the country, settlement workers fought city hall to get better schools and factory safety laws (see American Voices, p. 593). At the Henry Street Settlement in New York, Lillian Wald developed a system of visiting nurses to improve health in tenement wards. Mary McDowell, head of the University of Chicago Settlement, operated a citizenship school for recent immigrants.

Settlement work served as a springboard for other projects. Hull House worker Julia Lathrop, for example, investigated the plight of teenagers caught in the criminal justice system. She drafted a proposal for separate juvenile courts and persuaded Chicago to adopt it. Pressuring the city to experiment with better rehabilitation strategies for juveniles convicted of crime, Lathrop created a model for juvenile court systems across the United States. Other settlement workers went on to prominent national reform careers. Jane Addams and Florence Kelley of Hull House became two of America's most famous advocates for children, labor, women's rights, and international peace.

Settlements were an early, crucial proving ground for the emerging profession of social work, which transformed the provision of public welfare. Social workers rejected the older model of private Christian charity, dispensed by well-meaning middle-class people to those in need. Instead, social workers defined themselves as caseworkers who served as advocates of social justice. Like many reformers of their era, they allied themselves with the new social sciences, such as sociology and economics, and undertook statistical surveys and other systematic methods for gathering facts. Social work proved to be an excellent opportunity for educated women who sought professional careers. By 1920, women made up 62 percent of U.S. social workers.

Cities and National Politics

Despite the work of reformers, the problems of the industrial city grew more rapidly than remedies for them could be found. To overcome the ills of industrialization — which wrought transformations at the national and even global level — city governments needed allies in state and national politics. That urgent need was made clear in New York City by a shocking event on March 25, 1911. On that Saturday afternoon, just before quitting time, a fire broke out at the Triangle Shirtwaist Company. It quickly spread through the three floors the company occupied at the top of a ten-story building. Panicked workers discovered that, despite fire safety laws, employers had locked the emergency doors to prevent theft. Dozens of Triangle workers, mostly young immigrant women, were trapped in the flames. Many leaped to their deaths; the rest never reached the windows. The average age of the 146 people who died was just nineteen.

AMERICAN VOICES

Tracking Down Lead Poisoning   DR. ALICE HAMILTON

Alice Hamilton (1869–1970) studied medicine over the objections of her socially prominent family. When she finally landed a job teaching pathology in Chicago, Dr. Hamilton moved into Jane Addams's Hull House. That experience launched her on a pioneering career in industrial medicine — one of the many paths to social reform opened up by settlement-house work.

When I look back on the Chicago of 1897 I can see why life in a settlement seemed so great an adventure. It was all so new, this exploring of the poor quarters of a big city. . . . To settle down to live in the slums of a great city was a piece of daring as great as trekking across the prairie in a covered wagon. . . .

It was also my experience at Hull House that aroused my interest in industrial diseases. Living in a working-class quarter, coming in contact with laborers and their wives, I could not fail to hear tales of the dangers that working-men faced, of cases of carbon-monoxide gassing in the great steel mills, of painters disabled by lead palsy, of pneumonia and rheumatism among the men in the stockyards. . . .

At the time I am speaking of [1910] Professor Charles Henderson . . . persuaded [the governor] to appoint an Occupational Disease Commission, the first time a state had ever undertaken such a survey. . . . We were staggered by the complexity of the problem we faced and we soon decided to limit our field almost entirely to the occupational poisons . . . lead, arsenic, brass, carbon monoxide, the cyanides, and turpentine. Nowadays [1943], the list involved in a survey of the painters' trade alone is many times as long as that.

But to us it seemed far from a simple task. We could not even discover what were the poisonous occupations in Illinois. . . .

There was nothing to do but begin with trades we knew were dangerous and hoped that, as we studied them, we would discover others less well known. My field was to be lead. . . .

One case, of colic and double wristdrop [paralysis of the wrist muscles, causing the hand to droop], which was discovered in the Alexian Brothers' Hospital, took me on a pretty chase. The man, a Pole, said he had worked in a sanitary-ware factory, putting enamel on bathtubs. . . . The management assured me that no lead was used in the coatings and invited me to inspect the workroom. . . . Completely puzzled, I made a journey to the Polish quarter to see the palsied man and heard from him I had not even been in the enameling works, only the one for final touching up. The real one was far out on the Northwest Side. I found it and discovered that enameling means sprinkling a finely ground enamel over a red hot tub. . . . The air is thick with enamel dust . . . rich in red oxide of lead. A specimen . . . proved to contain as much as 20 per cent soluble lead — that is, lead that will pass into solution in the human stomach. Thus I nailed down the fact that sanitary-ware enameling was a dangerous lead trade. . . .

SOURCE: *Exploring the Dangerous Trades: The Autobiography of Alice Hamilton* (Boston: Little, Brown and Co., 1943), 60, 114, 118–121.

The Triangle Fire

Artist John Sloan's drawing captures better than any photograph the horror of the 1911 Triangle fire. According to observers, a number of young workers, having no other way to escape the flames, chose to fall to their deaths in each other's arms. The fireman who cannot bear to watch may be a product of Sloan's imagination, but the anguish he felt is true enough: When the fire trucks arrived, they did not have the equipment to save anyone. Not only were the ladders too short, but the safety nets were too weak — the bodies simply shot right through to the ground. *Harper's Weekly*, May 8, 1915.

Shocked by this horrific event, New Yorkers responded across lines of class, religion, and ethnicity. Many remembered that, only a year earlier, shirtwaist workers had walked off the job to protest abysmal safety and working conditions — and that the owners of Triangle, among other employers, had broken the strike. Facing public demands for action, New York State appointed a factory commission that developed a remarkable program of labor reform: fifty-six laws dealing with such issues as fire hazards, unsafe machines, and wages and working hours for women and children. The chairman and vice chairman of the commission were Robert F. Wagner and Alfred E. Smith, both Tammany Hall politicians then serving in the state legislature. They established the commission, participated fully in its work, and marshaled party regulars to pass the proposals into law — all with the approval of Tammany. The labor code that resulted was the most advanced in the United States. Tammany's response to the Triangle fire showed that it was conceding to reform: The social and economic problems of the industrial city had outgrown the power of party machines. Only stronger state and national laws could bar industrial firetraps, alleviate sweatshop conditions, and improve slums. Machine politicians like Wagner and Smith saw that Tammany had to change or die.

The political aftermath of the Triangle fire demonstrated how challenges posed by industrial cities pushed politics in new directions, not only by transforming urban government but also by helping to build broader movements for reform. At the end of the Civil War, the nation's political and cultural standard had been set by native-born, rural, Protestant, and middle-class Americans. Over the decades that followed, people had thronged to the great cities from rural areas and from countries around the world. They helped build America into a global industrial power. In the process, they created an electorate that was far more ethnically, racially, and religiously diverse then ever before. This diversity was most obvious in the cities.

In the era of industrialization, some rural and native-born commentators warned that immigrants were "inferior breeds" who would "mongrelize" American culture. But urban political leaders defended cultural pluralism, expressing their appreciation — even admiration — for Southern and Eastern European immigrants, Catholics and Jews who sought a better life in the United States. At the same time, urban reformers worked to improve the conditions of work, housing, and daily living for the diverse residents of American cities. It is not surprising, then, that cities played a pivotal role in national efforts to remedy the ills of industrialization. City problems, and the innovative solutions proposed by urban leaders, held a central place in the national consciousness as Americans turned to the task of progressive reform.

▶ If you had lived in a large American city in the post–Civil War decades, might you have joined any of the reform movements working to improve public health, morals, and welfare? If not, why not? If so, which ones, and why?

▶ What effect did the Triangle fire have on politics? Why do you think its impact was so wide-ranging?

SUMMARY

After 1865, American cities grew at an unprecedented rate, and urban populations swelled with workers from rural areas and abroad. To move burgeoning populations around the city, cities pioneered innovative forms of mass transit. Skyscrapers came to mark urban skylines, and new electric lighting systems encouraged nightlife. Neighborhoods divided along class and ethnic lines, with white middle-class people moving out to new suburban communities. Working-class city dwellers lived in crowded, shoddily built tenements. Immigrants developed new ethnic cultures in their neighborhoods, while racism followed African American migrants from country to city. At the same time, new forms of popular urban culture bridged class and ethnic lines, challenging traditional sexual norms and gender roles. Popular journalism rose to prominence and helped build rising sympathy for reform.

Industrial cities confronted a variety of new political challenges. Despite notable achievements, established machine governments could not address urban problems through traditional means. Forward-looking politicians took the initiative and implemented a range of political, labor, and social reforms. Urban reformers also launched campaigns to address public health, morals, and welfare. They did so through a variety of innovative institutions, most notably social settlements, which brought affluent Americans into working-class neighborhoods to learn, cooperate, and advocate on behalf of their neighborhoods. Such projects began to increase Americans' acceptance of urban diversity and their confidence in government's ability to solve the problems of industrialization.

> For additional primary sources from this period, see *Documents for America's History*, Seventh Edition.
>
> For Web sites, images, and documents related to topics and places in this chapter, visit *Make History* at **bedfordstmartins.com/henrettaconcise**.

For Further Exploration

On industrial cities see Sam Bass Warner, *Streetcar Suburbs* (1962); Carl Condit, *Rise of the New York Skyscraper* (1996); and Harold L. Platt, *The Electric City* (1991). On urban life see Gunther Barth, *City People* (1982); David Nasaw, *Going Out* (1993); Joanne Meyerowitz, *Women Adrift* (1988); Howard P. Chudacoff, *The Age of the Bachelor* (1999); Kathy Peiss, *Cheap Amusements* (1986); Tera Hunter, *To 'Joy My Freedom* (1997); and George Chauncey, *Gay New York* (1994). On popular music, see Richard Crawford, *America's Musical Life* (2001). Among many books on immigrant life see Susan Glenn, *Daughters of the Shtetl* (1990), and George Sanchez, *Becoming Mexican American* (1993).

On urban Progressivism see Maureen A. Flanagan, *America Reformed* (2007), John Buenker, *Urban Liberalism and Progressive Reform* (1973), and Eric Rauchway's *Blessed Among Nations* (2006). On the settlement movement, Jane Addams's *Twenty Years at Hull House* (1910) is a must; see also Allen Davis, *Spearheads for Reform* (1984); Elisabeth Lasch-Quinn, *Black Neighbors* (1993); Robert Handy, *The Social Gospel in America* (1966); and Ralph Luker, *The Social Gospel in Black and White* (1991).

On prostitution and campaigns against it, see Ruth Rosen, *The Lost Sisterhood* (1982). On the Triangle fire see David von Drehle, *Triangle: The Fire That Changed America* (2003), and Leon Stein, *The Triangle Fire* (1962).

Test Your Knowledge

For practice quizzes, activities, and other study tools, visit the Online Study Guide at **bedfordstmartins.com/henrettaconcise**.

TIMELINE

1866	▶ New York City contains cholera epidemic
1876	▶ Alexander Graham Bell invents telephone
1878	▶ Yellow fever epidemic in Memphis, Tennessee
1879	▶ First elevated railroad opened in Chicago
	▶ Edison invents incandescent light bulb
1885	▶ First skyscraper completed in Chicago
1887	▶ First electric trolley system built in Richmond, Virginia
1889	▶ Jane Addams and Ellen Gates Starr found Hull House in Chicago
1893	▶ Ragtime introduced to national audience at Chicago World's Fair

1897	▶ First subway line opened in Boston
1903	▶ National Trade Union League founded
1904	▶ Subway running the length of Manhattan completed
1906	▶ Food and Drug Administration established
1910	▶ Mann Act prohibits transportation of prostitutes across state lines
1911	▶ National Urban League founded
	▶ Triangle Shirtwaist Company fire in New York
1913	▶ Fifty-five-story Woolworth Building completed in New York

Whose Government? Politics, Populists, and Progressives

1880–1917

> Society is looking itself over, in our day, from top to bottom. . . . We are in a temper to reconstruct economic society.
>
> —Woodrow Wilson, 1913

"We are living in a grand and wonderful time," declared Kansas political organizer Mary E. Lease in 1891. "Men, women and children are in commotion, discussing the mighty problems of the day." She declared this "movement among the masses" to be based on the words of Jesus: "Whatsoever ye would that men should do unto you, do ye even so unto them." Between the 1880s and the 1910s, thousands of reformers like Lease confronted the problems of an industrializing nation. Lease herself stumped not only for the People's Party, which sought more government regulation of the economy, but also for the Knights of Labor, the Woman's Christian Temperance Union, and the woman suffrage movement. In addition, she advocated new initiatives in education and public health.

Between the end of Reconstruction and the start of World War I, prominent political reform movements focused on four main goals: making politics more effective, limiting the power of big business, ameliorating poverty, and promoting social justice. In the 1880s and 1890s, labor unions and farm radicals took the lead in critiquing the new industrial order and demanding change. Over time, more and more middle-class and elite Americans also took up the call, eventually earning the name **progressives**. On the whole, middle-class progressives proposed more limited measures than farmer and labor advocates did, but since they wielded more political clout, they often had greater success in winning passage of new laws. Thus, while their goals and tactics differed, both radicals and progressives played important roles in advancing reform.

Although historians call this era of political agitation and innovation the Progressive Era, no single group led the way. On the contrary, prominent reformers took opposing views on such questions as immigration policy, racial justice, women's rights, and imperialism. Most middle-class progressives were initially hostile to the sweeping critiques of capitalism advanced by farmer-labor movements and by socialists, but over time some adopted more radical ideas themselves. Dramatic changes in national politics also shaped the course of reform. Close party competition early in the era gave way

Coxey's Army on the March, 1894
During the severe depression of the 1890s, Ohio businessman Jacob Coxey organized unemployed men for a peaceful march to the U.S. Capitol, to plead for an emergency jobs program. They called themselves the Commonweal of Christ but won the nickname "Coxey's Army." Though it failed to win sympathy from Congress, the army's march on Washington — one of the nation's first — inspired similar groups to set out from many cities. Here, Coxey's group nears Washington, D.C. The man on horseback is Carl Browne, one of the group's leaders and a flamboyant publicist. As the marchers entered Washington, Coxey's seventeen-year-old daughter Mamie, dressed as the "Goddess of Peace," led the procession on a white Arabian horse. Library of Congress.

to Republican control between 1894 and 1910, followed by a period of Democratic-led progressivism during the presidency of Woodrow Wilson (1913–1919). Progressives gave their era its name, not because they acted as a unified force, but because they engaged in diverse, energetic movements to improve American life.

Reform Visions, 1880–1892

In the 1880s, radical farmers' groups and the Knights of Labor provided the most urgent, powerful challenge to industrialization (see Chapter 17). At the same time, groups like the Woman's Christian Temperance Union began to lay the groundwork for middle-class progressivism, especially among women (see Chapter 18). Though they had different goals, these groups confronted similar dilemmas as they entered the political arena. Should they work through existing political parties, or create new ones? Or should they instead generate pressure from the outside, through nonpartisan organizations? At different times, reformers tried all these strategies as they wrestled with the realities of post-Reconstruction politics.

Electoral Politics after Reconstruction

The collapse of Reconstruction ushered in a period of high voter turnout and fierce partisan conflict. Republicans and Democrats traded control of the Senate three times between 1880 and 1894, and control of the House five times (Table 20.1). The causes of this upheaval included northerners' disillusionment with Reconstruction and the resurgence of ex-Confederates, who regained a strong base in Congress. Dizzying population growth and the entry of new western states also changed the size and shape of Congress, contributing to political uncertainty.

Heated party competition drew Americans into the fray: Proportionately more voters turned out in presidential elections from 1876 to 1892 than at any other time in American history. The presidents of this era — Rutherford B. Hayes, James Garfield, Chester Arthur, Grover Cleveland, and Benjamin Harrison — are often remembered as colorless and ineffective. But they had limited room to maneuver in a period of extremely tight competition. Hayes and Harrison both won in the electoral college but lost the popular vote. In 1880, Garfield won the popular vote by a margin of less than 0.5 percent. Four years later, Cleveland won only 29,214 more votes than his opponent, James Blaine, while almost half a million voters rejected both major candidates (Map 20.1). With key states decided by razor-thin margins, both Republicans and Democrats engaged in vote buying, ballot-box stuffing, and other forms of fraud.

TABLE 20.1	Composition and Control of Congress, 1869–1897	
Congress	**Senate/House Seats**	**Entry of States and Shifts in Partisan Control**
41st; 1869–1871	68 / 226	1870: Last ex-Confederate states reenter Union
42nd; 1871–1873	74 / 243	
43rd; 1873–1875	74 / 292	1874 election: House control shifts to Democrats
		1876: Colorado enters Union
44th, 45th; 1875–1879	76 / 293	1878 election: Senate control shifts to Democrats
46th; 1879–1881	76 / 293	1880 election: House control shifts to Republicans
47th; 1881–1883	76 / 293	1882 election: Senate control shifts to Republicans
48th; 1883–1885	76 / 325	1884 election: House control shifts to Democrats
49th; 1885–1887	76 / 325	
50th; 1887–1889	76 / 325	1888 election: House control shifts to Republicans
		1889: Montana, North and South Dakota, and Washington enter Union
		1890: Idaho and Wyoming enter Union
51st; 1889–1891	88 / 332	1890 election: House control shifts to Democrats
52nd; 1891–1893	88 / 332	1892 election: Senate control shifts to Democrats
53rd; 1896–1895	88 / 356	1894 election: Control of both houses shifts to Republicans
		1896: Utah enters Union
54th; 1895–1897	90 / 357	

Republicans and Democrats traded control of both the Senate and the House of Representatives several times during the tumultuous era of Reconstruction and its aftermath. Equally striking were changes in the size of Congress, based on the nation's geographic expansion and rapid population growth. Note how the entry of new western states, as well as adjustments after each census (implemented soon after 1870, 1880, and 1890), increased the numbers of senators and representatives.

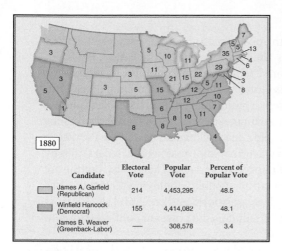

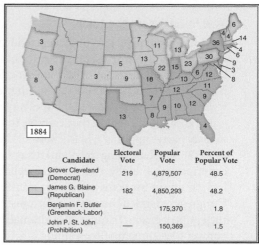

1880

Candidate	Electoral Vote	Popular Vote	Percent of Popular Vote
James A. Garfield (Republican)	214	4,453,295	48.5
Winfield Hancock (Democrat)	155	4,414,082	48.1
James B. Weaver (Greenback-Labor)	—	308,578	3.4

1884

Candidate	Electoral Vote	Popular Vote	Percent of Popular Vote
Grover Cleveland (Democrat)	219	4,879,507	48.5
James G. Blaine (Republican)	182	4,850,293	48.2
Benjamin F. Butler (Greenback-Labor)	—	175,370	1.8
John P. St. John (Prohibition)	—	150,369	1.5

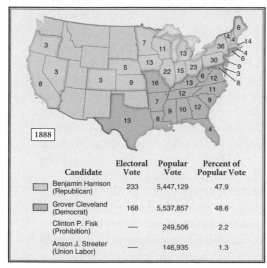

1888

Candidate	Electoral Vote	Popular Vote	Percent of Popular Vote
Benjamin Harrison (Republican)	233	5,447,129	47.9
Grover Cleveland (Democrat)	168	5,537,857	48.6
Clinton P. Fisk (Prohibition)	—	249,506	2.2
Anson J. Streeter (Union Labor)	—	146,935	1.3

MAP 20.1 The Presidential Elections of 1880, 1884, and 1888

The anatomy of hard-fought, narrowly won presidential campaigns is evident in this trio of electoral maps of the 1880s. First, note the equal division of the popular vote between Republicans and Democrats. Second, note the persistent pattern of electoral votes, as states overwhelmingly went to the same party in all three elections. Here, we can identify who determined the outcomes—"swing" states, such as New York and Indiana, whose vote shifted every four years and always in favor of the winning candidate.

Close elections inspired fierce party loyalty among many voters. As early as the 1880s, though, other Americans became frustrated with electoral politics. Republicans had enacted Emancipation and other major achievements, but after Reconstruction ended they gradually became defenders of the economic status quo. National leaders of the Democratic Party, meanwhile, at first resisted the idea that industrialization might signal the need to use government power in new ways. Disillusioned with both Republicans and Democrats, some reformers created new parties. For a brief moment in the early 1890s, it appeared that the new People's Party might displace Republicans in the South or Democrats in the West and become a major party in its own right. Though third-party strategies ultimately failed, they made for lively politics in the 1880s and 1890s. By putting important policy ideas on the table, new parties helped build national momentum for reform.

New Initiatives in the 1880s

One of the first federal reforms enacted in the post-Reconstruction years resulted from tragedy. On July 2, 1881, only four months after entering the White House, President James Garfield was shot. After lingering for several agonizing months, he died. Most historians now believe the assassin, Charles Guiteau, suffered from mental illness. But reformers at the time blamed the **spoils system**, arguing that Guiteau had killed Garfield out of disappointment in the scramble for **patronage**, the granting of government jobs to loyal party supporters. In the wake of Garfield's death, Congress passed the Pendleton Act (1883), establishing the nonpartisan Civil Service Commission to fill federal jobs by examination. Initially, civil service applied to only 10 percent of such jobs, but the act laid the groundwork for a sweeping transformation of public employment. By the 1910s, Congress extended the act to cover most federal positions, and cities and states across the country enacted similar laws, dramatically reducing the power of political parties to control government office holding.

Leaders of the civil service movement included many proponents of classical liberalism. At the time, the word *liberal* was used very differently than it is today. It described those Americans, especially former Republicans, who became disillusioned with Reconstruction and advocated more limited and professionalized government. Many had opposed President Ulysses S. Grant's reelection in 1872. In 1884, they again left the Republican Party because they could not stomach its scandal-tainted candidate, James Blaine. Liberal Republicans — ridiculed by their enemies as Mugwumps (fence-sitters who had their "mugs" on one side of the fence and their "wumps" on the other) — threw their support to Democrat Grover Cleveland. They believed Cleveland shared their vision of smaller government. After he entered the White House, Cleveland showed that to a large extent he did share their views. But in 1887, responding to pressure from farmer-labor advocates in the Democratic Party, he signed the Hatch Act and the Interstate Commerce Act (see Chapter 17), two major bills that expanded federal power. The Interstate Commerce Act, by establishing a national commission to investigate and regulate railroad shipping rates, set an important precedent for later regulation.

Railroad regulation and other such changes came slowly at the national level, in part because influential liberals pressed for smaller government, not more regulation. But political innovations also emerged in the states, driven in some places by farmer-labor radicalism, and in others by Republican reform energy that lingered past Reconstruction. Midwestern farmers had already secured state laws to regulate railroads and other key industries. Massachusetts, one of the most daring states, set new standards for free, compulsory schooling, including free textbooks, to help young people gain the education they needed to find jobs in the new industrial economy. The state's Bureau of Labor Statistics investigated workplace safety and published groundbreaking reports on unemployment. By 1887, Massachusetts had created an array of public regulatory commissions. New York passed similarly ambitious measures. While few states attempted such wide-ranging reforms, many created commissions to oversee key industries from banking to dairy farming.

By later standards, state commissions of the 1880s were weak and underfunded, but they represented pioneering steps in reform. Even when they lacked the legal power to protect public safety, the most dedicated, energetic commissioners served as public advocates, exposing unsafe or unjust practices and generating pressure for further laws. As early as 1879, reformers also created the national Conference of Charities (after 1884, the National Conference of Charities and Corrections) so that public officials and social scientists could exchange ideas and promote the best practices at state institutions. By 1900, regulations of the type pioneered by Massachusetts reformers and midwestern farm advocates began to spread nationwide.

Republican Activism | In 1888, after a decade of divided government, Republicans gained control of both Congress and the White House. They pursued an ambitious agenda that they believed would meet the needs of a modernizing nation, while seeking to preserve the legacy of Union victory. In 1890, Congress extended pensions to all Union veterans, whether or not they were disabled, to protect them from poverty in old age. Congress also yielded to the growing public outrage over trusts by passing a law to regulate interstate corporations. Though it proved difficult to enforce and was soon weakened by the Supreme Court, the Sherman Antitrust Act (1890) was the first federal attempt to forbid any "combination, in the form of trust or otherwise, or conspiracy, in restraint of trade."

President Benjamin Harrison also sought to protect black voting rights in the South. Warned during his campaign that the issue was politically risky, Harrison vowed that he would not "purchase the presidency by a compact of silence upon this question." He found allies in Congress. Massachusetts representative Henry Cabot Lodge drafted a bill to create a bipartisan federal elections board. Whenever 100 citizens, in any district or city of 20,000 or more, appealed for intervention, the board would investigate. If it found sufficient evidence of fraud or disenfranchisement, the board could work with federal courts to seat the rightful winner. Despite cries of outrage from southern Democrats — who warned that this so-called force bill meant "Negro supremacy" — the House passed the measure.

But the bill met deep resistance in the Senate. Northern liberals, who wanted the "best men" to rule through professional expertise, thought it provided for too much democracy. Urban machine bosses denounced the threat of federal interference in the cities. Southerners threatened to boycott northern products if the law went into effect, frightening manufacturers. Most damaging of all was the opposition of Republicans from the trans-Mississippi West. With the entry of ten new states since 1863, and thus twenty new U.S. senators, westerners had gained enormous clout. Senator William Stewart of Nevada, who had southern family ties, claimed that Lodge's proposal would bring "monarchy or revolution." He and his allies killed the bill by a single vote.

The defeat was a devastating blow to those who sought to defend black voting rights. In the verdict of one furious Republican leader who supported Lodge's proposal, the episode marked the demise of the party of Emancipation. "Think of it," he fumed. "Nevada, barely a respectable *county*, furnished two senators to betray the Republican Party and the rights of citizenship." In fact, many of the Republicans' 1890 programs — including Lodge's bill, even though it never became law — proved unpopular. In a sweeping repudiation of Republican policies, Democrats took control of the House in the 1890 elections. Two years later, by the largest margin seen in twenty years, they reelected Grover Cleveland to the presidency for his nonconsecutive second term. Congress abandoned all further attempts to enforce fair elections in the South.

The Populist Program

When Democrats took power in Washington, they faced rising pressure from rural voters in the South and West who had organized the Farmers' Alliance. Some savvy politicians responded quickly, as they had done in passing the Interstate Commerce Act. Iowa Democrats, for example, took up some of farmers' demands, forestalling the creation of a separate farmer-labor party in that state. But other politicians listened to Alliance pleas and did nothing. It was a response they came to regret.

In Kansas, a state chock-full of Union veterans and railroad boosters, Republicans dominated the political scene. They treated the Kansas Farmers' Alliance with contempt. In a breakthrough election in 1890, the alliance joined with the state Knights of Labor and created the People's Party. They stunned the nation by capturing four-fifths of the lower house of the Kansas legislature and most of the state's congressional seats. The victory electrified Knights of Labor and Farmers' Alliance members across the country. In July 1892, after conferences in Cincinnati and St. Louis, delegates from these groups met at Omaha, Nebraska, and formally created the national People's Party. They nominated former Union general and Greenback-Labor leader James B. Weaver for president. In November, the Populists, as they became known, captured a million votes and carried four western states.

In recognizing an "irrepressible conflict between capital and labor," the Populists split from the mainstream parties, calling for a stronger state that would adopt new measures to protect ordinary Americans. "We believe," declared their Omaha Platform in 1892, "that the power of government — in other words, of the people — should be expanded as rapidly and as far as the good sense of an intelligent people and the teachings of experience shall justify, to the end that oppression, injustice and poverty should eventually cease in the land." Populists called for public ownership of railroad and telegraph systems, protection of land and natural resources from monopoly and foreign ownership, a federal income tax on the highest incomes, and a looser monetary policy to help borrowers.

Though farmers' votes were its chief instrument of victory, the People's Party attracted support from other groups. Labor planks won the movement a strong base among such groups as Alabama steelworkers and Rocky Mountain miners. Antiliquor and woman suffrage leaders, including Frances Willard and Elizabeth Cady Stanton, attended the party's organizing conferences in 1891 and 1892, hoping that Populists would adopt their causes, but they were disappointed. In addition to divisions among reformers with different goals and priorities, the bitter legacies of the Civil War also hampered the party. Southern Democrats warned that the Populists were Radical Republicans in disguise; northeastern Republicans claimed that southern "Pops" were ex-Confederates plotting another round of treason. In the midst of these heated debates, the Populists and their opponents suddenly confronted a national economic crisis.

▶ What factors shaped party politics after the end of Reconstruction? In the 1880s, what important measures did federal and state governments implement?

▶ What were the origins of the People's Party? How did it exemplify dissatisfaction with the two established parties?

The Political Earthquakes of the 1890s

Hitting in 1893 and lingering almost to the turn of the century, the severe depression of the 1890s transformed American politics. In 1894 and 1896, voters outside the South voted overwhelmingly for Republicans who promised safety and prosperity. These elections destroyed the rising People's Party and ended the era of close party competition in national elections. The shift shaped politics for decades to come, creating both opportunities and challenges for reformers. In the South, meanwhile, Democrats moved from being the leading political party to becoming virtually the *only* political party. The resulting formal disenfranchisement and segregation of African Americans left a bitter legacy that lasted for generations.

Depression and Reaction

At the time of Grover Cleveland's inauguration in March 1893, farm foreclosures and railroad bankruptcies were signaling economic trouble, as hard times in Europe caused investors there to pull money out of the United States. Only a few weeks after Cleveland entered the White House, the Pennsylvania and Reading Railroad went bankrupt, followed soon afterward by the National Cordage Company. Investors panicked, and the stock market crashed. Europeans who had invested in the United States called back their money. By July, major banks had drained their reserves and "suspended," unable to give depositors access to their money. By year's end, 500 banks and thousands of other businesses went under. "Boston," one observer remembered, "grew suddenly old, haggard, and thin." The unemployment rate quickly soared above 20 percent.

For Americans who had lived through the terrible 1870s, the depression looked grimly familiar. Even fresher in the public mind were recent labor uprisings, including the 1886 Haymarket bombing and the 1892 showdown at Homestead — followed, during the depression's first year, by a massive Pennsylvania coal strike and a Pullman railroad boycott that ended with bloody clashes between angry crowds and the U.S. Army. Prosperous Americans were terrified of a nationwide uprising of workers making a desperate stand for survival. They also feared the farmer-labor movement that had organized its political revolt through the People's Party. Would the United States hold together amid the crisis?

In the summer of 1894, another protest jolted Americans. Radical reformer Jacob Coxey of Ohio proposed that the U.S. government hire the unemployed to fix the nation's roads. In 1894, he organized hundreds of jobless men — nicknamed "Coxey's Army" — to carry out a peaceful march to Washington to appeal for the program. Though public works of the kind Coxey proposed would become a central part of the New Deal in the 1930s, in the 1890s many Americans viewed Coxey as a dangerous extremist. Public alarm grew when other spontaneous marches followed the one led by Coxey. In some towns and cities, marchers found warm support and offers of aid. In others, police and property owners drove the marchers away at gunpoint. Coxey was stunned by what happened on May 1, when his group reached Capitol Hill: He was arrested and jailed for trespassing on the grass. Coxey's marchers went home hungry.

The public blamed hard times and political upheaval not only on radicals like Coxey but also on the Democrats who held power. Any president would have been hard-pressed to cope, but Grover Cleveland made a particularly bad hash of it. Cleveland was out of step with his party on a major issue: expansion of federal coinage to include silver as well as gold. Advocates of "free silver" ("free" because, under this plan, the U.S. Mint would not charge a fee for minting silver coins) believed the policy would expand the U.S. money supply, encourage borrowing, and stimulate industry. But Cleveland was a firm advocate of the gold standard; the money supply should not be expanded, he believed, but should remain tied solely to the nation's reserves of gold. After 1893, neither collapsing prices nor a groundswell of free-silver sentiment in his own party budged Cleveland. With gold reserves dwindling, in 1895 he made a secret arrangement with a syndicate of bankers led by John Pierpont Morgan to arrange gold purchases to replenish the Treasury. Morgan helped maintain America's gold supply — preserving the gold standard — and in doing so turned a tidy profit. Cleveland's deal, once discovered, enraged his fellow Democrats. South Carolina orator Ben Tillman vowed to go to Washington and "poke old Grover with a pitchfork," thus earning him the nickname "Pitchfork Ben."

As the 1894 midterm elections loomed, Democrats tried to distance themselves from Cleveland. But on Election Day, large numbers of voters chose the Republicans, who promised to support business, put down social unrest, and bring back prosperity. In western states, voters turned Populists out of office. In the Midwest and Mid-Atlantic states, voters handed the Democrats crushing defeats. In the next congressional session, Republicans controlled the House by a margin of 245 to 105. The election began sixteen years of Republican dominance in national politics.

Democrats and the "Solid South"

In the South, the only region where Democrats gained strength in the 1890s, the People's Party met defeat for distinctive reasons. After the rollback of Reconstruction, while some states adopted poll taxes and other measures to limit voting, African Americans in other states had continued to vote in significant numbers. As long as Democrats competed for (and sometimes bought) black votes, the possibility remained that other parties could win African Americans' loyalty. The People's Party proposed new measures to help farmers and wage earners — an appealing message for poverty-stricken people of both races. Some white Populists went out of their way to forge cross-racial ties. "The accident of color can make no difference in the interest of farmers, croppers, and laborers," argued Georgia Populist Tom Watson. "You are kept apart that you may be separately fleeced of your earnings."

Such Populist appeals threatened the foundations of elite southern politics. As ex-Confederates had done during Reconstruction, Democrats struck back, calling themselves the "white man's party" and denouncing Populists for promoting "Negro rule." From Georgia to Texas, many white farmers, tenants, and wage earners ignored such appeals and continued to support the Populists in large numbers. Democrats found they could put down the Populist threat only through fraud and violence. "We had to do it!" one Georgia Democrat later explained, admitting that he had stuffed ballot boxes and threatened black voters. "Those damned Populists would have ruined the country."

Having suppressed the political revolt, Democrats vowed that white supremacy was nonnegotiable — but they looked for new ways to enforce it. As early as 1890, a state constitutional convention in Mississippi adopted a key innovation: an "understanding

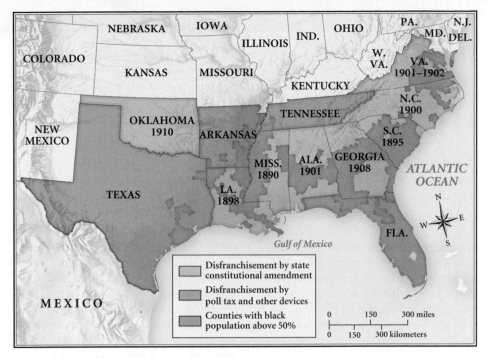

NEBRASKA IOWA OHIO PA. N.J.
ILLINOIS IND. MD. DEL.
COLORADO W. VA.
KANSAS MISSOURI VA.
KENTUCKY 1901–1902
N.C.
OKLAHOMA TENNESSEE 1900
NEW 1910 ARKANSAS S.C.
MEXICO 1895
MISS. ALA. GEORGIA
1890 1901 1908 ATLANTIC
OCEAN
TEXAS LA.
1898
FLA.
Gulf of Mexico
MEXICO

Disfranchisement by state
constitutional amendment

Disfranchisement by
poll tax and other devices

Counties with black
population above 50%

0   150   300 miles
0   150   300 kilometers

MAP 20.2 Disfranchisement in the New South
In the midst of the Populist challenge to Democratic one-party rule in the South, a movement to deprive blacks of the right to vote spread from Mississippi across the South. By 1910, every state in the region except Tennessee, Arkansas, Texas, and Florida had made constitutional changes designed to prevent blacks from voting, and these four states accomplished much the same result through poll taxes and other exclusionary methods. For the next half century, the political process in the South would be for whites only.

clause" that required would-be voters who appeared at registrars' offices to interpret a clause of the state constitution, with local Democratic officials deciding who met the standard. After the Populist uprising, such measures spread to other southern states. Louisiana's **grandfather clause**, which denied the vote to any man whose grandfather, in slavery days, had been unable to vote, was struck down by the U.S. Supreme Court. But in *Williams v. Mississippi* (1898), the Court allowed poll taxes and **literacy tests** to stand. By 1908, every southern state had adopted such measures.

The impact of disfranchisement can hardly be overstated (Map 20.2). In most of the South, voter turnout plunged, from above 70 percent to 34 percent or even lower. Not only blacks but also many poor whites ceased to vote. Since Democrats faced virtually no opposition, political activity shifted to the "white primaries," where Democratic candidates competed for party nominations. Some former Populists joined the Democrats in openly advocating white supremacy. The racial climate hardened. Segregation laws proliferated, barring blacks not only from white schools and railroad cars but also from hotels, parks, and public drinking fountains. Lynchings of African Americans increasingly occurred in broad daylight, with crowds of thousands gathering to watch (see American Voices, p. 608).

The Cause of Lynching   IDA B. WELLS

In the 1890s, African American journalist Ida B. Wells waged a lonely campaign against the extrajudicial murder of blacks. Wells was forced to flee Memphis after she publicly denounced the lynching of three friends. Their crime? They had dared to open a grocery store that drew customers from a white competitor. Most Americans believed interracial rape led to lynching. In a series of devastating pamphlets, Wells destroyed that myth. As in this passage from *Southern Horrors* (1892), Wells conducted careful research and often quoted from white Southern newspapers to make her case. Wells later helped founded the National Association for the Advancement of Colored People (NAACP).

There are many white women in the South who would marry colored men if such an act would not place them at once beyond the pale of society and within the clutches of the law. The miscegenation laws of the South only operate against the legitimate union of the races; they leave the white man free to seduce all the colored girls he can, but it is death to the colored man who yields to the force and advances of a similar attraction in white women. . . .

A few instances to substantiate the assertion that some white women love the company of the Afro-American will not be out of place. . . . Sarah Clark of Memphis loved a black man and lived openly with him. When she was indicted last spring for miscegenation, she swore in court that she was *not* a white woman. This she did to escape the penitentiary. . . . A young girl living on Poplar Street, who was discovered in intimate relations with a handsome mulatto young colored man, Will Morgan by name, stole her father's money to send the young fellow away from that father's wrath. She has since joined him in Chicago. . . .

There is hardly a town in the South which has not an instance of the kind which is well-known. . . . Hence there is a growing demand among Afro-Americans that the guilt or innocence of parties accused of rape be fully established. . . .

When the victim is a colored woman it is different. Last winter in Baltimore, Md., three white ruffians assaulted a Miss Camphor, a young Afro-American girl, while out walking with a young man of her own race. They held her escort and outraged the girl. It was a deed dastardly enough to arouse Southern blood, which gives its horror of rape as excuse for lawlessness, but she was an Afro-American. The case went to the courts, an Afro-American lawyer defended the men, and they were acquitted. . . .

Only *one-third* of the 728 victims to mobs have been charged with rape, to say nothing of those of that one-third who were innocent of the charge. . . . This cry [of rape] has had its effect. It has closed the heart, stifled the conscience, warped the judgment and hushed the voice of press and pulpit. . . . Even to the better class of Afro-Americans the crime of rape is so revolting they have too often taken the white man's word and given lynch law neither the investigation nor condemnation it deserved.

SOURCE: Ida B. Wells, *Southern Horrors and Other Writings*, ed. Jacqueline Jones Royster (Boston: Bedford/St. Martin's Press, 1997), 53–56, 58, 61.

Lynching in Texas

Lynchings peaked between 1890 and 1910; while most common in the South, they occurred in almost every state, from Oregon to Minnesota to New York. After many lynchings — such as this one in the town of Center, Texas, in 1920 — crowds posed to have their pictures taken. Commercial photographers often, as in this case, produced photographic post-cards to sell as souvenirs. What do we make of these gruesome rituals? Who is in the crowd, and who is not? What do we learn from the fact that this group of white men, some of whom may have been respon-sible for the lynching, felt comfortable having their photographs recorded with the body? The victim in this photograph, a young man named Lige Daniels, was seized from the local jail by a mob that broke down the prison door to kidnap and kill him. The inscription on the back of the postcard includes information about the killing, along with the instruc-tions "Give this to Bud From Aunt Myrtle." Private Collection.

The nature of this political counter-revolution can be illustrated by events in Grimes County, a cotton-growing area in eastern Texas where African Americans comprised more than half of the popula-tion. African American voters kept the local Republican Party going after Reconstruction and regularly sent black representatives to the Texas legislature. Many local white Populists proved immune to Democrats' taunts of "negro supremacy," and a Populist-Republican coalition swept the county elections in 1896 and 1898. But after their 1898 defeat, Democrats in Grimes County organized a secret brotherhood. They forcibly prevented African Americans from voting in town elections, shooting two black leaders in cold blood. The Populist sheriff proved unable to bring the murderers to justice. Reconstituted in 1900 as the White Man's Party, Demo-crats carried Grimes County by an overwhelming margin. Gunmen then laid siege to the Populist sheriff's office, killed his brother and a friend, and drove the wounded sheriff out of the county. The White Man's Party ruled Grimes County for the next fifty years.

The Election of 1896 and Its Aftermath

After their crushing defeats outside the South in 1894, Democrats astonished the coun-try by embracing parts of the radical farmer-labor program in the presidential election of 1896. They nominated young free-silver advocate William Jennings Bryan of Nebraska, who sealed his nomination with a passionate defense of farmers and an attack on the gold standard. "Burn down your cities and leave our farms," Bryan declared, "and your cities will spring up again as if by magic; but destroy our farms and the grass will grow in the streets of every city in the country." He ended with a vow: "You shall not crucify mankind on a cross of gold." Cheering delegates nominated Bryan on a platform that advocated free silver and a federal income tax on the wealthy that would replace **tariffs** as a source of revenue. The national Democratic Party, which had long defended **states' rights** and limited government, was moving toward a more activist stance.

Populists, reeling from their recent defeats, endorsed Bryan for president. But their power was waning. Bryan ignored them, running as a straight Democrat without ever acknowledging the People's Party nomination. Populist leader Tom Watson, who had wanted a separate, more radical program, observed that Democrats had cast the Populists as "Jonah while they play whale." The Populists never recovered from their electoral losses in 1894 or from Democrats' ruthless opposition in the South. By 1900, the party had largely faded. Rural voters pursued their reform efforts elsewhere, particularly through the newly energized Bryan wing of the Democrats.

Republicans' brilliant manager, Ohio manufacturer Mark Hanna, orchestrated an unprecedented fund-raising campaign in 1896 among corporate leaders. Republicans denounced Bryan's supporters as "revolutionary and anarchistic." Under Hanna's guidance, the party backed away from moral issues such as prohibition and invited new immigrants to join them. The Republican candidate William McKinley won handily

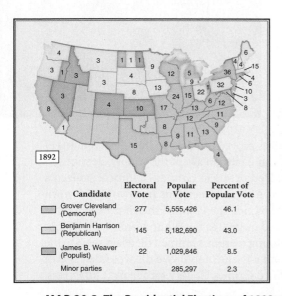

Candidate	Electoral Vote	Popular Vote	Percent of Popular Vote
Grover Cleveland (Democrat)	277	5,555,426	46.1
Benjamin Harrison (Republican)	145	5,182,690	43.0
James B. Weaver (Populist)	22	1,029,846	8.5
Minor parties	—	285,297	2.3

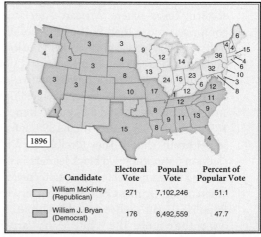

Candidate	Electoral Vote	Popular Vote	Percent of Popular Vote
William McKinley (Republican)	271	7,102,246	51.1
William J. Bryan (Democrat)	176	6,492,559	47.7

MAP 20.3 The Presidential Elections of 1892 and 1896

In the 1890s, the age of political stalemate came to an end. Students should compare the 1892 map with Map 20.1 (p. 601) and note especially Cleveland's breakthrough in the normally Republican states of the upper Midwest. In 1896, the pendulum swung in the opposite direction, with McKinley's consolidation of Republican control over the Northeast and Midwest far overbalancing the Democratic advances in the thinly populated western states. The 1896 election marked the beginning of sixteen years of Republican dominance in national politics.

(Map 20.3), with 271 electoral votes to Bryan's 176. McKinley had persuaded the nation that he would bring prosperity.

Nationwide, as in the South, the 1894–1896 realignment prompted a wave of political changes — but they were the kind of "reforms" that excluded voters rather than increasing democratic participation. As in the South, many northern states imposed literacy tests and restrictions on voting by new immigrants. Leaders of both major parties worked to shut out future threats from new movements like the Populists, making it more difficult for new parties to get their candidates listed on the ballot. In the wake of such laws, voter turnout declined. In all parts of the United States, the electorate narrowed in ways that favored the native born and wealthy.

Antidemocratic restrictions on voting helped, paradoxically, to foster democratic innovations. Having excluded or reduced the number of poor, African American, and immigrant voters, elite and middle-class reformers felt far more comfortable increasing the power of the voters who remained. Both major parties increasingly turned to the **direct primary**, asking voters (in most states, registered party members) rather than party leaders to choose nominees. Another measure that enhanced democratic participation was the Seventeenth Amendment to the Constitution (1913), which required that U.S. senators be chosen not by the state legislatures, but by popular vote. Though many states had already adopted the practice, southern states had resisted, since Democrats feared that it might give more power to their political foes. After disenfranchisement, such objections faded and the measure passed. Thus a gross injustice — disenfranchisement of blacks — helped pave the way for a measure that today enhances the direct voting power of all Americans. Such were the ironies of political reform in the wake of the upheaval of the 1890s.

The Courts Reject Reform

While the major political parties restricted suffrage, federal courts invalidated many of the regulatory laws that states had passed to protect workers and promote public welfare. As early as 1882, in the case of *In re Jacobs*, the New York State Court of Appeals struck down a public-health law that prohibited cigar manufacturing in tenements, arguing that such regulation exceeded the state's police powers. In *Lochner v. New York* (1905), the U.S. Supreme Court told New York State that it could not limit bakers' workdays to ten hours because that violated bakers' rights to make contracts. Judges found support for such rulings in the Fourteenth Amendment to the Constitution (1868), which prohibited states from depriving "any person of life, liberty, or property, without due process of law." The due process clause had been intended to protect the rights of former slaves, but the courts used it to shield contract rights. Judges argued that they were protecting workers' freedom *from* government regulation. Interpreted in this way, the Fourteenth Amendment became a powerful obstacle to state laws regulating private business.

Farmer and labor advocates, along with some urban progressives who supported stronger regulation of the economy, vehemently disagreed with such rulings. They believed judges, not state legislators, were overreaching their power. While courts treated employers and employees as equal parties, critics dismissed this as a "legal fiction."

"Modern industry has reduced 'freedom of contract' to a paper privilege," declared one labor advocate, "a mere figure of rhetoric." Supreme Court Justice Oliver Wendell Holmes Jr., dissenting in the *Lochner* decision, agreed. If the choice was between working and starving, he observed, how could bakers "choose" their hours of work? Employers set the rules, and employees' only alternatives were to work the specified hours or lose their jobs. Holmes's view, known as legal realism, eventually won judicial favor, but it only did so after years of progressive and labor activism.

Meanwhile, in its landmark decision in *Plessy v. Ferguson* (1896), the Supreme Court put the nation's stamp of approval on racial discrimination. The case was brought by civil rights advocates on behalf of Homer Plessy, a New Orleans resident who was one-eighth black. Ordered to move to the "colored" car of a Louisiana train, Plessy refused and was arrested. Advocates hoped to challenge the growing number of southern **Jim Crow** laws, which segregated whites and blacks in hotels, trains, streetcars, and even cemeteries. The Court ruled that such segregation did not violate the Fourteenth Amendment as long as blacks had access to accommodations equal to those of whites. This "separate but equal" doctrine — like the Court's ruling on bakers' work hours — protected theoretical rights while ignoring reality. Segregated facilities in the South were flagrantly unequal; state funding for African American schools, for example, lagged far behind that for whites. Segregation was clearly discriminatory, but the Court allowed it to stand. Of all the decisions of the 1890s, *Plessy* had perhaps the most powerful and long-lasting impact. Though the Supreme Court became friendlier to economic regulation after 1900, *Plessy* remained in place until 1954, when the *Brown v. Topeka Board of Education* ruling finally struck down segregation.

▶ What were the political consequences of the economic crisis of the 1890s? What role did the federal courts play in the political transformations of the 1890s?

▶ What was the impact of measures, both in the South and elsewhere, to restrict the vote?

Reform Reshaped, 1901–1917

William McKinley was a powerful presence in the White House, but he was no reformer. He won the 1896 campaign on a promise to restore order and prosperity, and many affluent Americans greeted his victory with profound relief. Amid the crisis of the 1890s, the nation's leading journals dismissed labor unions as "wild-eyed radicals" and Populists as ignorant "hayseeds." McKinley's victory was widely understood as a triumph for business, especially for industrial titans who had contributed heavily to his campaign.

But the depression of the 1890s, by subjecting millions of ordinary Americans to severe hardship, had dramatically illustrated the problems industrialization had created. By the turn of the twentieth century, more and more prosperous citizens acknowledged that government needed to play a more active role in the economy. At the same time, the very success of McKinley's campaign managers — who spent more than $3.5 million, versus Bryan's $300,000 — raised unsettling questions about the power of corporations and the use of money in politics. Once the crisis of the 1890s passed, middle-class Americans proved increasingly willing to embrace progressive ideas. This process accelerated after a shocking assassination brought a reformer to the presidency.

Teddy Roosevelt and the "Square Deal"
When William McKinley ran for president in 1896, he sat on his front porch in Canton, Ohio, and received delegations of voters. That was not Theodore Roosevelt's way. He was a vigorous campaigner, and used the office of the presidency brilliantly to mobilize public opinion and to assert his leadership. The preeminence of the presidency in American public life began with Roosevelt's administration. Here, at the height of his crusading power, Roosevelt stumps from a train in the 1904 election. Library of Congress.

Theodore Roosevelt in the White House

In 1900, William McKinley easily won his second political face-off against Democrat William Jennings Bryan. Only six months into his second term, however, on September 14, 1901, the president was shot as he attended the Pan-American Exposition in Buffalo, New York. He died eight days later. The murderer, Leon Czolgosz, was influenced by anarchist thinkers and inspired by recent assassinations in Europe. McKinley's violent death was another warning, many Americans felt, of the threat posed by radical immigrants (even though Czolgosz was American-born). As the nation mourned its third murdered president in less than four decades, Vice President Theodore Roosevelt was sworn in as McKinley's replacement.

Roosevelt, born into a prominent family, had chosen an unconventional path. After graduating from Harvard, he plunged into politics, winning a seat as a New York assemblyman. In 1884, Roosevelt had joined Mugwump Republicans in opposing James Blaine's nomination. Disillusioned by the group's failure to steer the party in a reform direction, Roosevelt left politics and moved to a North Dakota ranch, creating a "frontier" persona that later served him well. But Roosevelt's cattle herd was wiped out in the blizzards of 1887. He returned east, winning appointments as a U.S. Civil Service commissioner, head of the New York City Police Commission, and McKinley's assistant secretary of the navy. An energetic presence in all these jobs, Roosevelt gained broad knowledge of the problems America faced at the municipal, state, and federal levels.

Roosevelt became a popular hero when he enlisted in the army during the War of 1898. Elected as New York's governor soon afterward, he asserted his faith in government's capacity to improve the lives of ordinary people. As governor, Roosevelt pushed through civil service reform and a tax on corporations. In an effort to neutralize this rising (and rather unpredictable) political star, Republican bosses chose Roosevelt as McKinley's running mate in 1900, hoping the vice presidency would be a political dead end. Instead, they suddenly found Roosevelt in the White House.

Roosevelt did not prove to be quite the rebel his critics feared. He was, after all, a Republican who had denounced the "extreme" views of Populists, and he blended reform with the needs of private enterprise. Roosevelt won fame as an environmentalist, for example, but many of his conservation policies had a strong pro-business bent. He increased the amount of land held in federal forest reserves and turned their management over to the new, independent U.S. Forest Service. But Roosevelt's forestry chief, Gifford Pinchot, insisted on fire suppression to maximize logging potential. In addition, Roosevelt lent his support to the Newlands Reclamation Act (1902), which had much in common with earlier Republican policies to promote economic development in the West. Under the Newlands Act, the federal government sold public lands to raise money for irrigation projects that expanded agriculture on arid lands. In funding such projects, however, Roosevelt not only met business needs but also fulfilled one of the demands of the unemployed men who had marched with Coxey's Army.

Antitrust Legislation | Despite his generally supportive attitude toward business, Roosevelt undertook some marked departures from his predecessors. During a bitter 1902 coal strike, he threatened to nationalize the big coal companies if their owners refused to negotiate with the miners' union. The owners hastily came to the table. Roosevelt also sought better enforcement of the Interstate Commerce Act and the Sherman Antitrust Act. In 1903, he pushed through the Elkins Act, which prohibited discriminatory railway rates that favored powerful customers. That same year, he created the Bureau of Corporations, empowered to investigate business practices and bolster the Justice Department's capacity to mount antitrust suits. The department had already filed such a suit against the Northern Securities Company, a combine of the railroad systems of the northwestern part of the country. In a landmark decision in 1904, the Supreme Court ordered Northern Securities dissolved.

That year, calling for every American to get what he called a "Square Deal," Roosevelt handily defeated a weak Democratic candidate, Alton B. Parker. Now president in his own right, Roosevelt stepped up his attack on the trusts. He regarded large-scale enterprise as the natural tendency of modern industry, but he hoped to identify and punish "malefactors of great wealth" who abused their power. In 1906, after much wrangling in Congress, Roosevelt won a major victory with the passage of the Hepburn Act, which enabled the Interstate Commerce Commission to set shipping rates.

At the time Roosevelt acted, trusts had partially protected themselves with the help of two friendly state legislatures. New Jersey and then Delaware had loosened their regulations, inviting trusts to incorporate under new state laws. As anticipated, dozens of large companies took up the offer and established headquarters in these states. With its Northern Securities ruling, however, the Supreme Court began to recognize federal authority to dissolve the most egregious monopolies. After 1908, Roosevelt left a powerful legacy to his successor, William Howard Taft. In its *Standard Oil* decision in 1911, the Supreme Court agreed with Taft's Justice Department that John D. Rockefeller's massive oil monopoly should be broken up into several competing companies. After this ruling, Taft's attorney general undertook antitrust actions against other giant companies.

Theodore Roosevelt was a man of contradictions whose presidency left a mixed legacy. An unabashed believer in what he called "Anglo-Saxon" superiority, Roosevelt nonetheless invited Booker T. Washington to dine at the White House, earning fierce criticism from white supremacists. Similarly, Roosevelt was an advocate of elite rule who called for the "best men" to enter politics, but he also defended the dignity of labor. Later in his public career, Roosevelt read and recommended works written by European socialists. This complex mix of condescension and social-justice activism was characteristic of many elite and middle-class progressives.

Grassroots Progressive Movements

In part, President Roosevelt provided reform leadership because he faced increasing pressure for government action. At the grassroots, farmer and labor leaders continued to demand stronger remedies for dangerous working conditions, low pay, and concentrated corporate power. Building on earlier movements such as civil service reform and the antiliquor cause, elite and middle-class progressives were also mobilizing for change. They concentrated on cleaning up government, protecting public health and safety, and launching crusades against the vice industry and political machines. Some toured other parts of the world, exchanging ideas with peers (see Voices from Abroad, p. 616).

Women and Reform As they had since the 1880s, women played prominent roles in reform. Justifying their work through maternalism — the claim that women should expand their motherly role in the public sphere — they focused on the welfare of working-class women and children. The National Congress of Mothers, founded in 1897, promoted better child-rearing techniques. Women also served as leaders in the National Child Labor Committee, created in 1907. The committee hired photographer Lewis Hine to record brutal conditions in mines and mills where children worked (see Hine's photograph on p. 521). Impressed with the committee's work, Theodore Roosevelt sponsored the White House Conference on Dependent Children, bringing national attention to child welfare. In 1912, momentum from the conference resulted in the creation of the Children's Bureau in the U.S. Labor Department.

As the bureau's creation showed, progressives were partly inspired by the emerging fields of social work and social science. Social scientists focused special attention on the plight of the urban poor. They argued that unemployment and crowded slums were not caused by individual laziness and ignorance, as elite Americans had long believed. Instead, wrote journalist Robert Hunter in his landmark study, *Poverty* (1904), such problems resulted from "miserable and unjust social conditions." A reform leader in Boston agreed. "How vain to waste our energies on single cases of relief," he declared, "when *society* should aim at removing the prolific sources of all the woe."

No one exemplified this new attitude more than Josephine Shaw Lowell, a Civil War widow from a prominent family. After years of struggling to aid poverty-stricken individuals in New York City, Lowell concluded that charity was not enough. In 1890, she helped found the New York Consumers' League, to improve the wages and working conditions of female clerks in the city's stores. The league encouraged shoppers to patronize only stores on the "White List" they issued, where wages and working conditions were known to be fair. The organization spread to other cities and by 1899 had become the National Consumers' League (NCL). At its head stood the outspoken Florence Kelley, a Hull House worker and, for a brief time, chief factory inspector of Illinois. Kelley believed that only government oversight could protect exploited workers. Under her crusading leadership, the NCL became a powerful advocate for protective legislation.

All the nations and people I had hitherto passed thro... resembled our own in their manners, customs and langu...

A Progressive Report from New Zealand

HENRY DEMAREST LLOYD

Henry Demarest Lloyd, a reform journalist who had written extensively on politics and economic justice, undertook a study tour of New Zealand in 1899. Discouraged by Populism's defeat in the United States, Lloyd was enthusiastic about New Zealand's sudden burst of reform legislation, which stemmed from an industrial strike in 1890 and a subsequent election that swept the Labor Party into office. Like Lloyd, many American officials and reformers learned from progressive initiatives in other parts of the industrializing world. They borrowed ideas ranging from municipal ownership of utilities to scientific forest management to workmen's compensation laws.

New Zealand democracy is the talk of the world to-day. It has made itself the policeman and partner of industry to an extent unknown elsewhere. It is the "experiment station" of advanced legislation. Reforms that others have been only talking about, New Zealand has done. . . .

Instead of escaping from the evils of the social order by going to a new country, the Englishmen who settled New Zealand found that they had brought all its problems with them. . . . The best acres were in the hands of monopolists. . . . The little farmer, forced by unjust and deliberately contrived laws to pay his own and his rich neighbor's taxes, had to sell out his little homestead to that neighbor for what he could get. The workingman, able to get neither land nor work, had to become a tramp. . . .

. . . [But] here is the record of ten years [of progressive legislation]:

The rich man, because rich, is made to pay more. . . . By compulsory arbitration the public gets for the guidance of public opinion all the facts as to disputes between labor and capital [and] puts an end of strikes and lockouts. . . .

For the unemployed the nation makes itself a labor bureau. It brings them and the employers together. It reorganizes its public works and land system so as to give land to the landless and work to the workless. . . . The state itself insures the working people against accident. . . . The nation's railroads . . . are used to redistribute unemployed labor, to rebuild industry shattered by calamity, to stimulate production by special rates to and from farms and factories, to give health and education to the school and factory population and the people generally by cheap excursions.

. . . Women are enfranchised. . . . On election day one can see the baby-carriage standing in front of the polls while the father and mother go in and vote — against each other if they choose.

Last of all, pensions are given to the aged poor.

. . . We are exhorted to take "one step at a time," and are assured that this is the evolutionary method. This theory does not fit the New Zealand evolution. . . . It was not merely a change in parties; it was a change in principles and institutions that amounted to nothing less than a social right-about-face. It was a New Zealand revolution.

SOURCE: Henry Demarest Lloyd, *Newest England: Notes of a Democratic Traveller to New Zealand* (New York: Doubleday, 1900), 1; 364; 368; 370–374.

One of the NCL's greatest triumphs was the Supreme Court's decision in *Muller v. Oregon* (1908), which upheld an Oregon law limiting the workday to ten hours for women. To win the case, the NCL recruited Louis Brandeis, a son of Jewish immigrants, who was widely known as "the people's lawyer" for his eagerness to take on vested interests. Brandeis's legal brief in the *Muller* case devoted only two pages to the constitutional issue of state "police powers." Instead, Brandeis rested his arguments on data gathered by the NCL describing the toll that long hours took on women's health. The "Brandeis brief" cleared the way for use of social-science research and other expert testimony in legal decisions.

By approving an expansive welfare role for the states, the *Muller* decision encouraged women's organizations to lobby for further reforms. Their achievements included the first law providing public assistance for single mothers with dependent children (Illinois, 1911) and the first minimum wage law for women (Massachusetts, 1912). The NCL, working with the National Child Labor Committee, also played a role in creation of the Children's Bureau, and later the Women's Bureau, in the U.S. Department of Labor.

But the *Muller* decision had significant drawbacks both for labor and for women's rights. Though critics noted that men as well as women suffered from long work hours, the *Muller* case did not protect men. Brandeis's brief treated all women as potential mothers, focusing on the state's interest in protecting their future children. Brandeis and his allies hoped this strategy would open the door to broader regulation of working hours. In its ruling, however, the Supreme Court seized on motherhood as the critical issue. It asserted that the female worker, because of her maternal function, was "properly placed in a class by herself, and legislation for her protection may be sustained, even when like legislation is not necessary for men and could not be sustained." This conclusion dismayed labor advocates and divided female reformers. In the 1920s, while some women's rights advocates continued to fight for more laws to protect working women, others protested against any "discrimination or restriction based upon sex."

Civil Rights | In the wake of the *Plessy* decision and southern disenfranchisement, African American leaders grappled with a distinct set of political challenges. Faced with the obvious deterioration of African American rights — and the indifference or hostility of most whites — a new generation of black leaders challenged the leadership of Tuskegee educator Booker T. Washington. Harvard-educated sociologist W. E. B. Du Bois called for a "talented tenth" of educated blacks to develop new strategies. "The policy of compromise has failed," wrote William Monroe Trotter, pugnacious editor of the *Boston Guardian*. "The policy of resistance and aggression deserves a trial." Ida Wells-Barnett, a fearless journalist who undertook a one-woman crusade against lynching, joined the call for new ideas.

In 1905, Du Bois and Trotter called a meeting at Niagara Falls — on the Canadian side, because no hotel on the U.S. side would admit blacks. The resulting Niagara Movement had a broad impact. The group's Niagara Principles called for full voting rights; an end to segregation; equal treatment in the justice system; and equal opportunity in education, jobs, health care, and military service. These principles, based on black pride and an uncompromising demand for full equality, guided the civil rights movement throughout the twentieth century.

Not long after the Niagara conference, a shocking atrocity brought public attention to the civil rights cause. In 1908, a bloody race riot broke out in Springfield, Illinois, hometown of Abraham Lincoln. Appalled by the violence against blacks, New York settlement worker Mary White Ovington called together a small group of sympathetic progressives. Their meeting led in 1909 to the creation of the National Association for the Advancement of Colored People (NAACP). Most leaders of the Niagara Movement soon joined, and W. E. B. Du Bois became editor of the NAACP journal, *The Crisis*. The fledgling NAACP found allies in the black churches and the National Association of Colored Women's Clubs. It also cooperated with the National Urban League (1911), a union of agencies that assisted black migrants in the North. Over the coming decades, these groups grew into a powerful force for racial justice.

Innovation in the States | As reform emerged at the local level, some states served as important seedbeds. Theodore Roosevelt dubbed Wisconsin a "laboratory of democracy" under energetic Republican governor Robert La Follette (1901–1905). La Follette promoted what he called the "Wisconsin Idea" — greater government intervention in the economy. To promote this goal, he relied heavily on experts

Robert M. La Follette

La Follette was transformed into a political reformer when, in 1891, a Wisconsin Republican boss attempted to bribe him to influence a judge in a railway case. As he described it in his autobiography, "Out of this awful ordeal came understanding; and out of understanding came resolution. I determined that the power of this corrupt influence . . . should be broken." This photograph captures him at the top of his form, expounding his progressive vision to a rapt audience of Wisconsin citizens at an impromptu street gathering. Library of Congress.

at the University of Wisconsin, particularly economists, for policy recommendations. La Follette combined respect for experts with a strong commitment to democracy. He won battles to restrict lobbying and give Wisconsin citizens the right of **recall** (voting to remove unpopular politicians from office) and **referendum** (voting directly on a proposed policy measure, rather than leaving it in the hands of elected legislators). Going on to a long career in the U.S. Senate, La Follette, like Roosevelt, advocated increasingly aggressive measures to protect workers and rein in corporate power.

Labor reforms also advanced steadily through state initiatives, most notably workmen's compensation laws. The U.S. industrial workplace was incredibly dangerous; coal miners, for example, died from cave-ins and explosions at a rate 50 percent higher than in German mines. Between 1910 and 1917, all the industrial states enacted insurance laws covering on-the-job accidents, so that workers' families would not starve if a breadwinner was injured or killed. Some states also experimented with so-called mothers' pensions or widows' pensions, which provided state assistance after a breadwinner's desertion or death. Mothers, however, were subjected to home visits to determine whether they were "deserving" of government aid; injured workmen were not, a pattern of gender discrimination that reflected the broader impulse to protect women, while treating them differently from men. Although mothers' pensions reached relatively small numbers of women, they laid the foundations for federal Aid to Dependent Children, an important component of the Social Security Act of 1935.

While federalism gave states considerable freedom to innovate, it hampered national reforms. In some states, for example, opponents of child labor won laws that barred young children from factory work and strictly regulated the hours and conditions of older children's labor. In the South, however, and in some industrial states like Pennsylvania, manufacturers fiercely resisted such laws — as did many working-class parents who relied on children's income to keep the family fed. A proposed U.S. constitutional amendment to abolish child labor won ratification in only four states. Tens of thousands of children continued to work in low-wage jobs, especially in the South. The same decentralized power that permitted innovation in Wisconsin also hampered the creation of national minimum standards for pay and conditions of work.

The Problem of Labor | The failure to pass labor laws reflected both Republican political control and unions' reluctance to engage in electoral politics. Leaders of the nation's dominant union, the American Federation of Labor, had long preached that workers should improve wages and working conditions through self-help. **Voluntarism**, as trade unionists called this doctrine, centered on strikes and direct negotiations with employers, not political action. But voluntarism began to weaken by the 1910s. As muckraking journalists exposed the plight of workers and progressive reformers came forward with solutions, labor leaders in state after state began to join the cause.

At the same time, the nation confronted a daring wave of labor militancy. In 1905, the Western Federation of Miners (WFM), led by fiery leaders like William D. "Big Bill" Haywood, joined with other radicals to create a new movement, the Industrial Workers of the World (IWW). The Wobblies, as they were called, were fervent supporters of the Marxist class struggle. As **syndicalists**, they believed that by resisting in the workplace and ultimately launching a **general strike**, workers could overthrow capitalism. A new society would emerge, run directly by workers. At its height, around 1916, the IWW had about 100,000 members. Though divided by internal conflicts, the group helped spark a number of local protests during the 1910s, including strikes of railcar builders in Pennsylvania; textile operatives in Lawrence, Massachusetts; rubber workers in Ohio; and miners in northern Minnesota.

Meanwhile, after midnight on October 1, 1910, an explosion ripped through the *Los Angeles Times* headquarters, killing twenty employees and wrecking the building. It turned out that John J. McNamara, a high official of the American Federation of Labor's Bridge and Structural Iron Workers Union, had planned the bombing against the fiercely anti-union *Times*. McNamara's brother and another union member had carried out the attack. The bombing created a sensation, as did the terrible Triangle Shirtwaist fire (see Chapter 19) and the IWW's high-profile strikes. What should be done? As the election of 1912 approached, the "labor question" moved high on the nation's agenda.

Taft and the Election of 1912

In 1908, President Theodore Roosevelt chose to retire. He bequeathed the Republican nomination to William Howard Taft, a talented administrator. Taft portrayed himself as "Roosevelt's man," though he maintained a closer relationship than his predecessor had with pro-business Republicans in Congress. Taft's Democratic opponent in 1908 was William Jennings Bryan. Eloquent as ever, Bryan attacked Republicans as the party of "plutocrats," men who used their wealth to buy political influence. He outdid Taft in urging tougher antitrust and pro-labor legislation, but Taft won comfortably.

In the wake of Taft's victory, however, rising pressure for national reform initiatives began to divide Republicans. Conservatives dug in against further reforms, while militant progressives within the party thought Roosevelt and his successor had not gone far enough. Reconciling these conflicting forces was a daunting task. For Taft it spelled disaster. Through various incidents he found himself on the opposite side of progressive Republicans, who began to call themselves Insurgents and plot their own path.

Returning from a yearlong safari in Africa, Roosevelt yearned to reenter the political fray. Taft's dispute with the Insurgents gave the former president the reason he needed. In a speech in Osawatomie, Kansas, in August 1910, Roosevelt made the case for what he called the New Nationalism. In modern America, he argued, property had to be controlled "to whatever degree the public welfare may require it." With this formulation, Roosevelt took up social justice issues, proposing a federal child labor law, more recognition of labor rights, and a national minimum wage for women. Pressed by friends like Jane Addams, Roosevelt also endorsed women's voting rights. Most radical was his attack on the legal system. Insisting that courts stood in the way of reform, Roosevelt proposed sharp curbs on their powers, even raising the possibility of popular recall of court decisions.

Early in 1912, Roosevelt announced himself as a Republican candidate for president, sweeping Insurgents into his camp. A bitter battle within the party ensued. Roosevelt won the states that held primary elections, but Taft controlled party caucuses elsewhere. Dominated by regulars, the Republican convention chose Taft. Roosevelt led his followers into what became known as the Progressive Party, offering his New Nationalism directly to the people. Though she harbored private doubts (especially about Roosevelt's mania for battleships), Jane Addams called the new party "the American exponent of a world-wide movement for juster social conditions." In a nod to Roosevelt's combative stance, the Progressive Party won the nickname "Bull Moose Party."

The Ludlow Massacre, 1914
Like his drawing of the Triangle Shirtwaist fire victims on page 594, this cover illustration for the popular socialist magazine *The Masses* is another demonstration of John Sloan's outrage at social injustice in progressive America. The drawing memorializes a tragic episode during a coal miners' strike at Ludlow, Colorado — the asphyxiation of women and children when the state militia torched the tent city of evicted miners — and the aftermath, an armed revolt by enraged miners. *The Masses*, June 1914.

Roosevelt was not the only rebel on the ballot in 1912. The major parties also faced a challenge from charismatic socialist Eugene V. Debs. In the 1890s, Debs had founded the American Railway Union (ARU), a broad-based union that included both skilled and unskilled workers. In 1894, amid the upheavals of depression and popular protest, the ARU had boycotted luxury Pullman sleeping cars, in support of a strike by workers at the Pullman Company. Railroad managers, claiming that the strike obstructed the U.S. mail, persuaded Grover Cleveland's administration to intervene against the union. The strike failed. Along with other ARU leaders, Debs served time in prison. The experience radicalized him, and in 1901 he launched the Socialist Party of America. Debs translated socialism into an American idiom, emphasizing the democratic process as a means to defeat capitalism. By the early 1910s, his party had secured a minor but persistent role in politics.

Both the Progressive and Socialist Parties drew strength from the West, a region with vigorous urban reform movements and a legacy of farmer-labor activism. The Progressive Party tapped California's reform governor, Hiram Johnson, as Roosevelt's running mate on the Progressive ticket. Watching the threats posed by the insurgent Progressive and Socialist Parties, Democrats were also keen to build on dramatic gains they had made in the 1910 midterm elections. Among their new generation of leaders was Virginia-born Woodrow Wilson, a political scientist who had served as president of Princeton University. As governor of New Jersey, Wilson had compiled an impressive reform record, including passage of a direct primary, workers' compensation, and utility regulation. In 1912, he won the Democratic presidential nomination.

Wilson possessed, to a fault, the moral certainty that characterized many elite progressives. Only gradually did he hammer out a coherent reform program, calling it the New Freedom. Wilson had much in common with Roosevelt. "The old time of individual competition is probably gone by," Wilson admitted, and he agreed on the need for more federal measures to restrict big business. But his program appeared less sweeping than Roosevelt's. "If America is not to have free enterprise," Wilson warned, "then she can have freedom of no sort whatever." He claimed that Roosevelt's program represented collectivism, whereas the New Freedom would preserve political and economic liberty.

With four candidates in the field — Taft, Roosevelt, Wilson, and Debs — the 1912 campaign generated intense excitement. But the division of former Republicans between Taft and Roosevelt made the results fairly easy to predict. Wilson won, though he received only 42 percent of the popular vote, and almost certainly would have lost if Roosevelt had not been in the race (Map 20.4). With his defense of free enterprise and his markedly southern racial views, Wilson appeared to be a rather old-fashioned choice. But with labor protests reaching new peaks of visibility and middle-class progressives gathering public support, Wilson faced intense pressure to act.

Wilson and the New Freedom

In his inaugural address, Wilson acknowledged that industrialization had precipitated a crisis. "There can be no equality or opportunity, the first essential of justice in the body politic," he said, "if men and women and children be not shielded . . . from the consequences of great industrial and social processes which they cannot alter, control, or singly cope with." Wilson was a Democrat, and labor interests and farmers made up important components of his party's base. Thus, though the Greenback-Labor and People's Parties had faded away, rural Democrats played a central role in the reforms achieved under Wilson. In an era of rising corporate power, such Democrats had come to believe that workers needed stronger government to intervene on their behalf.

Democrats continued to have an enormous blind spot: their opposition to African American rights, a position to which the national party adhered until 1948, and to which southern Democrats clung even longer. There was no hope, for example, that Democrats would pass federal antilynching legislation. But Republicans, who had had plenti-

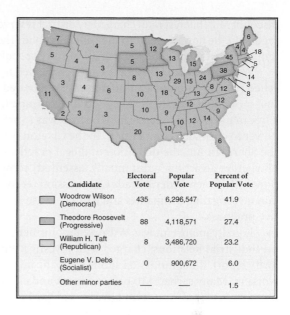

MAP 20.4 The Presidential Election of 1912

The 1912 election reveals why the two-party system is so strongly rooted in American politics — especially in presidential elections. The Democrats, though a minority party, won an electoral landslide because the Republicans divided their vote between Roosevelt and Taft. This result indicates what is at stake when major parties splinter. The Socialist Party candidate, Eugene V. Debs, despite a record vote of 900,000, received no electoral votes.

Candidate	Electoral Vote	Popular Vote	Percent of Popular Vote
Woodrow Wilson (Democrat)	435	6,296,547	41.9
Theodore Roosevelt (Progressive)	88	4,118,571	27.4
William H. Taft (Republican)	8	3,486,720	23.2
Eugene V. Debs (Socialist)	0	900,672	6.0
Other minor parties	—	—	1.5

ful opportunities, had also conspicuously failed to pass such a law. In 1912, the Progressive Party had refused to seat southern black delegates or take a stand for racial equality. While African Americans had no reason to vote for Democrats, they found few reasons to vote for Republicans or Progressives, either.

In other ways, Democrats were transforming themselves into a modern, state-building party. The Wilson administration achieved a series of landmark economic reforms. The most enduring was the federal income tax. This long-sought tax required a federal constitutional amendment, which was ratified by the states in February 1913. The next year, Congress used this new power to enact an income tax of 1 to 7 percent on Americans who had annual incomes of $4,000 or more. At a time when white male wageworkers might expect to make $800 per year, the tax affected less than 5 percent of households. Three years later, Congress followed it with an inheritance tax. These measures created an entirely new way to fund the federal government; they replaced Republicans' high tariff as the chief source of revenue, and tariff reduction benefited ordinary consumers. Over subsequent decades, especially between the 1930s and the 1970s, the income tax system markedly reduced America's extremes of wealth and poverty.

The new president also reorganized the nation's financial system to address problems caused by the absence of a central bank. The main function of central banks at the time was to back up commercial banks in case they could not meet their obligations. In the United States, the great private banks of New York assumed this role; if they weakened, the entire system could collapse. This had nearly happened in 1907, when the Knickerbocker Trust Company failed and caused a financial panic. The Federal Reserve Act of 1913 gave the nation a banking system more resistant to such panic. It created twelve district reserve banks funded and controlled by their member banks, with the central Federal Reserve Board to impose public regulation. The Federal Reserve had authority to issue currency — paper money based on assets held within the system — and to set the discount rate (interest rate) charged by district reserve banks to member banks. It thereby regulated the flow of credit to the general public. The act strengthened the banking system and, to a modest degree, reined in risky speculation on Wall Street.

Wilson and the Democratic Congress turned next to the trusts. In doing so, Wilson relied heavily on Louis D. Brandeis, the celebrated "people's lawyer." Brandeis denied that monopoly meant efficiency. On the contrary, he believed vigorous competition in a free market was most efficient. The trick was to prevent trusts from unfairly using their power to curb such competition. In the Clayton Antitrust Act of 1914, which amended the Sherman Act, the definition of illegal practices was left flexible, subject to the test of whether an action "substantially lessen[ed] competition or tend[ed] to create a monopoly." The new Federal Trade Commission received broad powers to decide what was fair, investigating companies and issuing "cease and desist" orders against anticompetitive practices.

Equally important was Wilson's appointment of the blue-ribbon U.S. Commission on Industrial Relations, charged with investigating the conditions of labor. In its majority report, the commission summed up the impact of industrialization on low-skilled workers. Many earned $10 or less a week and endured regular episodes of unemployment. Some faced long-term poverty and hardship, and they held "an almost universal conviction" that they were "denied justice." The commission concluded that the core reason for industrial violence was the ruthless anti-unionism of American employers. In its most important recommendation, the majority report called for federal laws protecting workers' right to organize and engage in collective bargaining. Though such laws were, in 1915, too radical to win passage, the commission's report helped set a new national agenda for labor rights that would come to fruition in the 1930s.

Guided by the revelations of this commission, President Wilson warmed up to labor. In 1915 and 1916, he championed a host of bills to benefit American workers. They included the Adamson Act, which established an eight-hour day for railroad workers; the Seamen's Act, which eliminated age-old abuses of merchant sailors; and a workmen's compensation law for federal employees. Wilson, despite his initial modest goals, had presided over a major expansion of federal authority, reflected in the steady growth of U.S. government offices during his term (Figure 20.1).

Progressive Legacies

In the post–Civil War era, millions of Americans understood that the political system needed to adjust to new industrial conditions. In the 1880s, radical farmer and labor advocates proposed sweeping limitations on industrial capitalism; though they exerted substantial pressure, especially within the Democratic Party after 1896, only a portion of their vision was fulfilled. By the turn of the twentieth century, economic reform gained increasing support from middle-class and elite progressives, especially in the cities. They tended to propose more modest measures, often shying away from democratic solutions in favor of expert commissions and political management by the "best men." But they held substantial clout.

Whether they were rural, working-class, or middle-class, reformers faced fierce opposition from powerful business interests. Whenever reformers managed, at last, to win a key regulatory law, they often found it struck down by hostile courts. Thus, the Pro-

FIGURE 20.1 The Federal Bureaucracy, 1890–1917
The surge in federal employment after 1900 mirrored the surge in government authority. Progressive initiatives at the local and state levels, along with pressure from grassroots reformers, led to new federal departments and bureaus, designed to oversee and regulate the economy and protect public welfare. Source: Wallace S. Sayre, ed., *The Federal Government Service* (Englewood Cliffs, NJ: Prentice-Hall, 1965).

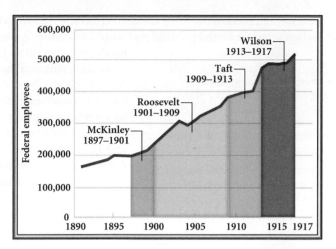

gressive Era in the United States should be understood partly by its limitations. Racial prejudice and increasing elitism warped the cause of reform; African Americans, their plight ignored by many white reformers, faced segregation and violence, and along with some immigrants and poor whites, they found themselves disenfranchised. Meanwhile, federal courts slowed down the progress of key reforms like state protections for labor. Divided power in a federalist system blocked the passage of uniform national laws on such key issues as child labor. Urgently needed social welfare programs, including national health insurance and old-age pensions — which became popular in Europe during these decades — scarcely made it onto the American agenda until the New Deal of the 1930s.

An international perspective suggests several reasons for the U.S. resistance to social welfare programs. Business interests in the United States were exceptionally successful and powerful, flush with recent expansion. And in general, during the era of industrialization, voters in countries with older, more native-born populations supported more robust government regulation and social welfare spending than did voters in countries with younger populations and large numbers of immigrants. Younger voters, understandably, seem to have been less concerned than older voters about health insurance and security in old age. Divisions within the American working class also played a role. Black, immigrant, and native-born white laborers often viewed one another as enemies or strangers rather than as members of a unified class with common interests. This helps explain why the Socialist Party drew, at its peak, less than 6 percent of the U.S. vote at a time when its counterparts in Finland, Germany, and France drew 40 percent or more. Lack of pressure from a strong, self-conscious workingmen's party led to more limited results in the United States.

But it would be wrong to underestimate the achievements of Progressive Era reformers. Over the course of several decades, they persuaded more and more comfortable, prosperous Americans that the industrial economy required stronger government regulation. Even the most cautious, elite progressives recognized that the United States had entered a new era. Giant multinational corporations overshadowed small businesses;

with immigrants and farmers' children crowding into vast cities, ties of kin and village melted away. Outdated political methods — from the "spoils system" to corrupt urban machines — would no longer do. Walter Lippman, a founding editor of the progressive magazine *The New Republic*, observed in 1914 that Americans found themselves with "no precedents to guide us, no wisdom that wasn't made for a simpler age." Progressives created new wisdom. Between 1883 and 1917, they drew the blueprints for a modern American state, one whose powers began to suit the needs of an industrial era. At the same time, a stronger, more assertive United States began to exercise new influence on the world stage.

▶ What types of progressive legislation passed in the early 1900s? To what extent were they the result of grassroots pressure? Of leadership by particular individuals and political parties?

▶ What factors explain the limits of progressive reform during this period?

SUMMARY

The Progressive Era emerged from the political turmoil of the 1880s and 1890s. In the 1880s, despite the limits imposed by close elections, federal and state governments managed to achieve important administrative and economic reforms. After 1888, Republican leaders undertook more sweeping efforts, including the Sherman Antitrust Act, but failed in a quest to protect black voting rights. In the South and West, the People's Party called for much stronger government intervention in the economy, but its radical program drew bitter Republican and Democratic resistance.

The depression of the 1890s brought a wave of political reaction. Labor unrest threw the nation into crisis, and Cleveland's intransigence over the gold standard cost the Democrats dearly in the 1894 and 1896 elections. While Republicans took over the federal government, southern Democrats restricted voting rights to build the "Solid South." Meanwhile, federal courts struck down regulatory laws and supported southern racial discrimination.

After McKinley's assassination, Roosevelt launched a program that balanced reform and private enterprise. At both the federal and state levels, Progressive reformers made extensive use of elite expertise. At the grassroots level, black and white reformers battled racial discrimination; women reformers worked on issues ranging from public health to women's working conditions; and labor activists tried to address the conditions that fueled persistent labor unrest. The election of 1912 split the Republicans, giving victory to Woodrow Wilson, who launched a Democratic program of economic and labor reform. Despite the limits of the Progressive Era, the reforms of this period laid the foundation for a modern American state.

For additional primary sources from this period, see *Documents for America's History*, Seventh Edition.

For Web sites, images, and documents related to topics and places in this chapter, visit *Make History* at **bedfordstmartins.com/henrettaconcise**.

For Further Exploration

On post-Reconstruction politics see H. Wayne Morgan, *From Hayes to McKinley* (1969) and Charles Calhoun, *Conceiving a New Republic* (2006). On liberals see Nancy Cohen, *The Reconstruction of American Liberalism* (2002). On rural reformers and labor see Elizabeth Sanders, *Roots of Reform* (1999) and Michael Kazin's biography of William Jennings Bryan, *A Godly Hero* (2006). On Populism, see Robert C. McMath's *American Populism* (1993) and Charles Postel's *The Populist Vision* (2007). Alexander Keyssar, *The Right to Vote* (2000), explores assaults on popular politics. On southern politics, the seminal book is C. Vann Woodward, *Origins of the New South, 1877–1913* (1951); a recent revision is Edward Ayers, *The Promise of the New South* (1992). On disenfranchisement see Michael Perman, *Struggle for Mastery* (2001), and J. Morgan Kousser, *The Shaping of Southern Politics* (1974).

On the crisis of the 1890s see Henry May, *Protestant Churches and Industrial America* (1949), R. Hal Williams, *Years of Decision* (1978), and Carlos Schwantes, *Coxey's Army* (1985). For the impact on labor, see William Forbath, *Law and the Shaping of the American Labor Movement* (1991). Bedford has issued helpful treatments of key Supreme Court decisions: *Plessy v. Ferguson*, ed. Brook Thomas (1997), and *Muller v. Oregon*, ed. Nancy Woloch (1996).

The literature on progressivism is voluminous. See Maureen Flanagan, *America Reformed* (2007); Robert D. Johnson, *The Radical Middle Class* (2003); Kathryn Kish Sklar, *Florence Kelley and the Nation's Work* (1995); Alan Dawley, *Changing the World* (2003); and Daniel Rogers, *Atlantic Crossings* (1998). A comparative treatment of Roosevelt and Wilson is John Milton Cooper's *The Warrior and the Priest* (1983).

Test Your Knowledge

For practice quizzes, activities, and other study tools, visit the Online Study Guide at **bedfordstmartins.com/henrettaconcise**.

TIMELINE

1881	► President James Garfield assassinated
1883	► Pendleton Act establishes the Civil Service Commission
1890	► Sherman Antitrust Act
	► People's Party created in Kansas
1893	► Economic depression begins
1894	► Coxey's Army marches on Washington, D.C.
1895	► John Pierpont Morgan arranges gold purchases to rescue U.S. Treasury
1896	► William McKinley wins presidency
	► *Plessy v. Ferguson* establishes "separate but equal" doctrine
1899	► National Consumers' League founded
1901	► Eugene Debs founds the Socialist Party of America

	► McKinley assassinated; Theodore Roosevelt assumes presidency
1902	► Newlands Reclamation Act
1903	► Elkins Act
1905	► Industrial Workers of the World founded
1906	► Hepburn Act
1908	► *Muller v. Oregon* limits women's work hours
1912	► Three-way election gives presidency to Woodrow Wilson
1913	► Seventeenth Amendment
	► Graduated income tax introduced
	► Federal Reserve Act
1914	► Clayton Antitrust Act

God has marked the
American people as His
chosen nation to finally
lead in the regeneration
of the world. This is the
divine mission of America,
and it holds for us all the
profit, all the glory, all the
happiness possible to man.

—Senator Albert J. Beveridge, arguing for
U.S. acquisition of the Philippines, 1900

When he accepted the Demo-cratic presidential nomination in 1900, William Jennings Bryan delivered a famous speech denouncing U.S. military occupation of overseas territories. "God Himself," Bryan declared, "placed in every human heart the love of liberty. . . . He never made a race of people so low in the scale of civilization or intelligence that it would welcome a foreign master." Two years earlier, the United States had helped Cuban rebels liberate their island from Spanish rule. Bryan and other Democrats had supported that cause, believing the United States was helping create an inde-pendent Cuba. By 1900, however, the political landscape had shifted. Republican pres-ident William McKinley was leading the United States in an ambitious plan of overseas expansion, which proved popular at home. McKinley's administration had asserted control over much of the Caribbean, claimed Hawaii as a territory, and sought to an-nex the Philippines. Bryan failed to convince a majority of the public that **imperialism** (the exercise of military, political, and economic power overseas) was the wrong path for the United States to take. He lost the 1900 election by a landslide, and the reelected McKinley moved forward with Philippine annexation.

In the longer run, however, Bryan's views were in some ways more influential than McKinley's. That became clear in the 1910s, when, despite initial efforts to remain neu-tral as European alliances battled each other in World War I, the United States became caught up in the catastrophic conflict. By the end of this horrific war, European nations' grip on their colonial empires was weakening. The United States ceased acquiring over-seas territories and pursued a different path. It developed an "informal empire," based on business interests rather than administrative control. President Woodrow Wilson, who in 1913 appointed Bryan as his first secretary of state, believed the United States should steer a middle course between revolutionary socialism and European-style imperialism.

American Soldiers on a French Battlefield, 1918
As the United States asserted its power on the world stage, American soldiers found themselves fighting on foreign battlefields. This 1918 photograph shows a few of the 1 million U.S. soldiers who joined French and British troops fighting on the brutal Western Front to defeat Germany in the Great War. More than 26,000 American soldiers lost their lives on the battlefield during World War I, and 95,000 were wounded. Library of Congress.

In Wilson's phrase, America would "make the world safe for democracy," while unapologetically working to foster global capitalism and advance U.S. economic interests. Critics argued that these goals constituted another form of imperialism, grounded in economic rather than administrative power. Advocates, however, established the dual goal of spreading democracy and capitalism as an enduring basis for American foreign policy.

From Expansion to Imperialism

Historians used to describe turn-of-the-twentieth-century U.S. imperialism as something new. Now they emphasize continuities between foreign policy in this era and the nation's relentless earlier expansion across the North American continent. Wars against native peoples had occurred almost continuously since the nation's founding; in the 1840s, the United States had taken one-third of Mexico. The United States never administered a large colonial empire, as did European powers like Spain, England, Belgium, and Germany, partly because the United States had a plentiful supply of natural resources in the American West. But policymakers went on a determined quest for global markets.

Industrialization and a modern navy gave the United States muscle; the economic crisis of the 1890s provided a spur.

Foundations of Empire

As they embarked on empire-building around 1900, American policymakers fulfilled a vision laid out three decades earlier by William Seward (secretary of state under presidents Abraham Lincoln and Andrew Johnson), who emphasized access to global markets as the key to power. Seward's ideas had won only limited support in the wake of the Civil War, but the severe economic depression of 1893 (see Chapter 20) brought Republicans into power and Seward's ideas back into vogue. Confronting high unemployment and mass protests, policymakers feared that American workers would embrace socialism or communism. The alternative, they believed, was to manufacture products for overseas markets in order to create jobs and prosperity at home.

Intellectual trends also favored imperialism. As early as 1885, in his popular book *Our Country*, Congregationalist minister Josiah Strong urged Protestants to proselytize overseas. He predicted that the American "Anglo-Saxon race" — "the representative, let us hope, of the largest liberty, the purest Christianity, the highest civilization, having developed particularly aggressive traits calculated to impress its institutions upon mankind" — would "spread itself over the earth." Such arguments were grounded in **American exceptionalism**, the idea that the United States had a destiny unique among nations to foster democracy and civilization.

As Strong's exhortation suggested, imperialists also drew on increasingly popular racial theories, which claimed that people of "Anglo-Saxon" descent — English and often German — were superior to all other peoples. "Anglo-Saxon" rule over foreign people of color made sense in an era when, at home, the Supreme Court sanctioned racial segregation, and many whites believed that native peoples were vanishing and black voters should be disenfranchised. Imperialists often linked white Americans' conquest of the North American continent with the drive for overseas power. Responding to critics of U.S. occupation of the Philippines, Theodore Roosevelt scoffed: If America ought to return the Philippines to Filipinos, he declared, then it was "morally bound to return Arizona to the Apaches." Imperialists also justified their views through racialized Social Darwinism. Josiah Strong, for example, predicted that with the lands of the globe fully occupied, a "competition of races" would ensue, based on "survival of the fittest."

Fear of ruthless competition drove the United States, like European nations, to invest in the latest weapons. American policymakers saw that the European powers were amassing steel-plated battleships and carving up Africa and Asia among themselves. In his book *The Influence of Sea Power upon History* (1890), U.S. naval officer Alfred T. Mahan urged the United States to enter the fray, observing that naval power had been essential to the growth of past empires. In 1890, Congress appropriated funds for three battleships. President Grover Cleveland continued this naval program.

Cleveland's secretary of state, Richard Olney, turned rising imperial interests into direct confrontation when he warned European powers away from Latin America, which he saw as the United States' rightful sphere of influence. Without consulting the nation of Venezuela, Olney suddenly demanded in July 1895 that Britain resolve a long-standing border dispute between Venezuela and Britain's neighboring colony, British

Guiana. Invoking the Monroe Doctrine, which stated that the Western Hemisphere was off-limits to further European colonization, Olney warned that the United States would brook no challenge to its interests. Startled, Britain agreed to arbitrate. American power was on the ascent.

The War of 1898

While Olney was intervening in Venezuela, events were unfolding in the Caribbean that would present the United States with a far greater opportunity to wield power. In February 1895, Cuban patriots mounted a major guerrilla war against Spain, which had lost most of its New World territories but had managed to hold on to the island of Cuba. The Spanish commander responded by rounding up Cuban civilians into concentration camps, where as many as 200,000 died of starvation, exposure, or dysentery. In the United States, William Randolph Hearst turned their plight into a cause célèbre. Hearst's campaign fed a surge of nationalism, especially among those who feared that American men were losing strength and courage amid the conditions of industrial society. The government should not pass up this opportunity, said Indiana senator Albert Beveridge, to "manufacture manhood." Congress called for Cuban independence.

President Cleveland had no interest in supporting the Cuban rebellion, but he worried over Spain's failure to end it. The war was disrupting trade and damaging American-owned sugar plantations on the island. An unstable Cuba was incompatible with America's strategic interests, which included a proposed canal whose Caribbean approaches would have to be safeguarded. Taking office in 1897, President William McKinley was inclined to take a tougher stance than Cleveland had. In September, the U.S. minister in Madrid informed Spain that it must ensure an "early and certain peace" or the United States would step in. At first, this hard line seemed to work: Spain's conservative regime fell, and a liberal government, taking office in October 1897, offered Cuba limited self-rule. But Spanish loyalists in Havana rioted against the proposal, while Cuban rebels held out for full independence.

On February 9, 1898, Hearst's *New York Journal* published a private letter in which Dupuy de Lôme, Spanish minister to the United States, belittled the McKinley administration. De Lôme resigned, but exposure of the letter intensified Americans' indignation toward Spain. The next week brought shocking news: The U.S. battle cruiser *Maine* had exploded and sunk in Havana harbor, with 260 seamen lost. "Whole Country Thrills with the War Fever," proclaimed the *New York Journal*. "Remember the *Maine* and to hell with Spain," became the chant across the country. Popular passions were now a major factor in the march toward war.

McKinley assumed that the sinking of the *Maine* had been accidental. Improbably, though, a U.S. naval board of inquiry blamed a mine, fueling public outrage. (Later investigators disagreed: The more likely cause was a faulty ship design that placed explosive munitions too close to coal bunkers, which were prone to fire.) No evidence linked Spain to the purported mine. But if a mine sank the ship, then Spain was responsible for not protecting the American vessel.

Hesitant business leaders now became impatient, believing that war was preferable to an unending Cuban crisis. On March 27, McKinley cabled an ultimatum to Madrid:

an immediate ceasefire in Cuba for six months and, with the United States as mediator, peace negotiations with the rebels. Spain, though desperate to avoid war, balked at McKinley's added demand that mediation must result in Cuban independence. On April 11, McKinley asked Congress for authority to intervene in Cuba "in the name of humanity, in the name of civilization, [and] in behalf of endangered American interests."

Historians long referred to the ensuing fight as the Spanish-American War, but that name ignores the central role of Cuban revolutionaries, who had started the war and hoped to achieve national independence. Therefore, many historians now call the three-way conflict the War of 1898. At the time, Americans widely admired Cuban rebels' aspirations for freedom; even so, the McKinley administration defeated a congressional attempt to recognize the rebel government. In response, Senator Henry M. Teller of Colorado added an amendment to the war bill, disclaiming any intention by the United States to occupy Cuba. The Teller Amendment reassured Americans that their country would uphold democracy abroad as well as at home. McKinley's expectations differed, however. He wrote privately, "While we are conducting war and until its conclusion, we must keep all we get; when the war is over we must keep what we want."

On April 24, 1898, Spain declared war on the United States. The news provoked full-blown war fever. Across America, young men enlisted for the fight. Theodore Roosevelt accepted a commission as lieutenant colonel of a cavalry regiment. Recruits poured into makeshift bases around Tampa, Florida, where confusion reigned. Rifles did not arrive; food was bad, sanitation worse. No provision had been made for getting troops to Cuba, so the government hastily collected a fleet of yachts and commercial boats. Fortunately, the small regular army was a disciplined, professional force, and its 28,000 seasoned troops provided a nucleus for the 200,000 volunteers. The navy was in better shape: Spain had nothing to match America's seven battleships and armored cruisers. The Spanish admiral bitterly predicted that his fleet would "like Don Quixote go out to fight wind-mills and come back with a broken head."

The first, decisive military engagement took place in the Pacific. This was the handi-work of Theodore Roosevelt, who, while still in the Navy Department, had gotten in-trepid Commodore George Dewey appointed commander of the Pacific fleet. In the event of war, Dewey had instructions to sail immediately for the Spanish-owned Philip-pines. When war was declared, Roosevelt confronted his surprised superior and pres-sured him into validating Dewey's instructions. On May 1, 1898, American ships cor-nered the Spanish fleet in Manila Bay and destroyed it. Manila, the Philippine capital, fell on August 13. Dewey's victory was critical. "We must on no account let the [Philip-pines] go," declared Senator Henry Cabot Lodge. McKinley and his advisors agreed. The United States now had a major foothold in the western Pacific.

Dewey's victory instantly directed policymakers' attention to the Hawaiian Islands. Nominally an independent nation, Hawaii had long been under American dominance, since its climate had attracted a horde of American sugarcane planters. An 1876 treaty between the United States and the island's monarch gave Hawaiian sugar tariff-free ac-cess to the American market, with Hawaii pledging to sign no such agreement with any other power. In 1887, Hawaii also granted a long-coveted lease for a U.S. naval base at Pearl Harbor. When Hawaii's access to the U.S. market was canceled by a new tariff in 1890, sugar planters revolted against the islands' ruler, Queen Liliuokalani, and

Sugarcane Plantation, Hawaii

More than 300,000 Asians from China, Japan, Korea, and the Philippines came to work in the Hawaiian sugarcane fields between 1850 and 1920. The hardships they endured are reflected in plantation work songs, such as this one by Japanese laborers:

> But when I came what I saw was Hell
> The boss was Satan
> The *lunas* [overseers] his helpers.

© Curt Teich Postcard Archives, Lake County Museum.

negotiated a treaty of annexation. But Grover Cleveland rejected the treaty when he entered office. He declared that it would violate America's "unbroken tradition" against acquiring territory overseas.

Dewey's victory delivered what the planters wanted: Hawaii acquired strategic value as a halfway station to the Philippines. In July 1898, Congress authorized the annexation of Hawaii. Further annexations then took on their own logic. The navy pressed for another coaling base in the central Pacific; that meant Guam, a Spanish island in the Marianas. A strategic base was needed in the Caribbean; that meant Puerto Rico. By early summer, before U.S. troops had fired a shot in Cuba, McKinley's broader war aims were crystallizing.

In Cuba, Spanish forces were depleted by the long guerrilla war. Though poorly trained and equipped, American forces had the advantages of a demoralized foe and knowledgeable Cuban allies. The main battle occurred on July 1 at San Juan Hill, near Santiago, where the Spanish fleet was anchored. Roosevelt's Rough Riders took the lead, but four African American regiments bore the brunt of the fighting. White observers credited much of the victory to the "superb gallantry" of these soldiers. Spanish troops retreated to a well-fortified second line, but U.S. forces were spared the test of a second assault. On July 3, the Spanish fleet in Santiago harbor tried a desperate run through the

American blockade and was destroyed. Days later, Spanish forces surrendered. American combat casualties had been few; most U.S. soldiers' deaths had resulted from malaria and yellow fever.

The Spoils of War

The United States and Spain quickly signed a preliminary peace agreement in which Spain agreed to liberate Cuba and cede Puerto Rico and Guam to the United States. But what would the United States do with the Philippines, an immense archipelago that lay more than 5,000 miles from California? Initially, the United States aimed to keep only Manila, because of its fine harbor. Manila was not defensible, however, without the whole of Luzon, the large island on which the city was located. After some deliberation, McKinley found a justification for annexing the whole Philippines. He decided that "we could not leave [the Filipinos] to themselves — they were unfit for self-rule."

This declaration provoked heated debate. Under the Constitution, argued Republican senator George F. Hoar, "no power is given to the Federal Government to acquire territory to be held and governed permanently as colonies" or "to conquer alien people and hold them in subjugation." Leading citizens and peace advocates, including Jane Addams and Mark Twain, enlisted in the anti-imperialist cause. Steel king Andrew Carnegie offered $20 million to purchase Philippine independence. Labor leader Samuel Gompers warned union members about the threat of competition from Filipinos working for low wages. Anti-imperialists, however, were a diverse lot. Some argued that Filipinos were perfectly capable of self-rule; others warned about the dangers of annexing 8 million Filipinos of an "inferior race." "No matter whether they are fit to govern themselves or not," declared one Missouri congressman, "they are not fit to govern us."

Beginning in late 1898, Anti-Imperialist Leagues sprang up around the country, but they never sparked a mass movement. McKinley's "splendid little war" was, in fact, immensely popular. Confronted with that political reality, Democrats waffled in their opposition. Their standard-bearer, William Jennings Bryan, decided not to stake his party's future on opposition to a policy that he believed to be irreversible. He threw his party into turmoil by declaring last-minute support for McKinley's proposed treaty. Having met military defeat, Spanish representatives had little choice. In the Treaty of Paris, Spain ceded the Philippines to the United States for a payment of $20 million.

But annexation was not as simple as U.S. policymakers had expected. On February 4, 1899 — two days before the Senate ratified the treaty — fighting broke out between American and Filipino patrols on the edge of Manila. Confronted by annexation, rebel leader Emilio Aguinaldo asserted his nation's independence and turned his guns on occupying American forces. Though Aguinaldo found it difficult to organize a mass-based resistance movement, the ensuing conflict between Filipino nationalists and U.S. troops far exceeded in length and ferocity the war just concluded with Spain. Fighting tenacious guerrillas, the U.S. Army resorted to the same tactics Spain had employed in Cuba: burning crops and villages and rounding up civilians. Atrocities became commonplace on both sides. In three years of warfare, 4,200 Americans and an estimated 200,000 Filipinos died; many of the latter were dislocated civilians, particularly children, who succumbed to malnutrition and disease.

Emilio Aguinaldo

At the start of the War of 1898, U.S. military leaders brought Filipino patriot Emilio Aguinaldo back from Singapore (where he had been living in exile) to foment a popular uprising that would help defeat the Spaniards. Aguinaldo came because he thought the Americans favored an independent Philippines. While it has remained a matter of dispute what assurances Aguinaldo received from the United States, differing intentions were the root cause of the Filipino insurrection against U.S. occupation, which proved far costlier in American and Filipino lives than the U.S. war with Spain that preceded it. © Bettmann/Corbis.

McKinley's convincing victory over William Jennings Bryan in 1900 suggested popular satisfaction with America's overseas adventure, even in the face of dogged Filipino resistance to U.S. rule. The fighting ended in 1902, and William Howard Taft, appointed as governor-general of the Philippines, sought to make the territory a model of road building and sanitary engineering. Yet misgivings lingered as Americans confronted the brutality of the war. Philosopher William James noted that the United States had destroyed "these islanders by the thousands, their villages and cities. . . . Could there be any more damning indictment," he asked, "of that whole bloated ideal termed 'modern civilization'?" (see American Voices, p. 637).

Constitutional issues also remained unresolved. The treaty, while guaranteeing freedom of religion to inhabitants of ceded Spanish territories, withheld any promise of citizenship. It was up to Congress to decide Filipinos' "civil rights and political status." In 1901, the Supreme Court upheld this provision in a set of decisions known as the Insular Cases. The Constitution, declared the court, did not automatically extend citizenship to people in acquired territories; Congress could decide. Puerto Rico, Guam, and the Philippines were thus marked as colonies, not future states. In accordance with a special commission set up by McKinley, the Jones Act of 1916 eventually committed the United States to Philippine independence but set no date. (The Philippines at last achieved independence in 1946.) Though the war's carnage had rubbed off some of the moralizing gloss, America's global aspirations remained intact.

▶ What economic and intellectual factors promoted U.S. imperialism in the late nineteenth century?

▶ What factors combined to precipitate the U.S. war with Spain in 1898, and then with Filipinos who resisted U.S. rule of their islands? What controversies at home did the war provoke?

AMERICAN VOICES

Making the Philippines Safe for Democracy
GENERAL ARTHUR MacARTHUR

General Arthur MacArthur was in on the action in the Philippines almost from the start.
He led one of the first units to arrive there in 1898 and in 1900 was reassigned back as
commander of the troops. After the insurrection had been put down, he appeared before a
Senate Committee to defend America's mission in the Philippines.

At the time I returned to Manila [May 1900] to assume the supreme command it seemed to me that . . . to doubt the wisdom of our [occupation] of the island was simply to doubt the stability of our own institutions . . . It seemed to me that our conception of right, justice, freedom, and personal liberty was the precious fruit of centuries of strife [and that] we must regard ourselves simply as the custodians of imperishable ideas held in trust for the general benefit of mankind. In other words, I felt that we had attained a moral and intellectual height from which we were bound to proclaim to all as the occasion arose the true message of humanity as embodied in the principles of our own institutions. . . .

To my mind the archipelago is a fertile soil upon which to plant republicanism. . . . We are planting the best traditions, the best characteristics of Americanism in such a way that they can never be removed from that soil. That in itself seems to me a most inspiring thought. . . .

Sen. Thomas Patterson: Do you mean that imperishable idea of which you speak is the right of self-government?

Gen. MacArthur: Precisely so; self-government regulated by law as I understand it in this Republic.

Sen. Patterson: Of course you do not mean self-government regulated by some foreign and superior power?

Gen. MacArthur: Well, that is a matter of evolution, Senator. We are putting these institutions there so they will evolve themselves just as here and everywhere else where freedom has flourished. . . .

Sen. Patterson: Do I understand your claim of right and duty to retain the Philippine Islands is based upon the proposition that they have come to us upon the basis of our morals, honorable dealing, and unassailable international integrity?

Gen. MacArthur: That proposition is not questioned by anybody in the world, excepting a few people in the United States. . . . We will be benefited, and the Filipino people will be benefited, and that is what I meant by the original proposition —

Sen. Patterson: Do you mean the Filipino people that are left alive?

Gen. MacArthur: I do not admit that there has been any unusual destruction of life in the Philippine Islands. . . . I doubt if any war — either international or civil, any war on earth — has been conducted with as much humanity, with as much careful consideration, with as much self-restraint, as have been the American operations in the Philippine Archipelago. . . .

SOURCE: Henry F. Graff, ed., *American Imperialism and the Philippine Insurrection* (Boston: Little, Brown, 1969), 137–139, 144–145.

A Power among Powers

No one appreciated America's emerging influence more than the man who, after the assassination of William McKinley, became president in 1901. Theodore Roosevelt was an avid student of world affairs who called on "all the civilized and orderly powers to insist on the proper policing of the world." He meant, in part, directing the affairs of "backward peoples." For Roosevelt, imperialism went hand in hand with domestic progressivism. He argued that a strong federal government, asserting itself both at home and abroad, would enhance economic stability and political order. Overseas, Roosevelt sought to arbitrate disputes and maintain a global balance of power, but also to assert U.S. interests.

The Open Door in Asia

American policymakers and business leaders had a burning interest in East Asian markets, but they were entering a crowded field. In the late 1890s, following Japan's victory in the Sino-Japanese War of 1894–1895, Japan, Russia, Germany, France, and Britain divided coastal China into spheres of influence. Fearful of being shut out, U.S. Secretary of State John Hay sent these powers a note in 1899, claiming the right of equal trade access — an "open door" — for all nations seeking to do business in China. The United States lacked leverage in Asia, and Hay's note elicited only noncommittal responses. But he chose to interpret this as acceptance of his position.

When a secret society of Chinese nationalists, known outside China as Boxers because of their pugnacious political stance, rebelled against foreign occupation in 1900, the United States sent 5,000 troops to join a multinational campaign to break the Boxers' siege of European government offices in Beijing. Hay took this opportunity to assert a second principle of the open door: China must be preserved as a "territorial and administrative entity." As long as the legal fiction of an independent China survived, American could claim equal access to that market.

In the same years, Europe and the United States were startled by an unexpected development: Japan emerged as East Asia's dominant power. A decade after its victory over China in the Sino-Japanese War of 1895, Japan responded to Russian rivalry for control of both the Korean Peninsula and Manchuria, in northern China, by attacking the czar's fleet at Russia's leased Chinese port. In a series of brilliant victories, the Japanese smashed the Russian forces. Westerners were shocked: For the first time, a European power had been defeated by a nation that was non-Western and non-white. Conveying both admiration and alarm, American cartoonists sketched Japan as a rising sun and as a martial artist knocking down the Russian giant. Roosevelt mediated a settlement in 1905.

Though he was contemptuous of other Asians, Roosevelt respected the Japanese, whom he called "a wonderful and civilized people." More important, he understood Japan's rising military might, and he aligned himself with the mighty. The United States approved Japan's "protectorate" over Korea in 1905 and, six years later, its seizure of full control. (Japan's victory over Russia prompted quite different responses from peoples subjected to European imperialism: It helped inspire nationalist uprisings in Iran, Turkey, and China, while in India and Indonesia, respectively, the British and Dutch faced new pressure from their colonial subjects for self-determination.) With Japan asserting harsh authority over Manchuria, the energetic Chinese diplomat Yüan Shih-k'ai tried to encourage the United States to intervene as a counterweight. But Roosevelt reviewed America's weak position in the Pacific and declined. He conceded that Japan had "a paramount interest in what surrounds the Yellow Sea." In 1908, the United States and Japan signed the Root-Takahira Agreement, confirming principles of free oceanic commerce and recognizing Japan's authority over Manchuria.

William Howard Taft entered the White House in 1909 convinced that the United States had been short-changed in Asia. He pressed for a larger role for American investors, especially in Chinese railroad construction. Eager to promote U.S. business interests abroad, he hoped that infusions of American capital would offset Japanese power. When the Chinese Revolution of 1911 toppled the Manchu dynasty, Taft supported the victorious Nationalists, who wanted to modernize their country and liberate it from Japanese domination. The United States had entangled itself in China and entered a long-term rivalry with Japan for power in the Pacific, a competition that would culminate thirty years later in World War II.

The United States in the Caribbean

Closer to home, European powers conceded Roosevelt's argument that the United States had a "paramount interest" in the Caribbean. In 1900, the United States consulted with Britain on building a canal across Central America. Britain — facing a rising military challenge from Germany, and entangled in a bloody war against Afrikaners in South Africa — welcomed a closer alliance with the United States and proved willing to give up some of its Latin American claims. In the Hay-Pauncefote Treaty (1901), Britain recognized the United States' sole right to build and fortify a Central American canal. Two years later, Britain helped resolve the last remaining U.S.-Canadian border disputes. No formal alliance emerged, but Anglo-American friendship was so firm that the British Admiralty designed its war plans on the assumption that America was "a kindred state." Roosevelt heartily agreed.

In facing rivals, Roosevelt famously argued that the United States should "speak softly and carry a big stick." By "big stick" he meant most of all naval power, and rapid access to two oceans required a canal. Freed by Britain's surrender of canal rights, Roosevelt persuaded Congress to authorize $10 million, plus future payments of $250,000 per year, to purchase from Colombia a six-mile strip of land across Panama, a Colombian province. Furious when Colombia rejected this proposal, Roosevelt contemplated outright seizure of Panama but settled on a more roundabout solution. Panamanians, long separated from Colombia by miles of remote jungle, chafed under Colombian rule. The United States lent covert assistance to an independence movement, triggering a bloodless revolution. On November 6, 1903, the United States recognized the new nation of Panama; two weeks later, it obtained a perpetually renewable lease on a canal zone. Roosevelt never regretted the venture, though in 1922 the United States paid Colombia $25 million as a kind of conscience money. To build the canal, the U.S. Army Corps of Engineers hired thousands of laborers, who cleared vast swamps, excavated 240 million cubic yards of earth, and constructed a series of immense locks. The project, a great engineering feat, took eight years. Opened in 1914, the Panama Canal gave the United States a commanding position in the Western Hemisphere.

Roosevelt was already working in other ways to strengthen U.S. control of the Caribbean. As a condition for its withdrawal from Cuba in 1902, for example, the United

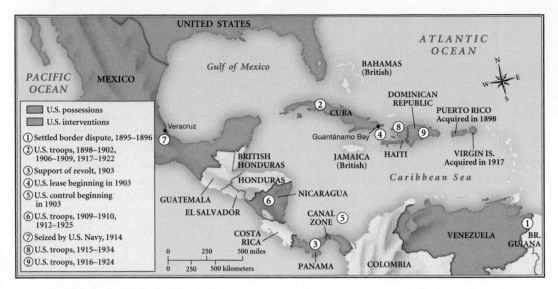

MAP 21.1 Policeman of the Caribbean

After the War of 1898, the United States vigorously asserted its interest in the affairs of its neighbors to the south. As the record of interventions shows, the United States truly became the "policeman" of the Caribbean.

States forced the newly independent island nation to accept a proviso in its constitution called the Platt Amendment. This blocked Cuba from making a treaty with any country except the United States and gave the United States the right to intervene in Cuban affairs if it saw fit. Cuba also granted the United States a lease on Guantánamo Bay (still in effect), where the U.S. Navy built a large base. It was a bitter pill for Cubans, who found that their hard-fought independence was stillborn.

Claiming that instability invited European intervention, Roosevelt announced in 1904 that the United States would police all parts of the Caribbean (Map 21.1). This so-called Roosevelt Corollary to the Monroe Doctrine actually turned that doctrine upside down: Instead of guaranteeing that the United States would protect its Latin American neighbors from European powers and help preserve their independence, it asserted the United States' unrestricted right to regulate Caribbean affairs. The Roosevelt Corollary was not a treaty; it was a unilateral declaration sanctioned only by America's military and economic might. Citing the corollary, the United States intervened regularly in Caribbean states over the next three decades.

Wilson and Mexico

Democratic president Woodrow Wilson criticized his predecessors' foreign policy decisions. In a speech soon after he took office in 1913, Wilson promised that the United States would "never again seek one additional foot of territory by conquest," but instead would advance "human rights, national integrity, and opportunity" abroad. This stance appealed to anti-imperialists in the Democratic base, including longtime supporters of William Jennings Bryan. But the new president soon showed that, when American interests called for it, his actions were not so different from those of Roosevelt and Taft.

Since the 1870s, Mexican dictator Porfirio Díaz had created a friendly climate for American investors who purchased Mexican railroads, plantations, mines, and much-coveted oil fields. By the early 1900s, however, Díaz feared the extraordinary power of these economic interests and began to nationalize — reclaim — key resources. Powerful American investors who faced the loss of their Mexican holdings began to back Francisco Madero, an advocate of constitutional government who was friendly to U.S. interests. In 1911, Madero forced Díaz to resign and proclaimed himself president. The revolution prompted thousands of poor Mexicans to mobilize rural armies and demand more radical change. At the same time, Madero's position was weak, and several strongmen sought to overthrow him. In February 1913, leading general Victoriano Huerta deposed and murdered Madero.

The Wilson administration became increasingly fearful that the unrest in Mexico threatened U.S. interests. Over the strong protests of Venustiano Carranza, the Mexican leader whom Wilson most favored, the United States threw its own forces into the emerging Mexican Revolution. On the pretext of a minor insult to the U.S. Navy, Wilson ordered U.S. occupation of the port of Veracruz on April 21, 1914, at the cost of 19 American and 126 Mexican lives. The Huerta regime crumbled. Carranza's forces, after nearly engaging the Americans themselves, entered Mexico City in triumph in August 1914. But despite Wilson's support of Carranza, his heavy-handed interference caused lasting mistrust.

Carranza's victory did not subdue all revolutionary activity in Mexico. In 1916, General Pancho Villa stirred up trouble on the U.S.-Mexico border, killing sixteen American civilians and raiding the town of Columbus, New Mexico. Wilson sent 11,000 troops under General John J. Pershing across the border after Villa. Soon Pershing's force resembled an army of occupation. Mexican public opinion demanded withdrawal, and armed clashes broke out between U.S. and Mexican troops. At the brink of war, both governments backed off, and U.S. forces withdrew. The following year, Carranza's government finally received official recognition from Washington. But U.S. policymakers had shown their intention to police not only the Caribbean and Central America but also Mexico when they deemed it necessary. The Caribbean Sea, as one commentator quipped, had become an "American lake."

▶ How did Japan challenge the influence of European powers and the United States in Asia? How did U.S. policymakers respond?

▶ How did U.S. policymakers justify their policies in the Caribbean? What influence did the United States assert there? In Mexico?

The United States in World War I

While competing imperial claims fostered conflicts around the globe, a war of unprecedented scale was brewing in Europe. Germany, a rising power, had humiliated France in the Franco-Prussian War of 1870; its subsequent military buildup terrified its neighbors.

To the east, the disintegrating Ottoman Empire was losing its grip on the Balkans, while European powers jockeyed to claim and defend their colonies in Africa, the Middle East, and Asia. Out of these conflicts, two rival power blocs emerged: the Triple Alliance (Germany, Austria-Hungary, and Italy) and the Triple Entente (Britain, France, and Russia). Within each alliance, national governments pursued their own interests but were bound to one another by both public and secret treaties.

Americans had no obvious stake in these developments. In 1905, when Germany suddenly challenged French control of Morocco, Theodore Roosevelt arranged an international conference to defuse the crisis. Germany got a few concessions, but France — with British backing — retained control of Morocco. At the time, the conference seemed a diplomatic triumph. One U.S. official boasted that America had kept peace by "the power of our detachment." Such optimism proved wildly off the mark. A war was about to begin that would cause untold suffering and transform global power relations — and the United States would not remain detached.

The Great War Begins, 1914–1917

The spark that ignited World War I came in the Balkans, where Austria-Hungary and Russia competed for control. Austria's 1908 seizure of the Ottoman provinces of Bosnia and Herzegovina, with their substantial Slavic populations, angered Russia and its ally, the independent Slavic state of Serbia. In response, Serbian revolutionaries recruited Bosnian Slavs, including university student Gavrilo Princip, to resist Austrian rule. In June 1914, in the city of Sarajevo, Princip assassinated Archduke Franz Ferdinand, heir to the Austro-Hungarian throne.

Like dominos falling, the system of European alliances rapidly pushed all the powers into war. Austria-Hungary blamed Serbia for the assassination and declared war on July 28. Russia, tied by secret treaty to Serbia, mobilized its armies against Austria-Hungary. Russia's move prompted Germany to declare war on Russia and its ally France. As a preparation for attacking France, Germany launched a brutal invasion of the neutral country of Belgium, which caused Great Britain to declare war on Germany. By August 4, most of Europe was at war. The Allies — Great Britain, France, and Russia — confronted the Central Powers of Germany and Austria-Hungary, joined in November by the Ottoman Empire.

Two major war zones emerged. Germany battled the British and French on the Western Front. Assisted by Austrians and Hungarians, Germany also fought Russia on the Eastern Front. Because most of the warring nations held colonial empires, the conflict spread to the Middle East, Africa, and China, throwing the future of those areas into question. Hoping to secure valuable colonies, Italy and Japan soon joined the Allied side, while Bulgaria linked up with the Central Powers.

The so-called Great War wreaked terrible devastation. New technology, some of it devised in the United States, made warfare deadlier than ever before. Every soldier carried a long-range, high-velocity rifle that could hit a target at 1,000 yards — a vast technical advancement over the 300-yard range of the rifles used in the U.S. Civil War. The machine gun was even more deadly. Its American-born inventor, Hiram Maxim, had moved to Great Britain in the 1880s to follow a friend's advice: "If you want to make your fortune, invent something which will allow those fool Europeans to kill each other more quickly."

These technological developments gave a tremendous advantage to soldiers in defensive positions. Once the German advance ran into French fortifications, it stalled. For four bloody years, millions of soldiers fought a **war of attrition** in heavily fortified trenches that cut across a narrow swath of Belgium and northeastern France. Soldiers hunkered in wet trenches for months on end. One side and then the other mounted attacks across the no-man's-land that lay between them, only to be mangled by barbed wire or mowed down by machine guns. Struggling to break the stalemate, Germany launched an attack at the Belgian city of Ypres in April 1915 that introduced a new nightmare: poison gas. As the Germans tried to break through French lines at Verdun between February and December 1916, they suffered 450,000 casualties. The French fared even worse, with 550,000 dead or wounded soldiers. It was all to no avail. From 1914 to 1918, the Western Front barely moved.

From Neutrality to War

At the outbreak of the Great War, President Woodrow Wilson called on Americans to be "neutral in fact as well as in name, impartial in thought as well as in action." If he kept the United States out of the conflict, Wilson reasoned, he could influence the postwar settlement, much as President Theodore Roosevelt had helped arbitrate the Russo-Japanese War in 1905. Even if Wilson had wanted to unite Americans behind the Allies, that would have been nearly impossible in 1914. Many Irish Americans viewed Britain as an enemy, resenting its continued occupation of Ireland. Millions of German Americans maintained ties to their homeland. Progressive-minded Republicans such as Senator Robert La Follette of Wisconsin vehemently opposed taking sides in a European fight, as did Socialists who condemned the war as a conflict among greedy capitalist empires. Two giants of American industry, Andrew Carnegie and Henry Ford, opposed the war. In December 1915, Ford sent a hundred men and women to Europe on a "peace ship" to urge an end to the conflict. "It would be folly," declared the *New York Sun*, "for the country to sacrifice itself to . . . the clash of ancient hatreds which is urging the Old World to destruction."

The Struggle to Remain Neutral | The United States, wishing to trade with all the warring nations, might have remained neutral if Britain had not held commanding power at sea. In September 1914, the British imposed a naval blockade on the Central Powers to cut off vital supplies of food and military equipment. The Wilson administration protested this infringement of the rights of neutral carriers but did not take action. Profit was one reason: A spectacular increase in U.S. trade with the Allies more than made up for lost commerce with Germany and Austria. Trade with Britain and France grew fourfold over the next two years, from $824 million to $3.2 billion in 1916; moreover, by 1917, U.S. banks had lent the Allies $2.5 billion. In contrast, American trade and loans to Germany stood then at a mere $56 million. This imbalance undercut U.S. neutrality, tying America's economic health to Allied victory. If Germany won and Britain and France defaulted on their debts, American companies would suffer catastrophic losses.

To challenge the British navy, Germany launched a devastating new weapon, the U-boat (short for *Unterseeboot*, "undersea boat," or submarine). In April 1915, the German embassy in Washington issued a warning that all ships flying the flags of Britain or its allies were liable to destruction. A few weeks later, a U-boat torpedoed the British luxury liner *Lusitania* off the coast of Ireland, killing 1,198 people, including 128 Americans. The attack on the passenger ship (which was later revealed to have been carrying munitions) incensed Americans. President Wilson sent strongly worded protests to Germany, but tensions had subsided by September, when Germany announced that U-boats would no longer attack passenger vessels without warning. Nonetheless, the *Lusitania* crisis prompted Wilson to reconsider his options. He quietly tried to mediate an end to the European conflict. Finding neither side seriously interested in peace, Wilson endorsed a $1 billion buildup of the U.S. Army and Navy in the fall of 1915.

American public opinion still ran strongly against entering the war, a fact that shaped the election of 1916. The reunited Republican Party rejected the belligerently prowar Theodore Roosevelt in favor of Supreme Court justice Charles Evans Hughes, a progressive former governor of New York. Democrats renominated Wilson, who campaigned on his domestic record and as the president who "kept us out of war." Wilson eked out a narrow victory; winning California by a mere 4,000 votes, he secured a slim majority in the electoral college.

America Enters the War | Despite Wilson's campaign slogan, events pushed him toward war. On February 1, 1917, Germany resumed unrestricted submarine warfare, a decision dictated by the impasse on the Western Front. In response, Wilson broke off diplomatic relations with Germany. A few weeks later, newspapers published an intercepted dispatch from the German foreign secretary, Arthur Zimmermann, to his minister in Mexico City. The note urged Mexico to join the Central Powers; Zimmermann promised that if the United States entered the war, Germany would help Mexico recover "the lost territory of Texas, New Mexico, and Arizona." With Pancho Villa's border raids still fresh in the public mind, this threat jolted American opinion. Meanwhile, German U-boats attacked American ships without warning, sinking three on March 18 alone.

On April 2, 1917, Wilson asked Congress for a declaration of war. He argued that Germany had trampled on American rights and imperiled its trade and citizens' lives. "We desire no conquest, no dominion," Wilson declared, "no material compensation for the sacrifices we shall freely make." Rather, reflecting his Protestant zeal and progressive idealism, Wilson promised that American involvement would make the world "safe for democracy." On April 6, the United States declared war on Germany. Reflecting the nation's divided views, the vote was far from unanimous. Six senators and fifty members of the House voted against entry, including Representative Jeannette Rankin of Montana, the first woman elected to Congress. "You can no more win a war than you can win an earthquake," Rankin said. "I want to stand by my country, but I cannot vote for war."

"Over There"

To Americans, Europe seemed a great distance away — "over there," in the lyrics of a popular song by George M. Cohan. Many assumed that the United States would simply provide munitions and economic aid. "Good Lord," exclaimed one U.S. senator to a Wilson administration official. "You're not going to send soldiers over there, are you?" But when General John J. Pershing asked how the United States could best support the Allies, the French commander put it bluntly: "Men, men, and more men."

In 1917, the U.S. Army numbered fewer than 200,000 soldiers. To field a fighting force, Congress instituted a military draft in May 1917. In contrast to the Civil War, when resistance was common, conscription went smoothly, partly because local, civilian-run draft boards played a central role in the new system. Still, draft registration demonstrated government's increasing power over ordinary citizens. On a single day — June 5, 1917 — more than 9.5 million men between the ages of twenty-one and thirty registered at their local voting precincts for possible military service.

President Wilson chose General Pershing to head the American Expeditionary Force (AEF), which had to be trained, outfitted, and carried across the submarine-infested Atlantic. Thus, the nation's first significant contribution to the war effort was safer shipping. When the United States entered the war, German U-boats were sinking 900,000 tons of Allied ships each month. By sending merchant and troop ships in armed convoys, the U.S. Navy cut that monthly rate to 400,000 tons by the end of 1917. With trench warfare grinding on, Allied commanders pleaded for American soldiers to fill their depleted units, but Pershing waited until the AEF reached full strength. As late as May 1918, the brunt of the fighting fell to the French and British.

The Allies' burden increased when the Eastern Front collapsed following the Bolshevik (Communist) Revolution in Russia in November 1917. To consolidate its power at home, the new Bolshevik government, led by Vladimir Ilych Lenin, sought peace with the Central Powers. In the Treaty of Brest-Litovsk, signed on March 3, 1918, Russia surrendered its sovereignty over vast parts of central Europe — including Russian Poland, Ukraine, and the Baltic provinces — in exchange for peace. Released from the fight against Germany, the Bolsheviks turned their attention to struggles against their domestic enemies, including supporters of the ousted tsar. Japan and several Allied countries, including the United States, sent troops into Russian ports to fight the Bolsheviks. But after a four-year civil war, Lenin's forces established full control over Russia and reclaimed Ukraine, the Caucasus, and other former Russian possessions. In 1922, the Communists created the Union of Soviet Socialist Republics (USSR), or Soviet Union.

Peace with Russia freed Germany to launch a major offensive on the Western Front. By May 1918, German troops advanced to within 50 miles of Paris. As Allied leaders called desperately for U.S. troops, Pershing at last committed about 60,000 men to help the French in the battles of Château-Thierry and Belleau Wood. With American soldiers arriving in massive numbers, Allied forces brought the German offensive to a halt in July; by September, they had forced a German retreat. Then Pershing pitted more than 1 million American soldiers against an outnumbered and exhausted German army in the Argonne forest. By early November, this attack had broken the German defense of a crucial rail hub at Sedan. The cost was high: 26,000 Americans killed and 95,000 wounded (Map 21.2). But the flood of American troops and supplies turned the tide. Recognizing the inevitability of defeat and facing popular uprisings at home, the German government signed an armistice on November 11, 1918. The Great War was over.

The American Fighting Force By the end of World War I, almost 4 million American men — popularly known as "doughboys" — wore U.S. uniforms, as did several thousand female nurses. The recruits reflected America's heterogeneity: One-fifth had been born outside the United States, and soldiers spoke forty-nine different languages. Though ethnic diversity worried some observers, most predicted that military service would promote immigrants' Americanization.

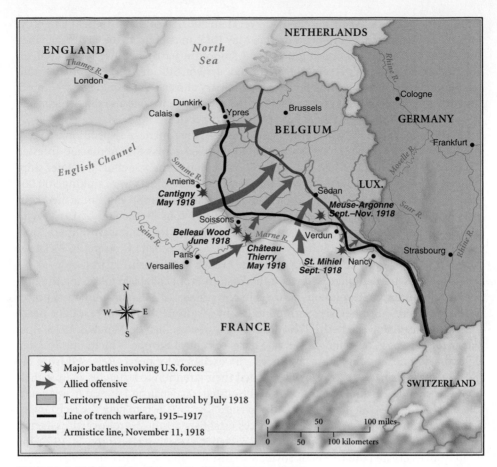

MAP 21.2 U.S. Participation on the Western Front, 1918

When American troops reached the European front in significant numbers in 1918, the Allied and Central Powers had been fighting a deadly war of attrition for almost four years. The influx of American troops and supplies helped to break the stalemate. Successful offensive maneuvers by the American Expeditionary Force included those at Belleau Wood and Château-Thierry and the Meuse-Argonne campaign.

More than 400,000 African American men enlisted, accounting for 13 percent of the armed forces. Their wartime experiences were often grim. They served in segregated units and were given the most menial tasks. Racial discrimination disrupted military efficiency and erupted in violence at several camps. The worst incident occurred in August 1917, when, after suffering a string of racial attacks, black members of the Twenty-fourth Infantry's Third Battalion rioted in Houston, killing 15 white civilians and police officers. The army tried 118 of the soldiers in military courts for mutiny and riot, hanged 19, and sentenced 63 to life in prison (see Voices from Abroad, p. 646).

Unlike African Americans, Native Americans served in integrated combat units. Racial stereotypes about Native Americans' prowess as warriors enhanced their military reputations, but it also prompted officers to assign them hazardous duties as

German Propaganda and Black Soldiers

Both sides distributed propaganda tracts, such as this German appeal to "Colored Soldiers." According to Charles Williams, who probed the lives of black recruits, the soldiers' reaction was, "We know what they say is true, but don't worry; we're not going over." The memoir of Bruce Wright, an African American volunteer, reveals both the truth of the German claims and the loyalty and hopes of the black soldiers.

To the Colored Soldiers of the U.S. Army,
Hello, boys, what are you doing over there? Fighting the Germans? Why? Have they ever done you any harm? Of course, some white folks and the lying English-American papers told you that the Germans ought to be wiped out for the sake of humanity and democracy. What is democracy? Personal freedom, all citizens enjoying the same rights socially and before the law. Do you enjoy the same rights as the white people do in America, the land of freedom and democracy? Or aren't you rather rated over there as second class citizens? Can you get into a restaurant where white people dine . . . or can you even ride in the South in the same street car with the white people? And how about the law? Is lynching and the most horrible cruelties connected therewith a lawful proceeding in a democratic country? . . .

Why, then, fight the Germans? . . . Come over to the German lines. You will find friends who will help you along.

I Bruce G. Wright joined Company L. of the sixth regiment Massachusetts National Guard June 15, 1917, at Camp Darling, Framingham Mass. . . . In November we broke camp to leave for the south. Arrived after a two days ride in regular pulman cars at Charlotte N.C. Camp Greene. Were the first colored soldiers seen south of the Mason & Dixon line in full equipment since 1865. The colored people used us fine and everything

went well for an *hour* or so. One of the crackers insulted one of our boys and the war began right then for us. We got plenty of practice for the "Boche" by fighting with the dirty crackers. . . . That night there was plenty of disturbance in the town [of] Charlotte and several crackers were bumped off. We lost no men but had some shot up so we had to carry them back to camp. Two days later we were moved out of Charlotte farther north. . . .

The dawn of that first day in the Argonne forest we got our very first look onto "No Mans Land" that we had heard & read so much about. Masses of barbed wire, skeletons of men, tin cans, rotted clothes and an awful smell greeted our eyes & noses. . . . lived in that living hell until late in August. . . . Twice before had the allies tried to take this sector known as the Champagne but were repulsed in each attack. But now [in September 1918] it was our lot and even though we heard of our own race of people being lynched every day back in the United States. We all wanted to do our best in hope that sooner it would be made easier for those at home. We kept saying to our selves we're fighting for "democracy."

SOURCES: Charles H. Williams, *Sidelights on Negro Soldiers* (Boston: B. J. Brimmer Co., 1923), 70–71; Tracey Lovette Spencer and James E. Spencer Jr., eds., "World War I As I Saw It," *Massachusetts Historical Review*, 9 (2007), 141, 144, 156–158.

Fighting the Flu

Influenza traversed the globe in 1918–1919, becoming a pandemic that killed as many as 50 million people. According to recent research, the flu began as a virus native to wild birds and then mutated into a form that passed easily from one human to another. In the United States, one-fifth of the population was infected and more than 500,000 civilians died — ten times the number of American soldiers who died in combat during World War I. In the United States, the flu virus spread with frightening speed, and the epidemic strained the resources of a public health system already fully mobilized for the war effort. In October 1918 alone, 200,000 Americans died. This photo shows doctors, army officers, and reporters who donned surgical masks and gowns before touring hospitals that treated influenza patients. ©Bettman/Corbis.

scouts, messengers, and snipers. Approximately 13,000, or 25 percent, of the United States' adult male Native American population served during the war. Roughly 5 percent of these soldiers died, compared to 2 percent for the military as a whole.

About two-thirds of American soldiers in France saw military action, but most escaped the horrors of sustained trench warfare. Still, during the brief period of American participation, 53,000 servicemen died in action. Another 63,000 died from disease, mainly the devastating influenza pandemic that began early in 1918 and, over the next two years, killed 50 million people worldwide. The nation's military deaths, though substantial, were only a tenth as many as those of the 500,000 American civilians who died of this terrible epidemic — not to mention the staggering 8 million soldiers lost by the Allies and Central Powers.

"Remember Your First Thrill of American Liberty"
Once the United States entered the Great War, government officials were eager to enlist all Americans in the battle against the Central Powers. They carefully crafted patriotic advertising campaigns that urged Americans to buy bonds, conserve food, enlist in the military, and join in the war effort in countless other ways. This poster targeted recent immigrants to the United States, reminding them that "American Liberty" carried with it the "Duty" to buy war bonds. Library of Congress.

War on the Home Front

In the United States, opponents of the war were in the minority. Most progressives hoped that Wilson's ideals, along with wartime demands for national unity, would renew Americans' attention to reform. Supporting the Allies did trigger an economic boom that benefited farmers and working people, and the federal government built an array of new agencies and programs. But the results bitterly disappointed progressives. Rather than enhancing democracy, World War I chilled the political climate as government agencies tried to enforce "100 percent loyalty."

Mobilizing the Economy American businesses made big bucks from World War I. As grain, weapons, and manufactured goods flowed to Britain and France, the United States became a creditor nation. Moreover, as the war drained British financial reserves, U.S. banks provided capital for investments around the globe. At the same time, government powers expanded, with new federal agencies overseeing almost every part of the economy.

The War Industries Board (WIB), established in July 1917, directed military production. After a fumbling start that showed the limits of voluntarism, the Wilson administration reorganized the board and placed Bernard Baruch, a Wall Street financier, at its head. Baruch was a superb administrator. Under his direction, the WIB allocated scarce resources among industries, ordered factories to convert to war production, set prices, and standardized procedures. Although he could compel compliance, Baruch preferred to win voluntary cooperation from industry. A man of immense charm, he usually succeeded — helped by the lucrative military contracts at his disposal. Despite higher taxes, corporate profits soared, as military production sustained a boom that continued until 1920.

Some federal agencies took dramatic measures. The Fuel Administration, for example, introduced daylight saving time to conserve coal and oil. The War Finance Corporation lent $1 billion to companies that converted to war production. In December 1917, the Railroad Administration seized control of the nation's chaotic hodgepodge of private railroads, seeking to facilitate rapid movement of troops and equipment — an experiment that had, at best, mixed results. To reassure railroads' stock- and bond-holders, the Railroad Administration guaranteed them a "standard return" and promised to return railroads to private control at war's end.

Perhaps the most successful wartime agency was the Food Administration, created in August 1917 and led by engineer Herbert Hoover. With the slogan "Food will win the war," Hoover convinced farmers to almost double their acreage of grain. This allowed a threefold rise in food exports to Europe. Among citizens, the Food Administration mobilized a "spirit of self-denial and self-sacrifice" rather than mandatory rationing. Female volunteers went from door to door to persuade housekeepers to observe "Wheatless" Mondays and "Porkless" Thursdays. Hoover, a Republican, emerged from the war as one of the nation's most admired public figures.

Promoting National Unity | During the war, suppressing dissent became a near obsession for President Wilson. In April 1917, Wilson formed the Committee on Public Information (CPI), a government propaganda agency headed by journalist George Creel. Professing lofty goals — educating citizens about democracy, assimilating immigrants, and ending the isolation of rural life — the committee set out to mold Americans into "one white-hot mass" of war patriotism. The CPI touched the lives of practically every civilian. It distributed seventy-five million pieces of literature and enlisted thousands of volunteers — "Four Minute Men" — to deliver short prowar speeches at movie theaters.

The CPI urged recent immigrants and long-established ethnic groups to become "One Hundred Percent Americans." German Americans bore the brunt of this campaign. Concert halls banned music by Beethoven, Bach, and other German composers. School districts shut down German-language programs. Hamburgers were renamed "liberty sandwiches." With posters exhorting citizens to root out German spies, a spirit of conformity pervaded the home front. A quasi-vigilante group, the American Protective League, mobilized about 250,000 self-appointed "agents," furnished them with badges issued by the Justice Department, and trained them to spy on neighbors and coworkers. In 1918, members of the league led violent raids against draft evaders and peace activists. Government propaganda helped fuel public mistrust of "hyphenated Americans" — a new term embracing Irish, Polish, Italian, and Jewish Americans — and helped rouse a nativist hysteria that would linger in the 1920s.

During the war, Congress passed two new laws to curb dissent. The Espionage Act of 1917 imposed stiff penalties for antiwar activities. The Sedition Act of 1918 prohibited any words or behavior that might "incite, provoke, or encourage resistance to the United States, or promote the cause of its enemies." Because these acts defined treason and sedition loosely, they led to the conviction of more than a thousand people. The Justice Department prosecuted members of the Industrial Workers of the World (IWW), whose opposition to militarism threatened to disrupt war production of lumber and copper. When a Quaker pacifist teacher in New York City refused to teach a prowar curriculum, she was fired for "conduct unbecoming a teacher." Socialist Party leader Eugene V. Debs was sentenced to ten years in jail for arguing that wealthy capitalists had started the conflict but forced workers to fight the battles.

Federal courts mostly supported the acts. In *Schenck v. United States* (1919), the Supreme Court upheld the conviction of a Socialist who was jailed for circulating pamphlets that urged army draftees to resist induction. The justices followed this with a similar decision in *Abrams v. United States* (1919), stating that authorities could prosecute speech that they believed to pose "a clear and present danger to the safety of the country." In an important dissent, however, Justices Oliver Wendell Holmes Jr. and Louis Brandeis objected to the *Abrams* decision. Though Holmes denied that he was changing his position on "clear and present danger," his questions about the definition of that phrase helped launch twentieth-century legal battles over free speech and civil liberties.

Great Migrations | World War I created new economic opportunities at home. Jobs in war industries drew thousands of people to the cities, including immigrants. For the first time, with so many men in uniform, jobs in heavy industry opened to African Americans. Well before the war, some southern blacks had moved to the North; wartime jobs accelerated the pace. During World War I, more than 400,000 African Americans moved to such cities as St. Louis, Chicago, New York, and Detroit, in what became known as the Great Migration. The rewards were great, and taking war jobs could be a source of patriotic pride. "If it hadn't been for the negro at that time," a Carnegie Steel manager later recalled, "we could hardly have carried on our operations."

Blacks in the North encountered considerable discrimination in jobs, housing, and education. But in the first flush of opportunity, most celebrated their escape from the repressive racism and low pay of the South. "It is a matter of a dollar with me and I feel that God made the path and I am walking therein," one woman reported to her sister back home. "Tell your husband work is plentiful here." "I just begin to feel like a man," wrote another migrant to a friend in Mississippi. "My children are going to the same school with the whites. . . . Will vote the next election and there isnt any 'yes sir' and 'no sir' — its all yes and no and Sam and Bill."

Wartime labor shortages also prompted Mexican Americans in California, Texas, New Mexico, and Arizona to leave farm labor for industrial jobs in rapidly growing southwestern cities. At the same time, continuing political instability in Mexico, combined with increased demand for farm workers in the United States, encouraged more Mexicans to move across the border. Between 1917 and 1920, at least 100,000 Mexicans entered the United States, and despite discrimination, large numbers stayed. If asked why, many might have echoed the words of an African American man who left New Orleans for Chicago: They were going "north for a better chance."

Jacob Lawrence: The Labor Agent in the South
This evocative painting shows how many African American workers found a route to opportunity: Northern manufacturers, facing severe wartime labor shortages, sent agents to the South to recruit workers. Agents often arranged loans to pay for train fare and other travel expenses; once laborers were settled and employed in the North, they repaid the loans from their wages. Here, a line of men waits for the agent to record their names in his open ledger. This panel, from the famous "Great Migration" series by African American painter Jacob Lawrence, was created in 1940. The bare tree in the background suggests the barrenness of economic prospects for impoverished rural blacks in the South; it also hints at the threat of lynching and racial violence. Digital Image © The Museum of Modern Art / Licensed by SCALA / Art Resource, NY.

Women were the largest group to take advantage of wartime employment opportunities. About 1 million women joined the paid labor force for the first time, while another 8 million gave up low-wage service jobs for higher-paying industrial work. Americans soon got used to the sight of female streetcar conductors, train engineers, and defense workers. Though most people expected these jobs to return to men in peacetime, the war created a new comfort level with women's work outside the home.

Women's Voting Rights

One of World War I's enduring legacies was woman suffrage. When the United States entered the war, the National American Woman Suffrage Association (NAWSA) threw the support of its 2 million members behind Wilson. Its president, Carrie Chapman Catt, declared that women had to prove their patriotism to advance the cause of suffrage. NAWSA members in thousands of communities promoted food conservation, aided war workers, and distributed emergency relief through organizations such as the Red Cross.

Alice Paul and the National Woman's Party (NWP) took a more confrontational approach. Paul was a Quaker who had worked in the settlement movement and earned a PhD in political science. As a lobbyist for NAWSA, Paul found her cause dismissed by congressmen, and in 1916 she founded the NWP. Inspired by militant British suffragists, the party began picketing the White House in July 1917. Standing as "Silent Sentinels" with suffrage banners, Paul and other NWP activists faced arrest for obstructing traffic and were sentenced to seven months in jail. They protested by going on a hunger strike, which prison authorities met with forced feeding. Public shock at the women's treatment put pressure on Wilson and drew attention to the suffrage cause.

Impressed by NAWSA's patriotism and worried by the NWP's militancy, the anti-suffrage Wilson reversed his position. In January 1918, he urged support for woman suffrage as a "war measure." The constitutional amendment quickly passed the House of Representatives; it took eighteen months to get through the Senate and another year to win ratification by the states. On August 26, 1920, Tennessee gave the Nineteenth Amendment the last vote it needed, becoming the only ex-Confederate state to ratify it. Seventy-two years after the women's rights convention at Seneca Falls, American women finally had full voting rights.

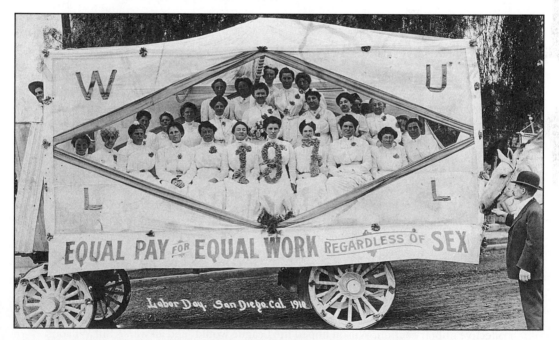

Wagon Decorated for the Labor Day Parade, San Diego, California, 1910
As the woman suffrage movement grew stronger in the years before and during World War I, working-class women played increasingly prominent and visible roles in its leadership. This Labor Day parade float, created by the Women's Union Label League of San Diego, showed that activists championed equal pay for women in the workplace as well as women's voting rights. "Union Label Leagues" urged middle-class shoppers to purchase only clothing with a union label, certifying that the item had been manufactured under safe conditions and the workers who made it had received a fair wage. San Diego Historical Society, Title Insurance Trust Collection.

In explaining why suffragists achieved victory, historians have debated the relative effectiveness of Catt's patriotic strategy and Paul's militant protests. Both played a role in persuading Wilson and Congress to act, but neither might have worked without the extraordinary impact of the Great War. Across the globe, before 1914, the only places where women had full suffrage were New Zealand, Australia, Finland, and Norway. After World War I, many nations moved to enfranchise women. The new Soviet Union acted first, in 1917, with Great Britain and Canada following in 1918; by 1920, the measure had passed in Germany, Austria, Poland, Czechoslovakia, and Hungary as well as the United States. Major exceptions were France and Italy, where women did not gain voting rights until after World War II, and Switzerland, which held out until 1971. Thus, while World War I introduced modern horrors on the battlefield — machine guns and poison gas — it brought more positive forms of modernization at home: new economic opportunities, urban growth, and women's political participation.

▶ When World War I broke out in Europe, what role did the United States hope to play as a neutral power? What factors undercut that neutrality?

▶ How did U.S. involvement affect the course of the war? In what ways did the war transform the economy, society, and politics of the United States?

The Treaty of Versailles

In January 1917, the idealistic Wilson had proposed "peace without victory," arguing that only "peace among equals" could last. Having achieved victory at an incredible price, Britain and France showed absolutely no interest in such a plan. But the immense devastation wrought by the war created popular pressure for an outcome that was just and enduring. Wilson scored a diplomatic victory at the Paris Peace Conference, held at Versailles in January 1919, when the Allies chose to base the negotiations on his Fourteen Points — a blueprint for peace that he had first presented a year earlier in a speech to the U.S. Congress.

Wilson's Fourteen Points embodied one important strand in American progressivism. They called for open diplomacy; "absolute freedom of navigation upon the seas"; arms reduction; removal of trade barriers; and national self-determination for peoples in the Austro-Hungarian, Russian, and German empires. Essential to Wilson's vision was the founding of an international regulatory body, eventually called the League of Nations, that would guarantee "independence and territorial integrity to great and small States alike." The League would mediate disputes, supervise arms reduction, and — according to the crucial Article X of its covenant — curb aggressor nations through collective military action. Wilson hoped the League would "end all wars." But Wilson's idealism had marked limitations — and at the negotiating table, his proposals met harsh realities.

The Fate of Wilson's Ideas

Though the conference at Versailles included ten thousand representatives from around the globe, leaders of France, Britain, and the United States dominated the proceedings.

When the Japanese delegation proposed a declaration that all races be treated equally, the Allies rejected it. Similarly, they ignored a global Pan-African Congress, organized by W. E. B. Du Bois and other black leaders, and they snubbed Arab representatives — even those who had been military allies during the war. Distrustful of the new Communist regime in Russia, the Allies deliberately excluded its representatives. Even Italy's prime minister, Vittorio Orlando — at first included among the influential "Big Four" — eventually withdrew from the conference, aggrieved at the way British and French leaders had marginalized him. Meanwhile, the Allies entirely barred Germany from the conference, choosing to impose conditions on their defeated foe. For Wilson's proposed "peace among equals," it was not a hopeful start.

European Allied leaders — most notably Prime Minister David Lloyd George of Great Britain and Premier Georges Clemenceau of France — imposed harsh punishments on Germany. Unbeknownst to the world at the time, Britain and France had already made secret agreements to divide up Germany's African colonies and take them as spoils of war. At Versailles, they also forced the defeated nation to pay $33 billion in reparations and to give up coal supplies, merchant ships, valuable patents, and even part of its territory along the French border. These requirements caused keen resentment and economic hardship in Germany. Over the following two decades they helped lead to World War II.

Given these conditions, it is a tribute to Wilson that he influenced the Treaty of Versailles as much as he did. He intervened repeatedly to soften harsh demands against Germany. Moreover, in accordance with the Fourteen Points, he worked with Clemenceau, Lloyd George, and Italy's Orlando to fashion nine new independent states. This string of nations, stretching from the Baltic Sea to the Mediterranean, was intended as a buffer to protect Western Europe from the new Communist Soviet Union; the plan also embodied Wilson's principle of self-determination for European states.

In other parts of the world, however, the Allies dismantled the Central Powers' colonial empires but did not create independent states; instead, they assigned themselves colonies to administer as "mandates." Because the war finished off the Ottoman Empire, France and England laid claim to Ottoman and German colonies in Africa and the Middle East. Japan took Germany's possessions in East Asia. France refused to give up its longstanding occupation of Indochina. Clemenceau's snub of future Vietnamese leader Ho Chi Minh, who sought representation at Versailles, had grave long-term consequences for both France and the United States.

The establishment of a British mandate, rather than an independent nation, in Palestine (now Israel) also proved crucial. During the war, British foreign secretary Sir Arthur Balfour had stated that his country would work to establish there a "national home for the Jewish people," with the condition that "nothing shall be done which may prejudice the civil and religious rights of existing non-Jewish communities in Palestine." Under the British mandate, thousands of Jews moved to Palestine and purchased land, in some cases evicting Palestinian tenants. As early as 1920, riots erupted between Jews and Palestinians — a situation that escalated, over the next two decades, far beyond British control.

Given these results, the Versailles treaty must be judged one of history's greatest catastrophes. Not only in Europe itself, but also in places as far-flung as Palestine and Indochina, it created the conditions for horrific future bloodshed. Balfour astutely described Clemenceau, Lloyd George, and Wilson as "three all-powerful, all-ignorant men, sitting there and carving up continents." Remarkably, however, Wilson remained optimistic as he returned to the United States — even though his health was beginning to fail. The president hoped the new League of Nations, authorized by the treaty, would moderate the terms of the settlement and secure a peaceful resolution of other disputes. For this to occur, American participation in the League was crucial. So Wilson set out to persuade the Senate to ratify the Treaty of Versailles.

Congress Rejects the Treaty

The outlook was not promising. Though major opinion makers and religious denominations supported the treaty, the Republican Party was openly hostile, and it held a majority in the Senate. One group, called the "irreconcilables," consisted of western Republicans, such as Hiram Johnson of California and Robert La Follette of Wisconsin, who opposed U.S. involvement in European affairs. Another group of Republicans, led by Senator Henry Cabot Lodge of Massachusetts, worried that Article X — the provision for collective security — would prevent the United States from pursuing an independent foreign policy. Was the nation, Lodge asked, "willing to have the youth of America ordered to war" by an international body? Wilson refused to accept any amendments, especially to placate Lodge, a hated political rival. "I shall consent to nothing," the president told the French ambassador. "The Senate must take its medicine."

To mobilize support for the treaty, Wilson embarked on an exhausting speaking tour. His impassioned defense of the League of Nations brought large audiences to tears, but the strain proved too much for the president. In Pueblo, Colorado, in September 1919, Wilson collapsed. A week later, back in Washington, he suffered a severe stroke that left one side of his body paralyzed. Wilson still urged Democratic senators to reject all Republican amendments. When the treaty came up for a vote in November 1919, it failed to win the required two-thirds majority; a second attempt, in March 1920, fell seven votes short.

The treaty was dead, and so was Wilson's leadership. The president never fully recovered from his stroke. During the final eighteen months of his administration, the government drifted as Wilson's physician, his wife, and various cabinet heads secretly took charge of routine work. The United States never ratified the Versailles treaty or joined the League of Nations. In turn, the weak League failed to do what Wilson had hoped. When Wilson died in 1924, his dream of a just and peaceful international order lay in ruins.

The impact of World War I on international politics can hardly be overstated. When the conflict began in 1914, European powers dominated the globe, but four brutal years of warfare shattered Europe's imperial supremacy. By 1918, the United States was no longer just a regional power; it was a major participant in world affairs. The war, and Wilson's energetic vision, forced Americans to confront big questions. How would the United States advance its interests? Could it serve as an independent force for peace — as William Jennings Bryan had put it, an "accepted arbiter of the world's disputes"? Having rejected the Versailles treaty, the United States appeared to turn its back on the world. But in laying claim to Hawaii and the Philippines, exerting its power in Latin America, and intervening in East Asia, the United States had already entangled itself deeply in imperial politics. The nation had gained too much economic control and diplomatic clout for isolation to be a realistic option. In the long term, World War I set the conditions for the United States to become a dominant twentieth-century power.

On the home front, the effect of World War I was no less dramatic. Wartime jobs and prosperity ushered in an era of exuberant consumerism, while the achievements of women's voting rights seemed to presage a new era of reform. But as peace returned, it became clear that the war would not further political reform. An ominous signal was Wilson's rejection of a plan by the War Industries Board to stabilize the economy during demobilization. This was a harbinger of things to come. Rather than embracing government activism, Americans of the 1920s proved eager to relinquish it. The war introduced, instead, a decade of political nativism, racism, and anticommunism.

▶ What were the flaws of the Treaty of Versailles? To what extent did Wilson succeed in influencing the development of the treaty?

▶ On balance, do you think U.S. entry into World War I had beneficial results that outweighed the costs? Why or why not?

SUMMARY

Between 1877 and 1918, the United States rose as a major economic and military power. Justifications for overseas expansion emphasized access to global markets, the importance of sea power, and the need to police international misconduct and trade. These justifications shaped U.S. policy toward European powers in Latin America, and victory in the War of 1898 enabled the United States to take control of former Spanish colonies in the Caribbean and Pacific. Victory, however, also led to a bloody conflict in the Philippines as the United States struggled to suppress Filipino resistance to American rule.

After 1899, the United States aggressively asserted its interests in Asia and Latin America. In China, the United States used the Boxer Rebellion to make good its claim to an "open door" to Chinese markets. Later, President Theodore Roosevelt strengthened relations with Japan, and his successor, William Howard Taft, supported U.S. business interests in China. In the Caribbean, the United States constructed the Panama Canal and regularly exercised the "right," claimed under the Roosevelt Corollary, to intervene in the affairs of states in the region. President Woodrow Wilson publicly disparaged the imperialism of his predecessors but repeatedly used the U.S. military to "police" Mexico.

At the outbreak of World War I, the United States asserted neutrality, but its economic ties to the Allies rapidly undercut that claim. In 1917, German submarine attacks drew the United States into the war on the side of England and France. Involvement in the war profoundly transformed the economy, politics, and society of the nation, resulting in an economic boom, mass migrations of workers to industrial centers, and the achievement of women's voting rights. At the Paris Peace Conference, Wilson attempted to implement his Fourteen Points. However, the designs of the Allies in Europe undermined the Treaty of Versailles, while Republican resistance at home prevented ratification of the treaty. Although Wilson's dream of a just international order failed, the United States had taken its place as a major world power.

For additional primary sources from this period, see *Documents for America's History*, Seventh Edition.

For Web sites, images, and documents related to topics and places in this chapter, visit *Make History* at **bedfordstmartins.com/henrettaconcise**.

For Further Exploration

Walter LaFeber's *The American Search for Opportunity, 1865–1913* (1993) is an excellent, up-to-date synthesis. LaFeber's influential *The New Empire* (1963) initiated scholarly debate on the quest for overseas markets as a driving force behind U.S. imperialism. Helpful on the Spanish-Cuban-American-Philippine conflict are Louis Pérez Jr., *The War*

TIMELINE

1890	▶ Congress appropriates funds for construction of modern battleships
1895	▶ United States arbitrates border dispute between Britain and Venezuela
	▶ Guerrilla war against Spanish rule begins in Cuba
1898	▶ War between United States and Spain
	▶ United States annexes territories in the Caribbean and Pacific
1899–1902	▶ Philippine War; United States pursues open-door policy in China
1900	▶ United States helps suppress Boxer Rebellion
1901	▶ Hay-Pauncefote Treaty
1902	▶ Platt Amendment
1903	▶ U.S. recognition of Panama's independence
1905	▶ Russo-Japanese War; Roosevelt mediates peace

1908	▶ Root-Takahira Agreement
1914	▶ Panama Canal opens
	▶ U.S. military actions in Mexico
	▶ World War I begins in Europe
1916	▶ Jones Act commits United States to Philippine independence
1917	▶ United States declares war on Germany and its allies; creates new agencies to mobilize economy and promote national unity
1918	▶ Sedition Act
	▶ World War I ends
1919	▶ *Schenck v. United States; Abrams v. United States*
	▶ Wilson introduces his Fourteen Points
	▶ Senate rejects the Treaty of Versailles
1920	▶ Nineteenth Amendment grants women suffrage
	▶ Senate again rejects the Treaty of Versailles

of 1898 (1998); Stuart Creighton Miller, *"Benevolent Assimilation"* (1982); Paul Kramer, *The Blood of Government* (2006); and Kristin Hoganson, *Fighting for American Manhood* (1998). On U.S. involvement in the Caribbean, see César Ayala, *American Sugar Kingdom* (1999); on the United States and Mexico, see John S. D. Eisenhower, *Intervention!* (1993); and on the Panama Canal, see Julie Greene, *The Canal Builders* (2009).

On World War I, see Hew Strachan, *The First World War* (2004), and visit **www.pbs.org/greatwar/index.html**. Frank Freidel's *Over There* (1990) offers soldiers' vivid firsthand accounts, while the home front is captured in Meirion Harries and Susie Harries, *The Last Days of Innocence* (1997), and David M. Kennedy, *Over Here* (1990). On the Great Migration, see James R. Grossman, *Land of Hope* (1999), and Joe William Trotter Jr., ed., *The Great Migration in Historical Perspective* (1991). On woman suffrage, see the essays in Jean H. Baker, ed., *Votes for Women* (2002); and on its consequences, see Nancy Cott, *The Grounding of Modern Feminism* (1987). On the influenza epidemic of 1918, see **www.archives.gov/exhibits/influenza-epidemic/index.html** and **www.pbs.org/wgbh/amex/influenza**.

Test Your Knowledge

For practice quizzes, activities, and other study tools, visit the Online Study Guide at **bedfordstmartins.com/henrettaconcise**.

We're in about the
rottenest period of
reaction that we have
had in many years.

—Hiram Johnson, former Progressive
governor of California

Margaret Sanger, a nurse who moved with her family to New York in 1911, immersed herself in the city's exciting political scene. She joined labor protests and the Socialist Party and volunteered in the immigrant wards of the Lower East Side. Horrified by women's suffering from constant pregnancies — and remembering her devout Catholic mother, who had died young after bearing eleven children — Sanger launched a crusade for what she called "birth control." Her column in the *New York Call*, "What Every Girl Should Know," soon garnered an indictment for violating obscenity laws. Sanger fled to England, where she spent fourteen months talking with sex radicals and economists studying overpopulation. After returning to the United States, Sanger opened the nation's first birth control clinic in Brooklyn, in 1916. Authorities shut it down, and Sanger spent a month in jail.

Sanger was in many ways a quintessential progressive reformer. She championed women's rights and believed birth control could solve urgent problems of industrialization and poverty. By the eve of World War I, she had launched a grassroots movement. Letters flooded in from across the country — some hostile, others begging for help. "Please send me one of your Papers on birth control, I have seven children and cannot afford any more," pleaded one woman. "Tell me how it is," demanded another, "that the wealthier class of people can get information like that and those that really need it, can't?" Allies set up clinics in St. Paul, Minnesota, and Ann Arbor, Michigan.

Yet, like many progressives, Sanger found herself on the defensive after World War I. Amid a postwar Red Scare that targeted the political left, Sanger's alliance with Socialists collapsed. Critics charged that birth control represented the most sinful and dangerous trends of modern society. Sanger had to respond to new political realities. To attract middle-class support, she emphasized expert, scientific approaches to birth control. Though she had previously advocated woman-to-woman educational networks, she now argued that only medical personnel should dispense contraception. Her new American Birth Control League cultivated support from eugenicists, who called for sterilization of the "unfit" and warned that darker races were reproducing more quickly than whites.

Celebrating the Fourth of July, 1926

This *Life* magazine cover celebrates two famous symbols of the 1920s: jazz music and the "flapper," in her droopy tights and scandalously short skirt, who loves to dance to its rhythms. The flags at the top record the latest slang expressions, including "so's your old man" and "step on it" ("it" being the accelerator of an automobile, in a decade when cars were America's hottest commodity). If you examine the bottom of the picture, you will also find a note of protest: While July 4, 1926, marked the 150th anniversary of the Declaration of Independence, *Life* says that Americans have had only "143 years of liberty"—followed by "seven years of Prohibition." Picture Research Consultants & Archives.

Sanger herself was eventually forced out of the league by leaders seeking to make the cause respectable.

In the 1920s, debates over Sanger's work mirrored larger struggles between tradition and modernity, faith and secularism, and rural and urban ways of life. World War I placed new emphasis on centralized planning and expert control, not grassroots democracy. After the war, political leaders abandoned two decades of trust busting and regulation and deferred to business interests. Political initiative shifted to groups that sought to keep out immigrants and preserve America's "racial purity." Millions turned their attention to radio shows, movies, cars, and other products of a thriving consumer culture. Americans wanted prosperity, not progressivism — at least until 1929, when the nation met up with the consequences of economic instability and excessive debt, through the shock of the Great Depression.

Conflicted Legacies of World War I

"The World War has accentuated all our differences," a journalist in the magazine *World's Work* observed. "It has not created those differences, but it has revealed and emphasized them." In the aftermath of the war, thousands of strikes revealed continuing class tensions. Violent race riots exposed determined white resistance to the rising expectations of African Americans, while an obsessive hunt for foreign radicals showed that ethnic pluralism would not win easy acceptance.

Racial Strife

African Americans emerged from World War I determined to insist on citizenship rights. Millions had loyally supported the war effort; 350,000 had served their country in uniform. The black man, one observer wrote, "realized that he was part and parcel of the great army of democracy. . . . With this realization came the consciousness of pride in himself as a man, and an American citizen." The Great Migration also drew hundreds of thousands of blacks from the South to Northern industrial cities, where they secured good wartime jobs and found they could vote, advocate for political reforms, and use their new economic clout to build community institutions and work for racial justice.

Across the United States, these trends sparked white violence. In the South, the number of lynchings rose from 48 in 1917 to 78 in 1919, including several murders of returning black soldiers in their military uniforms. Such incidents continued through the 1920s. A brutal lynching in the quiet railroad town of Rosewood, Florida, in 1921 prompted black residents to arm for self-defense. Mobs of furious whites responded by torching houses and hunting down black residents. Police and state authorities refused to intervene; completely destroyed, the town of Rosewood vanished from the map.

In northern and midwestern cities, the arrival of thousands of southern blacks deepened existing racial tensions. Blacks competed with whites — including recent immigrants — for scarce housing and jobs. Unionized white workers resented blacks who served as strikebreakers. Racism turned such economic and political conflicts into violent confrontations. Attacks on African Americans broke out in more than twenty-five cities. One of the deadliest riots occurred in 1917 in East St. Louis, Illinois, where nine whites and more than forty blacks died. Chicago endured five days of rioting in July 1919. By that September, the national death toll from racial violence had reached 120.

The oil boom town of Tulsa, Oklahoma, was the site of a particularly horrific incident in June 1921. Sensational, false news reports of an alleged rape helped incite white mobs who resented increasing black prosperity. Anger focused on the 8,000 residents of Tulsa's prosperous Greenwood district, locally known as "the black Wall Street." The white mob — helped by National Guardsmen, who arrested any residents who resisted — burned thirty-five blocks of Greenwood and killed several dozen African Americans. The city's leading paper acknowledged that "semi-organized bands of white men systematically applied the torch, while others shot on sight men of color." It took a decade for black residents, who refused to be driven out, to slowly rebuild Greenwood.

Erosion of Labor Rights

African Americans were not the only ones who faced challenges to hard-won recent gains. The war effort, overseen by a Democratic administration sympathetic to labor, had temporarily increased the size and power of labor unions. The National War Labor Board (NWLB), formed in April 1918, established an eight-hour day for war workers, with time-and-a-half pay for overtime, and endorsed equal pay for women. In return for a no-strike pledge, the NWLB also supported workers' right to organize. Membership in the American Federation of Labor (AFL) grew by a third, reaching more than 3 million by war's end. Workers' expectations rose as the war economy brought higher pay and better working conditions.

But when workers tried to maintain these standards after the war, employers cut wages and rooted out unions. These developments prompted a massive confrontation. In 1919, more than 4 million wage laborers — one in every five — went on strike, a proportion never since equaled. A walkout of shipyard workers in Seattle sparked a general strike that shut down the city. Another major strike disrupted the steel industry, as 350,000 workers demanded union recognition and an end to twelve-hour shifts. Elbert H. Gary, the head of United States Steel Corporation, refused to negotiate; he hired Mexican and African American strikebreakers and eventually broke the strike. Meanwhile, business leaders in rising industries, such as automobile manufacturing, resolutely resisted unions, leading to the creation of more and more non-unionized industrial jobs.

Public employees fared no better. Late in 1919, Boston's police force shocked many Americans by demanding a union and going on strike to get it. Massachusetts governor Calvin Coolidge won national fame by declaring, "There is no right to strike against the public safety by anybody, anywhere, anytime." Coolidge fired the entire police force, and the strike failed. A majority of the public supported the governor, and Republicans rewarded Coolidge by nominating him for the vice presidency in 1920.

Antilabor decisions by the Supreme Court were an important factor in unions' decline. In *Coronado Coal Company v. United Mine Workers* (1925), the Court ruled that a striking union could be penalized for illegal restraint of trade. The Court also struck down federal legislation regulating child labor; in *Adkins v. Children's Hospital* (1923), it voided a minimum wage for women workers in the District of Columbia, reversing many of the gains that had been achieved before World War I through the groundbreaking decision in *Muller v. Oregon* (see Chapter 20). Such decisions, along with aggressive anti-union campaigns, caused membership in labor unions to fall from 5.1 million in 1920 to 3.6 million in 1929 — only 10 percent of the nonagricultural workforce.

In place of unions, the 1920s marked the heyday of **welfare capitalism**, a system of labor relations that stressed management's responsibility for employees' well-being. Employers hoped this would build a loyal workforce and head off strikes and labor unrest. At a time when government unemployment compensation and Social Security did not exist, General Electric, U.S. Steel, and other large corporations offered workers health insurance and old-age pensions. But such plans covered only about 5 percent of the industrial workforce. In the tangible benefits that it offered workers, welfare capitalism had serious limitations.

The Red Scare

Many prosperous Americans sided with management in the upheavals of the postwar years. They blamed workers for the rapidly rising cost of living, which jumped nearly 80 percent between 1917 and 1919. The socialist outlook of some recent immigrants frightened native-born citizens, and the communist **ideology** of the Russian Bolsheviks terrified them. When Bolsheviks founded the Third International (or Comintern) in 1919, an organization intended to foster revolutions, some Americans began to fear that dangerous radicals were hiding everywhere. Hatred of Germans (disparaged as "Huns") was replaced by hostility toward Bolsheviks (labeled "Reds," after the color of Communist party badges and flags). Ironically, Communists remained few in number and had little political influence. Of the 50 million adults in the United States in 1920, no more than 70,000 belonged to either the fledgling U.S. Communist Party or the Communist Labor Party. The Industrial Workers of the World (IWW) had been weakened by wartime repression and internal dissent. Yet the public and the press blamed labor unrest on alien radicals.

In 1919, tensions mounted amid a series of threats and bombings. In April, alert postal workers discovered and defused thirty-four mail bombs addressed to government officials. In June, a bomb detonated outside the Washington townhouse of recently appointed attorney general A. Mitchell Palmer. Palmer escaped unharmed, but he used the incident to fan public fears. With President Woodrow Wilson incapacitated by stroke,

The Passion of Sacco and Vanzetti, **by Ben Shahn (1931–1932)**
Ben Shahn (1898–1969) came to the United States from Lithuania as a child and achieved fame as a social realist painter and photographer. Shahn used his art to advance his belief in social justice. In this painting, Sacco and Vanzetti lie dead and pale, hovered over by three distinguished Massachusetts citizens. These grim-faced men — holding lilies, a symbol of death — are Harvard University president A. Lawrence Lowell and the two other members of a commission appointed by the governor in 1927 to review the case. The commission concluded that the men were guilty, a finding that led to their execution. Judge Webster Thayer, who presided at the original trial in 1921, stands in the window in the background. Copyright Geoffrey Clements/Corbis, Copyright Estate of Ben Shahn/VAGA, New York.

Palmer had a free hand. He set up an antiradicalism division in the Justice Department and appointed his assistant J. Edgar Hoover to direct it; shortly afterward, it became the Federal Bureau of Investigation (FBI). Then, in November 1919, Palmer's agents stormed the headquarters of radical organizations. The dragnet captured thousands of aliens who had committed no crimes but who held anarchist or revolutionary beliefs. Lacking the protection of U.S. citizenship, many were deported without formal indictment or trial.

The "Palmer raids" peaked on a notorious night in January 1920, when federal agents invaded homes and meeting halls, arrested six thousand citizens and aliens, and denied the prisoners access to legal counsel. Then Palmer, ambitious for the presidency, overreached. He predicted that on May 1 a radical conspiracy would attempt to overthrow the U.S. government. State militia units and police went on twenty-four-hour alert to guard the nation against the alleged threat, but not a single incident occurred. As the summer of 1920 passed without major strikes or renewed bombings, the Red Scare began to abate.

Like other postwar legacies, however, antiradicalism persisted through the next decade. In May 1920, at the height of the Red Scare, police arrested Nicola Sacco, a shoemaker, and Bartolomeo Vanzetti, a fish peddler, for the murder of two men during a robbery of a shoe company in South Braintree, Massachusetts. Sacco and Vanzetti were Italian aliens and self-proclaimed anarchists who had evaded the draft. Convicted of the murders, Sacco and Vanzetti sat in jail for six years while supporters appealed their verdicts. In 1927, Judge Webster Thayer denied a motion for a new trial and sentenced them to death. Scholars still debate Sacco and Vanzetti's guilt or innocence. But it was clear that their trial was biased by prosecutors' emphasis on their ties to radical groups. The execution of Sacco and Vanzetti was one of the ugly scars left by the ethnic and political hostilities of the Great War.

▶ What factors contributed to racial and labor violence after the war?

▶ What factors, both international and domestic, contributed to the emergence of the Red Scare?

Politics in the 1920s

As the plight of labor suggested, the 1920s were a tough decade for the progressives who had gained ground before World War I. After a few early victories for reform, including the achievement of national woman suffrage, the dominant motif of the 1920s was limited government. At the grass roots, native-born white Protestants rallied against what they saw as big-city values and advocated such goals as immigration restriction. A series of Republican presidents placed responsibility for the nation's well-being in the hands of business interests. President Calvin Coolidge solemnly declared, "The man who builds a factory builds a temple. The man who works there worships there." The same theme prevailed in continued interventions in Latin America and elsewhere: The United States sought to reshape other nations' economies and finances to enhance American business needs.

Women in Politics

At the start of the 1920s, many progressive women hoped that the attainment of full voting rights would offer women new leverage to tackle industrial poverty. They created organizations like the Women's Joint Congressional Committee, a Washington-based advocacy group. The committee's greatest accomplishment was the first federally funded health-care legislation, the Sheppard-Towner Federal Maternity and Infancy Act (1921). Sheppard-Towner provided federal funds to subsidize medical clinics, prenatal education programs, and visiting nurses. Though opponents warned that the act would lead to socialized medicine, Sheppard-Towner improved health care for the poor and significantly lowered infant mortality rates. It also marked the first time that Congress designated federal funds to the states and encouraged them to administer a social welfare program.

Moved by the immense scale of suffering caused by World War I, some women joined the growing international peace movement. While diplomats conducted negotiations at Versailles, women peace advocates from around the world convened in Zurich and called on all nations to use their resources to end hunger and promote human welfare. The treaty negotiators in Paris ignored them, but the women activists organized for sustained opposition to war. In 1919, they created the Women's International League for Peace and Freedom (WILPF), whose leading members included Jane Addams. Through the 1920s and beyond, members of the WILPF denounced imperialism, stressed the suffering caused by militarism, and proposed social justice measures.

Despite such work, women's activism suffered major setbacks in the 1920s. The WILPF came under fierce attack during the Red Scare because of the presence of Socialist women among its ranks. And though women proved to be effective lobbyists, they had difficulty gaining access to posts in the Republican and Democratic parties. Finding that women did not vote as a bloc, politicians in both parties began to take their votes for granted. New reforms failed to gain support, and a key achievement was rolled back. Many congressmen had initially supported the Sheppard-Towner Act because they feared the voting power of women, but Congress ended the program in the late 1920s.

Republican "Normalcy"

With President Wilson ailing in 1920, Democrats nominated Ohio governor James M. Cox for president, on a platform calling for U.S. participation in the League of Nations and continuation of Wilson's progressivism. Republicans, led by their probusiness wing, tapped genial Ohio senator Warren G. Harding. In a dig at Wilson's sweeping idealism, Harding promised "not nostrums but normalcy." On Election Day he won in a landslide, beginning an era of Republican dominance that lasted until 1932.

Harding's most energetic appointee was Secretary of Commerce Herbert Hoover, well-known head of the wartime Food Administration. Under Hoover's direction, the Commerce Department helped create two thousand trade associations representing companies in almost every major industry. Government officials worked closely with the associations, providing statistical research, suggesting industry-wide standards, and promoting stable prices and wages. Hoover hoped that through voluntary business cooperation with government — an "associated state" — he could achieve what progressive reformers had sought through governmental regulation.

But more sinister links between government and corporate interests were soon revealed. When President Harding died suddenly of a heart attack in August 1923, evidence was just coming to light that parts of his administration were riddled with corruption. The worst scandal concerned the secret leasing of government oil reserves in Teapot Dome, Wyoming, and Elk Hills, California, to private companies. Secretary of the Interior Albert Fall was eventually convicted of taking $300,000 in bribes and became the first cabinet officer in U.S. history to serve a prison sentence.

Vice President Calvin Coolidge ascended to the presidency upon Harding's death. He maintained Republican dominance while offering, with his austere Yankee morality, a contrast to his predecessor's cronyism. Campaigning for election in his own right in 1924, Coolidge called for limited government, isolationism in foreign policy, and tax cuts for business. Rural and urban Democrats, deeply divided over such issues as prohibition and immigration restriction, deadlocked at their national convention; delegates cast 102 ballots before finally choosing John W. Davis, a Wall Street lawyer. Coolidge easily defeated Davis and staved off a challenge by Senator Robert M. La Follette of Wisconsin, who tried to resuscitate the Progressive Party. In the end, Coolidge received 15.7 million votes to Davis's 8.4 million and La Follette's 4.9 million.

For the most part, Republicans declined to carry forward progressive initiatives from the prewar years. The Republican-dominated Federal Trade Commission (FTC) failed to enforce antitrust laws. The Supreme Court, now headed by former Republican president William Howard Taft, refused to break up the mammoth U.S. Steel Corporation, despite evidence of its near-monopoly power. With the agricultural sector facing hardship, Congress sought to aid farmers with the McNary-Haugen bills of 1927 and 1928, which proposed a system of federal price supports for major crops. But President Coolidge opposed the bills as special-interest legislation and vetoed them both. While some state and municipal leaders continued to pursue ambitious agendas, they were shut out of power at the federal level.

Dollar Diplomacy

Political campaigns emphasized domestic issues in the 1920s, but the United States nonetheless remained deeply engaged in foreign affairs. Republican presidential administrations sought to advance U.S. business interests, especially by encouraging private banks to make foreign loans. Policymakers hoped such loans would stimulate growth and increase demand for U.S. products in developing markets. Bankers, though, wanted government assurance of repayment in countries that they perceived as weak or unstable.

U.S. officials acted to provide such assurance. In 1922, for example, when American banks offered an immense loan to Bolivia (at a hefty profit), State Department officials pressured the South American nation to accept it. The diplomats also forced Bolivia to agree to financial oversight by a commission under the banks' control. A similar arrangement was reached with El Salvador's government in 1923, though efforts to broker such deals in Honduras and Guatemala fell through. Where stronger action was needed, the United States intervened militarily, often to force repayment of debt. The U.S. Marines occupied Nicaragua almost continuously from 1912 to 1933, the Dominican Republic from 1916 to 1924, and Haiti from 1915 to 1934.

In these lengthy military deployments Americans came to think of the occupied countries as essentially U.S. possessions, much like Puerto Rico and the Philippines. Sensational memoirs by marines who had served in Haiti popularized the island as the "American Africa." White Americans became fascinated by *vodou* (voodoo) and other Haitian religious customs, reinforcing their view of Haitians as either dangerous savages or childlike people who needed U.S. guidance and supervision. One commander testified that his troops saw themselves as "trustees of a huge estate that belonged to minors. . . . The Haitians were our wards."

At home, critics denounced loan guarantees and military interventions as **dollar diplomacy**. The term was coined in 1924 by Samuel Guy Inman, a Disciples of Christ missionary who had toured U.S.-occupied Haiti and the Dominican Republic. "The United States," Inman declared, "cannot go on destroying with impunity the sovereignty of other peoples, however weak." African American leaders also denounced the Haitian occupation. On behalf of the Women's International League for Peace and Freedom and the International Council of Women of the Darker Races, a delegation conducted a fact-finding tour of Haiti in 1926. Their report exposed, among other things, the sexual exploitation of Haitian women by U.S. soldiers.

By the late 1920s, dollar diplomacy was on the defensive, in keeping with a broader mood of isolationism and disgust with international affairs. At the same time, political leaders became frustrated with their poor results. Dollar diplomacy usually managed to get loans repaid, securing bankers' profits. But the loans often ended up in the pockets of local elites; U.S. policies failed to build broad-based prosperity overseas. Military intervention could have even more dire results. In Haiti, the marines crushed peasant protests and helped the Haitian elite consolidate its power. U.S. occupation thus helped create the conditions for harsh dictatorships that Haitians endured through the rest of the twentieth century.

Culture Wars

By 1929, ninety-three U.S. cities had populations of more than 100,000. New York City's population exceeded 7 million, and Los Angeles's had exploded to 1.2 million. The lives and beliefs of urban Americans — including millions of recent immigrants — often differed dramatically from those in small towns and farming areas. Native-born rural Protestants, faced with a dire perceived threat, rallied in the 1920s to protect what they saw as American values.

Religion in | Rural and native-born Protestants started the decade with the achieve-
   Politics | ment of a longtime goal: national prohibition of liquor (see Chapter 18).
   | Wartime anti-German prejudice was a major spur. Since major breweries like Pabst and Busch were owned by German Americans, many citizens decided it was unpatriotic to drink beer. Mobilizing the economy for war, Congress also limited brewers' and distillers' use of barley, hops, and other scarce grains, causing consumption to decline. The nation's decades-long prohibition campaign culminated with Congress's passage of the Eighteenth Amendment in 1917. Ratified in 1919 by nearly every state and effective in January 1920, the amendment prohibited the "manufacture, sale, or trans-

portation of intoxicating liquors" anywhere in the United States. Though widely circumvented in urban speakeasies and other illegal drinking sites, the amendment remained in force until its repeal in 1933. Defenders hailed the Eighteenth Amendment as a victory for health, morals, and Christian values.

At the state and local levels, controversy erupted as fundamentalist Protestants sought to mandate school curricula based on the biblical account of creation. In 1925, Tennessee's legislature outlawed the teaching of "any theory that denies the story of the Divine creation of man as taught in the Bible, [and teaches] instead that man has descended from a lower order of animals." The American Civil Liberties Union (ACLU), which had been formed during the Red Scare to protect free speech rights, challenged the Tennessee law's constitutionality. The ACLU intervened in the trial of John T. Scopes, a high school biology teacher who taught the theory of evolution to his class and faced a jail sentence for doing so. The case attracted national attention because Clarence Darrow, a famous criminal lawyer, defended Scopes, while William Jennings Bryan, the three-time Democratic presidential candidate, spoke for the prosecution.

Journalists dubbed the Scopes case "the monkey trial." This label referred both to Darwin's argument that human beings and other primates share a common ancestor and to the circus atmosphere at the trial, which was broadcast live over a Chicago radio station. (Proving that sophisticated urbanites had their own bitter prejudices, acerbic critic H. L. Mencken dismissed anti-evolutionists as "gaping primates of the upland valleys," implying that they had not evolved.) The jury took only eight minutes to deliver its verdict: guilty. Though the Tennessee Supreme Court later overturned Scopes's conviction, the controversial law remained on the books for more than thirty years.

Nativism | Many native-born Protestants saw unrestricted immigration as the primary cause of cultural and religious disputes. A nation of 105 million people had added more than 23 million immigrants over the previous four decades. The newcomers included many Catholics and Jews from Southern and Eastern Europe, whom one Maryland congressman referred to as "indigestible lumps" in the "national stomach." Such **nativism**, which recalled hostility toward the Irish and Germans in the 1840s and 1850s, was widely shared.

Resurgent nativism fueled a momentous shift in immigration policy. "America must be kept American," President Coolidge declared in 1924. Congress had banned Chinese immigration in 1882, and Theodore Roosevelt had negotiated a so-called gentleman's agreement that limited Japanese immigration in 1907. Now nativists charged that there were also too many European immigrants, some of whom undermined Protestantism and imported anarchism, socialism, and other radical doctrines. Responding to these concerns, Congress passed emergency immigration restrictions in 1921 and a permanent measure three years later. The National Origins Act (1924) used thirty-four-year-old census data to establish a baseline: in the future, annual immigration from each country could not exceed 2 percent of that nationality's U.S. population as it had stood in 1890. Since only small numbers of Italians, Greeks, Poles, Russians, and other Southern and Eastern European immigrants had arrived before 1890, the law drastically limited immigration from those places. In 1929, Congress imposed even more restrictive quotas, setting a cap of 150,000 immigrants per year from Europe and continuing to ban most immigrants from Asia.

The new laws, however, permitted unrestricted immigration from the Western Hemisphere. Latin Americans arrived in increasing numbers, finding jobs in the West that had gone to Asian immigrants before exclusion. More than 1 million Mexicans entered the United States between 1900 and 1930, including many during World War I. Nativists lobbied Congress to cut this flow; so did labor leaders, who argued that impoverished migrants lowered wages for other American workers. But Congress heeded the pleas of employers, especially farmers in Texas and California, who wanted cheap labor. Only the coming of the Great Depression cut off migration from Mexico.

Other expressions of nativism emerged at the state level. In 1913, by an overwhelming majority, California's legislature had passed a law declaring that "aliens ineligible to citizenship" could not own "real property." The law aimed to exclude Asians, especially Japanese immigrants, from owning land, though some had lived in the state for decades and built up prosperous farms. In the wake of World War I, California tightened these laws, making it increasingly difficult for Asian immigrant families to establish themselves. California, Washington, and Hawaii also severely restricted schools that taught Japanese language, history, and culture to young Japanese Americans. California, for example, passed a law forbidding any Japanese school from operating more than one hour per day; textbooks could make no references to samurai warriors, emperors, or other "controversial" elements of Japanese history. Relentless hostility, which denied Asians both citizenship and land rights, left Japanese Americans in a vulnerable position at the outbreak of World War II, when anti-Japanese hysteria swept the United States.

The Klan Revived | The 1920s also brought a nationwide rebirth of the Ku Klux Klan (KKK), the white supremacist group formed in the post–Civil War South. Soon after the premiere of *Birth of a Nation* (1915), a popular film that glorified the Reconstruction-era Klan, a group of southerners gathered on Georgia's Stone Mountain to revive the group. With its blunt motto, "Native, white, Protestant supremacy," the Klan recruited supporters across the country. KKK members did not limit their harassment to blacks but targeted Catholics and Jews as well, with physical intimidation, arson, and economic boycotts. The KKK also turned to politics, and hundreds of Klansmen won election to local offices and state legislatures (Map 22.1).

At the height of its power, the Klan wielded considerable political clout and counted more than three million members, including many women (see American Voices, p. 671). The Klan's mainstream appeal was illustrated by President Woodrow Wilson's public praise for *Birth of a Nation*. Though it declined nationally after 1925, robbed of a potent issue by passage of the anti-immigration bill, the Klan remained strong in the South, and pockets of KKK activity persisted in all parts of the country. Klan activism also lent a menacing cast to other political issues. Some local Klansmen, for example, cooperated with members of the Anti-Saloon League to enforce prohibition laws through threats and violent attacks.

The Election of 1928 | Conflicts over race, religion, and ethnicity created the climate for a stormy presidential election in 1928. Democrats had traditionally drawn strength from white voters in the South and immigrants in the North. In the 1920s, however, these groups divided over prohibition, immigration restriction, and the Klan. By 1928, the northern urban wing gained firm control. Democrats nominated Governor

The Fight for Americanism   HIRAM WESLEY EVANS

Hiram Wesley Evans was a Texas dentist and the Grand Wizard of the Ku Klux Klan, which boasted a nationwide membership of 3 million. He published this defense of the Klan in *The North American Review*, a leading journal of opinion. Like fascist movements in Italy and Germany, the Klan focused on racial identity. For the KKK, real Americans were those of Nordic (north European) descent; all others were "aliens," including those of southern or central European ancestry (Italian, Spanish, Polish, Czech, etc.) and those with Jewish or African forebears.

We are a movement of the plain people, very weak in the matter of culture, intellectual support, and trained leadership. We are demanding, and we expect to win, a return of power into the hands of the everyday, not highly cultured, not overly intellectualized, but entirely unspoiled and not de-Americanized, average citizen of the old stock. . . .

This is undoubtedly a weakness. It lays us open to the charge of being hicks and "rubes" and "drivers of second-hand Fords." We admit it. Far worse, it makes it hard for us to state our case and advocate our crusade in the most effective way, for most of us lack skill in language. . . .

To understand the Klan, then, it is necessary to understand the character and present mind of the mass of old-stock Americans. The mass, it must be remembered, as distinguished from the intellectually mongrelized "Liberals."

These are. . . . a blend of various peoples of the so-called Nordic race . . . which, with all its faults, has given the world almost the whole of modern civilization. . . . These Nordic Americans for the last generation have found themselves increasingly uncomfortable. . . .

Finally came the moral breakdown that has been going on for two decades. . . . All our traditional moral standards went by the boards or were so disregarded that they ceased to be binding. The sacredness of our Sabbath, of our homes, of chastity, and finally even of our right to teach our own children in our own schools fundamental facts and truths were torn away from us. . . . One more point about the present attitude of the old-stock American: he has revived and increased his long-standing distrust of the Roman Catholic Church. . . . [which is] the chief leader of alienism, and the most dangerous alien power with a foothold inside our boundaries. . . .

The Ku Klux Klan . . . is an organization which gives expression, direction and purpose to the most vital instincts, hopes, and resentments of the old-stock Americans, provides them with leadership, and is enlisting and preparing them for militant, constructive action toward fulfilling their racial and national destiny. . . . a definite crusade for Americanism! . . .

There are three of these great racial instincts. . . . These are the instincts of loyalty to the white race, to the traditions of America, and to the spirit of Protestantism, which has been an essential part of Americanism ever since the days of Roanoke and Plymouth Rock. They are condensed into the Klan slogan: "Native, white, Protestant supremacy."

SOURCE: Hiram Wesley Evans, "The Klan's Fight for Americanism," *The North American Review*, 223 (March 1926), 37–39.

MAP 22.1 Ku Klux Klan Politics and Violence in the 1920s

Unlike the Reconstruction-era Klan, the Klan of the 1920s was geographically dispersed and had substantial strength in the West and Midwest as well as in the South. Although the Klan is often thought of as a rural movement, some of the strongest "klaverns" were in Chicago, Los Angeles, Atlanta, Detroit, and other large cities. The organization's members operated as vigilantes in areas where they were strong; elsewhere, their aggressive tactics triggered riots between Klansmen and their ethnic and religious targets.

Al Smith of New York, the first presidential candidate to reflect the aspirations of the urban working class. The grandson of Irish peasants, Smith had risen through New York City's Democratic machine and had become a dynamic reformer. But Smith offended many small-town and rural Americans. He spoke in a heavy New York accent and sported a brown derby that highlighted his ethnic working-class origins. Middle-class reformers questioned his ties to Tammany Hall; temperance advocates opposed him as a "wet." The governor's greatest handicap was his religion. Although Smith insisted that his Catholic beliefs would not affect his duties as president, many Protestant leaders opposed him. "No Governor can kiss the papal ring and get within gunshot of the White House," vowed a Methodist bishop from Buffalo.

Smith proved no match for the Republican nominee, Secretary of Commerce Herbert Hoover, an outstanding administrator who embodied the technological promise of the modern age. Women who had mobilized for Hoover's food conservation campaigns during World War I enlisted as "Hoover Hostesses," inviting friends to their homes to hear the candidate's radio speeches. Enjoying the benefit of eight years of Republican prosperity, Hoover promised voters that individualism and cooperative endeavors would

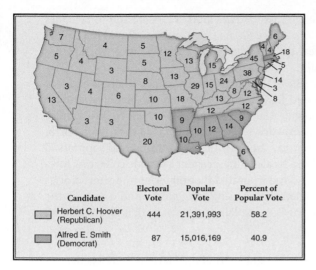

MAP 22.2 The Presidential Election of 1928
Historians still debate the extent to which 1928 was a critical election — an election that produced a significant realignment in voting behavior. Although the Republican Herbert Hoover swept the popular and the electoral votes, Democrat Alfred E. Smith won majorities not only in the South, his party's traditional stronghold, but also in Rhode Island, Massachusetts, and (although it is not evident on this map) all of the large cities of the North and Midwest. In subsequent elections, the Democrats won even more votes among African American and European ethnic groups and, until 1980, were the nation's dominant political party.

Candidate	Electoral Vote	Popular Vote	Percent of Popular Vote
Herbert C. Hoover (Republican)	444	21,391,993	58.2
Alfred E. Smith (Democrat)	87	15,016,169	40.9

banish poverty. He won a major victory, receiving 58 percent of the popular vote to Smith's 41 percent and an overwhelming 444 electoral votes to Smith's 87 (Map 22.2).

Because many southern Protestants refused to vote for a Catholic, Hoover carried five ex-Confederate states, breaking the Democratic "Solid South" for the first time since Reconstruction. Despite his resounding defeat, though, Smith carried the industrialized states of Massachusetts and Rhode Island. He also carried the nation's twelve largest cities — suggesting that urban voters were moving into the Democratic camp.

▶ To what extent was Republicans' foreign policy during the 1920s consistent with their domestic agenda?

▶ How did grassroots conflicts over race, religion, and immigration shape politics in the 1920s?

Intellectual Modernism

Before World War I, dramatic forms of modernism had emerged in art and literature. In the 1920s, these became — like political campaigns — sites of struggle between modernity and tradition, secularism and faith. The horrors of the war prompted many American intellectuals, like their European counterparts, to question long-standing assumptions about civilization, progress, and the alleged superiority of Western cultures over so-called primitive ways of life. Some of these intellectual movements — such as the Harlem Renaissance — emerged from the social and economic upheavals that the Great War had wrought at home.

Harlem in Vogue

As the Great Migration tripled New York's black population in the decade after 1910, Harlem stood as "the symbol of liberty and the Promised Land to Negroes everywhere," as one black minister put it. Talented black artists and writers flocked to the district, where they broke with genteel traditions and asserted ties to Africa. Poet Langston Hughes drew on African American music in *The Weary Blues* (1926), a groundbreaking collection of poems. He captured the upbeat spirit of the Harlem Renaissance when he asserted, "I am a Negro — and beautiful."

Like Hughes, other writers and artists of the Harlem Renaissance championed race pride. Claude McKay, Jean Toomer, and Jessie Fauset explored the black experience and represented in fiction what philosopher Alain Locke called the "New Negro." Painter Jacob Lawrence, who had grown up in crowded tenement districts of the urban North, used bold shapes and vivid colors to portray the daily life, aspirations, and suppressed anger of African Americans. Author Zora Neale Hurston spent a decade collecting folklore in the South and the Caribbean and incorporated that material into short stories and novels. This creative work embodied the ongoing struggle to find a way, as the influential black intellectual W. E. B. Du Bois explained, "to be both a Negro and an American."

Jazz | To millions of Americans, the most notable part of the Harlem Renaissance was jazz. Though the origins of the word *jazz* are unclear, many historians believe it was a slang term for sexual intercourse — an etymology that makes sense, given the association of early jazz with urban vice districts. As a musical form, jazz coalesced in New Orleans and other parts of the South before World War I. Borrowing from blues, ragtime, and other popular forms, jazz musicians developed an ensemble style in which individual performers, keeping a rapid ragtime beat, improvised over and around a basic melodic line. The majority of early jazz musicians were black, but white performers, some of whom had more formal training, injected elements of European concert music.

In the 1920s, as jazz spread nationwide, musicians developed its signature mode of performance, the improvised solo. The key figure in this development was cornetist and trumpeter Louis Armstrong. A native of New Orleans, Armstrong learned his craft while playing in the saloons and brothels of Storyville, the city's vice district. Armstrong showed an inexhaustible capacity for melodic invention. His dazzling solos inspired other musicians to try solos. The white trumpeter Bix Beiderbecke, for example, pioneered an influential bright-toned style. By the late 1920s, soloists had become the celebrities of jazz, thrilling audiences with their improvisational skills (see Voices from Abroad, p. 676).

As jazz spread, it generally followed the routes of the Great Migration from the South to northern and western cities, where it met consumers primed to receive it. Before World War I, ragtime and other forms of dance music had created broad, enthusiastic audiences for African American music. Most cities had plentiful venues where jazz could be featured. By the 1920s, radio also helped popularize jazz, as the emerging record industry churned out records of the latest tunes. New York became the hub of this commercially lucrative jazz. While the New Orleans style persisted in Chicago, attracting enthusiasts across racial lines, New York's jazz, which featured less syncopation and fewer blues inflections, had more mainstream appeal. White listeners flocked to theaters, ballrooms, and expensive clubs to hear the "Harlem sound" from the orchestras of Duke Ellington and other stars. Yet those who hailed "primitive" black music rarely suspended their racial condescension: Visiting a mixed-race club became known as "slumming."

All That Jazz

Born in Florida in 1892, Augusta Fells Savage arrived in New York to study in 1921 and remained to take part in the Harlem Renaissance. Widowed at a young age, and struggling to support her parents and young daughter, Savage faced both racism and poverty. Much of her work has been lost, because she sculpted in clay and could not afford to cast in bronze. Savage began to speak out for racial justice after she was denied, on the basis of her race, a fellowship to study in Paris. In 1923, she married a close associate of UNIA leader Marcus Garvey. Archives of American Art/ Smithsonian Institution.

Through jazz, the recording industry began to develop products specifically aimed at urban working-class blacks. The breakthrough came in 1920, when Otto K. E. Heinemann, a producer who sold immigrant records in Yiddish, Swedish, and other languages, recorded singer Mamie Smith performing "Crazy Blues." This smash hit prompted big recording labels like Columbia and Paramount to develop "race records" for black audiences. Yet, while its marketing reflected the segregation of American society at large, jazz brought black music to the center stage of American culture. It became the era's signature music, so much so that novelist F. Scott Fitzgerald dubbed the 1920s the "Jazz Age."

All the nations and people I had hitherto passed throu
resembled our own in their manners, customs and langu

**VOICES
FROM
ABROAD**

Europeans Encounter American Jazz   LEO VAUCHANT

U.S. involvement in World War I carried American jazz to Europe. After the war, some discharged African American soldiers chose to remain in France. Many of these veterans were musicians who quickly found work in Parisian nightclubs performing for war-weary audiences ready for the pleasures of this new music, which was soon adopted by forward-looking European musicians. French drummer and trombonist Leo Vauchant became a noted jazz musician in Paris. He also studied classical composition and later, after emigrating to the United States, wrote scores for Hollywood films. Here he recalls the Parisian jazz scene as he experienced it after World War I.

I loved those black guys. . . . There was always a pianist and a drum set and so we played. Mitchell formed a Tempo Club above Joe Zelli's club and I was the only white guy in that outfit. . . . They accepted me because I played their way, you know. They enjoyed that. It was a challenge — learning their way of playing. I found it novel. I liked the way they approached dance music. It was rhythmical, and the tempo never varied within the tune. Whereas, when the French would play, there was no sense of beat. They were playing things with rubato — there was no dance beat. It didn't swing. It didn't move. . . .

[On Sunday evenings in Paris, after playing an afternoon show] there was nothing to do. So I'd go somewhere to jam. I'd go to the Abbaye Thélème or Zelli's — anywhere. I knew all the musicians so I could go where I wanted. Most of the trombone players were guys that sat there and played from the stocks. So I could go anywhere and be welcome. I wouldn't go to the big places. I'd go to the little clubs and sometimes there'd be black Americans and we'd play till about five o'clock in the morning.

I was always especially glad to play with the black guys. It was always better to play with them. In the first place I liked to speak English. Talking about jazz in French always seemed to me to be ridiculous. It didn't ring true. "Hey, stay in B flat for the first ending." That meant something. The language has a lot to do with it. In America, even today, musicians dress differently, talk differently, they even shake hands differently. . . . I wanted to come to America so much, you've no idea.

To the blacks, life in Europe was like heaven, I can tell you, . . . being able to go any place, and live where they wanted. Also they were looked up to as stars. And that must have been pretty pleasant after life in the States. A lot of French guys resented the blacks going off with their women. But every guy I knew found himself a white broad. . . . They met them as hostesses who danced with them.

SOURCE: Chris Goddard, *Jazz Away from Home* (New York: Paddington Press, 1979), 274, 262.

Marcus Garvey and the UNIA | Harlem produced not only a tremendous burst of artistic creativity but also broad political aspirations. It was no accident that the Universal Negro Improvement Association (UNIA), which arose in the 1920s to mobilize African American workers, was based in Harlem. The UNIA's charismatic leader, Jamaican-born Marcus Garvey, championed black separatism. Garvey urged followers to move to Africa, arguing that peoples of African descent would never be treated justly in white-run countries.

The UNIA grew rapidly in the early 1920s and soon claimed four million followers, including many recent migrants to northern industrial centers. It published a newspaper, *Negro World*, opened "liberty halls" in northern cities, and solicited funds for the Black Star Line steamship company, which Garvey intended to trade with the West Indies and carry American blacks back to Africa. But the UNIA declined as quickly as it had risen. In 1925, Garvey was imprisoned for mail fraud because of his solicitations for the Black Star Line. President Coolidge commuted his sentence but ordered his deportation to Jamaica. Without Garvey's leadership, the movement collapsed.

The UNIA left a legacy of activism, however, especially among working-class blacks. Garvey and his followers represented an emerging **pan-Africanism**: They argued that people of African descent, in all parts of the world, had a common destiny and should cooperate in political action. Black men's military service in Europe during World War I, the Pan-African Congress that had sought representation at the treaty table, protests against the U.S. occupation of Haiti, and modernist experiments in literature and the arts all contributed to this emerging transnational consciousness. One African American historian wrote in 1927: "The grandiose schemes of Marcus Garvey gave to the race a consciousness such as it had never possessed before. The dream of a united Africa, not less than a trip to France, challenged the imagination, and the soul of the Negro experienced a new sense of freedom."

Critiquing American Life

Paralleling the defiant creativity of Harlem, other artists and intellectuals of the 1920s registered various types of dissent. Some had experienced firsthand the shock and devastation of World War I, an experience so searing that American writer Gertrude Stein dubbed those who survived it the "Lost Generation." Novelist John Dos Passos railed at the obscenity of "Mr. Wilson's war" in *The Three Soldiers* (1921). Ernest Hemingway's novels *The Sun Also Rises* (1926) and *A Farewell to Arms* (1929) portrayed the futility and dehumanizing consequences of war. Such work linked American writers to European counterparts such as Siegfried Sassoon, Rebecca West, and Erich Maria Remarque, who explored the devastating impact of trench warfare. In a broad sense, the cataclysm of World War I challenged intellectuals' belief in progress. In his influential poem *The Waste Land* (1922), American expatriate T. S. Eliot, living in Britain, evoked the shattered fragments of a civilization in ruins.

The war also accelerated a literary trend of exploring the dark side of the human psyche. In such dramas as *Desire Under the Elms* (1924), for example, playwright Eugene O'Neill offered a Freudian view of humans' raw, ungovernable sexual impulses. O'Neill first made his mark with *The Emperor Jones* (1920), which appealed to Americans' fascination with Haiti. Telling the story of a black dictator driven from power by an uprising of his people, *The Emperor Jones* offered an ambiguous message. The drama's black protagonist was played not by the customary white actors made up in blackface, but by African Americans who won acclaim for their performances. W. E. B. Du Bois called the popular Broadway drama "a splendid tragedy." But many blacks were dissatisfied with the play's primitivism; one actor who played Emperor Jones altered the script to omit the offensive word *nigger*. The white crowds who made *The Emperor Jones* a hit, much like those who flocked to Harlem's jazz clubs, indulged their fascination with "primitive" sexuality while projecting those traits onto people of African descent.

In a decade of conflict between traditional and modern worldviews, many writers exposed what they saw as the hypocrisy of small-town and rural life. The most savage critic of conformity was Sinclair Lewis, whose novel *Babbitt* (1922) depicted the disillusionment of an ordinary small-town salesman. *Babbitt* was widely denounced as un-American; *Elmer Gantry* (1927), a satire about a greedy evangelical minister on the make, provoked even greater outrage. But critics found Lewis's work superb, and in 1930 he became the first American to win the Nobel Prize for literature. Even more famous was F. Scott Fitzgerald's *The Great Gatsby* (1925), which offered a scathing indictment of Americans' mindless pursuit of pleasure and material wealth.

▶ What were the origins of jazz, and what role did it play in the culture of the 1920s?

▶ What criticisms of mainstream culture did modernist American writers offer in the 1920s?

From Boom to Bust

Spurred by rapid expansion during the war, American business thrived in the 1920s. Corporations expanded more and more into overseas markets, while at home the decade brought the flowering of a national consumer culture that emphasized leisure and amusement. But some sectors of the economy, notably agriculture, never recovered from a sharp recession in the wake of World War I. Meanwhile, close observers worried over the rapid economic growth and easy credit that fueled the "Roaring Twenties." Their fears proved well-founded. In 1929, these factors helped trigger the Great Depression.

Business after the War

By the 1920s, large-scale corporations headed by chief executive officers (CEOs) had replaced individual- or family-run enterprises as the major form of American business organization. Through successive waves of consolidation, the two hundred largest businesses came to control almost half of the country's nonbanking corporate wealth by 1929. The greatest number of mergers occurred in rising industries such as chemicals (with DuPont emerging as the leader) and electrical appliances (General Electric). Rarely did any single corporation monopolize an entire field; rather, an **oligopoly** of a few major producers tended to dominate each market. At the same time, mergers between Wall Street banks enhanced the role of New York City as the financial center of the United States and, increasingly, the world. U.S. companies exercised growing international power. Seeking cheaper livestock, giant American meatpackers opened plants in Argen-

Bananas
... a good mixer
with every fruit that grows

Oranges, apples, grapefruit, pineapples, pears, melons, grapes—all these and many others—blend perfectly with bananas. The distinctive flavor of the banana, when added to a fruit cup, a fruit salad, or any fruit combination, brings out the flavor of the other fruits and makes them taste better.

"EAT plenty of fresh fruits" is now an accepted principle of diet—and the mere sight of mellow, luscious bananas is an invitation to serve many delicious and nourishing fruit combinations.

All year round from the tropics ... Easter, Fourth of July, Thanksgiving, Christmas—every season, every day— bananas are available. Thanks to the nearness and all-year-round productiveness of the tropics, they always can be had at your grocery or fruit store.

Children crave the temptingly flavored banana instinctively. And it is well that they do, for bananas are one of the most important energy-producing foods. Doctors and dietitians consider the banana not only one of the most valuable foods, but also one of the most easily digested ... as beneficial for grown-ups as for children.

Serve bananas with other fruits, with cereals, with milk or cream ... or serve them plain. But always be sure they are fully ripe (generously flecked with brown spots). If they are not at the proper stage of ripeness when you buy them, let them ripen at room temperature. Never place them in the ice-box.

UNIFRUIT BANANAS
Reg. U. S. Pat. Off.
A United Fruit Company Product
Imported and Distributed by Fruit Dispatch Company
17 Battery Place, New York, N. Y.

"Ripe bananas are good for little children."

American Companies Abroad

United Fruit was one of the many American companies that found opportunities for investment in South America in the 1920s and introduced tropical foods to the United States. The company used elaborate and informative color advertisements to sell its products. Bananas were sufficiently exotic that the ads explained to consumers how to tell when bananas were ripe and how to store them ("Never place them in the ice-box"). Duke University Library, Special Collections.

tina. The United Fruit Company developed plantations in Costa Rica, Honduras, and Guatemala. General Electric set up production facilities in Latin America, Asia, and Australia. Republican "dollar diplomats" in Washington worked to support such enterprises.

Immediately after World War I, however, the United States experienced a series of economic shocks. They began with rampant inflation, as prices jumped by one-third in 1919 alone. Then came a sharp two-year recession that raised unemployment to

10 percent. Finally, the economy began to grow smoothly and more Americans began to benefit from the success of corporate enterprise. Between 1922 and 1929, the gross domestic product grew from $74 billion to $103 billion; in the same years, national per capita income rose an impressive 24 percent. Consumer goods, particularly the automobile, sparked this expansion. Not only did the products themselves create growth, but manufacturing cars and refrigerators required huge quantities of steel, chemicals, and oil.

Despite the boom, the U.S. economy had areas of significant weakness throughout the 1920s. Agriculture, which still employed one-fourth of all American workers, never fully recovered from the postwar recession. Once Europe's economy revived, its farmers flooded world markets with grain and other farm products, causing agricultural prices to fall. Other industries, including coal and textiles, languished for similar reasons. As a consequence, many rural Americans shared little of the decade's prosperity. The bottom 40 percent of American families earned an average annual income of only $725 (about $9,100 today). Many, especially rural tenants and sharecroppers, languished in conditions of poverty and malnutrition.

Consumer Culture

In homes across the country, middle-class Americans during the 1920s sat down to a breakfast of Kellogg's corn flakes. They got into Ford Model Ts to go to work or to shop at Safeway. In the evening, families gathered around their radios to listen to such popular programs as *Great Moments in History*; on weekends, they might go to see the newest Charlie Chaplin film at the local theater. By 1929, 40 percent of American households owned a radio. At the same time, electric refrigerators and vacuum cleaners came into use in affluent homes. If one judged from the advertisements in *Good Housekeeping, The Saturday Evening Post*, and other popular magazines, all Americans wore fashionable clothes and drove the latest model cars. That, of course, was not true, but the advertising industry reached new levels of ambition and sophistication, entering what one historian calls the era of the "aggressive hard sell." The 1920s gave birth, for example, to fashion modeling and style consulting. "Sell them their dreams," one radio announcer urged advertisers in 1923. "People don't buy things to have things. . . . They buy hope — hope of what your merchandise will do for them."

In practice, the question of who participated in consumer culture was contested. It was no accident that white mobs in the Tulsa race riot plundered radios and phonograph players from the homes of prosperous African Americans: The clear message was that whites deserved such items and blacks did not. But neither prosperity nor poverty was limited by race. Surrounded by exhortations to indulge in luxuries, millions of working-class Americans — white, black, Latino, immigrant, or native-born — barely squeaked by, with wives and mothers often taking paid work to provide basic necessities. In times of crisis, some families sold all their furniture, starting with pianos and phonograph players and continuing, if necessary, with dining tables and beds. In the Los Angeles suburb of South Gate, white working-class men secured jobs in the steel, automobile, and tire industries, but urban prices were high and families often found it difficult to make ends meet. Self-help was the watchword as husbands and wives pinched pennies, bartered with neighbors, and used their yards to raise large vegetable gardens, rabbits, and chickens.

When every dollar counted, the lure of consumer culture often created friction. Married women resented husbands who spent discretionary cash at the ballpark and expected wives to make do. Generational conflicts emerged, especially when wage-earning children challenged the long-standing expectation that their pay should go "all to mother." In St. Louis, a Czech-born woman was exasperated when her son and daughter stopped contributing to their room and board and pooled their wages to buy a car. In Los Angeles, one fifteen-year-old girl spent her summer earning $2 a day sorting tiles at a local factory. Planning to enroll in business school, she spent the resulting $75 on "a black coat with a red fox collar, costing $40," as well as shoes and other ready-made clothes. Her brother reported that "Mom is angry at her for 'squandering' so much money."

Poor and affluent families often had one thing in common: They stretched their incomes by taking advantage of new forms of borrowing, such as auto loans and installment plans. "Buy now, pay later," said the ads, and millions did—a factor that contributed to the country's broad economic overextension in the 1920s. Anyone, no matter how rich, could get into debt, but consumer credit was particularly perilous for those living on the economic margins. In Chicago, one Lithuanian man casually described his neighbor's financial situation: "She ain't got no money. Sure she buys on credit, clothes for the children and everything." Such borrowing turned out to be a contributing factor to the bust in 1929.

The Automobile │ No possession typified national consumer culture more than the automobile, a showpiece of modern consumer capitalism that revolutionized American economic and social life. Mass production of cars played a major role in the boom of the 1920s. In a single year, 1929, Americans spent $2.58 billion on automobiles. By the end of the decade, they owned 23 million cars—about 80 percent of the world's automobiles—or an average of one car for every six people.

The exuberant expansion of the auto industry rippled through the economy, with both positive and negative results. It stimulated the steel, petroleum, chemical, rubber, and glass industries and, directly or indirectly, provided jobs for 3.7 million workers. Highway construction became a billion-dollar-a-year enterprise, financed by federal subsidies and state gasoline taxes. Car ownership spurred the growth of suburbs and, in 1924, the first suburban shopping center: Country Club Plaza outside Kansas City, Missouri. But cars were expensive, and most Americans bought them on credit. This created risks not only for buyers but for the whole economy. Borrowers who could not pay off car loans lost their entire investment in their cars, and if they defaulted, banks were left holding unpaid loans. Amid the boom of the 1920s, however, such a scenario seemed remote.

Cars changed the way Americans spent their leisure time, as proud drivers took their machines on the road. An infrastructure of gas stations, motels, and drive-in restaurants soon catered to drivers. Cars also changed the dating patterns of young Americans. A Model T offered more privacy than did the family living room or front porch and contributed to increased sexual experimentation among the young. Though early cars were hardly comfortable places for sex, manufacturers learned to accommodate the market. The suggestive Playboy car was advertised, in 1923, as designed for the woman who "can do with eleven hundred pounds of steel and action when he's going high, wide

Automobiles at Jacksonville Beach, Florida, 1923
The automobile transformed Americans' leisure pursuits. As proud car owners took to the road in ever-larger numbers, the "vacation" became a summer staple. Auto travel created a booming business in gas stations, roadside motels, campgrounds, and sightseeing destinations. A Florida vacation — once reserved for wealthy northeasterners who had traveled to Miami's exclusive hotels by first-class railcar — became an attainable luxury for middle-class and even some working-class families. © Curt Teich Postcard Archives, Lake County Museum.

and handsome." The Jewett, introduced in 1925, even had a fold-down bed — for camping on the road, or for other pleasures.

Railroad travel began to falter as automobiles became central to tourism. The American Automobile Association, founded in 1902, estimated that in 1929 almost a third of the population took vacations by car, patronizing "autocamps" and cabins. Already, by 1923, there were 247 autocamps in Colorado alone. "I had a few days after I got my wheat cut," reported one Kansas farmer, "so I just loaded my family . . . and lit out." One elite Californian complained that automobile travel was no longer "aristocratic and exclusive." "All the mechanics, the clerks and their wives and sweethearts," observed a reporter, "driving through the Wisconsin lake country, camping at Niagara, scattering tin cans and pop bottles over the Rockies, made those places taboo for bankers and chairmen of the board."

In rural areas, cars contributed to a consolidation of churches, schools, and post offices: These could now be reached over longer distances, so fewer were needed. The automobile also stimulated intercommunity leagues for softball and other activities — as well as an insatiable interest in movies and other commercial pleasures. It was hard to find any corner of the United States untouched by the automobile. Rural southern blacks, if they could get use of a car, found they could travel three counties away and secure a loan that white bankers in their own county might be reluctant to offer. Whites in South Dakota were "amazed to see Sioux Indians whirl into town in family automobiles." An anthropologist in California found, to his surprise, that men among the Pit River Achumawi people were well prepared to disassemble and repair the engine on his Model T.

Hollywood | Movies, which had their roots in the short silent films shown in turn-of-the-century nickelodeons, formed a second centerpiece of consumer culture in the 1920s. By 1910, the moviemaking industry had moved to southern California to take advantage of cheap land, sunshine, and varied scenery within easy reach. The large studios — United Artists, Paramount, and Metro-Goldwyn-Mayer — were run mainly by Eastern European Jewish immigrants. Adolph Zukor, for example, arrived in the United States from a Hungarian Jewish shtetl in the 1880s. Starting in Chicago with fur sales, Zukor and a partner set up five-cent theaters in Manhattan. "I spent a good deal of time watching the faces of the audience," Zukor recalled. "With a little experience I could see, hear, and 'feel' the reaction to each melodrama and comedy." Founding Paramount Pictures, Zukor sought to produce high-quality, feature-length films. He succeeded, in part, by signing famous rising stars.

By the end of World War I, Hollywood reigned as movie capital of the world, producing nearly 90 percent of all films. New feature-length movies, exhibited in large, ornate theaters, attracted middle-class as well as working-class audiences. Early stars such as Charlie Chaplin, Mary Pickford, and Douglas Fairbanks became idols who set national trends in clothing and hairstyles. In Chicago, young Mexican American men sported sideburns like those of screen star Rudolph Valentino; they called each other "sheik," a reference to one of Valentino's famous roles. Thousands of young women followed the lead of actress Clara Bow, Hollywood's famous flapper, who flaunted her boyish figure. Decked out in knee-length skirts, flappers shocked the older generation by smoking and wearing makeup.

Flappers represented only a tiny minority of women, but thanks to the movies and advertising, they became an influential symbol of women's sexual and social emancipation. In cities, young immigrant women eagerly bought American makeup and the latest flapper fashions and went dancing to jazz. Jazz stars helped popularize the style among working-class African Americans. Mexican American teenagers joined the trend, though they usually found themselves under the watchful eyes of *la dueña*, the chaperone. One *corrido* (ballad) commented sarcastically on the results:

> The girls of San Antonio
> Are lazy at the *metate*.
> They want to walk out bobbed-haired,
> With straw hats on.
> The harvesting is finished,
> So is the cotton;
> The flappers stroll out now
> For a good time.

American radio and film had an immediate global impact, and politicians grasped the potential benefits for the United States. In 1919, with government support, General

The Appeal of the Movies, 1921

Advertising in *Ladies' Home Journal* in May 1921, Paramount Pictures suggested that the local movie theater could bring families closer together. Eager to make the show, father and son help the women of the family clean up after supper so they can drive together to the theater. Picture Research Consultants & Archives.

Electric spearheaded the creation of Radio Corporation of America (RCA), to expand U.S. presence in foreign radio markets. During the 1920s, RCA — which had a federal appointee on its board of directors — emerged as a major provider of radio transmission in Latin America and East Asia. Meanwhile, by 1925, American films made up 95 percent of the movies screened in Britain, 80 percent in Latin America, and 70 percent in France. When Britain and Germany instituted quotas, requiring that the number of imported films not exceed the number of domestic ones, Hollywood studios set up European subsidiaries to churn out hundreds of "quota quickies," allowing the flow of imports to continue unchecked.

As European and Latin American audiences embraced the American movie industry, critics understood it as a serious cultural challenge. Protestant missionaries with "pious brochures," one Frenchman noted gloomily, had been replaced by their "more cheerful offspring," who now deluged the world with "blond movie stars." But, he added, both groups were "equally devoted to spreading the American way of life." As early as 1920, movie stars Douglas Fairbanks and Mary Pickford were greeted by immense crowds when they visited London and Paris on their honeymoon. The State Department, tracking their trip, arranged for the couple to gain extra publicity by meeting with European royalty. The United States was experimenting with what historians call **soft power** — the exercise of popular cultural influence — as radio and movies exuberantly celebrated the American Dream.

The Coming of the Great Depression

Toward the end of the decade, strains on the economy began to show. By 1927, consumer lending had become the tenth-largest business in the country, topping $7 billion a year. Increasing numbers of Americans also bought into the stock market, often with unrealistic expectations. One Yale professor proclaimed that stocks had reached a "permanently high plateau"; a General Motors executive assured readers of *Ladies' Home Journal* that if they saved $15 a month and bought stocks, in two decades they would have $80,000. Corporate profits were so high that some companies, fully invested in their own operations, plowed excess earnings into the stock market. Other market players compounded risk by purchasing on margin. This meant, for example, that an investor spent $20 of his own money and borrowed $80 to buy a $100 share of stock, expecting to pay back the loan as the stock rose rapidly in value. Such a strategy raked in gains as long as the economy grew, jobs were plentiful, and the stock market climbed. But those conditions did not last.

Yet even when the stock market crashed, in a series of plunges between October 25 and November 13, 1929, few onlookers understood the magnitude of the crisis. Deep, cyclical depressions had been a familiar part of the industrializing economy since at least the panic of the 1830s; in a **business cycle** such depressions tended to follow periods of rapid growth and speculation. A sharp downturn had occurred recently, in 1921, without triggering long-term disaster. The market rose again in late 1929 and early 1930, and while a great deal of money had been lost, most Americans hoped the aftermath of the crash would be brief. In fact, the nation had entered the Great Depression. Over the next four years, industrial production fell by 37 percent, and construction plunged by 78 percent. Prices for crops and other raw materials, already low, fell by half. By 1932, unemployment had reached a staggering 24 percent.

A precipitous drop in consumer spending helped deepen the crisis. Having bought on credit, and now facing hard times, consumers cut back dramatically, creating a vicious cycle of falling demand and forfeited loans. In late 1930, several major banks went under, victims of overextended credit and reckless management. As industrial production slowed, a much larger wave of bank failures occurred in 1931. These bank failures caused an even more severe shock. Since the government did not insure bank deposits, savings in failed banks simply vanished. Some people with steady jobs and comfortable savings suddenly found themselves unemployed and penniless.

The Great Depression was, in part, a global crisis that emerged from the aftermath of World War I. By shattering Europe politically and economically, the war had destabilized international systems of trade and finance. Britain's central bank had long played a key role in managing the international financial system; the heavy cost of the war prevented it from resuming that role. In addition, the war disrupted the international gold standard. The United States and most European nations had long tied the value of their currencies to gold. This system had worked fairly well before the crisis of World War I, but it was vulnerable during economic downturns, when foreign financiers withdrew their investments and demanded gold payments.

While many factors caused the Great Depression, adherence to the gold standard was a major factor in its length and severity in the United States. Faced with economic catastrophe, both Britain and Germany abandoned the gold standard in 1931; when they did so, their economies began a modest recovery. A similar pattern held for other industrialized and developing countries. But the Hoover administration argued that such a move would cause irreparable damage to trade and the value of the dollar. Thus the Federal Reserve, the central banking system that had been created in 1913, was forced to do two contradictory things at once: try to revive the economy and protect the nation's gold supply. The United States finally left the gold standard in 1933, under Franklin D. Roosevelt's administration. This, and Roosevelt's resuscitation of banks, stimulated a partial recovery between 1933 and 1937. But by that time, the crisis had achieved catastrophic dimensions. Billions had been lost in bank and business failures, and the economy had stalled completely. Partial recovery brought unemployment down from 25 to a "mere" 14 percent.

Adhering to their long-standing faith in high protective tariffs, Republicans not only protected the gold standard but also enacted the Smoot-Hawley Tariff of 1930, hoping to stimulate domestic manufacturing. Historians are divided on whether the tariff worsened the depression, but it certainly did not help. It triggered retaliatory tariffs in other countries, as governments worldwide struggled to protect their own industries. Adopting a more helpful measure, in 1932, President Hoover created the Reconstruction Finance Corporation to provide loans to banks, railroads, and utilities. The administration also slashed taxes, and Hoover exhorted state and local governments to employ the jobless on public projects (though he and Congress proved unwilling to enact such measures at the federal level). Overall, though, Republicans clung to the belief that depressions were healthy and self-regulating. Treasury Secretary Andrew Mellon suggested that the downturn would help Americans "work harder" and "live a more moral life."

Thus, while the Great Depression began mere months after Hoover took office, the conditions that worsened it unfolded gradually over his presidential term. By the early 1930s, comprehending the magnitude of the crisis, Americans looked back wistfully on the previous decade of prosperity. In the 1920s, business had boomed and politics had been so placid that people chuckled when President Coolidge disappeared on extended fishing trips. In the following decade, Americans still flocked to the movies when they could afford it, eager to see light-hearted comedies that would help them forget their woes. But they now wanted bold action in Washington. In 1932, voters replaced Herbert Hoover with Democrat Franklin D. Roosevelt. Republicans, who had held solid majorities in both houses of Congress as late as 1931, found themselves swept out of power. Faced with the cataclysm of the Great Depression, Americans transformed their government and created a modern welfare state.

▶ How did the automobile exemplify both the opportunities and the risks of 1920s consumer culture?

▶ What domestic and global factors triggered the Great Depression? What accounted for its length and severity? What steps did Hoover take to address the crisis?

SUMMARY

Although involvement in the Great War (World War I) strengthened the United States economically and diplomatically, it also left the nation profoundly unsettled. Racial tensions exploded after the war as African Americans sought to pursue new opportunities and assert their rights. Meanwhile, labor unrest grew as employers cut wages and sought to break unions. Labor's power declined sharply in the war's aftermath, while anxieties over radicalism and immigration also prompted the nationwide Red Scare.

The politics of the 1920s brought a backlash against prewar progressivism. The efforts of women reformers to advance a reform agenda met very limited success. Republican administrations pursued pro-business "normalcy" at home and "dollar diplomacy" abroad. Prohibition and the Scopes trial demonstrated the influence religion could exert on public policy, while rising nativism fueled a resurgent Ku Klux Klan and led to sweeping new restrictions on immigration.

Postwar alienation found artistic expression in new forms of modernism, which denounced the dehumanizing effects of the war and criticized American materialism and hypocrisy. Spreading throughout the nation from New Orleans, jazz appealed to elite and popular audiences alike. Black artists and intellectuals of the Harlem Renaissance, including many who were inspired by pan-African ideas, explored the complexities of African American life.

During the 1920s, business thrived and a booming consumer culture, exemplified by the automobile and Hollywood films, created new forms of leisure, influencing daily life and challenging older sexual norms. However, the risky speculation and easy credit of the period undermined the foundations of the economy. After the 1929 crash, these factors, along with a range of interconnected global conditions, plunged the United States into the Great Depression.

For additional primary sources from this period, see *Documents for America's History*, Seventh Edition.

For Web sites, images, and documents related to topics and places in this chapter, visit *Make History* at **bedfordstmartins.com/henrettaconcise.**

TIMELINE

1912	► United States occupies Nicaragua	**1923**	► *Adkins v. Children's Hospital*
1913	► Henry Ford introduces moving assembly line		► President Harding dies; Calvin Coolidge assumes presidency
1915	► New Ku Klux Klan founded	**1924**	► National Origins Act
	► United States occupies Haiti		► Coolidge wins presidential election
1916	► United States occupies Dominican Republic		► First suburban shopping center opens in Kansas City, Missouri
1917	► Race riot in East St. Louis, Illinois	**1925**	► *Coronado Coal Company v. United Mine Workers*
1919	► Race riot in Chicago		► Scopes "monkey trial"
	► Boston police strike		► Height of new Ku Klux Klan's power
	► Palmer raids		► Marcus Garvey deported
	► Women's International Committee for Peace founded		► F. Scott Fitzgerald's *The Great Gatsby*
1920	► Height of Red Scare	**1927**	► Sacco and Vanzetti executed
	► Sacco and Vanzetti arrested	**1928**	► Herbert Hoover wins presidency
	► Eighteenth Amendment takes effect	**1929**	► Stock market crashes precipitate Great Depression
	► Warren Harding wins presidency	**1930**	► Smoot-Hawley Tariff
	► Eugene O'Neill's *The Emperor Jones*	**1932**	► Franklin D. Roosevelt elected president
1921	► Race riots in Rosewood, Florida, and Tulsa, Oklahoma	**1933**	► United States abandons gold standard
	► Sheppard-Towner Federal Maternity and Infancy Act		

For Further Exploration

Lynn Dumenil, *The Modern Temper* (1995), offers a good overview of the 1920s; see also Michael Parris, *Anxious Decades* (1992). On Margaret Sanger see Linda Gordon, *The Moral Property of Women* (2002); on race riots, Scott Ellsworth, *Death in a Promised Land* (1982), and Michael D'Orso, *Like Judgement Day* (1996). On nativism see David M. Reimers, *Unwelcome Strangers* (1998), and Noriko Asato, *Teaching Mikadoism* (2006).

For politics, consult Ellis Hawley, *The Great War and the Search for a Modern Order* (1979), and Lee Nash, ed., *Understanding Herbert Hoover* (1987). Emily S. Rosenberg covers foreign relations in *Spreading the American Dream* (1982) and *Financial Missionaries to the World* (2003). On U.S. involvement in Haiti, see Mary A. Renda, *Taking Haiti* (2001). On the Harlem Renaissance see David Levering Lewis, *When Harlem Was in Vogue* (1979), and on Marcus Garvey, **www.pbs.org/wgbh/amex/garvey**.

An overview of consumer credit is Martha L. Olney, *Buy Now, Pay Later* (1991). On working-class and immigrant families see Susan Porter Benson, *Household Accounts* (2007), Becky Nicolaides, *My Blue Heaven* (2002), Vicki Ruíz, *From Out of the Shadows* (1998), and Gabriela Arredondo, *Mexican Chicago* (2008). On the impact of cars see James J. Flink, *The Automobile Age* (1988), and Michael L. Berger, *The Devil Wagon in God's Country* (1979). On the coming of the Great Depression a groundbreaking book is Barry Eichengreen, *Golden Fetters* (1992). For a broad view of the crash see **www.pbs.org/wgbh/amex/crash**.

Test Your Knowledge

For practice quizzes, activities, and other study tools, visit the Online Study Guide at **bedfordstmartins.com/henrettaconcise**.

6 The Modern State and the Age of Liberalism

1929–1973

"What Rome was to the ancient world," proclaimed the influential journalist Walter Lippmann in 1945, "America is for the world of tomorrow." Lippmann believed that the United States, having emerged from World War II triumphant, was poised to play a leading role in world affairs. What Lippman underestimated were the challenges, global and domestic, confronting the postwar United States. In this Part 6, covering the years 1929–1973, we track how the United States responded to the depression by creating a modern welfare state, enlarged that state to fight a war on three continents, and then entered a prolonged period of international tension and conflict known as the Cold War. These developments were intertwined with the predominance of liberalism in American politics. One might think of an "age of liberalism" in this era, encompassing the social welfare liberalism of the New Deal and the rights liberalism of the 1960s — inspired by the modern civil rights movement — both of which came to fall under the larger umbrella of Cold War liberalism.

ECONOMY In response to the Great Depression, President Franklin Roosevelt's New Deal expanded federal responsibility for the welfare of ordinary citizens, sweeping away much of the laissez-faire individualism that dominated earlier eras. Wartime measures went even further, as the government mobilized the entire economy and tens of millions of citizens to fight the Axis Powers. After the war, prodded by liberal ideas about the good that government can do, legislators from both political parties helped create the largest middle class in the nation's history, through such measures as the GI Bill, subsidies for suburban homeownership, and educational initiatives. More than ever, the American economy was driven by mass consumption and the accompanying process of suburbanization. Poverty, however, affected nearly one-third of Americans in the 1960s. The lack of economic opportunity became a driving force in the civil rights movement and in the Great Society under President Lyndon Johnson.

DIPLOMACY Faced with the rise of fascist powers in Europe and Japan and of isolationist sentiment at home, the Roosevelt administration steered a middle course. In the late 1930s, it began to send aid to its traditional ally Great Britain without committing U.S. military forces. This strategy kept the nation out of the brewing wars in Europe and the Pacific until late 1941. When the United States officially joined World War II, it entered into a "Grand Alliance" with England and the Soviet Union. That alliance proved impossible to sustain after 1945, as the United States and the Soviet Union became competitors to shape postwar Europe, Asia, and the developing world. The resulting Cold War lasted four decades, during which the United States extended an unprecedented political and military reach onto every continent.

POLITICS The New Deal set the tone for American politics throughout this period. Though Democrats and Republicans differed over key issues — such as the power of the labor movement — there was broad agreement that a modern welfare state was necessary to regulate the economy and provide a basic safety net for the nation's citizens. Anticommunism was another unifying force. Political leaders from both parties sought to contain communism abroad and isolate "subversives" at home. The result was "Cold War liberalism," a centrist politics that rejected radicalisms of both the left and the right. By the late 1960s, however, Cold War liberalism was under attack from the antiwar and civil rights movements on the left and new conservative groups on the right. The liberal coalition fractured and split, and by the 1970s a new conservative age had dawned.

SOCIETY A defining characteristic of the "age of liberalism" was the growth of the American middle class. Rising wages, increasing access to higher education, and the availability of suburban homeownership raised living standards and allowed more Americans than ever to afford consumer goods. Suburbanization transformed the nation's cities, and the Sunbelt led the nation in population growth. But the new prosperity had mixed results. Cities declined and new racial and ethnic ghettoes formed. These conditions, alongside continued southern segregation, helped to fuel the civil rights movement, a decades-long effort to ensure equal opportunity for African Americans. Adopting the civil rights model, women, Mexican Americans and other Latino groups, Native Americans, and gays and lesbians helped spawn a "rights" revolution.

CULTURE Two powerful forces shaped American culture in this era: the advent of television and the youth-centered baby boom. By the mid-1950s, nearly every household in the country had a television. Americans increasingly experienced defining events — the Cuban Missile Crisis, the assassination of President Kennedy, and the Vietnam War, for instance — through television. Through this new medium, the advertising industry attained an unprecedented power to create consumer desire and shape purchasing habits. Meanwhile, baby boom children embraced new musical forms (rock 'n' roll, rhythm and blues, and the folk revival, especially), experimented with countercultural sexual values, and forged a "youth culture" that remains influential to this day.

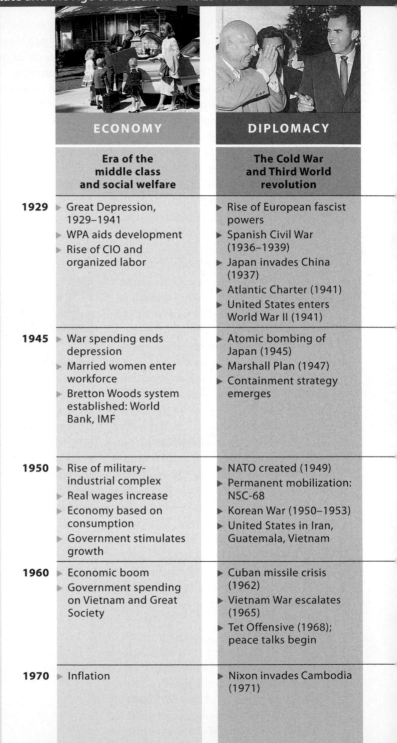

	ECONOMY	DIPLOMACY
	Era of the middle class and social welfare	**The Cold War and Third World revolution**
1929	▶ Great Depression, 1929–1941 ▶ WPA aids development ▶ Rise of CIO and organized labor	▶ Rise of European fascist powers ▶ Spanish Civil War (1936–1939) ▶ Japan invades China (1937) ▶ Atlantic Charter (1941) ▶ United States enters World War II (1941)
1945	▶ War spending ends depression ▶ Married women enter workforce ▶ Bretton Woods system established: World Bank, IMF	▶ Atomic bombing of Japan (1945) ▶ Marshall Plan (1947) ▶ Containment strategy emerges
1950	▶ Rise of military-industrial complex ▶ Real wages increase ▶ Economy based on consumption ▶ Government stimulates growth	▶ NATO created (1949) ▶ Permanent mobilization: NSC-68 ▶ Korean War (1950–1953) ▶ United States in Iran, Guatemala, Vietnam
1960	▶ Economic boom ▶ Government spending on Vietnam and Great Society	▶ Cuban missile crisis (1962) ▶ Vietnam War escalates (1965) ▶ Tet Offensive (1968); peace talks begin
1970	▶ Inflation	▶ Nixon invades Cambodia (1971)

POLITICS	SOCIETY	CULTURE
Rise and fall of the liberal consensus	**Social movements and the rights revolution**	**Consumer culture and its critics**
▸ Franklin Roosevelt elected president (1932) ▸ First New Deal (1933) ▸ Second New Deal (1935) ▸ Social welfare liberalism	▸ Bonus Army (1932) ▸ Social Security created (1935) ▸ Rural electrification ▸ Federal Housing Authority (1937)	▸ Documentary impulse in arts ▸ WPA assists artists
▸ Truman's Fair Deal ▸ Loyalty-Security Program ▸ Taft-Hartley Act (1947) ▸ Truman reelected (1948)	▸ Imprisonment of Japanese Americans ▸ Segregation in armed services ▸ Rural blacks and whites migrate to cities for war jobs ▸ Early civil rights organizing	▸ Film industry aids war effort ▸ Rationing curbs consumer spending
▸ Cold War liberalism ▸ McCarthyism and Red Scare ▸ Eisenhower's liberal Republicanism	▸ Treaty of Detroit (1950) ▸ *Brown v. Board of Education* (1954) ▸ Montgomery bus boycott (1955)	▸ Growth of suburbia and Sunbelt ▸ Height of baby boom ▸ Jazz, Bebop, the Beats ▸ Youth culture develops
▸ Kennedy's New Frontier ▸ Kennedy assassinated (1963) ▸ War on Poverty; Great Society ▸ Nixon elected (1968)	▸ March on Washington (1963) ▸ Civil Rights legislation (1964, 1965) ▸ Student and antiwar activism ▸ Black Power	▸ Shopping malls and fast food ▸ Baby boomers swell college enrollment ▸ Hippie counterculture
▸ Nixon landslide (1972)	▸ Revival of women's movement ▸ Conservative resurgence	▸ Consumer-safety movement

I hope relief will be coming
soon and action not just
paper talk. . . . I hope that
Wall Street will never have
the power again to cause
such a panic.

—Anonymous resident of Pottstown,
Pennsylvania; letter to Herbert Hoover,
October 30, 1930

In his inaugural address in March 1933, President Franklin Delano Roosevelt did not hide the country's precarious condition. "A host of unemployed citizens face the grim problem of existence," he said, "and an equally great number toil with little return. Only a foolish optimist can deny the dark realities of the moment." Roosevelt, his demeanor sincere and purposeful, saw both despair and determination as he looked out over the country. "This nation asks for action, and action now." From Congress he would request "broad Executive power to wage a war against the emergency, as great as the power that would be given to me if we were in fact invaded by a foreign foe." With these words, Roosevelt launched a program of federal activism — which he called the New Deal — that would change the nature of American government.

The New Deal represented a new form of liberalism, a fresh interpretation of the ideology of individual rights that had long shaped the character of American society and politics. Classical nineteenth-century liberals believed that, to protect those rights, government should be small and relatively powerless. However, the "regulatory" liberals of the early twentieth century had safeguarded individual freedom and opportunity by strengthening state and federal control over large businesses and monopolies. New Deal activists went much further: Their **social-welfare liberalism** expanded individual rights to include minimum standards of economic security. Beginning in the 1930s and continuing through the 1960s, they increased the responsibility of the national government for the welfare of ordinary citizens. Their efforts did not go unchallenged. Conservative critics of the New Deal charged that its program of "big government" and "social welfare" was both paternalistic and dangerous — a threat to individual responsibility and personal freedom. This division between the advocates and the critics of the New Deal shaped American politics for the next half century.

Before Roosevelt became president, between the onset of the depression in 1929 and the election of 1932, the "dark realities of the moment" wore down American society.

The New Deal
This Federal Arts Project poster from 1936 captured the spirit of the New Deal under President Franklin Roosevelt. Roosevelt and other "New Dealers" hoped to get people working again during the depths of the Great Depression, raise their spirits, and help rebuild the national infrastructure. Library of Congress.

Rising unemployment, shuttered businesses, failing banks, and home foreclosures tore at the nation's social fabric. As crisis piled upon crisis, and the federal government's initiatives under President Hoover proved weak and ineffectual, Americans had to reconsider more than the role of government in economic life: They had to rethink many of the principles of individualism and free enterprise that had guided so much of the nation's history.

The Early Years of the Depression, 1929–1932

The American economy went rapidly downhill between 1929 and 1932. U.S. gross domestic product fell almost by half, from $103.1 billion to $58 billion. Consumption dropped by 18 percent, construction by 78 percent, and private investment by 88 percent. Nearly 9,000 banks closed their doors, and 100,000 businesses failed. Corporate profits fell from $10 billion to $1 billion. Most tellingly, unemployment rose to 25 percent. Fifteen million people were out of work by 1933, and many who had jobs took wage cuts. "Hoover made a souphound outa me!" sang jobless harvest hands in the Southwest.

Down and Out: Life in the Great Depression

Not all Americans were devastated by the depression; the middle class did not disappear, and the rich lived in their accustomed luxury. But more Americans than ever were without gainful employment or means of support. Incomes plummeted among workers in the cities and among farmers in rural areas. In September 1931, with unemployment hovering around 17 percent, Salt Lake City ran out of money. Barbers traded haircuts for onions and Idaho potatoes. Laborers put in a day's work for payment in eggs, peaches, or pork. The depression years are filled with such stories. The down and out did what they could to survive. "We do not dare to use even a little soap," wrote a jobless Oregonian, "when it will pay for an extra egg, a few more carrots for our children." "I would be only too glad to dig ditches to keep my family from going hungry," wrote a North Carolina man. By almost any standard, the depression was the worst national crisis since the Civil War.

Where did people turn in these years? The first line of defense was private charity, especially churches and synagogues. But by the winter of 1931, these institutions were overwhelmed, unable to keep pace with the extraordinary need. Only eight states provided any unemployment insurance, and it was minimal. There was no public support for the aged — the elderly, statistically among the poorest citizens, relied on their grown children. Few Americans had any retirement savings. Soup kitchens, bread lines, and the helping hands of neighbors were appreciated, but they could not permanently lift the millions whom the depression had wiped out.

Even if they fell short of being wiped out, Americans had to adapt to depression conditions. Couples delayed marriage and reduced the number of children they conceived. As a consequence, the marriage rate fell to a historical low, and the birthrate dropped from 97 births per 1,000 women to 75 by 1933. Limiting reproduction was a couple's decision, but often the responsibility for birth control fell to women. It "was one of the worst problems of women whose husbands were out of work," one Californian told a reporter. Women also endured additional burdens. Campaigns against hiring married women were common, on the theory that available jobs should go to male breadwinners. Three-quarters of the school districts in the country banned married women from being hired as teachers. Despite such restrictions, female employment increased during the decade of the 1930s, as women expanded their financial contributions to their families in the face of hard times.

Depression conditions respected no national or regional boundaries, though the severity of economic contraction varied from place to place. Germany had preceded the United States into depression in 1928, and its economy, burdened by World War I reparation payments, had been brought to its knees by 1929. France, Britain, Argentina, Poland, and Canada were hard hit as well (see Voices from Abroad, p. 698). Within the United States, there were regional variations. Southern states generally fared better, having fewer manufacturing establishments than northern states — although agricultural wages plummeted in the South. Bank failures tended to be concentrated in farming states in the Midwest and Plains. Regions dependent on timber, mining, and other resource extraction industries experienced a steeper downturn than regions with more mixed economies. In northern industrial cities and the southern states, the unemployment rate among African American men was double that of white men. Among African American women it was triple that of white women. The depression, and the lives the crisis changed, touched every corner of the country.

Herbert Hoover Responds

President Hoover responded to the downturn by drawing on two powerful American traditions. The first was the belief that economic outcomes were the product of individual character. Success went to those who deserved it. People's fate was in their own hands, not in the workings of the market. The second tradition held that through voluntary action, the business community could regulate itself. Reflecting these ideologies, Hoover asked Americans to tighten their belts and work hard. Following the stock market crash, he cut federal taxes in an attempt to boost private spending and corporate investment. "Any lack of confidence in the economic future or the strength of business in the United States is foolish," Hoover assured the country in late 1929.

But the president recognized that voluntarism might not be enough, given the depth of the crisis, and he proposed government action as well. He called on state and local governments to provide jobs by investing in public projects. And in 1931, he secured an unprecedented increase of $700 million in federal spending for public works. Hoover's most innovative program was the Reconstruction Finance Corporation (RFC), which stimulated economic activity by providing federal loans to railroads, banks, and other businesses. This plan might have worked, but the RFC lent money too cautiously. By the end of 1932, after a year in operation, it had loaned out only 20 percent of its $1.5 billion in funds. Like most federal initiatives under Hoover, the RFC was not nearly aggressive enough given the severity of the depression.

Hoover was as unlucky as any American president. Few chief executives could have survived the downward economic spiral of 1929–1932, but Hoover's reluctance to break with the philosophy of limited government and his insistence that recovery was always just around the corner contributed to his unpopularity. Unemployment during the depression was simply too massive for private charities and local governments to handle. By 1932, Americans perceived Hoover, despite his many accomplishments, as insensitive to the depth of the country's economic woes. The nation had come a long way since the depressions of the 1870s and 1890s, when no one except the most radical figures, such as Jacob Coxey, called for direct federal aid to the unemployed (see Chapter 20).

All the nations and people I had hitherto passed throu
resembled our own in their manners, customs and langua

A British Historian Looks at the Great Depression
DENIS W. BROGAN

Denis Brogan, a professor at Cambridge University in England, was a noted critic of the United States. In a book written in the 1950s, Brogan looked back at the descent into the Great Depression between 1929 and 1932 and explained the significance of Franklin Roosevelt's election from a European perspective.

It is now nearly thirty-five years since I first visited the United States, and in that time I have returned repeatedly. . . . In the course of these visits I have been more than once in every region of the country, and have lived stretches of time in all of them except the Deep South. Thus my view of the promise, achievements, and limitations of American life has changed continually over the past generation or more, as the United States itself has changed. . . .

The success of the United States was limited, so the critics thought, to the more crude forms of material advancement, to central heating, a car in every garage, the creation of a mass market supplied by crude if popular artifacts like the Model T Ford. The life that was satisfied by these material achievements was drab and spiritually uninteresting. . . .

Then came the great debacle. No event . . . has so colored the European view of the United States as "the Depression." The first news of the crash of 1929 was not ill received. There was not only a marked feeling of *Schadenfreude* at the snub that destiny had given to the overconfident masters of the new world, but also a widespread belief that the extravagant gambling of the New York market was one of the chief causes of our ills. . . .

In the depression years more people fled America than entered it. The emigrants were embittered, disillusioned. Their stories of bread lines, of apple sellers, of the savagery of the police (including Ford's muscle men), of the cruelties of the primitive social services, revived all the old suspicions of a country in which the rich, ruthless, callous, savage, ruled . . .

American politics was seen as not only sterile but positively immoral and dangerous. Criticism of the existing political order and of the Republican Party grew to a great height outside the United States. Mr. Hoover's moralism was as much disliked as his positive policy. . . . And it is safe to say that the election of F. D. Roosevelt was welcomed in every country of Europe as good news almost overshadowing the nomination of Adolf Hitler as Chancellor of the German Reich.

SOURCE: Denis W. Brogan, "From England," in *As Others See Us: The United States Through Foreign Eyes*, ed. Franz M. Joseph (Princeton, NJ: Princeton University Press, 1959), 3–10.

Compared with previous chief executives — and in contrast to his popular image as a "do-nothing" president — Hoover had responded to the national emergency with government action on an unprecedented scale. But the nation's needs were even more unprecedented, and Hoover's programs failed to meet them.

Rising Discontent

As the depression deepened, the American vocabulary now included "Hoovervilles" (shantytowns where people lived in packing crates) and "Hoover blankets" (newspapers). Bankrupt farmers banded together to resist the bank agents and sheriffs who tried to evict them from their land. To protest low prices for their goods, thousands of farmers joined the Farm Holiday Association, which cut off supplies to urban areas by barricading roads and dumping milk, vegetables, and other foodstuffs onto the roadways.

Layoffs and wage cuts led to violent industrial strikes. When coal miners in Harlan County, Kentucky, went on strike over a 10 percent wage cut in 1931, the mine owners called in the state's National Guard, which crushed the union. A 1932 confrontation between workers and security forces at the Ford Motor Company's giant River Rouge factory outside Detroit left five workers dead and fifty with serious injuries. A photographer had his camera shot from his hands, and fifteen policemen were clubbed or stoned. Such examples abounded.

Veterans staged the most publicized — and most tragic — protest. In the summer of 1932, the so-called Bonus Army, a determined group of 15,000 unemployed World War I veterans, hitchhiked to Washington to demand immediate payment of pension awards that were due to be paid in 1945. "We were heroes in 1917, but we're bums now," one veteran complained bitterly. While their leaders unsuccessfully lobbied Congress, the Bonus Army set up camps near the Capitol building. Hoover called out regular army troops under the command of General Douglas MacArthur. MacArthur forcefully evicted the marchers and burned their main encampment to the ground. When newsreel footage showing the U.S. Army attacking and injuring veterans reached movie theaters across the nation, Hoover's popularity plunged. In another measure of how the country had changed since the 1890s, what Americans had applauded when done to Coxey in 1894 was condemned in 1932.

The 1932 Election

Despite rising discontent, the national mood was mixed as the 1932 election approached. Many Americans had internalized the ideal of the self-made man and blamed themselves for their economic hardships. Despair, not anger, characterized their mood. Others, out of work for a year or more, perhaps homeless, felt the deeper stirrings of frustration and rage. Regardless of their circumstances, most Americans believed that something altogether *new* had to be tried — whatever that might be. The Republicans, reluctant to dump an incumbent president, unenthusiastically renominated Hoover. The Democrats turned to New York governor Franklin Delano Roosevelt, whose state had initiated innovative relief and unemployment programs.

Roosevelt, born into a wealthy New York family, was a distant cousin to former president Theodore Roosevelt, whose career he emulated. After attending Harvard College and Columbia University, Franklin Roosevelt served as assistant secretary of the navy during World War I (as Theodore Roosevelt had done before the War of 1898). Then, in 1921, a crippling attack of polio left both of his legs paralyzed for life. Strongly supported by his wife, Eleanor, he slowly returned to public life and campaigned successfully for the governorship of New York in 1928 and again in 1930. In campaigning for the presidency in 1932, Roosevelt pledged vigorous action but gave no indication as to what that might be, arguing simply that "the country needs and, unless I mistake its temper, the country demands bold, persistent experimentation." He won easily, receiving 22.8 million votes to Hoover's 15.7 million.

Elected in November, Roosevelt would not begin his presidency until March 1933. (The Twentieth Amendment, ratified in 1933, set subsequent inaugurations for January 20.) Meanwhile, Americans suffered through the worst winter of the depression.

▶ Why did President Hoover respond to the economic emergency as he did?

▶ What problems in the economy and society of the United States were exposed by the Great Depression?

Unemployment continued to climb, and in three major industrial cities in Ohio, it was staggering: 50 percent in Cleveland, 60 percent in Akron, and 80 percent in Toledo. Private charities and public relief agencies reached only a fraction of the needy. The nation's banking system was so close to collapse that many state governors closed banks temporarily to avoid further withdrawals. By March 1933, the nation had hit rock bottom.

The New Deal Arrives, 1933–1935

Ironically, the ideological differences between Herbert Hoover and Franklin Roosevelt were not vast. Both leaders wished to maintain the nation's economic institutions and social values, to save capitalism while easing its worst downturns. Both believed in a balanced government budget and extolled the values of hard work, cooperation, and sacrifice. But Roosevelt's personal charm, political savvy, and willingness to experiment made him immensely popular and far more effective than Hoover. Most Americans felt a kinship with their new president, calling him simply "FDR." His New Deal programs put people to work and restored hope for the nation's future. "The New Deal was so abruptly different it was startling," remarked a seasoned Washington journalist.

Roosevelt and the First Hundred Days

A wealthy aristocrat from a patrician family, Roosevelt was an unlikely figure to inspire millions of ordinary Americans. But inspire them he did. His close rapport with the American people was critical to his political success. More than 450,000 letters poured into the White House in the week after his inauguration. The president's masterful use of the new medium of radio, especially his "fireside chats," made him an intimate presence in people's lives. Thousands of citizens felt a personal relationship with FDR, saying, "He gave me a job" or "He saved my home" (see American Voices, p. 701).

Roosevelt's charisma, coupled with the national economic emergency, allowed him to broaden further the presidential powers that Theodore Roosevelt and Woodrow

Ordinary People Respond to the New Deal

Franklin Roosevelt's fireside chats and relief programs prompted thousands of Americans to write directly to him and his wife, Eleanor. Mrs. M. H. A. worked in the County Court House in Eureka, California; R. A., a sixty-nine-year-old man, was an architect and builder in Lincoln, Nebraska; and M. A., a woman, held a low-level salaried position in a corporation.

June 14, 1934
Dear Mrs. Roosevelt:
My husband and I are a young couple of very simple, almost poor families. We married eight years ago on the proverbial shoe-string but with a wealth of love. . . . But with the exception of two and one-half months work with the U.S. Coast and Geodetic Survey under the C.W.A. [Civil Works Administration], my husband has not had work since August, 1932.

My salary could continue to keep us going, but I am to have a baby. . . .

We have always stood on our own feet and been proud and happy. But you are a mother and you'll understand this crisis.

Very sincerely yours,
Mrs. M. H. A.

May 19/34
Dear Mrs Roosevelt:
In the Presidents inaugral address delivered from the capitol steps the afternoon of his inauguration he made mention of The Forgotten Man, and I with thousands of others am wondering if the folk who was borned here in America some 60 or 70 years a go are this Forgotten Man, the President had in mind, if we are this Forgotten Man then we are still Forgotten. . . .

First we have grown to what is termed Old Age, this befalls every man.

Second, . . . we are confronted on every hand with the young generation, taking our places, this of corse is what we have looked forward to in training our children. But with the extra ordinary crisese which left us helpless and placed us in the position that our fathers did not have to contend with. . . .

Yours very truly.
R. A.

Jan. 18, 1937
[Dear Mrs. Roosevelt:]
I . . . was simply astounded to think that anyone could be nitwit enough to wish to be included in the so called social security act if they could possibly avoid it. Call it by any name you wish it, in my opinion, (and that of many people I know) [it] is nothing but downright stealing. . . .

I am not an "economic royalist," just an ordinary white collar worker at $1600 per [year — about $23,600 in 2011]. Please show this to the president and ask him to remember the wishes of the forgotten man, that is, the one who dared to vote against him. We expect to be tramped on but we do wish the stepping would be a little less hard.
M. A.

SOURCES: Robert S. McElvaine, *Down and Out in the Great Depression* (Chapel Hill: University of North Carolina Press, 1983), 54–55; Michael P. Johnson, ed., *Reading the American Past*, 4th ed., 2 vols. (Boston: Bedford/St. Martin's, 2009), 2: 171; Robert D. Marcus and David Burner, eds., *America Firsthand*, 7th ed. (Boston: Bedford/St. Martin's, 2007), 184.

Wilson had expanded previously. To draft legislation and policy, he relied heavily on financier Bernard Baruch and a "Brains Trust" of professors from Columbia, Harvard, and other leading universities. Roosevelt turned as well to his talented cabinet, which included Harold L. Ickes, secretary of the interior; Frances Perkins at the Labor Department; Henry A. Wallace at Agriculture; and Henry Morgenthau Jr., secretary of the Treasury. These intellectuals and administrators attracted hundreds of highly qualified recruits to Washington. Inspired by the idealism of the New Deal, many of them would devote their lives to public service and the principles of social-welfare liberalism.

Roosevelt could have done little, however, without a sympathetic Congress. The 1932 election had swept Democratic majorities into both the House and Senate, giving the new president the lawmaking allies he needed. The political tide had turned against the Republicans in full. The first months of FDR's administration produced a whirlwind of activity on Capitol Hill. In a legendary session, known as the "Hundred Days," Congress enacted fifteen major bills that focused primarily on four problems: banking failures, agricultural overproduction, the business slump, and soaring unemployment. Derided by opponents as an "alphabet soup" because of the many abbreviations they spawned (CCC, WPA, AAA, etc.), the new policies and agencies were more than bureaucracies: They represented the first blush of a new American state.

Banking Reform | The weak banking system placed a drag on the entire economy, curtailing consumer spending and business investment. Widespread bank failures had cut into the savings of nearly nine million families, and panicked account holders raced to withdraw their funds. On March 5, 1933, the day after his inauguration, FDR declared a national "bank holiday"— closing all the banks — and called Congress into special session. Four days later, Congress passed the Emergency Banking Act, which permitted banks to reopen if a Treasury Department inspection showed that they had sufficient cash reserves.

In his first Sunday night fireside chat, to a radio audience of sixty million, the president reassured citizens of the safety of their money. When the banking system reopened on March 13, deposits exceeded withdrawals, restoring stability to the nation's basic financial institutions. "Capitalism was saved in eight days," quipped Roosevelt's advisor Raymond Moley. Four thousand banks had collapsed in the months prior to Roosevelt's inauguration; only sixty-one closed their doors in all of 1934. A second banking law, the Glass-Steagall Act, further restored public confidence by creating the Federal Deposit Insurance Corporation (FDIC), which insured deposits up to $2,500 (and now insures them up to $250,000) and prohibited banks from making risky, unsecured investments. And in a move with profound symbolic importance, Roosevelt removed the U.S. Treasury from the gold standard, which allowed the Federal Reserve to lower interest rates — it had been *raising* rates since 1931, which had only deepened the downturn.

Agriculture and Manufacturing | Roosevelt and the New Deal Congress next turned to agriculture and manufacturing. The national government had long assisted farmers through cheap prices for land, Department of Agriculture programs, and low-interest loans. But the Agricultural Adjustment Act (AAA) began direct governmental regulation of the farm economy. To solve the problem of overproduction, which lowered prices, the AAA provided cash subsidies to farmers who cut production

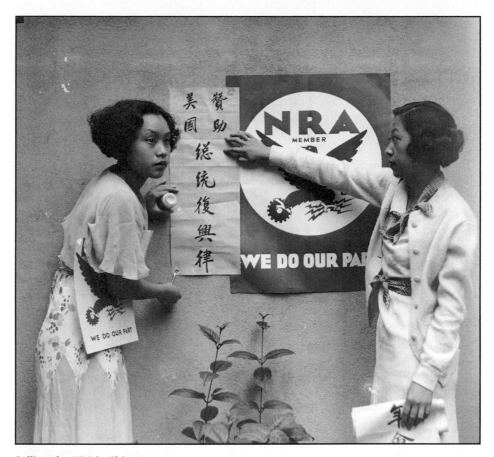

Selling the NRA in Chinatown
To mobilize support for its program, the National Recovery Administration (NRA) distributed millions of posters to businesses and families, urging them to display its symbol, the Blue Eagle, in shops, factories, and homes. Here Constance King and Mae Chinn of the Chinese YMCA affix a poster (and a Chinese translation) to a shop in San Francisco that is complying with the NRA codes. © Copyright Bettmann / Corbis.

of seven major commodities: wheat, cotton, corn, hogs, rice, tobacco, and dairy products. The hope was that farm prices would rise as production fell.

By dumping cash in farmers' hands, the AAA briefly stabilized the farm economy. But the act's benefits were not evenly distributed. Subsidies went primarily to the owners of large- and medium-sized farms, who often cut production by reducing the amount of land they rented to tenants and sharecroppers. In Mississippi, one plantation owner received $26,000 from the federal government, while thousands of black sharecroppers living in the same county received only a few dollars in relief payments.

In manufacturing, the New Deal attacked declining production with the National Industrial Recovery Act. A new government agency, the National Recovery Administration (NRA), set up separate self-governing private associations in six hundred industries. Each industry — ranging from large corporations producing coal, cotton textiles, and steel to small businesses making pet food and costume jewelry — regulated itself by agreeing on a code of prices and production quotas. Because large companies usually ran these associations, the NRA solidified its power at the expense of smaller enterprises and consumer interests.

The AAA and the NRA were designed to rescue the nation's productive industries and stabilize the economy. The measures had positive effects in some regions, but most historians agree that, overall, they did little to end the depression.

Unemployment Relief | The Roosevelt administration next addressed the problems of massive unemployment. By 1933, local governments and private charities had exhausted their resources and were looking to Washington for assistance. Although Roosevelt wanted to avoid a budget deficit, he asked Congress to provide relief for millions of unemployed Americans. In May, Congress established the Federal Emergency Relief Administration (FERA). Directed by Harry Hopkins, a hard-driving social worker from New York, the FERA provided federal funds for state relief programs.

Roosevelt and Hopkins had strong reservations about the "dole," the nickname for government welfare payments. As Hopkins put it, "I don't think anybody can go year after year, month after month, accepting relief without affecting his character." To support the traditional values of individualism, the New Deal put people to work. Early in 1933, Congress established the Public Works Administration (PWA), a construction program, and several months later, Roosevelt created the Civil Works Administration (CWA) and named Hopkins its head. Within thirty days, Hopkins had put 2.6 million men and women to work; at its peak in 1934, the CWA provided jobs for 4 million Americans repairing bridges, building highways, and constructing public buildings. A stopgap measure to get the country through the winter of 1933–1934, the CWA lapsed in the spring, when Republican opposition compelled New Dealers to abandon it. A more long-term program, the Civilian Conservation Corps (CCC), mobilized 250,000 young men to do reforestation and conservation work. Over the course of the 1930s, the "CCC boys" built thousands of bridges, roads, trails, and other structures in state and national parks, bolstering the national infrastructure (Map 23.1).

Housing Crisis | Millions of Americans also faced the devastating prospect of losing their homes. The 1920s' economic expansion had produced the largest inflationary housing bubble in American history to that point. In the early 1930s, as home prices collapsed and banks closed, homeowners were dragged down with them. More than half a million Americans lost their homes between 1930 and 1932, and in cities such as Cleveland and Indianapolis, half of all home mortgage holders faced possible foreclosure. In response, Congress created the Home Owners Loan Corporation (HOLC) to refinance home mortgages. In just two years of operation, the HOLC helped more than a million Americans retain their homes. The Federal Housing Act of 1934 would extend this program under a new agency, the Federal Housing Administration (FHA). Together, the HOLC, the FHA, and the subsequent Housing Act of 1937 permanently changed the mortgage system and set the foundation for the broad expansion of homeownership in the post–World War II decades (see Chapter 26).

When an exhausted Congress recessed in June 1933, at the end of the Hundred Days, it had enacted Roosevelt's agenda: banking reform, recovery programs for agri-

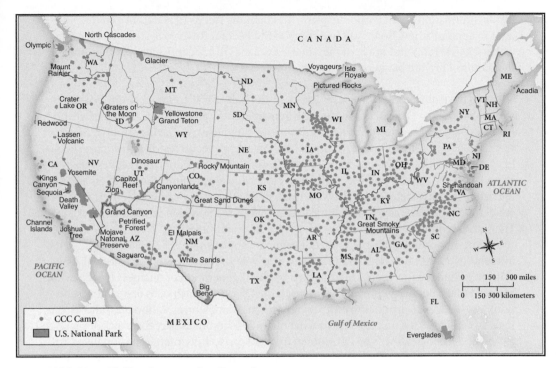

MAP 23.1 Civilian Conservation Corps Camps

The Civilian Conservation Corps (CCC) gave hope to unemployed young men during the Great Depression. The first camp opened in Big Meadows, Virginia, in July 1933, and by the end of the decade CCC camps had appeared across the length of the country, located in rural, mountainous, and forested regions alike. Young men constructed bridges and roads, built hiking trails, erected public campgrounds, and performed other improvements. By the early 1940s, the CCC had planted 3 billion trees, among its many other contributions to the national infrastructure.

culture and industry, public works, and unemployment relief. Few presidents had won the passage of so many measures in so short a time. The new agencies established in Washington were far from perfect and had their critics on both the radical left and the conservative right. But the vigorous actions taken by Roosevelt and Congress had halted the downward psychological spiral of the Hoover years, stabilized the financial sector, and sent a message of hope from the nation's political leaders. For all that, however, they did not break the grip of the depression.

The New Deal under Attack

As New Dealers waited anxiously for the economy to revive, Roosevelt turned his attention to the reform of Wall Street, where reckless speculation and overleveraged buying of stocks had helped trigger the financial panic of 1929. In 1934, Congress established the Securities and Exchange Commission (SEC) to regulate the stock market. The commission had broad powers to determine how stocks and bonds were sold to the public, to set rules for margin (credit) transactions, and to prevent stock sales by those with inside information about corporate plans. The Banking Act of 1935 authorized the president to appoint a new Board of Governors of the Federal Reserve System, placing control of interest rates and other money-market policies in a federal agency rather than in the hands of private bankers.

Critics on the Right | Such measures exposed the New Deal to attack from economic conservatives — also known as the political right. A man of wealth, Roosevelt saw himself as the savior of American capitalism, declaring simply, "To preserve we had to reform." Many bankers and business executives disagreed. To them, FDR became "That Man," a traitor to his class. In 1934, Republican business leaders joined with conservative Democrats in the Liberty League to fight the "reckless spending" and "socialist" reforms of the New Deal. Reflecting their outlook, Herbert Hoover condemned the NRA as a "state-controlled or state-directed social or economic system." That, declared the former president, was "tyranny, not liberalism."

More important than the Liberty League in opposing the New Deal, because its influence would stretch far into the post–World War II decades, was the National Association of Manufacturers (NAM). Sparked by a new generation of business leaders who believed that a publicity campaign was needed to "serve the purposes of business salvation," the NAM was producing radio programs, motion pictures, billboards, and direct mail by the late 1930s. In response to what many conservatives perceived as Roosevelt's antibusiness policies, the NAM promoted free enterprise and unfettered capitalism. After World War II, the NAM would emerge as one of the staunchest critics of liberalism and would forge alliances with influential postwar conservative politicians such as Barry Goldwater and Ronald Reagan.

For its part, the Supreme Court repudiated many of the cornerstones of the early New Deal. In May 1935, in *Schechter v. United States*, the Court unanimously ruled the National Industrial Recovery Act unconstitutional because it delegated Congress's power to make laws to the executive branch and extended federal authority to intrastate (in contrast to interstate) commerce. Roosevelt protested but watched helplessly as the Court struck down more New Deal legislation: the Agricultural Adjustment Act, the Railroad Retirement Act, and the Frazier-Lemke Act (intended to provide debt relief).

Critics on the | If business leaders and the Supreme Court thought that the New Deal
Populist Left | had gone too far, many ordinary Americans believed it had not gone
| far enough. Among these were public figures who, in the tradition of American populism, sought to place government on the side of ordinary citizens against corporations and the wealthy. Francis Townsend, a doctor from Long Beach, California, spoke for the nation's elderly, most of whom had no pensions and feared poverty in their old age. In 1933, Townsend proposed the Old Age Revolving Pension Plan, which would give the considerable sum of $200 a month (about $3,300 today) to citizens over the age of sixty. To receive payments, the elderly would have to retire from their jobs, opening their positions to younger workers. Townsend Clubs sprang up across the country, mobilizing mass support for old-age pensions.

Father Charles Coughlin also challenged Roosevelt's leadership and attracted a large following, especially in the Midwest. A Catholic priest in Detroit, Coughlin had turned to the radio in the mid-1920s to enlarge his pastorate. By 1933, an astonishing 40 million

Americans listened regularly to his broadcasts. Coughlin, known as the "Radio Priest," initially supported the New Deal but turned against it when Roosevelt refused to nationalize the banking system and expand the money supply. To promote his own ideas on money and banking, Coughlin organized the National Union for Social Justice.

The most direct political threat to Roosevelt came from Louisiana senator Huey Long. As the Democratic governor of Louisiana from 1928 to 1932, the flamboyant Long had achieved stunning popularity. He increased taxes on corporations, lowered the utility bills of consumers, and built new highways, hospitals, and schools. To push through these measures, Long seized almost dictatorial control of the state government. Now a U.S. Senator, Long broke with the New Deal in 1934 and, like Townsend and Coughlin, established a national movement. His Share Our Wealth Society maintained that because wealth was so unequally distributed, millions of ordinary families lacked the funds to buy goods and thereby keep the factories humming. Long's society advocated a tax of 100 percent on all income over $1 million and on all inheritances over $5 million. He hoped that this populist program would carry him into the White House.

That prospect encouraged conservatives, who hoped that a split between New Dealers and populist reformers might return the Republican Party, and its ideology of limited government and free enterprise, to political power. In fact, Roosevelt feared that Townsend, Coughlin, and Long might join forces to form a third party. He had to respond or risk the political unity of the country's liberal forces.

▶ What were the main programs of the New Deal's Hundred Days? How were they different from reforms in the early decades of the century?

▶ Who were the New Deal's major critics, and what were their alternative programs?

The Second New Deal and the Redefining of Liberalism, 1935–1938

As attacks on the New Deal increased, Roosevelt and his advisors moved to the left. Historians have labeled this shift in policy the Second New Deal. Roosevelt now openly criticized the "money classes," proudly stating, "We have earned the hatred of entrenched greed." He also moved decisively to counter the rising popularity of Townsend, Coughlin, and Long by adopting parts of their programs. The administration's Revenue Act of 1935 proposed a substantial tax increase on corporate profits and higher income and estate taxes on the wealthy. When conservatives attacked this legislation as an attempt to "soak the rich," Congress moderated its tax rates. But FDR was satisfied. He had met the Share Our Wealth Society's proposal with a wealth plan of his own.

The Welfare State Comes into Being

The Revenue Act symbolized the administration's new outlook. Unlike the First New Deal, which focused on economic recovery, the Second New Deal emphasized social justice and the creation of a safety net: the use of the federal government to enhance the power of working people and to guarantee the economic security and welfare of the old, the disabled, and the unemployed. The resulting welfare state — a term applied to industrial democracies that adopted some form of government-guaranteed social safety net — fundamentally changed American society.

The Wagner Act and Social Security | The first beneficiary of Roosevelt's move to the left was the labor movement. Section 7(a) of the National Industrial Recovery Act (NIRA) had given workers the right to organize unions, producing a dramatic growth in rank-and-file militancy and leading to a strike wave in 1934. When the Supreme Court voided the NIRA in 1935, labor unions called for new legislation that would allow workers to organize and bargain collectively with employers. Named for its sponsor, Senator Robert F. Wagner of New York, the Wagner Act (1935) upheld the right of industrial workers to join unions. The act outlawed many practices that employers had used to suppress unions, such as firing workers for organizing activities. It established the National Labor Relations Board (NLRB), a federal agency with the authority to protect workers from employer coercion and to guarantee collective bargaining.

A second initiative, the Social Security Act of 1935, had an even greater impact. Other industrialized societies, such as Germany and Britain, had created national old-age pension systems at the turn of the century, but American reformers had failed to secure a similar program in the United States. The Townsend and Long movements now pressed Roosevelt to act, giving political muscle to pension proponents within the administration. Also pressuring the president were children's welfare advocates concerned about the fate of fatherless families. The resulting Social Security Act had three main provisions: old-age pensions for workers; a joint federal-state system of compensation for unemployed workers; and a program of payments to widowed mothers and the blind, deaf, and disabled. Roosevelt, however, limited the reach of the legislation. Knowing that compulsory pension and unemployment legislation alone would be controversial, he refused to include a provision for national health insurance, fearing it would doom the entire bill.

The Social Security Act was a milestone in the creation of an American welfare state. Never before had the federal government assumed such responsibility for the well-being of a substantial portion of the citizenry. Social Security, as old-age pensions were known, became one of the most popular government programs in American history. On the other hand, the assistance program for widows and children known as Aid to Dependent Children (ADC) became one of its most controversial measures. ADC covered only 700,000 youngsters in 1939; by 1994, its successor, Aid to Families with Dependent Children (AFDC), enrolled 14.1 million Americans. A minor program during the New Deal, AFDC grew enormously in the 1960s and remained a cornerstone of the welfare state, if a contentious and controversial one, until it was eliminated under President Clinton in 1996.

New Deal Liberalism | The Second New Deal created what historians call New Deal liberalism. Classical liberalism held individual liberty to be the foundation of a democratic society, and the word *liberal* had traditionally denoted support for free-market policies and weak government. Roosevelt and his advisors, along with intellectuals such as education reformer John Dewey and economist John Maynard Keynes, disagreed. They countered that, to preserve individual liberty, government must assist

Labor on the March

Trade unions were among the most active and vocal organizations of the 1930s. Organized labor led a number of major strikes between 1934 and 1936 in various industries. None was more important to the future of trade unions than the sit-down strike at General Motors in Flint, Michigan, in 1936. It was this strike that compelled GM to recognize the United Auto Workers (UAW). After this strike had spread to Chevrolet, more than seventy-five women (workers and the wives of workers) clashed with company police. © Bettmann/Corbis.

the needy and guarantee the basic welfare of citizens. This liberal welfare state was opposed by inheritors of the nineteenth-century ideology of laissez-faire capitalism, who gradually became known as conservatives. These two visions of liberty and government — with liberals on one side and conservatives (as classical liberals came to be known) on the other — would shape American politics for the next half century.

From the outset, however, New Dealers wrestled with potentially fatal racial politics. Franklin Roosevelt and the Democratic Party depended heavily on white voters in the South, who were determined to keep African Americans poor and powerless. But many Democrats in the North and West — centers of New Deal liberalism — opposed racial discrimination. This meant, ironically, that the nation's most liberal political forces and some of its most conservative political forces existed side by side in the same political party.

From Reform to Stalemate

Roosevelt's first term had seen an extraordinary expansion of the federal state. The great burst of government action between 1933 and 1935 was unequaled in the nation's history (and would be matched only by Congress and President Lyndon Johnson in 1965–1966 — see Chapter 28). Roosevelt's second term, however, was characterized by a series of political entanglements and economic bad news that stifled further reform.

The 1936 Election FDR was never enthusiastic about public relief programs. But with the election of 1936 on the horizon and 10 million Americans still out of work, he won funding for the Works Progress Administration (WPA). Under the energetic direction of Harry Hopkins, the WPA employed 8.5 million Americans between 1935 and 1943. The agency's workers constructed or repaired 651,087 miles of road, 124,087 bridges, 125,110 public buildings, 8,192 parks, and 853 airports. Although the WPA was an extravagant operation by 1930s standards, it reached only about one-third of the nation's unemployed.

As the 1936 election approached, new voters joined the Democratic Party. Many had personally benefited from New Deal programs such as the WPA or knew people who had. One was Jack Reagan, a down-on-his-luck shoe salesman (and the father of future president Ronald Reagan), who took a job as a federal relief administrator in Dixon, Illinois, and became a strong supporter of the New Deal. In addition to voters such as Reagan, Roosevelt could count on a powerful coalition of organized labor, midwestern farmers, white ethnic groups, northern blacks, and middle-class families concerned about unemployment and old-age security. He also commanded the support of intellectuals and progressive Republicans. With difficulty, the Democrats held on to the votes of their white southern constituency as well.

Republicans recognized that the New Deal was too popular to oppose directly, so they chose as their candidate the progressive governor of Kansas, Alfred M. Landon. Landon accepted the legitimacy of many New Deal programs but stridently criticized their inefficiency and expense. He also pointed to authoritarian regimes in Italy and Germany, directed by Benito Mussolini and Adolph Hitler, respectively, and hinted that FDR harbored similar dictatorial ambitions. These charges fell on deaf ears. Roosevelt's victory in 1936 was one of the biggest landslides in American history. The assassination of Huey Long by a Louisiana political rival in September 1935 had eliminated the threat of a serious third-party challenge. Roosevelt received 60 percent of the popular vote and carried every state except Maine and Vermont. Organized labor, in particular, mobilized on behalf of FDR, donating money, canvassing door-to-door, and registering hundreds of thousands of new voters. The *New Republic*, a liberal publication, boasted that "it was the greatest revolution in our political history." The New Deal was at high tide.

"I see one-third of a nation ill-housed, ill-clad, ill-nourished," the president declared in his second inaugural address in January 1937. But any hopes that FDR had for expanding the liberal welfare state were quickly dashed. Within a year, staunch opposition to Roosevelt's initiatives arose in Congress, and a sharp recession undermined confidence in his economic leadership.

Court Battle and Economic Recession Roosevelt's first setback came when he surprised the nation by asking for fundamental changes to the Supreme Court. In 1935, the Court had struck down a series of New Deal measures by the narrow margin of 5 to 4. With the Wagner Act, the Tennessee Valley Authority, and Social Security all coming up on appeal with the Court, the future of the New Deal slate of programs rested in the hands of a few elderly, conservative-minded judges. To diminish their influence, the president proposed adding a new justice to the Court for every member over the age of seventy. Roosevelt's opponents protested that he was trying to "pack" the Court. After a bitter, months-long debate, Congress rejected this blatant attempt to alter the judiciary to the president's advantage.

If Roosevelt lost the battle, he went on to win the war. Swayed in part by the president's overwhelming electoral victory in the 1936 election, the Court upheld the Wagner and Social Security Acts. Moreover, a series of timely resignations allowed Roosevelt to reshape the Supreme Court after all. His new appointees — who included the liberal-leaning and generally pro–New Deal Hugo Black, Felix Frankfurter, and William O. Douglas — viewed the Constitution as a "living document" that had to be interpreted in the light of present conditions.

The so-called Roosevelt recession of 1937–1938 dealt another blow to the president. From 1933 to 1937, gross domestic product had grown at a yearly rate of about 10 percent, bringing industrial output and real income back to 1929 levels. Unemployment had declined from 25 percent to 14 percent. "The emergency has passed," declared Senator James F. Byrnes of South Carolina. Acting on this assumption, Roosevelt slashed the federal budget. Following the president's lead, Congress cut the WPA's funding in half, causing layoffs of about 1.5 million workers, and the Federal Reserve, fearing inflation, raised interest rates. These measures halted recovery. The stock market responded by dropping sharply, and unemployment jumped to 19 percent. Quickly reversing course, Roosevelt began once again to spend his way out of the recession by boosting funding for the WPA and resuming public works projects.

Although improvised, this spending program accorded with the theories of John Maynard Keynes, a visionary British economist of the first part of the twentieth century. Keynes transformed economic policymaking in capitalist societies by arguing that government intervention could smooth out the highs and lows of the business cycle through **deficit spending** and the manipulation of interest rates, which determined the money supply. Though it had been sharply criticized by Republicans and conservative Democrats in the 1930s, **Keynesian economics** gradually won wider acceptance as defense spending during World War II finally ended the Great Depression.

A reformer rather than a revolutionary, Roosevelt had preserved capitalism and liberal individualism — even as he transformed them in significant ways. He had met the challenge to American capitalism and democratic institutions posed by the Great Depression. At the same time, conservatives had reclaimed a measure of power in Congress, and those who believed the New Deal had created an intrusive federal bureaucracy kept reform in check after 1937. Throughout Roosevelt's second term, a conservative coalition composed of southern Democrats, rural Republicans, and industrial interests in both parties worked to block or impede social legislation. By 1939, the era of change was over.

▶ How did the Second New Deal differ from the first? What were FDR's reasons for changing course?

▶ Describe Keynesian economic policies. How important were they to the New Deal?

The New Deal's Impact on Society

Whatever the limits of the New Deal, it had a tremendous impact. Its ideology of social-welfare liberalism fundamentally altered Americans' relationship to their government and provided assistance to a wide range of ordinary people: the unemployed, the elderly, workers, and racial minorities. In doing so, New Dealers created a sizable federal bureaucracy: The number of civilian federal employees increased by 80 percent between 1929 and 1940, reaching a total of 1 million. The expenditures — and deficits — of the federal government grew at an even faster rate. In 1930, the Hoover administration spent $3.1 billion and had a surplus of almost $1 billion; in 1939, New Dealers expended $9.4 billion and ran a deficit of nearly $3 billion (still small by later standards). But the New Deal represented more than figures on a balance sheet. Across the country, the new era in government inspired democratic visions among ordinary citizens.

A People's Democracy

In 1939, writer John La Touche and musician Earl Robinson produced "Ballad for Americans." A patriotic song, it called for uniting "everybody who's nobody . . . Irish, Negro, Jewish, Italian, French, and English, Spanish, Russian, Chinese, Polish, Scotch, Hungarian, Litvak, Swedish, Finnish, Canadian, Greek, and Turk, and Czech and double Czech American." The song captured the democratic aspirations that the New Deal had awakened. Millions of ordinary people believed that the nation could, and should, become more egalitarian. Influenced by the liberal spirit of the New Deal, Americans from all walks of life seized the opportunity to push for change in the nation's social and political institutions.

Organized Labor | Demoralized and shrinking during the 1920s, labor unions increased their numbers and clout during the New Deal, thanks to the Wagner Act. "The era of privilege and predatory individuals is over," labor leader John L. Lewis declared. By the end of the decade, the number of unionized workers had tripled to 23 percent of the nonagricultural workforce. A new union movement, led by the Congress of Industrial Organizations (CIO), promoted "industrial unionism"— organizing all the workers in an industry, from skilled machinists to unskilled janitors, into a single union. American Federation of Labor (AFL), representing the other major group of unions, favored organizing workers on a craft-by-craft basis. Both federations dramatically increased their membership in the second half of the 1930s.

Labor's new vitality translated into political action and a long-lasting alliance with the Democratic Party. The CIO helped fund Democratic campaigns in 1936, and its political action committee became a major Democratic contributor during the 1940s. These successes were real but limited. The labor movement did not become the dominant force in the United States that it was in Europe, and unions never enrolled a majority of American wageworkers. Employer groups such as the National Association of Manufacturers and the Chamber of Commerce, vehemently anti-union, remained powerful forces in American business life. After a decade of gains, organized labor remained an important, but secondary, force in American industry.

Women and the New Deal | The New Deal did not directly challenge gender inequities. The high point of first-wave feminism, the ratification of the Nineteenth Amendment in 1920, had long passed. Women's advocates struggled for the attention of policymakers, who saw the depression primarily as a crisis of male breadwinners. New Deal measures generally enhanced women's welfare, but few addressed their needs and concerns directly. The Roosevelt administration did welcome women into the higher ranks of government. Frances Perkins, the first woman named to a cabinet post, served as secretary of labor throughout Roosevelt's presidency. While relatively few, female appointees often worked to open up other opportunities in government for talented women.

The most prominent woman in American politics was the president's wife, Eleanor Roosevelt. In the 1920s, she had worked to expand positions for women in political parties, labor unions, and education. A tireless advocate for women's rights, during her years in the White House, Mrs. Roosevelt emerged as an independent public figure and the most influential First Lady in the nation's history. Descending deep into coal mines to view working conditions, meeting with African Americans seeking antilynching laws, and talking to people on breadlines, she became the conscience of the New Deal, pushing her husband to do more for the disadvantaged. "I sometimes acted as a spur," Mrs. Roosevelt later reflected, "even though the spurring was not always wanted or welcome."

Without the intervention of Eleanor Roosevelt, Frances Perkins, and other prominent women, New Deal policymakers would have largely ignored the needs of women. A fourth of the National Recovery Act codes set a lower minimum wage for women than for men performing the same jobs, and only 7 percent of the workers hired by the Civil Works Administration were female. The Civilian Conservation Corps excluded women entirely. Women fared better under the Works Progress Administration; at its peak, 405,000 women were on the payroll. Most Americans agreed with such policies. When Gallup pollsters in 1936 asked people whether wives should work outside the home when their husbands had jobs, 82 percent said no. Such sentiment reflected a persistent belief in women's secondary status in public life.

African Americans under the New Deal Across the nation, but especially in the South, African Americans held the lowest-paying jobs and faced harsh social and political discrimination. Though FDR did not fundamentally change this fact, he was the most popular president among black Americans since Abraham Lincoln. African Americans held 18 percent of WPA jobs, although they constituted 10 percent of the population. The Resettlement Administration, established in 1935 to help small farmers and tenants buy land, actively protected the rights of black tenant farmers. Black involvement in the New Deal, however, could not undo centuries of racial subordination, nor could it change the overwhelming power of southern whites in the Democratic Party.

Nevertheless, black Americans received significant benefits from New Deal relief programs. Help from New Deal agencies and a belief that the White House cared about their plight caused a momentous shift in African Americans' political allegiance. Since the Civil War, African Americans had staunchly supported the Republican Party, the party of Abraham Lincoln, the Great Emancipator. Even in the Depression year of 1932, they overwhelmingly supported Republican candidates. But in 1936, as part of the tidal wave of national support for FDR, northern blacks gave Roosevelt 71 percent of their votes. African American voters have remained solidly Democratic ever since.

African Americans supported the New Deal partly because the Roosevelt administration appointed a number of black people to federal office, and an informal "black cabinet" of prominent African American intellectuals advised New Deal agencies. Among the most important appointees was Mary McLeod Bethune. Born in 1875 in South

Scottsboro Defendants

The 1931 trial in Scottsboro, Alabama, of nine black youths accused of raping two white women became a symbol of the injustices African Americans faced in the South's legal system. Denied access to an attorney, the defendants were found guilty after a three-day trial, and eight were sentenced to death. When the U.S. Supreme Court overturned their convictions in 1932, the International Labor Defense organization hired noted criminal attorney Samuel Leibowitz to argue the case. Leibowitz eventually won the acquittal of four defendants and jail sentences for the rest. This 1933 photograph, taken in a Decatur jail, shows Leibowitz conferring with Haywood Patterson, in front of the other eight defendants. Brown Brothers.

Carolina to former slaves, Bethune founded Bethune-Cookman College and served during the 1920s as president of the National Association of Colored Women. She joined the New Deal in 1935, confiding to a friend that she "believed in the democratic and humane program" of FDR. Americans, Bethune observed, had to become "accustomed to seeing Negroes in high places." Bethune had access to the White House and pushed continually for New Deal programs to help African Americans.

But there were sharp limits on the New Deal in regard to race. Roosevelt did not go further in support of black rights, because of both his own racial blinders and his need for the votes of the white southern Democrats in Congress. Most New Deal programs reflected prevailing racial attitudes. Civilian Conservation Corps camps segregated blacks, and most NRA codes did not protect black workers from discrimination. Both Social Security and the Wagner Act explicitly excluded domestic and agricultural workers, the two categories where most African Americans labored in the 1930s. Roosevelt also refused to support legislation making lynching a federal crime, which was one of the most pressing demands of African Americans in the 1930s. Between 1882 and 1930, more than 2,500 African Americans were lynched by white mobs in the southern states; statistically, one man, woman, or child was murdered every week for fifty years. But despite pleas from black leaders, and from Mrs. Roosevelt herself, FDR feared that southern white Democrats would block his other reforms in retaliation for such legislation.

If lynching embodied southern lawlessness, southern law was not much better. In an infamous 1931 case in Scottsboro, Alabama, nine young black men were accused of rape by two white women hitching a ride on a freight train. The women's stories contained many inconsistencies, but within weeks a white jury had convicted all nine defendants; eight received the death sentence. After the U.S. Supreme Court overturned the sentences because the defendants had been denied adequate legal counsel, five of the men were again convicted and sentenced to long prison terms. Across the country, the Scottsboro Boys, as they were known, inspired solidarity within African American communities. Among whites, the Communist Party took the lead in publicizing the case — and was one of the only white organizations to do so — helping to support the Scotts- boro Defense Committee, which raised money for legal efforts on the defendants' behalf.

In southern agriculture, where many sharecroppers were black while landowners and government administrators were white, the Agricultural Adjustment Act hurt rather than helped the poorest African Americans. White landowners collected government subsidy checks but refused to distribute payments to their sharecroppers. Such practices forced 200,000 black families off the land. Some black farmers tried to protect them- selves by joining the Southern Tenant Farmers Union (STFU), a biracial organization founded in 1934. "The same chain that holds you hold my people, too," an elderly black farmer reminded his white neighbors. But landowners had such economic power and such support from local sheriffs that the STFU could do little.

The biggest obstacle to fundamental change, however, was political. In the South, Democrats had a monopoly on power, and they remained wedded to white supremacy. They resisted any government action that would overturn racial segregation. As a re- sult, Roosevelt and other New Dealers had to trim their proposals of measures that would substantially benefit African Americans. FDR could not afford to lose the sup- port of powerful southern senators, many of whom held influential committee posts in Congress. A generation of African American leaders came of age inspired by the New Deal's democratic promise. But it remained just a promise. Another thirty years would pass before black Americans would gain an opportunity to reform U.S. racial laws and practices.

Indian Policy | New Deal reformers seized the opportunity to implement their vision for the future of Native Americans. The results were decidedly mixed. Indian peoples had long been one of the nation's most disadvantaged and powerless groups. In 1934, the average individual Indian income was only $48 per year, and the Native American unemployment rate was three times the national average. The plight of Native Americans won the attention of the commissioner of the Bureau of Indian Affairs (BIA), John Collier, a progressive intellectual and staunch critic of the past practices of the BIA. Collier understood what Indian peoples had long known: that the government's decades-long policy of forced assimilation, prohibition of Indian reli- gions, and the taking of Indian lands had left most tribes poor, isolated, and without basic self-determination.

Collier helped to write and push through Congress the Indian Reorganization Act of 1934, sometimes called the Indian New Deal. On the positive side, the law reversed the Dawes Act of 1887 (see Chapter 16) by promoting Indian self-government through formal constitutions and democratically elected tribal councils. A majority of Indian peoples — some 181 tribes — accepted the reorganization policy, but 77 declined to par- ticipate, primarily because they preferred the traditional way of making decisions by consensus rather than majority vote. Through the new law, Indians won a greater degree of religious freedom, and tribal governments regained their status as semisovereign dependent nations. When the latter policy was upheld by the courts, Indian people gained a measure of leverage that would have major implications for native rights in the second half of the twentieth century.

Like so many other federal Indian policies, however, the "Indian New Deal" was far from an uncomplicated blessing. For some peoples, the model of self-government the act imposed proved incompatible with tribal traditions and languages. The Papagos of southern Arizona, for instance, had no words for *budget* or *representative*, and made no linguistic distinctions among *law, rule, charter*, and *constitution*. In another case, the nation's largest tribe, the Navajos, rejected the BIA's new policy, in large part because the government was simultaneously reducing Navajo livestock to protect the Boulder Dam project. In theory, the new policy gave Indians a much greater degree of self-determination. In practice, however, although some tribes did benefit, the BIA and Congress did not stop interfering in internal Indian affairs and retained financial control of reservation governments.

Struggles in the West | By the 1920s, agriculture in California had become a big business — intensive, diversified, and export-oriented. Large-scale corporate-owned farms produced specialty crops — lettuce, tomatoes, peaches, grapes, and cotton — whose staggered harvests allowed the use of transient laborers. Thousands of workers, immigrants from Mexico and Asia and white migrants from the midwestern states, trooped from farm to farm and from crop to crop during the long picking season. Some migrants settled in the rapidly growing cities along the West Coast, especially the sprawling metropolis of Los Angeles.

Under both Hoover and FDR, the federal government promoted the "repatriation" of Mexican citizens — their deportation to Mexico. Between 1929 and 1937, approximately half a million people of Mexican descent were deported. But historians estimate that more than 60 percent of these were legal U.S. citizens, making the government's actions constitutionally questionable. Many Mexican farm laborers left voluntarily as the depression deepened. They knew that most local officials would not provide them with relief assistance. Virtually every immigrant Mexican family in the United States in the early 1930s confronted the decision of whether to leave or stay.

Despite the deportations, many Mexican Americans benefited from the New Deal and generally held Roosevelt and the Democratic Party in high regard. People of Mexican descent, like other Americans, took jobs with the WPA and the CCC, or received relief in the worst years of the depression. The National Youth Administration (NYA), which employed young people from families on relief and sponsored a variety of school programs, was especially important in southwestern cities. In California, the Mexican American Movement (MAM), a youth-focused organization, received assistance from liberal New Dealers. New Deal programs did not improve the migrant farm labor system under which so many people of Mexican descent labored, but Mexicans joined the New Deal coalition in large numbers because of the Democrats' commitment to ordinary Americans. "Franklin D. Roosevelt's name was the spark that started thousands of Spanish-speaking persons to the polls," noted Los Angeles activist Beatrice Griffith.

Men and women of Asian descent — mostly from China, Japan, and the Philippines — formed a small minority of the American population but were a significant presence in some western cities and towns. Immigrants from Japan and China had long faced discrimination. A California law of 1913 prohibited them from owning land. Japanese farmers, who specialized in fruit and vegetable crops, circumvented this restriction by putting land titles in the names of their American-born children. As the depression cut farm prices and racial discrimination excluded young Japanese Americans from nonfarm jobs, about 20 percent of the immigrants returned to Japan.

Chinese Americans were less prosperous than their Japanese counterparts. Only 3 percent of Chinese Americans worked in professional and technical positions, and discrimination barred them from most industrial jobs. In San Francisco, most Chinese worked in small businesses: restaurants, laundries, and firms that imported textiles and ceramics. During the depression, they turned for assistance to Chinese social organizations such as *huiguan* (district associations) and to the city government; in 1931, about one-sixth of San Francisco's Chinese population was receiving public aid. But few Chinese benefited from the New Deal. Until the repeal of the Exclusion Act in 1943, Chinese immigrants were classified as "aliens ineligible for citizenship" and therefore were excluded from most federal programs.

Because Filipino immigrants came from a U.S. territory, they were not affected by the ban on Asian immigration enacted in 1924. During the 1920s, their numbers swelled to about 50,000, many of whom worked as laborers on large corporate-owned farms. As the depression cut wages, Filipino immigration slowed to a trickle, and it was virtually cut off by the Tydings-McDuffie Act of 1934. The act granted independence to the Philippines (which since 1898 had been an American colony), classified all Filipinos in the United States as aliens, and restricted immigration from the Philippines to fifty people per year.

Reshaping the Environment

Attention to the land and natural resources was a dominant motif of the New Deal, and the shaping of the landscape was among its most visible legacies. Franklin Roosevelt and Interior Secretary Harold Ickes saw themselves as conservationists in the tradition of FDR's cousin, Theodore Roosevelt. In an era before environmentalism, FDR practiced what he called the "gospel of conservation." The president cared first and foremost about making the land — and other natural resources, such as trees and water — better serve human needs. National policy stressed scientific management of the land and ecological balance. Preserving wildlife and wilderness were of secondary importance. Under Roosevelt, the federal government both responded to acute environmental crises and aggressively reshaped how natural resources, especially water, were used in the United States.

The Dust Bowl | Among the most hard-pressed citizens during the depression were farmers fleeing the "dust bowl" of the Great Plains. Their land had taken a beating. Between 1930 and 1941, a severe drought afflicted the semiarid states of Oklahoma, Texas, New Mexico, Colorado, Arkansas, and Kansas. Farmers in these areas had stripped the land of its native vegetation, which destroyed the delicate ecology of the plains. To grow wheat and other crops, they had pushed agriculture beyond the natural limits of the soil and climate, making their land vulnerable, in times of drought, to wind erosion of the topsoil. When the winds came, huge clouds of thick dust rolled over the land, turning the day into night. This ecological disaster prompted a mass exodus. At least 350,000 "Okies" (so called whether or not they were from Oklahoma) loaded their belongings into cars and trucks and headed to California. John Steinbeck's novel *The Grapes of Wrath* (1939) immortalized them, and New Deal photographer Dorothea Lange's haunting images of California migrant camps made them the public face of the depression's human toll.

Poor land practices, Roosevelt and Ickes believed, made for poor people. Under their direction, government agencies tackled the dust bowl's human causes. Agents from the newly created Soil Conservation Service, for instance, taught farmers to prevent soil erosion by tilling hillsides along the contours of the land. They also encouraged (and sometimes paid) farmers to take certain commercial crops out of production and plant soil-preserving grasses instead. One of the U.S. Forest Service's most widely publicized programs was the Shelterbelts, the planting of 220 million trees running north along the 99th meridian from Abilene, Texas, to the Canadian border. Planted as a windbreak, the trees also prevented soil erosion. Ultimately, agencies from the CCC to the U.S. Department of Agriculture lent their expertise to establishing sound farming practices in the plains.

Tennessee Valley Authority | The most extensive New Deal environmental undertaking was the Tennessee Valley Authority (TVA), which Roosevelt imagined as the first step in modernizing the South. Funded by Congress in 1933, the TVA integrated flood control, reforestation, inexpensive electricity generation, and agricultural and industrial development, including the production of chemical fertilizers. The dams and their hydroelectric plants provided cheap electric power for homes and factories as well as ample recreational opportunities for the valley's residents. The massive project won praise around the world (Map 23.2).

The TVA was an integral part of the Roosevelt administration's effort to keep farmers on the land by enhancing the quality of rural life. The Rural Electrification Administration (REA), established in 1935, was also central to that goal. Fewer than one-tenth of the nation's 6.8 million farms had electricity. The REA addressed this problem by promoting nonprofit farm cooperatives that offered loans to farmers to install power lines. By 1940, 40 percent of the nation's farms had electricity; a decade later, 90 percent did. Electricity brought relief from the drudgery and isolation of farm life. Electric irons, vacuum cleaners, and washing machines eased women's burdens, and radios brightened the lives of the entire family. Along with the automobile and the movies, electricity broke down the barriers between urban and rural life.

Grand Coulee | As the nation's least populated but fastest-growing region, the West benefited enormously from the New Deal's attention to the environment. With the largest number of state and federal parks in the country, the West gained countless trails, bridges, cabins, and other recreational facilities, laying the groundwork for the post–World War II expansion of western tourism. On the Colorado River, Boulder Dam (later renamed Hoover Dam) was completed in 1935 with Public Works Administration (PWA) funds; the dam generated power for the region's growing cities such as Las Vegas, Los Angeles, and Phoenix.

The largest project in the West, however, took shape in an obscure corner of Washington State, where the PWA and the Bureau of Reclamation built the Grand Coulee Dam on the Columbia River. When it was completed in 1941, Grand Coulee was the largest electricity-producing structure in the world, and its 150-mile lake provided irrigation for the state's major crops: apples, cherries, pears, potatoes, and wheat. Inspired by the dam and the modernizing spirit of the New Deal, folk singer Woody Guthrie wrote a song about the Columbia. "Your power is turning our darkness to dawn," he sang, "so roll on, Columbia, roll on!"

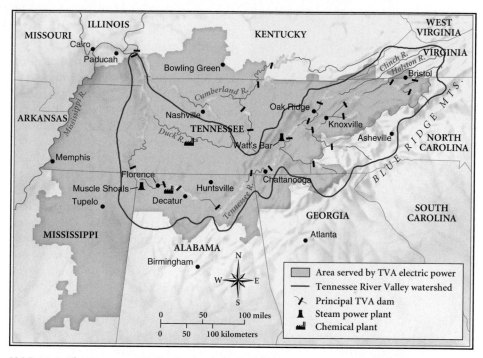

MAP 23.2 The Tennessee Valley Authority, 1933–1952

The Tennessee Valley Authority was one of the New Deal's most far-reaching environmental projects. Between 1933 and 1952, the TVA built twenty dams and improved five others, taming the flood-prone Tennessee River and its main tributaries. The cheap hydroelectric power generated by the dams brought electricity to industries as well as hundreds of thousands of area residents, and artificial lakes provided extensive recreational facilities. Widely praised at the time, the TVA came under attack in the 1970s for its practice of strip mining and the pollution caused by its power plants and chemical factories.

New Deal projects that enhanced people's enjoyment of the natural environment can be seen today throughout the country. CCC and WPA workers built the famous Blue Ridge Parkway, which connects the Shenandoah National Park in Virginia with the Great Smoky Mountains National Park in North Carolina. In the West, government workers built the San Francisco Zoo, Berkeley's Tilden Park, and the canals of San Antonio. The Civilian Conservation Corps helped to complete the East Coast's Appalachian Trail and the West Coast's Pacific Crest Trail through the Sierra Nevada. In state parks across the country, cabins, shelters, picnic areas, lodges, and observation towers stand as monuments to the New Deal ethos of recreation coexisting with nature.

The New Deal and the Arts

In response to the Great Depression, many American writers and artists redefined their relationship to society. Never had there been a decade, critic Malcolm Cowley suggested in 1939, "when literary events followed so closely on the flying coat-tails of social events." New Deal administrators encouraged artists to create projects that would be of interest to the entire community, not just the cultured elite. "Art for the millions"

Grand Coulee Dam

This photo shows workers hitching a ride on a 13-ton conduit as it is lowered into place on the Grand Coulee Dam in Washington State. Dozens of dams were constructed under New Deal programs, but none more majestic than Boulder Dam (renamed Hoover Dam in 1947) and Grand Coulee. Built to harness the Columbia River, Grand Coulee would ultimately provide electric power to northwestern cities and new irrigation waters for Washington's farms and orchards. Library of Congress.

became a popular New Deal slogan and encouraged the painting of murals in hundreds of public buildings.

The Federal Art Project, an arm of the WPA, gave work to many young artists who would become the twentieth century's leading painters, muralists, and sculptors. Jackson Pollock, Alice Neel, Willem de Kooning, and Louise Nevelson all received support. The Federal Music Project and Federal Writers' Project (FWP) employed 15,000 musicians and 5,000 writers, respectively. Among the latter were Saul Bellow, Ralph Ellison, and John Cheever, future novelists of great stature. The FWP collected oral histories, including two thousand narratives by former slaves. The black folklorist and novelist Zora Neale Hurston finished three novels while in the Florida FWP, among them *Their Eyes Were Watching God* (1937). Richard Wright won the 1938 *Story* magazine prize for the best tale by a WPA writer and went on to complete *Native Son* (1940), a searing novel about white racism. Similarly, the Federal Theatre Project (FTP) nurtured such talented directors, actors, and playwrights as Orson Welles, John Huston, and Arthur Miller.

The WPA arts projects reflected a broad cultural trend known as the "documentary impulse." Documentary artists focused on actual events that were relevant to people's lives and presented them in ways that engaged the interest and emotions of the audience. This trend influenced practically every aspect of American culture: literature, photography, art, music, film, dance, theater, and radio. It is evident in novels such as John Steinbeck's *The Grapes of Wrath* and in John Dos Passos's *USA* trilogy (1930–1936), which used actual newspaper clippings and headlines in its fictional story. New photojournalism magazines, including *Life* and *Look*, carried this documentary approach into millions of living rooms.

The Legacies of the New Deal

The New Deal addressed the Great Depression by restoring hope and promising security. FDR and Congress created a powerful social-welfare state that took unprecedented responsibility for the well-being of American citizens. During the 1930s, millions of people began to pay taxes directly to the Social Security Administration, and more than one-third of the population received direct government assistance from federal programs, including old-age pensions, unemployment compensation, farm loans, relief work, and mortgage guarantees. New legislation regulated the stock market, reformed the Federal Reserve System, and subjected business corporations to federal regulation. The New Deal's pattern of government involvement in social life would persist for the rest of the twentieth century. In the 1960s, Lyndon Johnson and the "Great Society" Congress dramatically expanded social-welfare programs, most of which remained intact in the wake of the "Reagan Revolution" of the 1980s.

Like all other major social transformations, the New Deal was criticized both by those who thought it did too much and by those who believed it did too little. Conservatives, who prioritized limited government and individual freedom, pointed out that the New Deal state intruded deeply into the personal and financial lives of the citizenry. Conversely, advocates of social-welfare liberalism complained that the New Deal's safety net had many holes: no national health-care system, welfare programs that excluded domestic workers and farm laborers, and the fact that state governments often limited the benefits distributed under New Deal programs.

Whatever the merits of its critics, there is no question that the New Deal transformed the American political landscape. From 1896 to 1932, the Republican Party had commanded the votes of a majority of Americans. That changed as Franklin Roosevelt's magnetic personality and innovative programs brought millions of voters into the Democratic fold. Democratic recruits included first- and second-generation immigrants from southern and central Europe — Italians, Poles, Slovaks, and Jews — as well as African American migrants to northern cities. Organized labor aligned itself with a Democratic administration that had recognized unions as a legitimate force in modern industrial life. The elderly and the unemployed, assisted by the Social Security Act, likewise supported FDR. This New Deal coalition of ethnic groups, city dwellers, organized labor, blacks, and a cross-section of the middle class formed the nucleus of the northern Democratic Party and supported additional liberal reforms in the decades to come.

▶ In what ways did the New Deal assist African Americans and in what ways did it not? How do you explain these effects?

▶ What was the New Deal's long-term legacy?

SUMMARY

We have seen how Franklin Delano Roosevelt's First New Deal focused on stimulating recovery, providing relief to the unemployed, and regulating banks and other financial institutions. The Second New Deal was different. Influenced by the persistence of the depression and the growing popularity of Huey Long's Share the Wealth proposals, Roosevelt promoted social-welfare legislation that provided Americans with economic security.

We also explored the impact of the New Deal on various groups of citizens, especially African Americans, women, and unionized workers. Our survey paid particular attention to the lives of the Mexicans, Asians, and Okies who worked in the farms and factories of California. Because of New Deal assistance, the members of those groups gravitated toward the Democratic Party. The party's coalition of ethnic workers, African Americans, farmers, parts of the middle classes, and white southerners gave FDR and other Democrats a landslide victory in 1936.

Finally, we examined the accomplishments of the New Deal. In 1933, New Deal programs resolved the banking crisis while preserving capitalist institutions. Subsequently, these programs expanded the federal government and, through the Social Security system, farm subsidy programs, and public works projects, launched federal policies that were important to nearly every American. Great dams and electricity projects sponsored by the Tennessee Valley Authority, the Works Progress Administration in the West, and the Rural Electrification Administration permanently improved the quality of life for the nation's citizens.

For additional primary sources from this period, see *Documents for America's History*, Seventh Edition.

For Web sites, images, and documents related to topics and places in this chapter, visit *Make History* at **bedfordstmartins.com/henrettaconcise**.

For Further Exploration

Robert S. McElvaine, *The Great Depression* (1984), and Amity Shlaes, *The Forgotten Man: A New History of the Great Depression* (2007), provide a general treatment of the Great Depression and New Deal. Katie Louchheim, ed., *The Making of the New Deal: The Insiders Speak* (1983), portrays important New Dealers. Robert S. McElvaine's *Down and Out in the Great Depression* (1983) contains letters written by ordinary people. For audio versions of Studs Terkel's interviews, visit the Chicago Historical Society Web site at **www.studsterkel.org/index.html**. John Steinbeck, *The Grapes of Wrath* (1939); Josephine Herbst, *Pity Is Not Enough* (1933); and Richard Wright, *Native Son* (1940), are classic Depression-era novels. On African Americans in the depression, see Harvard Sitkoff, *A New Deal for Blacks: The Emergence of Civil Rights as a National Issue* (1978). For two extensive collections of 1930s materials, see the "New Deal Network" at **newdeal.feri.org** and "America in the 1930s" at **xroads.virginia.edu/~1930s/home_1.html**, which includes clips from radio programs. A good all-around New Deal site for teachers is **newdeal.feri .org/classrm/a.htm**. Also, see the wonderful collection of government-commissioned art at **www.archives.gov/exhibits/new_deal_for_the_arts**. The Library of Congress multimedia presentation "Voices from the Dust Bowl" can be viewed at **memory.loc.gov/ ammem/afctshtml/tshome.html**; a superb collection of photographs covering the years 1935–1945 can be found at **lcweb2.loc.gov/ammem/fsowhome.html** and **memory.loc .gov/ammem/fsahtml/fahome.html**. The slave narratives collected by the Federal Writer's Project can be found at **memory.loc.gov/ammem/snhtml**.

Test Your Knowledge

For practice quizzes, activities, and other study tools, visit the Online Study Guide at **bedfordstmartins.com/henrettaconcise**.

TIMELINE

1931–1937	▶ Scottsboro case: trials and appeals
1932	▶ Bonus Army marches on Washington, D.C.
	▶ Franklin Delano Roosevelt elected president
1933	▶ FDR's inaugural address and first fireside chats
	▶ Emergency Banking Act begins the Hundred Days
	▶ Civilian Conservation Corps (CCC) created
	▶ Agricultural Adjustment Act (AAA)
	▶ National Industrial Recovery Act (NIRA)
	▶ Tennessee Valley Authority (TVA) established
	▶ Townsend Clubs promote Old Age Revolving Pension Plan
	▶ Twenty-first Amendment repeals Prohibition
1934	▶ Securities and Exchange Commission (SEC) created
	▶ Tenant Farmers Union (STFU) founded
	▶ Indian Reorganization Act
	▶ Senator Huey Long promotes Share Our Wealth Society
	▶ Father Charles Coughlin founds National Union for Social Justice
1935	▶ Supreme Court voids NRA in *Schechter v. United States*
	▶ National Labor Relations (Wagner) Act
	▶ Social Security Act creates old-age pension system
	▶ Works Progress Administration (WPA) created
	▶ Huey Long assassinated
	▶ Rural Electrification Administration (REA) established
	▶ Supreme Court voids Agricultural Adjustment Act
	▶ Congress of Industrial Organizations (CIO) formed
1936	▶ General Motors sit-down strike
	▶ Landslide reelection of FDR marks peak of New Deal power
1937	▶ FDR's Supreme Court plan fails
1937–1938	▶ "Roosevelt recession" raises unemployment
1938	▶ Fair Labor Standards Act (FLSA)
1939	▶ Federal Theatre Project terminated

The World at War

1937–1945

The Battle of Britain is about to begin. . . . Hitler knows that he will have to break us in this island or lose the war. . . . If we fail, then the whole world, including the United States, including all that we have known and cared for, will sink into the abyss of a new Dark Age.

—British Prime Minister Winston Churchill, 1940

The Second World War was the defining international event of the twentieth century. Battles raged across six of the world's seven continents and all of its oceans. It killed 50 million human beings and left hundreds of millions of others wounded. When it was over, the industrial economies and much of the infrastructure of Europe and East Asia lay in ruins. Waged with both technologically advanced weapons and massive armies, the war involved every industrialized power in Europe, North America, and Asia, as well as dozens of smaller nations, many of them colonies of the industrialized countries.

The military conflict began on two continents: in Asia with Japan's 1937 invasion of China across the Sea of Japan, and in Europe with the 1939 blitzkrieg (lightning war) conducted by superbly engineered German tanks across the plains of Poland. It ended in 1945 after American planes dropped two atomic bombs, the product of stunning yet ominous scientific breakthroughs, on the Japanese cities of Hiroshima and Nagasaki. In between these demonstrations of technological prowess and devastating power, huge armies confronted and destroyed one another in the fields of France, the forests and steppes of Russia, the river valleys of China, the volcanic islands of the Pacific, and the sandy deserts of North Africa.

"Armed defense of democratic existence is now being gallantly waged in four continents," President Franklin Delano Roosevelt told the nation in January 1941. After remaining on the sidelines for several years, the United States would soon commit to that "armed defense." Both FDR and British prime minister Winston Churchill came to see the war as a defense of democratic values from the threat posed by German, Italian, and Japanese fascism. For them, the brutal conflict was the "good war." When the grim reality of the Jewish Holocaust came to light, U.S. participation in the war seemed even more just. But there was another side to the war. As much as it represented a struggle between democracy and fascism, it was also inescapably a war to maintain British, French, and Dutch control of colonies in Africa, India, the Middle East, and Southeast Asia. By 1945, democracy in the industrialized world had been preserved, and a new Euro-American alliance had taken hold; the future of the vast European colonial empires, however, remained unresolved.

On the U.S. domestic front, World War II brought an end to the Great Depression, hastened profound social changes, and expanded the scope and authority of the federal government. Race relations and gender roles shifted under the weight of wartime protest, migration, and labor shortages. The pace of urbanization increased as millions of Americans uprooted themselves and moved hundreds or thousands of miles to join the military or to take a war job. These developments, which were accelerations of social transformations already under way, would have repercussions far into the postwar decades.

At the same time, federal laws and practices established during the war — universal taxation of incomes, a huge military establishment, and multibillion-dollar budgets, to name but a few — became part of American life. So, too, did the active participation of the United States in international politics and alliances, an engagement intensified by the unresolved issues of the wartime alliance with the Soviet Union and the postwar fate of colonized nations. A robust American state, the product of a long, hard-fought war, would remain in place to fight an even longer, more expensive, and potentially more dangerous Cold War.

The Road to War

The Great Depression disrupted economic life around the world and brought the collapse of traditional political institutions. In response, an antidemocratic movement known as fascism, which had originated in Italy during the 1920s, developed in Germany, Spain, and Japan. By the mid-1930s, these nations had instituted authoritarian, militaristic governments led by powerful dictators: Benito Mussolini in Italy, Adolf Hitler in Nazi Germany, Francisco Franco in Spain, and, after 1940, Hideki Tojo in Japan. As early as 1936, President Roosevelt warned that other peoples had "sold their heritage of freedom" and urged Americans to work for "the survival of democracy" both at home and abroad. Hampered at first by strong isolationist sentiment, by 1939 FDR was leading the nation toward war against the fascist powers.

Fascism was sharply at odds with the capitalist democracies of Europe and the United States, as well as with the communist Soviet Union. Fascism, as established in Germany by Hitler, combined a centralized, authoritarian state, a doctrine of Aryan racial supremacy, and intense nationalism in a call for the spiritual reawakening of the German people. Fascist leaders worldwide disparaged parliamentary government, independent labor movements, and individual rights. They opposed both the economic collectivism of the Soviet Union — where, in theory, the state managed the economy to ensure social equality — and the competitive capitalist economies of the United States and Western Europe. Fascist movements arose around the world in the 1930s — the closest in the United States was the Ku Klux Klan — but managed to achieve power in only a handful of countries. Those countries were at the center of global war making in the 1930s.

The Rise of Fascism

World War II had its roots in the settlement of World War I (see Chapter 21). Germany struggled under the harsh terms of the Treaty of Versailles, and Japan and Italy had their dreams of overseas empires thwarted by the treaty makers. Faced with the expansive ambitions and deep resentments of those countries, the League of Nations, the collective security system established at Versailles, proved unable to maintain the existing international order.

Japan and Italy | The first challenge came from Japan. To become an industrial power, Japan required raw materials and overseas markets. Like the Western European powers and the United States before it, Japan embarked on a program of military expansion in pursuit of colonial possessions. In 1931, its troops occupied Manchuria, an industrialized province in northern China, and in 1937, the Japanese launched a full-scale invasion of China. In both instances, the League of Nations condemned Japan's actions but did nothing to stop them.

Japan's defiance of the League encouraged a fascist leader half a world away: Italy's Benito Mussolini, who had come to power in 1922. Il Duce (The Leader), as Mussolini was known, had long denounced the Versailles treaty, which denied Italy's claim on German and Turkish colonies in Africa and the Middle East. As in Japan, the Italian fascists desired overseas colonies for raw materials, markets, and national prestige. In 1935, Mussolini invaded Ethiopia, one of the few remaining independent countries in Africa. Ethiopian emperor Haile Selassie appealed to the League of Nations, but the League's verbal condemnation and limited sanctions did not stop Italy's forces, which took control of Ethiopia in 1936.

Hitler's Germany | It was Germany that posed the gravest threat to the existing world order. Huge World War I reparation payments, economic depression, fear of communism, labor unrest, and rising unemployment fueled the ascent of Adolf Hitler and his National Socialist (Nazi) Party. When Hitler became chancellor of Germany in 1933, the Reichstag (the German legislature) granted him dictatorial powers to deal with the economic crisis. Using that emergency authority, Hitler outlawed other political parties, arrested many of his political rivals, and took the title of *führer* (leader). Now under unchallenged Nazi control, the Reichstag invested all legislative power in Hitler's hands.

Hitler's goal was nothing short of European domination and world power, as he had made clear in his book *Mein Kampf* (*My Struggle*), first published in 1925. His writings outlined his plans to overturn the territorial settlements of the Versailles treaty, unite Germans living throughout central Europe in a great German fatherland, and annex large areas of Eastern Europe. The "inferior races" who lived in these regions — Jews, Gypsies, and Slavs — would be removed or subordinated to the German "master race."

Adolf Hitler

Adolf Hitler salutes German troops during a parade at the Nazi Party's annual congress at Nuremberg. German fascism reveled in great public spectacles, such as the famous Nuremberg rallies held every year between the early 1920s and the late 1930s. Hitler used these mass rallies, at which tens and sometimes hundreds of thousands of soldiers and civilians gathered, to build wide support for his policies of aggressive militarism abroad and suppression of Jews and other minorities at home. Getty Images.

A virulent anti-Semite, Hitler had long blamed Jews for Germany's problems. Once in power, he began a sustained and brutal persecution of Jews, which expanded into a campaign of extermination in the early 1940s.

Hitler's strategy for restoring Germany's military power and lost territories was to escalate his objectives in a series of small steps, daring Britain and France to go to war to stop him each time. In 1935, Hitler began to rearm Germany, in violation of the Versailles treaty. No one stopped him. In 1936, he sent troops into the Rhineland, a demilitarized zone under the terms of Versailles. Once again, France and Britain took no action. Later that year, Hitler and Mussolini formed the Rome-Berlin Axis, a political and military alliance between the two fascist nations. Also in 1936, Germany signed a pact to create a military alliance with Japan against the Soviet Union.

Isolationists versus Interventionists

As Hitler pushed his initiatives in Europe, which was mired in economic depression as deeply as the United States, the Roosevelt administration faced widespread isolationist sentiment at home. In part, this desire to avoid European entanglements reflected disillusion with American participation in World War I. In 1934, Gerald P. Nye, a progressive Republican senator from North Dakota, launched an investigation into the profits of munitions makers during that war. Nye's committee concluded that arms manufacturers (popularly labeled "merchants of death") had maneuvered President Wilson into World War I.

Although Nye's committee failed to prove its charge against weapon makers, its factual findings prompted Congress to pass a series of acts to prevent the nation from being drawn into another overseas war. The Neutrality Act of 1935 imposed an embargo on selling arms to warring countries and declared that Americans traveling on the ships of belligerent nations did so at their own risk. In 1936, Congress banned loans to belligerents, and in 1937 it imposed a "cash-and-carry" requirement: If a warring country wanted to purchase nonmilitary goods from the United States, it had to pay cash and carry them in its own ships, keeping the United States out of potentially dangerous naval warfare.

Among the general public, there was little enthusiasm for war. Isolationist sentiment was vocalized by a wide variety of different groups. Many isolationists looked to Ohio senator Robert Taft, who despised and distrusted Roosevelt. Taft believed that overseas entanglements would draw the United States closer to Europe, which he viewed as a decadent society unworthy of emulation. Another conservative group, the National Legion of Mothers of America, combined isolationism with anticommunism, Christian morality, and even anti-Semitism. Most isolationists came from among conservatives, but some progressives (or liberals) opposed America's potential involvement in the war on pacifist or moral grounds. Whatever their philosophies, ardent isolationists and a disinterested public forced Roosevelt to be cautious in his approach to the brewing war.

The Popular Front | Other Americans, notably writers, intellectuals, and liberal social activists, responded to the rise of fascism in Europe by advocating U.S. intervention. Some joined the American Communist Party, which had taken the lead in opposing fascism and had increased its membership as the depression revealed flaws in the capitalist system. Between 1935 and 1938, Communist Party membership peaked at about 100,000 in the United States, drawn from a wide range of social groups, including African American civil rights activists and even a few New Deal administrators. Many intellectuals did not join the party but considered themselves "fellow travelers." They sympathized with the party's objectives and supported various left-wing groups and causes.

The courting of intellectuals, union members, and liberals reflected a shift in the strategy of the Communist Party. Fearful of German and Japanese aggression, the Soviet leaders instructed Communists in Western Europe and the United States to join in a coalition of opponents to fascism known as the Popular Front. The Popular Front threw its support behind various international causes — supporting the Loyalists in their fight against fascist leader Francisco Franco in the Spanish Civil War (1936–1939), for example, even as the United States, France, and Britain remained neutral. In time, however, many supporters in the United States grew uneasy with the Popular Front because of the rigidity of its Communist associates and the cynical brutality and political repression under Soviet leader Joseph Stalin. Nevertheless, Popular Front activists were among a small but vocal group of Americans encouraging Roosevelt to take a more determined stand against European fascism.

The Failure of Appeasement | Encouraged by the weak worldwide response to the invasions of China, Ethiopia, and the Rhineland, and emboldened by British and French neutrality during the Spanish Civil War, Hitler grew more aggressive in 1938. He sent troops to annex German-speaking Austria while making clear his intention to seize part of Czechoslovakia. Because Czechoslovakia had an alliance with France, war seemed imminent. But at the Munich Conference in September 1938, Britain and France again capitulated, agreeing to let Germany annex the Sudetenland — a German-speaking border area of Czechoslovakia — in return for Hitler's pledge to seek no more territory. The agreement, declared British prime minister Neville Chamberlain, guaranteed "peace for our time." Hitler drew a different conclusion, telling his generals: "Our enemies are small fry. I saw them in Munich."

Within six months, Hitler's forces had overrun the rest of Czechoslovakia and were threatening to march into Poland. Realizing that their policy of appeasement — capitulating to Hitler's demands — had been disastrous, Britain and France warned Hitler that further expansion meant war. Then, in August 1939, Hitler and Stalin shocked the world by signing a mutual nonaggression pact. For Hitler, this pact was crucial, as it meant that Germany would not have to wage a two-front war against Britain and France in the west and Russia in the east. On September 1, 1939, Hitler launched a blitzkrieg against Poland. Two days later, Britain and France declared war on Germany. World War II had officially begun.

Two days after the European war started, the United States declared its neutrality. But President Roosevelt made no secret of his sympathies. When war broke out in 1914, Woodrow Wilson had told Americans to be neutral "in thought as well as in action." FDR, by contrast, said: "This nation will remain a neutral nation, but I cannot ask that every American remain neutral in thought as well." The overwhelming majority of Americans — some 84 percent, according to a poll in 1939 — supported Britain and France rather than Germany, but most did not want to be drawn into another European war.

At first, the need for U.S. intervention seemed remote. After the German conquest of Poland in September 1939, calm settled over Europe. Then, on April 9, 1940, German forces invaded Denmark and Norway. In May, the Netherlands, Belgium, Luxembourg, and France were invaded. On June 14, German troops occupied Paris, and Hitler's armies marched along the Champs-Élysées. The final shock came on June 22, 1940, when France surrendered. Britain stood alone against Hitler's plans for domination of Europe.

War Arrives | What *Time* magazine would later call America's "thousand-step road to war" had already begun. After a bitter battle in Congress in 1939, Roosevelt won a change in the neutrality laws to allow the Allies to buy arms as well as nonmilitary goods on a cash-and-carry basis. Interventionists, led by journalist William Allen

White and his Committee to Defend America by Aiding the Allies, became increasingly vocal. In response, in 1940 isolationists formed the America First Committee (AFC), with well-respected figures such as the aviator Charles Lindbergh and Senator Gerald Nye speaking on the AFC's behalf, to keep the nation out of the war.

Because of the efforts of America Firsters, Roosevelt continued to act cautiously in 1940 as he moved the United States closer to involvement. The president did not want war, but he believed that most Americans "greatly underestimate the serious implications to our own future," as he confided to William Allen White. In May, Roosevelt created the National Defense Advisory Commission and brought two prominent Republicans, Henry Stimson and Frank Knox, into his cabinet as secretaries of war and the navy, respectively. During the summer, the president traded fifty World War I destroyers to Great Britain in exchange for the right to build military bases on British possessions in the Atlantic, circumventing neutrality laws by using an executive order to complete the deal. In October, a bipartisan vote in Congress approved a large increase in defense spending and instituted the first peacetime draft in American history. "We must be the great arsenal of democracy," FDR declared.

As the war in Europe and the Pacific expanded, the United States was preparing for the 1940 presidential election. The crisis had convinced Roosevelt that he should seek an unprecedented third term. The Republicans nominated Wendell Willkie of Indiana, a former Democrat who supported many New Deal policies. The two parties' platforms differed only slightly. Both pledged aid to the Allies, and both candidates promised not to "send an American boy into the shambles of a European war," as Willkie put it. Willkie's spirited campaign resulted in a closer election than those of 1932 or 1936; nonetheless, Roosevelt won 55 percent of the popular vote.

Having been reelected, Roosevelt now undertook to persuade Congress to increase aid to Britain, whose survival he viewed as key to American security. In January 1941, he delivered one of the most important speeches of his career. Defining "four essential human freedoms"— freedom of speech, freedom of religion, freedom from want, and freedom from fear — Roosevelt cast the war as a noble defense of democratic societies. He then linked the fate of democratic regimes in Western Europe with the new welfare state at home. Sounding a decidedly New Deal note, Roosevelt pledged to end "special privileges for the few" and to preserve "civil liberties for all." Americans, Roosevelt suggested, must continue to democratize their own society while steadfastly supporting Britain. His words inspired people far beyond the shores of the United States: in Africa, India, and Asia. Like President Wilson's speech championing national self-determination at the close of World War I, Roosevelt's "Four Freedoms" speech outlined a liberal international order with appeal well beyond its intended European and American audiences.

Two months later, in March 1941, with Britain no longer able to pay cash for arms, Roosevelt convinced Congress to pass the Lend-Lease Act. The legislation authorized the president to "lease, lend, or otherwise dispose of" arms and equipment to Britain or any other country whose defense was considered vital to the security of the United States. When Hitler abandoned his nonaggression pact with Stalin and invaded the Soviet Union in June 1941, the United States promptly extended lend-lease to the Soviets. The implementation of lend-lease marked the unofficial entrance of the United States into the European war.

Roosevelt underlined his support for the Allied cause by meeting in August 1941 with British prime minister Winston Churchill (who had succeeded Chamberlain in 1940). Their joint press release, which became known as the Atlantic Charter, provided the ideological foundation of the Western cause. Drawing from Wilson's Fourteen Points and Roosevelt's Four Freedoms, the charter called for economic collaboration, national self-determination, and guarantees of political stability after the war to ensure "that all men in all the lands may live out their lives in freedom from fear and want." It would become the basis for a new American-led transatlantic alliance after the war's conclusion.

In the fall of 1941, the reality of U.S. involvement in the war drew closer. By September, Nazi U-boats and the American Navy were exchanging fire in the Atlantic, though the conflict remained largely unknown to the American public. With isolationists still a potent force, Roosevelt hesitated to declare war and insisted that the United States would defend itself only against a direct attack. But behind the scenes, the president openly discussed American involvement with close advisors and considered war inevitable.

The Attack on Pearl Harbor

The crucial provocation came not from Germany but from Japan. After Japan invaded China in 1937, Roosevelt had denounced "the present reign of terror and international lawlessness" and suggested that aggressors be "quarantined" by peace-loving nations. Despite such rhetoric, the United States refused to intervene when Japanese troops sacked the city of Nanjing, massacred 300,000 Chinese residents, and raped thousands of women.

Without a counterweight, the imperial ambitions of Japan's military officers expanded. In 1940, General Hideki Tojo became war minister. After concluding a formal military alliance with Germany and Italy, Tojo dispatched Japanese troops to occupy the northern section of the French colony of Indochina (present-day Vietnam, Cambodia, and Laos). Tojo's goal, supported by Emperor Hirohito, was to create a "Greater East Asia Co-Prosperity Sphere," run by Japan and stretching from the Korean Peninsula south to Indonesia. Like Germany and Italy, Japan sought to match the overseas empires of Britain, France, Holland, and the United States.

The United States responded to the invasion of Indochina by restricting trade with Japan, especially aviation-grade gasoline and scrap metal. Roosevelt hoped that these economic sanctions would deter Japanese aggression. But in July 1941, Japanese troops occupied the remainder of Indochina. Roosevelt then froze Japanese assets in the United States and instituted an embargo on all trade with Japan, including vital oil shipments that accounted for almost 80 percent of Japanese consumption.

Meanwhile, in October 1941, General Tojo had become prime minister and had accelerated secret preparations for war against the United States. By November, American military intelligence knew that Japan was planning an attack but did not know where it would occur. Early on Sunday morning, December 7, 1941, Japanese bombers attacked Pearl Harbor in Hawaii, killing more than 2,400 Americans. They destroyed or heavily damaged eight battleships, three cruisers, three destroyers, and almost two hundred airplanes.

Although the assault was devastating, it united the American people. Calling December 7 "a date which will live in infamy," President Roosevelt asked Congress for a declaration of war against Japan. The Senate voted unanimously for war, and the House concurred by a vote of 388 to 1. The lone dissenter was Jeannette Rankin of Montana, a committed pacifist — she also voted against entry into World War I — and the first female member of Congress. Three days later, Germany and Italy declared war on the United States, which in turn declared war on the Axis powers. The long shadows of two wars, one in Europe and one in Asia, had at long last converged over the United States.

▶ Why did the United States wait until 1941, after nearly every European nation had fallen to Germany, to enter World War II?

▶ What were the sources of American political isolationism?

Organizing for Victory

The task of fighting on a global scale brought a dramatic increase in the power of the federal government. Coordinating the changeover from civilian to military production, raising an army, and assembling the necessary workforce required a huge expansion in government authority and bureaucracy. When Congress passed the War Powers Act in December 1941, it gave President Roosevelt unprecedented control over all aspects of the war effort. This act marked the beginning of what historians call the **imperial presidency**: the far-reaching use (and sometimes abuse) of executive authority during the latter part of the twentieth century.

Financing the War

A prominent British economic historian has argued that "the Great Depression was without doubt the most important macroeconomic [large-scale structural] event of the twentieth century; the mobilization of the American economy in World War II is a close second." Defense mobilization ended the Great Depression. Between 1940 and 1945, the annual gross national product doubled, after-tax profits of American businesses nearly doubled, and farm output grew by one-third. Federal spending on war production powered this advance. By late 1943, two-thirds of the economy was directly involved in the war effort. The government paid for these military expenditures by raising taxes and borrowing money. The Revenue Act of 1942 expanded the number of people paying income taxes from 3.9 million to 42.6 million. Taxes on personal incomes and business profits paid half the cost of the war. The government borrowed the rest, both from wealthy Americans and from ordinary citizens, who invested in long-term Treasury bonds (war bonds).

Financing and coordinating the war effort required far-reaching cooperation between government and private business. The number of civilians employed by the government increased almost fourfold, to 3.8 million — a far higher rate of growth than that during the New Deal. The powerful War Production Board (WPB) awarded defense contracts, allocated scarce resources — such as rubber, copper, and oil — for military uses, and persuaded businesses to convert to military production. For example, it encouraged Ford and General Motors to build tanks rather than cars by granting generous tax write-offs for re-equipping existing factories and building new ones. In other instances, the board approved "cost-plus" contracts, which guaranteed a profit, and allowed corporations to keep new steel mills, factories, and shipyards after the war. Such government subsidies of defense industries would intensify during the Cold War and continue to this day.

To secure maximum production, the WPB preferred to deal with major corporations rather than with small businesses. The nation's fifty-six largest corporations received three-fourths of the war contracts; the top ten received one-third. The best-known contractor was Henry J. Kaiser. Already highly successful from building roads in California and the Hoover and Grand Coulee dams, Kaiser went from government construction work to navy shipbuilding. At his shipyard in Richmond, California, he revolutionized ship construction by applying Henry Ford's techniques of mass production. To meet wartime production schedules, Kaiser broke the work process down into small, specialized tasks that newly trained workers could do easily. Soon, each of his work crews was building a "Liberty Ship," a large vessel to carry cargo and troops to the war zone, every two weeks. The press dubbed him the "Miracle Man."

Central to Kaiser's success were his close ties to federal agencies. The government financed the great dams that he built during the depression, and the Reconstruction Finance Corporation lent him $300 million to build shipyards and manufacturing plants during the war. Working together in this way, American business and government turned out a prodigious supply of military hardware: 86,000 tanks; 296,000 airplanes; 15 million rifles and machine guns; 64,000 landing craft; and 6,500 cargo ships and naval vessels. The sheer productivity of the U.S. economy, as much as or more than its troops, proved the decisive factor in the war's outcome. The system of allotting contracts, along with the suspension of antitrust prosecutions during the war, created huge corporate enterprises. By 1945, the largest one hundred American companies produced 70 percent of the nation's industrial output. These same corporations would form the core of what came to be known as the nation's "military-industrial complex" in the Cold War era (see Chapter 25).

Mobilizing the American Fighting Force

The expanding federal bureaucracy also had a human face. To fight the war, the government began to mobilize tens of millions of soldiers, civilians, and workers — coordinated on a scale unprecedented in U.S. history. During World War II, the armed forces of the United States enlisted more than fifteen million men and women. In no other military conflict have so many American citizens, from such different backgrounds, served in the armed services. They came from every region and economic station: black sharecroppers from Alabama; white farmers' sons from the Midwest; the sons and daughters of European, Mexican, and Caribbean immigrants; native men from Navajo and Choctaw reservations and other tribal communities; women from every state in the nation; and Hollywood celebrities. From urban, rural, and suburban areas, from working-class and middle-class backgrounds — they all served in the military.

In contrast to its otherwise democratic character, the American army segregated the nearly one million African Americans in uniform. The National Association for the Advancement of Colored People (NAACP) and other civil rights groups reprimanded the government, saying "A Jim Crow army cannot fight for a free world," but the military continued to separate African Americans and assign them menial duties. In contrast, Native Americans and Mexican Americans were never officially segregated; they rubbed elbows with the sons of European immigrants and native-born soldiers from all regions of the country.

Among the most instrumental soldiers were the Native American "code talkers." In the Pacific theater, native Navajo speakers communicated orders to fleet commanders. Japanese intelligence could not decipher the code, based on the Navajo language, which fewer than fifty non-Navajos in the world understood. At the battle of Iwo Jima, for instance — one of the war's fiercest — Navajo code talkers, working around the clock, sent and received more than eight hundred messages without error. In the European theater, army commanders used Comanche, Choctaw, and Cherokee speakers to thwart the Nazis and pass crucial military commands back and forth on the battlefield. No Axis nation ever broke the codes devised by Native Americans.

Approximately 350,000 American women enlisted in the armed services. About 140,000 served in the Women's Army Corps (WAC), and 100,000 served in the navy's Women Accepted for Volunteer Emergency Service (WAVES). One-third of the nation's registered nurses, almost 75,000 overall, volunteered for military duty. In addition, about 1,000 Women's Airforce Service Pilots (WASPs) ferried planes and supplies in non-combat areas. The armed forces limited the duties assigned to women, however. Female officers could not command men, and WACs and WAVES were barred from combat duty, although nurses of both sexes served close to the front lines, risking capture or death. Most of the jobs that women did in the military — clerical work, communications, and health care — resembled women's jobs in civilian life.

These Americans from dramatically different walks of life were viewed by an admiring nation as citizen-soldiers. Dating from the War of Independence, the citizen-soldier ideal held that citizens, especially adult men, owed a military obligation to community and country. Soldiers fought to preserve the nation. While in combat, however, soldiers also fought for more personal, less abstract reasons: for their comrades and their loved ones, and simply to survive and return home. After visiting troops, the actor Alan Ladd revealed that soldiers preferred movies with "street scenes, normal people on the streets, women who look like their mothers, wives, sweethearts." Why? Because they "bring them near home," Ladd said.

Workers and the War Effort

As millions of working-age citizens joined the military, the nation faced a critical labor shortage. As a result, substantial numbers of women and African Americans joined the industrial workforce, taking jobs unavailable to them prior to the conflict. Unions, benefiting from the demand for labor, negotiated higher wages and improved conditions for America's workers. By 1943, with the economy operating at full capacity, the breadlines and double-digit unemployment of the 1930s were a memory.

Rosie the Riveter
Women workers install fixtures and assemblies to a tail fuselage section of a B-17 bomber at the Douglas Aircraft Company plant in Long Beach, California. To entice women to become war workers, the War Manpower Commission created the image of "Rosie the Riveter," later immortalized in posters and by a Norman Rockwell illustration on the cover of the *Saturday Evening Post*. A popular 1942 song celebrating Rosie went: "Rosie's got a boyfriend, Charlie/Charlie, he's a marine/Rosie is protecting Charlie/Working overtime on the riveting machine." Even as women joined the industrial workforce in huge numbers (half a million in the aircraft industry alone), they were understood as fulfilling a nurturing, protective role. Library of Congress.

Rosie the Riveter | Government officials and corporate recruiters urged women to take jobs in defense industries, creating a new image of working women. "Longing won't bring him back sooner . . . GET A WAR JOB!" one poster urged, while artist Norman Rockwell's famous "Rosie the Riveter" illustration beckoned to women from the cover of the *Saturday Evening Post*. The government directed its publicity at housewives, but many working women gladly abandoned low-paying "women's jobs" as domestic servants or secretaries for higher-paying work in the defense industry. Suddenly, the nation's factories were full of women working as airplane riveters, ship welders, and drill-press operators (see American Voices, p. 736). Women made up 36 percent of the labor force in 1945, compared with 24 percent at the beginning of the war. War work did not free women from traditional expectations and limitations, however. Women often faced sexual harassment on the job and usually received lower wages than men did. In shipyards, women with the most seniority and responsibility earned $6.95 a day, whereas the top men made as much as $22.

Women in the Wartime Workplace

During World War II, millions of men served in the armed forces and millions of women worked in war-related industries. A generation later, some of these women workers recounted their wartime experiences to historians in oral interviews. Peggy Terry grew up in Paducah, Kentucky, and worked in defense plants in Kentucky and Michigan. Sarah Killingsworth, an African American, grew up in Clarksville, Tennessee. During the war, after taking a variety of jobs, she ended up working in the women's restroom of a defense plant.

Peggy Terry: The first work I had after the Depression was at a shell-loading plant in Viola, Kentucky. It is between Paducah and Mayfield. They were large shells: anti-aircraft, incendiaries, and tracers. . . . We made the fabulous sum of thirty-two dollars a week [about $452 in 2011]. To us it was just an absolute miracle. Before that, we made nothing. . . .

The war just widened my world. Especially after I came up to Michigan. . . . We made ninety dollars a week [about $1,273 in 2011]. We did some kind of testing for airplane radios. Ohh, I met all those wonderful Polacks. They were the first people I'd ever known that were any different from me. A whole new world just opened up. I learned to drink beer like crazy with 'em. They were all very union-conscious. I learned a lot of things that I didn't even know existed. . . .

Sarah Killingsworth: The war started and jobs kinda opened up for women that the men had. I took a job at a shoe-repair place on Wilshire Boulevard. Cleanin' shoes and dyin' shoes, the same thing that men did. They started takin' applications at Douglas, to work in a defense plant.

I didn't want a job on the production line. I heard so many things about accidents, that some girls got their fingers cut off or their hair caught in the machines. I was frightened. All I wanted to do was get in the factory, because they were payin' more than what I'd been makin'. Which was forty dollars a week, which was pretty good considering I'd been makin' about twenty dollars a week. When I left Tennessee I was only makin' two-fifty a week, so that was quite a jump.

I got the job workin' nights in the ladies rest room, which wasn't hard. We had about six rest rooms to do. They [assembly-line workers] would stay up all night and they would be sleeping. . . . We would watch out for them, so their supervisor wouldn't miss 'em. . . .

I do know one thing, this place was very [racially] segregated when I first come here. Oh, Los Angeles, you just couldn't go and sit down like you do now. You had certain places you went. You had to more or less stick to the restaurants and hotels where black people were. It wasn't until the war that it really opened up. 'Cause when I come out here it was awful, just like bein' in the South.

I was relating this to my daughter last night. What am I gonna relate to my children? "You young people are makin' money and really doin' well," I says. "You would never go through the hardships that I went through to get where I am today."

SOURCE: Excerpted from Studs Terkel, *"The Good War": An Oral History of World War II* (New York: Pantheon, 1984), 102–115.

Wartime work thus remained bittersweet for women. The majority remained clustered in low-wage service jobs. Child care was hard to come by, despite the largest government-sponsored child care program in history. When the men came home from war, Rosie the Riveter was usually out of a job. Government propaganda, which during the war years had badgered women to "take a war job," now reversed course and encouraged them back into the home — where, it was implied, their true calling lay in raising families and standing behind the returning soldiers. But many married women refused, or could not afford, to put on aprons and stay home. Women's participation in the paid labor force rebounded by the late 1940s and continued to rise over the rest of the twentieth century, bringing major changes in family life (see Chapter 26).

Wartime Civil Rights | Among African Americans, a new mood of militancy prevailed during the war. Pointing to parallels between anti-Semitism in Germany and racial discrimination in the United States, black leaders waged the Double V campaign: victories over Nazism abroad and racism at home. "This is a war for freedom. Whose freedom?" the renowned black leader W. E. B. Du Bois asked. If it meant "the freedom of Negroes in the Southern United States," Du Bois answered, "my gun is on my shoulder."

Even before Pearl Harbor, black labor activism was on the rise. In 1940, only 240 of the nation's 100,000 aircraft workers were black, and most of them were janitors. African American leaders demanded that the government require defense contractors to hire more blacks. When Washington took no action, A. Philip Randolph, head of the Brotherhood of Sleeping Car Porters, the largest black labor union in the country, announced plans for a march on Washington in the summer of 1941.

Roosevelt was not a strong supporter of civil rights, but he wanted to avoid public protest and a disruption of the nation's war preparations. So the president made a deal: He issued Executive Order 8802, and in June 1941 Randolph canceled the march. The order prohibited "discrimination in the employment of workers in defense industries or government because of race, creed, color, or national origin" and established the Fair Employment Practices Commission (FEPC). Mary McLeod Bethune called the wartime FEPC "a refreshing shower in a thirsty land." This federal commitment to black employment rights was unprecedented but limited: It did not affect segregation in the armed forces, and the FEPC could not enforce compliance with its orders.

Nevertheless, wartime developments laid the groundwork for the civil rights revolution of the 1960s. The NAACP grew ninefold, to 450,000 members, by 1945. In Chicago, James Farmer helped to found the Congress of Racial Equality (CORE) in 1942, a group that would become known nationwide in the 1960s for its direct-action protests such as sit-ins. The FEPC inspired black organizing against employment discrimination in hundreds of cities and workplaces. This combination of government action and black militancy was the framework within which the civil rights movement advanced on multiple fronts in the postwar years.

Mexican Americans, too, challenged long-standing practices of discrimination and exclusion. Throughout much of the Southwest, it was still common to see signs reading "No Mexicans Allowed," and Mexican American workers were confined to menial, low-paying jobs. There was no single Mexican American counterpart to the NAACP, but several organizations, including the League of United Latin American Citizens (LULAC) and the Congress of Spanish Speaking Peoples, pressed the government and private employers to end anti-Mexican discrimination. Workers themselves, often in Congress of Industrial Organization (CIO) unions such as the Cannery Workers and Shipyard Workers, also led efforts to enforce the equal employment mandate of the FEPC.

Exploitation persisted, however. To meet wartime labor demands, the U.S. government brought tens of thousands of Mexican contract laborers into the United States under the Bracero Program. Paid little and treated poorly, the braceros (who took their name from the Spanish *brazo*, "arm") highlighted the oppressive conditions of farm labor in the United States. After the war, the federal government continued to be a willing participant in labor exploitation, bringing hundreds of thousands of Mexicans into the United States to perform low-wage work in agriculture. Future Mexican American civil rights leaders Dolores Huerta and Cesar Chavez began to fight this labor system in the 1940s.

Organized Labor During the war, unions solidified their position as the most powerful national voice on behalf of American workers, an extension of their gains under the New Deal. By 1945, almost 15 million workers belonged to a union, up from 9 million in 1939. Representatives of the major unions made a no-strike pledge for the duration of the war, and Roosevelt rewarded them by creating the National War Labor Board (NWLB), composed of representatives of labor, management, and the public. The NWLB established wages, hours, and working conditions and had the authority to seize manufacturing plants that did not comply.

Despite these arrangements, many Americans felt cheated as consumer prices rose and corporate profits soared. In 1943, John L. Lewis led more than half a million United Mine Workers out on strike, demanding a higher wage increase than that recommended by the NWLB. Congress responded by passing (over Roosevelt's veto) the Smith-Connally Labor Act of 1943, which allowed the president to prohibit strikes in defense industries and forbade political contributions by unions. Congressional hostility would continue to hamper the union movement in the postwar years. Organized labor would emerge from World War II more powerful than at any time in U.S. history. But its business and corporate opponents, too, would emerge from the war with new strength.

Politics in Wartime

In one of his most farsighted speeches — his 1944 State of the Union address — FDR called for a second Bill of Rights, one that would guarantee all Americans access to education and jobs, adequate food and clothing, and decent housing and medical care. Like his Four Freedoms speech, this was a call to extend the New Deal by broadening the rights to individual security and welfare guaranteed by the government. The answer to his call, however, would have to wait for the war's conclusion. Congress created new government benefits only for military veterans, known as GIs (short for "government issue"). The Servicemen's Readjustment Act (1944), an extraordinarily influential program popularly known as the "GI Bill of Rights," provided education, job training, medical care, pensions, and mortgage loans for men and women who had served in the armed forces.

The president's call for social legislation sought to reinvigorate the New Deal political coalition. In the election of 1944, Roosevelt once again headed the Democratic ticket.

But party leaders, aware of FDR's health problems and anxious to find a middle-of-the-road successor, dropped Vice President Henry Wallace from the ticket. They feared that Wallace's outspoken support for labor, civil rights, and domestic reform would alienate southern Democrats. In his place they chose Senator Harry S. Truman of Missouri. A straight-talking, no-nonsense politician, Truman was a product of the Democratic machine in Kansas City.

The Republicans nominated Governor Thomas E. Dewey of New York. Dewey accepted the general principles of welfare state liberalism domestically and favored internationalism in foreign affairs, and so attracted some of Roosevelt's supporters. But a majority of voters preferred political continuity. Roosevelt received 53.5 percent of the nationwide vote and 60 percent in cities of more than 100,000 people, where labor unions and working-class voters of all backgrounds strongly supported Democratic candidates. The Democratic coalition retained its hold on government power, and the era of Republican political dominance (1896–1932) slipped further into the past.

> ▶ In what ways did World War II contribute to the growth of the federal government? How did it foster what historians now call the military-industrial complex?
>
> ▶ What impact did war mobilization have on women, racial minorities, and organized labor?

Life on the Home Front

The United States escaped the physical devastation that ravaged Europe and East Asia, but the war profoundly changed the country. Americans welcomed wartime prosperity but shuddered when they saw a Western Union boy on his bicycle, fearing that he carried a War Department telegram reporting the death of someone's son, husband, or father. Citizens also grumbled about annoying wartime regulations and rationing but accepted that their lives would be different "for the duration."

"For the Duration"

People on the home front took on wartime responsibilities. They worked on civilian defense committees, recycled old newspapers and scrap material, and served on local rationing and draft boards. About twenty million backyard "victory gardens" produced 40 percent of the nation's vegetables. Various federal agencies encouraged these efforts, especially the Office of War Information (OWI), which disseminated news and promoted patriotism. The OWI urged advertising agencies to link their clients' products to the war effort, arguing that patriotic ads would not only sell goods but also "invigorate, instruct and inspire" the citizenry.

Popular culture, especially the movies, reinforced connections between the home front and the war effort. Hollywood producers, directors, and actors offered their talents to the War Department. Director Frank Capra created a documentary series titled *Why We Fight* to explain war aims to conscripted soldiers. Movie stars such as John Wayne, Anthony Quinn, and Spencer Tracy portrayed the heroism of American fighting men in numerous films, such as *Guadalcanal Diary* (1943) and *Thirty Seconds over Tokyo*

(1945). Demand was so great that many theaters operated around the clock to accommodate defense workers on the swing and night shifts. In this pre-television era, newsreels accompanying the feature films kept the public up to date on the war, as did on-the-spot radio broadcasts by Edward R. Murrow and other well-known commentators.

For many Americans, the major inconvenience during the war years was the shortage of consumer goods. Federal agencies subjected almost everything Americans ate, wore, or used to rationing or regulation. The first major scarcity was rubber. The Japanese conquest of Malaysia and Dutch Indonesia cut off 97 percent of America's imports of that essential raw material. To conserve rubber for the war effort, the government rationed tires, so many of the nation's 30 million car owners put their cars up on blocks. As more people walked, they wore out their shoes. In 1944, shoes were rationed to two pairs per person a year, half the prewar usage. By 1943, the government was regulating the amount of meat, butter, sugar, and other foods Americans could buy. Most citizens cooperated with the complicated rationing and coupon system, but at least one-quarter of the population bought items on the black market, especially meat, gasoline, cigarettes, and nylon stockings.

One thing not in short supply was money. Workers earned higher take-home pay, despite wage freezes, than at any point since the 1920s. "Money came easy, and they spent it easy," one worker observed. Much of it was earned as overtime, with shipyards and other manufacturers running operations around the clock. "There were no more weekends or nights. It was just twenty-four hours a day, seven days a week," a California shipyard worker explained.

Migration and the Wartime City

The war determined where people lived. When husbands entered the armed services, their families often followed them to training bases or points of debarkation. Civilians moved to take high-paying defense jobs. About 15 million Americans changed residences during the war years, half of them moving to another state. One of them was Peggy Terry, who grew up in Paducah, Kentucky; worked in a shell-loading plant in nearby Viola; and then moved to a defense plant in Michigan. There, she recalled, "I met all those wonderful Polacks [Polish Americans]. They were the first people I'd ever known that were any different from me. A whole new world just opened up."

As the center of defense production for the Pacific war, California experienced the largest share of wartime migration. The state welcomed nearly three million new residents and grew by 53 percent during the war. "The Second Gold Rush Hits the West," announced the *San Francisco Chronicle* in 1943. One-tenth of all federal dollars flowed into California, and the state's factories turned out one-sixth of all war materials. People went where the defense jobs were: to Los Angeles, San Diego, and cities around San Francisco Bay. Some towns grew practically overnight; within two years of the opening of the huge Kaiser Corporation shipyard in Richmond, California, the town's population had quadrupled. Other industrial states — notably New York, Illinois, Michigan, and Ohio — also attracted both federal dollars and migrants on a large scale.

The growth of war industries accelerated patterns of rural-urban migration. Cities across the country grew by leaps and bounds, as factories, shipyards, and other defense work drew millions of citizens from small towns and rural areas. This newfound mobility, coupled with people's distance from their hometowns, loosened the authority of traditional institutions and made wartime cities vibrant and exciting. Around-the-clock work shifts kept people on the streets night and day, and jazz clubs, dance halls, and night-clubs proliferated, fed by the ready cash of war workers.

Racial Conflict | Migration and the relaxing of social boundaries meant that people of different racial and ethnic groups rubbed elbows in the booming cities. More than one million African Americans left the rural South for California, Illinois, Michigan, Ohio, and Pennsylvania — a continuation of the Great Migration earlier in the century (see Chapter 21). As blacks and whites competed for jobs and housing, racial conflicts broke out in more than a hundred cities during 1943. The worst violence took place in Detroit. In June 1943, a riot incited by southern-born whites and Polish Americans against African Americans left thirty-four people dead and hundreds injured.

Zoot-Suit Youth in Los Angeles
During a four-day riot in June 1943, servicemen in Los Angeles attacked young Latino men wearing distinctive zoot suits, which were widely viewed as emblems of gang membership and a delinquent youth culture. The police response was to arrest scores of zoot-suiters. Here, a group of handcuffed young Latino men is about to board a Los Angeles County Sheriff's bus to make a court appearance. Note the wide-legged pants that taper at the ankle, a hallmark of the zoot suit. The so-called "zoot-suit riot" was evidence of cracks in wartime unity on the home front. Library of Congress.

New Urban Communities

Folk singer Pete Seeger performs at the opening of the Washington, D.C., labor canteen in 1944, sponsored by the Congress of Industrial Organizations (CIO). Wartime migration brought people from across the country to centers of industry and military operations. Migration opened new possibilities for urban communities. African American neighborhoods grew dramatically; urban populations grew younger and more mobile; and gay and lesbian communities began to flourish and become more visible. The Granger Collection, New York.

Racial conflict struck the West as well. In Los Angeles, male Hispanic teenagers formed pachuco (youth) gangs. Many dressed in "zoot suits"— broad-brimmed felt hats, thigh-length jackets with wide lapels and padded shoulders, pegged trousers, and clunky shoes; they wore their long hair slicked down and carried pocket knives on gold chains. Pachucas (young women) favored long coats, huarache sandals, and pompadour hairdos. Other working-class teenagers in Los Angeles and elsewhere took up the zoot-suit style to underline their rejection of middle-class values. To many adults, the zoot suit symbolized juvenile delinquency. Rumors circulating in Los Angeles in July 1943 that a pachuco gang had beaten an Anglo (white) sailor set off a four-day riot. Anglo servicemen roamed through Mexican American neighborhoods and attacked zoot-suiters, taking special pleasure in slashing their pegged pants.

Gay and Lesbian Community Formation Wartime migration to urban centers created new opportunities for gay men and women to establish communities. Widespread hostility toward and suspicion of gays and lesbians kept the majority of them silent and their sexuality hidden. Religious morality and social convention prevented the recognition of homosexuality as normal and natural. During the war, however, cities such as New York, San Francisco, Los Angeles, Chicago, and even

Kansas City, Buffalo, and Dallas developed vibrant gay neighborhoods, sustained in part by a sudden influx of migrants and the relatively open wartime atmosphere. These communities became centers of the gay rights movement of the 1960s and 1970s (see Chapter 29).

The military tried to screen out homosexuals but had little success. Once in the services, homosexuals found opportunities to participate in a gay culture often more extensive than that in civilian life. In the last twenty years, historians have documented extensive communities of gay and lesbian soldiers in the World War II military. Some "came out under fire," as one historian put it, but most kept their sexuality hidden from authorities, because army officers, doctors, and psychiatrists treated homosexuality as a psychological disorder that was grounds for dishonorable discharge.

Japanese Removal

Unlike World War I, which evoked widespread harassment of German Americans, World War II produced relatively little condemnation of Euro-Americans. Federal officials held about 5,000 potentially dangerous German and Italian aliens during the war. Despite the presence of small but vocal groups of Nazi sympathizers and Mussolini supporters, German American and Italian American communities were largely left in peace during the war. The relocation and temporary imprisonment of Japanese immigrants and Japanese American citizens was a glaring exception to this otherwise tolerant record on the home front. Immediately after the attack on Pearl Harbor, the West Coast remained calm. Then, as residents began to fear spies, sabotage, and further attacks, California's long history of racial animosity toward Asian immigrants surfaced. Local politicians and newspapers whipped up hysteria against Japanese Americans, who numbered only about 112,000, had no political power, and lived primarily in small enclaves in the Pacific coast states.

Early in 1942, President Roosevelt responded to anti-Japanese fears by issuing Executive Order 9066, which gave the War Department the authority to force Japanese Americans from their West Coast homes and hold them in relocation camps for the rest of the war. Although there was no disloyal or seditious activity among the evacuees, few public leaders opposed the plan. "A Jap's a Jap," snapped General John DeWitt, the officer charged with defense of the West Coast. "It makes no difference whether he is an American citizen or not."

The relocation plan shocked Japanese Americans, more than two-thirds of whom were Nisei; that is, their parents were immigrants, but they were native-born American citizens. Army officials gave families only a few days to dispose of their property. Businesses that had taken a lifetime to build were liquidated overnight (see Voices from Abroad, p. 744). The War Relocation Authority moved the prisoners to hastily built camps in desolate areas in California, Arizona, Utah, Colorado, Wyoming, Idaho, and Arkansas. Ironically, the Japanese Americans who made up one-third of the population of Hawaii, and presumably posed a greater threat because of their numbers and proximity to Japan, were not imprisoned. They provided much of the unskilled labor in the island territory, and the Hawaiian economy could not have functioned without them.

Cracks soon appeared in the relocation policy. A labor shortage in farming led the government to furlough seasonal agricultural workers from the camps as early as 1942.

VOICES FROM ABROAD

Japanese Relocation   MONICA ITOI SONE

As Monica Itoi Sone discovered, her legal status as an American citizen did not keep her from being treated like an unwelcome foreigner. Her autobiography, *Nisei Daughter* (1953), tells the story of the relocation and internment of Japanese Americans during World War II.

We felt fortunate to be assigned to a room at the end of the barracks because we had just one neighbor to worry about. The partition wall separating the rooms was only seven feet high with an opening of four feet at the top, so at night, Mrs. Funai next door could tell when Sumi was still sitting up in bed in the dark, putting her hair up. "Mah, Sumi-chan," Mrs. Funai would say through the plank wall, "are you curling your hair tonight again? Do you put it up every night?" Sumi would put her hands on her hips and glare defiantly at the wall.

The block monitor, an impressive Nisei who looked like a star tackle with his crouching walk, came around the first night to tell us that we must all be inside our room by nine o'clock every night. At ten o'clock, he rapped at the door again, yelling, "Lights out!" and Mother rushed to turn the light off not a second later.

Throughout the barracks, there were a medley of creaking cots, whimpering infants and explosive night coughs. Our attention was riveted on the intense little wood stove which glowed so violently I feared it would melt right down to the floor. We soon learned that this condition lasted for only a short time, after which it suddenly turned into a deep freeze. Henry and Father took turns at the stove to produce the harrowing blast which all but singed our army blankets, but did not penetrate through them. As it grew quieter in the barracks, I could hear the light patter of rain. Soon I felt the "splat! splat!" of raindrops digging holes into my face. The dampness on my pillow spread like a mortal bleeding, and I finally had to get out and haul my cot toward the center of the room. . . .

I remembered the wire fence encircling us, and a knot of anger tightened in my breast. What was I doing behind a fence like a criminal? If there were accusations to be made, why hadn't I been given a fair trial? Maybe I wasn't considered an American anymore. My citizenship wasn't real, after all. Then what was I? . . .

I was certainly not a citizen of Japan as my parents were. On second thought, even Father and Mother were more alien residents of the United States than Japanese nationals for they had little tie with their mother country. In their twenty-five years in America, they had worked and paid their taxes to their adopted government as any other citizen.

Of one thing I was sure. The wire fence was real. I no longer had the right to walk out of it. It was because I had Japanese ancestors. It was also because some people had little faith in the ideas and ideals of democracy. They said that after all these were but words and could not possibly insure loyalty. . . .

SOURCE: Monica Itoi Sone, *Nisei Daughter* (Boston: Little, Brown & Co., 1953), 176–178.

About 4,300 students were allowed to attend colleges outside the West Coast military zone. Another route out of the camps was enlistment in the armed services. The 442nd Regimental Combat Team, a unit composed almost entirely of Nisei volunteers, served with distinction in Europe.

Gordon Hirabayashi was among the Nisei who actively resisted incarceration. A student at the University of Washington, Hirabayashi was a religious pacifist who had registered with his draft board as a conscientious objector. He refused to report for evacuation and turned himself in to the FBI. "I wanted to uphold the principles of the Constitution," Hirabayashi later stated, "and the curfew and evacuation orders which singled out a group on the basis of ethnicity violated them." Tried and convicted in 1942, he appealed his case to the Supreme Court in *Hirabayashi v. United States* (1943). In that case and in *Korematsu v. United States* (1944), the Court allowed the removal of Japanese Americans from the West Coast on the basis of "military necessity" but avoided ruling on the constitutionality of the incarceration program. The Court's refusal to rule directly on the relocation program underscored the fragility of civil liberties in wartime. Congress issued a public apology in 1988 and awarded $20,000 to each of the eighty thousand surviving Japanese Americans who had once been internees.

▶ What was the impact of World War II on the everyday life of the majority of Americans?

▶ How do you explain the decision to temporarily hold virtually all Americans of Japanese birth or ancestry?

Fighting and Winning the War

World War II was a war for control of the world. Had the Axis powers triumphed, Germany would have dominated, either directly or indirectly, all of Europe and much of Africa and the Middle East; Japan would have controlled most of East and Southeast Asia. To prevent this outcome, which would have crippled democracy in Europe and restricted American power to the Western Hemisphere, the Roosevelt administration took the United States to war. American intervention, the extraordinary endurance of Britain, and the profound civilian and military sacrifices of the Soviet Union decided the outcome of the conflict and shaped the character of the postwar world.

Wartime Aims and Tensions

Great Britain, the United States, and the Soviet Union were the key actors in the Allied coalition. China, France, and other nations played crucial but smaller roles. The leaders who came to be known as the Big Three — President Franklin Roosevelt, Prime Minister Winston Churchill of Great Britain, and Premier Joseph Stalin of the Soviet Union — set military strategy. However, Stalin was not a party to the Atlantic Charter, which Churchill and Roosevelt had signed in August 1941, and disagreed fundamentally with some of its precepts, such as a capitalist-run international trading system. Another major disagreement among the Allies related to military strategy and timing. The Big Three made defeating Germany (rather than Japan) the top military priority, but differed over how best to do it. In 1941, a massive German force had invaded the Soviet Union and advanced to the outskirts of Leningrad, Moscow, and Stalingrad before being halted in early 1942 by hard-pressed Russian troops. To relieve pressure on the Soviet Army, Stalin wanted the British and Americans to open a second front with a major invasion of Germany through France.

Roosevelt informally assured Stalin that the Allies would comply in 1942, but the British opposed an early invasion, and American war production was not yet sufficient to support it. For eighteen months, Stalin's pleas went unanswered, and the Soviet Union bore the brunt of the fighting — in the 1943 Battle of Kursk alone, the Soviet Army suffered 860,000 casualties, several times what the Allies would suffer for the first two months of the European campaign after D-Day. Then, at a conference of the Big Three in Tehran, Iran, in November 1943, Churchill and Roosevelt agreed to open a second front in France within six months in return for Stalin's promise to join the fight against Japan. Both sides adhered to this agreement, but the long delay angered Stalin, who became increasingly suspicious of American and British intentions.

The War in Europe

Throughout 1942, the Allies suffered one defeat after another. German armies pushed deep into Soviet territory, advancing through the wheat fields of the Ukraine and the rich oil fields of the Caucasus. Simultaneously, German forces began an offensive in North Africa aimed at seizing the Suez Canal. In the Atlantic, U-boats relentlessly devastated American convoys carrying oil and other vital supplies to Britain and the Soviet Union.

Over the winter of 1942–1943, however, the tide began to turn in favor of the Allies. In the epic Battle of Stalingrad, Soviet forces not only decisively halted the German advance, but allowed the Russian army to push westward (Map 24.1). By early 1944, Stalin's troops had driven the German army out of the Soviet Union. Meanwhile, as Churchill's temporary substitute for a second front in France, the Allies launched a major counteroffensive in North Africa. Between November 1942 and May 1943, Allied troops under the leadership of General Dwight D. Eisenhower and General George S. Patton defeated the German Afrika Korps, led by General Erwin Rommel.

From Africa, the Allied command followed Churchill's strategy of attacking the Axis through its "soft underbelly": Sicily and the Italian peninsula. Faced with an Allied invasion, the Italian king ousted Benito Mussolini's fascist regime in July 1943. But German troops, which far outmatched the Allies in skill and organization, took control of Italy and strenuously resisted the Allied invasion. American and British divisions took Rome only in June 1944 and were still fighting German forces in northern Italy when the European war ended in May 1945 (Map 24.2). Churchill's southern strategy proved a time-consuming and costly mistake.

D-Day | The long-promised invasion of France came on D-Day, June 6, 1944. That morning, the largest armada ever assembled moved across the English Channel under the command of General Eisenhower. When American, British, and Canadian soldiers hit the beaches of Normandy, they suffered terrible casualties but secured a beachhead. Over the next few days, more than 1.5 million soldiers and thousands of tons of military supplies and equipment flowed into France. Much to the Allies' advantage,

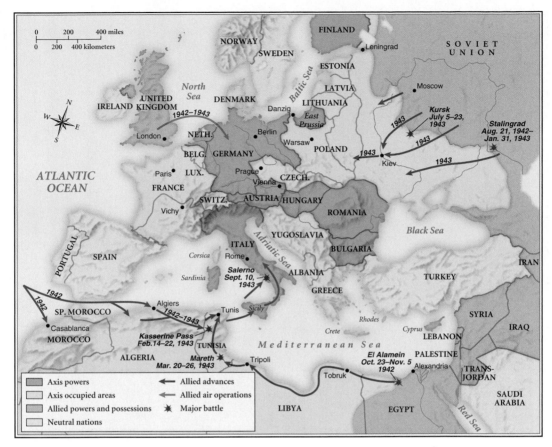

MAP 24.1 World War II in Europe, 1941–1943
Hitler's Germany reached its greatest extent in 1942, by which time Nazi forces had occupied Norway, France, North Africa, central Europe, and much of western Russia. The tide of battle turned in late 1942 when the German advance stalled at Leningrad and Stalingrad. By early 1943, the Soviet Army had launched a massive counterattack at Stalingrad, and Allied forces had driven the Germans from North Africa and launched an invasion of Sicily and the Italian mainland.

they never faced more than one-third of Hitler's Wehrmacht (armed forces), because the Soviet Union continued to hold down the Germans on the eastern front. In August, Allied troops liberated Paris; by September, they had driven the Germans out of most of France and Belgium. Meanwhile, long-range Allied bombers attacked German cities such as Hamburg and Dresden as well as military and industrial targets. The air campaign killed some 305,000 civilians and soldiers, and injured another 780,000 — a grisly reminder of the war's human brutality.

The Germans were not yet ready to give up, however. In December 1944, they mounted a final offensive in Belgium, the so-called Battle of the Bulge, before being pushed back across the Rhine River into Germany. As American and British troops

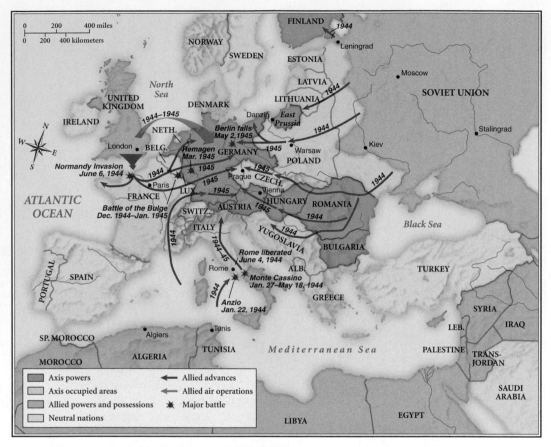

MAP 24.2 World War II in Europe, 1944–1945

By the end of 1943, the Russian Army had nearly pushed the Germans out of the Soviet Union, and by June 1944, when the British and Americans finally invaded France, the Russians had liberated eastern Poland and most of southeastern Europe. By the end of 1944, British and American forces were ready to invade Germany from the west, and the Russians were poised to do the same from the east. Germany surrendered on May 7, 1945.

drove toward Berlin from the west, Soviet troops advanced east through Poland. On April 30, 1945, as Russian troops massed outside Berlin, Hitler committed suicide; on May 7, Germany formally surrendered.

The Holocaust | As Allied troops advanced into Poland and Germany in the spring of 1945, they came face-to-face with Hitler's "final solution" for the Jewish population of Germany and the German-occupied countries: the extermination camps in which 6 million Jews had been put to death, along with another 6 million Poles, Slavs, Gypsies, homosexuals, and others deemed "undesirables." Photographs of the Nazi death camps at Buchenwald, Dachau, and Auschwitz showed bodies stacked like cordwood and survivors so emaciated that they were barely alive. Quickly published in *Life*

The Living Dead

When Allied troops advanced into Germany in the spring of 1945, they discovered the existence of what had long been rumored — concentration camps, Adolf Hitler's "final solution" for the Jews of Nazi-dominated Europe. In this picture from the Wöbbelin concentration camp — liberated by the 82nd Airborne Division and 8th Infantry Division of the U.S. Army — emaciated inmates are being taken to a hospital. In the days before the Allied troops reached the camp, one thousand of the five thousand prisoners had been allowed to starve to death. National Archives.

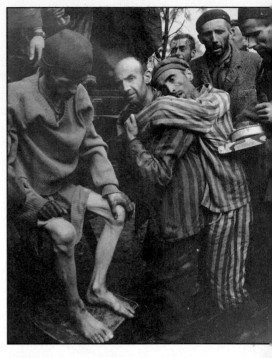

and other mass-circulation magazines, the photographs horrified the American public and the world.

The Nazi persecution of German Jews in the 1930s was widely known in the United States. But when Jews had begun to flee Europe, the United States refused to relax its strict immigration laws to take them in. In 1939, when the SS *St. Louis*, a German ocean liner with nearly a thousand Jewish refugees aboard, sought permission from President Roosevelt to dock at an American port, FDR had refused. Its passengers' futures uncertain, the *St. Louis* was forced to return to Europe. American officials, along with those of most other nations, continued this exclusionist policy during World War II as the Nazi regime extended its control over millions of Eastern European Jews.

Among the various factors that inhibited American action, the most important was widespread anti-Semitism: in the State Department, Christian churches, and the public at large. The legacy of the immigration restriction legislation of the 1920s and the isolationist attitudes of the 1930s also discouraged policymakers from assuming responsibility for the fate of the refugees. Taking a narrow view of the national interest, the State Department allowed only 21,000 Jewish refugees to enter the United States during the war. But the War Refugee Board, which President Roosevelt established in 1944 at the behest of Secretary of the Treasury Henry Morgenthau, helped move 200,000 European Jews to safe havens in other countries.

The War in the Pacific

Winning the war against Japan was every bit as arduous as waging the campaign against Germany. After crippling the American battle fleet at Pearl Harbor, the Japanese quickly expanded into the South Pacific, with seaborne invasions of Hong Kong, Wake Island, and Guam. Japanese forces then advanced into Southeast Asia, conquering the Solomon Islands, Burma, and Malaya and threatening Australia and India. By May 1942, they had forced the surrender of U.S. forces in the Philippine Islands and, in the Bataan "death march," caused the deaths of 10,000 American prisoners of war.

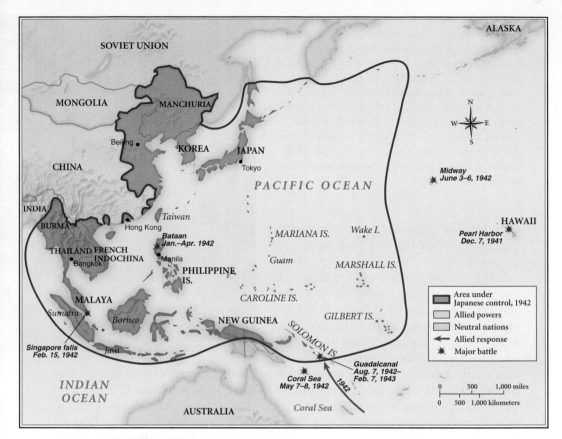

MAP 24.3 World War II in the Pacific, 1941–1942

After the attacks on Pearl Harbor in December 1941, the Japanese rapidly extended their domination in the Pacific. The Japanese flag soon flew as far east as the Marshall and Gilbert islands and as far south as the Solomon Islands and parts of New Guinea. Japan also controlled the Philippines, much of Southeast Asia, and parts of China, including Hong Kong. By mid-1942, American naval victories at the Coral Sea and Midway stopped further Japanese expansion.

At that dire moment, American naval forces scored two crucial victories. These were possible because the attack on Pearl Harbor had crippled American battleships but left all aircraft carriers unscathed. In the Battle of the Coral Sea, off southern New Guinea in May 1942, they halted the Japanese offensive against Australia. Then, in June, at the Battle of Midway Island, the American navy inflicted serious damage on the Japanese fleet. In both battles, dive-bombers launched from American aircraft carriers provided the margin of victory. The U.S. military command, led by General Douglas MacArthur and Admiral Chester W. Nimitz, now took the offensive in the Pacific (Map 24.3). For the next eighteen months, American forces advanced slowly toward Japan, taking one island after another in the face of determined Japanese resistance. In October 1944, MacArthur and Nimitz began the reconquest of the Philippines by winning the Battle of Leyte Gulf, a massive naval encounter in which the Japanese lost practically their entire fleet (Map 24.4).

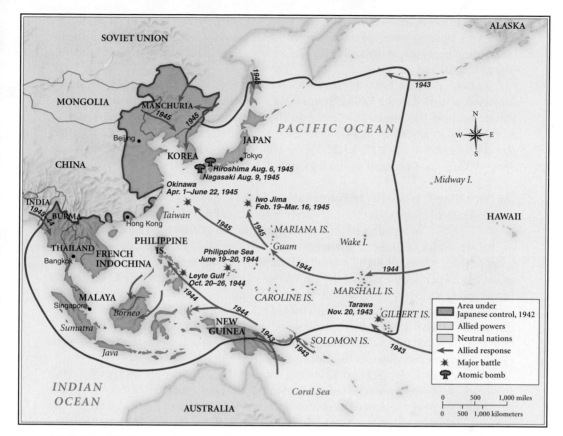

MAP 24.4 World War II in the Pacific, 1943–1945

Allied forces retook the islands of the central Pacific in 1943 and 1944 and ousted the Japanese from the Philippines early in 1945. Carrier-launched planes had started bombing Japan itself in 1942, but the capture of these islands gave U.S. bombers more bases from which to strike Japanese targets. As the Soviet Army invaded Japanese-occupied Manchuria in August 1945, U.S. planes took off from one of the newly captured Mariana Islands to drop the atomic bombs on Hiroshima and Nagasaki. The Japanese offered to surrender on August 10.

By early 1945, victory over Japan was in sight. Japanese military forces had suffered devastating losses, and American bombing of the Japanese homeland had killed 330,000 civilians and crippled the nation's economy. The bloodletting on both sides was horrendous. On the small islands of Iwo Jima and Okinawa, tens of thousands of Japanese soldiers fought to the death, killing 13,000 U.S. Marines and wounding 46,000 more. Desperate to halt the American advance and short on ammunition, Japanese pilots flew suicidal kamikaze missions, crashing their bomb-laden planes into American ships.

Among the grim realities of war in the Pacific was the conflict's racial overtones. The long tradition of anti-Asian sentiment in the United States was reawakened by the attack on Pearl Harbor. In the eyes of many Americans, the Japanese were "yellow monkeys," an inferior race whose humanity deserved minimal respect. Racism was evident among the Japanese as well. Their brutal attacks on China (including the rape of Nanjing), their forcing of Korean "comfort women" to have sex with soldiers, and their treatment of American prisoners in the Philippines flowed from their own sense of racial superiority. Anti-Japanese attitudes in the United States would subside in the 1950s as the island nation became a trusted ally. But racism would again play a major role in the U.S. war in Vietnam in the 1960s.

As the American Navy advanced on Japan in the late winter of 1945, President Roosevelt returned to the United States from a meeting of the Big Three at Yalta, a resort in southern Ukraine on the Black Sea. The sixty-three-year-old president was a sick man, visibly exhausted by his 14,000-mile trip and suffering from heart failure and high blood pressure. On April 12, 1945, during a short visit to his vacation home in Warm Springs, Georgia, Roosevelt suffered a cerebral hemorrhage and died.

The Manhattan Project | When Harry Truman assumed the presidency, he learned for the first time about the top-secret Manhattan Project, which was on the verge of testing a new weapon: the atomic bomb. By the 1930s, building on the earlier work of European physicists, scientists theorized that the fission (breaking apart of the nucleus) of highly processed uranium atoms would unleash tremendous amounts of energy. Working at the University of Chicago in December 1942, Enrico Fermi and Leo Szilard, refugees from fascist Italy and Nazi Germany, produced the first controlled atomic chain reaction. With the aid of German-born refugee Albert Einstein, the greatest theorist of modern physics and a scholar at Princeton, they persuaded Franklin Roosevelt to develop an atomic weapon, warning that German scientists were also working on such nuclear reactions.

The Manhattan Project cost $2 billion, employed 120,000 people, and involved the construction of thirty-seven installations in nineteen states — with all of its activity hidden from Congress, the American people, and even Vice President Truman. Directed by General Leslie Graves and scientist J. Robert Oppenheimer, the nation's top physicists assembled the first bomb in Los Alamos, New Mexico, and successfully tested it on July 16, 1945. Overwhelmed by its frightening power, as he witnessed the first mushroom cloud, Oppenheimer recalled the words from the *Bhagavad Gita*, one of the great texts of Hindu scripture: "I am become Death, the Destroyer of Worlds."

Three weeks later, President Truman ordered the dropping of atomic bombs on two Japanese cities: Hiroshima on August 6 and Nagasaki on August 9. Why Truman gave this order, and what its implications were, have long been the subject of scholarly and popular debate. The principal reason was straightforward: Truman and his American advisors, including Secretary of War Henry Stimson and Army Chief of Staff General George Marshall, believed that Japan's military leaders would never surrender unless their country was utterly devastated. Moreover, at the Potsdam Conference in July, the Allies had agreed that only the "unconditional surrender" of Japan was acceptable — the same terms under which Germany and Italy had been defeated. To win such a surrender, it looked as if an invasion of Japan itself would be necessary. Stimson and Marshall told Truman that an invasion of mainland Japan would produce between half a million and a million Allied casualties.

Before giving the order to drop the atomic bomb, Truman considered other options. His military advisors rejected the most obvious alternative: a nonlethal demonstration of the bomb's awesome power, on a remote island in the Pacific, for instance. If such a demonstration failed — not out of the question, since the bomb had been tested only

The Big Three at Yalta
With victory in Europe at hand, Roosevelt journeyed in February 1945 to Yalta, on the Black Sea, and met for what would be the final time with Churchill and Stalin. The leaders discussed the important and controversial issues of the treatment of Germany, the status of Poland, the creation of the United Nations, and Russian entry into the war against Japan. The Yalta agreements mirrored a new balance of power and set the stage for the Cold War. Franklin D. Roosevelt Library.

once — it would embolden Japan further. A detailed advance warning designed to scare Japan into surrender was also rejected as unlikely to succeed. Given the tenacity with which Japan had fought in the Pacific, the Americans simply believed that nothing short of massive devastation or a successful invasion would lead Japan's military leadership to surrender. After all, the deaths of more than 100,000 Japanese civilians in the U.S. fire-bombing of Tokyo and other cities in the spring of 1945 had brought Japan no closer to surrender.

Two final considerations were not lost on Truman's inner circle. The first was Stalin and the Soviet Union. At Potsdam, Truman had hoped to surprise Stalin with news of "a new weapon of unusual, destructive force" (Truman kept the nature of this weapon secret). However, Stalin's spy network had already informed him of the bomb's success-ful test, and he showed no shock at this announcement. Disagreements at Yalta had foreshadowed approaching U.S.-Soviet conflict over plans for the postwar world, and Truman hoped that use of the bomb might make Stalin think twice about resisting

American initiatives. Second, Stimson, Marshall, and Truman were well aware of the moral implications, both of the bomb's development and of its use against Japan. Historical documents reveal that these discussions took place. Moral objections were not minimized, but they were overruled by the argument that an invasion would spill far more blood, both Allied and Japanese.

In any event, the atomic bombs achieved the immediate goal. The deaths of 100,000 people at Hiroshima and 60,000 at Nagasaki prompted the Japanese government to surrender unconditionally on August 10 and to sign a formal agreement on September 2, 1945. Fascism had been defeated, thanks to a fragile alliance between the capitalist nations of the West and the communist government of the Soviet Union. The coming of peace would strain and then destroy the victorious coalition. Albert Einstein, who had urged Roosevelt to pursue the bomb, found after its use that he was less optimistic. "The unleashed power of the atom has changed everything save our modes of thinking," he wrote in 1946. "And thus we drift toward unparalleled catastrophe."

Planning the Postwar World

As Allied forces neared victory in Europe and advanced toward Japan in the Pacific in February 1945, Roosevelt, Churchill, and Stalin had met in Yalta. Roosevelt focused on maintaining Allied unity, which he saw as the key to postwar peace and stability. But two sets of issues, the fates of the British and French colonial empires, and of the nations of Central and Eastern Europe, divided the Big Three. An independence movement in British India, led by Mohandas K. Gandhi (also known by the honorific Mahatma, "great-souled"), had gathered strength and caused friction between Roosevelt, who favored Indian independence, and Churchill, intent on preserving British rule.

An equally serious conflict was created by Stalin's insistence that Russian national security required pro-Soviet governments in Central and Eastern Europe. Roosevelt pressed for an agreement that guaranteed self-determination and democratic elections in Poland and neighboring countries. However, given the presence of Soviet troops in those nations, FDR had to accept a pledge from Stalin to hold "free and unfettered elections" at a future time. The three leaders agreed to divide Germany into four administrative zones, each controlled by one of the four allied powers (the United States, Great Britain, France, and the Soviet Union), and to similarly partition the capital city, Berlin, which was located in the middle of the Soviet zone.

At Yalta, the Big Three had also agreed to establish an international body to replace the discredited League of Nations. They decided that the new organization, to be known as the United Nations, would have both a General Assembly, in which all nations would be represented, and a Security Council comprised of the five major Allied powers — the United States, Britain, France, China, and the Soviet Union — and six other nations elected on a rotating basis. They determined that the five permanent members of the Security Council should have veto power over decisions of the General Assembly. Roosevelt, Churchill, and Stalin announced that the United Nations would convene in San Francisco on April 25, 1945.

► Evaluate the tensions among the Allies over military strategy and postwar territorial issues.

► Explain why the United States used atomic weapons against Japan.

SUMMARY

The rise of fascism in Germany, Italy, and Japan led to the outbreak of World War II. Initially, the American public insisted on noninvolvement. But by 1940, President Roosevelt was mobilizing support for military preparedness and intervention. The Japanese attack on Pearl Harbor in December 1941 brought the nation fully into the conflict. War mobilization dramatically expanded the federal government. It also boosted geographical and social mobility as women, rural whites, and southern blacks took up work in new defense plants in California and elsewhere. Government rules assisted both the labor movement and the African American campaign for civil rights. However, religious and racial animosity caused the exclusion of Jewish refugees and the internment of 112,000 Japanese Americans.

As our account shows, by 1942 Germany and Japan had almost won the war. But in 1943, the Allies took the offensive — with advances by the Soviet Army in Europe and the American Navy in the Pacific — and by the end of 1944, Allied victory was all but certain. The United States emerged from the war with an undamaged homeland, sole possession of the atomic bomb, and a set of unresolved diplomatic disputes with the Soviet Union that would soon lead to the four-decade-long Cold War.

For additional primary sources from this period, see *Documents for America's History*, Seventh Edition.

For Web sites, images, and documents related to topics and places in this chapter, visit *Make History* at **bedfordstmartins.com/henrettaconcise**.

For Further Exploration

The standard military history of World War II is Henry Steele Commager's *The Story of World War II*, as expanded and revised by Donald L. Miller (1945; revisions 2001). Fifty-three personal stories of war appear in *War Stories: Remembering World War II* (2002), edited by Elizabeth Mullener. An engaging overview of war on the home front is John Morton Blum, *V Was for Victory* (1976). The National Archives Administration at **www.archives.gov/exhibit_hall/index.html** has two World War II sites: "A People at War" and "Powers of Persuasion: Poster Art from World War II." Powerful novels inspired by the war include John Hersey, *A Bell for Adano* (1944); James Jones, *From Here to Eternity* (1951); and Norman Mailer, *The Naked and the Dead* (1948).

The Library of Congress exhibit "Women Come to the Front: Journalists, Photographers, and Broadcasters During World War II" at **lcweb.loc.gov/exhibits/wcf/wcf0001.html** records the contributions of women during World War II. Sherna B. Gluck, *Rosie the Riveter Revisited* (1988), offers compelling accounts by women war workers. Many sites cover the Japanese internment. For interviews with detainees and thousands of images, go to **www.densho.org/densho.asp**. The Library of Congress site presents "Suffering Under a Great Injustice," a haunting exhibition of Ansel Adams's photographs of the

TIMELINE

1933	► Adolf Hitler becomes chancellor of Germany	**1942**	► Allied defeats in Europe and Asia
1935	► Italy invades Ethiopia		► Executive Order 9066 leads to Japanese internment camps
1935–1937	► U.S. Neutrality Acts		
1936	► Germany reoccupies Rhineland demilitarized zone		► Battles of Coral Sea and Midway halt Japanese advance
	► Rome-Berlin Axis established	**1942–1945**	► Rationing of scarce goods
	► Japanese-German pact against the Soviet Union	**1943**	► Race riots in Detroit and Los Angeles
1937	► Japan invades China		► Fascism falls in Italy
1938	► Munich conference	**1944**	► D-Day: Allied landing in France (June 6)
1939	► German-Soviet nonaggression pact		► GI Bill of Rights enacted
	► Germany invades Poland	**1945**	► Yalta Conference (February)
	► Britain and France declare war on Germany		► Battles of Iwo Jima and Okinawa
1940	► American conscription reinstated		► Harry S. Truman becomes president after Roosevelt's death (April 12)
	► Germany, Italy, and Japan form alliance		
1941	► Roosevelt gives Four Freedoms speech		► Germany surrenders (May 7)
	► Germany invades Soviet Union		► United Nations founded
	► Lend-Lease Act passed		► United States drops atomic bombs on Hiroshima and Nagasaki (August 6 and 9)
	► Fair Employment Practices Commission (FEPC) created		
	► Atlantic Charter issued		► Japan surrenders (August 10)
	► Japanese attack Pearl Harbor (December 7)		

Manzanar camp, at **memory.loc.gov/ammem/aamhtml**. The decision to drop the atomic bomb remains controversial. An excellent site is Lehigh University Professor Edward J. Gallagher's "The *Enola Gay* Controversy: How Do We Remember a War That We Won?" at **www.lehigh.edu/~ineng/enola**.

Test Your Knowledge

For practice quizzes, activities, and other study tools, visit the Online Study Guide at **bedfordstmartins.com/henrettaconcise**.

CHAPTER 25

Cold War America

1945–1963

The great majority of the American people understand very well that this war is not a war only, but an end and a beginning—an end to things known and a beginning of things unknown.

—Archibald MacLeish, 1943

In the autumn of 1950, a little-known California congressman named Richard Nixon stood before reporters in Los Angeles. Nixon was running for a U.S. Senate seat. His opponent, Helen Gahagan Douglas, was a Hollywood actress and a New Deal stalwart, having served three terms as a pro-Roosevelt Democrat in the House of Representatives. Nixon looked sternly into the eyes of reporters and told them that Douglas had cast "Communist-leaning" votes and that she was "pink right down to her underwear." Gahagan's voting record was in reality not much different from Nixon's. But the label stuck, and Nixon defeated the "pink lady" with nearly 60 percent of the vote. Tarring her with communism made her seem disloyal and un-American, and as a campaign tactic it worked.

A few months earlier, half a world away, U.S. tanks, planes, and artillery supplies had arrived in a region of Southeast Asia that most of the world knew as French Indochina. A French colony since the nineteenth century, Indochina (present-day Vietnam, Laos, and Cambodia) was home to an independence movement led by Ho Chi Minh and supported by the Soviet Union and China. In the summer of 1950, President Harry S. Truman authorized $15 million worth of military supplies to aid France, which was fighting Ho's army to keep possession of its Indochinese empire. "Neither national independence nor democratic evolution exists in any area dominated by Soviet imperialism," Secretary of State Dean Acheson warned ominously as he announced U.S. support for French imperialism.

Connecting these coincidental historical moments, one domestic and the other international, was a decades-old force in American life that gained renewed strength after World War II: anticommunism. The events in Los Angeles and Vietnam, however different on the surface, were part of the global geopolitical struggle between the United States and the Soviet Union known as the Cold War. Although it did not lead to any direct engagement on the battlefield, the Cold War inaugurated a half century of international

The Perils of the Cold War
In this detail of a 1948 Pulitzer Prize–winning cartoon, Rube Goldberg depicts the perilous nature of America's postwar peace — one that was based largely on the threat of nuclear annihilation. The Granger Collection.

tension and proxy wars during which either side, armed with nuclear weapons, might have tipped the entire world into oblivion.

Beginning in Europe before the final shots of World War II had been fired and extending to Asia, Latin America, the Middle East, and Africa by the mid-1950s, the

Cold War reshaped international relations across the globe. Imposing a new frame-work on the centuries-old pattern of rivalry between great powers, it pitted the capital-ist, democratic United States against the Communist, authoritarian Soviet Union. In that divided world, the fates of nations and peoples were rendered in stark either/or terms.

In the United States, the Cold War fostered suspicion of "subversives" in government, education, and the media. The arms race that developed between the two superpowers required Congress to boost military expenditures. The resulting **military-industrial complex** enhanced the power of the corporations that built rockets, bombs, planes, munitions, and electronic devices. In politics, the Cold War stifled liberal initiatives as the New Deal coalition tried to advance its domestic agenda in the shadow of anticom-munism. In all these ways, the line between the international and the domestic blurred — and that blurred line was an enduring legacy of the Cold War.

Containment in a Divided World

The Cold War began at the close of World War II in 1945 and ended in 1991 with the col-lapse and dissolution of the Soviet Union. While it lasted, two critical questions stood at the center of global history: Under what conditions, and in whose interest, would the European and Asian balances of political power be maintained? And how would the developing nations (the European colonies in Asia, the Middle East, and Africa) gain their independence and take their places on the world stage? Cold War rivalries framed the possible answers to both questions as they drew the United States into a prolonged engagement with world affairs, unprecedented in the nation's history, that continues to the present day.

The Cold War in Europe, 1945–1946

World War II set the basic conditions for the Cold War. With Germany and Japan de-feated and Britain and France exhausted, only two superpowers remained standing in 1945. Even had nothing else divided them, the United States and the Soviet Union would have jostled each other as they moved to fill the postwar vacuum of power. But, of course, the two countries were divided — by geography, by history, by ideology, and by strategic interest. President Franklin Roosevelt understood that maintaining the U.S.-Soviet alliance was an essential condition for postwar global stability. But he also be-lieved that permanent peace and long-term U.S. interests depended on the Wilsonian principles of collective security, self-determination, and free trade (see Chapter 21).

Yalta | At the Yalta Conference of February 1945, Roosevelt, British prime minister Winston Churchill, and Soviet premier Joseph Stalin faced the challenge of rec-onciling Wilsonian principles with U.S.-Soviet power realities. The Big Three agreed there to proceed with the United Nations, on the condition that the United States and the Soviet Union (along with Great Britain, France, and China) receive permanent seats, with veto rights, on the Security Council. The paramount problem at Yalta, however, was Eastern Europe. At the first meeting of the Big Three, at Tehran in 1943, Stalin had agreed to fol-low the British and American strategy to defeat Hitler, in exchange for assurances that he

East Meets West

With an "East Meets West" placard providing inspiration, Private Frank B. Huff of Virginia (on the right) and a Russian soldier shake hands. Huff was one of the first four Americans to contact the Russians when the two armies met at the River Elbe (seen in the background of this photo) in eastern Germany, on April 25, 1945. The goodwill in evidence in the spring of 1945, as Americans and Russians alike celebrated the defeat of Nazi Germany, would within two short years be replaced by Cold War suspicion and hostility. © Bettmann/Corbis.

could reshape the Soviet border with Poland. At Yalta, Roosevelt and Churchill agreed that Poland and its neighbors would fall under the Soviet "sphere of influence," thus meeting Stalin's demand for secure eastern borders. In Stalin's view, Soviet wartime sacrifices and the threat of future invasions through Europe entitled him to a buffer of client states on the USSR's western border — Russia had been invaded three times through Poland (by France once and Germany twice). But the Yalta agreement also called for "free and unfettered" elections to uphold the principle of democratic self-determination.

Such elections eventually took place in Finland, Hungary, Bulgaria, and Czechoslovakia, with varying degrees of democratic openness. This was not the case in Poland and Romania, where Stalin was determined to establish Communist governments and to punish wartime collaborators. As the largest Eastern European nation, Poland was "the big apple in the barrel," according to Roosevelt's secretary of state, Edward Stettinius. Because Stalin's armies occupied both Poland and Romania at the time of the Yalta Conference, Roosevelt and Churchill had little bargaining room. Stalin got the client regimes he desired there and would soon exert near-complete control over Bulgaria, Czechoslovakia, and Hungary as well. Stalin's unwillingness to honor self-determination for nations in Eastern Europe was, from the American point of view, the precipitating event of the Cold War.

Truman Steps In | Historians doubt that even the resourceful Roosevelt, had he lived, could have preserved the alliance with the Soviet Union. With Harry Truman as president, such a possibility grew ever more remote. Truman, who succeeded to the presidency in April 1945, was inexperienced in foreign affairs. Lacking Roosevelt's history of negotiating with the Soviet leader, Truman acted on blunt instinct to stand up to Stalin. "Unless Russia is faced with an iron fist and strong language," he said, "another war is in the making." At a meeting held shortly after he took office, the fledgling president berated the Soviet foreign minister, Vyacheslav Mikhaylovich Molotov, over the Soviets' failure to honor their Yalta agreements. Truman's tough talk may not have been diplomatic, but it pleased many Western European leaders, who feared Stalin nearly as much as they had Hitler.

Truman used what he called "tough methods" again that July at the Potsdam Conference, which had been called to take up postwar planning. After learning of the successful test of America's atomic bomb, Truman "told the Russians just where they got off and generally bossed the whole meeting," recalled Churchill. In the presidency only a few months, Truman had raised Cold War tensions another notch. Stalin, who secretly knew of the Manhattan Project, refused to back down and his suspicion of the West deepened when Truman failed to reveal the bomb's existence, saying only that the United States possessed "a new weapon of unusual, destructive force." On the American side, the bomb encouraged a certain swagger. It was unwise, warned the U.S. secretary of war, Henry L. Stimson, for the United States to try to negotiate with "this weapon rather ostentatiously on our hip."

Germany | Germany represented the biggest challenge of all. American officials believed that rebuilding the German economy was essential to the prosperity of democratic regimes throughout Western Europe — and to keeping ordinary Germans from turning again to Nazism. Stalin hoped merely to extract reparations from Germany in the form of industrial machines and goods. Unlike in Eastern Europe, in Germany the Americans, British, and French had troops on the ground and could force the compromise on Stalin of dividing Germany into zones of occupation (British, French, American, and Russian) with minimal reparations for the Soviet Union (Map 25.1). Stalin did not like it, but circumstances forced him to accept the compromise, which sharpened his resentment against the West.

The cities and fields of Europe had barely ceased to run with the blood of World War II before they were menaced again by the tense standoff between the Soviet Union and the United States. With Stalin intent on establishing a protective barrier of client states in Eastern Europe and the United States equally intent on reviving Germany and ensuring collective security throughout Europe, the points of agreement were few and far between.

The Containment Strategy

By 1947, the West had developed a clear strategy toward the Soviet Union that would become known as **containment**. The Soviet Union was expanding its reach: stationing troops in northern Iran, pressing Turkey for access to the Mediterranean, and

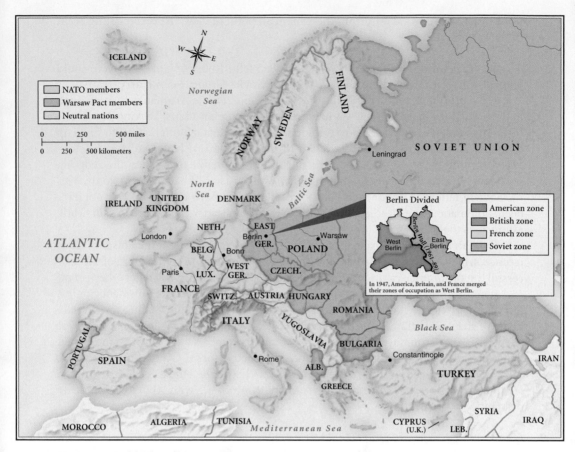

MAP 25.1 Cold War in Europe, 1955

This map vividly shows the Cold War division of Europe. The NATO countries (colored green) are allies of the United States; the Warsaw Pact countries (in purple) are allied to the USSR. At that point, West Germany had just been admitted to NATO, completing Europe's stabilization into two rival camps. But Berlin remained divided, and one can see from its location deep in East Germany why the former capital was always a flash point in Cold War controversies.

supporting Communist forces in a guerrilla war in Greece. To counter, the West would seek to contain Soviet expansion, limiting Stalin's influence to Eastern Europe while reconstituting industrial capitalism and democratic governments in Western Europe. The United States was wedded to the notion — dating to the Wilson administration — that communism and capitalism were incompatible on the world stage.

Toward an Uneasy Peace | American thinking was significantly advanced in February 1946 by American diplomat George F. Kennan, in an 8,000-word cable dubbed the "Long Telegram," sent from his post at the U.S. embassy in Moscow. Kennan argued that the Soviet Union was an "Oriental despotism" and that communism was just the "fig-leaf" justifying its aggression. The West's only recourse, Kennan wrote a year later in a famous *Foreign Affairs* article, was to meet the Soviets "with unalterable counter-force at every point where they show signs of encroaching upon the interests of a peaceful and stable world." Kennan called for "long-term, patient but firm and vigilant containment of Russian expansive tendencies." *Containment*, the key word, came to define America's evolving strategic stance toward the Soviet Union.

Kennan was confident that the Soviet system was inherently unstable and would — not in Stalin's lifetime, but eventually — collapse. Containment would work, Kennan believed, as long as the United States and its allies opposed Soviet expansion in all parts of the world. Kennan's attentive readers included Stalin himself, who quickly obtained a copy of the classified Long Telegram. The Soviet leader was equally suspicious of the West, seeing the United States as an imperialist aggressor determined to replace Great Britain as the world's dominant capitalist power. Just as Kennan thought that the Soviet system was despotic and unsustainable, Stalin believed that the West suffered from its own fatal weaknesses. Neither side completely understood or trusted the other, and each projected its worst fears onto the other.

In fact, Britain's influence in the world was declining. Exhausted by the war, facing enormous deficits and a collapsing economy at home, and confronted with determined independence movements in India and Egypt, Britain was on the wane as a global power. "The reins of world leadership are fast slipping from Britain's competent but now very weak hands," read a U.S. State Department report. "These reins will be picked up either by the United States or by Russia."

It did not take long for the reality of Britain's decline to resonate across the Atlantic. In February 1947, London informed Truman that it could no longer afford to support the anticommunists in Greece, where a bitter civil war had split the country. If the Communists won in Greece, Truman worried, that would lead to Soviet domination of the eastern Mediterranean and embolden Communist parties in France and Italy. In response, the president announced what came to be known as the Truman Doctrine. In a speech on March 12, he asserted an American responsibility "to support free peoples who are resisting attempted subjugation by armed minorities or by outside pressures." To that end, Truman proposed large-scale assistance for Greece and Turkey (then involved in a dispute with the Soviet Union over the Dardanelles, a strait connecting the Aegean Sea and the Sea of Marmara). "If we falter in our leadership, we may endanger the peace of the world," Truman declared. Despite the open-endedness of this military commitment, Congress quickly approved Truman's request for $300 million in aid to Greece and $100 million for Turkey.

Soviet expansionism was not the entire story. Europe was sliding into economic chaos. Already devastated by the war, in 1947 the continent was hit by the worst winter in memory. People were starving, credit was nonexistent, wages were stagnant, and the consumer market had collapsed. For both humanitarian and practical reasons, Truman's advisors believed something had to be done. A global depression might ensue if the European economy, the largest foreign market for American goods, did not recover. Worse, unemployed and dispirited Western Europeans might fill the ranks of the Communist Party, threatening political stability and the legitimacy of the United States. At Secretary of State George C. Marshall's behest, Kennan came up with a remarkable proposal: a massive infusion of American capital to help get the European economy back on its feet. Speaking at the Harvard University commencement in June 1947, Marshall urged the nations of Europe to work out a comprehensive recovery program based on U.S. aid.

This pledge of financial aid met significant opposition in Congress. Republicans castigated the Marshall Plan as a huge "international W.P.A." But in the midst of the congressional stalemate, on February 25, 1948, Stalin ordered a political coup in Czechoslovakia. In response, Congress rallied and voted overwhelmingly to approve funds for the Marshall Plan. Over the next four years, the United States contributed nearly $13 billion to a highly successful recovery effort that benefited both Western Europe and the United States (see Voices from Abroad, p. 765). European industrial production increased by 64 percent, and the appeal of Communist parties waned in the West. Markets for American goods grew stronger and helped foster an economic interdependence between Europe and the United States. Notably, however, the Marshall Plan intensified Cold War tensions. U.S. officials invited the Soviets to participate but insisted on certain restrictions that would virtually guarantee Stalin's refusal. When Stalin did refuse, ordering Soviet client states to do so as well, the onus of dividing Europe appeared to fall on the Soviet leader and deprived his threadbare partners of assistance they sorely needed.

East and West in the New Europe | The flash point for a hot war remained Germany, the most important industrial economy and most strategic land mass in Europe. When no agreement could be reached to unify the four zones of occupation into a single state, the Western allies consolidated their three zones in 1947. They then prepared to establish an independent federal German republic. Marshall Plan funds would jump-start economic recovery. Some of those funds were slated for West Berlin, in hopes of making the city a capitalist showplace 100 miles deep inside the Soviet zone.

Stung by the West's intention to create a German republic without Soviet input, in June 1948 Stalin blockaded all Allied traffic to West Berlin, which he perceived as an indefensible Western outpost. Instead of giving way, as Stalin had expected, Truman and the British were galvanized into action. "We are going to stay, period," Truman said plainly. For nearly a year, American and British pilots, who had been dropping bombs on Berlin only four years earlier, improvised an airlift that flew 2.5 million tons of food and fuel into the Western zones of the city — nearly a ton for each resident. The Berlin crisis was the closest the two sides came to actual war. Military officials reported to Truman that General Lucius D. Clay, the American commander in Berlin, was "drawn as tight as a steel spring." But Stalin backed down: On May 12, 1949, he lifted the blockade. West Berlin became a symbol of resistance to communism.

The crisis in Berlin persuaded Western European nations to forge a collective security pact with the United States. In April 1949, for the first time since the end of the American Revolution, the United States entered into a peacetime military alliance, the North Atlantic Treaty Organization (NATO). Under the NATO pact, twelve nations — Belgium, Canada, Denmark, France, Great Britain, Iceland, Italy, Luxembourg, the Netherlands, Norway, Portugal, and the United States — agreed that "an armed attack against one or more of them in Europe or North America shall be considered an attack against them all." In May 1949, those nations also agreed to the creation of the Federal Republic of Germany (West Germany), which joined NATO in 1955. In response, the Soviet

VOICES FROM ABROAD

Truman's Generous Proposal   JEAN MONNET

Jean Monnet was an eminent French statesman and a tireless promoter of postwar European union. As head of a French postwar planning commission, he helped oversee the dispersal of Marshall Plan funds, the importance of which he describes in his memoirs.

So we had at last concerted our efforts to halt France's economic decline; but now, once more, everything seemed to be at risk. Two years earlier [1947], we thought that we had plumbed the depths of material poverty. Now we were threatened with the loss of even basic essentials. . . . Our dollar resources were melting away at an alarming rate, because we were having to buy American wheat to replace the crops we had lost during the winter. . . . A further American loan was soon exhausted.

Nor was this grim situation confined to France. Britain too had come to the end of her resources. In February 1947 she had abruptly cancelled her aid to Greece and Turkey, whose burdens she had seemed able to assume in 1945. Overnight, this abrupt abdication gave the United States direct responsibility for part of Europe. Truman did not hesitate for a moment: with the decisiveness that was to mark his actions as President, he at once asked for credits and arms for both Turkey and Greece. . . . [Soon after], he announced the Truman Doctrine of March 12, 1947. Its significance was general: it meant that the United States would prevent Europe from becoming a depressed area at the mercy of Communist advance. On the very same day, the Four-Power Conference began in Moscow. There, for a whole month, George Marshall, Ernest Bevin, and Georges Bidault argued with Vyacheslav Molotov about all the problems of the peace, and above all about Germany.

When Marshall returned to Washington, he knew that for a long time there would be no further genuine dialogue with Stalin's Russia. The "Cold War," as it was soon to be known, had begun. . . . Information from a number of sources convinced Marshall and his Under-Secretary Dean Acheson that once again, as in 1941, the United States had a great historic duty. And once again there took place what I had witnessed in Washington a few years earlier: a small group of men brought to rapid maturity an idea which, when the Executive gave the word, turned into vigorous action. This time, it was done by five or six people, in total secrecy and at lightning speed. Marshall, Acheson, [William] Clayton, Averell Harriman, and George Kennan worked out a proposal of unprecedented scope and generosity. It took us all by surprise when we read the speech that George Marshall made at Harvard on June 5, 1947. Chance had led him to choose the University's Commencement Day to launch something new in international relations: helping others to help themselves.

SOURCE: Jean Monnet, *Memoirs*, trans. Richard Mayne (New York: Doubleday, 1978), 264–266.

Union set up the German Democratic Republic (East Germany); the Council for Mutual Economic Assistance (COMECON); and, in 1955, the Warsaw Pact, a military alliance for Eastern Europe whose members included Albania, Bulgaria, Czechoslovakia, East Germany, Hungary, Poland, Romania, and the Soviet Union. In these parallel steps, the two superpowers had institutionalized the Cold War through a massive division of the continent.

By the early 1950s, *West* and *East* were the stark markers of the new Europe. As Churchill had observed in 1946, the line dividing the two stretched "from Stettin in the Baltic to Trieste in the Adriatic," cutting off tens of millions of Eastern Europeans — and the ancient capitals Berlin, Belgrade, Bucharest, Budapest, Prague, Sofia, and Warsaw — from the rest of the continent. Stalin's tactics had been dictatorial and often ruthless, but they were not without reason. The Soviets acted out of the sort of self-interest that had long defined powerful nations — ensuring a defensive perimeter of friendly allies, seeking access to raw materials, and pressing the advantage that victory in war allowed.

Nuclear Diplomacy | The final stage in the foundational years of the Cold War came in September 1949, when the Soviet Union detonated an atomic bomb. With America's brief tenure as sole nuclear power over, Truman turned to the U.S. National Security Council (NSC), established by the National Security Act of 1947, for a strategic reassessment. In April 1950, the NSC delivered its report, known as NSC-68. Bristling with alarmist rhetoric, the document urged a crash program to maintain America's nuclear edge, including the development of a hydrogen bomb, a thermonuclear device that used atomic fission to fuse atoms, and which was a thousand times more destructive than the atomic bombs dropped on Japan. The United States exploded the first hydrogen bomb in 1954, but the Soviet Union exploded its own soon thereafter. Paradoxically, with the advent of the hydrogen bomb, the utility of nuclear devices as actual weapons shrank to zero. No political objective could possibly be worth the destructiveness of a thermonuclear exchange.

The "balance of terror" that now prevailed magnified the importance of conventional forces. Having demobilized its wartime army, the United States had treated the atomic bomb as the equalizer against the vast Soviet Army. Now the only credible deterrent was a stronger conventional military. To that end, NSC-68 called for increased taxes to finance "a bold and massive program of rebuilding the West's defensive potential to surpass that of the Soviet world." Truman was reluctant to commit to a major defense buildup, fearing that it would overburden the national budget. But shortly after NSC-68 was completed, events in Asia led him to reverse course.

Containment in Asia

In Asia, U.S. attention centered on Japan. As with Germany, American officials had come to believe that restoring Japan's economy, while limiting its military influence, was key to ensuring prosperity and containing communism in East Asia. After dismantling Japan's military, American occupation forces under General Douglas MacArthur drafted a democratic constitution and paved the way for the restoration of Japanese sovereignty in 1951. Considering the scorched-earth war that had just ended, this was a remarkable achievement, thanks partly to the imperious MacArthur but mainly to the Japanese, who

Communist China

People in Beijing raise their clenched fists in a welcoming salute for Chinese Communist forces entering the city after the Nationalists surrendered on January 31, 1949. The center portrait behind them is of General Mao Zedong, the leader of the Communist Party of China. Mao's victory in the civil war meant that from East Germany to the Pacific Ocean, much of the Eurasian land mass (including Eastern Europe, the Soviet Union, and China) was ruled by Communist governments. AP Images.

embraced peace and accepted U.S. military protection. However, events on the mainland proved much more difficult for the United States to shape to its advantage.

Civil War in China | A civil war had been raging in China since the 1930s as Communist forces led by Mao Zedong (Mao Tse-tung) contended for power with Nationalist forces under Jiang Jieshi (Chiang Kai-shek). Fearing a Communist victory, between 1945 and 1949 the United States provided $2 billion to Jiang's army. Pressing Truman to "save" China, conservative Ohio Republican senator Robert A. Taft predicted that "the Far East is ultimately even more important to our future peace than is Europe." By 1949, Mao's forces held the advantage. Truman reasoned that to save Jiang, the United States would have to intervene militarily, something the president was unwilling to do. He cut off aid and left the Nationalists to their fate. The People's Republic of China was formally established under Mao on October 1, 1949, and the remnants of Jiang's forces fled to Taiwan.

Both Stalin and Truman expected Mao to take an independent line, as the Communist leader Tito had just done in Yugoslavia. Mao, however, aligned himself with the Soviet Union, partly out of fear that the United States would re-arm the Nationalists and invade the mainland. As attitudes hardened, many Americans viewed Mao's success as a defeat for the United States. A pro-Nationalist "China lobby" accused Truman's State Department of being responsible for the "loss" of China. Sensitive to these charges, the Truman administration refused to recognize "Red China" and blocked China's admission to the United Nations. But the United States pointedly refused to guarantee Taiwan's independence, and in fact accepted the outcome on the mainland. (Since 1982, however, the United States has recognized Taiwanese sovereignty.)

The Korean War | The United States took a stronger stance in Korea, the narrow peninsula between China and the west coast of Japan. The United States and the Soviet Union had agreed at the close of World War II to occupy Korea jointly, temporarily dividing the former Japanese colony at the 38th parallel. As tensions rose in Europe, the 38th parallel hardened into a permanent demarcation line. The Soviets supported a Communist government, led by Kim Il Sung, in North Korea; the United States backed a right-wing Nationalist, Syngman Rhee, in South Korea. The two sides had waged low-level war since 1945, and both leaders were spoiling for a more definitive fight. However, neither Kim nor Rhee could launch an all-out offensive without the backing of his sponsor. Washington repeatedly said no, and so did Moscow. But Kim continued to press Stalin to permit him to reunify the nation. Convinced by the North Koreans that victory would be swift, the Soviet leader finally relented in the late spring of 1950.

On June 25, 1950, the North Koreans launched a surprise attack across the 38th parallel (Map 25.2). Truman immediately asked the U.N. Security Council to authorize a "police action" against the invaders. The Soviet Union was boycotting the Security Council to protest China's exclusion from the United Nations and could not veto Truman's request. With the Security Council's approval of a "peacekeeping force," Truman ordered U.S. troops to Korea. The rapidly assembled U.N. army in Korea was overwhelmingly American, with General Douglas MacArthur in command. At first, the North Koreans held a distinct advantage, occupying the entire peninsula except for the southeast corner around Pusan. But on September 15, 1950, MacArthur launched a surprise amphibious attack at Inchon, far behind the North Korean lines. Within two weeks, the U.N. forces controlled Seoul, the South Korean capital, and almost all the territory up to the 38th parallel.

The impetuous MacArthur ordered his troops across the 38th parallel and led them all the way to the Chinese border at the Yalu River. It was a major blunder, certain to draw China into the war. Sure enough, just after Thanksgiving, a massive Chinese counterattack forced MacArthur's forces into headlong retreat back down the Korean peninsula. Two months later, the American forces and their allies counterattacked, and pushed back to the 38th parallel. Then stalemate set in. With weak public support for the war in the United States, Truman and his advisors decided to work for a negotiated peace. MacArthur disagreed. In an inflammatory letter to the House minority leader, Republican Joseph J. Martin of Massachusetts, MacArthur denounced the Korean stalemate, declaring, "There is no substitute for victory." On April 11, 1951, Truman relieved MacArthur of his command. Truman's decision was highly unpopular, especially among conservative Republicans, but he had likely saved the nation from years of costly warfare with China.

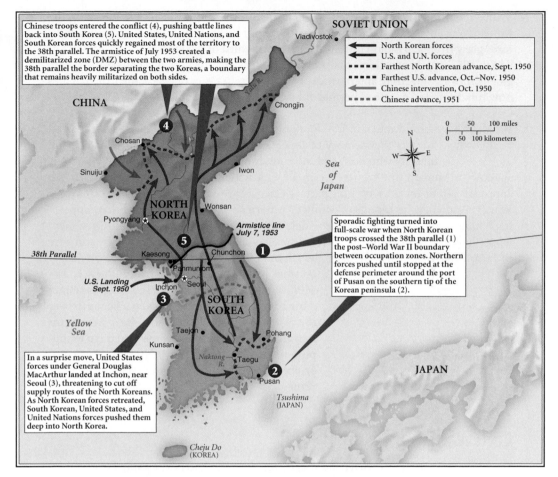

Chinese troops entered the conflict (4), pushing battle lines back into South Korea (5). United States, United Nations, and South Korean forces quickly regained most of the territory to the 38th parallel. The armistice of July 1953 created a demilitarized zone (DMZ) between the two armies, making the 38th parallel the border separating the two Koreas, a boundary that remains heavily militarized on both sides.

SOVIET UNION

⬅ North Korean forces
⬅ U.S. and U.N. forces
▪▪▪▪ Farthest North Korean advance, Sept. 1950
▪▪▪▪ Farthest U.S. advance, Oct.–Nov. 1950
⬅ Chinese intervention, Oct. 1950
▪▪▪▪ Chinese advance, 1951

Vladivostok

CHINA

Chongjin

④

Chosan

Sinuiju

Iwon

Sea of Japan

0   50   100 miles
0   50   100 kilometers

N
W   E
S

NORTH KOREA   Wonsan

Pyongyang

Armistice line July 7, 1953

⑤

38th Parallel   Kaesong   Chunchon   ①

Panmunjom

U.S. Landing Sept. 1950   Inchon   Seoul

③

SOUTH KOREA

Sporadic fighting turned into full-scale war when North Korean troops crossed the 38th parallel (1) the post–World War II boundary between occupation zones. Northern forces pushed until stopped at the defense perimeter around the port of Pusan on the southern tip of the Korean peninsula (2).

Yellow Sea

Taejon   Pohang

Kunsan

Naktong R.   Taegu

②

Pusan

In a surprise move, United States forces under General Douglas MacArthur landed at Inchon, near Seoul (3), threatening to cut off supply routes of the North Koreans. As North Korean forces retreated, South Korean, United States, and United Nations forces pushed them deep into North Korea.

Tsushima (JAPAN)

JAPAN

Cheju Do (KOREA)

MAP 25.2 The Korean War, 1950–1953

The Korean War, which the United States officially deemed a "police action," lasted three years and cost the lives of more than 36,000 U.S. troops. South and North Korean deaths were estimated at more than 900,000. Although hostilities ceased in 1953, the South Korean Military (with U.S. military assistance) and the North Korean Army continue to face each other across the demilitarized zone, more than fifty years later.

Notwithstanding MacArthur's dismissal, the war dragged on for more than two years. An armistice in July 1953, pushed by the newly elected president, Dwight D. Eisenhower, left Korea divided at the original demarcation line. North Korea remained firmly allied with the Soviet Union; South Korea signed a mutual defense treaty with the United States. It had been the first major proxy battle of the Cold War, in which the Soviet Union and United States took sides in a civil conflict. It would not be the last.

The Korean War had far-reaching consequences. Truman's decision to commit troops without congressional approval set a precedent for future undeclared wars. His refusal to unleash atomic bombs, even when American forces were reeling under a massive Chinese attack, set ground rules for Cold War conflict. The war also expanded American involvement in Asia, transforming containment into a truly global policy. Finally, the Korean War ended Truman's resistance to a major military buildup. Defense expenditures grew from $13 billion in 1950, roughly one-third of the federal budget, to $50 billion in 1953, nearly two-thirds of the budget. American foreign policy had become more global, more militarized, and more expensive. Even in times of peace, the United States now functioned in a state of permanent military mobilization.

The Munich Analogy | Behind much of U.S. foreign policy in the first two decades of the Cold War lay the memory of appeasement. The generation of politicians and officials who designed the containment strategy had come of age in the shadow of Munich, the conference in 1938 at which the Western democracies had appeased Hitler by offering him part of Czechoslovakia, paving the road to World War II. Applying the lessons of Munich, American presidents believed that "appeasing" Stalin (and subsequent Soviet rulers Nikita Khrushchev and Leonid Brezhnev) would have the same result: wider war. Thus in Germany, Greece, and Korea, and later in Iran, Guatemala, and Vietnam, the United States staunchly resisted the Soviets — or what it perceived to be Soviet influence. The Munich analogy strengthened the U.S. position in a number of strategic conflicts, particularly over the fate of Germany. But it also drew Americans into armed conflicts — and convinced them to support repressive, right-wing regimes — that compromised, as much as supported, stated American principles.

▶ Was the Cold War inevitable? Why or why not?

▶ How would you assess overall responsibility for the origins of the Cold War?

Cold War Liberalism

Harry Truman never intended to be a caretaker executive and never wanted to be a Cold War president. He had big plans. In September 1945, just fourteen days after Japan surrendered, Truman called for a dramatic expansion of the New Deal, fulfilling the "second Bill of Rights" that Roosevelt had proclaimed in his State of the Union Address in 1944 (see Chapter 24). Truman phrased his proposals in just that way, as rights expected by all Americans — the right to a "useful and remunerative" job, good housing, "adequate medical care," "protection from the economic fears of old age," and a "good education." In the end, his high hopes were crushed, and Truman went down in history not as a New Dealer, but as a Cold Warrior.

Truman and the Democratic Party of the late 1940s and early 1950s forged what historians call Cold War liberalism. They preserved the core programs of the New Deal welfare state, developed the containment policy to oppose Soviet influence throughout the world, and fought so-called subversives at home. But there would be no second act for the New Deal. The Democrats adopted this combination of moderate liberal policies and anticommunism — Cold War liberalism — partly by choice and partly out of necessity. A few high-level espionage scandals and the Communist outcomes in Eastern Europe and China reenergized the Republican Party, which forced Truman and the Democrats to occupy what historian Arthur Schlesinger called the "vital center" of American politics. However, Americans on both the progressive left and the conservative right remained dissatisfied with this development. Cold War liberalism was a practical centrist policy for a turbulent era. But it would not last.

Organized labor was a key force in Cold War liberalism. Stronger than ever, union membership swelled to more than 14 million by 1945. Determined to make up for their wartime sacrifices, unionized workers made aggressive demands and mounted major strikes in the automobile, steel, and coal industries after the war. Republicans responded. They gained control of the House in a sweeping repudiation of Democrats in 1946 and promptly passed — over Truman's veto — the Taft-Hartley Act (1947), an overhaul of the 1935 National Labor Relations Act. Antilabor legislators skillfully crafted changes in procedures and language that, over time, eroded the law's stated purpose of protecting the right of workers to organize and engage in collective bargaining. Unions especially disliked Section 14b, which allowed states to pass "right-to-work" laws prohibiting the union shop. Taft-Hartley effectively "contained" the labor movement. Trade unions would continue to support the Democratic Party, but the labor movement would not move into the largely non-union South and would not extend into the many American industries that remained unorganized.

Truman and the End of Reform

By 1947, most observers wouldn't have bet a nickel on Truman's political future. His popularity ratings had plummeted, and "To err is Truman" became a favorite political gibe. Republicans, seeking political advantage in the Cold War, blamed Truman for the Soviet takeover of Eastern Europe. Determined to govern as a Democratic reformer, Truman found his domestic programs stymied and his international efforts questioned and criticized.

The 1948 Election | Democrats would have dumped Truman in 1948 had they found a better candidate. But the party fell into disarray. The left wing split off and formed the Progressive Party, nominating Henry A. Wallace, an avid New Dealer whom Truman had fired as secretary of commerce in 1946 because of his vocal opposition to America's actions in the Cold War. A right-wing challenge came from the South. When northern liberals such as Mayor Hubert H. Humphrey of Minneapolis pushed through a strong civil rights platform at the Democratic convention, the southern delegations bolted and, calling themselves Dixiecrats, nominated for president South Carolina governor Strom Thurmond, an ardent supporter of racial segregation. The Republicans meanwhile renominated Thomas E. Dewey, the politically moderate governor of New York who had run a strong campaign against FDR in 1944.

Truman surprised everyone. He launched a strenuous cross-country speaking tour and hammered away at the Republicans for opposing progressive legislation and, in general, for running a "do-nothing" Congress. By combining these issues with attacks on the Soviet menace abroad, Truman began to salvage his troubled campaign. At his rallies, enthusiastic listeners shouted, "Give 'em hell, Harry!" Truman won, receiving 49.6 percent of the vote to Dewey's 45.1 percent.

Close observers could see in this remarkable election a foreshadowing of political turmoil. Truman occupied the center of a sprawling Democratic Party, the New Deal

Truman Triumphant

In one of the most famous photographs in U.S. political history, Harry S. Truman gloats over an erroneous headline in the November 3 *Chicago Daily Tribune*. Pollsters had predicted an easy victory for Thomas E. Dewey. Their primitive techniques, however, missed the dramatic surge in support for Truman during the last days of the campaign. © Bettmann/Corbis.

coalition forged under FDR. On his left were progressives, civil rights advocates, and anti–Cold War peace activists. On his right were segregationist white southerners, who opposed civil rights and were allied with Republicans on many economic and foreign policy issues. In 1948, Truman performed a delicate balancing act, largely retaining the support of Jewish and Catholic voters in the big cities, black voters in the North, and organized labor voters across the country. But Thurmond's strong showing — he carried four states in the Deep South — demonstrated the fragile nature of the Democratic Party's coalition and prefigured the revolt of the party's southern wing in the 1960s. On top of juggling the contending forces in his own party, Truman faced mounting pressure from Republicans to prove his anticommunist credentials and take a tough stand against the Soviet Union.

The Fair Deal | Despite having to perform a balancing act, Truman and progressive Democrats forged ahead. In 1949, reaching ambitiously to extend the New Deal, Truman proposed the Fair Deal: national health insurance, aid to education, a housing program, expansion of Social Security, a higher minimum wage, and a new agricultural program. In its attention to civil rights, the Fair Deal also reflected the growing role of African Americans in the Democratic Party. Congress, however, remained a huge stumbling block, and the Fair Deal fared poorly. The same conservative coalition that had blocked Roosevelt's initiatives in his second term continued the fight against Truman's. Cold War pressure did not help. The nation's growing paranoia over internal subversion weakened support for bold extensions of the welfare state. Truman's proposal for national health insurance, for instance, was a popular idea, with strong backing from organized labor. But it was denounced as "socialized medicine" by the American Medical Association and the insurance industry. In the end, the Fair Deal's only significant breakthrough, other than improvements to the minimum wage and Social Security, was the National Housing Act of 1949, which authorized the construction of 810,000 low-income units.

Red Scare: The Hunt for Communists

Cold War liberalism was premised on the grave domestic threat posed, many believed, by Communists and Communist sympathizers. Was there any significant Soviet penetration of the American government? Records opened after the 1991 disintegration of the Soviet Union — intelligence files in Moscow and, most important among U.S. sources, the intercepts of Soviet cables collected in a U.S. intelligence project code-named Venona — indicate that there was. Among American suppliers of information to Moscow were FDR's assistant secretary of the treasury, Harry Dexter White; FDR's administrative aide Laughlin Currie; a strategically placed midlevel group in the State Department (including Alger Hiss, who was with FDR at Yalta); and several hundred more, some identified only by code name, working in a range of government departments and agencies.

There have long been competing ways to view this espionage. Many of these enlistees in the Soviet cause had been bright young New Dealers in the mid-1930s, when the Soviet-backed Popular Front suggested that the lines separating liberalism, progressivism, and communism were permeable (see Chapter 24). At that time, the United States was not at war and never expected to be. And when war did come, the Soviet Union was an American ally. For critics of the informants, however, there remained the time between the Nazi-Soviet Pact and the German invasion of the Soviet Union, a nearly two-year period during which cooperation with the Soviet Union could be seen in a less positive light. Moreover, passing secrets to another country, even a wartime ally, was simply indefensible to many Americans. The lines between U.S. and Soviet interests blurred for some; for others, they remained clear and definite.

After World War II, however, most suppliers of information to the Soviets apparently ceased spying. For one thing, the professional apparatus of Soviet spying was dismantled or disrupted by American counterintelligence work. For another, most of the well-connected amateur spies moved on to other careers. The State Department official Alger Hiss, for example, was serving as head of the prestigious Carnegie Endowment for International Peace when he was accused in 1948 by Whittaker Chambers, a Communist-turned-informant, of having passed classified documents to him in the 1930s. Historians have thus developed a healthy skepticism about Soviet espionage in the United States after 1947, but this was not how many Americans saw it at the time. Legitimate suspicions and real fears, along with political opportunism, combined to fuel the national Red Scare, longer and more far-reaching than the one that followed World War I (see Chapter 21).

Loyalty-Security Program To insulate his administration against charges of Communist infiltration, Truman issued Executive Order 9835 on March 21, 1947, which created the Loyalty-Security Program. The order permitted officials to investigate any employee of the federal government (some 2.5 million people) for "subversive" activities. Representing a profound centralization of power, the order sent shock waves through every federal agency. Truman intended the order to apply principally to actions intended to harm the United States (sabotage, treason, etc.), but it was broad enough to allow anyone to be accused of subversion for the slightest reason — for marching in a Communist-led demonstration in the 1930s, for instance, or signing a petition calling for public housing. Along with suspected political subversives, thousands of gay men and lesbians were dismissed from federal employment in the 1950s, victims of an obsessive search for anyone deemed "unfit" for government work.

Following Truman's lead, many state and local governments, universities, political organizations, churches, and businesses undertook their own antisubversion campaigns, which often included loyalty oaths. In the labor movement, where Communists had served as organizers in the 1930s, charges of Communist domination led to the expulsion of a number of unions by the Congress of Industrial Organizations (CIO) in 1949. Civil rights organizations such as the National Association for the Advancement of Colored People (NAACP) and the National Urban League also expelled Communists and "fellow travelers," or Communist sympathizers. Thus, the Red Scare spread from the federal government to the farthest reaches of American organizational, cultural, and economic life.

HUAC | The Truman administration had legitimized the vague and malleable concept of "disloyalty." Others proved willing to stretch the concept even further, beginning with the House Un-American Activities Committee (HUAC), which Congressman Martin Dies of Texas and other conservatives had launched in 1938. After the war, HUAC helped spark the Red Scare by holding widely publicized hearings on alleged Communist infiltration in the movie industry. Appearing before HUAC, an actor named Ronald Reagan assured the committee, "I do not believe that the Communists have ever at any time been able to use the motion picture industry." However, a group of writers and directors dubbed the "Hollywood Ten" went to jail for contempt of Congress for refusing to testify about their past associations. Hundreds of other actors, directors, and writers whose names had been mentioned in the HUAC investigation were unable to get work, victims of an unacknowledged but very real blacklist honored by industry executives (see American Voices, p. 776).

Here, too, however, revelations from the Soviet archives have complicated the picture. Historians have mostly regarded the American Communist Party as a "normal" organization, acting in America's home-grown radical tradition. In some instances, this was the case. Communists were among the most effective trade union organizers in the labor movement, and the American Communist Party promoted black civil rights long before many other organizations did. But Soviet archives have also shown that the American party was not entirely independent — it was taking money and instructions from Moscow. When American Communists joined other organizations, they often pushed Moscow's agenda. Whether this constituted disloyalty or subversion remained a divisive question, easily manipulated for an unknowing public by anticommunist institutions such as HUAC and by determined individuals such as an unknown and undistinguished senator from the Upper Midwest.

McCarthyism | The meteoric career of Senator Joseph McCarthy of Wisconsin marked the finale of the Red Scare. In February 1950, McCarthy delivered a bombshell during a speech in Wheeling, West Virginia: "I have here in my hand a list of 205 . . . a list of names that were made known to the Secretary of State as being members of the Communist Party and who nevertheless are still working and shaping policy in the State Department." McCarthy later reduced his numbers, gave different figures in different speeches, and never released any names or proof. But he had gained the attention he sought.

For the next four years, from his position as chair of the Senate Permanent Subcommittee on Investigations, he waged a virulent smear campaign. Critics who disagreed with him exposed themselves to charges of being "soft" on communism. Truman called

McCarthy's charges "slander, lies, [and] character assassination" but could do nothing to curb him. Republicans, for their part, refrained from publicly challenging their most outspoken senator and, on the whole, were content to reap the political benefits. McCarthy's charges almost always targeted Democrats.

In early 1954, McCarthy overreached by launching an investigation into subversive activities in the U.S. Army. When lengthy hearings — the first of their kind broadcast on the new medium of television — brought McCarthy's tactics into the nation's living rooms, support for him plummeted. In December 1954, the Senate voted 67 to 22 to censure McCarthy for unbecoming conduct. He died from an alcohol-related illness three years later at the age of forty-eight, his name forever attached to a period of political repression of which he was only the most flagrant manifestation.

The Politics of Cold War Liberalism

As Election Day 1952 approached, the nation — just seven years removed from World War II — was embroiled in the tense Cold War with the Soviet Union and fighting a "hot" war in Korea. Though Americans gave the Republicans victory, radical change was not in the offing. The new president, Dwight D. Eisenhower, set the tone for what his supporters called modern Republicanism, an updated GOP approach that aimed at moderating, not dismantling, the New Deal state. Eisenhower and his supporters were more successors of FDR than of Herbert Hoover. Foreign policy revealed a similar continuity. Like their predecessors, Republicans saw the world in Cold War polarities.

Republicans rallied around Eisenhower, the popular former commander of Allied forces in Europe, but they remained deeply divided. On one side, party activists looked to Robert A. Taft of Ohio. The Republican leader in the Senate, Taft was a vehement opponent of the New Deal. A close friend of business, he particularly detested labor unions. Though an ardent anticommunist, the isolationist-minded Taft did not support the aggressive policy of containment pursued by Truman, and he sharply criticized U.S. participation in NATO. Taft ran for president three times, and though he was never the Republican nominee, he won the loyalty of conservative Americans who saw the welfare state as a waste and international affairs as dangerous foreign entanglements.

On the other side, moderate Republicans looked to men like Eisenhower and Nelson Rockefeller, who supported international initiatives such as the Marshall Plan and NATO and were willing to tolerate labor unions and the welfare state. Eisenhower was a man without a political past. Believing that democracy required the military to stand aside, he had never voted. Rockefeller, the scion of one of the richest families in America, was a Cold War internationalist. He served in a variety of capacities under Eisenhower, including as an advisor on foreign affairs. Having made his political name, Rockefeller was elected the governor of New York in 1959 and became the de facto leader of the liberal wing of the Republican party.

For eight years, between 1952 and 1960, Eisenhower steered a precarious course from the middle of the party, with conservative Taft Republicans on one side and liberal Rockefeller Republicans on the other. His popularity temporarily kept the two sides at bay, though staunch conservatives considered him a closet New Dealer. "Ike," as he was widely known, proved willing to work with the mostly Democratic-controlled congresses of those years. He signed bills increasing federal outlays for veterans' benefits,

Red Hunting on the Quiz Shows   MARK GOODSON

Active in the television industry from its earliest days, Mark Goodson was a highly successful producer whose game shows included *What's My Line?*, *To Tell the Truth*, and *Family
Feud*. In this interview, Goodson recalls his experience in the industry in the early 1950s at
the height of the McCarthy period.

I'm not sure when it began, but I believe
it was early 1950. At that point I had no
connection with the blacklisting that was
going on, although I heard about it in the
motion picture business and heard rumors
about things that had happened on other
shows, like *The Aldrich Family.* . . .

Soon afterwards, CBS installed a clear-
ance division. There wasn't any discussion.
We would just get the word — "drop that
person" — and that was supposed to be it.
Whenever I booked a guest or a panelist on
What's My Line? or *I've Got a Secret*, one of
our assistants would phone up and say,
"We're going to use so-and-so." We'd either
get the okay, or they'd call back and say,
"Not clear," or "Sorry, we can't use them." . . .
You were never supposed to tell the person
what it was about; you'd just unbook them.
They never admitted there was a blacklist. It
just wasn't done. . . .

Anna Lee was an English actress on a
later show of ours called *It's News to Me*. The
sponsor was Sanka Coffee, a product of
General Foods. The advertising agency was
Young & Rubicam. One day, I received a call
telling me we had to drop one of our panel-
ists, Anna Lee, immediately. They said she
was a radical, that she wrote a column for
the *Daily Worker*. They couldn't allow that
kind of stuff on the air. They claimed they
were getting all kinds of mail. It seemed
incongruous to me that this little English
girl, someone who seemed very conservative, would be writing for a Communist
newspaper. It just didn't sound right.

I took her out to lunch. After a little social
conversation, I asked her about her politics.
She told me that she wasn't political, except
she voted Conservative in England. Her
husband was a Republican from Texas.

I went to the agency and said, "You guys
are really off your rocker. Anna Lee is nothing close to a liberal." They told me, "Oh,
you're right. We checked on that. It's a different Anna Lee who writes for the *Daily
Worker*." I remember being relieved and
saying, "Well, that's good. You just made a
mistake. Now we can forget this." But that
wasn't the case. They told me, "We've still
got to get rid of her, because the illusion is
just as good as the reality. If our client continues to get the mail, no one is going to
believe him when he says there's a second
Anna Lee." At that point I lost it. I told them
their demand was outrageous. They could
cancel the show if they wanted to, but I
would not drop somebody whose only
crime was sharing a name. When I got back
to my office, there was a phone call waiting
for me. It was from a friend of mine at the
agency. He said, "If I were you, I would not
lose my temper like that. If you want to argue, do it quietly. After you left, somebody
said, 'Is Goodson a pinko?' "

S O U R C E : Griffin Fariello, *Red Scare* (New York:
Norton, 1995), 320–324.

housing, highway construction (see Chapter 26), and Social Security, and increased the minimum wage from 75 cents an hour to $1. He supported the creation of the new Department of Health, Education, and Welfare in 1957. Like Truman, Eisenhower accepted some government responsibility for economic performance, part of a broad liberal consensus in American politics in these years.

America under Eisenhower The power realities that had called forth containment guided Eisenhower's foreign policy. New developments, however, altered the tone of the Cold War. Stalin's death in March 1953 precipitated an intraparty struggle in the Soviet Union that lasted until 1956, when Nikita Khrushchev emerged as Stalin's successor. Khrushchev soon startled Communists around the world by denouncing Stalin and detailing his crimes and blunders. He also surprised Westerners by calling for "peaceful coexistence" and by dealing more flexibly with dissent in the Communist world. But the new Soviet leader had his limits, and when Hungarians rose up in 1956 to demand independence from Moscow, Khrushchev crushed the incipient revolution.

With no end to the Cold War in sight, Eisenhower turned his attention to limiting the cost of containment. The president hoped to economize by relying on a nuclear arsenal and skimping on expensive conventional forces. Under the "New Look" defense policy, the Eisenhower administration stepped up production of the hydrogen bomb and developed long-range bombing capabilities. The Soviets, however, matched the United States weapon for weapon. By 1958, both nations had intercontinental ballistic missiles. When an American nuclear submarine launched an atomic-tipped Polaris missile in 1960, Soviet engineers raced to produce an equivalent weapon.

Although confident in the international arena, Eisenhower started out a novice in domestic affairs. He did his best to set a less confrontational mood after the rancorous Truman years. He was reluctant to speak out against Joe McCarthy, and he was not a leader on civil rights. His acceptance of the welfare state, however, did not please the more conservative members of the Republican Party. Led by Taft and Arizona senator Barry Goldwater — and supported by the new conservative magazine *National Review* — conservatives began to revolt against liberal and moderate Republicans.

Democrats meanwhile maintained a strong presence in Congress but proved weak in presidential elections in the 1950s. In the two presidential contests of the decade, 1952 and 1956, Eisenhower defeated the admired but politically ineffectual liberal Adlai Stevenson. In the 1952 contest, Stevenson was hampered by the unpopularity of the Truman administration. The deadlocked Korean War and a series of scandals that Republicans dubbed "the mess in Washington" combined to give the war-hero general an easy victory. In 1956, Ike won an even more impressive victory over Stevenson, whose eloquent and learned speeches on liberalism led vice president Richard Nixon to call him an "egghead."

During Eisenhower's presidency, new political forces on both the right and the left had begun to stir. But they had not yet fully transformed the party system itself. Particularly at the national level, Democrats and Republicans seemed in broad agreement about the realities of the Cold War and the demands of a modern, industrial economy and welfare state. Indeed, respected commentators in the 1950s declared "the end of ideology" and wondered if the great political clashes that had wracked the

►What were the components of Cold War liberalism?

►Should recently revealed information about espionage in the American government affect how we evaluate McCarthyism?

1930s were gone forever. Below the apparent calm of national party politics lay profound differences among Americans over the direction of the nation. Those differences were most pronounced with regard to civil rights for African Americans. But a host of other issues had begun to emerge as controversial subjects that would soon starkly divide the country.

Containment in the Postcolonial World

The world scene was changing at a furious pace. New nations were emerging across the Middle East, Africa, and Asia, created in the wake of powerful anticolonial movements whose origins dated to before World War II. Between 1947 and 1962, the British, French, Dutch, and Belgian empires all but disintegrated in a momentous collapse of European global power. FDR had favored the idea of national self-determination, often to the fury of his British and French allies. He expected democracies to be established as new partners in an American-led, free-market world system. But when colonial revolts produced independent- or socialist-minded regimes in the so-called **Third World**, the Truman and Eisenhower administrations often treated them as pawns of the Soviet Union to be opposed at all costs.

The Cold War and Colonial Independence

The Eisenhower administration, concerned less about democracy than about stability, tended to support governments, no matter how repressive, that were overtly anticommunist. Some of America's staunchest allies — the Philippines, South Korea, Iran, Cuba, South Vietnam, and Nicaragua — were governed by dictatorships or right-wing regimes that lacked broad-based support. Moreover, Secretary of State John Foster Dulles often resorted to covert operations against governments that, in his opinion, were too closely aligned with the Soviets.

Believing that these emerging nations had to choose sides, the United States drew them into collective security agreements, with the NATO alliance in Europe as a model. Secretary of State Dulles orchestrated the creation of the Southeast Asia Treaty Organization (SEATO), which in 1954 linked America and its major European allies with Australia, New Zealand, Pakistan, the Philippines, and Thailand. An extensive system of defense alliances eventually tied the United States to more than forty other countries (Map 25.3). The United States also sponsored a strategically valuable defensive alliance between Iraq and Iran, on the southern flank of the Soviet Union.

For covert tasks, Dulles used the newly created (1947) Central Intelligence Agency (CIA), run by his brother, Allen Dulles. When Iran's nationalist premier, Mohammad Mossadegh, seized British oil properties in 1953, CIA agents helped depose him and, eventually, installed the young Mohammad Reza Pahlavi as shah of Iran. Iranian resentment of the 1953 Iranian coup, followed by twenty-five years of U.S. support for the shah, eventually led to the 1979 Iranian Revolution (see Chapter 30). In 1954, the CIA engi-

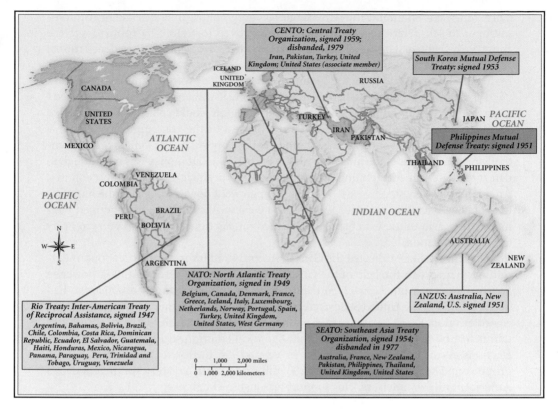

MAP 25.3 American Global Defense Treaties in the Cold War Era
The advent of the Cold War led to a major shift in American foreign policy — the signing of mutual defense treaties. Dating back to George Washington's call "to steer clear of permanent alliances with any portion of the foreign world," the United States had avoided treaty obligations that entailed the defense of other nations. As late as 1919, the U.S. Senate had rejected the principle of "collective security," the centerpiece of the League of Nations established by the Treaty of Versailles that ended World War I. But after World War II, in response to fears of Soviet global expansion, the United States entered defense alliances with much of the non-Communist world.

neered a coup in Guatemala against the democratically elected Jacobo Arbenz Guzmán, who had expropriated land owned by the American-owned United Fruit Company. Eisenhower specifically approved those CIA efforts and expanded the agency's mandate from gathering intelligence to intervening in the affairs of sovereign states.

Vietnam | But when covert operations and coups failed or proved impractical, the American approach to emerging nations could entangle the United States in deeper, more intractable conflicts. Such an instance was already unfolding on a distant stage, in a small country utterly unknown to most Americans: Vietnam. In August 1945, at the close of World War II, the Japanese occupiers of Vietnam surrendered to China in the north and Britain in the south. The Vietminh, the nationalist movement that had led the resistance against the Japanese, seized control in the north. But their leader, Ho

Chi Minh, was a Communist, and this single fact outweighed American and British commitment to self-determination. When France moved to restore its control over the country, the United States and Britain sided with their European ally. President Truman rejected Ho's plea to support the Vietnamese struggle for independence. As soon as France returned, in late 1946, the Vietminh resumed their war of national liberation.

Eisenhower picked up where Truman left off. If the French failed, Eisenhower argued, all non-Communist governments in the region would collapse. This so-called "domino theory" — which represented an extension of the containment doctrine — guided U.S. policy in Southeast Asia for the next twenty years. The United States eventually provided most of the financing for the French war, but money was not enough to defeat the determined Vietminh, who were fighting for the liberation of their country. After a fifty-six-day siege in early 1954, the French went down to defeat at the huge fortress of Dien Bien Phu. The result was the 1954 Geneva Accords, which partitioned Vietnam temporarily at the 17th parallel and called for elections within two years to unify the troubled nation.

The United States rejected the Geneva Accords and immediately set about undermining them. With the help of the CIA, a pro-American government took power in South Vietnam in June 1954. Ngo Dinh Diem, an anticommunist Catholic who had been residing in the United States, returned to Vietnam as premier. The next year, in a rigged election, Diem became president of an independent South Vietnam. Facing certain defeat by the popular Ho Chi Minh, Diem called off the scheduled reunification elections. As the last French soldiers left in March 1956, the Eisenhower administration propped up Diem with an average of $200 million a year in aid and a contingent of 675 American military advisors. This support was just the beginning.

The Middle East | If Vietnam was still of minor concern, the same could not be said of the Middle East, an area rich in oil and political complexity. The most volatile area was Palestine, populated by Arabs but also historically the ancient land of Israel and coveted by the Zionist movement as a Jewish national homeland. After World War II, many survivors of the Nazi extermination camps resettled in Palestine, which was still controlled by Britain under a World War I mandate. On November 29, 1947, the U.N. General Assembly voted to partition Palestine between Jewish and Arab sectors. When the British mandate ended, Zionist leaders proclaimed the state of Israel. A coalition of Arab nations known as the Arab League invaded, but Israel survived. Many Palestinians fled or were driven from their homes during the fighting. The Arab defeat left these people permanently stranded in refugee camps. President Truman recognized the new state, winning crucial support from Jewish voters in the 1948 election but alienating the Arab world.

Southeast of Palestine, Egypt gained independence from Britain in 1952. Two years later, Gamal Abdel Nasser emerged as the new Egyptian leader. He proclaimed a pan-Arab socialism designed to end the Middle East's colonial relationship with the West. Caught between the Soviet Union and the United States, Nasser sought an independent route. In 1956, he nationalized the Suez Canal, which was the lifeline for Western Europe's oil. Britain and France, in alliance with Israel, attacked Egypt and seized the canal. Taken by surprise and embarrassed because he had just condemned the Soviet invasion of Hungary, Eisenhower demanded that France and Britain pull back. Egypt reclaimed the Suez Canal and built the Aswan Dam on the Nile with Soviet support.

In early 1957, concerned about Soviet influence in the Middle East, the president announced the Eisenhower Doctrine, which stated that American forces would assist any nation in the region that required aid "against overt armed aggression from any nation controlled by International Communism." Invoking the doctrine later that year, Eisenhower helped King Hussein of Jordan put down a Nasser-backed revolt and propped up a pro-American government in Lebanon. The Eisenhower Doctrine was further proof of the global reach of containment, in this instance accentuated by the strategic need to protect the West's access to steady supplies of oil.

John F. Kennedy and the Cold War

Charisma, style, and personality — these, more than platforms and issues, were hallmarks of a new brand of politics in the early 1960s. This was John F. Kennedy's natural environment. Kennedy, a Harvard alumnus, World War II hero, and senator from Massachusetts, had inherited his love of politics from his grandfathers — colorful, and often ruthless, Irish Catholic politicians in Boston. Ambitious and deeply aware of style, the forty-three-year-old Kennedy made use of his many advantages to become, as novelist Norman Mailer put it, "our leading man." His one disadvantage — that he was Catholic in a country that had never elected a Catholic president — he masterfully neutralized. And thanks to both media advisors and his youthful attractiveness, Kennedy projected a superb television image.

At heart, however, Kennedy was a Cold Warrior who had come of age in the shadow of Munich, Yalta, and the McCarthy hearings. He projected an air of idealism, but his years in the Senate (1953–1960) had proved him to be a conventional Cold War politician. Once elected president, Kennedy would shape the nation's foreign policy by drawing both on his ingenuity and on old-style Cold War power politics.

The Election of 1960 and the New Frontier | Kennedy's Republican opponent in the 1960 presidential election, Eisenhower's vice president, Richard M. Nixon, was a seasoned politician and Cold Warrior himself. The great innovation of the 1960 campaign was a series of four nationally televised debates. Nixon, less photogenic than Kennedy, looked sallow and unshaven under the intense studio lights. Polls showed that television swayed political perceptions. Voters who heard the first debate on the radio concluded that Nixon had won, but those who viewed it on television favored Kennedy. Despite the edge Kennedy enjoyed in the debates, he won only the narrowest of electoral victories, receiving 49.7 percent of the popular vote to Nixon's 49.5 percent. Kennedy attracted Catholics, blacks, and the labor vote; his vice-presidential running mate, Texas senator Lyndon Baines Johnson, helped bring in southern Democrats. Yet only 120,000 votes separated the two candidates, and the shift of a few thousand votes in key states would have reversed the outcome.

Kennedy brought to Washington a cadre of young, ambitious newcomers, including Robert McNamara, a renowned systems analyst and former head of Ford Motor Company, as secretary of defense. A host of trusted advisors and academics flocked to

Washington to join the New Frontier. Included on the team as attorney general was Kennedy's younger brother Robert, who had made a name as a hard-hitting investigator of organized crime. But not everyone was enchanted. Kennedy's people "may be every bit as intelligent as you say," House Speaker Sam Rayburn told his old friend Lyndon Johnson, "but I'd feel a whole lot better about them if just one of them had run for sheriff once." Sure enough, the new administration immediately got into hot water.

Crises in Cuba and Berlin | In January 1961, the Soviet Union announced that it intended to support "wars of national liberation" wherever in the world they occurred. Kennedy took Soviet premier Nikita Khrushchev's words as a challenge, especially as they applied to Cuba, where in 1959 Fidel Castro had overthrown the right-wing dictator Fulgencio Batista and declared a revolution. Determined to keep Cuba out of the Soviet orbit, Kennedy followed through on Eisenhower administration plans to dispatch Cuban exiles to foment an anti-Castro uprising. The invaders, trained by the Central Intelligence Agency, were ill-prepared for their task. On landing at Cuba's Bay of Pigs on April 17, 1961, the force of 1,400 was crushed by Castro's troops. Kennedy had the good sense to reject CIA pleas for a U.S. air strike. Accepting defeat, Kennedy went before the American people and took full responsibility for the fiasco.

Already strained by the Bay of Pigs incident, U.S.-Soviet relations deteriorated further in June 1961 when Khrushchev stopped movement between Communist-controlled East Berlin and the city's western sector. Kennedy responded by dispatching 40,000 more troops to Europe. But in mid-August, to stop the exodus of East Germans, the Communist regime began constructing the Berlin Wall, policed by border guards under shoot-to-kill orders. The young president delivered a major speech in Berlin in June 1963 expressing solidarity with the city's residents. *"Ich bin ein Berliner!"* ("I am a Berliner!"), Kennedy pronounced. Until the 12-foot-high concrete barrier came down in 1989, it served as the supreme symbol of the Cold War.

The climactic Cold War confrontation came in October 1962. In a somber televised address on October 22, Kennedy revealed that U.S. reconnaissance planes had spotted Soviet-built bases for intermediate-range ballistic missiles in Cuba. Some of those weapons had already been installed, and more were on the way. Kennedy announced that the United States would impose a "quarantine on all offensive military equipment" on its way to Cuba. As the world held its breath waiting to see if the conflict would escalate into war, on October 25, ships carrying Soviet missiles turned back. After a week of tense negotiations, both sides made concessions: Kennedy pledged not to invade Cuba, and Khrushchev promised to dismantle the missile bases. Kennedy also secretly ordered U.S. missiles to be removed from Turkey, at Khrushchev's insistence. The risk of nuclear war, greater during the Cuban missile crisis than at any other time in the Cold War, prompted a slight thaw in U.S.-Soviet relations. As national security advisor McGeorge Bundy put it, both sides were chastened by "having come so close to the edge."

Kennedy and the World | Kennedy also launched a series of bold nonmilitary initiatives. One was the Peace Corps, which embodied a call to public service put forth in his inaugural address ("Ask not what your country can do for you, but what you can do for your country"). Thousands of men and women agreed to devote two or more years as volunteers for projects such as teaching English to Filipino school-

The Cuban Missile Crisis
During the 1962 Cuban Missile Crisis, President Kennedy meets with U.S. Army officials. Over two tense weeks, the world watched as the United States and the Soviet Union went to the brink of war when it became known that Soviet military officials had begun to construct nuclear weapons bases in Cuba, a mere 90 miles from the southern tip of Florida. Kennedy's threat to intercept Soviet missile shipments with American naval vessels forced the Cold War adversary to back down. © Corbis

children or helping African villagers obtain clean water. Exhibiting the idealism of the early 1960s, the Peace Corps was also a low-cost Cold War weapon intended to show the developing world that there was an alternative to Communism. Kennedy was also keen on space exploration. In a 1962 speech, he proposed that the nation commit itself to landing a man on the moon within the decade. The Soviets had already beaten the United States into space with the 1961 flight of cosmonaut Yuri Gagarin. Capitalizing on America's fascination with space, Kennedy persuaded Congress to increase funding for the National Aeronautics and Space Administration (NASA), enabling the United States to pull ahead of the Soviet Union. Kennedy's ambition was realized when U.S. astronauts arrived on the moon in 1969.

Making a Commitment in Vietnam

Despite slight improvements, U.S.-Soviet relations remained tense and containment the cornerstone of U.S. policy. When Kennedy became president, he inherited Eisenhower's commitment in Vietnam. Kennedy saw Vietnam in Cold War terms, but rather than practicing brinksmanship — threatening nuclear war to stop Communism — Kennedy sought what at the time seemed a more intelligent and realistic approach. He increased the amount of aid sent to the South Vietnamese military and dramatically expanded the role of U.S. Special Forces ("Green Berets") in training the South Vietnamese army in unconventional, small-group warfare tactics.

South Vietnam's corrupt and repressive Diem regime, propped up by Eisenhower since 1954, was losing ground in spite of American aid. By 1961, Diem's opponents, with backing from North Vietnam, had formed a revolutionary movement known as the National Liberation Front (NLF). NLF guerrilla forces — the Vietcong — found loyalty among peasants alienated by Diem's "strategic hamlet" program, which had uprooted entire villages and moved villagers into barbed-wire compounds. Too, Buddhists charged Diem, a Catholic, with religious persecution. Starting in May 1963, militant Buddhists staged dramatic demonstrations, including self-immolations recorded by American television news crews covering the activities of the 16,000 U.S. military personnel then in Vietnam.

The Buddhist self-immolations, carried by television to an uneasy global audience, powerfully illustrated the dilemmas embedded in U.S. policy in Vietnam. In order to ensure a stable southern government and prevent victory for Ho Chi Minh and the North, the United States had to support Diem's authoritarian regime. But the political repression used by the regime to quell massive opposition to Diem's rule simply made the regime more unpopular. Whether one supported U.S. involvement in Vietnam or not, the elemental paradox remained unchanged: In its efforts to win, the United States brought defeat ever closer.

Nothing proved that paradox more than the events of early November 1963. Having lost patience with Diem, Kennedy let it be known in Saigon that the United States would support a military coup. Kennedy's hope was that if the dictatorial Diem, now reviled throughout the south, could be replaced by a popular general or other military figure, a stable government — one strong enough to repel the NLF — would emerge. But when Diem was overthrown on November 1, the generals went further than Kennedy's team had anticipated and assassinated both Diem and his brother. This made the coup look less like an organic uprising and more like an American plot. South Vietnam fell into a period of chaos marked by a series of coups and defined by the increasing ungovernability of both the cities and countryside. Kennedy himself was assassinated in late November and would not live to see the grim results of Diem's murder: American engagement in a long and costly civil conflict in the name of fighting communism.

▶ How did America's deepening involvement in the Third World in the 1950s present the nation with a dilemma?

▶ Why did the United States support right-wing dictatorships?

SUMMARY

We have seen how the Cold War began as a conflict between the United States and the Soviet Union over Eastern Europe and the fate of Germany. Very early in the conflict, the United States adopted a strategy of containment. Although initially intended only for Europe, the containment strategy quickly expanded to Asia after China became a Communist state under Mao Zedong. The first effect of that expansion was the Korean

War, after which, under Dwight D. Eisenhower, containment of communism became America's guiding principle across the developing world — often called the Third World. Cold War tensions relaxed in the late 1950s but erupted again under John F. Kennedy, with the Cuban missile crisis, the building of the Berlin Wall, and major increases in American military assistance to South Vietnam. Cold War imperatives between 1945 and the early 1960s meant a major military buildup, a massive nuclear arms race, and unprecedented entanglements across the globe.

We have also seen how, on the domestic front, Harry S. Truman started out with high hopes for an expanded New Deal, only to be stymied by resistance from Congress and the competing demands of the Cold War. The greatest Cold War–inspired distraction, however, was a climate of fear over internal subversion by Communists that gave rise to McCarthyism. Truman's successor, Eisenhower, brought the Republicans back into power. Although personally conservative, Eisenhower actually proved a New Dealer in disguise. He declined to cut back on social welfare programs and broke new ground in federal spending on highways, scientific research, and higher education. When Eisenhower left office and Kennedy became president, it seemed that a "liberal consensus" prevailed, with old-fashioned, **laissez-faire** conservatism mostly marginalized in American political life.

For additional primary sources from this period, see *Documents for America's History*, Seventh Edition.

For Web sites, images, and documents related to topics and places in this chapter, visit *Make History* at **bedfordstmartins.com/henrettaconcise**.

For Further Exploration

On the Cold War from different perspectives, see John Lewis Gaddis, *The Cold War: A New History* (2005), and Thomas J. McCormick, *America's Half Century: United States Foreign Policy in the Cold War and After* (1989). On the Fair Deal, see Alonzo Hamby, *Beyond the New Deal: Harry S. Truman and American Liberalism* (1973). Jennifer Klein, in *For All These Rights* (2003), explains why the United States failed to develop a national health-care system. On McCarthyism, Ellen Schrecker, *Many Are the Crimes: McCarthyism in America* (1998), is excellent. For analysis of Soviet espionage, see John Earl Haynes and Harvey Klehr, *Venona: Decoding Soviet Espionage in America* (1999). David Halberstam's *The Fifties* (1993) offers a brief but searing account of CIA covert activities in Iran and Guatemala. A good starting point for Kennedy's presidency is W. J. Rorabaugh, *Kennedy and the Promise of the Sixties* (2002).

The Woodrow Wilson International Center has established the Cold War International History Project at **www.wilsoncenter.org/cwihp**. The Center for the Study of the Pacific Northwest's site, "The Cold War and Red Scare in Washington State," at **www.washington.edu/uwired/outreach/cspn/Website/Resources/Curriculum/ColdWar/ColdWarMain.html**, provides detailed information on how the Red Scare operated

TIMELINE

1945	▸ Yalta and Potsdam conferences
	▸ End of World War II
	▸ Senate approves U.S. participation in United Nations
1946	▸ George F. Kennan outlines containment policy
	▸ War begins between French and Vietminh over control of Vietnam
1947	▸ Truman Doctrine
	▸ House Un-American Activities Committee (HUAC) investigates film industry
	▸ Marshall Plan aids economic recovery in Europe
1948	▸ Communist coup in Czechoslovakia
	▸ State of Israel created
	▸ Stalin blockades West Berlin; Berlin airlift begins
1949	▸ North Atlantic Treaty Organization (NATO) founded
	▸ Soviet Union detonates atomic bomb
	▸ Mao Zedong establishes People's Republic of China
1950–1953	▸ Korean War
1950	▸ NSC-68 leads to nuclear buildup
	▸ Joseph McCarthy announces "list" of Communists in government
1952	▸ Dwight D. Eisenhower elected president
1953	▸ Joseph Stalin dies
1954	▸ Army-McCarthy hearings on army subversion
	▸ French defeat at Dienbienphu in Vietnam
	▸ Geneva Accords partition Vietnam
1956	▸ Crises in Hungary and at Suez Canal
1958	▸ National Aeronautics and Space Administration (NASA) established
1960	▸ John F. Kennedy elected president
1961	▸ Eisenhower warns nation against military-industrial complex
	▸ Kennedy orders the first contingent of Special Forces ("Green Berets") to Vietnam
1963	▸ Diem assassinated in South Vietnam

in one state. The Truman Library site's "1948 Whistle Stop Tour" feature is at **www .trumanlibrary.org/whistlestop/TruWhisTour/coverpge.htm**. "Korea + 50: No Longer Forgotten" is cosponsored by the Harry S. Truman and Dwight D. Eisenhower Presidential Libraries, at **www.trumanlibrary.org/korea**.

Test Your Knowledge

For practice quizzes, activities, and other study tools, visit the Online Study Guide at **bedfordstmartins.com/henrettaconcise**.

There was no obvious way
to tell a factory worker
from a business owner or
a professional man when
I grew up. Every house on
my block looked much
the same.

—D. J. Waldie, *Holy Land*, 1996

At the height of the Cold War, in 1959, U.S. vice president Richard Nixon debated Soviet premier Nikita Khrushchev on the merits of Pepsi-Cola, TV dinners, and electric ovens. Face-to-face at the opening of the American National Exhibit in Moscow, Nixon and Khrushchev strolled through a model American home, assembled to demonstrate the consumer products available to the typical citizen of the United States. Nixon explained to Khrushchev that although the Soviet Union may have had superior rockets, the United States was ahead in other areas, such as color television.

This was Cold War politics by other means — a symbolic contest over which country's standard of living was higher. What was so striking about the so-called kitchen debate was Nixon's insistence, to a disbelieving Khrushchev, that a modern home filled with shiny new refrigerators, toasters, televisions, and all manner of other consumer products was, rather than a luxury, accessible to the average American worker. "Any steelworker could buy this house," Nixon told the Soviet leader, who stood with other members of the politburo before cameras and reporters. Ever practical, Khrushchev noted, "Many things you've shown us are interesting but they are not needed in life." He added, condescendingly, "They are merely gadgets."

The kitchen debate settled little in the geopolitical rivalry between the United States and the Soviet Union. But it speaks to us across the decades because it reveals how Americans had come to see themselves by the late 1950s: as homeowners and consumers, as a people for whom the middle-class American dream was a commercial aspiration. The designers of the model home in Moscow, architect Andrew Geller and developer Herbert Sadkin, went on to build suburban developments on the East Coast, including the aptly named Leisurama on New York's Long Island. They were among legions of Americans — including architects, developers, advertising executives, and landscape designers — who created new middle-class tastes in the postwar decades.

The Middle-Class Family Ideal
A family eats breakfast at a campground in Zion National Park, Utah. Americans embraced a middle-class, nuclear family ideal in the postwar decades. Photo by Justin Locke / National Geographic / Getty Images.

The real story of the postwar period was the growing number of Americans who adopted those tastes. In the two decades following the end of World War II, nothing short of a new middle class was born in the United States. *Fortune* magazine estimated that in the 1950s the middle class — defined as families with more than $5,000 in annual earnings after taxes (about $40,000 today) — was increasing at the rate of 1.1 million people per year. Riding a wave of rising incomes, American dominance in the global economy, and Cold War federal spending, the postwar middle class enjoyed the highest standard of living in the world.

However, the success of the middle class could not hide deeper troubles. This was an era of neither universal conformity nor diminishing social strife. Jim Crow laws, contradictions in women's lives, cultural rebelliousness among young people, and changing sexual mores were only the most obvious sources of social tension. Suburban growth came at the expense of cities, hastening inner-city decay and exacerbating racial segregation. Nor was prosperity ever as widespread as the Moscow exhibit implied. The suburban lifestyle was beyond the reach of the working poor, the elderly, immigrants, Mexican Americans, and most African Americans — indeed, the majority of the country.

Economy: From Recovery to Dominance

The United States enjoyed enormous economic advantages at the close of World War II. While the Europeans and Japanese were still clearing the war's rubble, America stood poised to enter a postwar boom. As the only major industrial nation not devastated by war, the United States held an unprecedented global position. The American economy also benefited from an expanding internal market and heavy investment in research and development. Two additional developments stood out: One was that, for the first time in the nation's history, employers generally accepted collective bargaining, which for workers translated into rising wages, expanding benefits, and an increasing rate of home ownership. The other was that the federal government's outlays for military and domestic programs gave a huge boost to the economy.

Engines of Economic Growth

U.S. corporations, banks, and manufacturers so dominated the world economy that the postwar period has been called the Pax Americana (a Latin term meaning "American Peace" and harking back to the Pax Romana of the first and second centuries A.D.). So confident was he in the nation's growing power that during World War II, *Life* magazine publisher Henry Luce had immodestly predicted that the world was witnessing the dawning of the "American century." The preponderance of American economic power in the postwar decades, however, was not simply an artifact of the global war — it was not an inevitable development. Several key elements came together, internationally and at home, to propel three decades of unprecedented economic growth.

The Bretton Woods System American global supremacy rested partly on the economic institutions created at a United Nations conference in Bretton Woods, New Hampshire, in July 1944. The first of those institutions was the World Bank, created to provide loans for the reconstruction of war-torn Europe as well as for the development of former colonized nations — the so-called Third World or developing world. A second institution, the International Monetary Fund (IMF), was set up to stabilize currencies and provide a predictable monetary environment for trade, with the U.S. dollar serving as the benchmark. Third, in 1947, multinational trade negotiations resulted in the first General Agreement on Tariffs and Trade (GATT), which established an international framework for overseeing trade rules and practices.

The World Bank, the IMF, and GATT formed the cornerstones of the Bretton Woods system, which guided the world economy after the war. The Bretton Woods system served America's conception of an open-market global economy and complemented the nation's ambitious diplomatic aims in the Cold War. Anything less, Secretary of State Dean Acheson told Congress, would lead to "shrinking international trade, lower levels of living, and hostility between nations." The chief idea of the Bretton Woods system was to make American capital available, on cheap terms, to nations that adopted

The Kitchen Debate

At the American National Exhibition in Moscow in 1959, the United States put on display the technological wonders of American home life. When Vice President Richard Nixon visited, he and Soviet premier Nikita Khrushchev got into a heated debate over the relative merits of their rival systems, with the up-to-date American kitchen as a case in point. This photograph shows the debate in progress. Khrushchev is the bald man pointing his finger at Nixon. To Nixon's left stands Leonid Brezhnev, who would be Khrushchev's successor. Getty Images.

free-trade capitalist economies. Critics charged, rightly, that Bretton Woods favored the United States at the expense of recently independent countries, because the United States could dictate lending terms and stood to benefit as nations purchased more American goods.

The Military-Industrial Complex   A second engine of postwar prosperity was defense spending. In his final address to the nation in 1961, President Dwight D. Eisenhower spoke about the power of what he called the military-industrial complex, which by then employed 3.5 million Americans. Even though his administration had fostered this defense establishment, Eisenhower feared its implications: "We must guard against the acquisition of unwarranted influence, whether sought or unsought, by the military-industrial complex," he said. The military-industrial complex that Eisenhower identified had its roots in the business-government partnerships of World War II. After 1945, though the country was nominally at peace, the economy and the government operated in a state of perpetual readiness for war.

Based at the sprawling Pentagon in Arlington, Virginia, the Defense Department evolved into a massive bureaucracy. In the name of national security, defense-related industries entered into long-term relationships with the Pentagon. Some companies did so much business with the government that they in effect became private divisions of the Defense Department. Over 60 percent of the income of Boeing, General Dynamics, and Raytheon, for instance, came from military contracts, and the percentages were even higher for Lockheed and Republic Aviation. In previous peacetime years, military spending had constituted only 1 percent of gross domestic product (GDP); now it represented 10 percent. Economic growth was increasingly dependent on a robust defense sector.

As permanent mobilization took hold, science, industry, and the federal government became intertwined. Cold War competition for military supremacy spawned both an arms race and a space race. The United States and the Soviet Union each sought to develop more explosive bombs and more powerful rockets. Federal spending underwrote 90 percent of the cost of research for aviation and space, 65 percent for electricity and electronics, 42 percent for scientific instruments, and even 24 percent for automobiles. With the government footing the bill, corporations lost little time in transforming new technology into useful products. Backed by the Pentagon, for instance, IBM and Sperry Rand pressed ahead with research on integrated circuits, which later spawned the computer revolution.

When the Soviet Union launched the world's first satellite, *Sputnik*, in 1957, the startled United States went into high gear to catch up in the Cold War space competition. Alarmed that the United States was falling behind in science and technology, Eisenhower persuaded Congress to appropriate additional money for college scholarships and university research. The National Defense Education Act of 1958 funneled millions of dollars into American universities, helping institutions such as the University of California at Berkeley, Stanford University, the Massachusetts Institute of Technology, and the University of Michigan become the leading research centers in the world.

The defense buildup also created jobs — lots of them. Taking into account the additional positions created to serve and support defense workers, perhaps one American in seven owed his or her job to the military-industrial complex by the 1960s. But increased military spending also limited the resources for domestic social needs. Critics calculated the trade-offs: The money spent for a nuclear aircraft carrier and support ships could have paid for a subway system for Washington, D.C., while the cost of one Huey helicopter could have built sixty-six units of low-income housing.

Corporate Power | For over half a century, the consolidation of economic power into large corporate firms had characterized American capitalism. In the postwar decades, that tendency accelerated. By 1970, the top four U.S. automakers produced 91 percent of all motor vehicles sold in the country; the top four firms in tires produced 72 percent; those in cigarettes, 84 percent; and those in detergents, 70 percent. Eric Johnston, former president of the American Chamber of Commerce, declared that "we have entered a period of accelerating *bigness* in all aspects of American life." Expansion into foreign markets also spurred corporate growth. During the 1950s, U.S. exports nearly doubled, giving the nation a trade surplus of close to $5 billion in 1960. By the 1970s, such firms as Coca-Cola, Gillette, IBM, and Mobil made more than half their profits abroad.

To staff their bureaucracies, the postwar corporate giants required a huge white-collar army. A new generation of corporate chieftains emerged, operating in a complex environment that demanded long-range forecasting. Companies turned to the universities, which grew explosively after 1945. Postwar corporate culture inspired numerous critics, who argued that the obedience demanded of white-collar workers was stifling creativity and blighting lives. In *The Lonely Crowd* (1950), the sociologist David Riesman mourned a lost masculinity and contrasted the independent businessmen and professionals of earlier years with the managerial class of the postwar world. The sociologist William Whyte painted a somber picture of "organization men" who left the home "spiritually as well as physically to take the vows of organization life." Andrew Hacker, in *The Corporation Take-Over* (1964), warned that a small handful of such organization men "can draw up an investment program calling for the expenditure of several billions of dollars" and thereby "determine the quality of life for substantial segments of society."

Many of these "investment programs" relied on mechanization, or automation — another important factor in the postwar boom. From 1947 to 1975, worker productivity more than doubled across the whole of the economy. American factories replaced manpower with machines, substituting cheap fossil energy for human muscle. As industries mechanized, they could turn out products more efficiently and at lower cost. Mechanization did not come without social costs, however. Over the course of the postwar decades, millions of high-wage manufacturing jobs were lost as machines replaced workers, affecting entire cities and regions. Corporate leaders approved, but workers and their union representatives were less enthusiastic. "How are you going to sell cars to all of these machines?" wondered Walter Reuther, president of the United Auto Workers (UAW).

The Economic Record | The military-industrial complex produced an extraordinary economic record. America's annual GDP jumped from $213 billion in 1945 to more than $500 billion in 1960; by 1970, it exceeded $1 trillion. This sustained economic growth meant a 25 percent rise in real income for ordinary Americans between 1946 and 1959. Even better, the new prosperity featured low inflation. After a burst of high prices in the immediate postwar period, inflation slowed to 2 to 3 percent annually, and it stayed low until the escalation of the Vietnam War in the mid-1960s. Low inflation meant stable and predictable prices. Feeling secure about the future, Americans were eager to spend and rightly felt that they were better off than ever before. In 1940, 43 percent of American families owned their homes; by 1960, 62 percent did. In that period, moreover, income inequality dropped sharply. The share of total income going to the top tenth — the richest Americans — declined by nearly one-third from the 45 percent it had been in 1940. American society had become not only more prosperous but also more egalitarian.

However, the picture was not as rosy at the bottom, where tenacious poverty accompanied the economic boom. In *The Affluent Society* (1958), economist John Kenneth Galbraith argued that the poor were only an "afterthought" in the minds of economists and politicians, who largely celebrated the new growth. As Galbraith noted, one in thirteen families at the time earned less than $1,000 a year (about $7,500 in today's dollars). Four years later, in *The Other America* (1962), Michael Harrington chronicled "the economic underworld of American life," and a U.S. government study, echoing a well-known sentence from Franklin Roosevelt's second inaugural address ("I see one-third of a nation ill-housed, ill-clad, ill-nourished"), declared "one-third of the nation" to be poorly paid, poorly educated, and poorly housed. It appeared that in economic terms, as the top and the middle converged, the bottom remained far behind.

A Nation of Consumers

The most breathtaking development in the postwar American economy was the dramatic expansion of the domestic consumer market. The sheer quantity of consumer goods available to the average person was without precedent. In some respects, the postwar decades seemed like the 1920s all over again, with an abundance of new gadgets and appliances, a craze for automobiles, and new types of mass media. Yet there was a significant difference: In the 1950s, consumption became associated with citizenship. Buying things, once a sign of personal indulgence, now meant participating fully in American society and, moreover, fulfilling a social responsibility. What the suburban family consumed, asserted *Life* magazine in a photo essay, would help to ensure "full employment and improved living standards for the rest of the nation."

The GI Bill | The new ethic of consumption appealed to the postwar middle class, the driving force behind the expanding domestic market. Middle-class status was more accessible than ever before because of the Serviceman's Readjustment Act of 1944, popularly known as the GI Bill. In the immediate postwar years, more than half of all U.S. college students were veterans attending class on the government's dime. By the middle of the 1950s, 2.2 million veterans had attended college and another 5.6 million had attended trade school with government financing. The son of an Italian immigrant from Queens, New York, said simply: "It was a hell of a gift, an opportunity, and I've never thought of it any other way." Before the GI Bill, commented another, "I looked upon college education as likely as my owning a Rolls-Royce with a chauffeur."

Government financing of education helped make the U.S. workforce the best educated in the world in the 1950s and 1960s. American colleges, universities, and trade schools grew by leaps and bounds to accommodate the flood of students — and expanded again when the children of those students, the baby boomers, reached college age in the 1960s. At Rutgers University, enrollment went from 7,000 before the war to 16,000 in 1947; at the University of Minnesota, from 15,000 to more than 27,000. The GI Bill trained nearly half a million engineers; 200,000 doctors, dentists, and nurses; and 150,000 scientists (among many other professions). Better education meant higher earning power, and higher earning power translated into the consumer spending that drove the postwar economy. One observer of the GI Bill was so impressed with its achievements that he declared it responsible for "the most important educational and social transformation in American history."

The GI Bill stimulated the economy and expanded the middle class in another way: Home ownership increased under its auspices. Between the end of World War II and 1966, one of every five single-family homes built in the United States was financed through a GI Bill mortgage — 2.5 million new homes in all. In cities and suburbs across the country, the Veterans Administration (VA), which helped former soldiers purchase new homes with no down payment, sparked a building boom that created jobs in the construction industry and fueled consumer spending in home appliances and automobiles. Education

College on the GI Bill

In 1947 — the year this photo was taken of a crowded lecture hall at the University of Iowa — more than 6,000 of this university's 10,000 students (60 percent) were veterans whose education was financed by the GI Bill. Across the country, American universities were bursting at the seams from the massive enrollment of World War II veterans. Government financing of college education for these vets made the U.S. workforce one of the best educated in the world in the 1950s and 1960s. Margaret Bourke-White/Time Life Pictures/Getty Images.

and home ownership were more than personal triumphs for the families of World War II veterans (and Korean War veterans, after a new GI Bill was passed in 1952). They were concrete financial *assets* that helped lift more Americans than ever before into a mass-consumption-oriented middle class.

Trade Unions | Organized labor also expanded the ranks of the middle class. For the first time ever, trade unions and collective bargaining became major factors in the nation's economic life. In the past, organized labor had been confined to a narrow band of craft trades and a few industries, primarily coal mining, railroading, and the building and metal trades. The power balance shifted during the Great Depression, and by the time the dust settled after World War II, labor unions overwhelmingly represented America's industrial workforce. A question then arose: How would labor's power be used?

In late 1945, Walter Reuther of the UAW thought he knew. The youthful Reuther was thinking big, beyond a single company or even a single industry. He aimed at nothing less than a reshaped, high-wage economy. To jump-start it, he demanded a 30 percent wage hike from General Motors (GM) with no price increase for GM cars. When GM said it could not afford such largesse, Reuther demanded that the company "open the books" — a demand that company executives implacably resisted. The company endured a 113-day strike and soundly defeated the UAW. Having made its point, GM laid out its terms for a durable relationship. It would accept the UAW as a bargaining partner and guarantee GM workers an ever-higher living standard. The price was that the UAW abandon its assault on the company's "right to manage." Reuther accepted the company's terms and signed the five-year GM contract of 1950 — the Treaty of Detroit, it was called.

The Treaty of Detroit opened the way for a broader "labor-management accord" — not industrial peace, because the country still experienced many strikes, but general acceptance of collective bargaining as the method for setting the terms of employment. For industrial workers, the result was rising real income. The average worker with three dependents gained 18 percent in spendable real income in the 1950s. In addition, unions delivered greater leisure (more paid holidays and longer vacations) and, in a startling departure, a social safety net. In postwar Europe, America's allies were constructing welfare states. But having lost the bruising battle in Washington for national health care during Truman's presidency, American unions turned to the bargaining table. By the end of the 1950s, union contracts commonly provided pension plans and company-paid health insurance. Collective bargaining had become, in effect, the American alternative to the European welfare state and, as Reuther boasted, the passport into the middle class.

The labor-management accord, though impressive, was never as durable or universal as it seemed. Vulnerabilities lurked. For one thing, the sheltered domestic markets — the essential condition for generous contracts — were in fact quite fragile. In certain industries, the lead firms were already losing market share. Second, generally overlooked were the many unorganized workers with no middle-class passport — those consigned to unorganized industries, casual labor, or low-wage jobs in the service sector. A final vulnerability was the most basic: the abiding anti-unionism of American employers. At heart, managers regarded the labor-management accord as a negotiated truce, not a permanent peace. It was only a matter of time and the onset of a more competitive environment before the scattered anti-union forays of the 1950s turned into a full-scale counteroffensive. The postwar labor-management accord turned out to be a transitory event, not a permanent condition of American economic life.

Houses, Cars, and Children   Increased educational levels, growing home ownership, and higher wages all enabled more Americans than ever before to become what one historian has called members of a "consumer republic." But what did they buy? The postwar emphasis on nuclear families and suburbs provides the answer. In the emerging suburban nation, three elements came together to create patterns of consumption that would endure for decades: houses, cars, and children.

A feature in a 1949 issue of *McCall's*, a magazine targeting middle-class women, illustrates the connections. "I now have three working centers," a typical housewife explains. "The baby center . . . a baking center . . . and a cleaning center." Accompanying illustrations reveal the interior of the brand-new house, stocked with the latest consumer products: accessories for the baby's room; a new stove, oven, and refrigerator; and a washer and dryer, along with cleaning products and other household goods. The article does not mention automobiles, but the photo of the house's exterior makes the point clear: Father drives home from work in a new car.

Consumption for the home, including automobiles, drove the postwar American economy as much as, or more than, the military-industrial complex did. If we think like advertisers and manufacturers, we can see why. Between 1945 and 1970, more than 25 million new houses were built in the United States. Each required its own supply of new appliances, from refrigerators to lawn mowers. In 1955 alone, Americans purchased 4 million new refrigerators, and between 1940 and 1951 the sale of power mowers increased from 35,000 per year to more than 1 million. Moreover, as American industry discovered planned obsolescence — the encouragement of consumers to replace appliances and cars every few years — the home became a site of perpetual consumer desire.

Children also encouraged consumption. The baby boomers born between World War II and the late 1950s have consistently, throughout every phase of their lives, been the darlings of American advertising and consumption. When they were infants, companies focused on developing new baby products, from disposable diapers to instant formula. When they were toddlers and young children, new television programs, board games, fast food, TV dinners, and thousands of different kinds of toys came to market to supply the rambunctious youth. When they were teenagers, rock music, Hollywood films, and a constantly marketed "teen culture" — with its appropriate clothing, music, hairstyles, and other accessories — bombarded them. Remarkably, in 1956, middle-class American teenagers on average had a weekly income of more than $10, close to the weekly disposable income of an entire family a generation earlier.

Television | The emergence of commercial television in the United States was swift and overwhelming. In the realm of technology, only the automobile and the personal computer were its equal in transforming everyday life in the twentieth century. In 1947, there were 7,000 TV sets in American homes. A year later, the CBS and NBC radio networks began offering regular programming, and by 1950 Americans owned 7.3 million sets. Ten years later, 87 percent of American homes had at least one television set. Having conquered the home, television would soon become the principle mediator between the consumer and the marketplace.

Television advertisers mastered the art of creating desire and directing it toward consumption. TV stations, like radio stations before them, depended entirely on advertising for profits. The first television executives understood that as long as they sold viewers to advertisers they would stay on the air. Early corporate-sponsored shows (such as *General Electric Theater* and *U.S. Steel Hour*) and simple product jingles (such as "No matter what the time or place, let's keep up with that happy pace. . . . 7-Up your thirst away!") gave way by the early 1960s to slick advertising campaigns that used popular music, movie stars, sports figures, and stimulating graphics to captivate viewers.

By creating powerful visual narratives of pleasure and comfort, television revolutionized advertising and changed forever the ways products were sold to American, and global, consumers. On *Queen for a Day*, a show popular in the mid-1950s, women competed to see who could tell the most heartrending story of tragedy and loss. The winner was lavished with household products: refrigerators, toasters, ovens, and the like. In a groundbreaking advertisement for Anacin aspirin, a tiny hammer pounded inside the skull of a headache sufferer. Almost overnight, sales of Anacin increased by 50 percent.

What Americans saw on television, both in the omnipresent commercials and in the programming, was an overwhelmingly white, Anglo-Saxon, Protestant world of nuclear families, suburban homes, and middle-class life. A typical show was *Father Knows Best*, starring Robert Young and Jane Wyatt. Father left home each morning wearing a suit and carrying a briefcase. Mother was a full-time housewife and stereotypical female, prone to bad driving and tears. *The Honeymooners*, starring Jackie Gleason as a Brooklyn bus driver, and *The Life of Riley*, a situation comedy featuring a California aircraft worker, were rare in their treatment of working-class lives. *Beulah*, starring Ethel Waters and then Louise Beavers as the African American maid for a white family, and the comedic *Amos 'n' Andy* were the only shows featuring black actors in major roles. Black characters appeared mainly as sidekicks and servants, as with Rochester on Jack Benny's comedy show. Television was never a showcase for the breadth of American society. It was instead a vehicle for the transmission of a narrow range of middle-class tastes and values.

Religion and the Middle Class

In an age of anxiety about nuclear annihilation and the spread of "godless Communism," Americans yearned for a reaffirmation of faith. Church membership jumped from 49 percent of the population in 1940 to 70 percent in 1960. People flocked to the evangelical Protestant denominations, beneficiaries of a remarkable new crop of preachers. Most eloquent was the young Reverend Billy Graham, who made brilliant use of television, radio, and advertising. His massive 1949 revival in Los Angeles and his 1957 crusade at Madison Square Garden in New York, attended or viewed by hundreds of thousands of Americans, established Graham as the nation's leading evangelical.

Rather than clashing with the new middle-class ethic of consumption, the religious reawakening was designed to mesh with it. Preachers such as Graham and the California-based Robert Schuller told Americans that so long as they lived moral lives, they deserved the material blessings of modern life. No one was more influential

Billy Graham

Charismatic and inspiring, Billy Graham wore down shoe leather to bring Christian conversion to hundreds of thousands of Americans in the 1940s and 1950s, preaching to large crowds such as this one in Columbia, South Carolina. He also migrated onto the radio and television airwaves, using technology to reach even wider audiences. Graham used the Cold War to sharpen his message, telling Americans that "godless communism" was an inferior system, but that democracy in America required belief in god and a constant struggle against "sin." Photo by John Dominis/Time Life Pictures/Getty Images.

in this regard than the author Norman Vincent Peale, whose best-selling book *The Power of Positive Thinking* (1952) embodied the therapeutic use of religion as an anti-dote to life's trials and tribulations. Peale taught that with faith in God and "positive thinking," anyone could overcome obstacles and become a success. Graham, Schuller, Peale, and other 1950s evangelicals laid the foundation for the rise of the televangelists, who created popular television ministries in the 1970s.

The postwar purveyors of religious faith cast Americans as a righteous people op-posed to Communist atheism. When Julius and Ethel Rosenberg were sentenced to death in 1953, the judge criticized them for "devoting themselves to the Russian ideology of denial of God." Cold War imperatives drew Catholics, Protestants, and Jews into an in-fluential ecumenical movement that downplayed doctrinal differences. The phrase "under God" was inserted into the Pledge of Allegiance in 1954, and U.S. coins carried the words "In God We Trust" after 1956. These religious initiatives struck a dis-tinctly moderate tone, however, in comparison with the politicized evangelism that emerged in the wake of the sexual revolution and other developments in the 1960s and 1970s (see Chapter 29).

> ▶ How did the American economy benefit from World War II and the Cold War?
>
> ▶ What were the major factors in the expansion of the middle class in these decades?

A Suburban Nation

Prosperity — how much an economy produces, how much people earn — is more easily measured than is quality of life. During the 1950s, however, the American definition of the good life emerged with exceptional distinctness: a high value on consumption, a preference for suburban living, and a devotion to family and domesticity. In this sec-tion, we consider the second dimension of that definition: suburbanization. What drove the nation to abandon its cities for the suburbs, and what social and political conse-quences did this shift have?

The Postwar Housing Boom

Migration to the suburbs had been going on for a hundred years, but never before on the scale that the country experienced after World War II. Within a decade, farmland on the outskirts of cities filled up with tract housing and shopping malls. Entire coun-ties that had once been rural — such as San Mateo, south of San Francisco, or Passaic and Bergen in New Jersey, west of Manhattan — went suburban. By 1960, one-third of Americans lived in suburbs. Home construction, having ground to halt during the Great Depression, surged after the war. One-fourth of the country's entire housing stock in 1960 had not even existed a decade earlier.

William J. Levitt and the FHA | Two unique postwar developments remade the national housing mar-ket and gave it a distinctly suburban shape. First, an innovative Long Island building contractor, William J. Levitt, revolutionized suburban housing by applying mass-production techniques and turning out new homes at a dizzy-ing speed. Levitt's basic four-room house, complete with kitchen appliances, was priced at $7,990 in 1947 (about $76,000 today). Levitt did not need to advertise; word of mouth brought buyers flocking to his developments (all called Levittown) in New York, Pennsylvania, and New Jersey. Dozens of other developers were soon snapping up cheap farmland and building subdivisions around the country.

Even at $7,990, Levitt's homes would have been beyond the means of most young families had the traditional home-financing standard — half down and ten years to pay off the balance — still prevailed. That is where the second postwar development came in. The Federal Housing Administration (FHA) and the Veterans Administration (VA) — that is, the federal government — made the home mortgage market serve a broader range of Americans than ever before. After the war, the FHA insured thirty-year mortgages with as little as 5 percent down and interest at 2 or 3 percent. The VA was even more generous, requiring only a token $1 down for qualified ex-GIs. FHA and VA mortgages best explain why, after hovering around 45 percent for the previous half century, home ownership jumped to 60 percent by 1960.

What purchasers of suburban houses got, in addition to a good deal, were homogeneous communities. The developments contained few old people or unmarried adults. Even the trees were young. Levitt's company enforced regulations about maintaining lawns and not hanging out laundry on the weekends. Then there was the matter of race. Levitt's houses came with restrictive covenants prohibiting occupancy "by members of other than the Caucasian Race." (Restrictive covenants often applied to Jews and, in California, Asian Americans as well.)

After the war, the National Association for the Advancement of Colored People (NAACP), the Congress of Industrial Organization (CIO), and African American civil rights groups launched an ambitious campaign for open-housing ordinances in cities such as Detroit, New York, Philadelphia, and Oakland. White home owners rebelled, voting for racist politicians who promised to keep neighborhoods white by resisting what they called "Negro invasion." When politics failed, white home owners took matters into their own hands. In Chicago, Detroit, and other major northern cities, they bombed, set fires, threw bricks through windows, and employed other tactics to force black homebuyers out of certain neighborhoods. One California newspaper reported in 1948 that "faced with the great influx of colored population, [members of] the Caucasian race [would have] to protect their property values."

In *Shelley v. Kraemer* (1948), the Supreme Court outlawed restrictive covenants, but racial discrimination in housing changed little. The practice persisted long after *Shelley*, because the FHA and VA continued the policy of redlining: refusing mortgages to African Americans and members of other minority groups seeking to buy in white neighborhoods. Indeed, no federal law — or even court decisions like *Shelley* — actually prohibited racial discrimination in housing until Congress passed the Fair Housing Act in 1968.

Interstate Highways | Without automobiles, suburban growth on such a massive scale would have been impossible. Planners laid out subdivisions on the assumption that everybody would drive. And they did — to get to work, to take the children to Little League, to shop. With gas plentiful and cheap (15 cents a gallon), no one cared about the fuel efficiency of their V-8 engines or seemed to mind the elaborate tail fins and chrome that weighed down their cars. In 1945, Americans owned twenty-five million cars; by 1965, just two decades later, the number had *tripled* to seventy-five million (see Voices from Abroad, p. 801). American oil consumption followed, tripling as well between 1949 and 1972.

More cars required more highways, and the federal government obliged. In 1956, in a move that drastically altered America's landscape and driving habits, the National Interstate and Defense Highways Act authorized $26 billion over a ten-year period for the construction of a nationally integrated highway system — 42,500 miles (Map 26.1). Cast as a Cold War necessity, because broad highways made evacuating crowded cities easier in the event of a nuclear attack, the law changed American cities forever. An enormous public works program surpassing anything undertaken during the New Deal, federal highways made possible the massive suburbanization of the nation in the 1960s. Interstate highways rerouted traffic away from small towns, bypassed well-traveled main roads such as the cross-country Route 66, and cut wide swaths through old neighborhoods in the cities.

Fast Food and Shopping Malls Americans did not simply fill their new suburban homes with the latest appliances and gadgets; they also pioneered entirely new forms of consumption. Through World War II, downtowns had remained the center of retail sales and restaurant dining with their grand department stores, elegant eateries, and low-cost diners. As suburbanites abandoned big-city centers in the 1950s, ambitious entrepreneurs invented two new commercial forms that would profoundly shape the rest of the century: the shopping mall and the fast-food restaurant.

By the late 1950s, the suburban shopping center had become as much a part of the American landscape as the Levittowns and their imitators. A major developer of shopping malls in the Northeast called them "crystallization points for suburbia's community life." He romanticized the new structures as "today's village green," where "the fountain

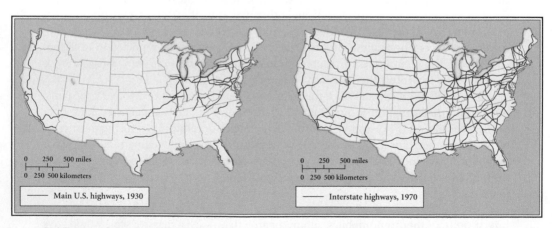

0   250   500 miles
0   250 500 kilometers

—— Main U.S. highways, 1930

0   250   500 miles
0   250 500 kilometers

—— Interstate highways, 1970

MAP 26.1 Connecting the Nation: The Interstate Highway System, 1930 and 1970
The 1956 Interstate and Defense Highways Act paved the way for an extensive network of federal highways throughout the nation. The act not only pleased American drivers and enhanced their love affair with the automobile but also benefited the petroleum, construction, trucking, real estate, and tourist industries. The new highway system promoted the nation's economic integration, facilitated the growth of suburbs, and contributed to the erosion of America's distinct regional identities.

VOICES FROM ABROAD

Everyone Has a Car   HANOCH BARTOV

One of Israel's foremost writers and journalists, Hanoch Bartov spent two years in the United States working as a correspondent for the newspaper *Lamerchav*. As a newcomer to Los Angeles in the early 1960s, he was both fascinated and appalled by Americans' love affair with the automobile.

Our immediate decision to buy a car sprang from healthy instincts. Only later did I learn from bitter experience that in California, death was preferable to living without one. Neither the views from the plane nor the weird excursion that first evening hinted at what I would go through that first week.

Very simple — the nearest supermarket was about half a kilometer south of our apartment, the regional primary school two kilometers east, and my son's kindergarten even farther away. A trip to the post office — an undertaking, to the bank — an ordeal, to work — an impossibility.

Truth be told: the Los Angeles municipality . . . does have public transportation. Buses go once an hour along the city's boulevards and avenues, gathering all the wretched of the earth, the poor and the needy, the old ladies forbidden by their grandchildren to drive, and other eccentric types. But few people can depend on buses, even should they swear never to deviate from the fixed routes. . . . There are no tramways. No one thought of a subway. Railroads — not now and not in the future. Why? Because everyone has a car. A man invited me to his house, saying, "We are neighbors, within ten minutes of each other." After walking for an hour and a half I realized what he meant — "ten minute drive within the speed limit." Simply put, he never thought I might interpret his remark to re-fer to the walking distance. The moment a baby sees the light of day in Los Angeles, a car is registered in his name in Detroit. . . .

At first perhaps people relished the freedom and independence a car provided. You get in, sit down, and grab the steering wheel, your mobility exceeding that of any other generation. No wonder people refuse to live downtown, where they can hear their neighbors, smell their cooking, and suffer frayed nerves as trains pass by bedroom windows. Instead, they get a piece of the desert, far from town, at half price, drag a water hose, grow grass, flowers, and trees, and build their dream house. . . .

. . . Why bother parking, getting out, getting in, getting up and sitting down, when you can simply "drive in"? Mailboxes have their slots facing the road, at the level of the driver's hand. That is how dirty laundry is deposited, electricity and water bills paid. That is how love is made, how children are taken to school. That is how the anniversary wreath is laid on the graves of loved ones. There are drive-in movies. And, yes, we saw it with our own eyes: drive-in churches. Only in death is a man separated from his car and buried alone.

SOURCE: Hanoch Bartov, "Measures of Affluence," in Oscar Handlin and Lilian Handlin, eds., *From the Outer World* (Cambridge, MA: Harvard University Press, 1997), 293–296.

in the mall has replaced the downtown department clock as the gathering place for young and old alike." Romanticism aside, suburban shopping centers worked perfectly in the world of suburban consumption; they brought "the market to the people instead of people to the market," commented the *New York Times*. In 1939, the suburban share of total metropolitan retail trade in the United States was a paltry 4 percent. By 1961, it was an astonishing 60 percent in the nation's ten largest metropolitan regions.

No one was more influential in creating suburban patterns of consumption than a Chicago-born son of Czech immigrants named Ray Kroc. A former jazz musician and traveling salesman, Kroc found his calling in 1954 when he acquired a single franchise of the little-known McDonald's Restaurant, based in San Bernardino, California. In 1956, Kroc invested in twelve more franchises and by 1958 owned seventy-nine. Three years later, Kroc bought the company from the McDonald brothers and proceeded to turn it into the largest chain of restaurants in the world. Based on inexpensive, quickly served hamburgers that hungry families could eat in the restaurant, in their cars, or at home, Kroc's vision transformed the way Americans consumed food.

Rise of the Sunbelt

Suburban living, although a nationwide phenomenon, was most at home in the Sunbelt (the southern and southwestern states), where taxes were low, the climate was mild, and open space allowed for sprawling subdivisions (Map 26.2). Florida added 3.5 million people, many of them retired, between 1940 and 1970. Texas profited from expanding petrochemical and defense industries. Most dramatic was California's growth, spurred especially by the state's booming defense-related aircraft and electronics industries. By 1970, California contained one-tenth of the nation's population and surpassed New York as the most populous state. At the end of the century, California's economy was among the top ten largest in the world — among *nations*.

A distinctive feature of Sunbelt suburbanization was its close relationship to the military-industrial complex. Building on World War II expansion, military bases proliferated in the South and Southwest in the postwar decades, especially in Florida, Texas, and California. In some instances, entire metropolitan regions — such as San Diego County, California, and the Houston area in Texas — expanded in tandem with nearby military outposts. Moreover, the aerospace, defense, and electronics industries were based largely in Sunbelt metropolitan regions.

Sunbelt suburbanization was best exemplified by Orange County, California. Southeast of Los Angeles, Orange County was until the 1940s mostly just that — a land of oranges, groves of them. But during World War II, boosters attracted new bases and training facilities for the marines, navy, and air force (then the army air corps). Cold War militarization and the Korean War kept those bases humming, and Hughes Aircraft, Autonetics, Ford Aeronautics, and other defense-related manufacturers built new plants in the sunny, sprawling groves. So did subdivision developers, who built so many new homes that the population of the county jumped from 130,760 in 1940 to 703,925 in 1960. Casting his eye on all this development in the early 1950s, an entrepreneurial filmmaker and cartoonist named Walt Disney chose Anaheim in Orange County as the place for a massive new amusement park. Disneyland was to the new generation of suburbanites what Coney Island had been to an earlier generation of urbanites.

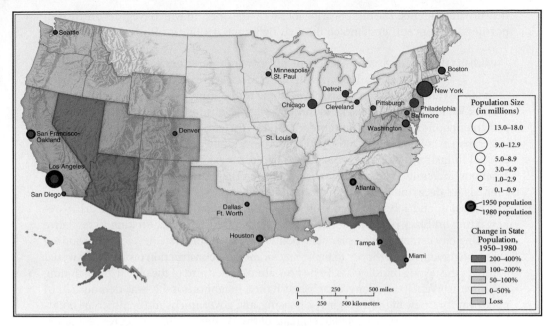

MAP 26.2 Shifting Population Patterns, 1950–1980
This map shows the two major, somewhat overlapping, patterns of population movement between 1950 and 1980. Most striking is the rapid growth of the Sunbelt states. All the states experiencing increases of over 100 percent in that period are in the Southwest, plus Florida. The second pattern involves the growth of metropolitan areas, defined as a central city or urban area and its suburbs. The central cities were themselves mostly not growing, however. The metropolitan growth shown in this map was accounted for by the expanding suburbs. And because Sunbelt growth was primarily suburban growth, that's where we see the most rapid metropolitan growth, with Los Angeles the clear leader.

Two Nations: Urban and Suburban

While middle-class whites flocked to the suburbs, an opposite stream of working-class migrants, many of them southern African Americans, moved into the cities. In the 1950s, the nation's twelve largest cities lost 3.6 million whites while gaining 4.5 million non-whites. These urban newcomers inherited a declining economy and a decaying infra-structure. To those enjoying prosperity, the "other America," as the social critic Michael Harrington called it, remained largely invisible. In 1968, however, a report by the National Advisory Commission on Civil Disorders (informally known as the Kerner Commission), delivered to President Lyndon Baines Johnson, warned that "our nation is moving toward two societies, one black, one white, separate and unequal."

American cities had long been the home of poverty, slum housing, and the hardships and cultural dislocations brought on by immigration from overseas or migration from rural areas. But postwar American cities, especially those in the industrial Northeast and Midwest, experienced these problems with new intensity. By the 1950s, the manufacturing sector was contracting, and mechanization was eliminating thousands upon thousands of unskilled and semiskilled jobs, the kind traditionally taken up by new urban residents. The disappearing jobs were the ones "in which Negroes are dispro-portionately concentrated," noted the civil rights activist Bayard Rustin.

The Urban Crisis | The intensification of poverty, the deterioration of older housing stock, and the persistence of racial segregation produced what many at the time called the urban crisis. Unwelcome in the shiny new suburbs built by men such as William J. Levitt, blacks found low-paying jobs in the city and lived in aging apartment buildings run by slumlords. Despite a thriving black middle class — indeed, larger than ever before — for those without resources, upward mobility remained elusive. Racism in institutional forms frustrated African Americans at every turn: housing re-strictions, increasingly segregated schools, and an urban infrastructure that stood under-funded and decaying as whites left for the suburbs.

Housing and job discrimination were compounded by the frenzy of urban re-newal that hit black neighborhoods in the 1950s and early 1960s. Seeking to revitalize declining city centers, urban planners, politicians, and real estate developers proposed razing blighted neighborhoods to make way for modern construction projects that would appeal to the fleeing middle class. In Boston, almost one-third of the old city — including the historic West End, a long-established Italian neighborhood — was demolished to make way for a new highway, high-rise housing, and government and commercial build-ings. In San Francisco, some 4,000 residents of the Western Addition, a predominantly black neighborhood, lost out to an urban renewal program that built luxury housing, a shopping center, and an express boulevard. Between 1949 and 1967, urban renewal na-tionwide demolished almost 400,000 buildings and displaced 1.4 million people.

The urban experts believed they knew what to do with the dislocated: relocate them to federally funded housing projects, an outgrowth of New Deal housing policy, now much expanded and combined with generous funding for slum clearance. However well intended, these grim projects too often took the form of cheap high-rise slums that iso-lated their inhabitants from surrounding neighborhoods. The impact was felt especially strongly among African Americans, who often found that public housing *increased* ra-cial segregation and concentrated the poor. The Robert Taylor Homes in Chicago, with twenty-eight buildings of sixteen stories each, housed 20,000 residents, almost all of them black. Despite the planners' wish to build decent affordable apartments, the huge complex became a notorious breeding ground for crime and hopelessness.

Urban | Despite the evident urban crisis, cities continued to attract immigrants
Immigrants | from abroad. Since the passage of the National Origins Act of 1924 (see Chapter 22), U.S. immigration policy had aimed mainly at keeping for-eigners out. But World War II and the Cold War began slowly to change American policy. The Displaced Persons Act of 1948 permitted the entry of approximately 415,000 Euro-peans, many of them Jewish refugees. In a gesture to an important war ally, the Chi-nese Exclusion Act was repealed in 1943. More far-reaching was the 1952 McCarran-Walter Act, which ended the exclusion of Japanese, Koreans, and Southeast Asians.

After the national-origins quota system went into effect in 1924, Mexico replaced Eastern and Southern Europe as the nation's labor reservoir. During World War II, the federal government introduced the Bracero Program to ease wartime labor shortages (see Chapter 24) and then revived it in 1951, during the Korean War. The federal govern-

Urban Crisis

This Pittsburgh neighborhood, photographed in 1955, typified what many came to call the "urban crisis" of the 1950s and 1960s. As suburbanization drew middle-class residents, investment, and jobs away from the core of older cities, those cities began to rot from the inside. Urban neglect left many working-class neighborhoods, increasingly occupied by the nation's poor, with few jobs, little industry, and dilapidated housing. W. Eugene Smith/Magnum Photos.

ment's ability to force workers to return to Mexico, however, was strictly limited. The Mexican population continued to grow, and by the time the Bracero Program ended in 1964, many of that group — an estimated 350,000 — had settled permanently in the United States. Braceros were joined by other Mexicans from small towns and villages, who immigrated to the United States to escape poverty or to earn money to return home and purchase land for farming.

As generations of immigrants had before them, Mexicans gravitated to major cities. Mostly, they settled in Los Angeles, Long Beach, San Jose, El Paso, and other southwestern cities. But many also went north, augmenting well-established Mexican American communities in Chicago, Detroit, Kansas City, and Denver. Although still important to American agriculture, Mexican Americans were employed in substantial numbers as industrial and service workers by 1960.

Another major group of Spanish-speaking migrants came from Puerto Rico. American citizens since 1917, Puerto Ricans enjoyed an unrestricted right to move to the mainland United States. Migration increased dramatically after World War II, when mechanization of the island's sugarcane agriculture pushed many Puerto Ricans off the land. Airlines began to offer cheap direct flights between San Juan and New York City. With the fare at about $50 (two weeks' wages), Puerto Ricans became America's first immigrants to arrive en masse by air. Most Puerto Ricans went to New York, where they settled first in East ("Spanish") Harlem and then scattered in neighborhoods across the city's five boroughs. This massive migration, which increased the Puerto Rican population to 613,000 by 1960, transformed the ethnic composition of the city. More Puerto Ricans now lived in New York City than in San Juan.

Cuban refugees constituted the third largest group of Spanish-speaking immigrants. In the six years after Fidel Castro's seizure of power in 1959 (see Chapter 25), an estimated 180,000 people fled Cuba for the United States. The Cuban refugee community grew so quickly that it turned Miami into a cosmopolitan, bilingual city almost overnight. Unlike other urban migrants, Miami's Cubans quickly prospered, in large part because they had arrived with money and middle-class skills.

Spanish-speaking immigrants — whether Mexican, Puerto Rican, or Cuban — created huge barrios in major American cities, where bilingualism flourished, the Catholic Church shaped religious life, and families sought to join the economic mainstream. Though distinct from one another, these Spanish-speaking communities remained largely segregated from white, or Anglo, neighborhoods and suburbs as well as from African American districts.

► How are we to explain the relationship between suburbanization and consumption?

► In what sense was the United States "two nations"?

Gender, Sex, and Family in the Era of Containment

Marriage, family structure, and gender roles had been undergoing significant changes since the turn of the twentieth century (see Chapter 18). Beginning in the nineteenth century, middle-class Americans increasingly saw marriage as "companionate," that is, based on romantic love and a lifetime of shared friendship. Companionate did not mean equal. In the mid-twentieth century, family life remained governed by notions of paternalism, in which men provided economic support and controlled the family's financial resources, while women cared for children and occupied a secondary position in public life.

The resurgent postwar American middle class was preoccupied with paternalism and its virtues. Everyone from professional psychologists to television advertisers and every organization from schools to the popular press celebrated nuclear families. Children were prized, and women's caregiving roles were valorized. This view of family life, and especially its emphasis on female "domesticity," was bolstered by Cold War politics. Americans who deviated from prevailing gender and sexual norms were not only viewed with scorn but were sometimes thought to be subversive and politically dangerous. The word *containment* could apply to the home as easily as to foreign policy. Sex had become politicized by the Cold War.

The model of domesticity so highly esteemed in postwar middle-class morality hid deeper, longer-term changes in the way marriage, gender roles, women's work, and even sex were understood. To comprehend the postwar decades, we have to keep in mind both the value placed on domesticity and the tumultuous changes surging beneath its prescriptions.

The Baby Boom

A popular 1945 song was called "Gotta Make Up for Lost Time," and Americans did just that. Two things were noteworthy about the families they formed after World War II: First, marriages were remarkably stable. Not until the mid-1960s did the divorce rate begin to rise sharply. Second, married couples were intent on having babies. Everyone expected to have several children — it was part of adulthood, almost a citizen's responsibility. After a century and a half of decline, the birthrate shot up. More babies were born between 1948 and 1953 than in the previous thirty years.

One of the reasons for this baby boom was that people were having children at the same time. A second was a drop in the average marriage age — down to twenty-two for men and twenty for women. Younger parents meant a bumper crop of children. Women who came of age in the 1930s averaged 2.4 children; their counterparts in the 1950s averaged 3.2 children. Such a dramatic turnaround reflected couples' decisions during the Great Depression to limit childbearing and couples' contrasting decisions in the postwar years to have more children. The baby boom peaked in 1957 and remained at a high level until the early 1960s. Far from "normal," all of these developments were anomalies, temporary reversals of long-standing demographic trends. From the perspective of the whole of the twentieth century, the 1950s and early 1960s stand out as exceptions to declining birthrates, rising divorce rates, and the steadily rising marriage age.

The passage of time revealed the ever-widening impact of the baby boom. When baby boomers competed for jobs during the 1970s, the labor market became tight. When career-oriented baby boomers belatedly began having children in the 1980s, the birthrate jumped. And in our own time, as baby boomers begin retiring, huge funding problems threaten to engulf Social Security and Medicare. The intimate decisions of so many couples after World War II continued to shape American life well into the twenty-first century.

Improving Health and Education | Baby boom children benefited from a host of important advances in public health and medical practice in the postwar years. Formerly serious illnesses became merely routine after the introduction of such "miracle drugs" as penicillin (introduced in 1943), streptomycin (1945), and cortisone (1946). When Dr. Jonas Salk perfected a polio vaccine in 1954, he became a national hero. The free distribution of Salk's vaccine in the nation's schools, followed in 1961 by Dr. Albert Sabin's oral polio vaccine, demonstrated the potential of government-sponsored public health programs.

The baby boom also gave the nation's educational system a boost. Postwar middle-class parents, America's first college-educated generation, placed a high value on education. Suburban parents approved 90 percent of school bond issues during the 1950s. By

1970, school expenditures accounted for 7.2 percent of the gross national product, double the 1950 level. In the 1960s, the baby boom generation swelled college enrollments. State university systems grew in tandem: the pioneering University of California, University of Wisconsin, and State University of New York systems added dozens of new campuses and offered students in their states a low-cost college education.

Dr. Benjamin Spock | To keep baby boom children healthy and happy, middle-class parents increasingly relied on the advice of experts. Dr. Benjamin Spock's *Common Sense Book of Baby and Child Care* sold one million copies every year after its publication in 1946. Spock urged mothers to abandon the rigid feeding and baby-care schedules of an earlier generation. New mothers found Spock's common-sense approach liberating. "Your little paperback is still in my cupboard, with loose pages, rather worn from use because I brought up two babies using it as my 'Bible,'" a California housewife wrote to Spock.

Despite his commonsense approach to child-rearing, Spock was part of a generation of psychological experts whose advice often failed to reassure women. If mothers were too protective, Spock and others argued, they might hamper their children's preparation for adult life. On the other hand, mothers who wanted to work outside the home felt guilty because Spock recommended that they be constantly available for their children. As American mothers aimed for the perfection demanded of them seemingly at every turn, many began to question these mixed messages. Some of them would be inspired by the resurgence of feminism in the 1960s.

Women, Work, and Family

Two powerful forces shaped women's relationships to work and family life in the postwar decades. One was the middle-class domestic ideal, which feminist Betty Friedan would later call the "feminine mystique." "The suburban housewife — she was the dream image of the young American women" in the 1950s, Friedan wrote. "She was healthy, beautiful, educated, concerned only about her husband, her children, her home." The second force was the job market. Most working-class women had to earn a paycheck to help their family. Despite their education, middle-class women found that jobs in the professions and business were dominated by men and often closed to them. For both groups, the market offered mostly "women's jobs" — in teaching, nursing, and other areas of the growing service sector — and little room for advancement (see American Voices, p. 809).

The idea that a woman's place was in the home was, of course, not new. The feminine mystique of the 1950s and 1960s — the idea that "the highest value and the only commitment for women is the fulfillment of their own femininity" — bore a remarkable similarity to the nineteenth century's notion of domesticity. The updated version drew on new elements of twentieth-century science and culture. Psychologists equated motherhood with "normal" female identity and suggested that career-minded mothers needed therapy. Television shows and movies depicted career women as social misfits. The postwar consumer culture also emphasized women's domestic role as purchasing agents for home and family. "Can a woman ever feel right cooking on a dirty range?" asked one advertisement.

Coming of Age in the Postwar Years

At the dawn of the postwar era, Americans faced new opportunities and new anxieties. Women faced new pressures to realize the ideal role of housewife and mother. And on the horizon lurked communism, which Americans feared but little understood. Below are two reactions to these postwar tensions, distinct experiences of coming of age in the 1940s and 1950s. Elizabeth Pope was an editor at *McCall's*, a major women's magazine. Susan Toth is a writer and scholar who grew up in Ames, Iowa, a small college town surrounded by cornfields.

Elizabeth Pope: Ever since World War II, when for the first time vast numbers of women were exposed to the seduction of a weekly pay check, more and more wives have been taking full-time jobs outside the home. Today, more than ten million — better than one of four — are working as homemakers and wage earners at the same time. . . .

Working women have been blamed for everything from juvenile delinquency to divorce. They have been charged with neglecting their babies, bulldozing their husbands, neglecting their homes. It's hard to think of a social problem ranging from inadequate breakfasts to world unrest which someone at some time or another hasn't dumped on their laps.

The question, of course, concerns not only the working women themselves, but every other member of their families, especially their children. There are more than five and a half million mothers of children under eighteen among the ranks of working wives. What happens to those children, big and little, when Mother goes out to work? . . .

Experts are unanimous in prefacing their answer to this question with the words, "That depends." It depends on what kind of person she is and why she gets a job, on how old the children are and what they are like, on the attitude of her husband and the family's financial situation. . . .

Susan Allen Toth: Of course, we all knew there was Communism. As early as sixth grade our teacher warned us about its

dangers. I listened carefully to Mr. Casper describe what Communists wanted, which sounded terrible. World domination. Enslavement. Destruction of our way of life. . . . I hung around school one afternoon hoping to catch Mr. Casper, whom I secretly adored, to ask him why Communism was so bad. He stayed in another teacher's room so late I finally scrawled my question on our blackboard: "Dear Mr. Casper, why is Communism so bad . . . Sue Allen" and went home. Next morning the message was still there. Like a warning from heaven it had galvanized Mr. Casper. He began class with a stern lecture, repeating everything he had said about dangerous Russians and painting a vivid picture of how we would all suffer if the Russians took over the city government in Ames. We certainly wouldn't be able to attend a school like this, he said, where free expression of opinion was allowed. At recess that day one of the boys asked me if I was a "dirty Commie": two of my best friends shied away from me on the playground; I saw Mr. Casper talking low to another teacher and pointing at me. I cried all the way home from school and resolved never to commit myself publicly with a question like that again.

SOURCES: Elizabeth Pope, "Is a Working Mother a Threat to the Home?" *McCall's* (July 1955), quoted in Sonya Michel and Robyn Muncy, eds., *Engendering America: A Documentary History, 1865 to the Present* (New York: McGraw Hill, 1999), 231–234. Susan Allen Toth, *Blooming: A Small-Town Girlhood* (Boston: Little, Brown and Company, 1978): 202–203.

The postwar domestic ideal held that women's principal economic contribution came through consumption — women shopped for the family. In reality, their contributions increasingly took them outside their homes and into the workforce. In 1954, married women made up half of all women workers. Six years later, the 1960 census reported a stunning fact: The number of mothers who worked had increased four times, and over one-third of these women had children between the ages of six and seventeen. In that same year, 30 percent of wives worked, and by 1970, it was 40 percent. For working-class women, in particular, the economic needs of their families demanded that they work outside the home.

Despite rising employment rates, occupational segmentation still haunted women. Until 1964, the classified sections of newspapers separated employment ads into "Help Wanted Male" and "Help Wanted Female." More than 80 percent of all employed women did stereotypical women's work as sales clerks, health-care technicians, waitresses, stewardesses, domestic servants, receptionists, telephone operators, and secretaries. In 1960, only 3 percent of lawyers and 6 percent of physicians were women — on the flip side, 97 percent of nurses and 85 percent of librarians were women. Along with women's jobs went women's pay, which averaged 60 percent of men's pay in 1963.

Contrary to stereotype, however, women's paid work was not merely supplementary. It helped lift families into the middle class. Even in the prosperous 1950s, many men found that their wages could not pay for what middle-class life demanded: cars, houses, vacations, and college education for the children. Many families needed more than one wage earner just to get by. Among married women, the highest rates of labor-force participation in the 1950s were found in families at the lower end of the middle class. Over the course of the postwar decades, from 1945 to 1965, more and more women, including married women, from all class backgrounds, entered the paid workforce.

How could American society steadfastly uphold the domestic ideal when so many wives and mothers were out of the house and at work? In many ways, the contradiction was hidden by the women themselves. Fearing public disapproval, women would explain their work in family-oriented terms — as a way to save money for the children's college education, for instance. Moreover, when women took jobs outside the home, they still bore full responsibility for child care and household management, contributing to the "double day" of paid work and family work. As one overburdened woman noted, she now had "two full-time jobs instead of just one — underpaid clerical worker and unpaid housekeeper." Finally, the pressures of the Cold War made strong nuclear families with breadwinning fathers and domesticated mothers symbols of a healthy nation. Americans wanted to believe this even if it did not perfectly describe the reality of their lives.

Sex and the Middle Class

In many ways, the two decades between 1945 and 1965 were a period of sexual conservatism that reflected the values of domesticity. At the dawn of the 1960s, going steady as a prelude to marriage was the fad in high school. College women had curfews and needed permission to see a male visitor. Americans married young; more than half of those who married in 1963 were under the age of twenty-one. After the birth control pill came on the market in 1960, few doctors prescribed it to unmarried women, and even married women did not enjoy unfettered access to contraception until the Supreme Court ruled it a "privacy" right in the 1965 decision *Griswold v. Connecticut*.

Both women and men were expected to channel their sexual desire strictly toward marriage. Men might temporarily escape such expectations, so long as their sexual adventures occurred prior to marriage and did not interfere with starting a family. Women faced much harsher social sanction, not to mention potential unwanted pregnancies, if they pursued similar adventures. Hugh Hefner, who founded *Playboy* magazine in 1953, created a countermorality of bachelorhood, a fictional world populated by "hip" men and sexually available women. Hefner was the exception that proved the rule: Marriage, not swinging bachelorhood, remained the destination for the vast majority of men. Millions of men read *Playboy*, but few adopted its fantasy lifestyle.

Beneath the surface of middle-class sexual morality, Americans were less repressed than confused. On the one hand, men and women were increasingly encouraged to embrace "sexual liberalism," in which sex was valued apart from its role in procreation. On the other hand, the notion of sex as an act of pleasure created anxieties Americans had yet to resolve, resulting in many unanswered questions: Should adults have sex before marriage? When was it appropriate for young men versus women to become sexually active? Should marriage itself define the boundaries of a person's sexual life? Was greater sexual freedom just another means of exploiting women? Should men have sex with, and could they love, other men? Could women?

The Kinsey Reports

Like the woman on the cover of this lighthearted 1953 book of photographs, many Americans reacted with surprise when Alfred Kinsey revealed the country's sexual habits. In his 1948 book about men and his 1953 book about women, Kinsey wrote about American sexual practices in the detached language of science. But it still made for salacious reading. Evangelical minister Billy Graham warned: "It is impossible to estimate the damage this book will do to the already deteriorated morals of America." Picture Research Consultants & Archives.

Alfred Kinsey Two controversial studies by an unassuming Indiana University zoologist named Alfred Kinsey forced questions about sexuality into the open. Kinsey and his research team published *Sexual Behavior in the Human Male* in 1948 and followed it up in 1953 with *Sexual Behavior in the Human Female* — an 842-page book that sold 270,000 copies in the first month after its publication. Taking a scientific, rather than moralistic, approach, Kinsey, who became known as "the sex doctor," documented the full range of sexual experiences of thousands of Americans. He broke numerous taboos, discussing such topics as masturbation, orgasms, homosexuality, and marital infidelity in the detached language of science.

Both studies confirmed that a sexual revolution, although a largely hidden one, had already begun to transform American society by the early 1950s. Kinsey estimated that 85 percent of white men had had sex prior to marriage, that more than 90 percent of men masturbated, and that more than 25 percent of married women had had sex outside of marriage by the age of forty. These were shocking public admissions in the late 1940s and early 1950s, and "hotter than the Kinsey report" became a national figure of speech. Kinsey was criticized by statisticians — because his samples were not randomly selected — and condemned even more fervently by religious leaders, who charged him with encouraging promiscuity and adultery. But his research opened a national conversation with profound implications for the future. Even if Kinsey's numbers were off, he helped Americans learn to talk more openly about sex.

The Homophile Movement | Among the most controversial of Kinsey's claims was that homosexuality was far more prevalent than most Americans believed. Although the American Psychiatric Association would officially define homosexuality as a mental illness in 1952, Kinsey's research found that 37 percent of men had engaged in some form of homosexual activity by early adulthood, as had 13 percent of women. Even more important, Kinsey claimed that 10 percent of American men were *exclusively* homosexual. These claims came as little surprise, but great encouragement, to a group of gay and lesbian activists who called themselves "homophiles." Organized primarily in the Mattachine Society (the first gay rights organization in the country, founded in 1951) and the Daughters of Bilitis (a lesbian organization founded in 1955), homophiles were a small but determined collection of activists who sought equal rights for gays and lesbians. "The lesbian is a woman endowed with all the attributes of any other woman," wrote the pioneer lesbian activist Del Martin in 1956. "The salvation of the lesbian lies in her acceptance of herself without guilt or anxiety."

Building on the urban gay and lesbian communities that had coalesced during World War II, homophiles sought to change American attitudes about same-sex love. They faced daunting obstacles, since same-sex sexual relations were illegal in every state and scorned, or feared, by most Americans. To combat prejudice and change the laws, homophile organizations cultivated a respectable, middle-class image. Members were encouraged to avoid bars and nightclubs, to dress in conservative shirts and ties (for men) and modest skirts and blouses (for women), and to seek out professional psychologists who would attest to their "normalcy." Only in the 1960s did homophiles begin to talk about the "homophile vote" and their "rights as citizens," laying the groundwork for the gay rights movement of the 1970s.

Youth Culture

One of the most striking developments in American family life in the postwar decades was the emergence of the teenager as a cultural phenomenon. In 1956, only partly in jest, the CBS radio commentator Eric Sevareid questioned "whether the teenagers will take over the United States lock, stock, living room, and garage." Sevareid was grumbling about American youth culture, a phenomenon first noticed in the 1920s and with its roots in the lengthening years of education, the role of peer groups, and the consumer tastes of teenagers.

Market research revealed a distinct teen market to be exploited. *Newsweek* noted with awe in 1951 that the aggregate of the $3 weekly spending money of the average teenager was enough to buy 190 million candy bars, 130 million soft drinks, and 230 million sticks of gum. Increasingly, advertisers targeted the young, both to capture their spending money and to exploit their influence on family purchases. Note the changing slogans for Pepsi-Cola: "Twice as much for a nickel" (1935), "Be sociable — have a Pepsi" (1948), "Now it's Pepsi for those who think young" (1960), and "the Pepsi Generation" (1965).

Hollywood movies played a large role in fostering a teenage culture. Young people made up the largest audience for motion pictures, and Hollywood studios learned over the course of the 1950s to cater to them. The success of films such as *The Wild One* (1953), starring Marlon Brando; *Blackboard Jungle* (1955), with Sidney Poitier; and *Rebel Without a Cause* (1955), starring James Dean, convinced movie executives that films directed at teenagers were worthy investments. "What are you rebelling against?" Brando is asked in *The Wild One*. "Whattaya got?" he replies. By the early 1960s, Hollywood had retooled its business model, shifting emphasis away from adults and families to teenagers. The "teenpic" soon included multiple genres: horror, rock 'n' roll, dangerous youth, and beach party, among others.

Rock 'n' Roll | What really defined the youth culture, however, was its music. Rejecting the romantic ballads of the 1940s, teenagers discovered rock 'n' roll, which originated in African American rhythm and blues. The Cleveland disc jockey Alan Freed took the lead in introducing white America to the black-created sound by playing what were called "race" records. "If I could find a white man who had the Negro sound and the Negro feel, I could make a billion dollars," a record company owner is quoted as saying. The performer who fit that bill was Elvis Presley, who rocketed into instant celebrity in 1956 with his hit records "Hound Dog" and "Heartbreak Hotel," covers of songs originally recorded by black artists such as Big Momma Thornton. Between 1953 and 1959, record sales increased from $213 million to $603 million, with rock 'n' roll as the driving force.

Many unhappy adults saw in rock 'n' roll music and teen movies an invitation to race mixing, rebellion, and a more flagrant sexuality. The media featured hundreds of stories on problem teens, and in 1955 a Senate subcommittee conducted a high-profile investigation of juvenile delinquency and its origins in the popular media. Denunciations only bounced off the new youth culture or, if anything, increased its popularity. Both Hollywood and the music industry had learned that youth rebellion sold tickets.

Cultural Dissenters | Youth rebellion was only one aspect of a broader discontent with the sometimes saccharine commercial culture of the 1950s. A great number of artists, jazz musicians, and writers embarked on powerful new experimental projects in a remarkable flowering of intensely personal, introspective art forms. In jazz, for instance, black musicians developed a hard-driving improvisational style known as bebop. Whether the "hot" bebop of saxophonist Charlie Parker or the more subdued "cool" West Coast sound of the trumpeter Miles Davis, postwar jazz was cerebral, intimate, and individualistic. As such, it stood in stark contrast to the commercialized, dance-oriented "swing" bands of the 1930s and 1940s.

Black jazz musicians found eager fans not only in the African American community but also among young white Beats, a group of writers and poets centered in New York and San Francisco who disdained middle-class materialism. In his poem "Howl" (1956), which became a manifesto of the Beat generation, Allen Ginsberg lamented: "I saw the best minds of my generation destroyed by madness, starving hysterical naked, / dragging themselves through the negro streets at dawn looking for an angry fix." In works such as Jack Kerouac's novel *On the Road* (1957), the Beats glorified spontaneity, sexual adventurism, drug use, and spirituality. The Beats were apolitical, but their cultural rebellion would, in the 1960s, inspire a new generation of young rebels disenchanted with both the political and cultural status quo.

▶ How would you explain the contradictions in postwar domesticity?

▶ What were the cultural expectations of men and women in the 1950s? How had they changed from the 1920s? The 1930s?

SUMMARY

We have explored how, at the same time it became mired in the Cold War, the United States entered an unparalleled era of prosperity in which a new middle class came into being. Indeed, the Cold War was one of the engines of prosperity. The postwar economy was marked by the dominance of big corporations and defense spending.

After years of depression and war-induced insecurity, Americans turned inward toward religion, home, and family. Postwar couples married young, had several children, and — if they were white and middle class — raised their children in a climate of suburban comfort and consumerism. The pro-family orientation of the 1950s celebrated traditional gender roles, even though millions of women entered the workforce in those years. Not everyone, however, shared in the postwar prosperity. Postwar cities increasingly became places of last resort for the nation's poor. Black migrants, unlike earlier immigrants, encountered an urban economy that had little use for them. Without opportunity, and faced by pervasive racism, many of them were on their way to becoming an American underclass, even as sparkling new suburbs emerged outside cities to house the new middle class. Many of the smoldering contradictions of the postwar period — Cold War anxiety in the midst of suburban domesticity, tensions in women's lives, economic and racial inequality — helped spur the protest movements of the 1960s.

For additional primary sources from this period, see *Documents for America's History*, Seventh Edition.

For Web sites, images, and documents related to topics and places in this chapter, visit *Make History* at **bedfordstmartins.com/henrettaconcise**.

For Further Exploration

Two engaging introductions to postwar society are Paul Boyer, *Promises to Keep* (1995), and David Halberstam, *The Fifties* (1993). John K. Galbraith, *The Affluent Society* (1958), is an influential contemporary analysis of the postwar economy. Nelson Lichtenstein, *State of the Union: A Century of American Labor* (2002), offers a searching account of the labor-management accord. The best book on consumer culture is Lizabeth Cohen, *A Consumers' Republic: The Politics of Mass Consumption in Postwar America* (2003). Elaine Tyler May, *Homeward Bound* (1988), is the classic introduction to postwar family life. On gender in the 1950s and 1960s, see Susan J. Douglas, *Where the Girls Are: Growing Up Female with the Mass Media* (1994), and James Gilbert, *Men in the Middle: Searching*

TIMELINE

1944
- Bretton Woods economic conference
- World Bank and International Monetary Fund (IMF) founded
- GI Bill (Servicemen's Readjustment Act)

1946
- First edition of Dr. Spock's *Baby and Child Care*

1947
- First Levittown built

1948
- Beginning of network television
- *Shelley v. Kraemer*
- Alfred Kinsey's *Sexual Behavior in the Human Male* published

1949
- Billy Graham revival in Los Angeles

1950
- Treaty of Detroit initiates labor-management accord

1951
- Bracero Program revived
- Mattachine Society founded

1952
- McCarran-Walter Act

1953
- Kinsey's *Sexual Behavior of the Human Female* published

1954
- Ray Kroc buys the first McDonald's franchise

1955
- AFL and CIO merge
- Daughters of Bilitis Founded

1956
- National Interstate and Defense Highways Act
- Elvis Presley's breakthrough records
- Allen Ginsberg's poem "Howl" published

1957
- Peak of postwar baby boom

1965
- *Griswold v. Connecticut*

for Masculinity in the 1950s (2005). A good guide to sex and sexuality in the period is Estelle Freedman and John D'Emilio, *Intimate Matters: A History of Sexuality in America* (1998). A good introduction to the complexity of the homophile movement is Marc Stein, *City of Sisterly and Brotherly Loves: Lesbian and Gay Philadelphia* (2000). For insightful essays on the impact of television, see Karal Ann Marling, *As Seen on TV* (1996). For youth culture, see William Graebner, *Coming of Age in Buffalo* (1990). On the urban crisis, see Thomas J. Sugrue, *The Origins of the Urban Crisis: Race and Inequality in Postwar Detroit* (1996). The Academy of American Poets has a "Brief Guide to the Beat Poets" page (which has links to other "Beat" poetry and prose resources) on their site: **www.poets.org/viewmedia.php/prmMID/5646**.

Test Your Knowledge

For practice quizzes, activities, and other study tools, visit the Online Study Guide at **bedfordstmartins.com/henrettaconcise**.

Walking into Freedom Land: The Civil Rights Movement

1941–1973

The way I see it, the test is on us now, those who believe in nonviolence and brotherhood. . . . We must build a foundation throughout the long hot summers and the long cold winters.

—Septima Clark, 1967

In June 1945, as the war in Europe was coming to a close, Democratic senator James O. Eastland of Mississippi stood on the floor of the U.S. Senate and brashly told his colleagues that "the Negro race is an inferior race." Flailing his arms, his tie askew from vigorous gesturing, Eastland ridiculed black troops. "The Negro soldier was an utter and dismal failure in combat," he said. "They have disgraced the flag of this country."

Eastland's assertions were untrue. Black soldiers had served honorably; many won medals for bravery in combat. All-black units, such as the 761st "Black Panther" Tank Battalion and the famous Tuskegee Airmen, were widely praised by military commanders, including General George Patton. But the fact remained that Eastland, and segregationists who shared his views, were a nearly unassailable force in Congress, able to block civil rights legislation, shape national opinion, and slander African Americans at will.

In the 1940s, two generations after W. E. B. Du Bois penned the indelible statement "The problem of the twentieth century is the problem of the color line," few white Americans believed in racial equality. Racial segregation remained firmly entrenched across the country, South and North. Much of the Deep South, like Eastland's home state of Mississippi, was a "closed society": Black people had no political rights and lived on the margins of white society, impoverished and exploited. Northern cities proved more hospitable to blacks, but schools, neighborhoods, and many businesses remained segregated and unequal in the North as well.

Across the nation, however, winds of change had begun to gather. Between World War II and the 1970s, slowly at first, and then with greater urgency in the 1960s, the civil rights movement swept aside the nationwide system of racial segregation. It could not sweep away racial inequality completely, but the movement constituted a "second Reconstruction" in which African American activism prompted a reshaping of the nation's laws and practices. Civil rights was the paradigmatic social movement of the twentieth

817

century — it provided inspiration for every subsequent social movement. Its model of nonviolent protest and its calls for self-determination inspired the New Left, the rebirth of feminism, the Chicano movement, the gay rights movement, the American Indian movement, and many others. Each of those movements was distinct, with unique goals, but all of them followed in the deep footprints left by black civil rights activists and organizations. Born in multiple communities, by the 1960s the movement was pushing for massive changes in American society and governing institutions.

Most important, the black-led civil rights movement, joined at key moments by Latinos, Asian Americans, and Native Americans, redefined *liberalism* amid titanic social upheaval. In the 1930s, New Deal liberalism had established a welfare state to protect citizens from economic hardship. The civil rights movement forged a new "rights liberalism": the notion that individuals require state protection from discrimination. This version of liberalism focused on identities — such as race or sex — rather than general social welfare, and as such would prove to be both a necessary expansion of the nation's ideals *and* a divisive concept that produced political backlash. Indeed, the quest for racial justice would contribute to a crisis of liberalism itself.

The Emerging Civil Rights Struggle, 1941–1957

As it took shape during World War II and the early Cold War, the battle against racial injustice proceeded along two tracks: at the grass roots and in governing institutions — federal courts, state legislatures, and ultimately the U.S. Congress. Labor unions, churches, and protest organizations such as the Congress of Racial Equality (CORE) inspired hundreds of thousands of ordinary citizens to join the movement. But grassroots struggle was not black citizens' only weapon. They also had the Bill of Rights and the Reconstruction amendments to the Constitution. Civil rights lived in those documents — especially in the Fourteenth Amendment, which guaranteed equal protection under the law to all U.S. citizens, and in the Fifteenth, which guaranteed the right to vote regardless of "race, color, or previous condition of servitude" — but had been ignored or violated by whites for nearly a century. The task was to restore the Constitution's legal force. Neither track — grassroots or legal/legislative — was entirely independent of the other. Together, they were the foundation of the fight for racial equality in the postwar decades.

Life under Jim Crow

Racial segregation and economic exploitation defined the lives of the majority of African Americans in the postwar decades. Numbering 15 million in 1950, African Americans were approximately 10 percent of the U.S. population. In the South, however, they constituted between 30 and 50 percent of the population of several states, such as South Carolina and Mississippi. Segregation, commonly known as Jim Crow (see Chapter 20), prevailed in every aspect of southern life. In southern states, where two-thirds of all African Americans lived in 1950, blacks could not eat in restaurants patronized by whites or use the same waiting rooms at bus stations. All forms of public transportation were rigidly segregated by custom or by law. Public parks and libraries were segregated. Even drinking fountains were labeled "White" and "Colored."

This system of segregation underlay economic and political structures that further marginalized and disempowered black citizens. Virtually no African American could work for city or state government, and the best jobs in the private sector were reserved for whites. Blacks worked "in the back," cleaning, cooking, stocking shelves, and loading trucks for the lowest wages. Rural African Americans labored in a sharecropping system that kept them stuck in poverty, often prevented them from obtaining an education, and offered virtually no avenue of escape. Politically, less than 20 percent of eligible black voters were allowed to vote, the result of poll taxes, literacy tests, intimidation, fraud, and the "white primary" (elections in which only whites could vote). This near-total disenfranchisement gave whites power disproportionate to their numbers — black people were one-third of the residents of Mississippi, South Carolina, and Georgia but had virtually no political influence in those states.

In the North, racial segregation in everyday life was less acute but equally tangible. Northern segregation took the form of a spatial system in which whites increasingly lived in suburbs or on the outskirts of cities, while African Americans were concentrated in downtown neighborhoods. The result was what many called ghettos: all-black districts characterized by high rents, low wages, and inadequate city services. Employment discrimination and lack of adequate training left many African Americans without any means of support. Few jobs other than the most menial were open to African Americans; journalists, accountants, engineers, and other highly educated men from all-black colleges and universities often labored as railroad porters because jobs commensurate with their skills remained for whites only. These conditions produced a self-perpetuating cycle that kept far too many black citizens trapped on the social margins.

It is customary in history textbooks to contrast Jim Crow racial segregation in the South with the relatively more open racial system of the North. To be certain, African Americans found greater freedom in the North and West. They could vote, participate in politics, and, at least after the early 1960s, enjoy equal access to public accommodations. But we err in thinking that racial segregation was *only* a southern problem or that poverty and racial discrimination were not also deeply entrenched in the North and West. In northern cities such as Detroit, Chicago, and Philadelphia, for instance, white home owners in the 1950s used various tactics — from police harassment to thrown bricks, burning crosses, bombs, and mob violence — to keep African Americans from living near them. Moreover, as we saw in Chapter 26, Federal Housing Authority (FHA) and bank redlining excluded African American home buyers from the all-white suburbs emerging around major cities. Racial segregation was a national, not regional, problem.

Origins of the Civil Rights Movement

Since racial discrimination had been part of American life for hundreds of years, why did the civil rights movement arise when it did? After all, the National Association for the Advancement of Colored People (NAACP), founded in 1909, had begun challenging racial segregation in a series of court cases in the 1930s. And other organizations, such as Marcus Garvey's United Negro Improvement Association in the 1920s, had attracted significant popular support. These precedents were important, but a series of factors came together in the middle of the twentieth century to make a broad and unique movement possible.

An important influence was World War II. "The Jewish people and the Negro people both know the meaning of Nordic supremacy," wrote the African American poet Langston Hughes in 1945. In the war against fascism, the Allies sought to discredit racist Nazi ideology. Committed to an antiracist ideology abroad, Americans increasingly condemned all forms of racism, even those at home. The Cold War placed added pressure on U.S. officials. "More and more we are learning how closely our democracy is under observation," President Harry S. Truman commented in 1947. To inspire other nations in the global standoff with the Soviet Union, Truman explained, "we must correct the remaining imperfections in our practice of democracy."

Among the most consequential factors was the growth of the urban black middle class. Historically small, the black middle class experienced robust growth after World War II. Its ranks produced most of the civil rights leaders: ministers, teachers, trade union representatives, attorneys, and other professionals. Churches, for centuries a sanctuary for black Americans, were especially important. Moreover, in the 1960s African American college students — part of the largest expansion of college enrollment in U.S. history — joined the movement, adding new energy and fresh ideas. With access to education, media, and institutions, this new middle class had more resources than ever before. Less dependent on white patronage, and therefore less vulnerable to white retaliation, middle-class African Americans were in a position to lead a movement for change.

Still other influences assisted the movement. Labor leaders were generally more equality-minded than the rank and file, but the United Auto Workers, the United Steel Workers, and the Communication Workers of America, among many other trade unions, were reliable allies at the national level. The new medium of television, too, played a crucial role. When television networks covered early desegregation struggles, such as the 1957 integration of Little Rock High School, Americans across the country saw the violence of white supremacy firsthand. None of these factors alone was decisive. None ensured an easy path. The civil rights movement faced enormous resistance and required dauntless courage and sacrifice from thousands upon thousands of activists for more than three decades. Ultimately, however, the movement changed the nation for the better and improved the lives of millions of Americans.

World War II: The Beginnings

During the war fought "to make the world safe for democracy," America was far from ready to extend full equality to its own black citizens. Black workers faced discrimination in wartime employment, and while more than a million black troops served in World War II, they were placed in segregated units commanded by whites. Both at home and abroad, World War II "immeasurably magnified the Negro's awareness of the disparity between the American profession and practice of democracy," NAACP president Walter White observed.

Executive Order 8802 | On the home front, activists pushed two strategies. First, A. Philip Randolph, whose Brotherhood of Sleeping Car Porters was the most prominent black trade union, called for a march on Washington in early 1941. Randolph planned to bring 100,000 protesters to the nation's capital if African Americans were not given equal opportunity in war jobs — then just beginning to expand with President Franklin Roosevelt's pledge to supply the Allies with materiel. To avoid a divisive protest, FDR issued Executive Order 8802, prohibiting racial discrimination in defense industries, and Randolph agreed to cancel the march. The resulting Fair Employment Practices Commission (FEPC) was weak, but it set an important precedent: federal action. Randolph's efforts showed that white leaders and institutions could be swayed by concerted African American action. It would be a critical lesson for the movement.

The Double V Campaign | A second strategy jumped from the pages of the *Pittsburgh Courier*, one of the foremost African American newspapers of the era. It was the brainchild of an ordinary cafeteria worker from Kansas. In a 1942 letter to the editor, James G. Thompson urged that "colored Americans adopt the double VV for a double victory" — victory over fascism abroad and victory over racism at home. Edgar Rouzeau, editor of the paper's New York office, agreed: "Black America must fight two wars and win in both." Instantly dubbed the Double V Campaign, Thompson's notion, with Rouzeau's backing, spread like wildfire through black communities across the country. African Americans would demonstrate their love of country by fighting the Axis Powers. But they would also demand, peacefully but emphatically, the defeat of racism at home. "The suffering and privation may be great," Rouzeau told his readers, "but the rewards loom even greater."

The Double V efforts met considerable resistance. In war industries, factories periodically shut down in Chicago, Baltimore, Philadelphia, and other cities because of "hate strikes": the refusal of white workers to labor with black workers. Detroit was especially tense. Referring to racial tension, *Life* magazine reported in 1942 that "Detroit is Dynamite. . . . It can either blow up Hitler or blow up America." In 1943, it nearly did the latter. On a hot summer day, whites from the city's ethnic neighborhoods taunted and beat African Americans in a local park. Three days of rioting ensued in

Wartime Workers

During World War II, hundreds of thousands of black migrants left the South, bound for large cities in the North and West. There, they found jobs such as the welding work done by these African American women at the Landers, Frary, and Clark plant in New Britain, Connecticut. Fighting employment discrimination during the war represented one of the earliest phases in the long struggle against racial segregation in the United States. Library of Congress.

which thirty-four people were killed, twenty-five of them black. Federal troops were called in to restore order.

Despite and because of such incidents, a generation was spurred into action during the war years. In New York City, employment discrimination on the city's transit lines prompted one of the first bus boycotts in the nation's history, led in 1941 by Harlem minister Adam Clayton Powell Jr. In Chicago, James Farmer and three other members of the Fellowship of Reconciliation (FOR), a nonviolent peace organization, founded the Congress of Racial Equality (CORE) in 1942. FOR and CORE adopted the philosophy of nonviolent disobedience espoused by Mahatma Gandhi. Meanwhile, after the war, hundreds of thousands of African American veterans used the GI Bill to go to college, trade school, or graduate school, placing them in a position to push against segregation. At the war's end, Powell affirmed that "the black man . . . is ready to throw himself into the struggle to make the dream of America become flesh and blood, bread and butter."

Cold War Civil Rights

Demands for justice persisted in the early years of the Cold War. African American efforts were propelled by symbolic victories to be certain — as when Jackie Robinson broke through the color line in major league baseball by joining the Brooklyn Dodgers in 1947 — but the growing black vote in northern cities proved more decisive. During World War II, more than a million African Americans migrated to northern and western cities, where they joined the Democratic Party of Franklin Roosevelt and the New Deal (Map 27.1). This newfound political leverage awakened northern liberals, who became allies of civil rights advocates. Ultimately, the Cold War produced mixed results, as the nation's commitment to anticommunism opened some avenues for civil rights while closing others.

Civil Rights and the New Deal Coalition | African American leaders had high hopes for President Truman, inheritor of the New Deal coalition. Although not opposed to using racist language himself, Truman supported civil rights on moral grounds. Moreover, he understood the growing importance of the small but often decisive black vote in key northern states such as New York, Illinois, and Michigan. Civil rights activists Randolph and Powell — along with vocal white liberals such as Hubert Humphrey, the mayor of Minneapolis, and members of Americans for Democratic Action (ADA), a liberal organization — pressed Truman to act.

With no support for civil rights in Congress, Truman turned to executive action. In 1946, he appointed the Presidential Committee on Civil Rights, whose 1947 report, "To Secure These Rights," called for robust federal action to ensure equality for African Americans. With the report fresh in his mind, in 1948 Truman issued an executive order desegregating employment in federal agencies and, under pressure from Randolph's Committee Against Jim Crow in Military Service, desegregated the armed forces. Truman then sent a message to Congress asking that all of the report's recommendations — including the abolition of poll taxes and the restoration of the Fair Employment Practices Commission — be made into law. It was the most aggressive, and politically boldest, call for racial equality by the leader of a major political party since Reconstruction.

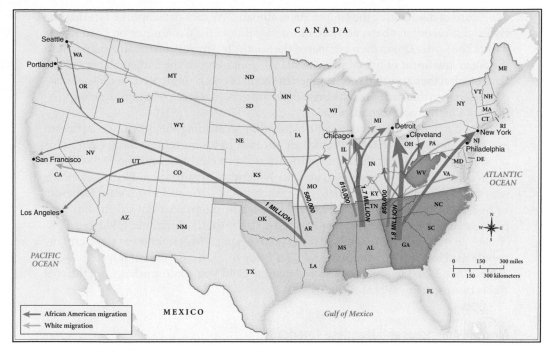

MAP 27.1 Internal Migrations

The migration of African Americans from the South to other regions of the country produced one of the most remarkable demographic shifts of the mid-twentieth century. Between World War I—which marked the start of the Great Migration—and the 1970s, more than 6 million blacks left the South. Where they settled in the North and West, they helped change the politics of entire cities and even states. Seeking black votes, which had become a key to victory in major cities, liberal Democrats and Republicans alike in New York, Illinois, California, and Pennsylvania, for instance, increasingly made civil rights part of their platform. In this way, migration advanced the political cause of black equality.

Truman's boldness was too much for southern Democrats. Under the leadership of Strom Thurmond, governor of South Carolina, white Democrats from the South formed the States' Rights Democratic Party, known popularly as the Dixiecrats, for the 1948 election (see Chapter 25). This brought into focus an internal struggle developing within the Democratic Party and its still-formidable New Deal coalition. Would the civil rights aims of the party's liberal wing alienate southern white Democrats, as well as many suburban whites in the North? It was the first hint of the discord that would eventually divide the Democratic Party in the 1960s.

Race and Anticommunism The Cold War shaped civil rights in both positive and negative terms. In a time of growing fear of Communist expansionism, Truman worried about America's image in the world. He reminded Americans that when whites and blacks "fail to live together in peace," that failure hurt "the cause of democracy itself in the whole world." Indeed, the Soviet Union used American racism as a means of discrediting the United States abroad. "We cannot escape the fact that our civil rights record has been an issue in world politics," the Committee on Civil Rights wrote. The Soviet Union even compared the South's treatment of African Americans to the Nazis' treatment of Jews. International tensions between the United States and the Soviet Union thus appeared to strengthen the hand of civil rights leaders, because Americans needed to demonstrate to the rest of the world that its race relations were improving (see Voices from Abroad, p. 825).

The Cold War strengthened one hand while weakening the other. McCarthyism and the hunt for subversives at home held the civil rights movement back. Civil rights opponents charged that racial integration was "communistic," and the NAACP was banned in many southern states as an "anti-American" organization. Black Americans who spoke favorably of the Soviet Union, such as the actor and singer Paul Robeson, or had been "fellow travelers" in the 1930s, such as the pacifist Bayard Rustin, were persecuted. Robeson, whose career was destroyed by such accusations, told House Un-American Activities Committee (HUAC) interrogators, "My father was a slave, and my people died to build this country, and I am going to . . . have a part of it just like you." The fate of people like Robeson showed that the Cold War could work *against* the civil rights cause just as easily as for it.

Mexican Americans and Japanese Americans

African Americans were the most prominent, but not the only, group in American society to organize against racial injustice in the 1940s. In the Southwest, from Texas to California, Mexican immigrants and Mexican Americans endured a "caste" system not unlike the Jim Crow system in the South. In Texas, for instance, poll taxes kept most Mexican American citizens from voting. Decades of discrimination by employers in agriculture and manufacturing — made possible by the constant supply of cheap labor from across the border — suppressed wages and kept the majority of Mexican Americans barely above poverty. Many lived in *colonias* or barrios, neighborhoods separated from Anglos and often lacking sidewalks, reliable electricity and water, and public services.

Developments within the Mexican American community set the stage for fresh challenges to these conditions in the 1940s. Labor activism in the 1930s and 1940s, especially in Congress of Industrial Organizations (CIO) unions with large numbers of Mexican Americans, improved wages and working conditions in some industries and produced a new generation of leaders. Additionally, more than 400,000 Mexican Americans served in World War II. Having fought for their country, many returned to the United States determined to challenge their second-class citizenship. Indeed, many historians consider World War II to be the seminal event in the emergence of the Mexican American civil rights movement. Additionally, a new Mexican American middle class began to take shape in major cities such as Los Angeles, San Antonio, El Paso, and Chicago, which, like the African American middle class, gave leaders and resources to the cause.

In Texas and California, Mexican Americans created new civil rights organizations in the postwar years. In Corpus Christi, Texas, World War II veterans founded the American GI Forum in 1948 to protest the poor treatment of Mexican American soldiers and veterans. Activists in Los Angeles created the Community Services Organization (CSO)

All the nations and people I had hitherto passed through resembled our own in their manners, customs and language

African Encounters with U.S. Racism
HAILOU WOLDE-GIORGHIS

Hailou Wolde-Giorghis was an Ethiopian student who visited the United States at the invitation of the State Department in the early 1960s.

"Negroes are dirty," say the whites, but in nearly all restaurants I saw Negro waiters and cooks. "They're lazy": I noticed that it is the Negro who does the hardest manual work. They are said to be uncultivated and are therefore denied access to culture. As George Bernard Shaw said, "The haughty American nation makes the Negro shine its shoes, and then demonstrates his physical and mental inferiority by the fact that he is a shoe-cleaner."

But why should this racism exist? Some will tell you that it's because the white man is ignorant of the Negro: he doesn't know him and has never tried to understand him. Why should the master bother to know his Negro cook? . . . The last and perhaps most important explanation of racism relates to the economy: the white worker is afraid of the competition represented by the Negro. The latter is offered all the degrading work, such as shining shoes and working as porters (at the airport in New York, for instance, I saw only one white porter). . . .

When speaking with an ex-racist or quite simply an honest Southerner, I noticed that when I spoke to him of certain injustices or of the white man's exploitation of the Negro, he would immediately ask me about Communism. In the South, for example, all anti-racist demonstrators are accused of being Communist. Therefore, in fighting the Negro the Southerner must also fight this twentieth-century "sickness." Nor is the United Nations exempted; it is "Communist," and if it is successfully to carry out its mission

it must first be purged of all Negro nations and all eastern countries. . . .

What is known as integration in the South is the ability of a Negro to enter a shop and buy a record, or the fact that, of ten thousand students enrolled in a university, two of them are Negroes. "A miracle!" they cry. Real integration, however, does not exist, not even in the North, and by real integration I mean interracial communication, complete equality in the strict sense of the word. Still another example drawn from the South: the manager of a television studio told me in frigid terms that he would not hire Negroes; there would be a scandal and all his sponsors would protest.

One of the consequences of this discrimination is obviously the Negro's economic situation; with the exception of a few wealthy Negroes in show business or sports, or businessmen (in Atlanta, for example, some of the most important banks are owned by Negroes), most belong to the lower class. I could talk here a little about the southern slums, which I personally saw, where thousands of Negroes are housed in quasi-military camps. I was told at great length — the way one profusely excuses oneself — that there were whites living in the same conditions. That is very possible, but I did not see any.

SOURCE: Hailou Wolde-Giorghis, "My Encounters with Racism in the United States," in *Views of America*, eds. Alan F. Westin et al. (New York: Harcourt, Brace, and World, 1966), 228–231.

the same year. Both groups arose to address specific local injustices (such as the segregation of military cemeteries), but they quickly broadened their scope to encompass political and economic justice for the larger community. Among the first young activists to work for the CSO were Cesar Chavez and Dolores Huerta, who would later found the United Farm Workers (UFW) and inspire the Chicano movement of the 1960s.

Activists also pushed for legal change. In 1947, five Mexican American fathers in California sued a local school district for placing their children in separate "Mexican" schools. The case, *Mendez v. Westminster School District*, never made it to the U.S. Supreme Court. But the Ninth Circuit Court ruled such segregation unconstitutional, laying the legal groundwork for broader challenges to racial inequality. Among those filing briefs in the case was the NAACP's Thurgood Marshall, who was then developing the legal strategy to strike at racial segregation against African Americans in the South. In another significant legal victory, the Supreme Court ruled in 1954 — just two weeks before the landmark *Brown v. Board of Education* decision — that Mexican Americans constituted a "distinct class" that could claim protection from discrimination.

Also on the West Coast, Japanese Americans accelerated their legal challenge to discrimination. Undeterred by rulings in the *Hirabayashi* (1943) and *Korematsu* (1944) cases upholding wartime imprisonment (see Chapter 24), the Japanese American Citizens League (JACL) filed lawsuits in the late 1940s to regain property lost during the war. The JACL also challenged the constitutionality of California's Alien Land Law, which prohibited Japanese immigrants from owning land, and successfully lobbied Congress to enable those same immigrants to become citizens — a right they were denied for fifty years. These efforts by Mexican and Japanese Americans enlarged the scope of civil rights beyond demands by African Americans and laid the foundation for a broader notion of racial equality in the postwar years.

The Legal Strategy and *Brown v. Board of Education*

With civil rights legislation blocked in Congress by southern Democrats throughout the 1950s, activists looked to the federal courts for a breakthrough. In the late 1930s, NAACP lawyers Thurgood Marshall, Charles Hamilton Houston, and William Hastie had begun preparing the legal ground in a series of cases challenging racial discrimination. The key was prodding the U.S. Supreme Court to use the Fourteenth Amendment's "equal protection" clause to overturn its 1898 ruling in *Plessy v. Ferguson*, which upheld racial segregation under the "separate but equal" doctrine.

Thurgood Marshall | Marshall was the great-grandson of slaves. Of modest origins, his parents instilled in him a faith in law and the Constitution. After his 1930 graduation from Lincoln University, a prestigious African American institution near Philadelphia, Marshall applied to the University of Maryland Law School. Denied admission because the school did not accept blacks, he enrolled at all-black Howard University. There Marshall met Houston, a law school dean, and the two forged a friendship and intellectual partnership that would change the face of American legal history. Marshall, with Houston's help, would argue most of the NAACP's landmark cases. In the late 1960s, President Johnson appointed Marshall to the Supreme Court — the first African American to have that honor.

Marshall, Houston, Hastie, and six other attorneys filed suit after suit, deliberately selecting each one from dozens of possibilities. The strategy was slow and time-consuming, but progress came. In 1936, Marshall and Hamilton won a state case that forced the University of Maryland Law School to admit qualified African Americans — a ruling of obvious significance to Marshall. Eight years later, in *Smith v. Allwright* (1944), Marshall convinced the U.S. Supreme Court that all-white primaries were unconstitutional. In 1950, with Marshall once again arguing the case, the Supreme Court ruled in *McLaurin v. Oklahoma* that universities could not segregate black students from others on campus. None of these cases produced swift or immediate changes in the daily lives of most African Americans, but they confirmed that civil rights attorneys were on the right track.

Brown v. Board of Education | The NAACP's legal strategy achieved its ultimate validation in a case involving Linda Brown, a black pupil in Topeka, Kansas, who had been forced to attend a distant segregated school rather than the nearby white elementary school. In *Brown v. Board of Education of Topeka*, Marshall argued that such segregation was unconstitutional because it denied Linda Brown the

School Desegregation in Little Rock, Arkansas
Less well known than the crisis at Little Rock's Central High School the same year, the circumstances at North Little Rock were nonetheless strikingly similar: white resistance to the enrollment of a handful of black students. In this photograph, white students block the doors of North Little Rock High School, preventing six African American students from entering on September 9, 1957. This photograph is noteworthy because it shows a striking new feature of southern racial politics: the presence of film and television cameras that broadcast these images to the nation and the world. AP Images.

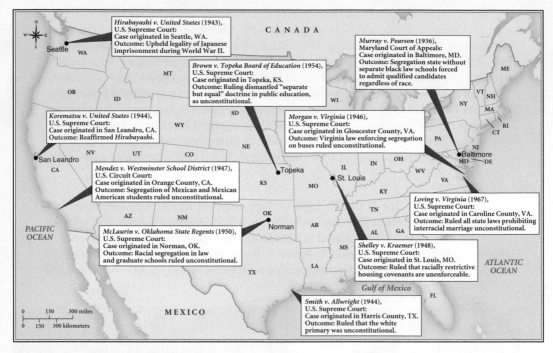

MAP 27.2 Desegregation Court Cases

Desegregation court battles were not limited to the South. Note the important California cases regarding Mexican Americans and Japanese Americans. Two seminal decisions, the 1948 housing decision in *Shelley v. Kraemer* and the 1954 school decision in *Brown v. Board of Education*, originated in Missouri and Kansas, respectively. This map helps show that racial segregation and discrimination were a national, not simply a southern, problem.

"equal protection of the laws" guaranteed by the Fourteenth Amendment (Map 27.2). In a unanimous decision on May 17, 1954, the Supreme Court agreed, overturning the "separate but equal" doctrine at last. Speaking for the Court, the new chief justice, Earl Warren, wrote: "We conclude that in the field of public education the doctrine of 'separate but equal' has no place. Separate educational facilities are inherently unequal." In an implementing 1955 decision known as *Brown II*, the Court declared simply that integration should proceed "with all deliberate speed."

In the South, however, Virginia senator Harry F. Byrd issued a call for "massive resistance." Calling May 17 "Black Monday," the Mississippi segregationist Tom P. Brady invoked the language of the Cold War to discredit the decision, assailing the "totalitarian government" that had rendered the decision in the name of "socialism and communism." That year, half a million southerners joined White Citizens' Councils dedicated to blocking school integration. Some whites revived the old tactics of violence and intimidation, swelling the ranks of the Ku Klux Klan to levels not seen since the 1920s. The "Southern Manifesto," signed in 1956 by 101 members of Congress, denounced the *Brown* decision as "a clear abuse of judicial power" and encouraged local officials to defy it. The white South had declared all-out war on *Brown*.

Enforcement of the Supreme Court's decision was complicated further by Dwight Eisenhower's presence in the White House — the president was no champion of civil rights. Eisenhower accepted the *Brown* decision as the law of the land, but he thought it a mistake. Ike was especially unhappy about the prospect of committing federal power to enforce the decision. A crisis in Little Rock, Arkansas, finally forced his hand. In September 1957, when nine black students attempted to enroll at the all-white Central High School, Governor Orval Faubus called out the National Guard to bar them. Angry white mobs appeared daily to taunt the students, chanting "Go back to the jungle." As the vicious scenes played out on television night after night, Eisenhower finally acted. He sent 1,000 federal troops to Little Rock and nationalized the Arkansas National Guard, ordering them to protect the black students. Eisenhower thus became the first president since Reconstruction to use federal troops to enforce the rights of African Americans. But Little Rock also showed that southern officials had more loyalty to local custom than to the law — a repeated problem in the post-*Brown* era.

▶ How did the NAACP go about developing a legal strategy to attack racial segregation?

▶ To what extent did the Supreme Court's decision in *Brown* bring about the change advocates had hoped for?

Forging a Protest Movement, 1955–1965

Declaring racial segregation integral to the South's "habits, traditions, and way of life," the Southern Manifesto signaled that many whites would not accept African American equality readily. As Americans had witnessed in Little Rock, the unwillingness of local officials to enforce *Brown* could render the decision invalid in practice. If legal victories would not be enough, citizens themselves, black and white, would have to take to the streets and demand justice. Following the *Brown* decision they did just that, forging a protest movement unique in the history of the United States.

Nonviolent Civil Disobedience

Brown had been the law of the land for barely a year when a single act of violence struck at the heart of black America. A fourteen-year-old African American from the South Side of Chicago, Emmett Till, was visiting relatives in Mississippi in the summer of 1955. Seen talking to a white woman in a grocery store ("Bye, baby," he reportedly said), Till was tortured and murdered under cover of night. His mutilated body was found at the bottom of a river, tied with barbed wire to a heavy steel cotton gin fan. Photos of Till's body in *Jet* magazine brought national attention to the heinous crime.

Two white men were arrested for Till's murder. During the trial, followed closely in African American communities across the country, the lone witness to Till's kidnapping — his uncle, Mose Wright — identified both killers. Feeling "the blood boil in hundreds of white people as they sat glaring in the courtroom," Wright said, "it was the first time in my life I had the courage to accuse a white man of a crime." Despite Wright's eyewitness testimony, the all-white jury found the defendants innocent. Afterward, *Look* magazine paid the two men $4,000 for their story. Safe from prosecution, they admitted to the murder. This miscarriage of justice—extreme even for the southern legal system—galvanized an entire generation of African Americans; no one who lived through the Till case ever forgot it.

Montgomery Buss Boycott In the wake of the Till case, civil rights advocates needed some good news. They received it three months later, as Southern black leaders embraced an old tactic put to new ends: nonviolent protest. On December 1, 1955, Rosa Parks, a seamstress in Montgomery, Alabama, refused to give up her seat on a bus to a white man. She was arrested and charged with violating a local segregation ordinance. Parks's act was not the spur-of-the-moment decision that it seemed: A woman of sterling reputation and a longtime NAACP member, she had been contemplating such an act for some time. Middle-aged and unassuming, Rosa Parks fit the bill perfectly for the NAACP's challenge against segregated buses.

Once the die was cast, the black community turned for leadership to the Reverend Martin Luther King Jr., the recently appointed pastor of Montgomery's Dexter Street Baptist Church. The son of a prominent Atlanta minister, King embraced the teachings of Mahatma Gandhi. Working closely, but behind the scenes, with Bayard Rustin, King studied nonviolent philosophy, which Rustin and others in the Fellowship of Reconciliation had first used in the 1940s. After Rosa Parks's arrest, King endorsed a plan proposed by a local black women's organization to boycott Montgomery's bus system. They were inspired by similar boycotts that had taken place in Harlem, New York, in 1941 and Baton Rouge, Louisiana, in 1953.

For the next 381 days, Montgomery's African Americans formed car pools or walked to work. "Darling, it's empty!" Coretta Scott King exclaimed to her husband as a bus normally filled with black riders rolled by their living room window on the first day of the boycott. The transit company neared bankruptcy, and downtown stores complained about the loss of business. But only after the Supreme Court ruled in November 1956 that bus segregation was unconstitutional did the city of Montgomery finally comply. "My feets is tired, but my soul is rested," said one woman boycotter.

The Montgomery bus boycott catapulted King to national prominence. In 1957, along with the Reverend Ralph Abernathy, he founded the Atlanta-based Southern Christian Leadership Conference (SCLC). The black church, long the center of African American social and cultural life, now lent its moral and organizational strength to the civil rights movement. Black churchwomen were a tower of strength, transferring the skills they had honed during years of church work to the fight for civil rights. The SCLC quickly joined the NAACP at the leading edge of the movement for racial justice.

Greensboro Sit-Ins The battle for civil rights entered a new phase in Greensboro, North Carolina, on February 1, 1960, when four black college students took seats at the whites-only lunch counter at the local Woolworth's five-and-dime store. This simple act was entirely the brainchild of the four students, who had discussed it in their dorm rooms over several preceding nights. A New York–based spokesman for Woolworth's said the chain would "abide by local custom," which meant refusing to serve African Americans at the lunch counter. The students were determined to "sit in" until they were served. For three weeks, they took turns sitting at the counters, quietly eating, doing homework, or reading. Taunted by groups of whites, pelted with food and other debris, the black students — often occupying more than sixty of the sixty-six seats — held strong. "I felt as though I had gained my manhood," recalled Franklin McCain, one of the "Greensboro Four." Although many were arrested, the tactic worked: The Woolworth's lunch counter was desegregated, and sit-ins quickly spread to other southern cities (see American Voices, p. 832).

Ella Baker and SNCC | Inspired by the developments in Greensboro and elsewhere, Ella Baker, an administrator with the SCLC, helped organize the Student Nonviolent Coordinating Committee (SNCC, pronounced "Snick") to facilitate student sit-ins. Rolling like a great wave across the Upper South, from North Carolina into Virginia, Maryland, and Tennessee, by the end of the year sit-ins had been launched in 126 cities. More than 50,000 people participated, and 3,600 were jailed. The sit-ins drew African American college students into the movement in significant numbers for the first time. Northern students formed solidarity committees and raised money for bail. SNCC quickly emerged as the most important student protest organization in the country and inspired a generation of students on college campuses everywhere.

Baker took a special interest in these students, because she found them receptive to her notion of participatory democracy. The granddaughter of slaves, Baker had moved to Harlem in the 1930s, where she worked for New Deal agencies and then the NAACP. She believed in nurturing leaders from the grass roots, encouraging ordinary people to

Ella Baker

Born in Virginia and educated at Shaw University in Raleigh, North Carolina, Ella Baker was one of the foremost theorists of grassroots, participatory democracy in the United States. Active all her life in the black freedom movement, in 1960 Baker cofounded the Student Nonviolent Coordinating Committee (SNCC). Her advocacy of leadership by ordinary, non-elite people often led her to disagree with the top-down movement strategy of Martin Luther King Jr. and other ministers of the Southern Christian Leadership Conference (SCLC). AP Images.

Thus I have given you, I think, the Substance of the Arguments on both sides of that great and important Question

Desegregating Lunch Counters FRANKLIN MCCAIN

Among the many challenges historians face is figuring out the processes by which long-oppressed ordinary people finally rise up and demand justice. During the 1950s, a liberating process was quietly under way among southern blacks, bursting forth dramatically in the Montgomery bus boycott of 1955 and then, by the end of the decade, emerging across the South. Franklin McCain was one of the four African American students at North Carolina A&T College in Greensboro, North Carolina, who sat down at the Woolworth's lunch counter on February 1, 1960, setting off a wave of student sit-ins that rocked the South and helped initiate a national civil rights movement.

The planning process was on a Sunday night, I remember it quite well. I think it was Joseph who said, "It's time that we take some action now. We've been getting together, and we've been, up to this point, still like most people we've talked about for the past few weeks or so—that is, people who talk a lot but, in fact, make very little action." After selecting the technique, then we said, "Let's go down and just ask for service." It certainly wasn't titled a "sit-in" or "sit-down" at that time. "Let's just go down to Woolworth's tomorrow and ask for service, and the tactic is going to be simply this: we'll just stay there."

. . . Once getting there . . . we did make purchases of school supplies and took the patience and time to get receipts for our purchases, and Joseph and myself went over to the counter and asked to be served coffee and doughnuts. As anticipated, the reply was, "I'm sorry, we don't serve you here." And of course we said, "We just beg to disagree with you. We've in fact already been served." . . . The attendant or waitress was a little bit dumbfounded, just didn't know what to say under circumstances like that. . . .

If it's possible to know what it means to have your soul cleansed—I felt pretty clean at that time. I probably felt better on that day than I've ever felt in my life. Seems like a lot of feelings of guilt or what-have-you suddenly left me, and I felt as though I had gained my manhood. . . . Not Franklin McCain only as an individual, but I felt as though the manhood of a number of other black persons had been restored and had gotten some respect from just that one day.

The movement started out as a movement of nonviolence and a Christian movement. . . . It was a movement that was seeking justice more than anything else and not a movement to start a war. . . . We knew that probably the most powerful and potent weapon that people have literally no defense for is love, kindness. That is, whip the enemy with something that he doesn't understand. . . . The individual who had probably the most influence on us was Gandhi. . . . Yes, Martin Luther King's name was well-known when the sit-in movement was in effect, but . . . no, he was not the individual we had uppermost in mind when we started the sit-in movement.

SOURCE: Clayborne Carson et al., eds., *The Eyes on the Prize Civil Rights Reader* (New York: Viking, 1991), 114–116.

stand up for their rights rather than to depend on charismatic figureheads. "My theory is, strong people don't need strong leaders," she once said. Nonetheless, Baker nurtured a generation of young activists in SNCC, including Stokely Carmichael, Anne Moody, John Lewis, and Diane Nash, who went on to become some of the most important civil rights leaders in the United States. Decentralized, nonhierarchical, and based on grass-roots input and involvement, participatory democracy inspired many of the most vocal social movements of the 1960s.

Freedom Rides | Emboldened by SNCC's sit-in tactics, in 1961 the Congress of Racial Equality (CORE) organized a series of what were called Freedom Rides on interstate bus lines throughout the South. The aim was to call attention to blatant violations of recent Supreme Court rulings against segregation in interstate commerce. The activists who signed on — mostly young, both black and white — knew that they were taking their lives in their hands. They found courage in song, as civil rights activists had begun to do across the country, with lyrics such as "I'm taking a ride on the Greyhound bus line. . . . Hallelujah, I'm traveling down freedom's main line!"

Courage they needed. Club-wielding Klansmen attacked the buses when they stopped in small towns. Outside Anniston, Alabama, one bus was fire-bombed; the Freedom Riders escaped only moments before it exploded. Some riders were then brutally beaten. Freedom Riders and news reporters were also viciously attacked by Klansmen in Birmingham and Montgomery. Despite the violence, state authorities refused to intervene. "I cannot guarantee protection for this bunch of rabble rousers," declared Governor John Patterson of Alabama.

Once again, local officials' refusal to enforce the law left the fate of the Freedom Riders in Washington's hands. The new president, John F. Kennedy, was cautious about civil rights. Despite a campaign commitment, he failed to deliver on a civil rights bill. Elected by a thin margin, Kennedy believed that he could ill afford to lose the support of powerful southern Senators. But civil rights was unlike other domestic issues. Its fate was going to be decided not in the halls of Congress, but on the streets of southern cities. Although President Kennedy discouraged the Freedom Rides, beatings shown on the nightly news forced Attorney General Robert Kennedy to dispatch federal marshals. Civil rights activists thus learned the value of nonviolent protest that provoked violent white resistance.

The victories so far had been limited, but the groundwork had been laid for a civil rights offensive that would transform the nation. The NAACP's legal strategy had been followed closely by the emergence of a major protest movement. And now civil rights leaders focused their gaze on Congress.

Legislating Civil Rights, 1963–1965

The first civil rights law in the nation's history came in 1875 during Reconstruction (see Chapter 15). Its provisions had long been ignored, and for nearly ninety years new civil rights legislation was blocked or filibustered by southern Democrats in Congress. Only a weak, largely symbolic act was passed in 1957 during the Eisenhower administration. But by the early 1960s, with legal precedents in their favor and nonviolent protest awakening the nation, civil rights leaders believed the time had come for a serious civil rights bill. The challenge was getting one through a still-reluctant Congress.

The Battle for Birmingham | The road to such a bill began when Martin Luther King Jr. called for demonstrations in "the most segregated city in the United States": Birmingham, Alabama. King and the SCLC needed a concrete victory in Birmingham to validate their strategy of nonviolent protest. In May 1963, thousands of black marchers tried to picket Birmingham's department stores. Eugene "Bull" Connor, the city's public safety commissioner, ordered the city's police troops to meet the marchers with violent force: snarling dogs, electric cattle prods, and high-pressure fire hoses. Television cameras captured the scene for the evening news.

While serving a jail sentence for leading the march, King, scribbling in pencil on any paper he could find, composed one of the classic documents of nonviolent civil disobedience: "Letter from Birmingham Jail." "Why direct action?" King asked. "There is a type of constructive, nonviolent tension that is necessary for growth." The civil rights move-

The Battle of Birmingham

One of the hardest-fought desegregation struggles of the early 1960s took place in April and May of 1963, in Birmingham, Alabama. In response to the daily rallies and peaceful protests, authorities cracked down, arresting hundreds. They also employed tactics such as those shown here, turning fire hoses on young, nonviolent student demonstrators, and using police dogs to intimidate peaceful marchers. These protests, led by Martin Luther King Jr. and broadcast on television news, prompted President Kennedy to introduce a civil rights bill in Congress in June 1963. © Bob Adelman/Corbis.

ment sought, he continued, "to create such a crisis and establish such a creative tension." Grounding his actions in equal parts Christian brotherhood and democratic liberalism, King argued that Americans confronted a moral choice: They could "preserve the evil system of segregation" or take the side of "those great wells of democracy . . . the Constitution and the Declaration of Independence."

Outraged by the brutality in Birmingham and embarrassed by King's imprisonment for leading a nonviolent march, President Kennedy decided that it was time to act. On June 11, 1963, after newly elected Alabama governor George Wallace barred two black students from the state university, Kennedy denounced racism on national television and promised a new civil rights bill. Many black leaders felt Kennedy's action was long overdue, but they nonetheless hailed this "Second Emancipation Proclamation." That night, Medgar Evers, president of the Mississippi chapter of the NAACP, was shot in the back in his driveway in Jackson by a white supremacist. Evers's martyrdom became a spur to further action.

The March on Washington and the Civil Rights Act To marshal support for Kennedy's bill, civil rights leaders adopted a tactic that A. Philip Randolph had first advanced in 1941: a massive demonstration in Washington. Under the leadership of Randolph and Bayard Rustin, thousands of volunteers across the country coordinated carpools, "freedom buses," and "freedom trains," and on August 28, 1963, delivered a quarter of a million people to the Lincoln Memorial for the officially named March on Washington for Jobs and Freedom. "We are the advance guard of a massive moral revolution for jobs and freedom," Randolph said to open the program.

Although other people primarily did the planning, Martin Luther King Jr. was the public face of the march. It was King's dramatic "I Have a Dream" speech, beginning with his admonition that too many black people lived "on a lonely island of poverty" and ending with the exclamation from a traditional black spiritual — "Free at last! Free at last! Thank God almighty, we are free at last!" — that captured the nation's imagination. The sight of 250,000 blacks and whites marching solemnly together marked the high point of the civil rights movement and confirmed King's position as the leading spokesperson for the cause.

To have any chance of getting the civil rights bill through Congress, King, Randolph, and Rustin knew they had to sustain this broad coalition of blacks and whites. They could afford to alienate no one. Reflecting a younger, more militant set of activists, however, SNCC member John Lewis had prepared a more provocative speech for that afternoon. Lewis wrote, "The time will come when we will not confine our marching to Washington. We will march through the South, through the Heart of Dixie, the way Sherman did." Signaling a growing restlessness among black youth, Lewis warned: "We shall fragment the South into a thousand pieces and put them back together again in the image of democracy." Fearing the speech would alienate white supporters, Rustin and others implored Lewis to tone down his rhetoric. With only minutes to spare before he stepped up to the podium, Lewis agreed. He delivered a more conciliatory speech, but his conflict with march organizers signaled an emerging rift in the movement.

Although the March on Washington galvanized public opinion, it changed few congressional votes. Southern senators continued to block Kennedy's legislation. Georgia senator Richard Russell, a leader of the opposition, refused to support any bill that would "bring about social equality and intermingling and amalgamation of the races." Then, suddenly, tragedies piled up, one on another. In September, white supremacists bombed a Baptist church in Birmingham, killing four black girls in Sunday school. Less than two months later, Kennedy himself lay dead, the victim of assassination.

On assuming the presidency, Lyndon Johnson made passing the civil rights bill a priority. A southerner and former Senate majority leader, Johnson was renowned for his fierce persuasive style and tough political bargaining. Using equal parts moral leverage, the memory of the slain JFK, and his own brand of hardball politics, Johnson overcame the filibuster. In June 1964, Congress approved the most far-reaching civil rights law since Reconstruction. The keystone of the Civil Rights Act, Title VII, outlawed discrimination in employment on the basis of race, religion, national origin, and sex. Another section guaranteed equal access to public accommodations and schools. The law granted new enforcement powers to the U.S. attorney general and established the Equal Employment Opportunity Commission to implement the prohibition against job discrimination.

Freedom Summer | The Civil Rights Act was a law with real teeth, but it left untouched the obstacles to black voting rights. So protesters went back into the streets. In 1964, in the period that came to be known as Freedom Summer, black organizations mounted a major campaign in Mississippi. The effort drew several thousand volunteers from across the country, including nearly one thousand white college students from the North. Led by the charismatic SNCC activist Robert Moses, the four major civil rights organizations (SNCC, CORE, NAACP, and SCLC) spread out across the state. They established freedom schools for black children and conducted a major voter registration drive. So determined was the opposition that only about twelve hundred black voters were registered that summer, at a cost of four murdered civil rights workers and thirty-seven black churches bombed or burned.

The murders strengthened the resolve of the Mississippi Freedom Democratic Party (MFDP), which had been founded during Freedom Summer. Banned from the "whites only" Mississippi Democratic Party, MFDP leaders were determined to attend the 1964 Democratic National Convention in Atlantic City, New Jersey, as the legitimate representatives of their state. Inspired by Fannie Lou Hamer, a former sharecropper turned civil rights activist, the MFDP challenged the most powerful figures in the Democratic Party, including Lyndon Johnson, the Democrats' presidential nominee. "Is this America?" Hamer asked bluntly. When party officials seated the white Mississippi delegation and refused to recognize the MFDP, civil rights activists left, convinced that the Democratic Party would not change. Demoralized, Moses told television reporters: "I will have nothing to do with the political system any longer."

Selma and the Voting Rights Act | Martin Luther King Jr. and the SCLC did not share Moses's skepticism. They believed that another confrontation with southern injustice could provoke further congressional action. In March 1965, James Bevel of the SCLC called for a march from Selma, Alabama, to the state capital, Montgomery, to protest the murder of a voting-rights activist. As soon as the six hundred marchers left Selma, crossing over the Edmund Pettus Bridge, mounted state troopers attacked them with tear gas and clubs. The scene was shown on national television that

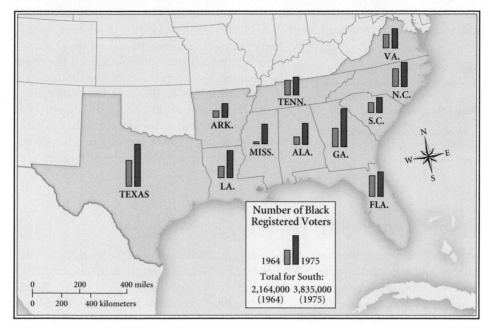

MAP 27.3 Black Voter Registration in the South, 1964 and 1975

After passage of the Voting Rights Act of 1965, black registration in the South increased dramatically. The bars on the map show the number of blacks registered in 1964, before the act was passed, and in 1975, after it had been in effect for ten years. States in the Deep South, such as Mississippi, Alabama, and Georgia, had the biggest increases.

night, and the day became known as Bloody Sunday. Calling the episode "an American tragedy," President Johnson went back to Congress.

The Voting Rights Act, which passed on August 6, 1965, outlawed the literacy tests and other devices that prevented blacks from registering to vote, and authorized the attorney general to send federal examiners to register voters in any county where registration was less than 50 percent. Together with the Twenty-fourth Amendment (1964), which outlawed the poll tax in federal elections, the Voting Rights Act enabled millions of blacks to vote for the first time since the Reconstruction era.

In the South, the results were stunning. In 1960, only 20 percent of blacks had been registered to vote; by 1971, registration reached 62 percent (Map 27.3). Moreover, across the nation the number of black elected officials began to climb, quadrupling from 1,400 to 4,900 between 1970 and 1980 and doubling again by the early 1990s. Most of those elected held local offices — from sheriff to county commissioner — but nonetheless embodied a shift in political representation nearly unimaginable a generation earlier. As Hartman Turnbow, a Mississippi farmer who risked his life to register in 1964, later declared, "It won't never go back where it was."

Something else would never go back either: the liberal New Deal coalition. By the second half of the 1960s, the liberal wing of the Democratic Party had won its battle with the conservative, segregationist wing. Democrats had embraced the civil rights movement and made African American equality a cornerstone of a new "rights" liberalism.

But over the next generation, between the 1960s and the 1980s, southern whites and many conservative northern whites would respond by switching to the Republican Party. Strom Thurmond, the segregationist senator from South Carolina, symbolically led the revolt by renouncing the Democrats and becoming a Republican in 1964. The New Deal coalition — which had joined working-class whites, northern African Americans, urban professionals, and white southern segregationists together in a fragile political alliance since the 1930s — was beginning to crumble.

▶ What factors explain the rise of the civil rights protest movement? Why was nonviolent civil disobedience the chosen tactic?

▶ In what ways did white resistance hinder the movement? In what ways did it help?

Beyond Civil Rights, 1966–1973

Activists had long known that Supreme Court decisions and new laws do not automatically produce changes in society. But in the mid-1960s, civil rights advocates confronted a more profound issue: Perhaps even *protests* were not enough. In 1965, Bayard Rustin wrote of the need to move "from protest to politics" in order to build institutional black power. Some black leaders, such as the young SNCC activists Stokely Carmichael, Frances Beal, and John Lewis, grew frustrated with the slow pace of reform and the stubborn resistance of whites. Still others believed that addressing black poverty and economic disadvantage remained the most important objective. Neither new laws nor long marches appeared capable of meeting these varied and complex challenges.

The conviction that civil rights alone were incapable of guaranteeing equality took hold in many minority communities in this period. African Americans were joined by Mexican Americans, Puerto Ricans, and American Indians. They came at the problem of inequality from different perspectives, but each group asked a similar question: As crucial as legal equality was, how much did it matter if most people of color remained in or close to poverty, if white society still regarded nonwhites as inferior, and if the major social and political institutions in the country were run by whites? Black leaders and representatives of other nonwhite communities increasingly asked themselves these questions as they searched for ways to build on the significant achievements of the civil rights decade of 1954–1965.

Black Nationalism

Seeking answers to these questions led many African Americans to embrace black nationalism. The philosophy of black nationalism signified many things in the 1960s. It could mean anything from pride in one's community to total separatism, from building African American–owned businesses to wearing dashikis in honor of African traditions. Historically, nationalism had emphasized the differences between blacks and whites as well as black people's power (and right) to shape their own destiny. In the late nineteenth century, nationalists founded the Back to Africa movement, and in the 1920s the nationalist Marcus Garvey inspired African Americans to take pride in their racial heritage (see Chapter 22).

In the early 1960s, the leading exponent of black nationalism was the Nation of Islam, which fused a rejection of Christianity with a strong philosophy of self-improvement. Black Muslims, as they were known, adhered to a strict code of personal behavior; men were recognizable by their dark suits, white shirts, and ties, women by their long dresses and head coverings. Black Muslims preached an apocalyptic brand of Islam, anticipating the day when Allah would banish the white "devils" and give the black nation justice. Although its full converts numbered only about ten thousand, the Nation of Islam had a wide popular following among African Americans in northern cities.

Malcolm X | The most charismatic Black Muslim was Malcolm X (the X stood for his African family name, lost under slavery). A spellbinding speaker, Malcolm preached a philosophy of militant separatism, although he advocated violence only for self-defense. Hostile to mainstream civil rights organizations, he caustically referred to the 1963 March on Washington as the "Farce on Washington." Malcolm said plainly, "I believe in the brotherhood of man, all men, but I don't believe in brotherhood with anybody who doesn't want brotherhood with me." Malcolm had little interest in changing the minds of hostile whites. Strengthening the black community, he believed, represented a surer path to freedom and equality.

In 1964, after a power struggle with founder Elijah Muhammad, Malcolm broke with the Nation of Islam. While he remained a black nationalist, he moderated his antiwhite views and began to talk of a class struggle uniting poor whites and blacks. Following an inspiring trip to the Middle East, where he saw Muslims of all races worshipping together, Malcolm formed the Organization of Afro-American Unity to promote black pride and to work with traditional civil rights groups. But he got no further. On February 21, 1965, Malcolm X was assassinated while delivering a speech in Harlem. Three Black Muslims were later convicted of his murder.

Black Power | A more secular brand of black nationalism emerged in 1966 when SNCC and CORE activists, following the lead of Stokely Carmichael, began to call for black self-reliance under the banner of Black Power. Advocates of Black Power asked fundamental questions: If alliances with whites were necessary to achieve racial justice, as King believed they were, did that make African Americans dependent on the good intentions of whites? If so, could black people trust those good intentions in the long run? Increasingly, those inclined toward Black Power believed that African Americans should build economic and political power in their own communities. Such power would translate into a less dependent relationship with white America. "For once," Carmichael wrote, "black people are going to use the words they want to use — not the words whites want to hear."

Spurred by the Black Power slogan, African American activists turned their attention to the poverty and social injustice faced by so many black people. President Johnson had declared the War on Poverty, and black organizers joined, setting up day-care centers, running community job training programs, and working to improve housing and health care in the inner cities. In major cities such as Philadelphia, New York, Chicago, and Pittsburgh, activists sought to open jobs in police and fire departments and in construction and transportation to black workers, who had been excluded from these occupations for decades. Others worked to end police harassment — a major problem in urban black communities — and to help black entrepreneurs to receive small-business loans. CORE leader Floyd McKissick explained, "Black Power is not Black Supremacy; it is a united Black Voice reflecting racial pride."

The attention to racial pride led some African Americans to reject white society and to pursue more authentic cultural forms. In addition to focusing on economic disadvantage, Black Power emphasized black pride and self-determination. Blacks subscribing to these beliefs wore African clothing, chose natural hairstyles, and awakened an interest in black history, art, and literature. The Black Arts movement thrived, and musical tastes shifted from the crossover sounds of Motown to the soul music of Philadelphia, Memphis, and Chicago.

Black Panther Party | One of the most radical nationalist groups was the Black Panther Party, founded in Oakland, California, in 1966 by two college students, Huey Newton and Bobby Seale. A militant self-defense organization dedicated to protecting African Americans from police violence, the Panthers took their cue from the slain Malcolm X. They vehemently opposed the Vietnam War and declared their affinity for Third World revolutionary movements and armed struggle. In their manifesto, "What We Want, What We Believe," the Panthers outlined their Ten Point Program for black liberation.

The Panthers' organization spread to other cities in the late 1960s, where members undertook a wide range of community-organizing projects. Their free breakfast program for children and their testing program for sickle-cell anemia, an inherited disease with a high incidence among African Americans, were especially popular. However, the Panthers' radicalism and belief in armed self-defense resulted in violent clashes with police. Newton was charged with murdering a police officer, several Panthers were killed by police, and dozens went to prison. Moreover, under its domestic counterintelligence program, the Federal Bureau of Investigation (FBI) had begun disrupting party activities.

Young Lords | Among those inspired by the Black Panthers were Puerto Ricans in New York. Their vehicle was the Young Lords Organization (YLO), later renamed the Young Lords Party. Like the Black Panthers, YLO activists sought self-determination for Puerto Ricans, both those in the United States and those on the island in the Caribbean. In practical terms, the YLO focused on improving neighborhood conditions: City garbage collection was notoriously poor in East Harlem, where most Puerto Ricans lived, and slumlords had allowed the housing to deteriorate to a near-intolerable level. Women in the YLO were especially active, publicizing sterilization campaigns against Puerto Rican women and fighting to improve access to health care. As was true of so many nationalist groups, immediate victories for the YLO were few, but their dedicated community organizing produced a generation of leaders (many of whom later went into politics) and awakened community consciousness.

The New Urban Politics | Black Power also inspired African Americans to work within the political system. By the mid-1960s, black residents neared 50 percent of the population in several major American cities — such as Atlanta, Cleveland, Detroit, and Washington, D.C. Black Power in these cities was not abstract; it counted in real votes. Residents of Gary, Indiana, and Cleveland, Ohio, elected the first black mayors of large cities in 1967. Richard Hatcher in Gary and Carl Stokes in Cleveland helped forge a new urban politics in the United States. Their campaign teams registered thousands of black voters and made alliances with enough whites to create a working majority. Many saw Stokes's victory, in particular, as heralding a new day. One Stokes campaign staffer summed up its importance: "If Carl Stokes could run for mayor in the eighth largest city in America, then maybe who knows. We could be senators. We could be anything we wanted."

Having met with some political success, in 1972 black leaders gathered in Gary for the National Black Political Convention. In a meeting that brought together radicals, liberals, and centrists, debate centered on whether to form a third political party. Hatcher recalled that many in attendance believed "there was going to be a black third party." In the end, however, delegates decided to "give the Democratic Party one more chance." Instead of creating a third party, the convention issued the National Black Political Agenda, which included calls for community control of schools in black neighborhoods, national health insurance, and the elimination of the death penalty.

By the end of the century, black elected offcials had become commonplace in major American cities. There were forty-seven African American big-city mayors by the 1990s, and blacks had led most of the nation's most prominent cities: Atlanta, Chicago, Detroit, Los Angeles, New York, Philadelphia, and Washington, D.C. These politicians had translated black power not into a rejection of white society but into a revitalized liberalism that would remain an indelible feature of urban politics for the rest of the century.

Poverty and Urban Violence

Black Power was not, fundamentally, a violent political ideology. But violence did play a decisive role in the politics of black liberation in the mid-1960s. Too many Americans, white and black, had little knowledge or understanding of the rage that existed just below the surface in many poor northern black ghettos. That rage boiled over in a wave of riots that struck the nation's cities in mid-decade. The first "long hot summer" began in July 1964 in New York City when police shot a black criminal suspect in Harlem. Angry youths looted and rioted there for a week. Over the next four years, the volatile issue of police brutality set off riots in dozens of cities.

In August 1965, the arrest of a young black motorist in the Watts section of Los Angeles sparked six days of rioting that left thirty-four people dead. "There is a different type of Negro emerging," one riot participant told investigators. "They are not going to wait for the evolutionary process for their rights to be a man." The riots of 1967, however, were the most serious, engulfing twenty-two cities in July and August. Forty-three people were killed in Detroit alone, nearly all of them black, and $50 million worth of property was destroyed. President Johnson called in the National Guard and U.S. Army troops, many of them having just returned from Vietnam, to restore order.

Johnson, who believed that the Civil Rights Act and the Voting Rights Act had immeasurably helped African Americans, was stunned by the rioting. Despondent at the news from Watts, "he refused to look at the cables from Los Angeles," recalled one aide. Virtually all black leaders condemned the rioting, though they understood its origins in poverty and deprivation. At a meeting in Watts, Martin Luther King Jr. admitted that he had "failed to take the civil rights movement to the masses of the people," such as those in the Los Angeles ghetto. His appearance appeased few. "We don't need your dreams; we need jobs!" one heckler shouted at King.

Following the gut-wrenching riots of 1967, Johnson appointed a presidential commission, headed by Illinois governor Otto Kerner, to investigate the causes of the violence. Released in 1968, the Kerner Commission Report was a searing look at race in America, the most honest and forthright government document about race since the Presidential Committee on Civil Rights' 1947 report "To Secure These Rights." "Our nation is moving toward two societies," the Kerner Commission Report concluded, "one black, one white — separate and unequal." The report did not excuse the brick-throwing, fire-bombing, and looting of the previous summers, but it placed the riots in sociological context. Shut out of white-dominated society, impoverished African Americans felt they had no stake in the social order. Pushed to the margins, many believed that violence was their only way to push back.

Stirred by turmoil in the cities, and seeing the limitations of his civil rights achievements, Martin Luther King Jr. began to expand his vision beyond civil rights to confront the deep-seated problems of poverty and racism in America as a whole. He began to criticize President Johnson and Congress for prioritizing the war in Vietnam over the fight against poverty at home, and he began to plan a massive movement called the Poor People's Campaign to fight economic injustice. To advance that cause, he went to Memphis, Tennessee, to support a strike by predominantly black sanitation workers. There, on April 4, 1968, he was assassinated by escaped white convict James Earl Ray. King's death set off a further round of urban rioting, with major violence breaking out in more than a hundred cities.

Tragically, King was murdered before achieving the transformations he sought: an end to racial injustice and a solution to poverty. The civil rights movement had helped set in motion permanent, indeed revolutionary, changes in American race relations. Jim Crow segregation ended, federal legislation ensured black Americans' most basic civil rights, and the white monopoly on political power in the South was broken. However, by 1968, the fight over civil rights had also divided the nation. The Democratic Party was splitting, and a new conservatism was gaining strength. Many whites felt that the issue of civil rights was receiving too much attention, to the detriment of other national concerns. The riots of 1965, 1967, and 1968 further alienated many whites, who blamed the violence on the inability of Democratic officials to maintain law and order.

Rise of the Chicano Movement

Mexican Americans had something of a counterpart to Martin Luther King: Cesar Chavez. In Chavez's case, however, economic struggle in community organizations and the labor movement had shaped his approach to mobilizing society's disadvantaged. He and Dolores Huerta had worked for the Community Service Organization (CSO), a California group founded in the 1950s to promote Mexican political participation and civil rights. Leaving that organization in 1962, Chavez concentrated on the agricultural region around Delano, California. With Huerta, he organized the United Farm Workers (UFW), a union for migrant workers.

Huerta was a brilliant organizer, but it was the deeply spiritual and ascetic Chavez who embodied the moral force behind what was popularly called La Causa. A 1965 grape pickers' strike led the UFW to call a nationwide boycott of table grapes, bringing Chavez huge publicity and backing from the AFL-CIO. In a bid for attention to the struggle, Chavez staged a hunger strike in 1968, which ended dramatically after twenty-eight days with Senator Robert F. Kennedy at his side to break the fast. Victory came in 1970 when California grape growers signed contracts recognizing the UFW.

Mexican Americans shared some civil rights concerns with African Americans — especially access to jobs — but they also had unique concerns: the status of the Spanish language in schools, for instance, and immigration policy. Mexican Americans had been politically active since the 1940s, aiming to surmount factors that obstructed their political involvement: poverty, language barriers, and discrimination. Their efforts began to pay off in the 1960s, when the Mexican American Political Association (MAPA) mobilized support for John F. Kennedy and worked successfully with other organizations to elect Mexican American candidates such as Edward Roybal of California and Henry González of Texas to Congress. Two other organizations, the Mexican American Legal Defense Fund (MALDF) and the Southwest Voter Registration and Education Project, carried the fight against discrimination to Washington, D.C., and mobilized Mexican Americans into an increasingly powerful voting bloc.

Younger Mexican Americans grew impatient with civil rights groups such as MAPA and MALDF, however. The barrios of Los Angeles and other western cities produced the militant Brown Berets, modeled on the Black Panthers (who wore black berets). Rejecting their elders' assimilationist approach (i.e., a belief in adapting to Anglo society), fifteen hundred Mexican American students met in Denver in 1969 to hammer out a new political and cultural agenda. They proclaimed a new term, *Chicano* (and its feminine form, *Chicana*), to replace *Mexican American*, and later organized a political party, La Raza Unida (The United Race), to promote Chicano interests. Young Chicana feminists formed a number of organizations, including Las Hijas (The Daughters), which organized women both on college campuses and in the barrios. In California and many southwestern states, students staged demonstrations to press for bilingual education, the hiring of more Chicano teachers, and the creation of Chicano studies programs. By the 1970s, dozens of such programs were offered at universities throughout the region.

The American Indian Movement

American Indians, inspired by the Black Power and Chicano movements, organized to address their unique circumstances. Numbering nearly 800,000 in the 1960s, native people were exceedingly diverse — divided by language, tribal history, region, and degree of integration into American life. As a group, they shared a staggering unemployment rate — ten times the national average — and were the worst off in housing, disease rates, and access to education. Native people also had an often troubling relationship with the federal government. In the 1960s, the prevailing spirit of protest swept through Indian communities. Young militants challenged their elders in the National Congress of American Indians. Beginning in 1960, the National Indian Youth Council (NIYC), under the slogan "For a Greater Indian America," promoted the notion of all Indian people as a single ethnic group. The effort to both unite Indians and celebrate individual tribal culture proved a difficult balancing act.

Native American Activism

In November 1969, a group of Native Americans, united under the name "Indians of all Nations," occupied Alcatraz Island in San Francisco Bay. They claimed the land under a nineteenth-century treaty, but their larger objective was to force the federal government — which owned the island — to address the long-standing grievances of native peoples, including widespread poverty on reservations. Shown here is the view along the gunwale of the boat carrying Tim Williams, a chief of the Klamath River Hurek tribe, in full ceremonial regalia, to the island. Ralph Crane/Time Life Pictures/Getty Images.

The NIYC had substantial influence within tribal communities, but two other organizations, the militant Indians of All Tribes (IAT) and American Indian Movement (AIM), attracted more attention in the larger society. These groups embraced the concept of Red Power, and beginning in 1968 staged escalating protests to draw attention to Indian concerns. In 1969, members of the IAT occupied the deserted federal penitentiary on Alcatraz Island in San Francisco Bay and proclaimed: "We will purchase said Alcatraz Island for twenty-four dollars in glass beads and red cloth, a precedent set by the white man's purchase of a similar island [Manhattan] about 300 years ago." In 1972, AIM members joined the Trail of Broken Treaties, a march sponsored by a number of Indian groups. When AIM activists seized the headquarters of the hated Bureau of Indian Affairs in Washington, D.C., and ransacked the building, older tribal leaders denounced them.

However, AIM managed to focus national media attention on Native American issues with a siege at Wounded Knee, South Dakota, in February 1973. The site of the infamous 1890 massacre of the Sioux, Wounded Knee was situated on the Pine Ridge reservation, where young AIM activists had culti- vated ties to sympathetic elders. For more than two months, AIM members occupied a small col- lection of buildings, surrounded by a cordon of FBI agents and U.S. marshals. Several gun battles left two dead, and the siege was finally brought to a ne- gotiated end. Although upsetting to many white onlookers and Indian elders alike, AIM protests attracted widespread mainstream media coverage and spurred government action on tribal issues.

▶ How would you characterize the different forms that the Black Power movement took?

▶ What were the advantages and disadvantages of calls among minority groups for racial or ethnic pride and independence from white America?

SUMMARY

Both African Americans and other people of color who fought for civil rights from World War II through the early 1970s sought equal rights and economic opportunity. For most of the first half of the twentieth century, African Americans faced a harsh Jim Crow system in the South and a segregated, though more open, society in the North. Segregation was held in place by a widespread belief among whites in black inferiority and by a southern political system that denied African Americans the vote. In the South- west and West, Mexican Americans, Native Americans, and Americans of Asian descent faced discriminatory laws and social practices that marginalized them.

The civil rights movement attacked racial inequality in three ways. First, the move- ment sought equal standing for all Americans, regardless of race, under the law. This required patient work through the judicial system and the more arduous task of win- ning congressional legislation, such as the Civil Rights Act of 1964 and the Voting Rights Act of 1965. Second, grassroots activists, using nonviolent protest, pushed all levels of government (from city to federal) to abide by Supreme Court decisions (such as *Brown v. Board of Education*) and civil rights laws. Third, the movement sought to open eco- nomic opportunity for minority populations. This was embodied in the 1963 March on Washington for Jobs and Freedom. Ultimately, the civil rights movement was success- ful in establishing the principle of legal equality, but its participants encountered more considerable odds in ending poverty and creating meaningful, widespread economic opportunity.

Limitations in the civil rights model of social change led black activists — along with Mexican Americans, Native Americans, and others — to adopt a more nationalist stance after 1966. Nationalism stressed creating political and economic power in com- munities of color themselves, taking pride in one's racial heritage, and refusing to allow whites to define cultural standards.

For additional primary sources from this period, see *Documents for America's History*, Seventh Edition.

For Web sites, images, and documents related to topics and places in this chapter, visit *Make History* at **bedfordstmartins.com/henrettaconcise**.

For Further Exploration

Historical work on the civil rights movement is rich and broad. For useful overviews, see Thomas J. Sugrue, *Sweet Land of Liberty: The Forgotten Struggle for Civil Rights in the North* (2008); Taylor Branch, *Parting the Waters: America in the King Years, 1954–63* (1988); and Peniel Joseph, *Waiting 'til the Midnight Hour: A Narrative History of Black Power in America* (2006). For powerful biographies of central activists, see John D'Emilio, *Lost Prophet: The Life and Times of Bayard Rustin* (2003); Barbara Ransby, *Ella Baker and the Black Freedom Movement* (2003); and David J. Garrow, *Bearing the Cross: Martin Luther King, Jr., and the Southern Christian Leadership Conference* (1986). For thoughtful case studies, see Charles Payne, *I've Got the Light of Freedom: The Organizing Tradition and the Mississippi Freedom Struggle* (1995), and William Chafe, *Civilities and Civil Rights: Greensboro, North Carolina, and the Black Struggle for Freedom* (1980). On women in the movement, see Bettye Collier-Thomas and V. P. Franklin, eds., *Sisters in the Struggle: African American Women in the Civil Rights–Black Power Movement* (2001). On the Mexican American and Chicano movements, see Ian F. Haney López, *Racism on Trial: The Chicano Fight for Justice* (2003). The Internet offers numerous resources. The Civil Rights in Mississippi Digital Archive, at **www.lib.usm.edu/~spcol/crda**, offers 150 oral histories relating to Mississippi. Audio clips are also included, as are short biographies, photographs, newsletters, FBI documents, and arrest records.

Test Your Knowledge

For practice quizzes, activities, and other study tools, visit the Online Study Guide at **bedfordstmartins.com/henrettaconcise**.

TIMELINE

1941	▶ A. Philip Randolph proposes march on Washington
	▶ Roosevelt issues Executive Order 8802
1942	▶ Double V campaign launched
1943	▶ Congress of Racial Equality (CORE) founded
1947	▶ "To Secure These Rights" published
	▶ Jackie Robinson integrates major league baseball
	▶ *Mendez v. Westminster School District*
1948	▶ States' Rights Democratic Party (Dixiecrats) founded
1954	▶ *Brown v. Topeka Board of Education*
1955	▶ Emmett Till murdered (August)
	▶ Montgomery Bus Boycott (December)
1956	▶ "Southern Manifesto" issued against *Brown* ruling
1957	▶ Integration of Little Rock High School
	▶ Southern Christian Leadership Council (SCLC) founded
1960	▶ Greensboro, North Carolina, sit-ins (February)

	▶ Student Non-Violent Coordinating Committee (SNCC) founded
1961	▶ Freedom Rides (May)
1963	▶ Demonstrations in Birmingham, Alabama
	▶ March on Washington for Jobs and Freedom
1964	▶ Civil Rights Act passed by Congress
	▶ Freedom Summer
1965	▶ Voting Rights Act passed by Congress
	▶ Malcolm X assassinated (February 21)
	▶ Riot in Watts neighborhood of Los Angeles (August)
1966	▶ Black Panther Party founded
1967	▶ Riots in Detroit and Newark
1968	▶ Martin Luther King Jr. assassinated (April 4)
	▶ Fair Housing Act passed by Congress
1969	▶ Young Lords founded
	▶ Occupation of Alcatraz
1972	▶ National Black Political Convention
	▶ "Trail of Broken Treaties" protest

Uncivil Wars:
Liberal Crisis and
Conservative Rebirth

1964–1972

> The nation of the well-off must be able to see through the wall of affluence and recognize the alien citizens on the other side. And there must be vision in the sense of purpose, of aspiration. . . . there must be a passion to end poverty, for nothing less than that will do.
>
> —Michael Harrington, *The Other America*

The civil rights movement stirred American liberals and pushed them to initiate bold new government policies to advance racial equality. That progressive spirit inspired an even broader reform agenda that came to include women's rights, new social programs for the poor and the aged, job training, environmental laws, and a host of educational and other social benefits for the middle class. All told, Congress passed more liberal legislation between 1964 and 1972 than in any period since the 1930s. The great bulk of it came during the 1965–1966 legislative session, one of the most active in American history. Liberalism was at high tide.

It did not stay there long. Liberals quickly came under assault from two directions. First, young activists became frustrated with slow progress on civil rights and rebelled against the Vietnam War. They accused the liberal establishment, represented by President Lyndon Baines Johnson, of imperial overreach in Southeast Asia. At the Democratic National Convention in 1968 in Chicago, police teargassed and clubbed antiwar demonstrators, who screamed (as the TV cameras rolled), "The whole world is watching!" Some of them had been among the idealistic youth exhorted into action by Kennedy's inaugural address and the civil rights movement. Now they detested everything that Cold War liberalism stood for. Inside the convention hall, the proceedings were chaotic, the atmosphere poisonous, the delegates bitterly divided over Vietnam.

A second assault on liberalism came from conservatives, who began to find their footing after being marginalized during the 1950s. Conservatives opposed the dramatic expansion of the federal government under Johnson and disdained the "permissive society" they believed liberalism had unleashed. Advocating law and order, belittling welfare, and resisting key civil rights reforms, conservatives leaped back to political life in the late sixties. Their champion was Barry Goldwater, a Republican senator from Arizona, who warned that "a government big enough to give you everything you want is also big enough to take away everything you have."

The clashing of left, right, and center made the eight years in between the passage of the 1964 Civil Rights Act and the 1972 landslide reelection of Richard Nixon one of the most contentious, complicated, and explosive eras in American history. There were thousands of marches and demonstrations; massive new federal programs aimed at achieving civil rights, ending poverty, and extending the welfare state; and new voices among women, blacks, and Latinos demanding to be heard. With heated, vitriolic rhetoric on all sides, these developments overlapped with political assassinations and violence both overseas and at home. All of it coincided in these extraordinary years. Civil rights leader John Lewis captured the urgency of the time when he said, simply, "Wake up, America!"

In this chapter, we undertake to explain how the passionate rekindling of liberal reform under the twin auspices of the civil rights movement and the leadership of President Johnson gave way in short order to a profound liberal crisis and the resurgence of conservatism.

The Great Society: Liberalism at High Tide

In May 1964, Lyndon Johnson, president for barely six months, delivered the commencement address at the University of Michigan. Johnson offered his audience a grand and inspirational vision of a new liberal age. "We have the opportunity to move not only toward the rich society and the powerful society," Johnson continued, "but upward to the Great Society." As the sun-baked graduates listened, Johnson spelled out what he meant: "The Great Society rests on abundance and liberty for all. It demands an end to poverty and racial injustice." Even this, Johnson declared, was just the beginning. He would push to renew American education, rebuild the cities, and restore the natural environment. Ambitious — even audacious — Johnson's vision was a New Deal for a new era. From that day forward, the president would harness his considerable political skills in an effort to make the vision a reality. A tragic irony, however, was that he held the presidency at all.

John F. Kennedy's Promise

In 1961, three years before Johnson's Great Society speech, John F. Kennedy declared at his inauguration: "Let the word go forth from this time and place, to friend and foe alike, that the torch has been passed to a new generation of Americans." He challenged his fellow citizens to "ask what you can do for your country," an inspiring call to service that many Americans took to heart. The British journalist Henry Fairley called Kennedy's activism "the politics of expectation." Over time, the expectations Kennedy embodied, combined with his ability to inspire a younger generation, laid the groundwork for an era of liberal reform.

Tragically, he would not live to see that era. On November 22, 1963, Kennedy went to Texas on a political trip. As he and his wife, Jacqueline, rode in an open car past the

Texas School Book Depository in Dallas, he was shot through the head and neck by a sniper. He died within the hour. (The accused killer, Lee Harvey Oswald, a twenty-four-year-old loner, was himself killed while in custody a few days later by an assassin, a Dallas nightclub owner named Jack Ruby.) Before Air Force One left Dallas to take the president's body back to Washington, a grim-faced Lyndon Johnson was sworn in, making the transition from vice president to president.

Kennedy's youthful image, the trauma of his assassination, and the nation's sense of loss contributed to a powerful Kennedy mystique. His canonization after death capped what had been an extraordinarily stage-managed presidency. An admiring country saw in Jack and Jackie Kennedy an ideal American marriage (though JFK was, in fact, an obsessive womanizer); in Kennedy the epitome of robust good health (though he was actually afflicted by Addison's disease); and in the Kennedy White House a glamorous world of high fashion and celebrity. No other presidency ever matched the Kennedy aura, but every president after him embraced the idea that image mattered as much as reality in conducting a politically effective presidency.

Lyndon B. Johnson and the Liberal Resurgence

In many ways, Lyndon Johnson was the opposite of Kennedy. A seasoned Texas politician and longtime Senate leader, Johnson was most at home in the back rooms of power. He was a rough-edged character who had scrambled his way up, without too many scruples, to wealth and political eminence. But he never forgot his modest, hill-country origins or lost his sympathy for the downtrodden. Johnson lacked the Kennedy style, but he capitalized on Kennedy's assassination, applying his astonishing energy and negotiating skills to bring to fruition several of Kennedy's stalled programs and many more of his own, in the ambitious Great Society.

On assuming the presidency, Johnson promptly pushed for civil rights legislation as a memorial to his slain predecessor (see Chapter 27). His motives were complex. As a southerner who had previously opposed civil rights for African Americans, Johnson wished to prove that he was more than a regional figure — he would be the president of all the people. He also wanted to make a mark on history, telling Martin Luther King Jr. and other civil rights leaders to lace up their sneakers because he would move so fast on civil rights they would be running to catch up. Politically, the choice was risky. Johnson would please the Democratic Party's liberal wing, but because most northern blacks already voted Democratic, the party would gain few additional votes. Moreover, southern white Democrats would likely revolt, dividing the party at a time when Johnson's legislative agenda most required unanimity. But Johnson pushed ahead, and the 1964 Civil Rights Act stands, in part, as a testament to the president's political risk-taking.

War on Poverty | More than civil rights, what drove Johnson hardest was his determination to "end poverty in our time." The president called it a national disgrace that in the midst of plenty, one-fifth of all Americans — hidden from most people's sight in Appalachia, urban ghettos, migrant labor camps, and Indian reservations — lived in poverty. Many had fallen through the cracks and were not served by New Deal–era welfare programs. But, Johnson declared, "for the first time in our history, it is possible to conquer poverty."

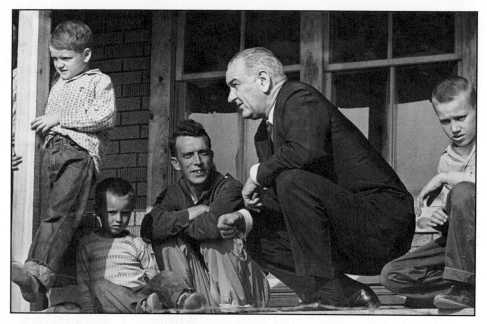

The Great Society
President Lyndon Johnson toured poverty-stricken regions of the country in 1964. Here he visits with Tom Fletcher, a father of eight children in Martin County, Kentucky. Johnson envisioned a dramatic expansion of liberal social programs, both to assist the needy and to strengthen the middle class, that he called the "Great Society." © Bettmann/Corbis.

The Economic Opportunity Act of 1964, which created a series of programs to reach these Americans, was the president's answer — what he called the War on Poverty. Head Start provided free nursery schools to prepare disadvantaged preschoolers for kindergarten. The Job Corps and Upward Bound provided young people with training and employment. Volunteers in Service to America (VISTA), modeled on the Peace Corps, offered technical assistance to the urban and rural poor. An array of regional development programs aimed at spurring economic growth in impoverished areas.

One of the most controversial features of the War on Poverty was the Community Action Program (CAP), which encouraged the poor to demand a voice in the decisions that affected their lives. CAP organizers, allied with lawyers employed by the federally funded Legal Services Program, pressed city and state governments to expand social programs and devote more resources to impoverished citizens. This often brought them into conflict with Democratic officials in large cities, splitting two constituencies of the New Deal coalition.

The 1964 Election | With the Civil Rights Act passed and his War on Poverty initiatives off the ground, Johnson turned his attention to the upcoming presidential election. Not content to govern in Kennedy's shadow, he wanted a national mandate of his own. Privately, Johnson cast himself less as a copy of Kennedy than as the heir of Franklin Roosevelt and the expansive liberalism of the 1930s. Johnson had come to

Congress for the first time in 1937 and had long admired FDR's political skills. He reminded his advisors never to forget "the meek and the humble and the lowly," because "President Roosevelt never did."

In the 1964 election, Johnson faced Republican Barry Goldwater of Arizona. An archconservative, Goldwater ran on an anticommunist, antigovernment platform, offering "a choice, not an echo" — meaning he represented a genuinely conservative alternative to liberalism rather than the echo of liberalism offered by the moderate wing of the Republican Party (see Chapter 25). Goldwater campaigned against the Civil Rights Act of 1964 and promised a more vigorous Cold War foreign policy. Among those supporting him was former actor Ronald Reagan, whose speech on behalf of Goldwater at the Republican convention, called "A Time for Choosing," made him a rising star in the party.

But Goldwater's strident foreign policy alienated voters. "Extremism in the defense of liberty is no vice," he told Republicans at the convention. Moreover, there remained strong national sentiment for Kennedy. Telling Americans that he was running to fulfill Kennedy's legacy, Johnson and his running mate, Hubert H. Humphrey of Minnesota, won in a landslide. In the long run, Goldwater's candidacy marked the beginning of a grassroots conservative revolt that would eventually transform the Republican Party. In the short run, however, Johnson's sweeping victory gave him a popular mandate and, equally important, the filibuster-proof Senate majority he needed to push the Great Society forward.

Great Society Initiatives | One of Johnson's first successes was breaking the congressional deadlock on education and health care. Passed in April 1965, the Elementary and Secondary Education Act authorized $1 billion in federal funds for teacher training and other educational programs. Standing in his old Texas schoolhouse, Johnson, a former teacher, said: "I believe no law I have signed or will ever sign means more to the future of America." Six months later, Johnson signed the Higher Education Act, providing federal scholarships for college students. Johnson also had the votes he needed to achieve some form of national health insurance. He proposed two new programs: Medicare, a health plan for the elderly funded by a surcharge on Social Security payroll taxes, and Medicaid, a health plan for the poor paid for by general tax revenues and administered by the states.

Also high on the Great Society's agenda was environmental reform. President Johnson pressed for an expanded national park system, improvement of the nation's air and water, protection for endangered species, stronger land-use planning, and highway beautification. Hardly pausing for breath, Johnson oversaw the creation of the Department of Housing and Urban Development (HUD); won funding for hundreds of thousands of units of public housing; made new investments in urban rapid transit such as the new Washington, D.C., Metro and the Bay Area Rapid Transit (BART) system in San Francisco; ushered new child safety and consumer protection laws through Congress; and helped create the National Endowment for the Arts and the National Endowment for the Humanities to support the work of artists, writers, and scholars.

It even became possible, at this moment of reform zeal, to tackle the nation's discriminatory immigration policy. The Immigration Act of 1965 abandoned the quota system that favored northern Europeans, replacing it with numerical limits that did not discriminate among nations. To promote family reunification, the law also stipulated that close relatives of legal residents in the United States could be admitted outside the numerical limits, an exception that especially benefited Asian and Latin American immigrants. Since 1965, Asian and Latin American immigrants have become increasingly visible in American society (see Chapter 31).

Assessing the | The Great Society had mixed results. The proportion of Americans living
Great Society | below the poverty line dropped from 20 percent to 13 percent between
1963 and 1968. Medicare and Medicaid, the most enduring of the Great Society programs, helped millions of elderly and poor citizens afford necessary health care. Further, as millions of African Americans moved into the middle class, the black poverty rate fell by half.

Conservatives, however, gave more credit for these changes to the decade's booming economy than to government programs. In the final analysis, the Great Society dramatically improved the financial situation of the elderly, reached millions of children, and increased the racial diversity of American society and workplaces. However, entrenched poverty remained, racial segregation in the largest cities worsened, and the national distribution of wealth remained highly skewed. In relative terms, the bottom 20 percent remained as far behind as ever. In these arenas, the Great Society made little progress.

The Women's Movement Reborn

The new era of liberal reform reawakened the American women's movement. Inspired by the civil rights movement and legislative advances under the Great Society, but frustrated by the lack of attention both gave to women, feminism sprang back to life as a mass movement. Refusing to allow women's needs to be sidelined, feminists entered the political fray and demanded not simply inclusion, but a rethinking of national priorities.

Labor | The women's movement had not languished entirely in the postwar years.
Feminists | Feminist concerns were kept alive in the 1950s and early 1960s by working
women, who campaigned for such things as maternity leave and equal pay for equal work. One historian has called these women "labor feminists," because they belonged to unions and fought for equality and dignity in the workplace. "It became apparent to me why so many employers could legally discriminate against women — because it was written right into the law," said one female labor activist.

Labor feminists were responding to the times. More women — including married women (40 percent by 1970) and mothers with young children (30 percent by 1970) — were working outside the home than ever before. But they encountered a labor market in which their contributions were undervalued. Moreover, most working women faced the "double day": they were expected to earn a paycheck and then return home to domestic labor. One woman put the problem succinctly: "The working mother has no 'wife' to care for her children."

National Organization for Women

Kathryn F. Clarenbach (left) and Betty Friedan (right) announced a "Bill of Rights for Women in 1968" to be presented to candidates in that election year. Clarenbach was the first chairwoman of the National Organization for Women (NOW) and Friedan the organization's first president. NOW became a fixture of the women's movement and the leading liberal voice for women's legal and social equality. © Bettmann/Corbis.

Betty Friedan and the National Organization for Women	When Betty Friedan's indictment of suburban domesticity, *The Feminine Mystique*, appeared in 1963, it targeted a different audience: college-educated, middle-class women who found themselves stifled by their domestic routine. Tens of thousands of women read Friedan's book — in which she identified "the problem that has no name" — and thought, "She's talking about me." *The Feminine Mystique* became a runaway best-

seller. Friedan persuaded middle-class women that they needed more than the convenience foods, improved diapers, and better laundry detergents that magazines and television urged them to buy. To live rich and fulfilling lives, they needed education and work outside the home.

Paradoxically, the domesticity described in *The Feminine Mystique* was already crumbling. After the postwar baby boom, women were again having fewer children, aided now by the birth control pill, first marketed in 1960. And as states liberalized divorce laws, more women were divorcing. Educational levels were also rising: By 1970, women made up 42 percent of the college population. All of these changes undermined traditional gender roles and enabled women to embrace *The Feminine Mystique*'s liberating prescriptions.

Government action also made a difference. In 1961, Kennedy appointed the Presidential Commission on the Status of Women, which issued a 1963 report documenting job and educational discrimination. The same year, Congress passed the Equal Pay Act, which established the principle of equal pay for equal work. A bigger breakthrough resulted from sheer happenstance. Hoping to derail the pending Civil Rights Act of 1964, a key conservative congressman added the word *sex* to the categories protected against discrimination. The act passed anyway, and to great national surprise, women suddenly had a powerful legal tool for fighting sex discrimination.

To force compliance with the new act, Friedan and others founded the National Organization for Women (NOW) in 1966. Modeled on the NAACP, NOW intended to be a civil rights organization for women, with the aim of bringing "women into full participation in . . . American society now, exercising all the privileges and responsibilities thereof in truly equal partnership with men." Under Friedan's leadership, membership grew to fifteen thousand by 1971, and NOW became, like the NAACP, a powerful voice for equal rights.

One of the ironies of the 1960s was the enormous strain that all of this liberal activism placed on the New Deal coalition. Faced with often competing demands from the civil rights movement, feminists, the poor, labor unions, conservative southern Democrats, the suburban middle class, and urban political machines, the old Rooseveltian coalition had begun to fray. Johnson hoped that the New Deal coalition was strong enough to negotiate competing demands among its own constituents while simultaneously resisting conservative attacks. In 1965, that still seemed possible. It would not remain so for long.

▶ What were the key components of the Great Society?

▶ What accounted for the resurgence of feminism in the 1960s?

The War in Vietnam, 1963–1968

As the accelerating rights revolution placed strain on the Democratic coalition, the war in Vietnam divided the country. In a CBS interview before his death, Kennedy remarked that it was up to the South Vietnamese whether "their war" would be won or lost. But the young president had already placed the United States on a course that would make retreat difficult. Like other presidents, Kennedy believed that giving up in Vietnam would weaken America's "credibility." Withdrawal "would be a great mistake," he said. It is impossible to know how JFK would have managed Vietnam had he lived. What is known is that when Kennedy gave the approval for the coup that cost president Ngo Dinh Diem his life (see Chapter 25), South Vietnam tumbled into political chaos.

Escalation under Johnson

Just as Kennedy had inherited Vietnam from Eisenhower, so Lyndon Johnson inherited Vietnam from Kennedy. Johnson's inheritance was more burdensome, however, for by now, only massive American intervention could prevent the collapse of South Vietnam (Map 28.1). Johnson, like Kennedy, was a subscriber to the Cold War tenets of global

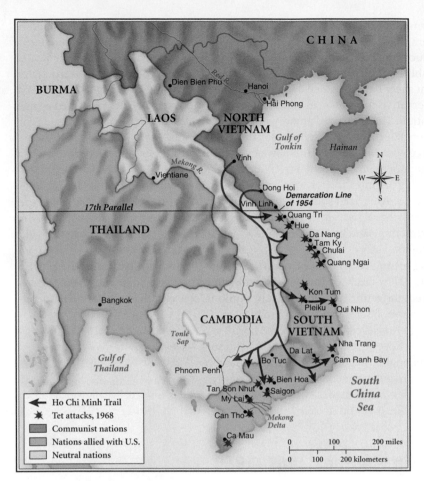

MAP 28.1 The Vietnam War, 1968

The Vietnam War was a guerrilla war, fought in skirmishes rather than set-piece battles. Despite repeated airstrikes, the United States was never able to halt the flow of North Vietnamese troops and supplies down the Ho Chi Minh Trail, which wound through Laos and Cambodia. In January 1968, Vietcong forces launched the Tet offensive, a surprise attack on cities and provincial centers across South Vietnam. Although the attackers were pushed back with heavy losses, the Tet offensive revealed the futility of American efforts to suppress the Vietcong guerrillas and marked a turning point in the war.

containment. "I am not going to lose Vietnam," he vowed on taking office. "I am not going to be the President who saw Southeast Asia go the way China went."

Gulf of Tonkin | It did not take long for Johnson to place his stamp on the war. During the summer of 1964, the president got reports that North Vietnamese torpedo boats had fired on the U.S. destroyer *Maddox* in the Gulf of Tonkin. In the first attack, on August 2, the damage inflicted was limited to a single bullet hole; a second attack, on August 4, later proved to be only misread radar sightings. It didn't matter if it was a real or imagined attack; Johnson believed a wider war was inevitable and issued a call to arms, sending his national approval rating from 42 to 72 percent. In the entire Congress, only two senators voted against his request for authorization to "take all necessary measures to repel any armed attack against the forces of the United States and to prevent further aggression." The Gulf of Tonkin Resolution, as it became known, gave Johnson the freedom to conduct operations in Vietnam as he saw fit.

Despite his mandate, Johnson was initially cautious about revealing his plans to the American people. "I had no choice but to keep my foreign policy in the wings . . . ," Johnson later said. "I knew that the day it exploded into a major debate on the war, that day would be the beginning of the end of the Great Society." So he ran in 1964 on the pledge that there would be no escalation — no American boys fighting Vietnam's fight. Privately, he doubted the pledge could be kept.

The New American Presence With the 1964 election safely behind him, Johnson began an American takeover of the war in Vietnam. The escalation, beginning in the early months of 1965, took two forms: deployment of American ground troops, and the intensification of bombing against North Vietnam.

On March 8, 1965, the first marines waded ashore at Da Nang. By 1966, more than 380,000 American soldiers were stationed in Vietnam; by 1967, 485,000; and by 1968, 536,000. The escalating demands of General William Westmoreland, the commander of U.S. forces, and Robert McNamara, the secretary of defense, pushed Johnson to Americanize the ground war in an attempt to stabilize South Vietnam. "I can't run and pull a Chamberlain at Munich," Johnson privately told a reporter in early March 1965, referring to the British prime minister who appeased Hitler in 1938.

In the meantime, Johnson authorized Operation Rolling Thunder, a massive bombing campaign against North Vietnam. Over the entire course of the war, the United States dropped twice as many tons of bombs on Vietnam as the Allies had dropped in both Europe and the Pacific during the whole of World War II. To McNamara's surprise, the bombing had little effect on the Vietcong's ability to wage war in the South. The North Vietnamese quickly rebuilt roads and bridges, and moved munitions plants underground. Instead of destroying the morale of the North Vietnamese, Operation Rolling Thunder hardened their will to fight. The massive commitment of troops and air power devastated Vietnam's countryside, however. After one harsh but not unusual engagement, a commanding officer reported, that "it became necessary to destroy the town in order to save it" — a statement that came to symbolize the terrible logic of the war.

The Johnson administration gambled that American superiority in personnel and weaponry would ultimately triumph. This strategy was inextricably tied to political considerations. For domestic reasons, policymakers searched for an elusive middle ground between all-out invasion of North Vietnam, which included the possibility of war with China, and disengagement. "In effect, we are fighting a war of attrition," said General Westmoreland. "The only alternative is a war of annihilation."

Public Opinion and the War

Johnson, who remained cautious in 1964, gradually grew more confident that his Vietnam policy had the support of the American people. Both Democrats and Republicans

Letters to Dr. Spock

The Vietnam War was among the most controversial wars in American history. It divided the country politically and split one generation from another. One of the war's foremost critics was Dr. Benjamin Spock, who was famous in the 1940s and 1950s for writing the child-rearing guidebook, *The Common Sense Book of Baby and Child Care*, used by so many parents to raise their baby-boomer children. Spock received thousands of letters in the 1960s in response to his antiwar activism. Here are two.

May 10, 1967

Dear Dr. Spock,

I have read with great interest your efforts to tell people the truth about our involvement in Vietnam. I certainly approve of everything you said on the Merv Griffin show and was glad that he gave you the time to present it on TV.

I'm sure that many people in the United States feel the same way, but other than write to our Congressman and the President, we don't know what to do about it. I certainly know how my Congressmen feel about the war and president Johnson tells us he's for peace, when he's continually escalating the war. I am a Democrat, but would *never again* vote for Mr. Johnson or Mr. Humphrey . . . What have we to vote for? Is any candidate going to come out AGAINST the war or some settlement for peace? Is there anyone who really wants peace?

I have a son, who is 17 and will soon be 18. (By the way, your little paperback is still in my cupboard, with loose pages, rather worn from use because I brought up two babies using it as my "Bible.") I don't want my son to fight in Vietnam for a cause that I don't believe in. I didn't work so hard to keep him good, bring him up to do right, keep him healthy and well . . . to have him go the jungles of Asia in the pretense of keeping democracy there.

M. C. [female]

January 28, 1968

Dr. Spock,

My name is [name deleted], a junior in high school, and the daughter of an Air Force sgt. I watched your interview today on Meet the Press. It aroused me somewhat. My father is in Vietnam on the U.S.S. Ranger working for the navy and our country. . . . My boyfriend is also in Vietnam, on the U.S.S. Canberra. Certainly I don't like the draft, as most Americans dislike sending their fathers, husbands, boyfriends, brothers, and friends off to war and perhaps to die. But . . . they are dying for their country and for what they love and believe in. . . .

Every week I get letters from my boyfriend telling me how good it makes them all feel to be fighting for us, yes us, you and me. But he says that the moral[e] needs lifting over there. I can certainly see why. There they are fighting and many of them dying while alot of punks are protesting the war and the draft. It makes some of them wonder if the fighting is worth it. . . .

You are older and perhaps wiser than I, but it could be that you can't see things as clearly from your point of view as I can from mine.

Cordially yours,

L. D. [female]

SOURCE: Michael S. Foley, ed., *Dear Dr. Spock: Letters about the Vietnam War to America's Favorite Baby Doctor* (New York: New York University Press, 2005), 87, 137.

approved Johnson's escalation in Vietnam, and so did public opinion polls in 1965 and 1966. But then opinion began to shift.

Every night, Americans saw on their television screens the carnage of war, including dead and wounded Americans. One such incident occurred in the first months of fighting in 1965. Television reporter Morley Safer witnessed a marine unit burning the village of Cam Ne to the ground. "Today's operation is the frustration of Vietnam in miniature," Safer explained. America can "win a military victory here, but to a Vietnamese peasant whose home is [destroyed] it will take more than presidential promises to convince him that we are on his side."

With such firsthand knowledge of the war, journalists began to write about a "credibility gap." The Johnson administration, they charged, was concealing bad news about the war's progress. In February 1966, television coverage of hearings by the Senate Foreign Relations Committee (chaired by J. William Fulbright, an outspoken critic of the war) raised further questions about the administration's policy. Johnson complained to his staff in 1966 that "our people can't stand firm in the face of heavy losses, and they can bring down the government." Economic problems put Johnson even more on the defensive. The Vietnam War cost taxpayers $27 billion in 1967, pushing the federal deficit from $9.8 billion to $23 billion. By then, military spending had set in motion the inflationary spiral that would plague the U.S. economy throughout the 1970s.

Out of these troubling developments, an antiwar movement began to crystallize. Its core, in addition to long-standing pacifist groups, comprised a new generation of peace activists such as SANE (the National Committee for a Sane Nuclear Policy), which in the 1950s had protested atmospheric nuclear testing. After the escalation in 1965, the activist groups were joined by student groups, clergy, civil rights advocates, even Dr. Benjamin Spock, whose book on child care had helped raise many of the students (see American Voices, p. 858). Although they were a diverse lot, these opponents of the war shared a skepticism about U.S. policy in Vietnam. They charged variously that intervention was antithetical to American ideals; that an independent, anticommunist South Vietnam was unattainable; and that no American objective justified the suffering that was being inflicted on the Vietnamese people (see Voices from Abroad, p. 860).

Rise of the Student Movement

College students, many of them inspired by the civil rights movement, helped lead the antiwar movement. In Ann Arbor, Michigan, they founded Students for a Democratic Society (SDS) in 1960. Two years later, forty students from Big Ten and Ivy League universities held the first national SDS convention in Port Huron, Michigan. Tom Hayden penned a manifesto, the Port Huron Statement, expressing students' disillusionment with the nation's consumer culture and the gulf between rich and poor. "We are people of this generation," Hayden wrote, "bred in at least modest comfort, housed now in universities, looking uncomfortably to the world we inherit." These students rejected Cold War foreign policy, including but not limited to the Vietnam conflict.

The New Left | The founders of SDS referred to their movement as the New Left to distinguish themselves from the Old Left — Communists and Socialists of the 1930s and 1940s. As New Left influence spread, it hit major university towns first — places such as Ann Arbor, Michigan; Madison, Wisconsin; and Berkeley, California.

Vietnam and the World Freedom Struggle
CHE GUEVARA

Ernesto "Che" Guevara was a middle-class, medically trained Argentinean who enlisted in Castro's Cuban Revolution and became a world icon of guerrilla resistance.

This is the painful reality: Vietnam, a nation representing the aspirations and the hopes for victory of the entire world of the disinherited, is tragically alone. . . .

And — what grandeur has been shown by this people! What stoicism and valor in this people! And what a lesson for the world their struggle holds!

It will be a long time before we know if President Johnson ever seriously thought of initiating some of the popular reforms necessary to soften the sharpness of the class contradictions that are appearing with explosive force and more and more frequently.

What is certain is that the improvements announced under the pompous label of the Great Society have gone down the drain in Vietnam.

The greatest of the imperialist powers feels in its own heart the drain caused by a poor, backward country; and its fabulous economy feels the effect of the war. . . .

And for us, the exploited of the world, what should our role be in this? . . .

Our part, the responsibility of the exploited and backward areas of the world, is to eliminate the bases sustaining imperialism — our oppressed peoples, from whom capital, raw materials, technicians and cheap labor are extracted, and to whom new capital, means of domination, arms and all kinds of goods are exported, submerging us in absolute dependence.

The fundamental element of this strategic goal will be, then, the real liberation of the peoples, a liberation that will be obtained through armed struggle in the majority of cases, and which, in the Americas, will have almost unfailingly the property of becoming converted into a socialist revolution.

In focusing on the destruction of imperialism, it is necessary to identify its head, which is none other than the United States of North America. . . .

The adversary must not be underestimated; the North American soldier has technical ability and is backed by means of such magnitude as to make him formidable. He lacks the essential ideological motivation which his most hated rivals of today have to the highest degree — the Vietnamese soldiers. . . .

Over there, the imperialist troops encounter the discomforts of those accustomed to the standard of living which the North American nation boasts. They have to confront a hostile land, the insecurity of those who cannot move without feeling that they are walking on enemy territory; death for those who go outside of fortified redoubts; the permanent hostility of the entire population.

All this continues to provoke repercussions inside the United States; it is going to arouse a factor that was attenuated in the days of the full vigor of imperialism — the class struggle inside its own territory.

SOURCE: Ernesto Guevara, *Che Guevara Speaks* (New York: Pathfinder Press, 1967), 144–159.

One of the first major demonstrations erupted in the fall of 1964 at the University of California at Berkeley after administrators banned student political activity on university property. In protest, student organizations formed the Free Speech Movement and organized a sit-in at the administration building. Some students had just returned from Freedom Summer in Mississippi, radicalized by their experience. Mario Savio spoke for many when he compared the conflict in Berkeley to the civil rights struggle in the South: "The same rights are at stake in both places — the right to participate as citizens in a democratic society and to struggle against the same enemy." Emboldened by the Berkeley movement, students across the nation were soon protesting their universities' academic policies and then, more passionately, the Vietnam War.

One spur to student protest was the military's Selective Service System, which in 1967 abolished automatic student deferments. To avoid the draft, some young men enlisted in the National Guard or applied for conscientious objector status; others dodged the draft by leaving the country, most often for Canada or Sweden. In public demonstrations, opponents of the war burned their draft cards, picketed induction centers, and on a few occasions broke into Selective Service offices and destroyed records. Antiwar demonstrators numbered in the tens or, at most, hundreds of thousands — a small fraction of American youth — but they were vocal, visible, and determined.

Students were on the front lines as the campaign against the war escalated. The 1967 Mobilization to End the War brought 100,000 protesters into the streets of San Francisco, while more than a quarter million followed Martin Luther King Jr. from Central Park to the United Nations in New York. Another 100,000 marched on the Pentagon. President Johnson absorbed the blows and counterpunched — "The enemy's hope for victory . . . is in our division, our weariness, our uncertainty," he proclaimed — but it had become clear that Johnson's war, as many began calling it, was no longer uniting the country.

Young Americans for Freedom | The New Left was not the only political force on college campuses. Conservative students were less noisy but more numerous. For them, the 1960s was not about protesting the war, staging student strikes, and idolizing Black Power. Inspired by the group Young Americans for Freedom (YAF), conservative students asserted their faith in "God-given free will" and their fear that the federal government "accumulates power which tends to diminish order and liberty." The YAF, the largest student political organization in the country, defended free enterprise and supported the war in Vietnam. Its founding principles were outlined in "The Sharon Statement," drafted (in Sharon, Connecticut) the same year the SDS was formed, and inspired young conservatives who would play important roles in the Reagan administration in the 1980s.

The Counterculture | While the New Left organized against the political and economic system and the YAF defended it, many other young Americans embarked on a general revolt against authority and middle-class respectability. The "hippie" — identified by ragged blue jeans or army fatigues, tie-dyed T-shirts, beads, and long unkempt hair — symbolized the new counterculture. With roots in the 1950s Beat culture of New York's Greenwich Village and San Francisco's North Beach, the 1960s counterculture initially turned to folk music for its inspiration. Pete Seeger set the tone

Jimi Hendrix at Woodstock
The three-day outdoor Woodstock concert in August 1969 was a defining moment in the rise of the counterculture. The event attracted 400,000 young people to Bethel, New York, for a weekend of music, drugs, and sex. Jimi Hendrix closed the show early Sunday morning with an electrified version of "The Star-Spangled Banner." More overtly political than most counterculture music, Hendrix's solo guitar rendition featured sound effects that seemed to evoke the violence of the Vietnam War. Michael Wadleigh, who directed the 1970 documentary *Woodstock*, called Hendrix's performance "his challenge to American foreign policy." Allan Koss/The Image Works.

for the era's idealism with songs such as the 1961 antiwar ballad "Where Have All the Flowers Gone?" In 1963, the year of the civil rights demonstrations in Birmingham and President Kennedy's assassination, Bob Dylan's "Blowin' in the Wind" reflected the impatience of people whose faith in America was wearing thin. Joan Baez emerged alongside Dylan and pioneered a folk sound that inspired a generation of female musicians.

By the mid-1960s, other winds of change in popular music came from the Beatles, four working-class Brits whose awe-inspiring music — by turns lyrical and driving — spawned a commercial and cultural phenomenon known as Beatlemania. American youths' embrace of the Beatles — as well as even more rebellious bands such as the Rolling Stones, the Who, and the Doors — deepened the generational divide between young people and their elders. So did the recreational use of drugs — especially marijuana and the hallucinogen popularly known as LSD or acid — which was celebrated in popular music.

For a brief time, adherents of the counterculture believed that a new age was dawning. In 1967, the "world's first Human Be-In" drew 20,000 people to Golden Gate

Park in San Francisco. That summer — called the Summer of Love — San Francisco's Haight-Ashbury, New York's East Village, and Chicago's Uptown neighborhoods swelled with young drop-outs, drifters, and teenage runaways whom the media dubbed "flower children." Although most young people had little interest in all-out revolt, media coverage made it seem as though all of American youth was rejecting the nation's social and cultural norms.

▶ What difficulties did the United States face in fighting a war against North Vietnam and the Vietcong in South Vietnam?

▶ Contrast the positions taken by SDS, the YAF, and the counter-culture. How can we account for the differences?

Days of Rage, 1968–1972

By 1968, a sense of crisis gripped the country. Riots in the cities, campus unrest, and a nose-thumbing counterculture escalated into a general youth rebellion that seemed on the verge of tearing America apart. Calling 1968 "the watershed year for a generation," SDS founder Tom Hayden wrote that it "started with legendary events, then raised hopes, only to end by immersing innocence in tragedy." It was perhaps the most shocking year in the postwar decades. Violent clashes both in Vietnam and back home in the United States combined with political assassinations to produce a palpable sense of despair and hopelessness.

Blood in the Streets

President Johnson had gambled in 1965 on a quick victory in Vietnam, before the po-litical cost of escalation came due. But there was no quick victory. North Vietnamese and Vietcong forces fought on, the South Vietnamese government repeatedly collapsed, and American casualties mounted. By early 1968, the death rate of U.S. troops had reached several hundred a week. Johnson and his generals kept insisting that there was "light at the end of the tunnel." Facts on the ground showed otherwise.

The Tet Offensive | On January 30, 1968, the Vietcong unleashed a massive, well-coordinated assault in South Vietnam. Timed to coincide with Tet, the Vietnamese new year, the offensive struck thirty-six provincial capitals and five of the six ma-jor cities, including Saigon, where the Vietcong nearly overran the U.S. embassy. In strictly military terms, the Tet offensive was a failure, with very heavy Vietcong losses. But psy-chologically, the effect was devastating. Television brought into American homes shock-ing live images: the American embassy under siege, and the Saigon police chief placing a pistol to the head of a Vietcong suspect and executing him.

The Tet offensive made a mockery of official pronouncements that the United States was winning the war. How could an enemy on the run manage such a large-scale, com-plex, and coordinated attack? Just before Tet, a Gallup poll found that 56 percent of Americans considered themselves "hawks" (supporters of the war), while only 28 percent identified with the "doves" (war opponents). Three months later, doves outnumbered hawks 42 to 41 percent. Without embracing the peace movement, many Americans simply concluded that the war was unwinnable. The Tet offensive undermined Johnson and discredited his war policies. When the 1968 presidential primary season got under way in March, antiwar senators Eugene McCarthy of Minnesota and Robert Kennedy of New York, JFK's brother, challenged Johnson for the Democratic nomination. Discouraged, perhaps even physically exhausted, on March 31 Johnson stunned the nation by announcing that he would not seek reelection.

Political Assassinations | Americans had barely adjusted to the news that a sitting president would not stand for reelection when, on April 4, James Earl Ray's bullet felled Martin Luther King Jr. in Memphis. Riots erupted in more than a hundred cities. The worst of them, in Baltimore, Chicago, and Washington, D.C., left dozens dead and hundreds of millions of dollars in property damaged or destroyed. The violence on the streets of Saigon had found an eerie parallel on the streets of the United States.

One city that did not erupt was Indianapolis. There, Robert Kennedy, in town campaigning in the Indiana primary, gave a quiet, somber speech to the black community on the night of King's assassination. Americans could continue to move toward "greater polarization," Kennedy said, "black people amongst blacks, white amongst whites," or "we can replace that violence . . . with an effort to understand, compassion and love." Kennedy sympathized with African Americans' outrage at whites, but he begged them not to strike back in retribution. Impromptu and heartfelt, Kennedy's speech was a plea to follow King's nonviolent example, even as the nation descended into greater violence.

But two months later, having emerged as the front-runner for the Democratic nomination, Kennedy, too, would be gone. On June 5, as he was celebrating his victory in the California primary over Eugene McCarthy, Kennedy was shot to death by a young Palestinian named Sirhan Sirhan. Amid the national mourning for yet another political murder, one newspaper columnist declared that "the country does not work anymore." *Newsweek* asked, "Has violence become a way of life?" Kennedy's assassination was a calamity for the Democratic Party because only he had seemed able to surmount the party's fissures over Vietnam. In the space of eight weeks, American liberals had lost two of their most important national figures, King and Kennedy. A third, Johnson, was unpopular and politically damaged. Without these unifying leaders, the crisis of liberalism had become unmanageable.

The Antiwar Movement and the 1968 Election

Before their deaths, Martin Luther King Jr. and Robert Kennedy had spoken eloquently against the Vietnam War. To antiwar activists, however, bold speeches and marches had not produced the desired effect. "We are no longer interested in merely protesting the war," declared one. "We are out to stop it." They sought nothing short of an immediate American withdrawal. Their anger at Johnson and the Democratic Party — fueled by news of the Tet offensive, the murders of King and Kennedy, and the general youth rebellion — had radicalized the movement.

Democratic Convention In August, at the Democratic National Convention in Chicago, the political divisions generated by the war consumed the party. Thousands of protesters descended on the city. The most visible group, led by Jerry Rubin and Abbie Hoffman, a remarkable pair of troublemakers, claimed to represent the Youth International Party. To mock those inside the convention hall, these "Yippies" nominated a pig, Pigasus, for president. Their stunts were geared toward maximum media exposure, but a far more numerous and serious group of activists had come to Chicago to demonstrate against the war — they staged what many came to call the Siege of Chicago.

Democratic mayor Richard J. Daley ordered the police to break up the demonstrations. Several nights of skirmishes between protesters and police culminated on the evening of the nominations. In what an official report later described as a "police riot," police officers attacked protesters with tear gas and clubs. As the nominating speeches proceeded, television networks broadcast scenes of the riot, cementing a popular impression of the Democrats as the party of disorder. "They are going to be spending the next four years picking up the pieces," one Republican said gleefully. Inside the hall, the party dispiritedly nominated Hubert H. Humphrey, Johnson's vice president. The delegates approved a middle-of-the-road platform that endorsed continued fighting in Vietnam while urging a diplomatic solution to the conflict.

Richard Nixon On the Republican side, Richard Nixon had engineered a remarkable political comeback. After losing the presidential campaign in 1960 and the California gubernatorial race in 1962, he won the Republican presidential nomination in 1968. Sensing Democratic weakness, Nixon and his advisors believed there were two groups of voters ready to switch sides: northern working-class voters and southern whites.

Tired of the antiwar movement, the counterculture, and urban riots, northern blue-collar voters, especially Catholics, had drifted away from the Democratic Party. Growing up in the Great Depression, these families were admirers of FDR and perhaps even had his picture on their living-room wall. But times had changed over three decades. To show how much they had changed, the social scientists Ben J. Wattenberg and Richard Scammon profiled blue-collar workers in their study *The Real Majority* (1970). Consider, Wattenberg and Scammon asked their readers, a forty-seven-year-old machinist's wife from Dayton, Ohio: "[She] is afraid to walk the streets alone at night . . . She has a mixed view about blacks and civil rights." Moreover, they wrote, "she is deeply distressed that her son is going to a community junior college where LSD was found on campus." Such northern blue-collar families were once reliable Democratic voters, but their political loyalties were increasingly up for grabs — a fact Republicans knew well.

George Wallace Working-class anxieties over student protests and urban riots were first exploited by the outlandish governor of Alabama, George C. Wallace. Running in 1968 as a third-party presidential candidate, Wallace traded on his fame as a segregationist governor. He had tried to stop the federal government from desegregating the University of Alabama in 1963, and he was equally obstructive during the Selma crisis of 1965. Appealing to whites in both the North and the South, Wallace called for "law and order" and claimed that mothers on public assistance were, thanks to Johnson's Great Society, "breeding children as a cash crop."

Wallace's hope was that by carrying the South, he could deny a major candidate an electoral majority and force the election into the House of Representatives. That strategy failed, as Wallace finished with just 13.5 percent of the popular vote. But he had defined hot-button issues — liberal elitism, welfare policies, and law and order — that became hallmarks among the next generation of mainstream conservatives.

The Southern Strategy | Nixon offered a subtler version of Wallace's populism. He adopted what his advisors called the "southern strategy," which aimed at attracting southern white voters still smarting over the civil rights gains by blacks. Nixon won over the key southerner, Democrat-turned-Republican senator Strom Thurmond of South Carolina, the 1948 Dixiecrat presidential nominee. Nixon informed Thurmond that while formally he had to support civil rights, his administration would go easy on enforcement. He also campaigned against the antiwar movement. He pledged to represent the "quiet voice" of the "great majority of Americans, the forgotten Americans, the nonshouters, the nondemonstrators."

These strategies worked. Nixon received 43.4 percent of the vote to Humphrey's 42.7 percent, defeating him by a scant 500,000 votes out of the 73 million that were cast. But the numerical closeness of the race could not disguise the devastating blow to the Democrats. Humphrey received almost 12 million fewer votes than had Johnson in 1964. The white South largely abandoned the Democratic Party, an exodus that would accelerate in the 1970s. In the North, Nixon and Wallace made significant inroads among traditionally Democratic voters. New Deal Democrats lost the unity of purpose that had served them for thirty years. A nation exhausted by months of turmoil and violence had chosen a new direction. Nixon's victory in 1968 foreshadowed — and helped propel — a national electoral realignment in the coming decade.

The Nationalist Turn

Vietnam and the increasingly radical youth rebellion intersected with the turn toward nationalism by young African American and Chicano activists. As we saw in Chapter 27, the Black Power and Chicano movements broke with the liberal "rights" politics of an older generation of leaders. These new activists expressed fury at the poverty and white racism that were beyond the reach of civil rights laws; they also saw Vietnam as an unjust war against other people of color.

In this spirit, the Chicano Moratorium Committee organized demonstrations against the war. Chanting "Viva la Raza, Afuera Vietnam" ("Long live the Chicano people, Get out of Vietnam!"), 20,000 Mexican Americans marched in Los Angeles in August 1970. At another rally, Cesar Chavez said: "For the poor it is a terrible irony that they should rise out of their misery to do battle against other poor people." He and other Mexican American activists charged that the draft was biased against the poor — like most wars in history, Vietnam was, in the words of one retired army colonel, "a poor boy's fight."

Among African Americans, the Black Panther Party and the National Black Antiwar Antidraft League spoke out against the war. "Black Americans are considered to be the world's biggest fools," Eldridge Cleaver of the Black Panther Party wrote in his typically acerbic style, "to go to another country to fight for something they don't have for them-

Chicano Moratorium

Between 1969 and 1970, Mexican American activists — who increasingly used the term *Chicano* to describe themselves — held a series of antiwar rallies in California. Known as the Chicano Moratorium (meaning a moratorium on war), the protests were galvanizing events in the emergence of the Chicano movement. On August 29, 1970, when 30,000 people marched in East Los Angeles, confrontations with the police led to violence — four marchers were killed, including the journalist Ruben Salazar. Los Angeles Public Library.

selves." Muhammad Ali, the most famous boxer in the world, refused to be inducted in the army. Sentenced to prison, Ali was eventually acquitted on appeal. But his action cost him his heavyweight title, and for years he was not allowed to box in the United States.

Women's Liberation

Among women, 1968 also marked a break with the past. The late 1960s spawned a new brand of feminism: women's liberation. These feminists were primarily younger, college-educated women fresh from the New Left, antiwar, and civil rights movements. Those movements' male leaders, they discovered, considered women little more than pretty helpers who typed memos and fetched coffee. Women who tried to raise feminist issues at civil rights and antiwar events were shouted off the platform with jeers such as "Move on, little girl, we have more important issues to talk about here than women's liberation."

Fed up with second-class status, and well versed in the tactics of organization and protest, women radicals broke away and organized on their own. Unlike the National Organization for Women (NOW), the women's liberation movement was loosely structured, comprising an alliance of collectives in New York, San Francisco, Boston, and other big cities and college towns. "Women's lib," as it was dubbed by a skeptical media, went public in 1968 at the Miss America pageant. Demonstrators carried posters of women's bodies labeled as slabs of beef — implying that society treated them as meat. Mirroring the identity politics of Black Power activists and the self-dramatization of the counterculture, women's liberation sought an end to the denigration and exploitation of women. "Sisterhood is powerful!" read one women's liberationist manifesto. The national Women's Strike for Equality in August 1970 brought hundreds of thousands of women into the streets of the nation's cities for marches and demonstrations.

By that year, new terms such as *sexism* and *male chauvinism* had become part of the national vocabulary. As converts flooded in, the two branches of the women's movement began to converge. Radical women realized that key feminist goals — child care, equal pay, and reproduction rights — could best be achieved in the political arena. At the same time, more traditional activists, exemplified by Betty Friedan, developed a broader view of women's oppression. They came to understand that women required more than equal opportunity: The culture that regarded women as nothing more than sexual objects and helpmates to men had to change as well. Although still largely white and middle class, feminists began to think of themselves as part of a broad social crusade.

"Sisterhood" did not unite all women, however. Rather than joining white-led women's liberation organizations, African American and Latina women continued to work within the larger framework of the civil rights movement. New groups such as the Combahee River Collective and the National Black Feminist Organization arose to speak for the concerns of African American women. They criticized sexism but were reluctant to break completely with black men and the struggle for racial equality. Chicana feminists came from Catholic backgrounds in which motherhood and family were held in high regard. "We want to walk hand in hand with the Chicano brothers, with our children, our *viejitos* [elders], our Familia de la Raza," one Chicana feminist wrote. Black and Chicana feminists embraced the larger movement for women's rights but carried on their own struggles to address specific needs in their communities.

One of the most important contributions of women's liberation was to raise awareness about what feminist Kate Millett called "sexual politics." Liberationists argued that unless women had control over their own bodies, they could not freely shape their destinies. They campaigned for reproductive rights, especially access to abortion, and railed against a culture that blamed women in cases of sexual assault and turned a blind eye to sexual harassment in the workplace.

Meanwhile, women's opportunities expanded dramatically in higher education. Dozens of formerly all-male bastions such as Yale, Princeton, and the U.S. military academies admitted women undergraduates for the first time. Hundreds of colleges started women's studies programs, and the proportion of women attending graduate and pro-

Women's Liberation

Arguing that beauty contests were degrading to women, members of the National Women's Liberation Party staged a protest against the Miss America pageant held in Atlantic City, New Jersey, in September 1968. AP Images.

fessional schools rose markedly. With the adoption of Title IX in 1972, Congress broadened the 1964 Civil Rights Act to include educational institutions, prohibiting colleges and universities that received federal funds from discriminating on the basis of sex. By requiring comparable funding for sports programs, Title IX made women's athletics a real presence on college campuses.

Women also became increasingly visible in public life. Congresswomen Bella Abzug and Shirley Chisholm joined Betty Friedan and Gloria Steinem, the founder of *Ms.* magazine, to create the National Women's Political Caucus in 1971. Abzug and Chisholm, both from New York, joined Congresswomen Patsy Mink from Hawaii and Martha Griffiths from Michigan to sponsor equal rights legislation. Congress authorized child-care tax deductions for working parents in 1972 and in 1974 passed the Equal Credit Opportunity Act, which enabled married women to get credit, including credit cards and mortgages, in their own names.

Antiwar activists, black and Chicano nationalists, and women's liberationists had each challenged the Cold War liberalism of the Democratic Party. In doing so, they helped build on the "rights liberalism" forged first by the African American–led civil rights movement. But they also created rifts among competing parts of the former liberal consensus. Many Catholics, for instance, opposed abortion rights and other freedoms sought by women's liberationists. "Traditional Catholics simply do not accept that abortion is a simple matter to be left between a woman and her doctor," one Texas priest explained. Still other Democrats, many of them blue-collar trade unionists, believed that antiwar protesters were unpatriotic and that supporting one's government in time of war was a citizen's duty. The antiwar movement and the evolving rights liberalism of the sixties had made the old Democratic coalition increasingly unworkable. Women's liberationists introduced the new term *sexual politics* to the protest movements of the late 1960s.

Stonewall and Gay Liberation

The liberationist impulse transformed the gay rights movement as well. Homophile activists in the 1960s (see Chapter 26) had pursued rights by protesting, but they adopted the respectable dress and behavior they knew straight society demanded. Meanwhile, the vast majority of gay men and lesbians remained "in the closet." So many were closeted because homosexuality was illegal in the vast majority of states — sodomy statutes outlawed same-sex relations, and police used other morals laws to harass and arrest gay men and lesbians. In the late 1960s, however, inspired by the Black Power and women's movements, gay activists increasingly demanded immediate and unconditional recognition of their rights. A gay newspaper in New York bore the title *Come Out!*

The new gay liberation found multiple expressions in major cities across the country, but a defining event occurred in New York's Greenwich Village. Police had raided gay bars for decades, making arrests, publicizing the names of patrons, and harassing customers simply for being gay. When a local gay bar called the Stonewall Inn was raided by police in the summer of 1969, however, its patrons — including gay men, lesbians, transvestites, and transsexuals — rioted for two days, burning the bar and battling with police in the narrow streets of the Village. Decades of repression by police had taken their toll. Few commentators excused the violence, and the Stonewall riots were not repeated, but activists celebrated them as a symbolic demand for full citizenship. The gay liberation movement grew quickly after Stonewall. Local gay and lesbian organizations proliferated, and activists began pushing for nondiscrimination ordinances and consensual sex laws at the state level. By 1975, the National Gay Task Force and other national organizations lobbied Congress, served as media watchdogs, and advanced suits in the courts. Despite all the activity, progress was slow; in most arenas of American life, gays and lesbians did not enjoy the same legal protections and rights as other Americans.

▶ In what ways did 1968 represent a turning point in postwar history? In what ways did it represent a continuation of the status quo?

▶ How did Black Power, Chicano, women's liberation, and gay liberation groups break with earlier liberal politics?

Richard Nixon and the Politics of the Silent Majority

Lyndon Johnson and the Democratic Party proved ill equipped to navigate Vietnam abroad and the antiwar movement and the counterculture at home. Richard Nixon, in contrast, showed himself to be an effective manipulator of the nation's unrest through carefully timed speeches and strategic displays of moral outrage. A centrist by nature and temperament, Nixon was not part of the conservative Goldwater wing of the Republican Party. Although his presidency ultimately ended ignobly, he laid the groundwork for the conservative resurgence of the 1980s.

In late 1969, following a massive antiwar rally in Washington, President Nixon gave a televised speech in which he referred to his supporters as the "silent majority." It was classic Nixonian rhetoric. In a single phrase, he summed up a generational and cultural struggle, placing himself on the side of ordinary Americans against the rabble-rousers and troublemakers. It was an oversimplification, but the label *silent majority* stuck, and Nixon had defined a political phenomenon. For the remainder of his presidency, Nixon cultivated the impression that he was the defender of a reasonable middle ground under assault from the radical left.

Nixon's War in Vietnam

When it came to Vietnam, Nixon picked up where Johnson had left off. Abandoning Vietnam, Nixon insisted, would damage America's "credibility" and make the country seem "a pitiful, helpless giant." Nixon wanted peace, but only "peace with honor." The North Vietnamese were not about to oblige him. The only outcome acceptable to them was a unified Vietnam under their control.

Vietnamization and Cambodia | To neutralize criticism at home, Nixon began delegating the ground fighting to the South Vietnamese. Under this new policy of "Vietnamization," American troop levels dropped from 543,000 in 1968 to 334,000 in 1971 to barely 24,000 by early 1973. American casualties dropped correspondingly. But the killing in Vietnam continued. As Ellsworth Bunker, the U.S. ambassador to Vietnam, noted cynically, it was just a matter of changing "the color of the bodies."

Far from abating, however, the antiwar movement intensified. In November 1969, half a million demonstrators staged a huge protest in Washington. On April 30, 1970, as part of a secret bombing campaign against Vietminh (Vietnamese liberation army) supply lines, American troops destroyed enemy bases in neutral Cambodia. When news of the invasion of Cambodia came out, American campuses exploded in outrage — and, for the first time, students died. On May 4, 1970, at Kent State University in Ohio, panicky National Guardsmen fired into an antiwar rally, wounding eleven students and killing four. At Jackson State College in Mississippi, Guardsmen stormed a dormitory, killing two black students. More than 450 colleges closed in protest. Across the country, the spring semester was essentially canceled.

My Lai Massacre | Meanwhile, one of the worst atrocities of the war had become public. In 1968, U.S. Army troops had executed nearly five hundred people in the South Vietnamese village of My Lai, including a large number of women and children. The massacre was known only within the military until 1969, when journalist Seymour Hersh broke the story and photos of the massacre appeared in *Life* magazine, discrediting the United States around the world. Americans, *Time* observed, "must stand in the larger dock of guilt and human conscience." Despite the involvement of high-ranking officers in the My Lai massacre and its cover-up, only one soldier, a low-ranking enlisted man named William Calley, was convicted.

Believing that Calley had been made a fall guy for official U.S. policies that inevitably brought death to innocent civilians, a group called Vietnam Veterans Against the War publicized other atrocities committed by U.S. troops. In a controversial protest in 1971, they turned in their combat medals at demonstrations outside the U.S. Capitol. "Here's my merit badge for murder," one vet said. Supporters of the war called the veterans cowards and un-American, but their heartfelt protest exposed the deep personal torment that the war had caused many soldiers.

Détente | As protests continued at home, Nixon pursued two strategies to achieve his declared "peace with honor," one diplomatic and the other brutal. First, he sought détente (a lessening of tensions) with the Soviet Union and a new openness with China. In a series of meetings between 1970 and 1972, Nixon and Soviet premier Leonid Brezhnev resolved tensions over Cuba and Berlin and signed the first Strategic Arms Limitation Treaty (SALT I), the latter a symbolic step toward ending the Cold War arms race. Heavily influenced by his national security advisor, the Harvard professor Henry Kissinger, Nixon believed that he could break the Cold War impasse that had kept the United States from productive dialogue with the Soviet Union.

Then, in 1972, Nixon visited China, becoming the first sitting U.S. president to do so. In a televised weeklong trip, the president pledged better relations with China and declared that the two nations — one capitalist, the other Communist — could peacefully coexist. This was the man who had risen to prominence in the 1950s by railing against the Democrats for "losing" China and by hounding Communists and fellow travelers. The president's impeccable anticommunist credentials gave him the political cover to travel to Beijing. He remarked genially to Mao: "Those on the right can do what those on the left only talk about." Praised for his efforts to lessen Cold War tensions, Nixon also had tactical objectives in mind. He hoped that by befriending both the Soviet Union and China, he could play one against the other and strike a better deal over Vietnam at the ongoing peace talks in Paris. His second strategy, however, would prove less praiseworthy and cost more lives.

Exit America | In April 1972, in an attempt to strengthen his negotiating position, Nixon ordered B-52 bombing raids against North Vietnam. A month later, he approved the mining of North Vietnamese ports, something Johnson had never dared to do. The North Vietnamese were not isolated, however: Supplies from China and the Soviet Union continued, and the Vietcong fought on.

With the 1972 election approaching, Nixon sent Henry Kissinger back to the Paris peace talks, initiated under Johnson. In a key concession, Kissinger accepted the presence of North Vietnamese troops in South Vietnam. North Vietnam then agreed to an interim arrangement whereby the Saigon government would stay in power while a special commission arranged a final settlement. With Kissinger's announcement that "peace is at hand," Nixon got the election lift he wanted, but the agreement was then sabotaged by General Nguyen Van Thieu, the South Vietnamese president. So Nixon, in one final spasm of bloodletting, unleashed the two-week "Christmas bombing," the most savage of the entire war. On January 27, 1973, the two sides signed the Paris Peace Accords.

Nixon hoped that with massive U.S. aid, the Thieu regime might survive. But Congress was in revolt. It refused appropriations for bombing Cambodia after August 15,

1973, and gradually cut back aid to South Vietnam. In March 1975, North Vietnamese forces launched a final offensive, and on April 30, Vietnam was reunited. Saigon, the South Vietnamese capital, was renamed Ho Chi Minh City, after the founding father of the Communist regime.

The collapse of South Vietnam in 1975 embodied a powerful, and tragic, historical irony. The Paris Peace Accords produced an outcome little different from what would likely have resulted from the unification vote in 1954 (see Chapter 25). In other words, America's most disastrous military adventure of the twentieth century barely altered the geopolitical realities in Southeast Asia. The Hanoi regime called itself Communist but never intended to be a satellite of any country, least of all China, Vietnam's ancient enemy.

Many paid a steep price for the Vietnam War. America's Vietnamese friends lost jobs and property, spent years in "reeducation" camps, or had to flee the country. Millions of Vietnamese had died in a decade of war, which included some of the most intensive aerial bombing of the twentieth century. In next-door Cambodia, the maniacal Khmer Rouge, followers of Cambodia's ruling Communist Party, took over and murdered 1.7 million people in bloody purges. And in the United States, more than 58,000 Americans had sacrificed their lives, and 300,000 had been wounded. On top of the war's $150 billion price tag, slow-to-heal internal wounds divided the country, and Americans increasingly lost confidence in their political leaders.

The 1972 Election

Political realignments have been infrequent in American history. One occurred between 1932 and 1936, when many Republicans, despairing over the Great Depression, had switched sides and voted for FDR. The years between 1968 and 1972 were another such pivotal moment. This time, it was Democrats who abandoned their party.

After the 1968 elections, the Democrats fell into disarray. Bent on sweeping away the party's old guard, reformers took over, adopting new rules that granted women, blacks, and young people delegate seats "in reasonable relation to their presence in the population." In the past, an alliance of urban machines, labor unions, and ethnic groups — the heart of the New Deal coalition — dominated the nominating process. But at the 1972 convention, few of the party faithful qualified as delegates under the changed rules. The crowning insult came when the convention rejected the credentials of Chicago mayor Richard Daley and his delegation, seating instead an Illinois delegation led by Jesse Jackson, a firebrand young black minister and former aide to Martin Luther King Jr.

Capturing the party was one thing; beating the Republicans was quite another. Party reforms opened the door for George McGovern, a left-liberal South Dakota senator and favorite of the antiwar and women's movements, to capture the nomination. But McGovern took a number of missteps, including failing to mollify key party backers such as the AFL-CIO, which, for the first time in memory, refused to endorse the Democratic ticket. A weak campaigner, McGovern was also no match for Nixon, who pulled out all the stops. Using the advantages of incumbency, Nixon gave the economy a well-timed lift and proclaimed (prematurely) a cease-fire in Vietnam. Nixon's appeal to the "silent majority" — people who "care about a strong United States, about patriotism, about moral and spiritual values" — was by now well honed. Court decisions mandating the busing of white students to desegregate public schools in major cities fueled resentment among white parents and thus gave Nixon another populist campaign issue.

Nixon won in a landslide, receiving nearly 61 percent of the popular vote and carrying every state except Massachusetts and the District of Columbia. The returns revealed how fractured traditional Democratic voting blocs had become. McGovern received only 38 percent of the big-city Catholic vote and lost 42 percent of self-identified Democrats overall. The 1972 election marked a pivotal moment in the country's shift to the right. The full effect of that shift was delayed, however, by the president's soon-to-be-discovered self-inflicted wounds.

Watergate and the Fall of a President

On June 17, 1972, something strange happened at Washington's Watergate office/apartment/hotel complex. Early that morning, five men carrying wiretapping equipment were apprehended there while they were breaking into the headquarters of the Democratic National Committee (DNC). Queried by the press, a White House spokesman dismissed the episode as "a third-rate burglary attempt." Pressed further, Nixon himself denied any White House involvement in "this very bizarre incident." In fact, the two masterminds of the break-in, G. Gordon Liddy and E. Howard Hunt, were former FBI and CIA agents currently working for Nixon's Committee to Re-elect the President (CREEP).

The Watergate burglary was no isolated incident. It was part of a broad pattern of abuse of power by a White House obsessed with its enemies. Liddy and Hunt, CREEP operatives on the White House payroll, were part of a clandestine squad, known as the "plumbers," that Nixon had established to plug administration "leaks" and do other nasty jobs. The two plumbers were soon arranging illegal wiretaps at DNC headquarters, part of a campaign of "dirty tricks" against the Democrats. Nixon's siege mentality best explains his fatal misstep. He could have dissociated himself from the break-in by firing his guilty aides or even just by letting justice take its course. But it was election time, and Nixon did not trust his political future to such a strategy. Instead, he arranged hush money for the burglars and instructed the CIA to stop an FBI investigation into the affair. This was obstruction of justice, a criminal offense.

Nixon kept the lid on until after the election, but in early 1973, one of the Watergate burglars, the security chief for CREEP, began to talk. In the meantime, two reporters at the *Washington Post*, Carl Bernstein and Bob Woodward, uncovered CREEP's illegal slush fund and its links to key White House aides. In May 1973, a Senate investigating committee began holding nationally televised hearings, at which Assistant Secretary of Commerce Jeb Magruder confessed his guilt and implicated former attorney general John Mitchell, White House counsel John Dean, and others. Dean, in turn, implicated Nixon. Just as startling, a former White House aide revealed that Nixon had installed a secret taping system in the Oval Office.

Under enormous pressure, Nixon eventually released some of the tapes, but there was a highly suspicious eighteen-minute gap in one of them. Finally, on June 23, 1974, the Supreme Court ordered Nixon to release the unexpurgated tapes. Lawyers found in them incontrovertible evidence that the president had ordered the cover-up. By then, the House Judiciary Committee was already considering articles of impeachment. Certain of being convicted by the Senate, Nixon became, on August 9, 1974, the first U.S.

president to resign his office. The next day, Vice President Gerald Ford was sworn in as president. Ford, the Republican minority leader in the House of Representatives, had replaced Vice President Spiro Agnew, who had himself resigned in 1973 for accepting kickbacks while governor of Maryland. A month after he took office, Ford stunned the nation by granting Nixon a "full, free, and absolute" pardon.

Congress pushed back, passing a raft of laws against the abuses of the Nixon administration: the War Powers Act (1973), which reined in the president's ability to deploy U.S. forces without congressional approval; amendments strengthening the Freedom of Information Act (1974), which gave citizens access to federal records; the Ethics in Government Act (1978); and the Foreign Intelligence Surveillance Act (1978), which prohibited domestic wiretapping without a warrant. However, it can be said that these measures curbed the growth of presidential powers, and of secret sectors of the federal government largely beyond public control, only in the short run.

▶ How was President Nixon's Vietnam policy different from President Johnson's?

▶ Were Nixon's actions in the Watergate scandal the product of an "imperial presidency" as much as an individual president? Why or why not?

SUMMARY

In this chapter, we saw how, under the combined pressures of the Vietnam War and racial and cultural conflict, the New Deal coalition fractured and split. Following John Kennedy's assassination in 1963, Lyndon Johnson advanced the most ambitious liberal reform program since the New Deal, securing not only civil rights legislation but also an array of programs in education, medical care, transportation, environmental protection, and, above all, his War on Poverty. But the Great Society fell short of its promise as Johnson escalated the American involvement in Vietnam.

The war bitterly divided Americans. Galvanized by the carnage of war and the draft, the antiwar movement spread rapidly among young people, and the spirit of rebellion spilled beyond the war. The New Left challenged the corporate dominance of society, while the more apolitical counterculture preached personal liberation through sex, drugs, music, and personal transformation. Women's liberationists broke from the New Left and raised a new set of concerns about society's sexism.

In 1968, the nation was rocked by the assassinations of Martin Luther King Jr. and Robert F. Kennedy and a wave of urban riots, fueling a growing popular desire for law and order. Adding to the national disquiet was the Democratic National Convention that summer, divided by the Vietnam War and under siege by rioting in the streets. The stage was set for a new wave of conservatism to take hold of the country, contributing to the resurgence of the Republican Party under Richard Nixon between 1968 and 1972. President Nixon ended the war in Vietnam, but only after five years had elapsed and enormous casualties accrued. Nixon's presidency ended abruptly when the Watergate scandal forced his resignation.

For additional primary sources from this period, see *Documents for America's History*, Seventh Edition.

For Web sites, images, and documents related to topics and places in this chapter, visit *Make History* at **bedfordstmartins.com/henrettaconcise.**

For Further Exploration

A good starting point for understanding Lyndon Johnson is Robert Dallek, *Flawed Giant* (1998). On the Great Society, see G. Calvin Mackenzie and Robert Weisbrot, *The Liberal Hour: Washington and the Politics of Change in the 1960s* (2008). On Vietnam, the basic

TIMELINE

1963	▶ John F. Kennedy assassinated; Lyndon B. Johnson assumes presidency
1964	▶ Civil Rights Act
	▶ Economic Opportunity Act inaugurates War on Poverty
	▶ Free Speech Movement at Berkeley
	▶ Gulf of Tonkin Resolution
1965	▶ Immigration Act abolishes national quota system
	▶ Voting Rights Act
	▶ Medicare and Medicaid programs established
	▶ Operation Rolling Thunder escalates bombing campaign (March)
	▶ First U.S. combat troops arrive in Vietnam
1967	▶ Hippie counterculture's "Summer of Love"
	▶ 100,000 march in antiwar protest in Washington, D.C. (October)

1968	▶ Tet offensive begins (January)
	▶ Martin Luther King Jr. and Robert F. Kennedy assassinated
	▶ Riot at Democratic National Convention in Chicago (August)
	▶ Women's liberation protest at Miss America pageant
	▶ Richard Nixon elected president
1969	▶ Stonewall riot (June)
1970	▶ National Women's Strike for Equality
1972	▶ Watergate break-in (June 17)
	▶ Nixon wins a second term (November 7)
1973	▶ Senate Watergate hearings
1974	▶ Nixon resigns presidency (August 9)

history is Marilyn Young, *The Vietnam Wars, 1945–1990* (1991). A terrific collection of analysis and documents is in Marvin E. Gettleman et al., eds., *Vietnam and America: A Documented History* (1995). A vivid account of dissent in the 1960s is Maurice Isserman and Michael Kazin, *America Divided: The Civil War of the 1960s* (1999). On the women's movement, see Ruth Rosen, *The World Split Open* (2000), and Kimberly Springer, *Living for the Revolution* (2005). *Takin' It to the Streets* (1995), edited by Alexander Bloom and Wini Breines, offers an array of documents that encompass the war, counterculture, civil rights, feminism, and gay liberation. Memoirs of Vietnam are numerous. Phillip Caputo's *A Rumor of War* (1977) and Ron Kovic's *Born on the Fourth of July* (1976) are powerful examples. On President Nixon and political realignment, see Bruce Schulman, *The Seventies* (2001), and for a fascinating look at Watergate, see Michael Schudson, *Watergate in American Memory* (1992). The John F. Kennedy Library and Museum's site at **www.jfklibrary.org** provides a large collection of records from Kennedy's presidency, including transcripts and recordings of JFK's speeches, a database of his executive orders, and a number of other resources. A useful Vietnam site that includes state papers and official correspondence from 1941 to the fall of Saigon in 1975 is at **www.mtholyoke .edu/acad/intrel/vietnam.htm**.

Test Your Knowledge

For practice quizzes, activities, and other study tools, visit the Online Study Guide at **bedfordstmartins.com/henrettaconcise**.

Global Capitalism and the End of the American Century

1973–2011

For historians, the recent past can be a challenge to evaluate and assess. Insufficient time has passed for scholars to weigh the significance of events and to determine which developments will have a lasting effect and which are more fleeting. Nevertheless, the period between the early 1970s and our own day has begun to emerge in the minds of historians with some clarity. Scholars generally agree on the era's three most significant developments: the resurgence of political conservatism, the end of the Cold War, and the globalization of communications and the economy. What Henry Luce had named the "American Century" — in his call for the United States to assume global leadership in the decades after World War II — came decisively to an end in the last quarter of the twentieth century and the first decade of the twenty-first. The United States lost its role as the world's dominant economy, faced rising competition from a united Europe and a surging China, and experienced a wide-ranging and divisive internal debate over its own values and priorities. Part 7 remains necessarily a work in progress, because events continue to unfold, but through equal parts conflict, struggle, and ingenuity, Americans collectively created a new era in national history after the 1960s.

The 1970s constituted a crucial transitional period between the aggressive liberalism of Lyndon Johnson's Great Society and the forthright conservatism of the Reagan era. Under Ronald Reagan, elected president in 1980, the conservative agenda combined reducing the regulatory power of the federal government, shrinking the welfare state created by liberal Democrats during the New Deal and Great Society, and expanding the military. Evangelical Christians and conservative lawmakers challenged abortion rights, feminism, and gay rights, and brought other social issues into the political arena, setting off controversies that sharply divided the American people and produced what many called a "culture war."

Between 1989 and 1991, the four-decade Cold War came to a stunning halt. The Soviet Union and its satellite communist regimes in Eastern Europe collapsed. The result was, in the words of President George H. W. Bush, a "new world order." Without a credible rival, the United States emerged in the 1990s as the lone military "superpower" in the world. In the absence of a clear Cold War enemy, the

United States intervened in civil wars, worked to disrupt terrorist activities, and provided humanitarian aid — but on a case-by-case basis, guided more by pragmatism than principle. The foremost region that occupied U.S. attention was the Middle East, where strategic interest in oil supplies remained paramount. Between 1991 and 2011, U.S. armed forces fought three wars in the region — two in Iraq and one in Afghanistan — and became even more deeply embedded in its politics.

 **ECONOMY** The long post–World War II expansion of the American economy came to an end in the early 1970s. Deindustrialization eliminated much of the nation's manufacturing base. Wages stagnated. Inflation skyrocketed. In the 1980s and 1990s, however, productivity increased, military spending boosted production, and new industries — such as computer technology — emerged. These developments led to renewed economic growth for much of the last two decades of the twentieth century. More and more, though, the economy produced *services* rather than *goods*. Americans increasingly bought products manufactured overseas, in China, Southeast Asia, and Latin America. The end of the Cold War had made possible this global expansion of capitalism, as multinational corporations moved production to low-wage countries.

 **SOCIETY** American society grew increasingly heterogeneous in this era. Immigrants from Latin America, Asia, and Africa contributed to a new racial and national diversity — the impact of changes in immigration law made in 1965. In the wake of the civil rights and women's and gay rights movements, American workplaces and educational institutions grew more diverse. These changes did not come without controversy, however. Some Americans believed that what they considered traditional culture and the family were under assault. Even as it grew more diverse, American society became more economically unequal. Conservative tax policies, deindustrialization, the decline of unions, and globalization all contributed to a widening inequality between the wealthiest Americans and the middle class and poor.

 **TECHNOLOGY AND SCIENCE** Americans experienced radical changes in their day-to-day lives because of developments in science and technology. In just over three decades, computers, cell phones, satellite and cable television, and the Internet revolutionized everyday life. These dramatic changes boosted economic productivity in the United States and around the world and made the globalization of commerce and trade possible. With new technologies came new questions and challenges: Would the Internet facilitate the export of middle-class jobs? Would enhanced surveillance techniques allow the government to monitor the activities of ordinary people? Would cell phones and computers allow terrorist networks to organize complex operations? The new world of technology altered virtually every aspect of American life.

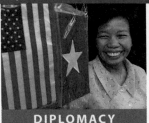

POLITICS	DIPLOMACY
Conservative ascendancy	**End of the Cold War and rising conflict in the Middle East**
1972 ▸ Endangered Species Act (1973) ▸ Watergate scandal; Nixon resigns (1974) ▸ Jimmy Carter elected president (1976) ▸ Tax revolt in California (1978)	▸ Paris Peace Accords end Vietnam War (1973) ▸ Camp David Accords between Egypt and Israel (1978) ▸ Iranian Revolution (1979); hostage crisis (1979–1981)
1980 ▸ New Right helps elect Ronald Reagan president (1980) ▸ Reagan tax cut (1981) ▸ Reagan reduces government regulation ▸ G. H. W. Bush elected president (1988)	▸ Reagan begins arms buildup ▸ Intermediate Nuclear Forces Treaty (1988) ▸ Berlin Wall comes down (1989)
1990 ▸ Bill Clinton elected president (1992) ▸ Republican resurgence (1994) ▸ Welfare reform (1996) ▸ Clinton impeached and acquitted (1998–1999)	▸ Persian Gulf War (1990) ▸ USSR breaks apart; end of Cold War ▸ Al Qaeda bombs World Trade Center (1993) ▸ U.S. peacekeeping forces in Bosnia (1995)
2000 ▸ George W. Bush narrowly elected president (2000) ▸ USA Patriot Act (2002) ▸ Barack Obama elected first African American president (2008) ▸ Health care reform passed (2010) ▸ Tea Party movement (2009–2010)	▸ Al Qaeda attacks World Trade Center and Pentagon (2001) ▸ United States and allies oust Taliban from Afghanistan (2002) ▸ U.S. invasion of Iraq (2004) ▸ North Korea tests a nuclear weapon; stalemate with Iran over nuclear program

ECONOMY	SOCIETY	TECHNOLOGY AND SCIENCE
Globalization and increasing social inequality	**Increasing diversity and culture wars**	**The information and digital revolutions**
▸ Arab oil embargo (1973–1974) ▸ Inflation surges, while economy stagnates (stagflation) ▸ New York City nears bankruptcy (1975) ▸ Chrysler bankruptcy averted by federal bailout (1979)	▸ *Roe v. Wade* (1973) ▸ STOP ERA fights Equal Rights Amendment ▸ *Bakke v. University of California* limits affirmative action (1978) ▸ Harvey Milk assassinated (1978)	▸ Microsoft founded by Bill Gates and Paul Allen (1975) ▸ Apple Computers founded (1976)
▸ National debt begins to rise ▸ Revival of military-industrial complex with military buildup ▸ Recession (1981–1982) followed by strong growth (1982–1987)	▸ Rise in Latino and Asian immigration ▸ AIDS epidemic begins (1981) ▸ Renewed emphasis on material success and the "rich and famous" ▸ *Webster v. Reproductive Health Services* (1989)	▸ Cable News Network (CNN) founded (1980) ▸ Apple IIe personal computer introduced (1983) ▸ Compact discs and cell phones invented
▸ Recession (1990–1991) ▸ Debt reduction and new technology spark economic growth and productivity rise ▸ NAFTA ratified (1993)	▸ Pat Buchanan declares "cultural war" (1992) ▸ Battles over homosexuality and abortion ▸ Defense of Marriage Act (1998)	▸ Internet gains in popularity ▸ Popularization of e-mail ▸ Biotech revolution ▸ Telecommunications Act deregulates media ▸ Google founded (1998)
▸ Bush tax cuts ▸ China purchases increasing amounts of U.S. debt ▸ Stock market and housing bubbles ▸ Great Recession (2007–2010)	▸ More than a dozen states ban gay marriage ▸ Baby boomer retirements begin; crisis forecast in Social Security ▸ Unemployment exceeds 10 percent	▸ Broadband and wireless access grows ▸ iPod introduced (2001) ▸ Global warming becomes a scientific consensus

CHAPTER 29

The Search for Order in an Era of Limits

1973–1980

I find people deeply concerned about the loss of stability, the loss of values in their lives.

—Jimmy Carter, 1976

Early in 1971, a new fictional character appeared on national television. Archie Bunker was a gruff blue-collar worker who berated his wife and bemoaned his daughter's marriage to a bearded hippie. Prone to bigoted and insensitive remarks, Archie and his wife Edith sang "Those Were the Days" at the opening of each episode of *All in the Family*, a half-hour situation comedy. The song celebrated a bygone era, when "girls were girls and men were men." Disdainful of the liberal social movements of the 1960s, Archie professed a conservative, hardscrabble view of the world.

Archie Bunker became a folk hero to many conservative Americans in the 1970s; he said what they felt. But his significance went beyond his politics. In its first three years on the air, *All in the Family* gave voice to a national search for order. Archie wrestled each week with a changing world. His feminist daughter, liberal-hippie son-in-law, and black neighbors brought that new world into Archie's modest home in Queens, New York. How would Archie, and by implication the viewer at home, make sense of the changing times? Not all Americans were as resistant to change as Archie. Most were ordinary, middle-of-the-road people confronting the aftermath of the tumultuous late 1960s and early 1970s. The liberal "rights revolution" of those years challenged Americans to think in new ways about race, gender roles, sexual morality, and the family. Vietnam and Watergate had compounded matters by producing a crisis of political authority. Something like an "old order" had seemingly collapsed. But what would take its place was not yet clear. There were as many questions as answers.

Alongside cultural dislocation and political alienation, the country confronted a series of distressing economic setbacks in the 1970s and early 1980s. In 1973, inflation began to climb at a pace unprecedented in the post–World War II decades, and economic growth slowed. An energy crisis, aggravated by American foreign policy in the Middle East, produced fuel shortages. Foreign competition in manufacturing brought less expensive, and often more reliable, goods into the U.S. market from nations such as Japan and West Germany. Both developments helped set off a round of plant closings and deindustrialization. The great economic ride enjoyed by the United States since World War II was over.

What distinguishes the period between the energy crisis and the beginning of President Nixon's second term (1973) and the election of Ronald Reagan to the presidency (1980) is the collective national search for order in the midst of economic crisis, political realignment, and rapid social change. Virtually all of the verities and touchstones of the postwar decades — Cold War liberalism, rising living standards, the nuclear family, sexual conservatism — had come under question, and most agreed on the urgency to act. For some, this search demanded new forms of liberal experimentation. For many others, it led instead to the conservatism of the emerging New Right.

An Era of Limits

Americans were deeply unsettled by the economic downturn of the early 1970s. Every major economic indicator — employment, productivity, growth — turned negative, and by 1973 the economy was in a tailspin. Inflation, brought on in part by military spending in Vietnam, proved especially difficult to control. When a Middle East embargo cut oil supplies in 1973, prices climbed even more. Unemployment remained high and productivity growth low until 1982. Overall, the 1970s represented the worst economic decade of the postwar period — what California governor Jerry Brown called an "era of limits." In this time of distress, Americans were forced to consider other limits to the growth and expansion that had long been markers of national progress. The environmental movement brought attention to the toxic effects of modern industrial capitalism on the natural world. As the urban crisis grew worse, several major cities verged on bankruptcy. Finally, political limits were reached as well: None of the presidents of the 1970s could reverse the nation's economic slide, though each spent years trying.

Energy Crisis

Modern economies run on oil. If the oil supply is drastically reduced, woe follows. Something like that happened to the United States in the 1970s. Once the world's leading oil producer, the United States had become heavily dependent on inexpensive imported oil, mostly from the Persian Gulf (Figure 29.1). American and European oil companies had discovered and developed the Middle Eastern fields early in the twentieth century, when much of the region was ruled by the British and French empires. When Middle Eastern states threw off the remnants of European colonialism, they demanded concessions for access to the fields. Foreign companies still extracted the oil, but now they did so under profit-sharing agreements with the Persian Gulf states. In 1960, these nations and other oil-rich developing countries formed a cartel (a business association formed to control prices), the Organization of Petroleum Exporting Countries (OPEC).

Conflict between Israel and the neighboring Arab states of Egypt, Syria, and Jordan politicized OPEC between 1967 and 1973. Following Israel's victory in the 1967 Six-Day War, Israeli-Arab tensions in the region grew closer to boiling over with each passing

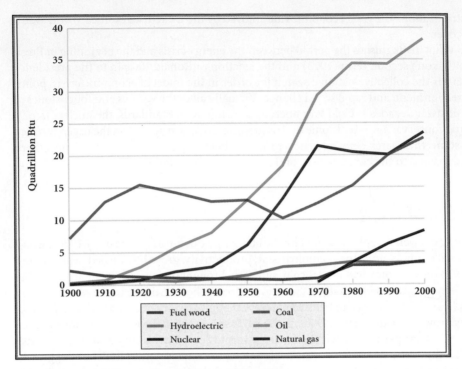

FIGURE 29.1 U.S. Energy Consumption, 1900–2000

Coal was the nation's primary source of energy until the 1950s, when it was surpassed by oil and natural gas. The revival of coal consumption after 1960 stemmed from new open-pit mining in the West that provided cheaper fuel for power plants. The decline in oil consumption in 1980 reflects the nation's response to the oil crisis of the 1970s, including, most notably, fuel-efficient automobiles. Nuclear energy became an important new fuel source, but after 1990 its contribution leveled off as a result of the safety concerns triggered by the Three Mile Island incident (see p. 886). Source: *World Almanac* 2002.

year. In the 1973 Yom Kippur War, Egypt and Syria invaded Israel to regain territory lost in the 1967 conflict. Israel prevailed, but only after being resupplied by an emergency American airlift. Resentful of U.S. support for Israel, the Arab states in OPEC declared an oil embargo in October 1973. Gas prices in the United States quickly jumped by 40 percent, and heating oil prices by 30 percent. Demand outpaced supply, and Americans found themselves parked for hours in mile-long lines at gasoline stations for much of the winter of 1973–1974. Oil had become a political weapon, and the West's vulnerability stood revealed.

The United States scrambled to meet its energy needs in the face of the oil shortage. Just two months after the OPEC embargo began, Congress imposed a national speed limit of 55 miles per hour to conserve fuel. Americans began to buy smaller, more fuel-efficient cars such as Volkswagens, Toyotas, and Datsuns (later Nissans) — while sales of Detroit-made cars (now nicknamed "gas guzzlers") slumped. With one of every six jobs in the country generated directly or indirectly by the auto industry, the effects rippled across the economy. Compounding the distress was the raging inflation set off by the oil shortage; prices of basic necessities, such as bread, milk, and canned goods, rose by nearly 20 percent in 1974 alone. "THINGS WILL GET WORSE," one newspaper headline warned, "BEFORE THEY GET WORSE."

Environmentalism

The energy crisis drove home the realization that the earth's resources are not limitless. Such a notion was also at the heart of the era's revival of environmentalism. The environmental movement was an offshoot of sixties activism, but it had numerous historical precedents: the preservationist, conservationist, and wilderness movements of the late nineteenth century; the conservationist ethos of the New Deal; and anxiety about nuclear weapons and overpopulation in the 1940s. Three of the nation's leading environmental organizations — the Sierra Club, the Wilderness Society, and the Natural Resources Council — were founded in 1892, 1935, and 1942, respectively. Environmental activists in the 1970s extended the movement's deep roots through renewed efforts to ensure a healthy environment and access to unspoiled nature.

The movement had received a hefty push back in 1962 when biologist Rachel Carson published *Silent Spring*, a stunning analysis of the pesticide DDT's toxic impact on the human and natural food chains. A succession of galvanizing issues followed in the late 1960s. The Sierra Club successfully fought two dams in 1966 that would have flooded the Grand Canyon. And in 1969, there were three major developments: An offshore drilling rig spilled millions of gallons of oil off the coast of Santa Barbara; the Cuyahoga River near Cleveland burst into flames because of the accumulation of flammable chemicals on its surface; and Friends of the Everglades opposed an airport that threatened plants and wildlife in Florida. With these events serving as catalysts, environmentalism became a certifiable mass movement on the first Earth Day, April 22, 1970, when 20 million citizens gathered in communities across the country to express their support for a cleaner, healthier planet.

Environmental Protection Agency Earlier that year, on the heels of the Santa Barbara oil spill, Congress passed the National Environmental Policy Act, which created the Environmental Protection Agency (EPA). A bipartisan bill with broad support, including that of President Nixon, the law required developers to file environmental impact statements assessing the effect of their projects on ecosystems. A spate of new laws followed: the Clean Air Act (1970), the Occupational Health and Safety Act (1970), the Water Pollution Control Act (1972), and the Endangered Species Act (1973).

The Democratic majority in Congress and the Republican president generally found common ground on these issues, and *Time* magazine wondered if the environment was "the gut issue that can unify a polarized nation." Despite the broad popularity of the movement, however, *Time*'s prediction was not borne out. Corporations resented environmental regulations, as did many of their workers, who believed that tightened standards threatened their jobs. "IF YOU'RE HUNGRY AND OUT OF WORK, EAT AN ENVIRONMENTALIST," read one labor union's bumper sticker. By the 1980s, environmentalism starkly divided Americans, with proponents of unfettered economic growth on one side and environmental activists preaching limits on the other.

Nuclear Power | An early foreshadowing of those divisions came in the brewing con-
troversy over nuclear power. Electricity from the atom — what could
be better? That was how Americans had greeted the arrival of power-generating nuclear
technology in the 1950s. By 1974, U.S. utility companies were operating forty-two nuclear power plants, with a hundred more planned. Given the oil crisis, nuclear energy
might have seemed a godsend; unlike coal- or oil-driven plants, nuclear operations produced no air pollutants.

Environmentalists, however, publicized the dangers of nuclear power plants: A reactor meltdown would be catastrophic, and so, in slow motion, would the dumping of
the plants' radioactive waste, which would generate toxic levels of radioactivity for hundreds of years. These fears seemed to be confirmed in March 1979, when the reactor core
at the Three Mile Island nuclear plant near Harrisburg, Pennsylvania, came close to meltdown. More than 100,000 people fled their homes. A prompt shutdown saved the plant,
but the near-catastrophe enabled environmentalists to win the battle over nuclear energy.
After the incident at Three Mile Island, no new nuclear plants were authorized, though
a handful with existing authorization were built in the 1980s. Today, nuclear reactors account for 20 percent of all U.S. power generation — substantially less than several European nations, but still fourth in the world.

Economic Transformation

In addition to the energy crisis, the economy was beset by a host of longer-term problems. Government spending on the Vietnam War and the Great Society made for a growing federal deficit and spiraling inflation. In the industrial sector, the country faced
more robust competition from West Germany and Japan. America's share of world trade
dropped from 32 percent in 1955 to 18 percent in 1970 and was headed downward. As
a result, in a blow to national pride, nine Western European countries had surpassed the
United States in per capita gross domestic product (GDP) by 1980. Many of these economic woes highlighted a broader, multigenerational transformation in the United States:
from an industrial-manufacturing economy to a postindustrial-service one. That transformation, which continues to this day, meant that the United States began to produce
fewer automobiles, appliances, and televisions and more financial, health-care, and
management consulting services — not to mention many millions of low-paying jobs
in the restaurant, retail, and tourist industries.

In the 1970s, the U.S. economy was hit simultaneously by unemployment, stagnant
consumer demand, and inflation — a combination called stagflation — which contradicted a basic principle taught by economists: Prices were not supposed to rise in a stagnant economy. For ordinary Americans, the reality of stagflation was a noticeable decline
in the standard of living, as discretionary income per worker dropped 18 percent between 1973 and 1982. None of the three presidents of the decade — Richard Nixon, Gerald
Ford, and Jimmy Carter — had much luck tackling stagflation. Nixon's New Economic
Policy was perhaps the most radical attempt. Nixon imposed temporary price and wage
controls in 1971 in an effort to curb inflation. Then he took an even bolder step: removing the United States from the gold standard, which allowed the dollar to float in international currency markets and effectively ended the Bretton Woods monetary system
established after World War II. The underlying weaknesses in the U.S. economy re-

mained, however. Ford, too, had little luck. His Whip Inflation Now (WIN) campaign urged Americans to cut food waste and do more with less, a noble idea but deeply unpopular among the American public. Carter's policies, considered in a subsequent section of this chapter, were similarly ineffective. The fruitless search for a new economic order was a hallmark of 1970s politics.

Deindustrialization | America's economic woes struck hardest at the industrial sector, which suddenly — shockingly — began to be dismantled. Worst hit was the steel industry, which for seventy-five years had been the economy's crown jewel. Unscathed by World War II, U.S. steel producers had enjoyed an open, hugely profitable field. But lack of serious competition left them without incentives to replace outdated plants and equipment. When the West German and Japanese steel industries rebuilt, they incorporated the latest technology. Foreign steel flooded into the United States during the 1970s, and the American industry was simply overwhelmed. Formerly titanic steel companies began a massive dismantling; virtually the entire Pittsburgh region, once

Deindustrialization
Increasing economic competition from overseas created hard times for American industry in the 1970s and 1980s. Many of the nation's once-proud core industries, such as steel, declined precipitously in these decades. This photo shows a steel factory in Youngstown, Ohio, that closed in 1980. The result of these closures was the creation of the so-called Rust Belt in the Northeast and Midwest (see Map 29.1). Richard Kalvar/Magnum Photos.

a national hub of steel production, lost its heavy industry in a single generation. By the mid-1980s, downsizing, automation, and investment in new technologies made the American steel industry competitive again — but it was a shadow of its former self, and it continues to struggle to this day.

The steel industry was the prime example of what became known as **deindustrialization**. The country was in the throes of an economic transformation that left it largely stripped of its industrial base. Steel was hardly alone. A swath of the Northeast and Midwest, the country's manufacturing heartland, became the nation's "Rust Belt" (Map 29.1), strewn with abandoned plants and distressed communities. The automobile, tire, textile, and other consumer durable industries (appliances, electronics, furniture, and the like) all started shrinking in the 1970s. In 1980, *Business Week* bemoaned "plant closings across the continent" and insisted on the "*re*industrialization of America."

Organized Labor in Decline | Deindustrialization threw many tens of thousands of blue-collar workers out of well-paid union jobs. One study followed 4,100 steelworkers left jobless by the 1977 shutdown of the Campbell Works of the Youngstown Sheet & Tube Co. Two years later, 35 percent had retired early at half pay; 10 percent had moved; 15 percent were still jobless, with unemployment benefits long gone; and 40 percent had found local work, but mostly in low-paying, service-sector jobs. In another instance, between 1978 and 1981, eight Los Angeles companies — including such giants as Ford, Uniroyal, and U.S. Steel — closed factories employing 18,000 workers. These Ohio and California workers, like hundreds of thousands of their counterparts across the nation, had fallen from their perch in the middle class.

Deindustrialization dealt an especially harsh blow to the labor movement, which had facilitated the postwar expansion of that middle class. In the early 1970s, as inflation hit, the number of strikes surged; 2.4 million workers participated in work stoppages in 1970 alone. However, industry argued that it could no longer afford union demands, and labor's bargaining power produced fewer and fewer concrete results. In these hard years, the much-vaunted labor-management accord of the 1950s, which raised profits and wages by passing costs on to consumers, went bust. Instead of seeking higher wages, unions now mainly fought to save jobs. Union membership went into steep decline, and by the mid-1980s organized labor represented less than 18 percent of American workers, the lowest level since the 1920s. The impact on liberal politics was huge. With labor's decline, a main buttress of the New Deal coalition was coming undone.

Urban Crisis Revisited | The economic downturn pushed already struggling American cities to the brink of fiscal collapse. Middle-class flight to the suburbs continued apace, and the "urban crisis" of the 1960s spilled into the "era of limits." Facing huge price inflation and mounting piles of debt — to finance social services for the poor and to replace disappearing tax revenue — nearly every major American city struggled to pay its bills in the 1970s. Surrounded by prosperous postwar suburbs, central cities seemingly could not catch a break.

New York, the nation's financial capital and its largest city, fared the worst. Its annual budget was in the billions, larger than that of most states. Unable to borrow on the tightening international bond market, New York neared collapse in the summer of 1975; bankruptcy was a real possibility. When Mayor Abraham Beame appealed to the federal

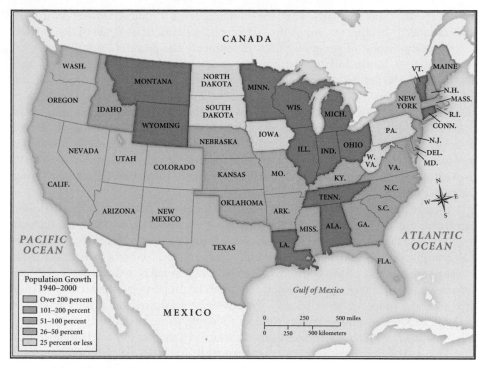

MAP 29.1 From Rust Belt to Sun Belt, 1940–2000

One of the most significant developments of the post–World War II era was the growth of the Sun Belt. Sparked by federal spending for military bases, the defense industry, and the space program, states of the South and Southwest experienced an economic boom in the 1950s. This growth was further enhanced in the 1970s, as the heavily industrialized regions of the Northeast and Midwest declined, and migrants from what was quickly dubbed the "Rust Belt" headed to the South and West in search of jobs.

government for assistance, President Ford refused. "Ford to City: Drop Dead" read the headline in the *New York Daily News*. Fresh appeals ultimately produced a solution: The federal government would lend New York money, and banks would declare a three-year moratorium on municipal debt. The arrangement saved the city from defaulting, but the mayor was forced to cut city services, freeze wages, and lay off workers. One pessimistic observer declared that "the banks have been saved, and the city has been condemned."

Cities faced declining fortunes in these years for many reasons, but one key was the continued loss of residents and businesses to nearby suburbs. In the 1970s alone, 13 million people (6 percent of the total U.S. population) moved to the suburbs. New suburban shopping centers opened weekly across the country, and other businesses — such as banks, insurance companies, and technology firms — increasingly sought suburban locations. More and more, people lived *and* worked in suburbs. In the San Francisco Bay area, 75 percent of all daily commutes were suburb-to-suburb, and 78 percent of New York's suburban residents worked in the suburbs. The 1950s "organization man," commuting downtown from his suburban home, had been replaced by the engineer, teacher, nurse, student, and carpenter who lived in one suburb and worked in another.

Tax Revolt and Economic Inequality Suburbanization and the economic crisis combined powerfully in what became known as the "tax revolt," a dramatic reversal of the postwar spirit of generous public investment. The premier example was California. Inflation pushed real estate values upward, and property taxes skyrocketed. Hardest hit were suburban property owners, along with retirees and others on fixed incomes, who suddenly faced unaffordable tax bills. Into this dire situation stepped Howard Jarvis, a conservative anti–New Dealer and a genius at mobilizing grassroots discontent. In 1978, Jarvis proposed Proposition 13, an initiative that would roll back property taxes, cap future increases for present owners, and require that all tax measures have a two-thirds majority in the legislature. Despite opposition by virtually the entire state leadership, including politicians from both parties, Californians voted overwhelmingly for Jarvis's measure.

Proposition 13 hobbled public spending in the nation's most populous state. Per capita funding of California public schools, once the envy of the nation, plunged from the top tier to the bottom, where it was second only to Mississippi. Moreover, Proposition 13's complicated formula benefited middle-class and wealthy homeowners at the expense of less-well-off citizens, especially those who depended heavily on public services. Businesses, too, came out ahead, because commercial property got the same protection as residential property. More broadly, Proposition 13 inspired tax revolts across the country and helped conservatives define an enduring issue: low taxes.

In addition to public investment, another cardinal marker of New Deal liberalism had been a remarkable decline in income inequality. In the 1970s, that trend reversed, and the wealthiest Americans, those among the top 10 percent, began to pull ahead again. As corporations restructured to boost profits during the 1970s slump, they increasingly laid off high-wage workers, paid the remaining workers less, and relocated overseas. Thus, upper-class Americans benefited, while blue-collar families who had been lifted into the middle class during the postwar boom increasingly lost out. An unmistakable trend was apparent by the end of the 1970s. The U.S. labor market was dividing in two: a vast, low-wage market at the bottom and a much narrower high-wage market at the top, with the middle squeezed smaller and smaller.

Politics in Flux, 1974–1980

A search for order characterized national politics in the 1970s as well. Liberals were in retreat, but conservatives had not yet put forth a clear alternative. Popular disdain for politicians, evident in declining voter turnout, deepened with Nixon's resignation in 1974. "Don't vote," read one bumper sticker in 1976. "It only encourages them." Watergate not only damaged short-term Republican prospects but also shifted the party's balance to the right. Despite mastering the populist appeal to the "silent majority," Nixon was never beloved by conservatives. His relaxation of tensions with the Soviet Union and his visit to communist China, in particular, won him no friends on the right. His disgraceful exit proved a boon to conservative Republicans, who proceeded to reshape the party in their image.

As for the Democrats, Watergate granted them a reprieve, a second chance at recapturing their eroding base. Backed by a public deeply disenchanted with politicians, especially scandal-tainted Republicans, congressional Democrats had an opportunity to repair the party's image. But any high-minded Democratic program that did not halt the nation's economic slide would not reverse the party's weakened position. The years in between Nixon's resignation and the election of Ronald Reagan in 1980 are thus best understood as a transitional period — the aggressive liberalism of the 1960s was losing national support, but nothing distinctly different had yet replaced it.

Watergate Babies   Less than a month into his presidency, which began when Nixon resigned on August 9, 1974, Gerald Ford did something unexpected: He officially pardoned Nixon. The decision saved the nation a prolonged and agonizing trial, which was Ford's rationale, but it was decidedly unpopular among the public. Pollster Louis Harris remarked that should a politician "defend that pardon in any part of this country, North or South, [he] is almost literally going to have his head handed to him." Democratic candidates in the 1974 midterm elections made Watergate and Ford's pardon their top issues. It worked. Seventy-five new Democratic members of the House came to Washington in 1975, many of them under the age of forty-five, and the press dubbed them "Watergate babies."

Young and reform-minded, the Watergate babies solidified huge Democratic majorities in both houses of Congress and quickly set to work. They eliminated the House Un-American Activities Committee (HUAC), which had investigated alleged Communists in the 1940s and 1950s and antiwar activists in the 1960s. In the Senate, Democrats reduced the number of votes needed to end a filibuster from 67 to 60 — a move intended to weaken the power of the minority to block legislation. In both houses, Democrats dismantled the existing committee structure, which had entrenched power in the hands of a few elite committee chairs. And in 1978, they passed the Ethics in Government Act, which forced political candidates to disclose financial contributions and limited the lobbying activities of former elected officials. Overall, the Watergate babies helped to decentralize power in Washington and bring greater transparency to American government.

In one of the great ironies of American political history, however, the post-Watergate reforms made government *less* efficient and *more* susceptible to special interests — the opposite of what had been intended. Under the new committee structure, smaller subcommittees proliferated, and the size of the congressional staff doubled to more than 20,000. A diffuse power structure actually gave lobbyists more places to exert influence. As the power of committee chairs weakened, influence shifted to party leaders, such as the Speaker of the House and the Senate majority leader. With little incentive to compromise, the parties grew more rigid, and bipartisanship became rare. Finally, filibustering, a seldom-used tactic largely employed by anti–civil rights southerners, increased in frequency. The Congress that we have come to know today — with its partisan rancor, its army of lobbyists, and its slow-moving response to public needs — came into being in the 1970s.

Political Realignment   Despite Democratic gains in 1974, the electoral realignment that had begun with Richard Nixon's presidential victories in 1968 and 1972 continued. As liberalism proved unable to stop runaway inflation or speed up economic growth, conservatism gained greater traction with the public. The postwar liberal economic formula — sometimes known as the Keynesian consensus — consisted of microadjustments to the money supply coupled with federal spending. When that formula failed to restart the economy in the mid-1970s, conservatives in Congress used this opening to articulate alternatives, especially economic deregulation and tax cuts.

On a grander scale, deindustrialization in the Northeast and Midwest and continued population growth in the Sunbelt were changing the political geography of the country. Power was shifting, incrementally but perceptibly, toward the West and South. As states with strong trade unions at the center of the postwar liberal political coalition — such as New York, Illinois, and Michigan — lost industry, jobs, and people, states with traditions of libertarian conservatism — such as California, Arizona, Florida, and Texas — gained greater political clout. The full impact of this shifting political geography would not be felt until the 1980s and 1990s, but its effects had become apparent by the mid-1970s.

Jimmy Carter: The Outsider as President   "Jimmy who?" was how journalists first responded when James Earl Carter, who had in turn been a naval officer, a peanut farmer, and the governor of Georgia, emerged from the pack to win the Democratic presidential nomination in 1976. When Carter told his mother that he intended to run for president, she had asked, "President of what?" Trading on Watergate and his down-home image, Carter pledged to restore morality to the White House. "I will never lie to you," he promised voters. Carter played up his credentials as a Washington

Jimmy Carter
President Jimmy Carter leans across the roof of his car to shake hands during a parade through Bardstown, Kentucky, in July 1979. The president needed all the support he could get. Inflation in 1979 was 11 percent, one of the highest annual rates in the postwar decades. A thoughtful man and a born-again Christian, Carter proved unable to solve the complex economic problems and international challenges of the late 1970s. Bob Daugherty/AP Images.

America's Crisis of Faith   FEI XIAOTONG

In the late 1970s, Fei Xiaotong, a Chinese scholar, wrote a series of essays entitled "Glimpses of America." In this passage, he responds to President Jimmy Carter's assertion in his famous "malaise" speech of 1979 that Americans faced a spiritual crisis.

I read in the newspaper that the energy crisis in the United States is getting worse and worse. I hear that after spending several days of quiet thought in his mountain retreat, President Carter decided that America's real problem is not the energy crisis but a "crisis of faith." The way it is told is that vast numbers of people have lost their faith in the present government and in the political system, and do not believe that the people in the government working with current government methods can solve the present series of crises. Even more serious, he believes that the masses have come to have doubts about traditional American values, and if this continues, in his opinion, the future of America is terrible to imagine. He made a sad and worried speech. . . .

In fact, loss of faith in the present social system on the part of the broad masses of the American people did not begin with the energy crisis. The spectacular advances in science and technology in America in the last decade or two and the unceasing rise in the forces of production are good. But the social system remains unchanged, and the relations of production are basically the same old capitalism. This contradiction between the forces of production and the relations of production has not lessened but become deeper. The ruling class, to be sure, still has the power to keep on finding ways of dealing with the endless series of crises, but the masses of people are coming increasingly to feel that they have fallen unwittingly into a situation where their fate is controlled by others, like a moth in a spiderweb, unable to struggle free. Not only the blacks of Harlem — who clearly are able to earn their own living but still have to rely on welfare to support themselves without dignity — but even well-off families in gardenlike suburban residences worry all day that some accident may suddenly rob them of everything. As the dependence of individuals on others grows heavier and heavier, each person feels in his heart that this society is no longer to be relied on. . . . Such a feeling is natural in a society like America's. Carter is right to call this feeling of helplessness a "crisis of faith," for it is a doubting of the present culture. Only he should realize that the present crisis has been long in the making and is already deep. . . .

These "Glimpses of America" essays may be brought to a close here, but to end with the crisis of faith does violence to my original intention. History is a stream that flows on and cannot be stopped. Words must be cut off, but history goes bubbling on. It is inconceivable that America will come to a standstill at any crisis point. I have full faith in the great American people and hope that they will continue to make even greater contributions to the progress of mankind.

SOURCE: R. David Arkush and Leo O. Lee, trans. and eds., *Land Without Ghosts: Chinese Impressions of America from the Mid-Nineteenth Century to the Present* (Berkeley: University of California Press, 1989), 271–280.

outsider, although he selected Senator Walter F. Mondale of Minnesota as his running mate, to ensure his ties to traditional Democratic voting blocs. Ford still might have prevailed, but his pardon of Nixon likely cost him enough votes in key states to swing the election to the Democratic candidate. Carter won with 50 percent of the popular vote to Ford's 48 percent.

For a time, Carter got some mileage as an outsider — the common man who walked to the White House after the inauguration and delivered fireside chats in a cardigan sweater. The fact that he was a born-again Christian also played well. But Carter's inexperience began to show. He made strange blunders, such as telling *Playboy* magazine that he had "looked upon a lot of women with lust." Most consequentially, his outsider strategy made for chilly relations with congressional leaders. Disdainful of the Democratic establishment, Carter relied heavily on inexperienced advisors from Georgia. And as a detail-oriented micromanager, he exhausted himself over the fine points of policy better left to his aides.

On the domestic front, Carter's big challenge was managing the economy. The problems that he faced defied easy solution. Most confounding was stagflation. If the government focused on inflation — forcing prices down by raising interest rates — unemployment became worse. If the government tried to stimulate employment, inflation became worse. None of the levers of government economic policy seemed to work. At heart, Carter was an economic conservative. He toyed with the idea of an "industrial policy" to bail out the ailing manufacturing sector, but he moved instead in a free-market direction by lifting the New Deal–era regulation of the airline, trucking, and railroad industries. Deregulation stimulated competition and cut prices, but it also drove firms out of business and hurt unionized workers.

The president's efforts proved ineffective at reigniting economic growth. Then, the Iranian Revolution curtailed oil supplies, and gas prices jumped again. In a major TV address, Carter lectured Americans about the nation's "crisis of the spirit." He called energy conservation "the moral equivalent of war" — or, in the media's shorthand, "MEOW," which aptly captured the nation's assessment of Carter's sermonizing. By then, his approval rating had fallen below 30 percent. And it was no wonder, given an inflation rate over 11 percent, failing industries, and long lines at the pumps. It seemed the worst of all possible economic worlds, and the first-term president could not help but worry about the political costs to him and his party (see Voices from Abroad, p. 893).

► Why did the environmental movement prove so divisive? Whose interests were threatened?

► What were the causes and effects of deindustrialization?

Reform and Reaction in the 1970s

Having lived through a decade of profound social and political upheaval — the Vietnam War, protests, riots, Watergate, recession — many Americans were exhausted and cynical by the mid-1970s. But while some retreated to private concerns, others took reform in new directions. Civil rights battles continued, the women's movement achieved some of its most far-reaching aims, and gay rights blossomed. These movements pushed the "rights revolution" of the 1960s deeper into American life. Others, however, pushed back. Social conservatives responded by forming their own organizations and resisting the emergence of what they saw as a permissive society.

Civil Rights in a New Era

When Congress banned job discrimination in the 1964 Civil Rights Act, the law required only that employers hire without regard to "race, color, religion, sex, or national origin." But after centuries of slavery and decades of segregation, would nondiscrimination bring African Americans into the economic mainstream? Many liberals thought not. They believed that government, universities, and private employers needed to take positive steps to open their doors to a wider, more diverse range of Americans — including other minority groups and women.

Affirmative Action | Among the most significant efforts to address the legacy of exclusion was affirmative action — procedures designed to take into account the disadvantaged position of minority groups after centuries of discrimination. First advanced by the Kennedy administration in 1961, affirmative action received a boost under President Lyndon Johnson, whose Labor Department fashioned a series of plans in the late 1960s to encourage government contractors to recruit underrepresented racial minorities. Women were added under the last of these plans, when pressure from the women's movement highlighted the problem of sex discrimination. By the early 1970s, affirmative action had been refined by court rulings that identified acceptable procedures: hiring and enrollment goals, special recruitment and training programs, and set-asides (specially reserved slots) for both racial minority groups and women.

Affirmative action, however, did not please many whites, who felt that the deck was being stacked against them. Much of the dissent came from conservative groups that had opposed civil rights all along. They charged affirmative action advocates with "reverse discrimination." Referring to Puerto Ricans and African Americans in an episode of *All in the Family*, Archie Bunker said that if they "want their rightful share of the American dream, let 'em go and hustle for it like I done," a common, if crudely stated, objection to affirmative action. Some liberal groups sought a middle position. In a widely publicized 1972 letter, Jewish organizations, seared by the memory of quotas that once kept Jewish students out of elite colleges, came out against all racial quotas but nonetheless endorsed "rectifying the imbalances resulting from past discrimination."

A major shift in affirmative action policy came in 1978. Allan Bakke, a white man, sued the University of California at Davis Medical School for rejecting him in favor of less-qualified minority-group candidates. Headlines across the country sparked anti-affirmative action protest marches on college campuses and vigorous discussion on television, radio, and in the White House. Ultimately, the Supreme Court rejected the medical school's quota system, which set aside 16 of 100 places for "disadvantaged" students. The Court ordered Bakke admitted but indicated that a more flexible affirmative action plan, in which race could be considered along with other factors, would still pass constitutional muster. *Bakke v. University of California* thus upheld affirmative action but, by rejecting a quota system, also called it into question. Future court rulings and state referenda, in the 1990s and 2000s, would further limit the scope of affirmative action. In particular, California voters passed Proposition 209 in 1996, prohibiting public institutions from using affirmative action to increase diversity in employment and education.

Busing | Another major civil rights objective — desegregating schools — produced even more controversy and fireworks. For fifteen years, southern states, by a variety of stratagems, had fended off court directives that they desegregate "with all deliberate speed." In 1968, only about one-third of all black children in the South attended schools with whites. At that point, the federal courts got serious and, in a series of stiff decisions, ordered an end to "dual school systems." Where schools remained highly segregated, the courts increasingly endorsed the strategy of busing students to achieve integration. Plans differed across the country. In some states, black children rode buses from their neighborhoods to attend previously all-white schools. In others, white children were bused to black or Latino neighborhoods. In an important 1971 decision, the Supreme Court upheld a countywide busing plan for Charlotte-Mecklenburg, a North Carolina school district. Despite local opposition, desegregation proceeded, and many cities in the South followed suit. By the mid-1970s, 86 percent of southern black children were attending school with whites. (In recent years, this trend has reversed.)

An Antibusing Confrontation in Boston
Where busing was implemented, it often faced stiff resistance. Many white communities resented judges dictating which children would attend which neighborhood school. In working-class Irish South Boston, mobs attacked African American students bused in from Roxbury in 1974. A police presence was required to keep South Boston High School open. When lawyer and civil rights activist Ted Landsmark tried to enter Boston's city hall during a 1976 antibusing demonstration, he was assaulted. Stanley Forman's Pulitzer Prize–winning photo for the Boston *Herald-American* — titled *The Soiling of Old Glory* — shows Joseph Rakes lunging at Landsmark with an American flag. Busing also had the perverse effect of speeding up "white flight" to city suburbs. Stanley Forman.

In the North, where segregated schooling was also a fact of life — arising from suburban residential patterns — busing orders proved less effective. Detroit dramatized the problem. To integrate Detroit schools would have required merging city and suburban school districts. A lower court ordered just such a merger in 1971, but in *Milliken v. Bradley* (1974), the Supreme Court reversed the ruling, requiring busing plans to remain within the boundaries of a single school district. Without including the largely white suburbs in busing efforts, however, achieving racial balance in Detroit, and other major northern cities, was all but impossible. Postwar suburbanization had produced in the North what law had mandated in the South: entrenched racial segregation of schools.

The Women's Movement and Gay Rights

Unlike the civil rights movement, whose signal achievements came in the 1960s, the women's and gay rights movements flourished in the 1970s. With three influential wings — radical, liberal, and "Third World" — the women's movement inspired both grassroots activism and legislative action across the nation. For their part, gay activists had further to go: They needed to convince Americans that same-sex relationships were natural and that gay men and lesbians deserved the same protection of the law as all other citizens. Neither movement achieved all of its aims in this era, but each laid a strong foundation for the future.

Women's Liberation | In the first half of the 1970s, the women's liberation movement reached its historic peak. Taking a dizzying array of forms — from lobbying legislatures to marching in the streets and establishing all-female collectives — women's liberation produced activism on the scale of the earlier black-led civil rights movement. Women's centers, as well as women-run child-care facilities, began to spring up in cities and towns. A feminist art and poetry movement flourished. Women challenged the admissions policies of all-male colleges and universities — opening such prestigious universities as Yale and Columbia and nearly bringing an end to male-only institutions of higher education. Female scholars began to transform higher education: by studying women's history, by increasing the number of women on college and university faculties, and by founding women's studies programs.

Much of women's liberation activism focused on the female body. Inspired by the Boston collective that first published *Our Bodies, Ourselves* — a groundbreaking book on women's health — the women's health movement founded dozens of medical clinics, encouraged women to become physicians, and educated millions of women about their bodies. To reform anti-abortion laws, activists pushed for remedies in more than thirty state legislatures. Women's liberationists founded the antirape movement, established rape crisis centers around the nation, and lobbied state legislatures and Congress to reform rape laws. Many of these endeavors and movements began as shoestring operations in living rooms and kitchens: *Our Bodies, Ourselves* was first published as a 35-cent mimeographed booklet, and the antirape movement began in small consciousness-raising groups that met in churches and community centers. By the end of the decade, however, all of these causes had national organizations and touched the lives of millions of American women.

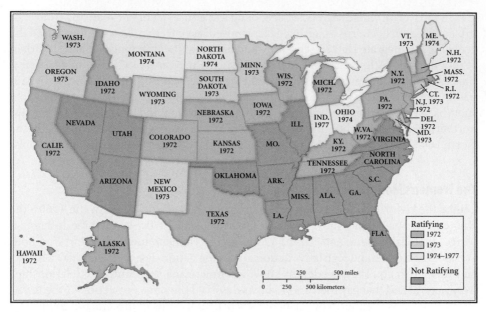

MAP 29.2 States Ratifying the Equal Rights Amendment, 1972–1977
The ratifying process for the Equal Rights Amendment (ERA) went smoothly in 1972 and 1973 but then stalled. The turning point came in 1976, when ERA advocates lobbied extensively, particularly in Florida, North Carolina, and Illinois, but failed to sway the conservative legislatures in those states. After Indiana ratified in 1977, the amendment still lacked three votes toward the three-fourths majority needed for adoption. Efforts to revive the ERA in the 1980s were unsuccessful, and it became a dead issue.

| Equal Rights Amendment | Buoyed by this flourishing of activism, the women's movement renewed the fight for an Equal Rights Amendment (ERA) to the Constitution. First |

introduced in 1923, the ERA stated, in its entirety, "Equality of rights under the law shall not be denied or abridged by the United States or any State on the basis of sex." Vocal congressional women, such as Patsy Mink (D-HI), Bella Abzug (D-NY), and Shirley Chisholm (D-NY), found enthusiastic male allies — among both Democrats and Republicans — and Congress adopted the amendment in 1972. Within just two years, thirty-four of the necessary thirty-eight states had ratified it, and the ERA appeared headed for adoption. But then, progress abruptly halted (Map 29.2).

Credit for putting the brakes on ERA ratification goes chiefly to a remarkable woman: Phyllis Schlafly, a lawyer long active in conservative causes. Despite her own flourishing career, Schlafly advocated traditional roles for women. The ERA, she proclaimed, would create an unnatural "unisex society," with women drafted into the army and forced to use single-sex toilets. Abortion, she alleged, could never be prohibited by law. Led by Schlafly's organization, STOP ERA, thousands of women mobilized, showing up at statehouses with home-baked bread and apple pies. As labels on baked goods at one anti-ERA rally expressed it: "My heart and hand went into this dough / For the sake of the family please vote no." It was a message that resonated widely, especially among those troubled by the rapid pace of social change (see American Voices, p. 899). The ERA never was ratified, despite a congressional extension of the deadline to June 30, 1982.

Debating the Equal Rights Amendment

The Equal Rights Amendment won congressional approval in 1972 and set off a furious debate when it was sent to the states for ratification. Lawyer and political activist Phyllis Schlafly was the most prominent opponent of the ERA; Elizabeth Duncan Koontz was a distinguished educator, and the first black woman to head the National Education Association.

Phyllis Schlafly: Women's magazines, the women's pages of newspapers, and television and radio talk shows have been filled for months with a strident advocacy of the "rights" of women to be treated on an equal basis with men in all walks of life. But what about the rights of the woman who doesn't want to compete on an equal basis with men? Does she have the right to be treated as a woman — by her family, by society, and by the law? . . .

The laws of every one of our 50 states now guarantee the right to be a woman — protected and provided for in her career as a woman, wife, and mother. The proposed Equal Rights Amendment will wipe out all our laws which — through rights, benefits, and exemptions — guarantee this right to be a woman. . . . Is this what American women want? Is this what American men want? . . .

There are two very different types of women lobbying for the Equal Rights Amendment. One group is the women's liberationists. Their motive is totally radical. They hate men, marriage, and children. They are out to destroy morality and the family. . . . There is another type of woman supporting the Equal Rights Amendment from the most sincere motives. It is easy to see why the business and professional women are supporting the Equal Rights Amendment—many of them have felt the keen edge of discrimination in their employment.

Elizabeth Duncan Koontz: A short time ago I had the misfortune to break my foot. . . . The pain . . . did not hurt me as much as when I went into the emergency room and the young woman upon asking me my name, the nature of my ailment, then asked me for my husband's social security number and his hospitalization number. I asked her what did that have to do with my emergency.

And she said, "We have to be sure of who is going to pay your bill." I said, "Suppose I'm not married, then." And she said, "Then give me your father's name." I did not go through that twenty years ago when I was denied the use of that emergency room because of my color.

I went through that because there is an underlying assumption that all women in our society are protected, dependent, cared for by somebody who's got a social security number and hospitalization insurance. Never once did she assume I might be a woman who might be caring for my husband, instead of him by me, because of some illness. She did not take into account the fact that one out of almost eight women heading families in poverty today [is] in the same condition as men in families and poverty. . . .

My greater concern is that so many women today . . . oppose the passage of the ERA very sincerely and . . . tell you without batting an eye, "I don't want to see women treated that way." And I speak up, "What way is that?" . . . Women themselves have been a bit misguided. We have mistaken present practice for law, and women have . . . assumed too many times that their present condition cannot change.

SOURCES: *The Phyllis Schlafly Report*, November 1972, 1–4. William A. Link and Marjorie Spruill Wheeler, eds. *The South in the History of the Nation* (Boston: Bedford/St. Martin's, 1999), 295–296.

Roe v. Wade | In addition to the ERA, the women's movement had identified another major goal: winning reproductive rights. Activists pursued two tracks: legislative and judicial. In the early 1960s, abortion was illegal in virtually every state. A decade later, thanks to intensive lobbying by women's organizations, liberal ministers, and physicians, a handful of states, such as New York, Hawaii, California, and Colorado, adopted laws making legal abortions easier to obtain. But progress after that was slow, and women's advocates turned to the courts. There was reason to be optimistic. The Supreme Court had first addressed reproductive rights in a 1965 case, *Griswold v. Connecticut. Griswold* struck down an 1879 state law prohibiting the possession of contraception as a violation of married couples' constitutional "right of privacy." Following the logic articulated in *Griswold*, the Court gradually expanded the right of privacy in a series of cases in the late 1960s and early 1970s.

Those cases culminated in *Roe v. Wade* (1973). In that landmark decision, the justices nullified a Texas law that prohibited abortion under any circumstances, even when the woman's health was at risk, and laid out a new national standard: Abortions performed during the first trimester were protected by the right of privacy. At the time and afterward, some legal authorities questioned whether the Constitution recognized any such privacy right and criticized the Court's seemingly arbitrary first-trimester timeline. Nevertheless, the Supreme Court chose to move forward, transforming a traditionally state-regulated policy into a national, constitutionally protected right.

For the women's movement, *Roe v. Wade* represented a triumph. For evangelical and fundamentalist Christians, Catholics, and conservatives generally, it was a bitter pill. In their view, abortion was, unequivocally, murder. These Americans, represented by groups such as the National Right to Life Committee, did not believe that something they regarded as immoral and sinful could be the basis for women's equality. Women's advocates responded that illegal abortions — common prior to *Roe* — were often unsafe procedures, which resulted in physical harm to women and even death. *Roe* polarized what was already a sharply divided public and mobilized conservatives to seek a Supreme Court reversal or, short of that, to pursue legislation that would strictly limit the conditions under which abortions could be performed. In 1976, they convinced Congress to deny Medicaid funds for abortions, an opening round in a campaign against *Roe v. Wade* that continues today.

Harvey Milk | The gay rights movement had achieved notable victories as well. These, too, proved controversial. More than a dozen cities had passed gay rights ordinances by the mid-1970s, protecting gay men and lesbians from employment and housing discrimination. One such ordinance in Dade County (Miami), Florida, sparked a protest led by Anita Bryant, a conservative Baptist and a television celebrity. Her "Save Our Children" campaign in 1977, which garnered national media attention, resulted in the repeal of the ordinance and symbolized the emergence of a conservative religious movement opposed to gay rights.

Across the country from Miami, developments in San Francisco looked promising for gay rights advocates, then turned tragic. No one embodied the combination of gay liberation and hard-nosed politics better than a San Francisco camera-shop owner named Harvey Milk. A closeted businessman in New York until he was forty, Milk arrived in San Francisco in 1972 and threw himself into city politics. Fiercely indepen-

Harvey Milk

In November 1977, Harvey Milk became the first openly gay man to be elected to public office in the United States, when he won a seat on the San Francisco Board of Supervisors. Shockingly, almost exactly a year from the day of his election, Milk was assassinated. © Bettmann/Corbis.

dent, he refused to work through the established channels of gay leadership in the city, believing that their behind-the-scenes style did more harm than good to the movement. Milk ran as an openly gay candidate for city supervisor (city council) twice and the state assembly once, both times unsuccessfully.

By mobilizing the "gay vote" into a powerful bloc, Milk finally won a supervisor seat in 1977. He was not the first openly gay elected official in the country — Kathy Kozachenko of Michigan and Elaine Noble of Massachusetts share that distinction — but he became a national symbol of emerging gay political power. Tragically, after he helped to win passage of a gay rights ordinance in San Francisco, he was assassinated — along with the city's mayor, George Moscone — by a disgruntled former supervisor named Dan White. When White was convicted of manslaughter rather than murder, five thousand gays and lesbians in San Francisco marched on city hall.

The Supreme Court and the Rights Revolution

The rights revolution found an ally in an unexpected place: the U.S. Supreme Court. The decision that stood as a landmark in the civil rights movement, *Brown v. Board of Education* (1954), triggered a larger judicial revolution. Following *Brown*, the Court increasingly agreed to hear human rights and civil liberties cases — as opposed to its previous focus on property-related suits. Surprisingly, this shift was led by the man whom President Dwight Eisenhower had appointed chief justice in 1953: Earl Warren. A popular Republican governor of California, Warren surprised many, including Eisenhower himself, with his robust advocacy of civil rights and civil liberties. The Warren Court lasted from 1954 until 1969 and established some of the most far-reaching liberal jurisprudence in U.S. history.

Law and Order and the Warren Court | Right-wing activists in the 1970s came to detest the Warren Court, which they accused of "legislating from the bench" and contributing to social breakdown. They pointed, for instance, to the Court's rulings that people who are arrested have a constitutional right to counsel (1963, 1964) and, in *Miranda v. Arizona* (1966), that arrestees have to be informed by police of their right to remain silent. Compounding conservatives' frustration was a series of decisions that liberalized restrictions on pornography. Trying to walk the fine line between censorship and obscenity, the Court ruled in *Roth v. United States* (1957) that obscene material had to be "utterly without redeeming social importance" to be banned. The "social importance" test, however, proved nearly impossible to define and left wide latitude for pornography to flourish. That measure was finally abandoned in 1972, when the Court ruled in *Miller v. California* that "contemporary community standards" were the rightful measure of obscenity. But *Miller*, too, had little effect on the pornographic magazines, films, and peep shows proliferating in the 1970s. Conservatives found these decisions especially distasteful, since the Court had also ruled that religious ritual of any kind in public schools — including prayers and Bible reading — violated the constitutional separation of church and state. To many religious Americans, the Court had taken the side of immorality over Christian values.

Supreme Court critics blamed rising crime rates and social breakdown on the Warren Court's liberal judicial record. Every category of crime was up in the 1970s, but especially disconcerting was the doubling of the murder rate since the 1950s and the 76 percent increase in burglary and theft between 1967 and 1976. Sensational crimes had always grabbed headlines, but now "crime" itself preoccupied politicians, the media, and the public. However, no one could establish a direct causal link between increases in crime and Supreme Court decisions, given myriad other social factors, including drugs, income inequality, enhanced statistical record-keeping, and the proliferation of guns. But when many Americans looked at their cities in the 1970s, they saw pornographic theaters, X-rated bookstores, and rising crime rates. Where, they wondered, was law and order?

The Burger Court | In response to what conservatives considered the liberal judicial revolution under the Warren Court, President Nixon came into the presidency promising to appoint "strict constructionists" (conservative-minded justices) to the bench. In three short years, between 1969 and 1972, he was able to appoint four new justices to the Supreme Court, including the new chief justice, Warren Burger. Surprisingly, despite the conservative credentials of its new members, the Burger Court refused to scale back the liberal precedents set under Warren. Most prominently, in *Roe v. Wade*

(1973) the Burger Court extended the "right of privacy" developed under Warren to include women's access to abortion. Few Supreme Court decisions in the twentieth century have disappointed conservatives more.

In a variety of cases, the Burger Court either confirmed previous liberal rulings or chose a centrist course. In 1972, for instance, the Court deepened its intervention in criminal procedure by striking down all existing capital punishment laws, in *Furman v. Georgia*. In response, Los Angeles police chief Ed Davis accused the Court of establishing a "legal oligarchy" that had ignored the "perspective of the average citizen." He and other conservatives vowed a nationwide campaign to bring back the death penalty — which was in fact shortly restored, in *Gregg v. Georgia* (1976). Other decisions advanced women's rights. In 1976, the Court ruled that arbitrary distinctions based on sex in the workplace and other arenas were unconstitutional, and in 1986 that sexual harassment violated the Civil Rights Act. These rulings helped women break employment barriers in the subsequent decades.

In all of their rulings on privacy rights, however, both the Warren and Burger Courts confined their decisions to heterosexuals. The justices were reluctant to move ahead of public attitudes toward homosexuality. Gay men and lesbians still had no legal recourse if state laws prohibited same-sex relations. In a controversial 1986 case, *Bowers v. Hardwick*, the Supreme Court upheld a Georgia sodomy statute that criminalized same-sex sexual acts. The majority opinion held that homosexuality was contrary to "ordered liberty" and that extending sexual privacy to gays and lesbians "would be to cast aside millennia of moral teaching." Not until 2003 (*Lawrence v. Texas*) would the court overturn that decision, recognizing for all Americans the right to sexual privacy.

▶ How did the idea of civil rights expand during the 1970s?

▶ How did the U.S. Supreme Court affect the extension or restriction of rights during the 1970s?

The American Family on Trial

In 1973, the Public Broadcasting System (PBS) aired a twelve-part television series that followed the life of a real American family. Producers wanted the show, called simply *An American Family*, to document how a middle-class white family coped with the stresses of a changing society. They did not anticipate that the family would dissolve in front of their cameras. Tensions and arguments raged, and in the final episode, Bill, the husband and father (who had had numerous extramarital affairs), moved out. By the time the show aired, the couple was divorced and Pat, the former wife, had become a single working mother with two sons.

An American Family captured a traumatic moment in the twentieth-century history of the family. Between 1965 and 1985, the divorce rate doubled, and children born in the 1970s had a 40 percent chance of spending part of their youth in a single-parent household. Moreover, as wages stagnated and inflation pushed prices up, more and more families depended on two incomes for survival. Furthermore, the women's movement and the counterculture had called into question traditional sex roles — father as provider and mother as homemaker — and middle-class baby boomers rebelled against what they saw as the puritanical sexual values of their parents' generation. In the midst of such rapid change, where did the family stand?

Working Families in the Age of Deindustrialization

One of the most striking developments of the 1970s and 1980s was the relative stagnation of wages. After World War II, hourly wages had grown steadily ahead of inflation, giving workers more buying power with each passing decade. By 1973, that trend had stopped in its tracks. The decline of organized labor, the loss of manufacturing jobs, and runaway inflation all played a role in the reversal. Hardest hit were blue-collar and pink-collar workers and those without college degrees.

Millions of wives and mothers had worked for wages for decades. But many Americans still believed in the "family wage": a breadwinner income, earned by men, sufficient to support a family. After 1973, fewer and fewer Americans had access to that luxury. Between 1973 and the early 1990s, every major income group except the top 10 percent saw their real earnings (accounting for inflation) either remain the same or decline. Over this period, the typical worker saw a 10 percent drop in real wages. To keep their families from falling behind, women streamed into the workforce. Between 1950 and 1994, the proportion of women ages 25 to 54 working for pay increased from 37 to 75 percent. Much of that increase occurred in the 1970s. Americans were fast becoming dependent on the two-income household.

The numbers tell two different stories of American life in these decades. On the one hand, the trends unmistakably show that women, especially in blue-collar and pink-collar families, *had* to work for wages to sustain their family's standard of living: to buy a car, pay for college, afford medical bills, support an aging parent, or simply pay the rent. Moreover, the number of single women raising children nearly doubled between 1965 and 1990. Women's paid labor was making up for the declining earning power or the absence of men in American households. On the other hand, women's real income overall grew during the same period. This increase reflected the opening of professional and skilled jobs to educated baby-boomer women. As older barriers began to fall, women poured into law and medicine, business and government, the sciences and engineering. Beneficiaries of feminism, these women pursued careers of which their mothers had only dreamed.

Workers in the National Spotlight For a brief period in the 1970s, the trials of working men and women made a distinct imprint on national culture. Reporters wrote of the "blue-collar blues" associated with plant closings and the hard-fought strikes of the decade. A 1972 strike at the Lordstown, Ohio, General Motors plant captivated the nation. Holding out not for higher wages but for better working conditions — the plant had the most complex assembly line in the nation — Lordstown strikers spoke out against what they saw as an inhumane industrial system. Across the nation, the number of union-led strikes surged, even as the number of Americans in the labor movement continued to decline. In Lordstown and most other sites of strikes and industrial conflict, workers won a measure of public attention but typically gained little economic ground.

Good Times

The popular 1970s sitcom *Good Times* examined how the "blue-collar blues" affected a working-class black family struggling to make ends meet in tough economic times. The show's theme song spoke of "temporary layoffs . . . easy credit ripoffs . . . scratchin' and surviving." Its actors, many of them classically trained, brought a realistic portrait of working-class African American life to television. © Bettmann/Corbis.

When Americans turned on their televisions in the mid-1970s, the most popular shows reflected the "blue-collar blues" of struggling families. *All in the Family* was joined by *The Waltons*, set during the Great Depression. *Good Times*, *Welcome Back Kotter*, and *Sanford and Son* dealt with poverty in the inner city. *The Jeffersons* featured an upwardly mobile black couple. *Laverne and Shirley* focused on young working women in the 1950s and *One Day at a Time* on working women in the 1970s making do after divorce. The most-watched television series of the decade, 1977's eight-part *Roots*, explored the history of slavery and the survival of African American culture and family roots despite the oppressive labor system. Not since the 1930s had American culture paid such close attention to working-class life.

The decade also saw the rise of musicians such as Bruce Springsteen, Johnny Paycheck, and John Cougar (Mellencamp), who became stars by turning the hardscrabble lives of people in small towns and working-class communities into rock anthems that filled arenas. Springsteen wrote songs about characters who "sweat it out in the streets of a runaway American dream," and, to the delight of his audience, Paycheck famously sang, "Take this job and shove it!" Meanwhile, on the streets of Harlem and the South Bronx in New York, young working-class African American men experimenting with dance and musical forms invented break dancing and rap music — styles that expressed both the hardship and the creativity of working-class black life in the deindustrialized American city.

Navigating the Sexual Revolution

The economic downturn was not the only force that placed stress on American families in this era. Another such force was what many came to call the "sexual revolution." Hardly revolutionary, sexual attitudes in the 1970s were, in many ways, a logical evolution of developments in the first half of the twentieth century. Beginning in the 1920s, Americans increasingly viewed sex as a component of personal happiness, distinct from reproduction. Attitudes toward sex grew even more lenient in the postwar decades, a fact reflected in the Kinsey studies of the 1940s and 1950s. By the 1960s, sex before marriage had grown more socially acceptable — an especially profound change for women — and frank discussions of sex in the media and popular culture had grown more common.

In that decade, three developments dramatically accelerated this process: the introduction of the birth control pill, the rise of the baby-boomer-led counterculture, and the influence of feminism. First made available in the United States in 1960, the birth control pill gave women an unprecedented degree of control over reproduction. By 1965, more than 6 million American women were taking advantage of this pharmaceutical advance. Rapid shifts in attitude accompanied the technological breakthrough. Middle-class baby boomers embraced a sexual ethic of greater freedom and, in many cases, a more casual approach to sex outside marriage. "I just feel I am expressing myself the way I feel at that moment in the most natural way," a female California college student, explaining her sex life, told a reporter in 1966. The rebellious counterculture encouraged this attitudinal shift by associating a puritanical view of sex with their parents' generation.

Finally, women's rights activists reacted to the new emphasis on sexual freedom in at least two distinct ways. For many feminists, the emphasis on casual sex seemed to perpetuate male privilege. They argued that while men could now freely explore numerous sexual relationships without social sanction, women remained trapped by a culture that still required them to be "innocent" and not to "sleep around" — the old double standard. Moreover, sexual harassment was all too common in the workplace, and the proliferation of pornography continued to commercialize women as sex objects. On the one hand, many feminists argued that the sexual revolution was by and for men. On the other hand, they remained optimistic that the new sexual ethic could free women from those older moral constraints. They called for a revolution in sexual *values*, not simply behavior, that would end exploitation and grant women the freedom to explore their sexuality on equal terms with men.

Sex and Popular Culture | In the 1970s, popular culture was suffused with discussions of the sexual revolution. Mass-market books with titles such as *Everything You Always Wanted to Know About Sex*, *Human Sexual Response*, and *The Sensuous Man* shot up the best-seller list. William Masters and Virginia Johnson became the most famous sex researchers since Alfred Kinsey by studying couples in the act of lovemaking. In 1972, English physician Alex Comfort published *The Joy of Sex*, a guidebook for couples that became one of the most popular books of the decade. Comfort made certain to distinguish his writing from pornographic exploitation. "Sex is the one place where we today can learn to treat people as people," he wrote.

Hollywood took advantage of the new sexual ethic by making films with explicit erotic content that pushed the boundaries of middle-class taste. Films such as *Midnight Cowboy* (1969), *Carnal Knowledge* (1971), and *Shampoo* (1974), the latter starring Hollywood's leading ladies' man, Warren Beatty, led the way. Throughout the decade, and into the 1980s, the Motion Picture Association of America (MPAA) scrambled to keep its guide for parents — the system of rating pictures G, PG, R, and X (and, after 1984, PG-13) — in tune with Hollywood's advancing sexual revolution.

On television, the popularity of social problem shows, such as *All in the Family*, and the fear of losing advertising revenue moderated the portrayal of sex in the early 1970s. However, in the second half of the decade networks both exploited and criticized the new sexual ethic. In frivolous, lighthearted shows such as the popular *Charlie's Angels*, *Three's Company*, and *The Love Boat*, heterosexual couples explored the often confusing, and usually comical, landscape of sexual morality. At the same time, between 1974 and 1981, the major networks produced more than a dozen made-for-TV movies about children in sexual danger — a sensationalized warning to parents of the potential threats to children posed by a less strict sexual morality.

Middle-Class Marriage | Many Americans worried that the sexual revolution threatened marriage itself. The notion of marriage as romantic companionship had defined middle-class norms since the early nineteenth century. It was also quite common throughout most of the twentieth century for Americans to see sexual satisfaction as a healthy part of the marriage bond. But what defined a healthy marriage in an age of rising divorce rates, changing sexual values, and feminist critiques of the nuclear family? Only a small minority of Americans rejected marriage outright; most continued to create monogamous relationships codified in marriage. But many came to believe that they needed help as marriage came under a variety of stresses — economic, psychological, and sexual.

A therapeutic industry arose in response. Churches and secular groups alike established marriage seminars and counseling services to assist couples in sustaining a healthy marriage. A popular form of 1960s psychotherapy, the "encounter group," was adapted to marriage counseling: Couples met in large groups to explore new methods of communicating. One of the most successful of these organizations, Marriage Encounter, was founded by the Catholic Church. It expanded into Protestant and Jewish communities in the 1970s and became one of the nation's largest counseling organizations. Such groups embodied another long-term shift in how middle-class Americans understood marriage. Spurred by both feminism and psychotherapeutic models that stressed self-improvement, Americans increasingly defined marriage not simply by companionship and sexual fidelity but also by the deeply felt emotional connection between two people.

Religion in the 1970s: The Fourth Great Awakening

For three centuries, American society has been punctuated by intense periods of religious revival — what historians have called "Great Awakenings" (see Chapters 4 and 8). These periods have seen rising church membership, the appearance of charismatic religious leaders, and the increasing influence of religion, usually of the evangelical variety, on society and politics. One such awakening, the fourth in U.S. history, took shape in the 1970s and 1980s. It had many elements, but one of its central features was a growing concern with the family.

In the 1950s and 1960s, many mainline Protestants had embraced the reform spirit of the age. Some of the most visible Protestant leaders were social activists who condemned racism and opposed the Vietnam War. Organizations such as the National Council of Churches — along with many progressive Catholics and Jews — joined with Martin Luther King Jr. and other African American ministers in the long battle for civil rights. Many mainline Protestant churches, among them the Episcopal, Methodist, and Congregationalist denominations, practiced a version of the "Social Gospel," the reform-minded Christianity of the early twentieth century.

Evangelical Resurgence Meanwhile, evangelical Protestantism survived at the grass roots. Evangelical churches emphasized an intimate, *personal* salvation (being "born again"); focused on a literal interpretation of the Bible; and regarded the death and resurrection of Jesus as the central message of Christianity. These tenets distinguished evangelicals from mainline Protestants as well as from Catholics and Jews, and they flourished in a handful of evangelical colleges, Bible schools, and seminaries in the postwar decades.

No one did more to keep the evangelical fire burning than Billy Graham. A graduate of the evangelical Wheaton College in Illinois, Graham cofounded Youth for Christ in 1945 and then toured the United States and Europe preaching the gospel. Following a stunning 1949 tent revival in Los Angeles that lasted eight weeks, Graham shot to national fame. His success in Los Angeles led to a popular radio program, but he continued to travel relentlessly, conducting old-fashioned revival meetings he called "crusades." A massive sixteen-week 1957 crusade held in New York City's Madison Square Garden made Graham, along with the conservative Catholic priest Fulton Sheen, one of the nation's most visible religious leaders.

Graham and other evangelicals in the 1950s and 1960s laid the groundwork for the Fourth Great Awakening. But it was the secular liberalism of the late 1960s and early 1970s that sparked the countervailing evangelical revival. Many Americans regarded feminism, the counterculture, sexual freedom, homosexuality, pornography, divorce, and legalized abortion not as distinct issues, but as a collective sign of moral decay in society. To seek answers and find order, more and more people turned to evangelical ministries, especially Southern Baptist, Pentecostal, and Assemblies of God churches. Numbers tell part of the story. As mainline churches lost about 15 percent of their membership between 1970 and 1985, evangelical church membership soared. The Southern Baptist Convention, the largest Protestant denomination, grew by 23 percent, while the Assemblies of God grew by an astounding 300 percent. *Newsweek* magazine declared 1976 "The Year of the Evangelical," and that November the nation made Jimmy Carter the nation's first evangelical president. In a national Gallup poll, 34 percent of Americans answered yes when asked, "Would you describe yourself as a 'born again' or evangelical Christian?"

Much of this astonishing growth came from the creative use of television. Graham had pounded the pavement and worn out shoe leather to reach his converts. But a new generation of preachers brought religious conversion directly into Americans' living rooms through television. These so-called televangelists built huge media empires through small donations from millions of avid viewers — not to mention advertising. Jerry Falwell's *Old Time Gospel Hour,* Pat Robertson's *700 Club,* and Jim and Tammy Bakker's *PTL (Praise the Lord) Club* were the leading pioneers in this televised race for American souls, but another half dozen — including Oral Roberts and Jimmy Swaggart — followed them onto the airwaves. Together, they made the 1970s and 1980s the era of Christian broadcasting.

Religion and the Family | Of primary concern to evangelical Christians was the family. Drawing on selected Bible passages, evangelicals believed that the nuclear family, and not the individual, represented the fundamental unit of society. The family itself was organized along paternalist lines: Father was breadwinner and disciplinarian; mother was nurturer and supporter. "Motherhood is the highest form of femininity," the evangelical author Beverly LaHaye wrote in an influential book on Christian women. Another popular Christian author declared, "A church, a family, a nation is only as strong as its men."

Evangelicals spread their message about the Christian family through more than the pulpit and television. They founded publishing houses, wrote books, established foundations, and offered seminars. Helen B. Andelin, for instance, a California housewife, produced a homemade book called *Fascinating Womanhood* that eventually sold more than 2 million copies. She used the book as the basis for her classes, which by the early 1970s had been attended by 400,000 women and boasted 11,000 trained teachers. *Fascinating Womanhood* was an evangelical response to the women's movement. Where the latter encouraged women to be independent and to seek equality with men, Andelin taught that "submissiveness will bring a strange but righteous power over your man." Andelin was but one of dozens of evangelical authors and educators who encouraged women to defer to men.

Evangelical Christians held that strict gender roles in the family would ward off the influences of an immoral society. Christian activists were especially concerned with sex education in public schools, the proliferation of pornography, legalized abortion, and the rising divorce rate. For them, the answer was to strengthen what they called "traditional" family structures. By the early 1980s, Christians could choose from among hundreds of evangelical books, take classes on how to save a marriage or how to be a Christian parent, attend evangelical churches and Bible study courses, watch evangelical ministers on television, and donate to foundations that promoted "Christian values" in state legislatures and the U.S. Congress.

Wherever one looked in the 1970s and early 1980s, American families were under strain. Nearly everyone agreed that the waves of social liberalism and economic transformation that swept over the nation in the 1960s and 1970s had destabilized society and, especially, family relationships. But Americans did not agree about how to *re*stabilize families. Indeed, different approaches to the family would further divide the country in the 1980s and 1990s, as the New Right would increasingly make "family values" a political issue.

▶ Why was there so much concern about the future of the family in the 1970s?

▶ How did evangelical Christianity influence American society in the 1970s and 1980s?

SUMMARY

For much of the 1970s, Americans struggled with economic problems, including inflation, energy shortages, income stagnation, and deindustrialization. These challenges highlighted the limits of postwar prosperity and forced Americans to consider lowering their economic expectations. In the midst of this gloomy economic climate, they also sought political and cultural resolutions to the upheavals of the 1960s. A movement for environmental protection, widely supported, led to new laws and an awareness of nature's limits. Meanwhile, the battle for civil rights entered a second stage, expanding to encompass women's rights and gay rights, the rights of alleged criminals and prisoners, and, in the realm of racial justice, focusing on the problem of producing concrete results rather than legislation. Many liberals cheered these developments, but another effect was to strengthen a new, more conservative social mood that began to challenge liberal values in politics and society more generally. Finally, we considered the multiple challenges faced by the American family in the 1970s and how a perception that the family was in trouble helped to spur an evangelical religious revival that would shape American society for decades to come.

For additional primary sources from this period, see *Documents for America's History*, Seventh Edition.

For Web sites, images, and documents related to topics and places in this chapter, visit *Make History* at **bedfordstmartins.com/henrettaconcise**.

For Further Exploration

Excellent overviews of the era include Rick Perlstein, *Nixonland: The Rise of a President and the Fracturing of America* (2008), and Bruce Schulman, *The Seventies: The Great Shift in American Culture, Society, and Politics* (2001). For documents on the Carter presidency, see Daniel Horowitz, *Jimmy Carter and the Energy Crisis of the 1970s* (2005). On the American environmental movement, see Kirkpatrick Sale, *The Green Revolution: The American Environmental Movement, 1962–1992* (1993). J. Anthony Lukas, *Common Ground* (1985), tells the story of the Boston busing crisis through the biographies of three families. Barbara Ehrenreich examines the backlash against feminism in *Hearts of Men* (1984). A sweeping treatment of *Roe v. Wade* is N. E. H. Hull and Peter Charles Hoffer, *Roe v. Wade: The Abortion Rights Controversy in American History* (2001). For a thought-provoking analysis of Christian broadcasting, see Jeffrey Hadden and Anson Shupe, *Televangelism: Power and Politics on God's Frontier* (1988).

The Oyez Project at Northwestern University, at **www.oyez.org/oyez/frontpage**, is an invaluable resource for more than one thousand Supreme Court cases, with audio transcripts, voting records, and summaries. For this period, see, for example, its materials on *Roe v. Wade, Bakke v. University of California*, and *Griswold v. Connecticut*. Documents from the Women's Liberation Movement, culled from the Duke University Special

TIMELINE

1970	▶ Earth Day first observed
	▶ Environmental Protection Agency established
1971	▶ *Swan v. Charlotte-Mecklenburg* approves countywide busing
	▶ First U.S. trade deficit in twentieth century
1972	▶ Equal Rights Amendment passed by Congress
	▶ Phyllis Schlafly founds STOP ERA
	▶ *Furman v. Georgia* outlaws death penalty
1973	▶ *Roe v. Wade* legalizes abortion
	▶ Endangered Species Act
	▶ Arab oil embargo; gas shortages
	▶ Period of high inflation begins
	▶ *San Antonio School District v. Rodriguez* rules property tax funding of schools constitutional
1974	▶ Nixon resigns over Watergate
	▶ Busing controversy in Boston
	▶ *Milliken v. Bradley* limits busing to school district boundaries
	▶ Congress imposes 55 mile-per-hour speed limit
1975	▶ New York nears bankruptcy
	▶ "Watergate babies" begin congressional reform
1976	▶ Jimmy Carter elected president
1978	▶ Proposition 13 reduces California property taxes
	▶ *Bakke v. University of California* limits affirmative action
	▶ Harvey Milk assassinated in San Francisco
1979	▶ Three Mile Island nuclear accident
	▶ Chrysler saved from bankruptcy by federal bailout
1980	▶ "Superfund" created to clean up toxic land sites

Collections Library, emphasize the women's movement of the late 1960s and early 1970s. This searchable site, at **scriptorium.lib.duke.edu/wlm**, includes books, pamphlets, and other written materials.

Test Your Knowledge

For practice quizzes, activities, and other study tools, visit the Online Study Guide at **bedfordstmartins.com/henrettaconcise**.

Conservative America Ascendant

1973–1991

Who's going to lock up that unbridled, excessive, uncontrolled federal government?

—Reverend James Robison, 1980

The decade of the 1970s saw Americans divided by the Vietnam War, wearied by social unrest, and unmoored by economic drift. As a result, many ordinary citizens developed a deep distrust of the muscular Great Society liberalism of the 1960s. Seizing political advantage amid the trauma and divisions, a revived Republican Party, led by the New Right, offered the nation a fresh way forward: economic deregulation, low taxes, Christian morality, and a reenergized Cold War foreign policy. The election of President Ronald Reagan in 1980 symbolized the ascendance of this new political formula, and the president himself helped define the era.

The New Right's rise was part of a larger development in the West in the 1980s. President Reagan in the United States and Prime Minister Margaret Thatcher in England, after decades of largely liberal government policies in both countries, asserted a renewed confidence in "free markets" and called for a smaller government role in economic regulation and social welfare. Reagan famously said, "Government is not the solution to our problem; government *is* the problem." Like the New Right generally, Reagan was profoundly skeptical of the liberal ideology that had informed American public policy since Franklin D. Roosevelt's New Deal. His presidency combined an economically conservative domestic agenda with aggressive anticommunism abroad. Reagan's foreign policy brought an end to **détente** — a lessening of tensions — with the Soviet Union (which had begun with Richard Nixon) and then, unexpectedly, a sudden thawing of U.S.-Soviet relations, laying the groundwork for the end of the Cold War.

Reagan defined the conservative ascendancy of the 1980s, but he did not create the New Right groundswell that brought him into office. Grassroots conservative activists in the 1960s and 1970s built a formidable right-wing movement that awaited an opportune political moment to challenge for national power. That moment came in 1980, when Democratic president Jimmy Carter's popularity plummeted as a result of his mismanagement of two national crises. Raging inflation and the Iranian seizure of U.S. hostages in Tehran undid Carter and provided an opening for the New Right, which would shape the nation's politics for the remainder of the twentieth century and the first decade of the twenty-first.

The Wall Comes Down

As the Communist government of East Germany collapsed, West Berliners showed their contempt for the wall dividing the city by defacing it with graffiti. Then, in November 1989, East and West Berliners destroyed huge sections of the wall with sledgehammers, an act of psychic liberation that symbolized the end of the Cold War. Alexandria Avakian/Woodfin Camp & Associates.

The Rise of the New Right

The Great Depression and World War II discredited the traditional conservative program of limited government at home and diplomatic isolationism abroad. Nevertheless, a right-wing faction survived within the Republican Party. Its adherents continued to oppose the New Deal but reversed their earlier isolationism. Conservatives pushed for military interventions against communism in Europe, Asia, and the developing world while calling for the broadest possible investigation of subversives at home. Heroes of the American right in the 1950s included J. Edgar Hoover, the head of the Federal Bureau of Investigation (FBI) and an outspoken anticommunist; General Douglas MacArthur, who advocated full-scale war with China; and Republican senator Robert A. Taft of Ohio, who accused the New Deal of "socialistic control of all property and income."

However, conservatives failed to devise policies that could win the allegiance of American voters in the two decades after World War II. Republicans by and large continued to favor party moderates, such as Dwight Eisenhower, Thomas Dewey, and Nelson Rockefeller. These were politicians, often called liberal Republicans, who supported much of the New Deal, endorsed the containment policy overseas, and generally steered a middle course through the volatile social and political changes of the postwar era. The conservative faction held out hope, however, that it might one day win the loyalty of a majority of Republicans and remake the party in its image. In the 1960s and 1970s, these conservatives invested their hopes for national resurgence in two dynamic figures: Barry Goldwater and Ronald Reagan. Together, the two carried the conservative banner until the national mood grew more receptive to right-wing appeals.

Barry Goldwater and Ronald Reagan: Champions of the Right

The personal odyssey of Ronald Reagan embodies the story of New Right Republican conservatism. Before World War II, Reagan was a well-known movie actor as well as a New Deal Democrat and admirer of Roosevelt. However, he turned away from liberalism, partly from self-interest (he disliked paying high taxes) and partly on principle. As head of the Screen Actors Guild from 1947 to 1952, Reagan had to deal with its Communist members, who formed the extreme left wing of the American labor movement. Dismayed by their hard-line tactics and goals, he became a militant anticommunist. After nearly a decade as a spokesperson for the General Electric Corporation, Reagan joined the Republican Party in the early 1960s and began speaking for conservative causes and candidates.

One of those candidates was archconservative Barry Goldwater, a Republican senator from Arizona. Confident in their power, centrist Republicans did not anticipate that grassroots conservatives could challenge the party's old guard and nominate one of their own for president: Goldwater himself. Understanding how they did so in 1964 brings us closer to comprehending the forces that propelled Reagan to the presidency a decade and a half later. Indeed, Reagan the politician came to national attention in 1964 with a televised speech at the Republican convention supporting Goldwater for the presidency. Reagan's address, titled "A Time for Choosing," secured his political future. Striking a dramatic tone, Reagan warned that if we "trade our freedom for the soup kitchen of the welfare state," the nation would "take the first step into a thousand years of darkness."

The Conscience of a Conservative | Like Reagan, Goldwater came from the Sunbelt, where citizens widely celebrated a libertarian spirit of limited government and great personal freedom. His 1960 book, *The Conscience of a Conservative*, set forth an uncompromising conservatism. In direct and accessible prose, Goldwater attacked the New Deal state, arguing that "the natural tendency of government [is] to expand in the direction of absolutism." The problem with the Republican Party, as he saw it, was that Eisenhower had been too accommodating to liberalism. When Ike told reporters that he was "liberal when it comes to human problems," Goldwater privately fumed.

After the appearance of *The Conscience of a Conservative*, a grassroots movement in support of Goldwater emerged in the Republican Party. By distributing his book widely and mobilizing activists at state party conventions, conservatives hoped to create such a groundswell of support that Goldwater could be "drafted" to run for president in 1964, something he reportedly did not wish to do. Meanwhile, Goldwater further enchanted conservatives with another book, *Why Not Victory?*, in which he criticized the containment policy — the strategy of preventing the spread of communism followed by both Democrats and Republicans since 1947 — as weak and defensive. It was, he complained, a policy of "timidly refusing to draw our own lines against aggression . . . unmarked by pride or the prospect of victory." Here was a politician saying exactly what conservatives wanted to hear.

Grassroots Conservatives | Because moderates controlled the Republican Party, winning the 1964 nomination for Goldwater required conservative activists to build their campaign from the bottom up. They found thousands upon thousands of Americans willing to wear down shoe leather for their political hero. Organizations such as the John Birch Society, Young Americans for Freedom, and the Liberty Lobby supplied an army of eager volunteers. They came from such conservative strongholds as Orange County, California, and the fast-growing suburbs of Phoenix, Dallas, Houston, Atlanta, and other Sunbelt cities. A critical boost came in the early spring of 1964, when conservatives outmaneuvered moderates at the state convention of the California Republican Party, which then enthusiastically endorsed Goldwater. The fight had been bruising, and one moderate Republican warned that "sinister forces are at work to take over the whole Republican apparatus in California."

Another spur to Goldwater backers was the appearance of a book by Phyllis Schlafly, who was then a relatively unknown conservative activist from the Midwest. Like Goldwater's own book, Schlafly's *A Choice Not an Echo* accused moderate Republicans of being Democrats in disguise (that is, an "echo" of Democrats). Schlafly, who reappeared in the national spotlight in the early 1970s to help halt the ratification of the Equal Rights Amendment, denounced the "Rockefeller Republicans" of the Northeast and encouraged the party to embrace a defiant conservatism. Contrasting Goldwater's "grassroots Republicans" with Rockefeller's "kingmakers," Schlafly hoped to "forestall another defeat like 1940, 1944, 1948, and 1960," Democratic victories all.

The conservative groundswell won the Republican nomination for Goldwater. However, his strident tone and militarist foreign policy were too much for a nation mourning the death of John F. Kennedy and still committed to liberalism. Democrat Lyndon B. Johnson defeated Goldwater in a historic landslide (see Chapter 28). Many believed that Goldwater conservatism would wither and die, but instead the nearly four million volunteers who had campaigned for the Arizona senator swung their support to Ronald Reagan. Skilled conservative political operatives such as Richard Viguerie, a Louisiana-born Catholic and antiabortion activist, applied new computer technology to political campaigning. Viguerie took a list of 12,000 Goldwater contributors and used computerized mailing lists to solicit campaign funds, drum up support for conservative causes, and get out the vote on election day. Conservatism was down but not out.

Backed financially by wealthy southern Californians and supported at the grass roots by Goldwaterites, Reagan won California's governorship in 1966 and again in 1970. His impassioned rhetoric supporting limited government and law and order — he vowed to "clean up the mess in Berkeley," referring to campus radicals — won broad support among citizens of the nation's most populous state. More significantly, it made him a force in national politics. His supporters believed that he was in line to succeed Nixon as the next Republican president. The Watergate scandal intervened, however, discrediting Nixon and making Gerald Ford the incumbent. After narrowly losing a campaign against Ford for the Republican presidential nomination in 1976, Reagan was forced to bide his time. When Ford lost to Carter in that year's election, Reagan was the party's brightest star and a near-lock to be the nominee in 1980.

Free-Market Economics and Religious Conservatism

The last phase of Reagan's rise was the product of several additional developments within the New Right. The burgeoning conservative movement increasingly resembled a three-legged stool. Each leg represented an ideological position and a popular constituency: anticommunism, free-market economics, and religious moralism. Uniting all three in a political coalition was no easy feat. Religious moralists demanded strong government action to implement their faith-based agenda, while economic conservatives favored limited government and free markets. Both groups, however, were ardent anticommunists — free marketeers loathed the state-directed Soviet economy, and religious conservatives despised the "godless" secularism of the Soviet state. In the end, the success of the New Right would come to depend on balancing the interests of economic and moral conservatives.

Since the 1950s, William F. Buckley, the founder and editor of the *National Review*, and Milton Friedman, the Nobel Prize–winning economist at the University of Chicago, had been the most prominent conservative intellectuals. Buckley famously wrote that his *National Review* "stands athwart history yelling Stop," meaning it opposed what he called "Liberal orthodoxy." Convinced that "the growth of government must be fought relentlessly," Buckley used the magazine to criticize liberal policy. For his part, Friedman became a national conservative icon with the publication of *Capitalism and Freedom* (1962), in which he argued that "economic freedom is . . . an indispensable means toward the achievement of political freedom." Friedman's free-market ideology, along with that of Friedrich von Hayek, another University of Chicago economist, was taken up by wealthy conservatives, who funded think tanks to disseminate market-based public policy ideas. The Heritage Foundation, the American Enterprise Institute, and the Cato Institute issued policy proposals and attacked liberal legislation and the permissive culture they claimed it had spawned. Followers of Buckley and Friedman envisioned themselves as crusaders, working against what one conservative called "the despotic aspects of egalitarianism."

The most striking addition to the conservative coalition was the Religious Right. Until the 1970s, most fundamentalist and evangelical Protestants worried about saving their souls and preparing for the Second Coming of Christ. Politics was an earthly concern of secondary interest. But the perception that American society had become immoral, combined with the influence of a new generation of popular ministers, made politics relevant. Conservative Protestants and Catholics joined together in a tentative alliance, as the Religious Right condemned divorce, abortion, premarital sex, and feminism. The route to a moral life and to "peace, pardon, purpose, and power," as one evangelical activist said, was "to plug yourself into the One, the Only One [God]."

Charismatic televangelists such as Pat Robertson and Jerry Falwell emerged as the champions of a morality-based political agenda during the late 1970s. Falwell, founder of Liberty University and host of the *Old Time Gospel Hour* television program, established the Moral Majority in 1979. Backed by behind-the-scenes conservative strategists such as Paul Weyrich, the Moral Majority boasted 400,000 members and $1.5 million in contributions in its first year. It would be the organizational vehicle for transforming the Fourth Great Awakening into a religious political movement. Falwell made no secret of his views: "If you want to know where I am politically," he told reporters, "I thought Goldwater was too liberal." Falwell was not alone. Phyllis Schlafly's STOP ERA, which became Eagle Forum in 1975, continued to advocate for conservative public policy; Focus on the Family was founded in 1977; and a succession of conservative organizations would emerge in the 1980s, including the Family Research Council.

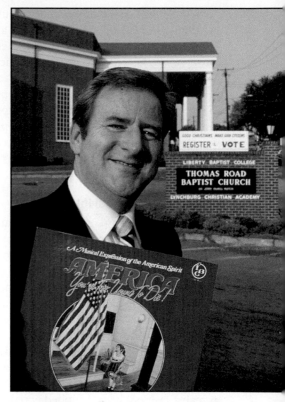

Jerry Falwell
The resurgence of evangelical religion in the 1970s was accompanied by a conservative movement in politics known as the Religious Right. Founded in 1979 by televangelist Jerry Falwell, the Moral Majority was one of the earliest Religious Right groups, committed to promoting "family values" and (as the title to the record album he is holding in this photo suggests) patriotism in American society and politics. Wally McNamee/Corbis.

The conservative message preached by Barry Goldwater and Ronald Reagan had appealed to few American voters in 1964. Then came the series of events that undermined support for the liberal agenda of the Democratic Party: the failed war in Vietnam; a judiciary that legalized abortion and pornography, enforced school busing, and curtailed public expression of religion; urban riots; and a stagnating economy. By the late 1970s, the New Right had developed a conservative message that commanded much greater popular support than Goldwater's program had. Religious and free-market conservatives joined with traditional anticommunist hard-liners — alongside whites opposed to black civil rights, affirmative action, and busing — in a broad coalition that attacked welfare-state liberalism, social permissiveness, and an allegedly weak and defensive foreign policy. Ronald Reagan expertly appealed to all of these conservative constituencies and captured the Republican presidential nomination in 1980 (see American Voices, p. 919). It had taken almost two decades, but the New Right appeared on the verge of winning the presidency.

The Carter Presidential Interregnum

First, the Republican Party had to defeat incumbent president Jimmy Carter. Carter's outsider status and his disdain for professional politicians had made him the ideal post-Watergate president. But his ineffectiveness as an executive also made him the perfect foil for Ronald Reagan. Indeed, Reagan and his New Right supporters could not have asked for a better predecessor: Carter's missteps opened the door for Reagan's election.

Carter had an idealistic vision of American leadership in world affairs. He presented himself as the anti-Nixon, a world leader who rejected Henry Kissinger's "realism" in favor of human rights and peacemaking. "Human rights is the soul of our foreign policy," Carter asserted, "because human rights is the very soul of our sense of nationhood." He established the Office of Human Rights in the State Department and withdrew economic and military aid from repressive regimes in Argentina, Uruguay, and Ethiopia — although, in realist fashion, he still funded equally repressive U.S. allies such as the Philippines and South Africa. In Latin America, Carter eliminated a decades-old symbol of Yankee imperialism by signing a treaty on September 7, 1977, turning control of the Panama Canal over to Panama (effective December 31, 1999). Carter's most important efforts came in forging an enduring, although in retrospect limited, peace in the intractable Arab-Israeli conflict. In 1978, he invited Israeli prime minister Menachem Begin and Egyptian president Anwar el-Sadat to Camp David, where they crafted a "framework for peace," under which Egypt recognized Israel and received back the Sinai Peninsula, which Israel had occupied since 1967.

Carter deplored what he called the "inordinate fear of Communism," but his efforts at improving relations with the Soviet Union foundered. His criticism of the Kremlin's record on human rights offended Soviet leader Leonid Brezhnev and slowed arms reduction negotiations. When, in 1979, Carter finally signed the second Strategic Arms Limitations Treaty (SALT II), limiting bombers and missiles, Senate hawks objected. Then, when the Soviet Union invaded Afghanistan that December, Carter suddenly endorsed the hawks' position and treated the invasion as a major crisis; he called it the "gravest threat to world peace since World War II." After ordering an embargo on wheat shipments to the Soviet Union and withdrawing SALT II from Senate consideration, Carter called for increased defense spending and declared an American boycott of the 1980 Summer Olympics in Moscow. In a fateful decision, he and Congress began providing covert assistance to anti-Soviet fighters in Afghanistan, some of whom, including Osama bin Laden, would metamorphose into anti-American Islamic radicals decades later.

Christianity and Public Life

Conservative Christians challenge the pluralism and secularism of modern social-welfare liberalism and seek to integrate religion into public life. Ronald Reagan's candidacy was strongly supported by Christian conservatives; he delivered these remarks to the National Association of American Evangelicals in 1983. A. Bartlett Giamatti, then president of Yale University (1978–1986), offered his remarks to Yale undergraduates in 1981.

President Ronald Reagan: I want you to know that this administration is motivated by a political philosophy that sees the greatness of America in you, her people, and in your families, churches, neighborhoods, communities — the institutions that foster and nourish values like concern for others and respect for the rule of law under God.

Now, I don't have to tell you that this puts us in opposition to, or at least out of step with, a prevailing attitude of many who have turned to a modern-day secularism, discarding the tried and time-tested values upon which our very civilization is based. No matter how well intentioned, their value system is radically different from that of most Americans. And while they proclaim that they're freeing us from superstitions of the past, they've taken upon themselves the job of superintending us by government rule and regulation. Sometimes their voices are louder than ours, but they are not yet a majority. . . .

Freedom prospers when religion is vibrant and the rule of law under God is acknowledged. When our Founding Fathers passed the First Amendment, they sought to protect churches from government interference. They never intended to construct a wall of hostility between government and the concept of religious belief itself.

A. Bartlett Giamatti: A self-proclaimed "Moral Majority," and its satellite or client groups, cunning in the use of a native blend of old intimidation and new technology, threaten the values [of pluralism and freedom]. . . .

From the maw of this "morality" come those who presume to know what justice for all is; come those who presume to know which books are fit to read, which television programs are fit to watch. . . . From the maw of this "morality" rise the tax-exempt Savonarolas who believe they, and they alone, possess the "truth." There is no debate, no discussion, no dissent. They know. . . . What nonsense.

What dangerous, malicious nonsense. . . .

We should be concerned that so much of our political and religious leadership acts intimidated for the moment and will not say with clarity that this most recent denial of the legitimacy of differentness is a radical assault on the very pluralism of peoples, political beliefs, values, forms of merit and systems of religion our country was founded to welcome and foster.

Liberty protects the person from unwarranted government intrusions into a dwelling or other private places. In our tradition the State is not omnipresent in the home. And there are other spheres of our lives and existence, outside the home, where the State should not be a dominant presence.

Freedom extends beyond spatial bounds. Liberty presumes an autonomy of self that includes freedom of thought, belief, expression, and certain intimate conduct.

SOURCES: Ronald Reagan, *Speaking My Mind: Selected Speeches* (New York: Simon & Schuster, 1989), 169–180. Yale University Archives.

Hostage | Carter's ultimate undoing came in Iran, however. The United States had long
Crisis | counted Iran as a faithful ally, a bulwark against Soviet expansion into the
Middle East and a steady source of oil. Since the 1940s, Iran had been ruled
by Mohammad Reza Shah Pahlavi. Ousted by a democratically elected parliament in
the early 1950s, the shah (king) sought and received the assistance of the U.S. Central
Intelligence Agency (CIA), which helped him reclaim power in 1953. American intervention soured Iranian views of the United States for decades. Notwithstanding his fine
words, Carter followed the same path in relations with Iran as his Cold War predecessors had, overlooking the crimes of Iran's CIA-trained secret police and ignoring mounting popular enmity toward the United States inside Iran. Early in 1979, a revolution drove
the shah into exile and brought a fundamentalist Shiite cleric, the Ayatollah Ruhollah
Khomeini, to power (Shiites represent one branch of Islam, Sunnis the other). When
the United States admitted the deposed shah into the country for cancer treatment,
Iranian students seized the U.S. embassy in Tehran, taking sixty-six Americans hostages. The captors demanded that the shah be returned to Iran for trial. Carter refused.
Instead, he suspended arms sales to Iran and froze Iranian assets in American banks.

For the next fourteen months, the hostage crisis paralyzed Carter's presidency.
Night after night, humiliating pictures of blindfolded American hostages appeared on
television newscasts. An attempt to mount a military rescue in April 1980 had to be
aborted because of equipment failures in the desert. Several months later, however, a
stunning development changed the calculus on both sides: Iraq, led by Saddam Hussein,
invaded Iran, officially because of a dispute over deep-water ports but also to prevent
the Shiite-led Iranian Revolution from spreading across the border into Sunni-run Iraq.
Desperate to focus his nation's attention on Iraq's invasion, Khomeini began to talk with
the United States about releasing the hostages. Difficult negotiations dragged on past the
American presidential election in November 1980, and the hostages were finally released
the day after Carter left office — a final indignity endured by a well-intentioned but ineffectual president.

The Election | President Carter's sinking popularity hurt his bid for reelection. When the
of 1980 | Democrats barely renominated him over his liberal challenger, Edward
(Ted) Kennedy of Massachusetts, Carter's approval rating was historically
low: A mere 21 percent of Americans believed that he was an effective president. The
reasons were clear: Economically, millions of citizens were feeling the pinch from stagnant wages, high inflation, crippling mortgage rates, and an unemployment rate of nearly
8 percent. In international affairs, the nation blamed Carter for his weak response to
Soviet expansion and the Iranians' seizure of American diplomats.

With Carter on the defensive, Reagan remained upbeat and decisive. "This is the
greatest country in the world," Reagan reassured the nation in his warm baritone voice.
"We have the talent, we have the drive. . . . All we need is the leadership." To emphasize
his intention to be a formidable international leader, Reagan hinted that he would take
strong action to win the hostages' return. To signal his rejection of liberal policies, he
declared his opposition to affirmative action and forced busing and promised to "get
the government off our backs." Most important, Reagan effectively appealed to the many
Americans who felt financially insecure. In a televised debate with Carter, Reagan empha-

sized the hardships facing working- and middle-class Americans in an era of stagflation and asked them: "Are you better off today than you were four years ago?"

In November, the voters gave a clear answer. They repudiated Carter, giving him only 41.0 percent of the vote. Independent candidate John Anderson garnered 6.6 percent (with a few minor candidates receiving fractions of a percent), and Reagan won with 50.7 percent of the popular vote. Moreover, the Republicans elected thirty-three new members of the House of Representatives and twelve new senators, which gave them control of the U.S. Senate for the first time since 1954. The New Right's long road to national power had culminated in an election victory that signaled a new political alignment in the country.

▶ Which were the key groups of the new Republican coalition? Were their goals complementary?

▶ In what ways was the New Right "reactive," responding to liberalism, and in what ways was it "proactive," asserting its own agenda?

The Dawning of the Conservative Age

By the time Ronald Reagan took office in 1981, conservatism commanded wider popular support than at any time since the 1920s. As the New Deal Democratic coalition continued to fragment, the Republican Party accelerated the realignment of the American electorate that had begun during the 1960s. Conservatism's ascendancy did more than realign the nation politically. Its emphasis on free markets, low taxes, and individual success shaped the nation's culture and inaugurated a conservative era. Reagan exhorted Americans, "Let the men and women of the marketplace decide what they want."

The Reagan Coalition

Reagan's decades in public life, especially his years working for General Electric, had equipped him to articulate conservative ideas in easily understandable aphorisms ("Concentrated power has always been the enemy of liberty," he said). Reagan was good at keeping the conservative message simple and straightforward. The core of the Republican Party remained the relatively affluent, white, Protestant voters who supported balanced budgets, opposed government activism, feared crime and communism, and believed in a strong national defense. Reagan Republicanism also attracted middle-class suburbanites and migrants to the Sunbelt states who endorsed the conservative agenda of combating crime and limiting social welfare spending. Suburban growth in particular, a phenomenon that reshaped metropolitan areas across the country in the 1960s and 1970s, benefited conservatives politically. Suburban traditions of privatization and racial homogeneity, combined with the amenities of middle-class comfort, made the residents of suburban cities more inclined to support conservative public policies.

This emerging Republican coalition was joined by a large and electorally key group of former Democrats that had been gradually moving toward the Republican Party since 1964: southern whites. Reagan capitalized on the "Southern Strategy" developed by Richard Nixon's advisors in the late 1960s. Many southern whites had lost confidence in the Democratic Party for a wide range of reasons, but one factor stood out: the party's support for civil rights. When Reagan came to Philadelphia, Mississippi, to deliver his first official speech as the Republican presidential nominee, his ringing endorsement of "states' rights" sent a clear message: He validated twenty-five years of southern opposition to federal civil rights legislation. Some of Reagan's advisors had warned him not to go to Philadelphia, the site of the tragic murder of three civil rights workers in 1964, but Reagan believed the opportunity to launch his campaign on a "states' rights" note too important. After 1980, southern whites would remain a cornerstone of the Republican coalition.

The Religious Right proved crucial to the Republican victory as well. Falwell's Moral Majority claimed that it had registered two million new voters for the 1980 election, and the Republican Party's platform reflected its influence. That platform called for a constitutional ban on abortion, voluntary prayer in public schools, and a mandatory death penalty for certain crimes. Republicans also demanded an end to court-mandated busing to achieve racial integration in schools, and, for the first time in forty years, opposed the Equal Rights Amendment. Within the Republican Party, conservatism had triumphed.

Reagan's broad coalition attracted the allegiance of another group dissatisfied with the direction of liberalism in the 1970s: blue-collar Catholics alarmed by antiwar protesters and rising welfare expenditures and hostile to feminist demands. Some observers saw these voters, which many called "Reagan Democrats," as coming from the "silent majority" that Nixon had swung into the Republican fold in 1968 and 1972. They lived in heavily industrialized midwestern states such as Michigan, Ohio, and Illinois, and had been a core part of the Democratic coalition for three decades. Reagan's victory in the 1980s thus hinged on both a revival of right-wing conservative activism and broad dissatisfaction with liberal Democrats — a dissatisfaction that had been building since 1968 but had been interrupted by the post-Watergate backlash against the Republican Party.

Conservatives in Power

The new president kept his political message clear and simple. "What I want to see above all," he remarked, "is that this country remains a country where someone can always get rich." Standing in the way, Reagan believed, was government. In his first year in office, Reagan and his chief advisor, James A. Baker III, quickly set new governmental priorities. To roll back the expanded liberal state, they launched a three-pronged assault on federal taxes, social welfare spending, and the regulatory bureaucracy. To prosecute the Cold War, they advocated a vast increase in defense spending and an end to détente with the Soviet Union. And to match the resurgent economies of Germany and Japan, they set out to restore American leadership of the world's capitalist societies and to inspire renewed faith in "free markets."

Reaganomics | To achieve its economic objectives, the new administration advanced a set of policies, quickly dubbed "Reaganomics," to increase the production (and thus the supply) of goods. The theory underlying supply-side economics, as this approach was called, emphasized investment in productive enterprises. According to supply-side theorists, the best way to bolster investment was to reduce the taxes paid by corporations and wealthy Americans, who could then use these funds to expand production. Supply-siders maintained that the resulting economic expansion would increase government revenues and offset the loss of tax dollars stemming from the original tax cuts. Meanwhile, the increasing supply would generate its own demand, as consumers stepped forward to buy ever more goods. Supply-side theory presumed — in fact, gambled — that future tax revenues would make up for present tax cuts. The idea had a growing list of supporters in Congress, led by an ex-professional football player from Buffalo named Jack Kemp. Kemp praised supply-side economics as "an alternative to the slow-growth, recession-oriented policies of the [Carter] administration."

Reagan took advantage of Republican control of the Senate, as well as high-profile allies such as Kemp, to win congressional approval of the 1981 Economic Recovery Tax Act (ERTA), a massive tax cut that embodied supply-side principles. The act reduced income tax rates for most Americans by 23 percent over three years. For the wealthiest Americans — those with millions to invest — the highest marginal tax rate dropped from 70 to 50 percent. The act also slashed estate taxes, levies on inheritances instituted during the Progressive Era to prevent the transmission of huge fortunes from one generation to the next. Finally, the new legislation trimmed the taxes paid by business corporations by $150 billion over a period of five years. As a result of ERTA, by 1986 the annual revenue of the federal government had been cut by $200 billion (nearly half a trillion in 2010 dollars).

David Stockman, Reagan's budget director, hoped to match this reduction in tax revenue with a comparable cutback in federal expenditures. To meet this ambitious goal, he proposed substantial cuts in Social Security and Medicare. But Congress, and even the president himself, rejected his idea; they were not willing to antagonize middle-class and elderly voters who viewed these government entitlements as sacred. As conservative columnist George Will noted ironically, "Americans are conservative. What they want to conserve is the New Deal." After defense spending, Social Security and Medicare were by far the nation's largest budget items; reductions in other programs would not achieve the savings the administration desired. This contradiction between New Right Republican ideology and political reality would continue to frustrate the party into the twenty-first century.

A more immediate embarrassment confronted conservatives, however. In a 1982 *Atlantic* article, Stockman admitted that supply-side theory was based on faith, not economics. To produce optimistic projections of higher tax revenue in future years, Stockman had manipulated the figures. Worse, Stockman told the *Atlantic* reporter candidly that supply-side theory was based on a long-discredited idea: the "trickle-down" notion that helping the rich would eventually benefit the lower and middle classes. Stockman had drawn back the curtain, much to Republicans' consternation, on the flawed reasoning of supply-side theory. But it was too late. The plan had passed Congress, and since Stockman could not cut major programs such as Social Security and Medicare, he had few options to balance the budget.

As the administration's spending cuts fell short, the federal budget deficit increased dramatically. Military spending contributed a large share of the growing **national debt.** But President Reagan remained undaunted. "Defense is not a budget item," he declared. "You spend what you need." To "make America number one again," Reagan and Defense Secretary Caspar Weinberger pushed through Congress a five-year, $1.2 trillion

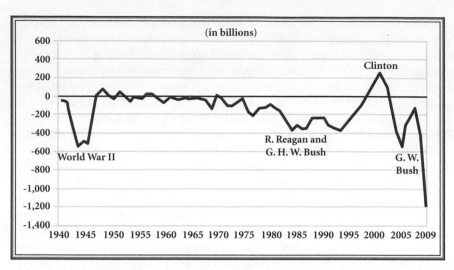

FIGURE 30.1 The Annual Federal Budget Deficit (or Surplus), 1940–2009

During World War II, the federal government incurred an enormous budget deficit. But between 1946 and 1965, it ran either an annual budget surplus or incurred a relatively small debt. The annual deficits rose significantly during the Vietnam War and the stagflation of the 1970s, but they really exploded between 1982 and 1994, in the budgets devised by the Ronald Reagan and George H. W. Bush administrations, and again between 2002 and 2005, in those prepared by George W. Bush. The Republican presidents increased military spending while cutting taxes, an enjoy-it-now philosophy that transferred costs to future generations of Americans. Source: National Priorities Project. See also *U.S. Budget for Fiscal Year 2010*, Historical Tables, Table 15.6.

military spending program. During Reagan's presidency, military spending accounted for one-fourth of all federal expenditures and contributed to rising annual budget deficits (the amount overspent by the government in a single year) and a skyrocketing national debt (the cumulative *total* of all budget deficits). By the time Reagan left office, the total federal debt had tripled, rising from $930 billion in 1981 to $2.8 trillion in 1989. The rising annual deficits of the 1980s contradicted Reagan's pledge of fiscal conservatism (Figure 30.1).

Deregulation | Advocates of Reaganomics believed that excessive regulation by federal agencies impeded economic growth. Deregulation of prices in the trucking, airline, and railroad industries had begun under President Carter in the late 1970s, but Reagan expanded the mandate to include cutting back on government protections of consumers, workers, and the environment. Some of the targeted federal bureaucracies, such as the U.S. Department of Labor, had risen to prominence during the New Deal; others, such as the Environmental Protection Agency (EPA) and the Occupational Safety and Health Administration (OSHA), had been created during the Johnson and Nixon administrations. Although these agencies provided many services to business corporations, they also increased their costs — by protecting the rights of workers, mandating safety improvements in factories, and requiring expensive equipment to limit the release of toxic chemicals into the environment. To reduce the reach of federal regulatory agencies, the Reagan administration cut their budgets, by an average of 12 percent.

Reagan also rendered regulatory agencies less effective by staffing them with leaders who were hostile to the agencies' missions. James Watt, an outspoken conservative who headed the Department of the Interior, attacked environmentalism as "a left-wing cult." Acting on his free-enterprise principles, Watt opened public lands for use by private businesses — oil and coal corporations, large-scale ranchers, and timber companies. Anne Gorsuch Burford, whom Reagan appointed to head the EPA, likewise disparaged environmentalists and refused to cooperate with Congress to clean up toxic waste sites under a program known as the Superfund. The Sierra Club and other environmental groups aroused enough public outrage about these appointees that the administration changed its position. During President Reagan's second term, he significantly increased the EPA's budget and added acreage to the National Wilderness Preservation System and animals and plants to the endangered species lists.

Ultimately, as these adjustments demonstrate, politics in the United States remained "the art of the possible." Savvy politicians know when to advance and when to retreat. Having attained two of his prime goals — a major tax cut and a dramatic increase in defense spending — Reagan did not seriously attempt to scale back big government and the welfare state. When he left office in 1989, federal spending stood at 22.1 percent of the gross domestic product (GDP) and federal taxes at 19 percent of GDP, both virtually the same as in 1981. In the meantime, though, the federal debt had tripled in size and the number of government workers had increased from 2.9 to 3.1 million. This outcome — so different from the president's rhetoric about balancing budgets and downsizing government — elicited harsh criticism from some conservative commentators. "There was no Reagan Revolution," one conservative noted. A former Reagan aide offered a more balanced assessment: "Ronald Reagan did far less than he had hoped . . . and a hell of a lot more than people thought he would."

Remaking the Judiciary | Historians continue to debate whether there was a "Reagan Revolution." Even if he did not achieve everything many of his supporters desired, however, Reagan left an indelible imprint on politics, public policy, and American culture. One place this imprint was felt in far-reaching ways was the judiciary, where Reagan and his attorney general, Edwin Meese, aimed at reversing the liberal judicial philosophy that had prevailed since the late 1950s. During his two terms, Reagan appointed 368 federal court judges — most of them with conservative credentials — and three Supreme Court justices: Antonin Scalia, Sandra Day O'Connor, and Anthony Kennedy. Ironically, the latter two turned out to be far less devoted to New Right conservatism than Reagan and his supporters imagined. O'Connor, the first woman to serve on the Court, shaped its decision making as a swing vote between liberals and conservatives. Kennedy also emerged as a judicial moderate, leaving Scalia as Reagan's only genuinely conservative appointee.

But Reagan also elevated Justice William Rehnquist, a conservative Nixon appointee, to the position of chief justice. Under Rehnquist's leadership (1986–2005), the Court's conservatives took an activist stance, limiting the reach of federal laws, ending court-ordered busing, and endorsing constitutional protection of property rights. However, on controversial issues such as individual liberties, abortion rights, affirmative action, and the rights of criminal defendants, the presence of O'Connor enabled the Court to resist the rightward drift and to maintain a moderate position. As a result, the justices scaled back, but did not usually overturn, the liberal rulings of the Warren and Burger Courts. In the controversial *Webster v. Reproductive Health Services* (1989), for instance, Scalia pushed for the justices to overturn the abortion-rights decision in *Roe v. Wade* (1973). O'Connor refused, but she nonetheless approved the constitutional validity of state laws that limited the use of public funds and facilities for abortions. A more conservative federal judiciary would remain a significant institutional legacy of the Reagan presidency.

AIDS | Another conservative legacy was the slow national response to one of the worst disease epidemics of the postwar decades. The human immunodeficiency virus (HIV), a deadly (though slow-acting) pathogen, developed in Africa when a chimpanzee virus jumped to humans; immigrants carried it to Haiti and then to the United States during the 1970s. In 1981, American physicians identified HIV as a new virus — one that caused a disease known as acquired immunodeficiency syndrome (AIDS). Hundreds of gay men, who were prominent among the earliest carriers of the virus, were dying of AIDS. Within two decades, HIV had spread worldwide, infected more than 50 million people of both sexes, and killed more than 20 million.

Within the United States, AIDS took nearly a hundred thousand lives in the 1980s — more than were lost in the Korean and Vietnam Wars combined. However, because its most prominent early victims were gay men, President Reagan, emboldened by New Right conservatives, hesitated in declaring a national health emergency. Some of Reagan's advisors asserted that this "gay disease" might even be God's punishment of homosexuals. Between 1981 and 1986, as the epidemic spread, the Reagan administration took little action — worse, it prevented the surgeon general, C. Everett Koop, from speaking forthrightly to the nation about the disease. Pressed by gay activists and prominent health officials from across the country, in Reagan's last years in office the administration finally began to devote federal resources to treatment for HIV and AIDS patients and research into possible vaccines. But the delay had proved costly, inhumane, and embarrassing.

Morning in America

During his first run for governor of California in 1966, Reagan held a revelatory conversation with a campaign consultant. "Politics is just like the movies," Reagan told him. "You have a hell of an opening, coast for a while, and then have a hell of a close." Reagan indeed had a "hell of an opening": one of the most lavish and expensive presidential inaugurations in American history in 1981 (and another in 1985). While some conservatives, including Goldwater, growled at the ostentatious display, Reagan showed that he was unafraid to celebrate wealth, luxury, and opulence, even with millions of American out of work. Moreover, the rest of Reagan's presidency closely corresponded to the simple formula he outlined in 1966.

Following his spectacular inauguration, Reagan quickly won passage of his tax reduction bill and launched his plan to bolster the Pentagon. But then a long "coasting" period descended on his presidency, during which he retreated on tax cuts and navigated a major foreign policy scandal. Finally, toward the end of his two-term presidency, Reagan found his "hell of a close," leaving office as major reforms — which he encour-

HIV/AIDS
The HIV/AIDS epidemic hit the United States in the early 1980s and remained a major social and political issue throughout the decade. Here, AIDS patients and their supporters participate in the 1987 March on Washington for Gay and Lesbian Rights, demanding that the Reagan administration commit more federal resources to finding a cure for the deadly disease. © Bettmann/Corbis.

aged from afar — had begun to tear apart the Soviet Union and bring an end to the Cold War. Through all the ups and downs, Reagan remained a master of the politics of symbolism, championing a resurgent American economy and reassuring the country that the pursuit of wealth was noble and that he had the reins of the nation firmly in hand.

Reagan's tax cuts had barely taken effect when he was forced to reverse course. High interest rates set by the Federal Reserve Board had cut the runaway inflation of the Carter years. But these rates — as high as 18 percent — sent the economy into a recession in 1981–1982 that put 10 million Americans out of work and shuttered 17,000 businesses. Unemployment neared 10 percent, the highest rate since the Great Depression. These troubles, combined with the booming deficit, forced Reagan to negotiate a tax *increase* with Congress in 1982 — to the loud complaints of supply-side diehards. The president's job rating plummeted, and in the 1982 midterm elections Democrats picked up twenty-six seats in the House of Representatives and seven state governorships.

Election of 1984 | Fortunately for Reagan, the economy had recovered by 1983, restoring the president's job approval rating just in time for the 1984 presidential election. During the campaign, Reagan emphasized the economic resurgence, touring the country promoting his tax policies and the nation's new prosperity. The Democrats nominated former vice president Walter Mondale of Minnesota. With strong ties to labor unions, ethnic and racial minority groups, and party leaders, Mondale epitomized the New Deal coalition. He selected Representative Geraldine Ferraro of New York as his running mate — the first woman to run on the presidential ticket of a major political party. Neither Ferraro's presence nor Mondale's credentials made a difference, however: Reagan won a landslide victory, losing only Minnesota and the District of Columbia. Still, Democrats retained their majority in the House and, in 1986, regained control of the Senate.

Reagan's 1984 campaign slogan, "It's Morning in America," projected the image of a new day dawning on a confident people. In Reagan mythology, the United States was an optimistic nation of small towns, close-knit families, and kindly neighbors. "The success story of America," he once said, "is neighbor helping neighbor." The mythology may not have reflected the *actual* nation — which was overwhelmingly urban and suburban, and in which the hard knocks of capitalism held down more than opportunity elevated — but that mattered little. Reagan's remarkable ability to produce positive associations and feelings, alongside robust economic growth after the 1981–1982 recession, helped make the 1980s a decade characterized both by both backward-looking nostalgia and aggressive capitalism.

Return to Prosperity | Between 1945 and the 1970s, the United States was the world's leading exporter of agricultural products, manufactured goods, and investment capital. Then American manufacturers lost market share, undercut by cheaper and better-designed products from Germany and Japan. By 1985, for the first time since 1915, the United States registered a negative balance of international payments. It now imported more goods and capital than it exported. The country became a debtor (rather than a creditor) nation. The rapid ascent of the Japanese economy to become the world's second largest was a key factor in this historic reversal (see Voices from Abroad, p. 929). More than one-third of the American annual trade deficit of $138 billion in the 1980s was from trade with Japan, whose corporations exported huge quantities of electronic goods and made nearly one-quarter of all cars bought in the United States. Reflecting these profits, Japan's Nikkei stock index tripled in value between 1965 and 1975 and then tripled again by 1985.

Meanwhile, American businesses grappled with a worrisome decline in productivity. Between 1973 and 1992, American productivity (the amount of goods or services per hour of work) grew at the meager rate of 1 percent a year — a far cry from the post–World War II rate of 3 percent. Because managers wanted to cut costs, the wages of most employees stagnated. Further, because of foreign competition, the number of high-paying, union-protected manufacturing jobs shrank. By 1985, more people in the United States worked for McDonald's slinging Big Macs than rolled out rails, girders, and sheet steel in the nation's steel industry. Middle-class Americans, baby boomers included, also found themselves with less economic security as corporations reduced the number, pay, and pensions of middle-level managers and accountants.

A brief return to competitiveness in the second half of the 1980s masked the steady long-term transformation of the economy that had begun in the 1970s. The nation's heavy industries — steel, autos, chemicals — continued to lose market share to global competitors. Nevertheless, the U.S. economy grew at the impressive average rate of 2 to 3 percent per year for much of the late 1980s and 1990s (with a short recession in 1990–1991). What had changed was the direction of growth and its beneficiaries.

Japan and America: Global Partners
YOICHI FUNABASHI

During the 1980s, Yoichi Funabashi lived in the United States as a columnist (and later bureau chief) for the *Asahi Shimbun*, one of Japan's most important daily newspapers.

As Japan struggled to rebuild itself after World War II, the charismatic Shigeru Yoshida, prime minister during the critical years of 1948 to 1952, called on the country to be a good loser. The Japanese have lost the war, he said, but they must not lose heart. Japan must cooperate with the United States, and pull itself out of misery and disgrace. The Japanese did indeed cooperate willingly with the Allied occupation — with the American (and British) "devils" whom they had been taught for years to despise to the very core of their souls. . . .

Postwar Japan went on to prove that it could indeed be a good loser. Under the new constitution promulgated under the guidance of the occupation, it has developed into a democratic country with a relatively moderate disparity between rich and poor and a stable, smoothly functioning political system. . . .

The Japanese-U.S. relationship has thus come to occupy a truly unique position in world history. Never before has a multiethnic, contract-based society and a homogenous, traditional society joined together to form such a powerful team. As global powers, Japan and the United Sates combined have a decisive impact on world politics; it follows that their future relations will largely determine the blueprints for multilateral cooperation and world stability in the coming century. . . .

Potential sources of bilateral friction are as numerous as ever: the trade imbalance, market liberalization, growing Japanese investment in the United States, heavy U.S. dependence on Japanese technology, and so on. Occasional outbursts of economic nationalism, or "revisionist" thinking are probably inevitable as the debate over these issues unfolds. . . .

Of far greater concern, however, is that Japanese-U.S. relations now face their gravest challenge since 1945. The end of the Cold War has drastically altered the global geopolitical and geoeconomic context that shaped Japanese-U.S. relations. Both countries now face the urgent need to redefine their relationship to suit the new context. . . .

Before they can build a strong bilateral relationship, Americans and Japanese must outgrow their obsession with being Number One. This psychological adjustment is absolutely necessary for both peoples. Projecting the nature of its own hierarchical society, Japan tends to view the rest of the world, it is said, in terms of ranking. This inclination fosters behavior patterns that are oriented more toward what to *be* than what to *do*. Japan is also overly conscious of itself as a late-starter, having entered modern international society only in the mid-nineteenth century, and this history has made catching up with and outpacing other countries a sort of national pastime. . . . It may be even more difficult for the United States, which dominated the free world during the Cold War, to make the psychological adjustments required to enter into a partnership with Japan that is truly equal. . . .

SOURCE: Yoichi Funabashi, "Japan and America: Global Partners," *Foreign Policy* 86 (Spring 1992): 24–39.

Increasingly, financial services, medical services, computer technology — *service* industries, broadly speaking — were the leading sectors of growth. This shift in the underlying foundation of the American economy, from manufacturing to service, from making *things* to producing *services*, would have long-term consequences for the global competitiveness of U.S. industries and the value of the dollar.

Culture of Success The economic growth of the second half of the 1980s popularized the materialistic values championed by the free marketeers. Every era has its capitalist heroes, but Americans in the 1980s celebrated wealth accumulation in ways unseen since the 1920s. When the president christened self-made entrepreneurs "the heroes for the eighties," he probably had people like Lee Iacocca in mind. Born to Italian immigrants and trained as an engineer, Iacocca rose through the ranks to become president of the Ford Motor Corporation. In 1978, he took over the ailing Chrysler Corporation and made it profitable again — by securing a crucial $1.5 billion loan from the U.S. government, pushing the development of new cars, and selling them on TV. His patriotic commercials in the 1980s echoed Reagan's rhetoric: "Let's make American mean something again." Iacocca's restoration would not endure, however: In 2009, Chrysler declared bankruptcy and was forced to sell a majority stake to the Italian company Fiat.

If Iacocca symbolized a resurgent corporate America, high-profile financial wheeler-dealers also captured Americans' imagination. One was Ivan Boesky, a white-collar criminal convicted of insider trading (buying or selling stock based on information from corporate insiders). "I think greed is healthy," Boesky told a business school graduating class. Boesky inspired the fictional film character Gordon Gekko, who proclaimed "Greed is good!" in 1987's *Wall Street*. A new generation of Wall Street executives, of which Boesky was one example, pioneered the leveraged buyout (LBO). In a typical LBO, a financier used heavily leveraged (borrowed) capital to buy a company, quickly restructured that company to make it appear spectacularly profitable, and then sold it at a higher price.

Americans had not set aside the traditional work ethic, but the Reagan-era public was fascinated with money and celebrity. (The documentary television show *Lifestyles of the Rich and Famous* began its run in 1984.) One of the most fascinating of money moguls was Donald Trump, a real estate developer who craved publicity. In 1983, the flamboyant Trump built the equally flamboyant Trump Towers in New York City. At the entrance of the $200 million apartment building stood two enormous bronze *T*'s, a display of self-promotion reinforced by the media. Calling him "The Donald," a nickname used by Trump's first wife, TV reporters and magazines commented relentlessly on his marriages, divorces, and glitzy lifestyle.

The Computer Revolution While Trump grabbed headlines and made splashy real estate investments, a handful of quieter, less flashy entrepreneurs was busy changing the face of the American economy. Bill Gates, Paul Allen, Steve Jobs, and Steve Wozniak were four entrepreneurs who pioneered the computer revolution in the late 1970s and 1980s. They took a technology that had been used exclusively for large-scale enterprises — the military and multinational corporations — and made it accessible to individual consumers. Scientists had devised the first computers for military purposes during World War II. Cold War military research subsequently funded the construction of large mainframe computers. But government and private-sector first-generation computers were bulky, cumbersome machines that had to be placed in large air-conditioned rooms.

Between the 1950s and the 1970s, concluding with the development of the microprocessor in 1971, each generation of computers grew faster and smaller. By the mid-1970s, a few microchips the size of the letter *O* on this page provided as much processing power as a World War II–era computer. The day of the personal computer (PC) had arrived. Working in the San Francisco Bay Area, Jobs and Wozniak founded Apple Computers in 1976 and within a year were producing small, individual computers that could be easily used by a single person. When Apple enjoyed success, other companies scrambled to get into the market. International Business Machines (IBM) offered its first personal computer in 1981, but Apple Corporation's 1984 Macintosh computer (later shortened to "Mac") became the first runaway commercial success for a personal computer.

Meanwhile, two former high school classmates, Gates, age nineteen, and Allen, age twenty-one, had set a goal in the early 1970s of putting "a personal computer on every desk and in every home." They recognized that software was the key. In 1975, they founded the Microsoft Corporation, whose MS-DOS and Windows operating systems soon dominated the software industry. By 2000, the company's products ran nine out of every ten personal computers in the United States and a majority of those around the world. Gates and Allen became billionaires, and Microsoft exploded into a huge company with 57,000 employees and annual revenues of $38 billion. In three decades, the computer had moved from a few military research centers to thousands of corporate offices and then to millions of peoples' homes. Ironically, in an age that celebrated free-market capitalism, government research and government funding had played an enormous role in the development of the most important technology since television.

▶ What were the key elements of Reagan's domestic policy? How did that policy reflect conservative ideology?

▶ What limits did Reagan face in promoting his policies? What were his successes and failures?

The End of the Cold War

Ronald Reagan entered office determined to confront the Soviet Union diplomatically and militarily. Backed by Republican and Democratic hard-liners alike, Reagan unleashed some of the harshest Cold War rhetoric since the 1950s, labeling the Soviet Union an "evil empire" and vowing that it would end up "on the ash heap of history." In a remarkable turnaround, however, by his second term Reagan had decided that this goal would be best achieved by actively cooperating with Mikhail Gorbachev, the reform-minded Russian Communist leader. The downfall of the Soviet Union in 1991 ended the nearly fifty-year-long Cold War, but a new set of foreign challenges quickly emerged.

U.S.-Soviet Relations in a New Era

When Reagan assumed the presidency in 1981, he broke with his immediate predecessors — Richard Nixon, Gerald Ford, and Jimmy Carter — in Cold War strategy. Nixon regarded himself as a "realist" in foreign affairs. That meant, above all, advancing the national interest without regard to ideology. Nixon's policy of détente with the Soviet Union and China embodied this realist view. President Carter endorsed détente and continued to push for relaxing Cold War tensions. This worked for a time, but the Soviet invasion of Afghanistan empowered hard-liners in the U.S. Congress and forced Carter to take a tougher line — which he did with the Olympic boycott and grain embargo. This was the relationship Reagan inherited in 1981: a decade of détente that had produced a noticeable relaxation of tensions with the Communist world, followed by a year of tense standoffs over Soviet advances into Central Asia, which threatened U.S. interests in the Middle East.

Reagan's Cold War Revival | Conservatives did not believe in détente. Neither did they believe in the containment policy that had guided U.S. Cold War strategy since 1947. Reagan and his advisors wanted to *defeat* the Soviet Union. His administration pursued a two-pronged strategy toward that end. First, it abandoned détente and set about rearming America. This buildup in American military strength, reasoned Secretary of Defense Caspar Weinberger, would force the Soviets into an arms race that would strain their economy and cause domestic unrest. Second, the president supported CIA initiatives to roll back Soviet influence in the developing world by funding anticommunist movements in Angola, Mozambique, Afghanistan, and Central America.

To accomplish this objective, Reagan supported repressive, right-wing regimes. Nowhere was this more conspicuous in the 1980s than in the Central American countries of Guatemala, Nicaragua, and El Salvador. Conditions were unique in each country but held to a pattern: The United States sided with military dictatorships and oligarchies if democratically elected governments or left-wing movements sought support from the Soviet Union. In Guatemala, this approach produced a brutal military rule — thousands of opponents of the government were executed or kidnapped. In Nicaragua, Reagan actively encouraged a coup against the left-wing Sandinista government, which had overthrown the U.S.-backed strongman Anastasio Somoza. And in El Salvador, the U.S.-backed government maintained secret "death squads," which murdered members of the opposition. In each case, Reagan blocked Soviet influence, but the damage done to local communities and to the international reputation of the United States, as in Vietnam, was great.

Iran-Contra | Reagan's determination to oppose left-wing movements in Central America engulfed his administration in a major scandal during the president's second term. For years, Reagan had denounced Iran as an "outlaw state" and a supporter of terrorism. But in 1985, he wanted its help. To win Iran's assistance in freeing two dozen American hostages held by Hezbollah, a pro-Iranian Shiite group in Lebanon, the administration sold arms to Iran without public or congressional knowledge. While this secret arms deal was diplomatically and politically controversial, the use of the resulting profits in Nicaragua was explicitly illegal. To overthrow the democratically elected Sandinistas, which the president accused of threatening U.S. business interests, Reagan ordered the CIA to assist an armed opposition group called the Contras (Map 30.1). Although Reagan praised the Contras as "freedom fighters," Congress worried that the president and other executive branch agencies were assuming war-making powers that

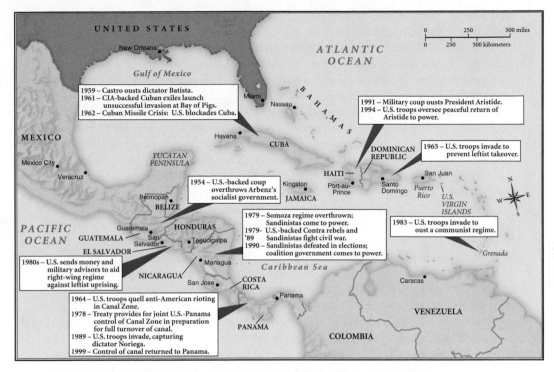

MAP 30.1 U.S. Involvement in Latin America and the Caribbean, 1954–2000

Ever since the Monroe Doctrine (1823), the United States has claimed a special interest in Latin America. During the Cold War, U.S. foreign policy throughout Latin America focused on containing instability and the appeal of communism in a region plagued by poverty and military dictatorships. Providing foreign aid was one approach to addressing social and economic needs, but the United States frequently intervened with military forces (or by supporting military coups) to remove unfriendly or socialist governments. The Reagan administration's support of the Contra rebels in Nicaragua, some of which was contrary to U.S. law, was one of those interventions.

the Constitution reserved to the legislature. In 1984, Congress banned the CIA and all other government agencies from providing any military support to the Contras.

Oliver North, a lieutenant colonel in the U.S. Marines and an aide to the National Security Council, defied that ban. With the tacit or explicit consent of high-ranking administration officials, including the president, North used the profits from the Iranian arms deal to assist the Contras. When asked whether he knew of North's illegal actions, Reagan replied, "I don't remember." Still swayed by Reagan's charm, the public accepted his convenient loss of memory. Nonetheless, the Iran-Contra affair not only resulted in the prosecution of North and several other officials but also jeopardized the president's reputation. The Iran-Contra scandal weakened Reagan domestically — he proposed no bold domestic policy initiatives in his last two years. But the president remained steadfastly engaged in international affairs, where events were unfolding that would bring a dramatic close to the Cold War.

Gorbachev | The Soviet system of state socialism and central economic planning had
and Soviet | transformed Russia from an agricultural to an industrial society between
Reform | 1917 and the 1950s. But it had done so inefficiently. Lacking the incentives
of a market economy, most enterprises hoarded raw materials, employed
too many workers, and did not develop new products. Except in military weaponry and
space technology, the Russian economy fell further and further behind those of capitalist societies, and most people in the Soviet bloc endured a low standard of living.
Moreover, the Soviet invasion of Afghanistan in 1979, like the American war in Vietnam,
turned out to be major blunder — an unwinnable war that cost vast amounts of money,
destroyed military morale, and undermined popular support of the government.

Mikhail Gorbachev, a relatively young Russian leader who became general secretary of the Communist Party in 1985, recognized the need for internal economic reform and an end to the war in Afghanistan. An iconoclast in Soviet terms, Gorbachev
introduced policies of *glasnost* (openness) and *perestroika* (economic restructuring),
which encouraged widespread criticism of the rigid institutions and authoritarian controls of the Communist regime. To lessen tensions with the United States, Gorbachev
met with Reagan in 1985, and the two leaders established a warm personal rapport. By
1987, they had agreed to eliminate all intermediate-range nuclear missiles based in
Europe. A year later, Gorbachev ordered Soviet troops out of Afghanistan, and Reagan
replaced many of his hard-line advisors with policymakers who favored a renewal of
détente. Reagan's sudden reversal with regard to the Soviet Union remains one of the
most intriguing aspects of his presidency. Many conservatives worried that their cowboy-
hero president had been duped by a duplicitous Gorbachev, but Reagan's gamble paid off:
The easing of tensions with the United States allowed the Soviet leader to press forward
with his domestic reforms.

As Gorbachev's efforts revealed the flaws of the Soviet system, the peoples of eastern
and central Europe demanded the ouster of their Communist governments. In Poland,
the Roman Catholic Church and its pope — Polish-born John Paul II — joined with Solidarity, the trade union movement, to overthrow the pro-Soviet regime. In 1956 and 1964,
Russian troops had quashed similar popular uprisings in Hungary and East Germany.
Now they did not intervene, and a series of peaceful uprisings — "Velvet Revolutions" —
created a new political order throughout the region. The destruction of the Berlin Wall in
1989 symbolized the end of Communist rule in Central Europe. Millions of television
viewers worldwide watched jubilant Germans knock down the hated wall. The cement
and barbed-wire barrier, which had divided the city since 1961, was a vivid symbol of
Communist repression and the Cold War division of Europe. Now East and West Berliners, young and old, danced on the remains of the forbidding wall. A new geopolitical
order in Europe was in the making.

Alarmed by the reforms, Soviet military leaders seized power in August 1991 and
arrested Gorbachev. But widespread popular opposition led by Boris Yeltsin, the president of the Russian Republic, thwarted their efforts to oust Gorbachev from office. This
failure broke the dominance of the Communist Party. On December 25, 1991, the Union
of Soviet Socialist Republics formally dissolved to make way for an eleven-member
Commonwealth of Independent States (CIS). The Russian Republic assumed leadership
of the CIS, but the Soviet Union was no more (Map 30.2). The collapse of the Soviet

Reagan and Gorbachev: Fellow Political Revolutionaries
Both Ronald Reagan and Mikhail Gorbachev changed the political outlook of their nations. As Reagan undermined social-welfare liberalism in the United States, Gorbachev challenged the rigidity of the Communist Party and state socialism in the Soviet Union. Although they remained ideological adversaries, by the mid-1980s the two leaders had established a personal rapport, which helped facilitate agreement on a series of arms reduction measures. © Bettmann/Corbis.

Union was the result of internal weaknesses of the Communist economy. External pressure from the United States played an important, though secondary, role.

"Nobody — no country, no party, no person — 'won' the cold war," concluded George Kennan, the architect in 1947 of the American policy of containment. The Cold War's cost was enormous, and both sides benefited greatly from its end. In 1956, Nikita

MAP 30.2 The Collapse of the Soviet Union and the Creation of Independent States, 1989–1991

The collapse of Soviet communism dramatically altered the political landscape of Central Europe and Central Asia. The Warsaw Pact, the USSR's answer to NATO, vanished. West and East Germany reunited, and the nations created by the Versailles treaty of 1919 — Estonia, Latvia, Lithuania, Poland, Czechoslovakia, Hungary, and Yugoslavia — reasserted their independence or split into smaller, ethnically defined nations. The Soviet republics bordering Russia, from Belarus in the west to Kyrgyzstan in the east, also became independent states, while remaining loosely bound with Russia in the Commonwealth of Independent States (CIS).

Khrushchev had told the United States, "We will bury you." For more than forty years, the United States had fought a bitter economic and ideological battle against that Communist foe, a struggle that exerted an enormous impact on American society. Taxpayers had spent some $4 trillion on nuclear weapons and trillions more on conventional arms, placing the United States on a permanent war footing and creating a massive military-industrial complex. The physical and psychological costs were equally high: radiation from atomic weapons tests, anticommunist witch hunts, and — most pervasive of all — a constant fear of nuclear annihilation. Of course, most Americans had no qualms about proclaiming victory, and advocates of free-market capitalism, particularly conservative Republicans, celebrated the outcome. The collapse of communism in Eastern Europe and the disintegration of the Soviet Union itself, they argued, demonstrated that they had been right all along.

A New Political Order at Home and Abroad

Ronald Reagan's role in facilitating the end of the Cold War was probably his most important achievement. Otherwise, his presidency left a mixed legacy. Despite his pledge to get the federal government "off our backs," he could not ultimately reduce its size or scope. Social Security and other entitlement programs remained untouched, and enormous military spending outweighed cuts in other programs. Determined not to divide the country, Reagan did not actively push controversial policies espoused by the Religious Right. He called for tax credits for private religious schools, restrictions on abortions, and a constitutional amendment to permit prayer in public schools, but he did not expend his political capital to secure these measures.

While Reagan failed to roll back the social welfare and regulatory state of the New Deal–Great Society era, he changed the dynamic of American politics. The Reagan presidency restored popular belief that America — and individual Americans — could enjoy increasing prosperity. And his antigovernment rhetoric won many adherents, as did his bold and fiscally dangerous tax cuts. One historian has summed up Reagan's domestic legacy as follows: "For the next twenty years at least, American policies would focus on retrenchment and cost-savings, budget cuts and tax cuts, deregulation and policy redefinitions." Social welfare liberalism, ascendant since 1933, remained intact but was now on the defensive — conservatives had changed the political conversation.

Election of 1988 | George H. W. Bush, Reagan's vice president and successor, was not beloved by conservatives, who did not see him as one of their own. But he possessed an insider's familiarity with government and a long list of powerful allies, accumulated over three decades of public service. Bush's route to the White House reflected the post-Reagan alignments in American politics. In the primaries, he faced a spirited challenge from Pat Robertson, the archconservative televangelist whose influence and profile had grown during Reagan's two terms. After securing the presidential nomination, which he won largely because of his fierce loyalty to Reagan, Bush felt compelled to select as his vice-presidential running mate an unknown and inexperienced Indiana senator, Dan Quayle. Bush hoped that Quayle would help secure the Christian "family values" vote. Robertson's challenge and Quayle's selection showed that the Religious Right had become a major force in Republican politics.

On the Democratic side, Jesse Jackson became the first African American to challenge for a major-party nomination, winning eleven states in primary and caucus voting. However, the much less charismatic Massachusetts governor, Michael Dukakis, emerged as the Democratic nominee. Dukakis, a liberal from the Northeast, proved unable to win back the constituencies Democrats had lost in the 1970s: southern whites, midwestern blue-collar Catholics, and middle-class suburbanites. Indeed, Bush's campaign manager, Lee Atwater, baited Dukakis by calling him a "card-carrying liberal," a not-so-subtle reference to J. Edgar Hoover's 1958 phrase "card-carrying communist." Bush won with 53 percent of the vote, a larger margin of victory than Reagan's in 1980. The election confirmed a new pattern in presidential politics that would last through the turn of the twenty-first century: Every four years, Americans would refight the battles of the 1960s, with liberals on one side and conservatives on the other.

Middle East | The end of the Cold War left the United States as the world's only military superpower and raised the prospect of a "new world order" dominated by the United States and its European and Asian allies. But American officials and diplomats now confronted an array of regional, religious, and ethnic conflicts that defied easy solutions. None were more pressing or more complex than those in the Middle East — the oil-rich lands stretching from Iran to Algeria. Middle Eastern conflicts would dominate the foreign policy of the United States for the next two decades, replacing the Cold War at the center of American geopolitics.

After Carter's success negotiating the 1979 Egypt-Israel treaty at Camp David, there were few bright spots in U.S. Middle Eastern diplomacy. In 1982, the Reagan administration supported Israel's invasion of Lebanon, a military operation intended to destroy the Palestine Liberation Organization (PLO). But when Lebanese militants, angered at U.S. intervention on behalf of Israel, killed 241 American marines, Reagan abruptly withdrew the forces. Three years later, Palestinians living in the Gaza Strip and along the West Bank of the Jordan River — territories occupied by Israel since 1967 — mounted an intifada, a civilian uprising against Israeli authority. In response, American diplomats stepped up their efforts to persuade the PLO and Arab nations to accept the legitimacy of Israel and to convince the Israelis to allow the creation of a Palestinian state. Neither initiative met with much success. Unable, or unwilling, to solve the region's most intractable problems and burdened by a history of support for undemocratic regimes in Middle Eastern countries, the United States was not seen by residents of the region as an honest broker.

Persian Gulf War | American interest in a reliable supply of oil from the region led the United States into a short but consequential war in the Persian Gulf in the early 1990s. Ten years earlier, in September 1980, the revolutionary Shiite Islamic nation of Iran, headed by Ayatollah Khomeini, came under attack from Iraq, a secular state headed by the ruthless dictator Saddam Hussein. The fighting was intense and long lasting — a war of attrition that claimed a million casualties. Reagan supported Hussein

Men — and Women — at War
Women played visible roles in the Persian Gulf War, comprising approximately 10 percent of the American troops. In the last decades of the twentieth century, increasing numbers of women chose military careers and, although prohibited from most fighting roles, were increasingly assigned to combat zones. Luc Delahaye/Sipa Press.

with military intelligence and other aid — in order to maintain supplies of Iraqi oil, undermine Iran, and preserve a balance of power in the Middle East. Finally, in 1988, an armistice ended the inconclusive war, with both sides still claiming the territory that sparked the conflict.

Two years later, in August 1990, Hussein went to war to expand Iraq's boundaries and oil supply. Believing (erroneously) that he still had the support of the United States, Hussein sent in troops and quickly conquered Kuwait, Iraq's small, oil-rich neighbor, and threatened Saudi Arabia, the site of one-fifth of the world's known oil reserves and an informal ally of the United States. To preserve Western access to oil, President George H. W. Bush sponsored a series of resolutions in the United Nations Security Council calling for Iraq to withdraw from Kuwait. When Hussein refused, Bush successfully prodded the UN to authorize the use of force, and the president organized a military coalition of thirty-four nations. Dividing mostly along party lines, the Republican-led House of Representatives authorized American participation by a vote of 252 to 182, and the Democratic-led Senate agreed by the close margin of 52 to 47.

The coalition forces led by the United States quickly won the war for the "liberation of Kuwait." To avoid a protracted struggle and retain French and Russian support for the UN coalition, Bush wisely decided against occupying Iraq and removing Saddam Hussein from power. Instead, he won passage of UN Resolution 687, which imposed economic sanctions against Iraq unless it allowed unfettered inspection of its weapons systems, destroyed all biological and chemical arms, and unconditionally pledged not to develop nuclear weapons. The military victory, the low incidence of American casualties, and the quick withdrawal produced a euphoric reaction at home. "By God, we've kicked the Vietnam syndrome once and for all," Bush gloated, and his approval rating shot up precipitously. But the president spoke too soon. Saddam Hussein remained a formidable power in the region. The dictator's alleged ambitions were one factor that, in March 2003, would cause Bush's son, President George W. Bush, to initiate another war in Iraq — one that would be much more protracted, expensive, and bloody for Americans and Iraqis alike.

Thus, the end of the Cold War brought not peace, but American militarism in the Middle East. For half a century, the United States and the Soviet Union had tried to divide the world into two rival economic and ideological blocs: communist and capitalist. The next decades promised a new set of struggles, one of them between a Western-led agenda of economic and cultural globalization and an anti-Western ideology of Muslim and Arab regionalism. Still more post–Cold War shifts were coming into view as well. One was the spectacular emergence of the European Union as a massive united trading bloc, economic engine, and global political force. Another was the equally spectacular economic growth in China, which was just beginning to take off in the early 1990s. The post–Cold War world promised to be a *multi*polar one, with great centers of power in Europe, the United States, and East Asia, and seemingly intractable conflict in the Middle East.

▶ What factors led to the end of the Cold War?

▶ Why did the United States intervene in the conflicts between Iraq and Iran, and between Iraq and Kuwait?

SUMMARY

This chapter examined two central developments of the years 1973–1991: the rise of the New Right in U.S. politics and the end of the Cold War. Each development set the stage for a new era in American life, one that stretches to our own day. Domestically, the New Right, which had been building in strength since the mid-1960s, criticized the "excessive" liberalism of the Great Society and the permissiveness conservative activists associated with feminism and the sexual revolution. Shifting their allegiance from Barry Goldwater to Ronald Reagan, right-wing Americans built a conservative movement from the ground up and in 1980 elected Reagan president. Advocating free-market econom- ics, lower taxes, and fewer government regulations, Reagan became a champion of the New Right. His record as president was more mixed than his rhetoric would suggest, how- ever. Reagan's initial tax cuts were followed by tax hikes. Moreover, he frequently dis- mayed the Christian Right by not pursuing their interests forcefully enough — especially regarding abortion and school prayer.

Reagan played a role in the ending of the Cold War. His massive military buildup in the early 1980s strained an already overstretched Soviet economy, which struggled to keep pace. Reagan then agreed to meet with Soviet leader Mikhail Gorbachev in sev- eral summits between 1985 and 1987. More important than Reagan's actions, however, were inefficiencies and contradictions in the Soviet economic structure itself. Combined with the forced military buildup and the disastrous war in Afghanistan, these strains led Gorbachev to institute the first significant reforms in Soviet society in half a century. The reforms stirred popular criticism of the Soviet Union, which formally collapsed in 1991.

For additional primary sources from this period, see *Documents for America's History*, Seventh Edition.

For Web sites, images, and documents related to topics and places in this chapter, visit *Make History* at **bedfordstmartins.com/henrettaconcise**.

For Further Exploration

James T. Patterson, *Restless Giant: The United States from Watergate to Bush v. Gore* (2005), provides a solid analysis of the 1980s and 1990s. For evangelical politics, see Frances FitzGerald, *Cities on a Hill* (1986), which has a section on Jerry Falwell and the Moral Majority; and William Martin, *With God on Our Side: The Rise of the Religious Right in America* (1996). On the rise of the New Right, see Lisa McGirr, *Suburban Warriors: The Origins of the New American Right* (2001). Two valuable overviews of the Reagan presi- dency are Lou Cannon, *President Reagan: The Role of a Lifetime* (2000), and Haynes Johnson, *Sleepwalking through History: America in the Reagan Years* (1992). John Greene, *The Presidency of George Bush* (2000), discusses the policies of the senior Bush.

On foreign policy, consult Richard A. Melanson, *American Foreign Policy Since the Vietnam War* (2005), and Raymond Garthoff, *The Great Transition: American-*

TIMELINE

1981	▶ Ronald Reagan becomes president
	▶ Republicans gain control of Senate
	▶ Economic Recovery Tax Act (ERTA) cuts taxes
	▶ Military expenditures increase sharply
	▶ Reagan cuts budgets of regulatory agencies
	▶ Sandra Day O'Connor appointed to the Supreme Court
1981–1989	▶ National debt triples
	▶ Emergence of New Right think tanks: Heritage Foundation, American Enterprise Institute, and the Cato Institute
	▶ United States assists Iraq in war against Iran (1980–1988)
1985	▶ Mikhail Gorbachev takes power in Soviet Union
1986	▶ Iran-Contra scandal weakens Reagan presidency
	▶ William Rehnquist named chief justice
1987	▶ United States and USSR agree to limit missiles in Europe
1988	▶ George H. W. Bush elected president
1989	▶ Destruction of Berlin Wall
	▶ "Velvet Revolutions" in Eastern Europe
	▶ *Webster v. Reproductive Health Services* limits abortion services
1990–1991	▶ Persian Gulf War
1991	▶ Dissolution of Soviet Union ends Cold War

Soviet Relations and the End of the Cold War (1994). Two fine Web sites that document various Cold War incidents are the National Security Archive, at **www.gwu.edu/ ~nsarchiv**, and the Cold War International History Project, at **www.wilsoncenter.org/ index.cfm?fuseaction=topics.home&topic_id=1409**. For the Gulf War, see Michael Gordon and Bernard Trainor, *The Generals' War: The Inside Story of the Conflict in the Gulf* (1995), and **www.pbs.org/wgbh/pages/frontline/gulf**, a site with maps, documents, and interviews with decision makers and soldiers.

Test Your Knowledge

For practice quizzes, activities, and other study tools, visit the Online Study Guide at **bedfordstmartins.com/henrettaconcise**.

National Dilemmas in a Global Society

1989-2011

Even a government as powerful as America's seems inadequate to crucial challenges—from the physical threat of terrorism to the economic wrenching of globalization. The political world, to many, seems out of joint.

—Michael Oreskes, Editor of the
International Herald Tribune, 2008

On the morning of September 11, 2001, two commercial airliners were deliberately flown into the World Trade Center in lower Manhattan, causing raging fires and bringing the towers to the ground. Millions of Americans, and many more people worldwide, watched live on television and the Internet as the towers collapsed. Simultaneously, a third plane was crashed into the Pentagon, and though passengers gained control of a fourth plane, it went down in rural western Pennsylvania. It took Federal Bureau of Investigation officials only a few hours to determine the identity of most of the hijackers, as well as the organization behind the murderous attacks — Al Qaeda. As elements of the shocking crime became clearer over the subsequent days, it was evident that the attacks had been directed from Al Qaeda bases in Afghanistan, where Osama bin Laden, a wealthy exile from Saudi Arabia, and Khalid Sheikh Mohammed, an American-educated jihadist originally from Kuwait, were protected by the Afghan government.

The attacks of September 11 symbolized the emergence of an anti-Western radical Islamic movement across much of the Middle East. But, tellingly, the attacks were made possible by the new era of globalization. Of the nineteen terrorists involved in the hijackings, fifteen were from Saudi Arabia, two were from the United Arab Emirates, one was from Egypt, and one was from Lebanon. Many had trained in Afghanistan, in guerrilla warfare camps operated by bin Laden. Four had gone to flight school in the United States itself. Several had lived and studied in Germany. They communicated with one another and with planners in Afghanistan through e-mail, Web sites, and cell phones. Al Qaeda sympathizers could be found among Muslims from Indonesia to Algeria. The most conspicuous crime of the twenty-first century, which left 2,900 people dead and sent waves of shock and anxiety through the American public, would have been impossible without the openness and interconnectivity that are central features of globalization.

The response, too, was global. Messages of sympathy and support poured into the United States from nearly every nation. Citizens of fifty-three different countries had perished in the World Trade Center, itself a symbol of the global financial and insurance industries. The world, quite literally, stood in shock. The emergence in the Middle East of a radical Muslim movement willing to use terrorism to inflict major damage on the United States and the West testified to the altered realities of global politics. The simple Cold War duality — communism versus capitalism — had for decades obscured regional, ethnic, and religious loyalties and conflicts. Those loyalties and conflicts moved to center stage in an era of globalization.

Globalization saw the rapid spread of capitalism around the world, huge increases in global trade and commerce, and a diffusion of communications technology, including the Internet, that linked the world's people to one another in ways unimaginable a generation earlier. Suddenly, the United States faced a dizzying array of opportunities and challenges, both at home and abroad. "Profound and powerful forces are shaking and remaking our world," said a young President Bill Clinton in his first inaugural address in 1993. He continued: "The urgent question of our time is whether we can make change our friend and not our enemy."

For Americans, the period between the Cold War (which devolved between 1989 and 1991) and our own day has been defined by twin dilemmas. The first relates to globalization. How should the United States engage in global trade and commerce? How should it relate diplomatically to emerging nations? How can it best confront radical Islamic terrorists? As the lone military superpower in a post–Cold War world of energetic capitalism, the United States has found it difficult to answer these vital questions. The second dilemma relates to domestic politics and the economy. In an era of conservative political dominance, how would the nation manage its cultural conflicts and ensure both economic opportunity and economic security for its citizens? As "profound and powerful forces" shook the world, these were, as the chapter title suggests, Americans' national dilemmas in a global society.

America in the Global Economy

On November 30, 1999, nearly 50,000 protesters took to the streets of Seattle, Washington. For much of the morning and afternoon, sometimes in pouring rain, they immobilized a wide swath of the city's downtown. Police, armed with pepper spray and arrayed in riot gear, worked feverishly to clear the clogged streets, get traffic moving, and usher well-dressed government ministers from around the world into a conference hall. Protesters jeered, chanted, and held hundreds of signs and banners aloft. A radical contingent joined the otherwise peaceful march, and a handful of them began breaking the windows of the chain stores they saw as symbols of global capitalism: Starbucks, Gap, Old Navy.

What had aroused such passion in the so-called Battle of Seattle? Globalization. The vast majority of Americans never surged into the streets, as had the Seattle protesters who tried to shut down this 1999 meeting of the World Trade Organization (WTO), but no American by the late 1990s could deny that developments in the global economy reverberated at home. In that decade, Americans rediscovered a long-standing truth:

The United States was not an island, but was linked in countless different ways to a global economy and society. Economic prosperity in the post–World War II decades had obscured for Americans this fundamental reality.

A question remained, however. In whose interest was the global economy structured? Many of the Seattle activists took inspiration from the five-point "Declaration for Global Democracy," issued by the nonprofit human rights organization Global Exchange during the WTO's Seattle meeting. "Global trade and investment," the declaration demanded, "must not be ends in themselves but rather the instruments for achieving equitable and sustainable development, including protections for workers and the environment." The declaration addressed other issues, such as inequality among nations, which called attention not to the mere *fact* of globalization but to the disparate *impact* of globalized trade and investment. Who benefited from globalization and who did not — such as the many impoverished citizens of the Middle East who turned to radical Islam for answers — were important questions in the new era.

The Rise of the European Union and China

During the Cold War, from 1945 through the late 1980s, the United States and the Soviet Union dominated the global balance of power. These two superpowers oversaw what observers called a bipolar world — two powerful poles, one capitalist and the other communist, around which global geopolitics were organized. Since the early 1990s, however, a multipolar world has emerged — with centers of power in Europe, Japan, China, and the United States, along with rising regional powers such as India and Brazil.

In 1992, the nations of Western Europe created the European Union (EU) and moved toward the creation of a single federal state, somewhat like the United States. By the end of the 1990s, the European Union embraced more than twenty countries and 450 million people — the third largest population in the world, behind China and India — and accounted for a fifth of all global imports and exports. In 2002, the EU introduced a single currency, the euro, which soon rivaled the dollar and the Japanese yen as a major international currency (Map 31.1). Militarily, however, the EU remained a secondary power. European countries preferred social programs to armies and posed no military challenge to the United States. An economic juggernaut and trading rival with a suspicion of warfare, the EU presented a number of new dilemmas for American officials.

So did China, a vast nation of 1.3 billion people that was the world's fastest-rising economic power in the first decade of the twenty-first century. Between 2000 and 2008, China *quadrupled* its gross domestic product (GDP). Economic growth rates during those years were consistently near 10 percent — higher than the United States achieved during its periods of furious economic growth in the 1950s and 1960s. The irony is that China could hardly have put up such impressive numbers without its symbiotic relationship with American consumers. Although still governed by the Communist Party, China embraced capitalism, and its factories produced inexpensive products for export, which Americans eagerly purchased — everything from children's toys and television sets to clothing, household appliances, and video games. Such a relationship is possible because China has deliberately kept its currency weak against the American dollar, ensuring that its exports remain cheap in the United States.

Beneficial to American consumers in the short run, the implications of this relationship for the future may be less promising. Two such implications stand out. First, as more

MAP 31.1 Growth of the European Community, 1951–2005

The European Community (EU) began in the 1950s as a loose organization of Western European nations. Over the course of the following decades, it created stronger common institutions, such as the European Parliament in Strasbourg, the EU Commission in Brussels, and the Court of Justice in Luxembourg. With the collapse of communism, the EU has expanded to include the nations of Eastern and Central Europe. It now includes twenty-seven nations and 450 million people.

and more goods that Americans buy are produced in China, the manufacturing base in the United States continues to shrink, costing jobs and adversely affecting communities. Second, China has kept its currency low against the dollar primarily by purchasing American debt. China now owns nearly 25 percent of total U.S. debt, more than any other nation. Many economists believe that it is unwise to allow a single country to wield so much influence over the U.S. currency supply. Should this relationship continue unchanged, Americans may find their manufacturing sector contracting even more severely in the coming decades.

An Era of Globalization

Over the centuries, Americans have depended on foreign markets to which they export their tobacco, cotton, wheat, and industrial goods, and have long received imported products and immigrants from other countries. But the intensity of international exchange has varied over time, as has Americans' awareness of that exchange. In the 1990s, both intensity and awareness were on the upswing. The end of the Cold War shattered barriers that had restrained international trade and impeded capitalist development of vast areas of the world. New communications systems — satellites, fiber-optic cables, global positioning networks — were shrinking the world's physical spaces to a degree unimaginable at the beginning of the twentieth century. Perhaps most important, global financial markets became integrated to an unprecedented extent, allowing investment capital to "flow" into and out of nations and around the world in a matter of moments. The global economy was entering a new phase.

International Organizations and Corporations | International organizations, many of them created in the wake of World War II, set the rules for capitalism's worldwide expansion. During the final decades of the Cold War, the leading capitalist industrial nations formed the Group of Seven (G7) to manage global economic policy. Russia joined in 1997, creating the Group of Eight (G8). The G8 nations — the United States, Britain, Germany, France, Italy, Japan, Canada, and Russia — largely controlled the major international financial organizations: the World Bank, the International Monetary Fund (IMF), and the General Agreement on Trades and Tariffs (GATT). In 1995, GATT evolved into the World Trade Organization (WTO), with nearly 150 participating nations.

As globalization accelerated, so did the integration of regional economies. To offset the economic clout of the European bloc, in 1993 the United States, Canada, and Mexico signed the North American Free Trade Agreement (NAFTA). This treaty, as ratified by the U.S. Congress, envisioned the eventual creation of a free-trade zone covering all of North America. In East Asia, the capitalist nations of Japan, South Korea, Taiwan, and Singapore consulted on economic policy; as China developed a quasi-capitalist economy and became a major exporter of manufactures, its Communist-led government joined their deliberations.

International organizations set the rules, but globalization was made possible by the proliferation of multinational corporations (MNCs). In 1970, there were 7,000 corporations with offices and factories in multiple countries; by 2000, the number had exploded to 63,000. Many of the most powerful MNCs were, and continue to be, American-based. Walmart, the biggest retailer in the United States, is also the world's largest corporation, with 1,200 stores in other nations and $32 billion in foreign sales. The McDonald's restaurant chain had 1,000 outlets outside the United States in 1980; twenty years later, there were nearly 13,000, and "McWorld" had become a popular shorthand term for globalization.

Globalization was driven by more than a quest for new markets. Corporations also sought ever-cheaper sources of labor. Many American MNCs closed their factories in the United States and outsourced manufacturing jobs to plants in Mexico, Eastern Europe, and especially Asia. The athletic sportswear firm Nike was a prime example. The company established manufacturing plants for its shoes and apparel in Communist Vietnam and China as well as in capitalist Indonesia. By the mid-1990s, Nike had 150 factories in Asia that employed more than 450,000 workers, most of whom received low wages, endured harsh working conditions, and had no health or pension benefits. Highly skilled jobs were outsourced as well.

A Nike Factory in China

In 2005, Nike produced its shoes and sportswear at 124 plants in China; additional factories were located in other low-wage countries. Most of the Chinese plants were run by subcontractors, who housed the workers — mostly women between the ages of sixteen to twenty-five — in crowded dormitories. The wages were low, about $3 a day, but more than the women could earn if they remained in their rural villages. AP Images.

Financial Deregulation

As trade restrictions among nations began to fall in the 1980s and 1990s, so did restrictions on investment. One of the principal differences between this new era of globalization and previous eras has been the opening of national financial and currency markets to investment from around the world. Global financial integration has been a hallmark of our time. The United States and Britain led the way. Both countries came under the sway of powerful political forces in the 1980s calling for the total deregulation of banks, brokerage houses, investment firms, and financial markets — letting the free market replace government oversight. Together, the United States and Britain led a quiet revolution in which investment markets around the world were gradually set free.

Financial deregulation led to spectacular profits for investors but produced a more fragile, crash-prone global economy. On the profit side, financial-industry profits in the United States rose from less than 10 percent of total business profits in the 1950s to more than 40 percent in the 1990s (Figure 31.1). But the costs were becoming clear as well: the bankruptcy of the American savings and loan industry in the 1980s; the "lost decade" in Japan in the 1990s; the near-bankruptcy of Russia in the late 1990s and of Argentina in 2001; the 1997 Asian financial crisis, centered in Thailand and Indonesia; and the collapse of nearly the entire global economy in 2008. These and other episodes dramatized the extraordinary risks that financial globalization has introduced.

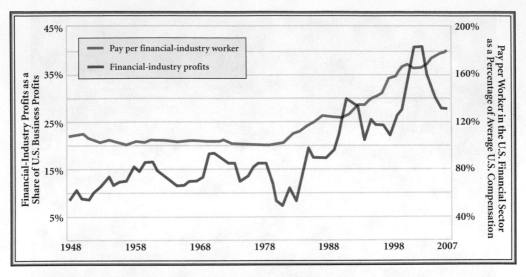

FIGURE 31.1 Financial-Industry Profits and Compensation
From the end of World War II until the late 1970s, financial markets (largely securities trading) accounted for less than 20 percent of the overall American economy. Since the 1970s, however, the financial industry has nearly doubled its share of economic activity, accounting for more than 40 percent of all U.S. business profits by the late 1990s. Financial sector salaries increased proportionally. Many economists doubt the wisdom of allowing securities trading to account for such a large share of economic activity, especially since U.S. manufacturing declined precipitously over these same decades.

The New Technology

The technological advances of the 1980s and 1990s changed the character of everyday life for millions of Americans, linking them with a global information and media environment unprecedented in world history. Not since television was introduced to American homes in the years following World War II had technology so profoundly changed the way people lived their lives. Personal computers, cell phones and smartphones, the Internet and the World Wide Web, the iPod, and other electronic devices and systems altered work, leisure, and access to knowledge in stunning ways. Like unimpeded trade, these advances in communications and personal technologies enhanced globalization.

During the 1990s, personal computers, which had emerged in the late 1970s, grew even more significant with the spread of the Internet and the World Wide Web. Like the computer itself, the Internet was the product of military-based research. During the late 1960s, the U.S. Department of Defense, in conjunction with the Massachusetts Institute of Technology, began developing a decentralized computer network, the Advanced Research Projects Agency Network (ARPANET). The Internet, which grew out of the ARPANET, was soon used by government scientists, academic specialists, and military contractors to exchange data, information, and electronic mail (e-mail). By the 1980s, the Internet had spread to universities, businesses, and the general public.

The debut in 1991 of the graphics-based World Wide Web — a collection of servers that allowed access to millions of documents, pictures, and other materials — enhanced the popular appeal and commercial possibilities of the Internet. By 2009,

75 percent of all Americans and more than one billion people worldwide used the Internet to send messages and view information. Businesses used the World Wide Web to sell their products and services; e-commerce transactions totaled $114 billion in 2003, $172 billion in 2005, and well over $200 billion by 2008. The Web proved instantly democratic, providing ordinary people with easy access to knowledge. For nearly two centuries, local public libraries had served that function; now, more and more material in libraries was instantly available in a home or an office.

Advances in electronic technology resulted in the rapid creation of new leisure and business products. The 1980s saw the introduction of videocassette recorders (VCRs), compact disc (CD) players, and inexpensive fax machines. By 2000, cameras took digital pictures that could be stored and transmitted on computers, and digital video discs (DVDs) had become the newest technology for viewing movies. Cellular telephones (cell phones), which also became available in the 1980s, ignited a communications revolution. By 2010, more than 80 percent of American adults carried one of these portable devices.

By the first decade of the twenty-first century, Americans had come to live in a world saturated with instantaneous electronic information. This total media environment left one of the most significant forms of media of the last four centuries struggling to survive: newspapers. As more and more Americans began to get their news from television and the Internet, advertising revenue migrated accordingly and newspapers suffered calamitously. Across the country, newspaper subscriptions were in freefall between 2000 and 2010, declining between 25 and 50 percent in various cities. Hundreds of newspapers — from small-town weeklies to major big-city dailies such as the *Rocky Mountain News* and the *Seattle Post-Intelligencer* — closed their doors in that decade. The printed newspaper, around since the 1660s, was expected to survive in some form, but few observers could predict what its rapid demise would mean in coming decades.

▶ What were the most important factors in globalization?

▶ In what ways has the United States benefited from globalization? In what ways has it not?

Politics and Partisanship in a New Era

Standing at the podium at the 1992 Republican National Convention, his supporters cheering by the thousands, Patrick Buchanan did not mince words. He had lost the nomination for president, but he still hoped to shape the party's message to voters. Buchanan was a former speechwriter for President Richard Nixon and a White House aide to President Ronald Reagan, and he remained a fiery opponent of the liberal social movements of the 1960s and 1970s. This election, he told the audience — including millions watching on television — "is about what we stand for as Americans." Citing Democratic support for abortion rights and the rights of lesbians and gay men, Buchanan claimed there was "a religious war going on in our country for the soul of America." It was, he emphasized, "a cultural war."

To Buchanan and other conservatives, the success of rights liberalism in the previous decades led to this "cultural war." For them, racial pluralism and "family values" — which was their term for issues related primarily to abortion and the status of women and gay Americans — remained hot-button concerns that could reliably energize conservative voters. Buchanan's war was another name for a long-standing political struggle, dating to the 1920s, between religious traditionalists and secular liberals (see Chapter 22). This time, however, Americans struggled over these questions in the long shadow of the sixties, which had taken on an exaggerated meaning in the nation's politics. Against the backdrop of globalization, American politics in the 1990s and early 2000s remained caught in a cycle of battles over the consequences of social upheaval during the sixties. The era's politics careened back and forth between contests over divisive social issues and concern over the nation's economic future.

An Increasingly Plural Society

Exact estimates vary, but demographers predict that at some point between 2040 and 2050 the United States will become a "majority-minority" nation: No single ethnic or racial group will be in the numerical majority. This is already the case in California, where in 2010 African Americans, Latinos, and Asians together constituted a majority of the state's residents. As this unmistakable trend became apparent in the 1990s, it fueled renewed debates over ethnic and racial identity and over public policies such as affirmative action.

New Immigrants
In the early years of the 2000s, more immigrants lived in the United States than at any time since the first decades of the twentieth century. Most came from Asia, Latin America, and Africa. Many, like those pictured here, started small businesses that helped revive the economies of urban and suburban neighborhoods across the country. © Bettmann/Corbis.

New Immigrants | According to the Census Bureau, the population of the United States grew from 203 million in 1970 to 280 million in 2000 (see American Voices, p. 953). Of that 77-million-person increase, immigrants accounted for 28 million, with legal entrants numbering 21 million and illegal entrants adding another 7 million (Figure 31.2). As a result, by 2000, 26 percent of California's population was foreign-born, as was 20 percent of New York's and 17 percent each of New Jersey's and Florida's. Relatively few immigrants came from Europe, which had dominated immigration to the United States between 1880 and 1924. The overwhelming majority — some 25 million — now came from Latin America (16 million) and East Asia (9 million) (Map 31.2).

This extraordinary inflow of immigrants was the unintended result of the Immigration and Nationality Act of 1965, one of the less well-known but most influential pieces of Great Society legislation. Known as the Hart-Celler Act, the legislation eliminated the 1924 quota system, which had favored northern Europe. In its place Congress created a more equal playing field among nations and a slightly higher total limit on immigration. The legislation also included provisions that eased the entry of immigrants who were professionals, scientists, and artists "of exceptional ability," or who possessed skills in high demand in the United States. Finally, a provision with far-reaching implications was included in the new law: Immediate family members of those already legally

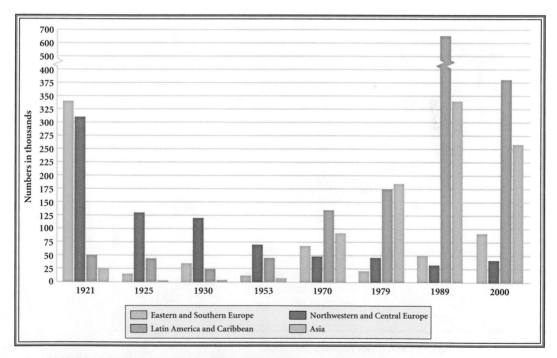

FIGURE 31.2 American Immigration, 1920–2000

Legislation inspired by nativism slowed the influx of immigrants after 1920, as did the dislocations brought on by economic depression and war in the 1930s and 1940s. Note the high rate of non-European immigration since the 1970s, the result of new eligibility rules in the Immigration Act of 1965 (see Chapter 28). The dramatic increase since 1980 in the number of migrants from Latin America and Asia reflects American economic prosperity, traditionally a magnet for migrants, and the rapid acceleration of illegal immigration.

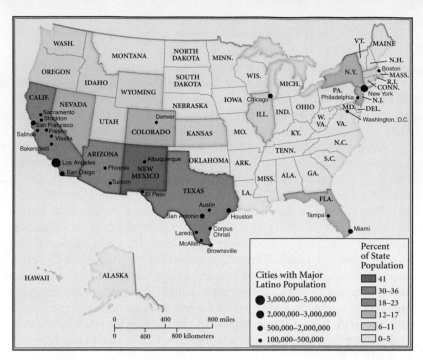

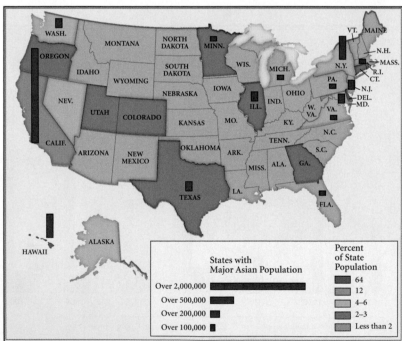

MAP 31.2 Hispanic and Asian Populations, 2000

In 2000, people of Hispanic descent made up more than 11 percent of the American population, and now outnumber African Americans as the largest minority group. Asian Americans accounted for an additional 4 percent of the population. Demographers predict that by the year 2050 only about half of the U.S. population will be composed of non-Hispanic whites. Note the high percentage of Hispanics and Asians in California and certain other states.

Cheap Labor: Immigration and Globalization

Petra Mata and Feiyi Chen are immigrants from low-wage countries who were "insourced"; on coming to the United States, they worked as low-paid garment workers. Then, their jobs were outsourced—sent abroad to even lower-paid workers as a result of free trade and globalization.

Petra Mata: My name is Petra Mata. I was born in Mexico. I have completed no more than the sixth grade in school. In 1969, my husband and I came to the U.S. believing we would find better opportunities for our children and ourselves. We first arrived without documents, then became legal, and finally became citizens. For years I moved from job to job until I was employed in 1976 by the most popular company in the market, Levi Strauss & Company. I earned $9.73 an hour and also had vacation and sick leave. Levi's provided me and my family with a stable situation, and in return I was a loyal employee and worked there for fourteen years.

On January 16, 1990, Levi's closed its plant in San Antonio, Texas, where I had been working, leaving 1,150 workers unemployed, a majority of whom were Mexican-American women. The company moved its factory to Costa Rica. . . .

As a result of being laid off, I personally lost my house, my method of transportation, and the tranquility of my home. My family and I had to face new problems. My husband was forced to look for a second job on top of the one he already had. He worked from seven in the morning to six at night. Our reality was very difficult. At that time, I had not the slightest idea what free trade was or meant. . . .

Our governments make agreements behind closed doors without participation from the working persons who are most affected by these decisions—decisions that

to my knowledge only benefit large corporations and those in positions of power. . . .

Feiyi Chen: My name is Feiyi Chen. I immigrated to the United States in December 1998 from China. I began my working career as a seamstress in a garment factory because I did not speak English and the garment manufacturing industry was one of the few employment opportunities available to me. I typically worked ten hours a day, six days a week, at a backbreaking pace. . . . I learned from some of the older garment workers that garment workers in San Francisco actually made a decent living before free trade lured many of the better-paying garment factories over to other countries and forced the smaller and rule-abiding factories to shut down because they could not compete with the low cost of production from neighboring countries. . . .

Working as a seamstress and an assembly worker has always been hard, but with so many of the factories leaving the country in search of cheaper labor, life for immigrant workers like myself is getting worse. For example, many garment workers who were paid one dollar for sewing a piece of clothing are now only making fifty cents for the same amount of work. There are a lot of garment workers who still work ten hours a day but make less than thirty dollars a day.

SOURCE: Christine Ahn, *Shafted: Free Trade and America's Working Poor* (Oakland, CA: Food First Books, 2003), 32–38.

resident in the United States were admitted outside of the total numerical limit. President Johnson signed the law at the base of the Statue of Liberty and said simply that immigrants would be admitted "on the basis of their skills and their close relationship to those already here."

American residents from Latin America and the Caribbean were best positioned to take advantage of the family provision. Millions of Mexicans came to the United States to join their families, and U.S. residents from El Salvador and Guatemala — tens of thousands of whom had arrived seeking sanctuary or asylum during the civil wars of the 1980s — and the Dominican Republic now brought their families to join them. Nationally, there were now more Latinos than African Americans. Many of these immigrants profoundly shaped the emerging global economy by sending substantial portions of their earnings, called remittances, back to family members in their home countries. In 2006, for instance, workers in the United States sent $23 billion to Mexico, a massive remittance flow that constituted Mexico's third-largest source of foreign exchange. Another $3 billion went to the Dominican Republic.

Asian immigrants came largely from China, the Philippines, South Korea, India, and Pakistan. In addition, 700,000 refugees came to the United States from Southeast Asia (Vietnam, Laos, and Cambodia) after the Vietnam War. This immigration signaled more than new flows of people into the United States. Throughout much of its history, the United States had oriented itself toward the Atlantic. Indeed, at the end of the nineteenth century, American secretary of state John Hay observed, "The Mediterranean is the ocean of the past; the Atlantic the ocean of the present." He added, presciently, "The Pacific [is] the ocean of the future." By the last decades of the twentieth century, Hay's future had arrived. As immigration from Asia increased, as Japan and China grew more influential economically, and as more and more transnational trade crossed the Pacific, commentators on both sides of the ocean began speaking of the Pacific Rim as an important new region.

Multiculturalism and Its Critics | Most new immigrants arrived under the terms of the 1965 law. But those who did not — and who thus became known as illegal aliens — stirred political controversy. In 1992, Patrick Buchanan, then campaigning for the Republican presidential nomination, warned Americans that their country was "undergoing the greatest invasion in its history, a migration of millions of illegal aliens a year from Mexico." Significantly, state governments led the efforts to deal with illegal immigration. In 1986, California voters overwhelmingly supported Proposition 63, which established English as the state's official language; seventeen other states followed suit. Eight years later, Californians approved Proposition 187, a ballot initiative forthrightly named "Save Our State," which barred illegal aliens from public schools, nonemergency care at public health clinics, and all other state social services. When a federal judge ruled that Proposition 187 was unconstitutional, supporters of the measure demanded that Congress take action to curtail legal immigration and expel illegal aliens — action that has yet to materialize.

Debates over post-1965 immigration looked a great deal like conflicts in the early decades of the century. Then, many native-born white Protestants worried that the largely Jewish and Catholic immigrants from Southern and Eastern Europe, along with African American migrants leaving the South, could not assimilate and threatened the "purity" of the nation. Although the conflicts looked the same, the cultural paradigm had shifted. In the earlier era, the melting pot — a term borrowed from the title of a 1908 play — became the metaphor for how American society would accommodate its new-found diversity. Some native-born Americans found solace in the melting-pot concept, because it implied that a single "American" culture would predominate. In the 1990s, how-ever, a different concept, multiculturalism, emerged to define social diversity. Americans, this concept suggested, were not a single people into whom others melted; rather, they comprised a diverse set of ethnic and racial groups living and working together. A shared set of public values held the multicultural society together, even as different groups main-tained unique practices and traditions.

Critics, however, charged that multiculturalism perpetuated ethnic chauvinism and conferred preferential treatment on minority groups. Many government policies, as well as a large number of private employers, for instance, continued to support affirmative ac-tion programs designed to bring African Americans, Latinos, and women into public- and private-sector jobs and universities in larger numbers. Conservatives argued that such governmental programs were deeply flawed, because they promoted "reverse dis-crimination" against white men and resulted in the selection and promotion of less-qualified applicants for jobs and educational advancement. Individualism, rather than multiculturalism, ought to prevail, they argued.

California stood at the center of the debate. In 1995, under pressure from Repub-lican governor Pete Wilson, the regents of the University of California scrapped their twenty-year-old policy of affirmative action. A year later, California voters approved Proposition 209, which outlawed affirmative action in state employment and public edu-cation. At the height of the 1995 controversy, President Bill Clinton delivered a major speech defending affirmative action. He reminded Americans that Richard Nixon, a Re-publican president, had endorsed affirmative action, and he concluded by saying the nation should "mend it," not "end it." However, as in the *Bakke* decision of the 1970s (see Chapter 29), it was the U.S. Supreme Court that spoke loudest on the subject. In two parallel 2003 cases, the Court invalidated one affirmative action plan at the University of Michigan but allowed racial preference policies that promoted a "diverse" student body. Thus, diversity became the law of the land, the constitutionally acceptable basis for af-firmative action. The policy had been narrowed but preserved.

Additional anxieties about a multicultural nation centered on language. In 1998, Silicon Valley software entrepreneur Ron Unz sponsored a California initiative calling for an end to bilingual education in public schools. Unz argued that bilingual education had failed because it did not adequately prepare Spanish-speaking students to succeed in an English-speaking society. The state's white, Anglo residents largely approved of the mea-sure; most Mexican American, Asian American, and civil rights organizations opposed it. When Unz's measure, Proposition 227, passed with a healthy 61 percent majority, it seemed to confirm the limits of multiculturalism in the nation's most diverse state.

Clashes over "Family Values"

If the promise of a multicultural nation was one contested political issue, another was the state of American families. New Right conservatives charged that the "abrasive ex-periments of two liberal decades," as a Reagan administration report put it, had eroded respect for marriage and what they had called, since the 1970s, "family values." They pointed to the 40 percent rate of divorce among whites and the nearly 60 percent rate of out-of-wedlock pregnancies among African Americans. To conservatives, there was a wide range of culprits: legislators who enacted liberal divorce laws, funded child care, and allowed welfare payments to unmarried mothers, as well as judges who condoned abortion and banished religious instruction from public schools.

Abortion | Abortion was central to the battles between feminists and religious conservatives, and a defining issue between Democrats and Republicans. Feminists who described themselves as "pro-choice" viewed the issue from the perspective of the pregnant woman; they argued that the right to a legal, safe abortion was crucial to her control over her body and life. Conversely, religious conservatives, who pronounced themselves "pro-life," viewed abortion from the perspective of the unborn fetus and claimed that its rights trumped those of the living mother. That is where the debate had stood since the U.S. Supreme Court's 1973 decision in *Roe v. Wade*. Both ideologies had roots in the American commitment to "life, liberty, and the pursuit of happiness." The questions remained: Whose life? Whose liberty? Whose definition of happiness?

By the 1980s, fundamentalist Protestants had assumed leadership of the antiabortion movement, which became increasingly confrontational and politically powerful. In 1987, the religious activist Randall Terry founded Operation Rescue, which mounted protests outside abortion clinics and harassed their staffs and clients. While such vocal protests took shape outside clinics, antiabortion activists also won state laws that limited public funding for abortions, required parental notification before minors could obtain abortions, and mandated waiting periods before any woman could undergo an abortion procedure. Such laws further restricted women's reproductive choices.

Homosexuality | The issue of homosexuality stirred equally deep passions — on all sides. As more gay men and women came out of the closet in the years after Stonewall (see Chapter 28), they demanded legal protections from discrimination in housing, education, and employment. Public opinion about these demands varied by region, but by the 1990s, many cities and states had indeed banned discrimination on the basis of sexual orientation. Gay rights groups also sought legal rights for same-sex couples — such as the eligibility for workplace health-care coverage — that were akin to those enjoyed by married heterosexuals. Many of the most prominent national gay rights organizations, such as the Human Rights Campaign, focused on full marriage equality: a legal recognition of same-sex marriage that was on par with opposite-sex marriages.

The Religious Right had long condemned homosexuality as morally wrong. Televangelist Pat Robertson, North Carolina senator Jesse Helms, activist Phyllis Schlafly, and other conservatives campaigned vigorously against measures that would extend rights to gays. Public opinion remained sharply divided. In 1992, Colorado voters approved an amendment to the state constitution that prevented local governments from enacting ordinances protecting gays and lesbians — a measure that the Supreme Court subsequently overturned as unconstitutional. That same year, however, Oregon voters defeated a more radical initiative that would have prevented the state from using any funds "to promote, encourage or facilitate" homosexuality. In 1998, Congress entered the fray by enacting the Defense of Marriage Act, which allowed states to refuse to recognize

Gay/Lesbian Rights

Nothing proved more controversial in the 1990s than lesbian and gay rights. Whether it was President Clinton's initiative to allow lesbians and gays to serve openly in the U.S. military or the state-level marriage equality movement, issues of sexuality were a central part of the decade's furious culture wars. Here, marchers, including the actress Cybill Shepherd, participate in the 1993 Gay Rights March in Washington, D.C. AP Images.

gay marriages or civil unions formed in other jurisdictions. More recently, gay marriage has been legalized in six states, including Massachusetts, Connecticut, and Vermont.

Culture Wars and the Supreme Court | Divisive rights issues increasingly came before the U.S. Supreme Court. Abortion led the way, with abortion rights activists challenging the constitutionality of the new state laws limiting access to the procedure. In *Webster v. Reproductive Health Services* (1989), the Supreme Court upheld the authority of state governments to limit the use of public funds and facilities for abortions. Then, in the important case of *Planned Parenthood of Southeastern Pennsylvania v. Casey* (1992), the court upheld a law requiring a twenty-four-hour waiting period prior to an abortion. Surveying these and other decisions, a reporter suggested that 1989 was "the year the Court turned right," with a conservative majority ready and willing to limit or invalidate liberal legislation and legal precedents.

This observation was only partly correct. The Court was not yet firmly conservative. Although the *Casey* decision upheld certain restrictions on abortions, it affirmed the "essential holding" in *Roe v. Wade* (1973) that women had a constitutional right to control their reproduction. Justice David Souter, appointed to the Court by President George H. W. Bush in 1990; voted with Reagan appointees Sandra Day O'Connor and

Anthony Kennedy to uphold *Roe*. Souter, like O'Connor, emerged as an ideologically moderate justice on a range of issues. Moreover, in a landmark decision, *Lawrence v. Texas* (2003), the Supreme Court limited the power of states to prohibit private homosexual activity between consenting adults. The Court had crept incrementally, rather than lurched, to the right while signaling its continued desire to remain within the broad mainstream of American public opinion.

The Clinton Presidency, 1993–2001

The culture wars contributed to a new, divisive partisanship in national politics. Rarely in the twentieth century had the two major parties so adamantly refused to work together. Also rare was the vitriolic rhetoric that politicians used to describe their opponents. The fractious partisanship was filtered through — or, many would argue, created by — the new twenty-four-hour cable news television networks, such as Fox News and CNN. Commentators on these channels, finding that nothing drew viewers like aggressive partisanship, increasingly abandoned their roles as conveyors of information and became entertainers and provocateurs.

That divisiveness was a hallmark of the presidency of William Jefferson Clinton. In 1992, Clinton, the governor of Arkansas, styled himself a "New Democrat" who would bring "Reagan Democrats" and middle-class voters back to the party. Only forty-six, he was an energetic, ambitious policy wonk — extraordinarily well informed about the details of public policy. To win the Democratic nomination in 1992, Clinton had to survive charges that he embodied the permissive social values conservatives associated with the 1960s: namely, that he dodged the draft to avoid service in Vietnam, smoked marijuana, and cheated repeatedly on his wife. The charges were damaging, but Clinton adroitly talked his way into the presidential nomination: He had charisma and a way with words. For his running mate, he chose Albert A. Gore, a senator from Tennessee. Gore was about the same age as Clinton, making them the first baby-boom national ticket as well as the nation's first all-southern major-party ticket.

President George H. W. Bush won renomination over his lone opponent, the conservative columnist Pat Buchanan. The Democrats mounted an aggressive campaign that focused on Clinton's domestic agenda: He promised a tax cut for the middle classes, universal health insurance, and a reduction of the huge Republican budget deficit. It was an audacious combination of traditional social-welfare liberalism and fiscal conservatism. For his part, Bush could not overcome voters' discontent with the weak economy and conservatives' disgust at his tax hikes. He received only 38.0 percent of the popular vote as millions of Republicans cast their ballots for independent businessman Ross Perot, who won more votes (19.0 percent) than any independent candidate since Theodore Roosevelt in 1912. With 43.7 percent of the vote, Clinton won the election. Still, there were reasons for him to worry. Among all post–World War II presidents, only Richard Nixon (in 1969) entered the White House with a comparably small share of the national vote.

New Democrats and Public Policy | As a self-proclaimed New Democrat, Clinton tried to steer a middle course through the nation's increasingly divisive partisanship. On his left was the Democratic Party's weakened but still vocal liberal wing. On his right were party moderates influenced by Reagan-era notions of reducing government regulation and the welfare state. Clinton's "third way," as he dubbed it, called

An Influential First Lady and Senator
Drawing inspiration from Eleanor
Roosevelt, Hillary Rodham Clinton
hoped the country was ready for a First
Lady who actively shaped policy. It
wasn't, or at least it wasn't ready for her
health-care plan. Subsequently, Hillary
Rodham Clinton assumed a less visible
role in administration policymaking. In
2000, and again in 2006, she won election to the U.S. Senate from New York.
In 2008, she nearly captured the Democratic nomination for president, and in
2009 was appointed secretary of state
by the man who defeated her in the
Democratic primaries (and who went on
to win the presidency), Barack Obama.
Robert Trippet/Sipa Press/AP Images.

for the new president to tailor his proposals to satisfy these two quite different — and
often antagonistic — political constituencies. Clinton had notable successes as well as
spectacular failures pursuing this course.

The spectacular failure came first. Clinton's most ambitious social-welfare goal was
to provide a system of health care that would cover all Americans and reduce the burden
of health-care costs on the larger economy. Although the United States spent a higher
percentage of its gross national product (GNP) on medical care than any other nation, it
was the only major industrialized country that did not provide government-guaranteed
health insurance to all citizens. It was an objective that had eluded every Democratic
president since Harry Truman.

Recognizing the potency of Reagan's attack on "big government," Clinton's health-
care task force — led by First Lady Hillary Rodham Clinton — proposed a system of "managed competition." Private insurance companies and market forces were to rein in health-
care expenditures. The cost of this system would fall heavily on employers, and many
smaller businesses campaigned strongly against it. So did the health insurance industry
and the American Medical Association, powerful lobbies with considerable influence in
Washington. By mid-1994, Democratic leaders in Congress declared that the Clintons'
universal health-care proposal was dead. Forty million Americans, or 15 percent of the
population, remained without health insurance coverage.

More successful was Clinton's plan to reduce the budget deficits of the Reagan-Bush
presidencies. In 1993, Clinton secured a five-year budget package that would reduce the
federal deficit by $500 billion. Republicans unanimously opposed the proposal because
it raised taxes on corporations and wealthy individuals, and liberal Democrats complained because it limited social spending. But shared sacrifice led to shared rewards.
By 1998, Clinton's fiscal policies had balanced the federal budget and begun to pay down
the federal debt — at a rate of $156 billion a year between 1999 and 2001. As fiscal sanity
returned to Washington, the economy boomed, thanks in part to the low interest rates
stemming from deficit reduction.

The Republican Resurgence | But the results of the 1993 budget package lay in the future. More immediately, the midterm election of 1994 confirmed that the Clinton presidency had not produced an electoral realignment: Conservatives still had a working majority. In a well-organized campaign, in which grassroots appeals to the New Right dominated, Republicans gained fifty-two seats in the House of Representatives, giving them a majority for the first time since 1954. They also retook control of the Senate and captured eleven governorships. Leading the Republican charge was Representative Newt Gingrich of Georgia, who revived calls for significant tax cuts, reductions in welfare programs, anticrime initiatives, and cutbacks in federal regulations. These initiatives had central components of the conservative-backed Reagan Revolution of the 1980s, but Gingrich believed that under the presidency of George H. W. Bush Republicans had not emphasized them enough.

In response to the massive Democratic losses in 1994, Clinton moved to the right. Claiming in 1996 that "the era of big government is over," he avoided expansive social-welfare proposals for the remainder of his presidency and sought Republican support for a centrist New Democrat program. The signal piece of that program was reforming the welfare system, a measure that saved relatively little money but carried a big ideological message. The Aid to Families with Dependent Children (AFDC) program provided annual payments to needy families. Still, many taxpaying Americans believed — with some supporting evidence — that AFDC perpetuated poverty by encouraging female recipients to remain on welfare rather than seek employment. In August 1996, the federal government abolished AFDC, achieving a long-standing goal of conservatives, when Clinton signed the Personal Responsibility and Work Opportunity Reconciliation Act. Liberals were furious with the president.

Clinton's Impeachment | Even with the concession on welfare, Clinton could not escape an opposition deeply hostile to his presidency. Following a relatively easy victory in the 1996 election, his second term unraveled when a sex scandal led to his impeachment. Clinton denied having had a sexual affair with Monica Lewinsky, a former White House intern. Independent prosecutor Kenneth Starr, a conservative Republican, concluded that Clinton had committed perjury and obstructed justice, and that these actions were grounds for impeachment. Viewed historically, Americans have usually defined "high crimes and misdemeanors" — the constitutional standard for impeachment — as involving a serious abuse of public trust that endangered the republic. In 1998, conservative Republicans favored a much lower standard because they did not accept Clinton's legitimacy as president. They vowed to oust him from office.

On December 19, the House of Representatives narrowly approved two articles of impeachment. Only a minority of Americans supported the House's action; according to a CBS News poll, 38 percent favored impeachment while 58 percent opposed it. Lacking public support, Republicans in the Senate fell well short of the two-thirds majority they needed to remove the president. But like Andrew Johnson, the only other president to be tried by the Senate, Clinton and the Democratic Party paid a high price for his acquittal. Preoccupied with defending himself, the president was unable to fashion a Democratic alternative to the Republicans' domestic agenda. The American public also paid a high price, because the Republicans' vendetta against Clinton drew attention away from pressing national problems.

Post–Cold War Foreign Policy

Politically weakened domestically after 1994, Clinton believed he could nonetheless make a difference on the international stage. There, post–Cold War developments gave him historic opportunities. The 1990s was a decade of stunning change in Europe and Central Asia. A great arc of newly independent states emerged as the Soviet empire collapsed — from Estonia in the far north of Europe, south through Georgia and Armenia in western Asia, and across Central Asia to Tajikistan on the border of China. The majority of the 142 million people living in those nations were poor, but the region had a sizable middle class — in countries such as Ukraine, Georgia, and Kazakhstan — and was rich in natural resources, especially oil and natural gas.

Among the challenges for the United States was the question of whether to support the admission of some of the new states, such as Ukraine, Georgia, and Armenia, into the North Atlantic Treaty Organization (NATO). Many observers believed, with some justification, that extending the NATO alliance into Eastern Europe, right up to Russia's western border, would damage U.S-Russian relations. However, Czechoslovakia, Poland, and Hungary were also eager to become NATO members — an outcome that would draw into the Western alliance three nations that Stalin had decisively placed in the Soviet sphere of influence at the close of World War II. Clinton encouraged NATO admission for those three countries but stopped short of advocating a broader expansion of the alliance during his terms in office. Nonetheless, by 2010, twelve new nations — most of them in Eastern Europe, and ten of them former members of the Warsaw Pact — had been admitted to the NATO alliance.

Two of the new NATO states, Slovenia and Croatia, emerged from an intractable set of conflicts that led to the dissolution of the communist nation of Yugoslavia. In 1992, the heavily Muslim province of Bosnia-Herzegovina declared its independence, but its substantial Serbian population refused to live in a Muslim-run multiethnic state. Slobodan Milosevic, the uncompromising Serbian nationalist, launched a ruthless campaign of "ethnic cleansing" to create a Serbian state. In November 1995, Clinton organized a NATO-led bombing campaign and peacekeeping effort, backed by 20,000 American troops, that ended the Serbs' vicious expansionist drive. Four years later, a new crisis emerged in Kosovo, another province of the Serbian-dominated Federal Republic of Yugoslavia. Again led by the United States, NATO intervened with air strikes and military forces to preserve Kosovo's autonomy. By 2008, seven independent nations had emerged from the wreckage of Yugoslavia.

America and the Middle East | No post–Cold War development proved more challenging than the emergence of radical Islamic movements in the Middle East. Muslim nations there had a long list of grievances against the West. Colonialism — both British and French — in the early decades of the twentieth century had been ruthless. A U.S.-sponsored overthrow of Iran's government in 1953 — and twenty-five years of American support for the Iranian shah — was also a sore point. America's support for Israel in the 1967 Six-Day War and the 1973 Yom Kippur War and its near-unconditional backing of Israel in the 1980s were particularly galling to Muslims. The region's religious and secular moderates complained about these injustices, but many of them had political and economic ties to the West, which constrained their criticism.

This left an opening for radical Islamic fundamentalists to build a movement based on fanatical opposition to Western imperialism and consumer culture. These groups interpreted the American presence in Saudi Arabia as signaling new U.S. colonial ambitions in the region. Clinton had inherited from President George H. W. Bush a defeated Iraq and a sizable military force — about 4,000 Air Force personnel — in Saudi Arabia. American fighter jets left Saudi Arabian air bases to fly regular missions over Iraq, enforcing a no-fly zone, where Iraqi planes were forbidden, and bombing select targets. Clinton also enforced a UN-sanctioned embargo on all trade with Iraq, a policy designed to constrain Saddam Hussein's military that ultimately denied crucial goods to the civilian population. Angered by the continued U.S. presence in Saudi Arabia, Muslim fundamentalists soon began targeting Americans. In 1993, radical Muslim immigrants set off a bomb in a parking garage beneath the World Trade Center in New York City, killing six people and injuring more than a thousand. Muslim terrorists used truck bombs to blow up U.S. embassies in Kenya and Tanzania in 1998, and they bombed the USS *Cole* in the Yemeni port of Aden in 2000.

The Clinton administration knew these attacks were the work of Al Qaeda, a network of radical Islamic terrorists organized by the wealthy Saudi exile Osama bin Laden. In February 1998, bin Laden had issued a call for holy war — a "*Jihad* against Jews and Crusaders,*"* in which it was said to be the duty of every Muslim to kill Americans and their allies. After the embassy attacks, Clinton ordered air strikes on Al Qaeda bases in Afghanistan, where an estimated 15,000 radical operatives had been trained since 1990. The strikes failed to disrupt this growing terrorist network, and when Clinton left office, the Central Intelligence Agency (CIA), the State Department, and the Pentagon were well aware of the potential threat posed by bin Laden's followers. That was where things stood on September 10, 2001.

► What were the battle lines in the cultural wars of the 1980s and 1990s? Why were those struggles so intense?

► What did Clinton mean when he said he was a New Democrat?

Into a New Century

As Americans enter the new century's second decade, they can reflect on two significant developments that have profoundly shaped their own day: the terrorist attack on the United States on September 11, 2001, and the election of the nation's first African American president, Barack Obama, on November 4, 2008. Too little time has passed for us to assess whether either event will be remembered as helping to define the twenty-first century. But both have indelibly marked our present. And both had distinct antecedents and still have profound implications.

The Ascendance of George W. Bush

The 2000 presidential election briefly offered the promise of a break with the intense partisanship of the final Clinton years. The Republican nominee, George W. Bush, the son of President George H. W. Bush, presented himself as an outsider, deploring Washington partisanship and casting himself as a "uniter, not a divider." His opponent, Al Gore —

Clinton's vice president — was a liberal policy specialist. The election of 2000 would join those of 1876 and 1960 as the closest and most contested in American history. Gore won the popular vote, amassing 50.9 million votes to Bush's 50.4 million but fell short in the electoral college, 267 to 271. Consumer- and labor-rights activist Ralph Nader ran as the Green Party candidate and drew away precious votes in key states that certainly would have carried Gore to victory.

Late on election night, the vote tally in Florida gave Bush the narrowest of victories. As was their legal prerogative, the Democrats demanded hand recounts in several counties. A month of tumult followed, until the U.S. Supreme Court, voting strictly along conservative/liberal lines, ordered the recount stopped and let Bush's victory stand. Recounting ballots without a consistent standard to determine "voter intent," the Court reasoned, violated the rights of Floridian voters under the Fourteenth Amendment's equal protection clause. As if acknowledging the frailty of this argument, the Court declared that *Bush v. Gore* was not to be regarded as precedent. But by making a transparently partisan decision, Justice John Paul Stevens warned in a dissenting opinion, the conservative majority undermined "the Nation's confidence in the judge as an impartial guardian of the rule of law."

Although Bush had positioned himself as a moderate, countertendencies drove his administration from the start. His vice president, the uncompromising conservative Richard Cheney, became, with Bush's consent, virtually a co-president. Bush also brought into the administration his campaign advisor, Karl Rove, whose advice made for an exceptionally politicized White House. Rove foreclosed the easygoing centrism of Bush the campaigner by arguing that a permanent Republican majority could be built on the party's conservative base. On Capitol Hill, Rove's hard line was reinforced by Tom DeLay, the House majority leader, who in 1995 had declared "all-out war" on the Democrats. To win that war, DeLay pushed congressional Republicans to endorse a fierce partisanship. The Senate, although more collegial, went through a similar hardening process. After 2002, with Republicans in control of both Congress and the White House, bipartisan lawmaking came to an end.

Tax Cuts | The domestic issue that most engaged President Bush, as it had Ronald Reagan, was taxes. Bush's Economic Growth and Tax Relief Act of 2001 had something for everyone. It slashed income tax rates, extended the earned income credit for the poor, and marked the estate tax to be phased out by 2010. A second round of cuts in 2003 targeted dividend income and capital gains. Bush's signature cuts — those favoring big estates and well-to-do owners of stocks and bonds — skewed the distribution of tax benefits upward (Table 31.1). Bush had pushed far beyond any other postwar president, even Reagan, in slashing federal taxes.

Critics warned that such massive tax cuts would plunge the federal government into debt. By 2006, federal expenditures had jumped 33 percent, at a faster clip than under any president since Lyndon Johnson. Huge increases in health-care costs were the main culprit. Two of the largest federal programs, Medicare and Medicaid — health care for the elderly and the poor, respectively — could not contain runaway medical costs. Midway through Bush's second term, the national debt stood at over $8 trillion — much of it owned by foreign investors, who also financed the nation's huge trade deficit. On top of that, staggering Social Security and Medicare obligations were coming due for retiring baby boomers. It seemed that these burdens would be passed on to future generations (Figure 31.3).

TABLE 31.1	Impact of the Bush Tax Cuts, 2001–2003					
Income in 2003	Taxpayers	Gross Income	Total Tax Cut	% Change in Tax Bill	Tax Bill	Tax Rate
Less than $50,000	92,093,452	$19,521	$435	—48%	$474	2%
$50,000 to 100,000	26,915,091	70,096	1,656	—21	6,417	9
$100,000 to 200,000	8,878,643	131,797	3,625	—17	18,281	14
$200,000 to 500,000	1,999,061	288,296	7,088	—10	60,464	21
$500,000 to 1,000,000	356,140	677,294	22,479	—12	169,074	25
$1,000,000 to 10,000,000	175,157	2,146,100	84,666	—13	554,286	26
$10,000,000 or more	6,126	25,975,532	1,019,369	—15	5,780,926	22

Source: New York Times, April 5, 2006.

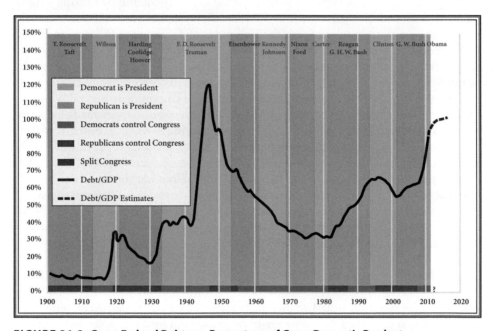

FIGURE 31.3 Gross Federal Debt as a Percentage of Gross Domestic Product
Economists argue that the best measure of a nation's debt is its size relative to the overall economy—that is, its percentage of gross domestic product (GDP). The size of the total U.S. debt declined from its World War II–high until the 1980s, when it increased dramatically under President Reagan. Since then, the debt has consistently increased as a percentage of GDP, aside from a small decline under President Clinton's deficit-reduction plans in the mid-1990s. Source: http://dshort.com.

September 11, 2001 How Bush's presidency might have fared in normal times is another of those unanswerable questions of history. As a candidate in 2000, George W. Bush had said little about foreign policy. He had assumed that his administration would rise or fall on his domestic program. But nine months into his presidency, an altogether different political scenario unfolded. On a sunny September

September 11, 2001
Photographers at the scene after a plane crashed into the north tower of New York City's World Trade Center found themselves recording a defining moment in the nation's history. When a second airliner approached and then slammed into the building's south tower at 9:03 A.M., the nation knew this was no accident. The United States was under attack. Of the 2,843 people killed on September 11, 2,617 died at the World Trade Center. Robert Clark/AURORA.

morning, nineteen Islamic terrorists from Al Qaeda hijacked four commercial jets and flew two of them into New York City's World Trade Center, destroying its twin towers and killing more than 2,900 people. A third plane crashed into the Pentagon, near Washington, D.C. The fourth, presumably headed for the White House or possibly the U.S. Capitol, crashed in Pennsylvania when the passengers fought back and thwarted the hijackers. As an outburst of patriotism swept the United States in the wake of the September 11 attacks, George W. Bush proclaimed a "war on terror" and vowed to carry the battle to Al Qaeda.

Operating out of Afghanistan, where they had been harbored by the fundamentalist Taliban regime, the elusive Al Qaeda briefly offered a clear target. In October 2001, the United States attacked — not with conventional forces, but by deploying military advisors and supplies that bolstered anti-Taliban rebel forces. While Afghani allies carried the ground war, American planes rained destruction on the enemy. By early 2002, this lethal combination had ousted the Taliban, destroyed Al Qaeda's training camps, and killed or captured many of its operatives. However, the big potential prize, Al Qaeda leader Osama bin Laden, had retreated to a mountain redoubt. Inexplicably, U.S. Special Operations forces failed to press the attack; bin Laden evidently bought off the local warlords and escaped over the border into Pakistan.

The Invasion of Iraq | Having unseated the Taliban in Afghanistan by early 2002, the Bush administration could have declared victory and relegated the unfinished business — tracking down the Al Qaeda remnants, stabilizing Afghanistan, and shaking up America's security agencies — to a postvictory operational phase. But President Bush had no such inclination. For him, the war on terror was not a metaphor, but the real thing: an open-ended war that required putting aside business as usual.

On the domestic side, Bush declared the terrorist threat too big to be contained by ordinary law-enforcement means. He wanted the government's powers of domestic surveillance placed on a wartime footing. With little debate, Congress passed the USA PATRIOT Act, granting the administration sweeping authority to monitor citizens and apprehend suspected terrorists. On the international front, Bush used the war on terror as the premise for a new policy of preventive war. Under international law, only an imminent threat justified a nation's right to strike first. Now, under the so-called Bush doctrine, the United States lowered the bar. It reserved for itself the right to act in "anticipatory self-defense." President Bush singled out Iran, North Korea, and Iraq — "an axis of evil" — as the targeted states.

Of the three, Iraq was the preferred mark. Officials in the Pentagon regarded Iraq as unfinished business, left over from the Gulf War of 1991. More grandly, they saw in Iraq an opportunity to unveil America's supposed mission to democratize the world. Iraqis, they believed, would abandon the tyrant Saddam Hussein and embrace democracy if given the chance. The democratizing effect would spread across the Middle East, toppling or reforming other unpopular Arab regimes and stabilizing the region. That, in turn, would secure the Middle East's oil supply, whose fragility Saddam's 1990 invasion of Kuwait had made all too clear. It was the oil, in the end, that was of vital interest to the United States (Map 31.3).

None of these considerations, either singly or together, met Bush's declared threshold for preventive war. So the president reluctantly acceded to the demand by America's anxious European allies that the United States go to the UN Security Council, which demanded that Saddam Hussein allow the return of the UN weapons inspectors expelled in 1998. Saddam surprisingly agreed. Nevertheless, anxious to invade Iraq for its own

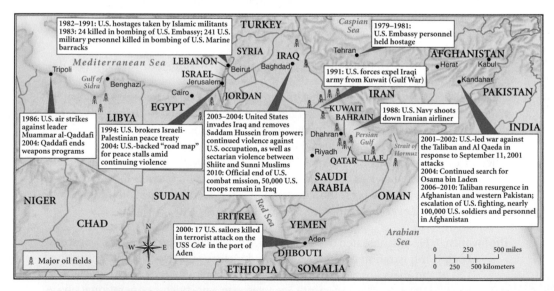

MAP 31.3 U.S. Involvement in the Middle East, 1979–2010

The United States has long played an active role in the Middle East, driven by the strategic importance of that region and, most important, by America's need to ensure a reliable supply of oil from the Persian Gulf states. This map shows the highlights of that troubled involvement, from the Tehran embassy hostage-taking in 1979 to the invasion and current occupation of both Iraq and Afghanistan.

reasons, the Bush administration geared up for war. Insisting that Iraq constituted a "grave and gathering danger" and ignoring its failure to secure a second, legitimizing UN resolution, Bush invaded in March 2003. America's one major ally in the rush to war was Great Britain. Relations with France and Germany became poisonous. Even neighboring Mexico and Canada condemned the invasion, and Turkey, a key military ally, refused transit permission, ruining the army's plan for a northern thrust into Iraq. As for the Arab world, it exploded in anti-American demonstrations.

The war began with massive air attacks. Within three weeks, American troops had taken the Iraqi capital. The regime collapsed, and its leaders went into hiding (Saddam Hussein was captured nine months later). Despite meticulous military planning, the Pentagon had made no provision for postconflict operations. Thousands of poor Iraqis looted everything they could get their hands on: stores, shops, museums, industrial plants, government offices, and military arsenals. The looting shattered the infrastructure of Iraq's cities, leaving them without reliable supplies of electricity and water. In the midst of this turmoil, an insurgency began, sparked by Sunni Muslims who had dominated Iraq under Saddam's Baathist regime (see Voices from Abroad, p. 968).

Iraq's Shiite majority, long oppressed by Saddam, at first welcomed the Americans, but extremist Shiite elements soon turned hostile and U.S. forces found themselves under fire from both sides. With the borders unguarded, Al Qaeda supporters flocked in from all over the Middle East, eager to do battle with the infidel Americans, bringing along a specialty of the jihad: the suicide bomber.

Popular insurgencies are a problem for superpowers. Blinded by their own nationalism, dominant nations tend to underestimate the strength of nationalism in other people. Lyndon Johnson discovered this in Vietnam. Soviet premier Leonid Brezhnev discovered it in Afghanistan. And George W. Bush rediscovered it in Iraq. The intractable fact is that the superpower's troops are invaders. Although it was hard for Americans to believe, that was how Iraqis of all stripes viewed the U.S. forces. Moreover, in a war against insurgents, no occupation force comes out with clean hands. In Iraq, that painful truth burst forth graphically in photographs showing American guards at Baghdad's Abu Ghraib prison abusing and torturing suspected insurgents. The ghastly images shocked the world. For Muslims, they offered final proof of American treachery. At that low point, in 2004, the United States had spent upward of $100 billion. More than 1,000 American soldiers had died, and 10,000 others had been wounded, many maimed for life. But if the United States pulled out, Iraq would descend into chaos. So, as Bush took to saying, the United States had to "stay the course."

The 2004 Election | As the 2004 presidential election approached, Rove, Bush's top advisor, theorized that stirring the culture wars and emphasizing patriotism and Bush's war on terror would mobilize conservatives and further entrench the Republican Party as the dominant power in Washington. Rove encouraged activists to place antigay initiatives on the ballot in key states to draw conservative voters to the polls; in all, eleven states would pass ballot initiatives that wrote bans on gay marriage equality into state constitutions that year. More conservative voters meant more votes for Bush. The Democratic nominee, Senator John Kerry of Massachusetts, was a Vietnam hero, twice wounded and decorated for bravery — in contrast to the president, who had spent the Vietnam years comfortably in the Texas Air National Guard. But when Kerry

A Strategy for the Iraq Insurgency
ABU MUSAB AL-ZARQAWI

From 2004 to June 2006, when he was killed by American forces, Abu Musab al-Zarqawi led the Al Qaeda–linked insurgency in Iraq. But al-Zarqawi was also engaged in a struggle inside the Islamic world. He was Sunni, and he regarded adherents of the other main branch of Islam, the Shiites, as heretical enemies as vile as the hated Westerners. Early in 2004, as he was taking up his struggle in Iraq, al-Zarqawi wrote the following letter, which outlined the deadly strategy of bombings and sectarian violence he proposed to follow. The letter should be read for what it reveals of the mind of the figure who, until his death, was more responsible than any other for plunging Iraq into chaos.

God favored the [Islamic] nation with jihad on His behalf in the land of Mesopotamia [the ancient name for Iraq]. . . . The Americans, as you know well, entered Iraq on a contractual basis to create the State of Greater Israel from the Nile to the Euphrates and that this Zionized American Administration believes that accelerating the creation of the State of [Greater] Israel will accelerate the emergence of the Messiah. It came to Iraq with all its people, pride, and haughtiness toward God and his Prophet. It thought that the matter would be somewhat easy. . . . But it collided with a completely different reality. The operations of the brother mujahidin [fighters] began from the first moment. . . . This forced the Americans to conclude a deal with the Shi'a, the most evil of mankind. The deal was concluded on [the basis that] the Shi'a would get two-thirds of the booty for having stood in the ranks of the Crusaders against the mujahidin.

[The Shi'a are] the insurmountable obstacle, the lurking snake, the crafty and malicious scorpion, the spying enemy, and the penetrating venom. . . . Shi'ism is the looming danger and the true challenge. "They are the enemy. Beware of them. Fight them. By God, they lie." History's message is validated by the testimony of the current situation, which informs most clearly that

Shi'ism is a religion that has nothing in common with Islam. . . .

America did not come to leave, and it will not leave no matter how numerous its wounds become and how much of its blood is spilled. It is looking to the near future, when it hopes to disappear into its bases secure and at ease and put the battlefields of Iraq into the hands of the foundling government with an army and police that will bring [the terror] of Saddam . . . back to the people. There is no doubt that the space in which we can move has begun to shrink and that the grip around the throats of the [Arab and Sunni] mujahidin has begun to tighten. With the deployment of soldiers and police, the future has become frightening. . . .

I come back and again say that the only solution is for us to strike the religious, military, and other cadres among the Shi'a with blow after blow until they bend to the Sunnis. . . . God's religion is more precious than lives and souls. When the overwhelming majority stands in the ranks of truth, there has to be sacrifice for this religion. Let blood be spilled.

SOURCE: Documents on Terrorist Abu Musab al-Zarqawi, 2004, www.personal.umich.edu/~jrcole/zarqawi/zarqawi.htm.

returned from service in Vietnam, he had joined the antiwar group Vietnam Veterans Against the War and in 1971 had delivered a blistering critique of the war to the Senate Armed Services Committee. In the logic of the culture wars, this made him vulnerable to charges of being weak and unpatriotic.

The Democratic convention in August was a tableau of patriotism, filled with waving flags, retired generals, and Kerry's Vietnam buddies. However, a sudden onslaught of slickly produced television ads by a group calling itself Swift Boat Veterans for Truth, falsely charging that Kerry had lied to win his medals, fatally undercut his advantage. Nor did it help that Kerry, as a three-term senator, had a lengthy record that was easily mined for hard-to-explain votes. Republicans tagged him a "flip-flopper," and the accusation, endlessly repeated, stuck. Nearly 60 percent of eligible voters — the highest percentage since 1968 — went to the polls. Bush beat Kerry, with 286 electoral votes to Kerry's 252. In exit polls, Bush did well among voters for whom moral "values" and national security were top concerns. Voters told interviewers that Bush made them feel "safer." Bush was no longer a minority president. He had won a clear, if narrow, popular majority.

Violence Abroad and Economic Collapse at Home

George Bush's second term was defined by crisis management. In 2005, Hurricane Katrina — one of the deadliest hurricanes in the nation's history — devastated New Orleans. Chaos ensued as floodwaters breached earthen barricades surrounding the city and covered low-lying neighborhoods in more than 10 feet of water. Many residents remained without food, drinking water, or shelter for days following the storm, and deaths mounted — the final death toll stood at more than 4,000. Initial emergency responses to the catastrophe by federal and local authorities were uncoordinated and inadequate. Because the hardest-hit parts of the city were poor and African American, Katrina had revealed the poverty and vulnerability at the heart of American cities.

The run of crises did not abate after Katrina. Increasing violence and a rising insurgency in Iraq made the war there even more unpopular in the United States in 2005 and 2006. In 2007, changes in U.S. military strategy helped quell some of the worst violence, but the war dragged into its fifth and sixth years under Bush's watch. A war-weary public grew impatient. Then, in 2008, the American economy began to stumble. By the fall, the Dow Jones Industrial Average had lost half its total value and major banks, insurance companies, and financial institutions were on the verge of collapse. The entire automobile industry was near bankruptcy. Millions of Americans lost their jobs, and the unemployment rate surged to 10 percent. Housing prices dropped by as much as 40 percent in some parts of the country, and millions of Americans defaulted on their mortgages. The United States had entered the worst economic recession since the 1930s, what soon became known as the Great Recession.

The 2008 presidential election took shape in that perilous context. In a historically remarkable primary season, the Democratic nomination was contested between the first woman and the first African American to be viable presidential contenders, Hillary Rodham Clinton and Barack Hussein Obama. In a close-fought contest, Obama had emerged by early summer as the nominee.

Meanwhile, the Bush administration confronted an economy in freefall. In September, less than two months before the election, Secretary of the Treasury Henry Paulson urged Congress to pass the Emergency Economic Stabilization Act, commonly referred to as the "bailout" of the financial sector. Passed in early October, the act dedicated $700 billion to rescuing many of the nation's largest banks and brokerage houses. Between Congress's actions and the independent efforts of the Treasury Department and the Federal Reserve, the U.S. government invested close to $1 trillion in saving the nation's financial system.

The Obama Presidency

During his campaign for the presidency against Republican senator John McCain, Barack Obama, a Democratic senator from Illinois, established himself as a unique figure in American politics. When he was attacked for his relationship with a fiery black minister, Obama gave one of the most honest and insightful speeches about race ever delivered by a major American politician. The son of an African immigrant-student and a young white woman from Kansas, Obama was raised in Hawaii and Indonesia, and he easily connected with an increasingly multiracial and multicultural America. A generation younger than Bill Clinton and George W. Bush, Obama (born in 1961) had not participated in the protests and counterculture of the 1960s and was not enmeshed in the ideological wars that followed. Obama seemed at once a product of the 1960s, especially civil rights gains, and outside its overheated conflicts.

Obama took the oath of office of the presidency on January 20, 2009, amid the deepest economic recession since the Great Depression and with the United States mired in two wars in the Middle East. From the podium, the new president recognized the crises and worried about "a nagging fear that America's decline is inevitable." But like all other presidents at the opening of their term, Obama hoped to strike an optimistic tone. Americans, he said, must "begin again the work of remaking America."

As the first African American president of the United States, Obama carried more than one immense burden. A nation that a mere two generations ago would not allow black Americans to dine with white Americans had elected a black man to the highest office. Obama himself was less taken with this historic accomplishment — which was also part of his deliberate strategy to downplay race — than with developing a plan to deal with the nation's innumerable challenges, at home and abroad. With explicit comparisons to Franklin Roosevelt, Obama used the "first hundred days" of his presidency to lay out an ambitious agenda: an economic stimulus package of federal spending to invigorate the economy; plans to draw down the war in Iraq and refocus American military efforts in Afghanistan; a reform of the nation's health insurance system; and new federal laws to regulate Wall Street.

The first objective, surprisingly, proved the easiest to accomplish; the others encountered enormous political and practical obstacles. In February, Congress passed the American Recovery and Reinvestment Act, an economic stimulus bill that provided $787 billion to state and local governments for schools, hospitals, and transportation projects — one of the largest single packages of government spending in U.S. history. But in the Middle East, Obama's promises to withdraw U.S. troops from Iraq and to turn the war in Afghanistan decisively against the Taliban insurgents have remained largely unfulfilled as of 2012.

Barack Obama

In 2008, Barack Obama became the first African American president in U.S. history. Here, presidential candidate Senator Obama shakes hands during the campaign with supporters near Philadelphia, Pennsylvania. © Bettmann/Corbis.

Political debate over the stimulus bill had been heated, with conservatives staunchly opposed. But that battle was a minor skirmish compared to what awaited Obama's health care proposal. Believing that he had learned from President Clinton's mistake in 1993 — drafting an entire bill in the White House and asking Congress simply to vote it up or down — Obama allowed congressional Democrats to put forth their own proposals. The president then worked to find Republican allies to support the first major reform of the nation's health care system since Medicare in 1965. None came forward. Conservatives within the president's own party — aided by a lobbying offensive from the insurance industry — ensured that the resulting Patient Protection and Affordable Care Act, passed by Congress on March 21, 2010, did not alter the private health care market and contained enough compromises that few could predict its long-term impact.

As debate over the health care bill dragged on, the Tea Party — a powerful new far-right oppositional group — emerged. Comprised of staunch conservatives opposed to any increase in government spending, the Tea Party represented a revival of the fiercely libertarian wing of the New Right. After Obama's "first hundred days," Tea Party activists increasingly set the tone of national political debate and emboldened the president's opponents. With little evidence that an economic recovery was under-way, and with unemployment hovering between 8 and 10 percent, Republicans scored a historic victory in the 2010 midterm elections. Democrats lost more than 60 con-gressional seats and their majority in the House. With a House majority in hand, Re-publicans endeavored to stymie any Democratic initiatives and to press their case for both budget and tax cuts. Their newfound power and determination were in evidence when they nearly forced the government to default on its debt obligations in order to compel Democrats to agree to further tax reductions.

It remains to be seen how the Obama presidency will affect American politics. From one vantage, Obama looks like the beneficiary of an electoral shift in a liberal di-rection. Since 1992, Democrats have won the popular vote in four of the five presidential elections, and Obama won a greater share of the popular vote (nearly 53 percent) than either Clinton (43 percent in 1992 and 49 percent in 1996) or Gore (48 percent in 2000). From another vantage, this shift toward liberalism appears contingent and fragile. Even with Democratic majorities in both houses of Congress to rival those of Roosevelt in 1937 and Johnson in 1965, Obama has not been able to generate political momentum for the kind of legislative advances achieved by those presi-dents. Moreover, the turnabout in the 2010 mid-term elections, combined with Obama's low ap-proval rating (less than 40 percent), suggests that amidst ongoing economic stagnation the elector-ate remains volatile and unpredictable. The history of Obama's presidency, and of the early twenty-first century more broadly, continues to unfold.

▶ In what ways was George H. W. Bush a political follower of Ronald Reagan? In what ways was he not?

▶ How would you compare the Iraq War with previous wars in U.S. history?

SUMMARY

This chapter has stressed how globalization — the worldwide flow of capital, goods, and people — entered a new phase after the end of the Cold War. The number of mul-tinational corporations, many of them based in the United States, increased dramati-cally, and people, goods, and investment capital moved easily across political boundar-ies. Financial markets, in particular, grew increasingly open and interconnected across the globe. Technological innovations strengthened the American economy and trans-formed daily life. The computer revolution and the spread of the Internet changed the ways in which Americans shopped, worked, learned, and stayed in touch with family and friends. Globalization facilitated the immigration of millions of Asians and Latin Americans into the United States.

In the decades since 1989, American life has been characterized by the dilemmas presented by the twin issues of globalization and divisive cultural politics. Conserva-tives spoke out strongly, and with increasing effectiveness, against multiculturalism and what they viewed as serious threats to "family values." Debates over women's rights, access to abortion, affirmative action, and the legal rights of homosexuals intensified.

The terrorist attacks of September 11, 2001, temporarily calmed the nation's increasingly bitter partisanship, but that partisanship was revived after President Bush's decision to invade Iraq (a nation not involved in the events of 9/11) in 2003 led to a protracted war. When Barack Obama was elected in 2008, the first African American president in the nation's history, he inherited two wars and the Great Recession, the most significant economic collapse since the 1930s. His, and the nation's, efforts to address these and other pressing issues — including the national debt and global warming — remain ongoing, unfinished business.

For additional primary sources from this period, see *Documents for America's History*, Seventh Edition.

For Web sites, images, and documents related to topics and places in this chapter, visit *Make History* at **bedfordstmartins.com/henrettaconcise**.

For Further Exploration

On globalization, see Alfred Eckes Jr. and Thomas Zeilin, *Globalization and the American Century* (2003). For discussions of recent growth in inequality, see Godfrey Hodgson, *More Equal Than Others* (2004). On American families and the culture wars, see Stephanie Coontz, *The Way We Never Were: American Families and the Nostalgia Trap* (1992); Susan Faludi, *Backlash: The Undeclared War against American Women* (1991); and Gertrude Himmelfarb, *One Nation, Two Cultures* (1999). For the Clinton years, consult William Berman, *From the Center to the Edge: The Politics and Policies of the Clinton Presidency* (2001), and Joe Klein, *The Natural: The Misunderstood Presidency of Bill Clinton* (2002). Richard A. Posner, *An Affair of State: The Investigation, Impeachment, and Trial of President Clinton* (1999), probes the legal aspects of Clinton's impeachment. For online materials on that subject, consult Jurist, the Law Professors' Network, at **jurist.law .pitt.edu/impeach.htm**. Information on all U.S. presidents is available at **www.ipl.org/ div/potus**. The literature on the presidency of George W. Bush, the September 11 attacks, and the Iraq War is already vast and growing. A good starting point is Richard A. Clarke, *Against All Enemies: Inside America's War on Terror* (2004), and Michael R. Gordon and Bernard R. Trainor, *Cobra II: The Inside Story of the Invasion and Occupation of Iraq* (2006). See the September 11 Digital Archive at **http://911digitalarchive.org/** for oral histories and both still and moving images from September 11. Barack Obama's first memoir, *Dreams from My Father: A Story of Race and Inheritance* (1995), makes compelling reading.

Test Your Knowledge

For practice quizzes, activities, and other study tools, visit the Online Study Guide at **bedfordstmartins.com/henrettaconcise**.

TIMELINE

1992	► Democratic moderate Bill Clinton elected president
	► *Planned Parenthood of Southeastern Pennsylvania v. Casey*
1993	► North American Free Trade Agreement (NAFTA)
1994	► Clinton fails to win health insurance reform but reduces budget deficit and national debt
	► Republicans gain control of Congress
1995	► U.S. troops enforce peace in Bosnia
1996	► Personal Responsibility and Work Opportunity Act reforms welfare system
1998	► Clinton impeached by House of Representatives
	► American intervention in Bosnia and Serbia
	► Defense of Marriage Act
1999	► Clinton acquitted by the Senate
	► World Trade Organization (WTO) protests

2000	► George W. Bush wins contested presidential election
2001	► Bush tax cuts
	► September 11, Al Qaeda terrorists attack World Trade Center and Pentagon
	► Congress passes USA PATRIOT Act
2002	► The United States unseats Taliban in Afghanistan
	► Bush declares Iran, North Korea, and Iraq "an axis of evil"
2003	► The United States invades Iraq in March
2004	► Torture at Abu Ghraib prison becomes public
	► Bush wins reelection
2007	► Great Recession begins
2008	► Barack Obama elected president
	► American Recovery and Reinvestment Act
2010	► Patient Protection and Affordable Care Act

Documents

The Declaration of Independence

In Congress, July 4, 1776,
The Unanimous Declaration of the
Thirteen United States of America

When in the Course of human events, it becomes necessary for one people to dissolve the political bands which have connected them with another, and to assume among the Powers of the earth, the separate and equal station to which the Laws of Nature and of Nature's God entitle them, a decent respect to the opinions of mankind requires that they should declare the causes which impel them to the separation.

We hold these truths to be self-evident, that all men are created equal, that they are endowed by their Creator with certain unalienable rights, that among these are Life, Liberty, and the pursuit of Happiness. That to secure these rights, Governments are instituted among Men, deriving their just powers from the consent of the governed. That whenever any Form of Government becomes destructive of these ends, it is the Right of the People to alter or to abolish it, and to institute new Government, laying its foundation on such principles and organizing its powers in such form, as to them shall seem most likely to effect their Safety and Happiness. Prudence, indeed, will dictate that Governments long established should not be changed for light and transient causes; and accordingly all experience hath shown, that mankind are more disposed to suffer, while evils are sufferable, than to right themselves by abolishing the forms to which they are accustomed. But when a long train of abuses and usurpations, pursuing invariably the same Object evinces a design to reduce them under absolute Despotism, it is their right, it is their duty, to throw off such Government, and to provide new Guards for their future security. — Such has been the patient sufferance of these Colonies; and such is now the necessity which constrains them to alter their former Systems of Government. The history of the present King of Great Britain is a history of repeated injuries and usurpations, all having in direct object the establishment of an absolute Tyranny over these States. To prove this, let Facts be submitted to a candid world.

He has refused his Assent to Laws, the most wholesome and necessary for the public good.

He has forbidden his Governors to pass Laws of immediate and pressing importance, unless suspended in their operation till his Assent should be obtained; and, when so suspended, he has utterly neglected to attend to them.

He has refused to pass other Laws for the accommodation of large districts of people, unless those people would relinquish the right of Representation in the Legislature, a right inestimable to them and formidable to tyrants only.

He has called together legislative bodies at places unusual, uncomfortable, and distant from the depository of their public Records, for the sole purpose of fatiguing them into compliance with his measures.

He has dissolved Representative Houses repeatedly, for opposing with manly firmness his invasions on the rights of the people.

He has refused for a long time, after such dissolutions, to cause others to be elected; whereby the Legislative powers, incapable of Annihilation, have returned to the People at large for their exercise; the State remaining in the mean time exposed to all the dangers of invasion from without and convulsions within.

He has endeavoured to prevent the population of these States; for that purpose obstructing the Laws of Naturalization of Foreigners; refusing to pass others to encourage their migrations hither, and raising the conditions of new Appropriations of Lands.

He has obstructed the Administration of Justice, by refusing his Assent to Laws for establishing Judiciary powers.

He has made Judges dependent on his Will alone, for the tenure of their offices, and the amount and payment of their salaries.

He has erected a multitude of New Offices, and sent hither swarms of Officers to harass our People, and eat out their substance.

He has kept among us, in times of peace, Standing Armies without the Consent of our legislature.

He has combined with others to subject us to a jurisdiction foreign to our constitution, and unacknowledged by our laws; giving his Assent to their Acts of pretended Legislation:

For quartering large bodies of armed troops among us:

For protecting them, by a mock Trial, from Punishment for any Murders which they should commit on the Inhabitants of these States:

For cutting off our Trade with all parts of the world:

For imposing taxes on us without our Consent:

For depriving us, in many cases, of the benefits of Trial by jury:

For transporting us beyond Seas to be tried for pretended offences:

For abolishing the free System of English Laws in a neighbouring Province, establishing therein an Arbitrary government, and enlarging its Boundaries so as to render it at once an example and fit instrument for introducing the same absolute rule into these Colonies:

For taking away our Charters, abolishing our most valuable Laws, and altering fundamentally the Forms of our Governments:

For suspending our own Legislatures, and declaring themselves invested with Power to legislate for us in all cases whatsoever.

He has abdicated Government here, by declaring us out of his Protection and waging War against us.

He has plundered our seas, ravaged our Coasts, burnt our towns, and destroyed the lives of our people.

He is at this time transporting large armies of foreign mercenaries to compleat the works of death, desolation, and tyranny, already begun with circumstances of Cruelty & perfidy scarcely paralleled in the most barbarous ages, and totally unworthy the Head of a civilized nation.

He has constrained our fellow Citizens taken Captive on the high Seas to bear Arms against their Country, to become the executioners of their friends and Brethren, or to fall themselves by their Hands.

He has excited domestic insurrections amongst us, and has endeavoured to bring on the inhabitants of our frontiers, the merciless Indian Savages, whose known rule of warfare, is an undistinguished destruction of all ages, sexes, and conditions.

In every stage of these Oppressions We have Petitioned for Redress in the most humble terms: Our repeated Petitions have been answered only by repeated injury. A Prince, whose character is thus marked by every act which may define a Tyrant, is unfit to be the ruler of a free people.

Nor have We been wanting in attention to our British brethren. We have warned them from time to time of attempts by their legislature to extend an unwarrantable jurisdiction over us. We have reminded them of the circumstances of our emigration and settlement here. We have appealed to their native justice and magnanimity, and we have conjured them by the ties of our common kindred to disavow these usurpations, which would inevitably interrupt our connections and correspondence. They too have been deaf to the voice of justice and of consanguinity. We must, therefore, acquiesce in the necessity, which denounces our Separation, and hold them, as we hold the rest of mankind, Enemies in War, in Peace Friends.

We, therefore, the Representatives of the United States of America, in General Congress, Assembled, appealing to the Supreme Judge of the world for the rectitude of our intentions, do, in the Name, and by Authority of the good People of these Colonies, solemnly publish and declare, That these United Colonies are, and of Right ought to be FREE AND INDEPENDENT STATES; that they are Absolved from all Allegiance to the British Crown, and that all political connection between them and the State of Great Britain, is and ought to be totally dissolved; and that as Free and Independent States, they have full Power to levy War, conclude Peace, contract Alliances, establish Commerce, and to do all other Acts and Things which Independent States may of right do. And for the support of this Declaration, with a firm reliance on the Protection of Divine Providence, we mutually pledge to each other our Lives, our Fortunes, and our sacred Honor.

John Hancock

Button Gwinnett	Thos. Heyward, Junr.	Charles Carroll
Lyman Hall	Thomas Lynch, Junr.	of Carrollton
Geo. Walton	Arthur Middleton	George Wythe
Wm. Hooper	Samuel Chase	Richard Henry Lee
Joseph Hewes	Wm. Paca	Th. Jefferson
John Penn	Thos. Stone	Benja. Harrison
Edward Rutledge		Thos. Nelson, Jr.

Francis Lightfoot Lee
Carter Braxton
Robt. Morris
Benjamin Rush
Benja. Franklin
John Morton
Geo. Clymer
Jas. Smith
Geo. Taylor
James Wilson
Geo. Ross
Caesar Rodney

Geo. Read
Thos. M'Kean
Wm. Floyd
Phil. Livingston
Frans. Lewis
Lewis Morris
Richd. Stockton
John Witherspoon
Fras. Hopkinson
John Hart
Abra. Clark
Josiah Bartlett

Wm. Whipple
Matthew Thornton
Saml. Adams
John Adams
Robt. Treat Paine
Elbridge Gerry
Step. Hopkins
William Ellery
Roger Sherman
Sam'el Huntington
Wm. Williams
Oliver Wolcott

Articles of Confederation and Perpetual Union

Agreed to in Congress, November 15, 1777; Ratified March 1781

BETWEEN THE STATES OF NEW HAMPSHIRE, MASSACHUSETTS BAY, RHODE ISLAND AND PROVIDENCE PLANTATIONS, CONNECTICUT, NEW YORK, NEW JERSEY, PENNSYLVANIA, DELAWARE, MARYLAND, VIRGINIA, NORTH CAROLINA, SOUTH CAROLINA, GEORGIA.*

Article 1

The stile of this confederacy shall be "The United States of America."

Article 2

Each State retains its sovereignty, freedom and independence, and every power, jurisdiction, and right, which is not by this confederation expressly delegated to the United States, in Congress assembled.

Article 3

The said states hereby severally enter into a firm league of friendship with each other for their common defence, the security of their liberties and their mutual and general welfare; binding themselves to assist each other against all force offered to, or attacks made upon them, or any of them, on account of religion, sovereignty, trade, or any other pretence whatever.

Article 4

The better to secure and perpetuate mutual friendship and intercourse among the people of the different states in this union, the free inhabitants of each of these states, paupers, vagabonds, and fugitives from justice excepted, shall be entitled to all privileges and immunities of free citizens in the several states; and the people of each State shall have free ingress and regress to and from any other State, and shall enjoy therein all the privileges of trade and commerce, subject to the same duties, impositions, and restrictions, as the inhabitants thereof respectively; provided, that such restrictions shall not extend so far as to prevent the removal of property, imported into any State, to any other State of which the owner is an inhabitant; provided also, that no imposition, duties, or restriction, shall be laid by any State on the property of the United States, or either of them.

If any person guilty of, or charged with treason, felony, or other high misdemeanor in any State, shall flee from justice and be found in any of the United States, he shall, upon demand of the governor or executive power of the State from which he fled, be delivered up and removed to the State having jurisdiction of his offence.

Full faith and credit shall be given in each of these states to the records, acts, and judicial proceedings of the courts and magistrates of every other State.

---

*This copy of the final draft of the Articles of Confederation is taken from the *Journals*, 9:907–25, November 15, 1777.

Article 5

For the more convenient management of the general interests of the United States, delegates shall be annually appointed, in such manner as the legislature of each State shall direct, to meet in Congress, on the 1st Monday in November in every year, with a power reserved to each State to recall its delegates, or any of them, at any time within the year, and to send others in their stead for the remainder of the year.

No State shall be represented in Congress by less than two, nor by more than seven members; and no person shall be capable of being a delegate for more than three years in any term of six years; nor shall any person, being a delegate, be capable of holding any office under the United States, for which he, or any other for his benefit, receives any salary, fees, or emolument of any kind.

Each State shall maintain its own delegates in a meeting of the states, and while they act as members of the committee of the states.

In determining questions in the United States, in Congress assembled, each State shall have one vote.

Freedom of speech and debate in Congress shall not be impeached or questioned in any court or place out of Congress: and the members of Congress shall be protected in their persons from arrests and imprisonments, during the time of their going to and from, and attendance on Congress, except for treason, felony, or breach of the peace.

Article 6

No State, without the consent of the United States, in Congress assembled, shall send any embassy to, or receive any embassy from, or enter into any conference, agreement, alliance, or treaty with any king, prince, or state; nor shall any person, holding any office of profit or trust under the United States, or any of them, accept of any present, emolument, office or title, of any kind whatever, from any king, prince, or foreign state; nor shall the United States, in Congress assembled, or any of them, grant any title of nobility.

No two or more states shall enter into any treaty, confederation, or alliance, whatever, between them, without the consent of the United States, in Congress assembled, specifying accurately the purposes for which the same is to be entered into, and how long it shall continue.

No state shall lay any imposts or duties which may interfere with any stipulations in treaties entered into by the United States, in Congress assembled, with any king, prince, or state, in pursuance of any treaties already proposed by Congress to the courts of France and Spain.

No vessels of war shall be kept up in time of peace by any State, except such number only as shall be deemed necessary by the United States, in Congress assembled, for the defence of such State or its trade; nor shall any body of forces be kept up by any State, in time of peace, except such number only as, in the judgment of the United States, in Congress assembled, shall be deemed requisite to garrison the forts necessary for the defence of such State; but every State shall always keep up a well regulated and disciplined militia, sufficiently armed and accoutred, and shall provide, and constantly have ready for use, in public stores, a due number of field pieces and tents, and a proper quantity of arms, ammunition and camp equipage.

No State shall engage in any war without the consent of the United States, in Congress assembled, unless such State be actually invaded by enemies, or shall have received certain advice of a resolution being formed by some nation of Indians to invade such State, and the danger is so imminent as not to admit of a delay till the United States, in Congress assembled, can be consulted; nor shall any State grant commissions to any ships or vessels of war, nor letters of marque or reprisal, except it be after a declaration of war by the United States, in Congress assembled, and then only against the kingdom or state, and the subjects thereof, against which war has been so declared, and under such regulations as shall be established by the United States, in Congress assembled, unless such State be infested by pirates, in which case vessels of war may be fitted out for that occasion, and kept so long as the danger shall continue, or until the United States, in Congress assembled, shall determine otherwise.

Article 7

When land forces are raised by any State for the common defence, all officers of or under the rank of colonel, shall be appointed by the legislature of each State respectively, by whom such forces shall be raised, or in such manner as such State shall direct; and all vacancies shall be filled up by the State which first made the appointment.

Article 8

All charges of war and all other expences, that shall be incurred for the common defence or general welfare, and allowed by the United States, in Congress assembled, shall be defrayed out of a common treasury, which shall be supplied by the several states, in proportion to the value of all land within each State, granted to or surveyed for any person, as such land and the buildings and improvements thereon shall be estimated according to such mode as the United States, in Congress assembled, shall, from time to time, direct and appoint.

The taxes for paying that proportion shall be laid and levied by the authority and direction of the legislatures of the several states, within the time agreed upon by the United States, in Congress assembled.

Article 9

The United States, in Congress assembled, shall have the sole and exclusive right and power of determining on peace and war, except in the cases mentioned in the 6th article; of sending and receiving ambassadors; entering into treaties and alliances, provided that no treaty of commerce shall be made, whereby the legislative power of the respective states shall be restrained from imposing such imposts and duties on foreigners as their own people are subjected to, or from prohibiting the exportation or importation of any species of goods or commodities whatsoever; of establishing rules for deciding, in all cases, what captures on land or water shall be legal, and in what manner prizes, taken by land or naval forces in the service of the United States, shall be divided or appropriated; of granting letters of marque and reprisal in times of peace; appointing courts for the trial of piracies and felonies committed on the high seas, and establishing courts for receiving and determining, finally, appeals in all cases of captures; provided, that no member of Congress shall be appointed a judge of any of the said courts.

The United States, in Congress assembled, shall also be the last resort on appeal in all disputes and differences now subsisting, or that hereafter may arise between two or more states concerning boundary, jurisdiction or any other cause whatever; which authority shall always be exercised in the manner following: whenever the legislative or executive authority, or lawful agent of any State, in controversy with another, shall present a petition to Congress, stating the matter in question, and praying for a hearing, notice thereof shall be given, by order of Congress, to the legislative or executive authority of the other State in controversy, and a day assigned for the appearance of the parties by their lawful agents, who shall then be directed to appoint, by joint consent, commissioners or judges to constitute a court for hearing and determining the matter in question; but, if they cannot agree, Congress shall name three persons out of each of the United States, and from the list of such persons each party shall alternately strike out one, the petitioners beginning, until the number shall be reduced to thirteen; and from that number not less than seven, nor more than nine names, as Congress shall direct, shall, in the presence of Congress, be drawn out by lot; and the persons whose names shall be so drawn, or any five of them, shall be commissioners or judges to hear and finally determine the controversy, so always as a major part of the judges who shall hear the cause shall agree in the determination; and if either party shall neglect to attend at the day appointed, without shewing reasons which Congress shall judge sufficient, or, being present, shall refuse to strike, the Congress shall proceed to nominate three persons out of each State, and the secretary of Congress shall strike in behalf of such party absent or refusing; and the judgment and sentence of the court to be appointed, in the manner before prescribed, shall be final and conclusive; and if any of the parties shall refuse to submit to the authority of such court, or to appear or defend their claim or cause, the court shall nevertheless proceed to pronounce sentence or judgment, which shall, in like manner, be final and decisive, the judgment or sentence and other proceedings begin, in either case, transmitted to Congress, and lodged among the acts of Congress for the security of the parties concerned: provided, that every commissioner, before he sits in judgment, shall take an oath, to be administered by one of the judges of the supreme or superior court of the State where the cause shall be tried, "well and truly to hear and determine the matter in question, according to the best of his judgment, without favour, affection, or hope of reward:" provided, also, that no State shall be deprived of territory for the benefit of the United States.

All controversies concerning the private right of soil, claimed under different grants of two or more states, whose jurisdictions, as they may respect such lands and the states which passed such grants, are adjusted, the said grants, or either of them, being at the same time claimed to have originated antecedent to such settlement of jurisdiction, shall, on the petition of either party to the Congress of the United States, be finally determined, as near as may be, in the same manner as is before prescribed for deciding disputes respecting territorial jurisdiction between different states.

The United States, in Congress assembled, shall also have the sole and exclusive right and power of regulating the alloy and value of coin struck by their own authority, or by that of the respective states; fixing the standard of weights and measures throughout the United States; regulating the trade and managing all affairs with the Indians not members of any of the states; provided that the legislative right of any State within its own limits be not infringed or violated; establishing and regulating post offices from one State to another throughout all the United States, and exacting such postage on the papers passing through the same as may be requisite to defray the expences of the said office; appointing all officers of the land forces in the service of the United States, excepting regimental officers; appointing all the officers of the naval forces, and commissioning all officers whatever in the service of the United States; making rules for the government and regulation of the said land and naval forces, and directing their operations.

The United States, in Congress assembled, shall have authority to appoint a committee to sit in the recess of Congress, to be denominated "a Committee of the States," and to consist of one delegate from each State, and to appoint such other committees and civil officers as may be necessary for managing the general affairs of the United States, under their direction; to appoint one of their number to preside; provided that no person be allowed to serve in the office of president more than one year in any term of three years; to ascertain the necessary sums of money to be raised for the service of the United States, and to appropriate and apply the same for defraying the public expences; to borrow money or emit bills on the credit of the United States, transmitting, every half year, to the respective states, an account of the sums of money so borrowed or emitted; to build and equip a navy; to agree upon the number of land forces, and to make requisitions from each State for its quota, in proportion to the number of white inhabitants in such State; which requisitions shall be binding; and thereupon, the legislature of each State shall appoint the regimental officers, raise the men, and cloathe, arm, and equip them in a soldier-like manner, at the expence of the United States; and the officers and men so cloathed, armed, and equipped, shall march to the place appointed and within the time agreed on by the United States, in Congress assembled; but if the United States, in Congress assembled, shall, on consideration of circumstances, judge proper that any State should not raise men, or should raise a smaller number than its quota, and that any other State should raise a greater number of men than the quota thereof, such extra number shall be raised, officered, cloathed, armed, and equipped in the same manner as the quota of such State, unless the legislature of such State shall judge that such extra number cannot be safely spared out of the same, in which case they shall raise, officer, cloathe, arm, and equip as many of such extra number as they judge can be safely spared. And the officers and men so cloathed, armed, and equipped, shall march to the place appointed and within the time agreed on by the United States, in Congress assembled.

The United States, in Congress assembled, shall never engage in a war, nor grant letters of marque and reprisal in time of peace, nor enter into any treaties or alliances, nor coin money, nor regulate the value thereof, nor ascertain the sums and expences necessary for the defence and welfare of the United States, or any of them: nor emit bills, nor borrow money on the credit of the United States, nor appropriate money, nor agree upon the number of vessels of war to be built or purchased, or the number of land or sea forces to be raised, nor appoint a commander in chief of the army or navy, unless nine states assent to the same; nor shall a question on any other point, except for adjourning from day to day, be determined, unless by the votes of a majority of the United States, in Congress assembled.

The Congress of the United States shall have power to adjourn to any time within the year, and to any place within the United States, so that no period of adjournment be for a longer duration than the space of six months, and shall publish the journal of their proceedings monthly, except such parts thereof, relating to treaties, alliances or military operations, as, in their judgment, require secrecy; and the yeas and nays of the delegates of each State on any question shall be entered on the journal, when it is desired by any delegate; and the delegates of a State, or any of them, at his, or their request, shall be furnished with a transcript of the said journal, except such parts as are above excepted, to lay before the legislatures of the several states.

Article 10

The committee of the states, or any nine of them, shall be authorized to execute, in the recess of Congress, such of the powers of Congress as the United States, in Congress assembled, by the consent of nine states, shall, from time to time, think expedient to vest them with; provided, that no power be delegated to the said committee, for the exercise of which, by the articles of confederation, the voice of nine states, in the Congress of the United States assembled, is requisite.

Article 11

Canada acceding to this confederation, and joining in the measures of the United States, shall be admitted into and entitled to all the advantages of this union; but no other colony shall be admitted into the same, unless such admission be agreed to by nine states.

The Constitution of the United States of America

Agreed to by Philadelphia Convention, September 17, 1787
Implemented March 4, 1789

We the People of the United States, in Order to form a more perfect Union, establish Justice, insure domestic Tranquility, provide for the common defence, promote the general Welfare, and secure the Blessings of Liberty to ourselves and our Posterity, do ordain and establish this Constitution for the United States of America.

Article I

Section 1. All legislative Powers herein granted shall be vested in a Congress of the United States, which shall consist of a Senate and a House of Representatives.

Section 2. The House of Representatives shall be composed of Members chosen every second Year by the People of the several States, and the Electors in each State shall have the Qualifications requisite for Electors of the most numerous Branch of the State Legislature.

No Person shall be a Representative who shall not have attained to the Age of twenty-five Years, and been seven Years a Citizen of the United States, and who shall not, when elected, be an Inhabitant of that State in which he shall be chosen.

Representatives and direct Taxes shall be apportioned among the several States which may be included within this Union, according to their respective Numbers, *which shall be determined by adding to the whole Number of free Persons, including those bound to Service for a Term of Years, and excluding Indians not taxed, three fifths of all other Persons.** The actual Enumeration shall be made within three Years after the first Meeting of the Congress of the United States, and within every subsequent Term of ten Years, in such Manner as they shall by Law direct. The Number of Representatives shall not exceed one for every thirty Thousand, but each State shall have at Least one Representative; and *until such enumeration shall be made, the State of New Hampshire shall be entitled to chuse three, Massachusetts eight, Rhode Island and Providence Plantations one, Connecticut five, New York six, New Jersey four, Pennsylvania eight, Delaware one, Maryland six, Virginia ten, North Carolina five, South Carolina five, and Georgia three.*

When vacancies happen in the Representation from any State, the Executive Authority thereof shall issue Writs of Election to fill such Vacancies.

The House of Representatives shall chuse their Speaker and other Officers; and shall have the sole Power of Impeachment.

Section 3. The Senate of the United States shall be composed of two Senators from each State, *chosen by the Legislature thereof,*† for six Years; and each Senator shall have one Vote.

Note: The Constitution became effective March 4, 1789. Provisions in italics are no longer relevant or have been changed by constitutional amendment.

*Changed by Section 2 of the Fourteenth Amendment.

†Changed by Section 1 of the Seventeenth Amendment.

Immediately after they shall be assembled in Consequence of the first Election, they shall be divided as equally as may be into three Classes. The Seats of the Senators of the first Class shall be vacated at the Expiration of the second Year, of the second Class at the Expiration of the fourth Year, and of the third Class at the Expiration of the sixth Year, so that one-third may be chosen every second Year; and if Vacancies happen by Resignation, or otherwise, during the Recess of the Legislature of any State, the Executive thereof may make temporary Appointments until the next Meeting of the Legislature, which shall then fill such Vacancies.*

No person shall be a Senator who shall not have attained to the Age of thirty Years, and been nine Years a Citizen of the United States, and who shall not, when elected, be an Inhabitant of that State for which he shall be chosen.

The Vice President of the United States shall be President of the Senate, but shall have no Vote, unless they be equally divided.

The Senate shall chuse their other Officers, and also a President pro tempore, in the absence of the Vice President, or when he shall exercise the Office of President of the United States.

The Senate shall have the sole Power to try all Impeachments. When sitting for that Purpose, they shall be on Oath or Affirmation. When the President of the United States is tried, the Chief Justice shall preside: And no Person shall be convicted without the Concurrence of two-thirds of the Members present.

Judgment in Cases of Impeachment shall not extend further than to removal from Office, and disqualification to hold and enjoy any Office of honor, Trust or Profit under the United States: but the Party convicted shall nevertheless be liable and subject to Indictment, Trial, Judgment and Punishment, according to Law.

Section 4. The Times, Places and Manner of holding Elections for Senators and Representatives, shall be prescribed in each State by the Legislature thereof; but the Congress may at any time by Law make or alter such Regulations, except as to the Places of Chusing Senators.

The Congress shall assemble at least once in every Year, and such Meeting shall be on the first Monday in December, unless they shall by Law appoint a different Day.†

Section 5. Each House shall be the Judge of the Elections, Returns and Qualifications of its own Members, and a Majority of each shall constitute a Quorum to do Business; but a smaller number may adjourn from day to day, and may be authorized to compel the Attendance of absent Members, in such Manner, and under such Penalties, as each House may provide.

Each House may determine the Rules of its Proceedings, punish its Members for disorderly Behavior, and, with the Concurrence of two-thirds, expel a Member.

Each House shall keep a Journal of its Proceedings, and from time to time publish the same, excepting such Parts as may in their Judgment require Secrecy; and the Yeas and Nays of the Members of either House on any question shall, at the Desire of one-fifth of those Present, be entered on the Journal.

---

*Changed by Clause 2 of the Seventeenth Amendment.
†Changed by Section 2 of the Twentieth Amendment.

Neither House, during the Session of Congress, shall, without the Consent of the other, adjourn for more than three days, nor to any other Place than that in which the two Houses shall be sitting.

Section 6. The Senators and Representatives shall receive a Compensation for their Services, to be ascertained by Law, and paid out of the Treasury of the United States. They shall in all Cases, except Treason, Felony and Breach of the Peace, be privileged from Arrest during their Attendance at the Session of their respective Houses, and in going to and returning from the same; and for any Speech or Debate in either House, they shall not be questioned in any other Place.

No Senator or Representative shall, during the Time for which he was elected, be appointed to any civil Office under the Authority of the United States, which shall have been created, or the Emoluments whereof shall have been increased, during such time; and no Person holding any Office under the United States, shall be a Member of either House during his Continuance in Office.

Section 7. All Bills for raising Revenue shall originate in the House of Representatives; but the Senate may propose or concur with Amendments as on other Bills.

Every Bill which shall have passed the House of Representatives and the Senate, shall, before it becomes a Law, be presented to the President of the United States; If he approve he shall sign it, but if not he shall return it, with his Objections to that House in which it shall have originated, who shall enter the Objections at large on their Journal, and proceed to reconsider it. If after such Reconsideration two-thirds of that House shall agree to pass the Bill, it shall be sent, together with the Objections, to the other House, by which it shall likewise be reconsidered, and if approved by two-thirds of that House, it shall become a Law. But in all such Cases the Votes of both Houses shall be determined by Yeas and Nays, and the Names of the Persons voting for and against the Bill shall be entered on the Journal of each House respectively. If any Bill shall not be returned by the President within ten Days (Sundays excepted) after it shall have been presented to him, the Same shall be a Law, in like Manner as if he had signed it, unless the Congress by their Adjournment prevent its Return, in which Case it shall not be a Law.

Every Order, Resolution, or Vote to which the Concurrence of the Senate and the House of Representatives may be necessary (except on a question of Adjournment) shall be presented to the President of the United States; and before the Same shall take Effect, shall be approved by him, or being disapproved by him, shall be repassed by two-thirds of the Senate and House of Representatives, according to the Rules and Limitations prescribed in the Case of a Bill.

Section 8. The Congress shall have Power To lay and collect Taxes, Duties, Imposts and Excises, to pay the Debts and provide for the common Defence and general Welfare of the United States; but all Duties, Imposts and Excises shall be uniform throughout the United States;

To borrow money on the credit of the United States;

To regulate Commerce with foreign Nations, and among the several States, and with the Indian Tribes;

To establish an uniform Rule of Naturalization, and uniform Laws on the subject of Bankruptcies throughout the United States;

To coin Money, regulate the Value thereof, and of foreign Coin, and fix the Standard of Weights and Measures;

To provide for the Punishment of counterfeiting the Securities and current Coin of the United States;

To establish Post Offices and post Roads;

To promote the Progress of Science and useful Arts, by securing for limited Times to Authors and Inventors the exclusive Right to their respective Writings and Discoveries;

To constitute Tribunals inferior to the supreme Court;

To define and punish Piracies and Felonies committed on the high Seas, and Offenses against the Law of Nations;

To declare War, grant Letters of Marque and Reprisal, and make Rules concerning Captures on Land and Water;

To raise and support Armies, but no Appropriation of Money to that Use shall be for a longer Term than two Years;

To provide and maintain a Navy;

To make Rules for the Government and Regulation of the land and naval Forces;

To provide for calling forth the Militia to execute the Laws of the Union, suppress Insurrections and repel Invasions;

To provide for organizing, arming, and disciplining the Militia, and for governing such Part of them as may be employed in the Service of the United States, reserving to the States respectively, the Appointment of the Officers, and the Authority of training the Militia according to the discipline prescribed by Congress;

To exercise exclusive Legislation in all Cases whatsoever, over such District (not exceeding ten Miles square) as may, by Cession of particular States, and the acceptance of Congress, become the Seat of Government of the United States, and to exercise like Authority over all Places purchased by the Consent of the Legislature of the State in which the Same shall be, for the Erection of Forts, Magazines, Arsenals, dock-Yards, and other needful Buildings; — And

To make all Laws which shall be necessary and proper for carrying into Execution the foregoing Powers, and all other Powers vested by this Constitution in the Government of the United States, or in any Department or Officer thereof.

Section 9. The Migration or Importation of such Persons as any of the States now existing shall think proper to admit, shall not be prohibited by the Congress prior to the Year one thousand eight hundred and eight but a tax or duty may be imposed on such Importation, not exceeding ten dollars for each Person.

The privilege of the Writ of Habeas Corpus shall not be suspended, unless when in Cases of Rebellion or Invasion the public Safety may require it.

No Bill of Attainder or ex post facto Law shall be passed.

*No capitation, or other direct, Tax shall be laid, unless in Proportion to the Census or Enumeration herein before directed to be taken.**

---

*Changed by the Sixteenth Amendment.

No Tax or Duty shall be laid on Articles exported from any State.

No Preference shall be given by any Regulation of Commerce or Revenue to the Ports of one State over those of another: nor shall Vessels bound to, or from, one State, be obliged to enter, clear, or pay Duties in another.

No Money shall be drawn from the Treasury, but in Consequence of Appropriations made by law; and a regular Statement and Account of the Receipts and Expenditures of all public Money shall be published from time to time.

No Title of Nobility shall be granted by the United States: And no Person holding any Office of Profit or Trust under them, shall, without the Consent of the Congress, accept of any present, Emolument, Office, or Title, of any kind whatever, from any King, Prince, or foreign State.

Section 10. No State shall enter into any Treaty, Alliance, or Confederation; grant Letters of Marque and Reprisal; coin Money; emit Bills of Credit; make any Thing but gold and silver Coin a Tender in Payment of Debts; pass any Bill of Attainder, ex post facto Law, or Law impairing the Obligation of Contracts, or grant any Title of Nobility.

No State shall, without the Consent of the Congress, lay any Imposts or Duties on Imports or Exports, except what may be absolutely necessary for executing its inspection Laws: and the net Produce of all Duties and Imposts, laid by any State on Imports or Exports, shall be for the Use of the Treasury of the United States; and all such Laws shall be subject to the Revision and Control of the Congress.

No State shall, without the Consent of the Congress, lay any duty of Tonnage, keep Troops, or Ships of War in time of Peace, enter into any Agreement or Compact with another State, or with a foreign Power, or engage in War, unless actually invaded, or in such imminent Danger as will not admit of delay.

Article II

Section 1. The executive Power shall be vested in a President of the United States of America. He shall hold his Office during the Term of four Years, and, together with the Vice President, chosen for the same Term, be elected, as follows:

Each State shall appoint, in such Manner as the Legislature thereof may direct, a Number of Electors, equal to the whole Number of Senators and Representatives to which the State may be entitled in the Congress; but no Senator or Representative, or Person holding an Office of Trust or Profit under the United States, shall be appointed an Elector.

The Electors shall meet in their respective States, and vote by Ballot for two Persons, of whom one at least shall not be an Inhabitant of the same State with themselves. And they shall make a List of all the Persons voted for, and of the Number of Votes for each; which List they shall sign and certify, and transmit sealed to the Seat of the Government of the United States, directed to the President of the Senate. The President of the Senate shall, in the Presence of the Senate and House of Representatives, open all the Certificates, and the Votes shall then be counted. The Person having the greatest Number of Votes shall be the President, if such Number be a Majority of the whole Number of Electors appointed; and if there be more than one who have such Majority, and have an equal Number of Votes, then the House of Representatives shall immediately chuse by Ballot one of them for President;

and if no Person have a Majority, then from the five highest on the List the said House shall in like Manner chuse the President. But in chusing the President, the Votes shall be taken by States, the Representation from each State having one Vote; a quorum for this Purpose shall consist of a Member or Members from two thirds of the States, and a Majority of all the States shall be necessary to a Choice. In every Case, after the Choice of the President, the Person having the greatest Number of Votes of the Electors shall be the Vice President. But if there should remain two or more who have equal Votes, the Senate shall chuse from them by Ballot the Vice President.*

The Congress may determine the Time of chusing the Electors, and the Day on which they shall give their Votes; which Day shall be the same throughout the United States.

No Person except a natural born Citizen, or a Citizen of the United States, at the time of the Adoption of this Constitution, shall be eligible to the Office of President; neither shall any Person be eligible to that Office who shall not have attained to the Age of thirty five Years, and been fourteen Years a Resident within the United States.

In Case of the Removal of the President from Office, or of his Death, Resignation, or Inability to discharge the Powers and Duties of the said Office, the same shall devolve on the Vice President, *and the Congress may by Law provide for the Case of Removal, Death, Resignation, or Inability, both of the President and Vice President, declaring what Officer shall then act as President, and such Officer shall act accordingly, until the Disability be removed, or a President shall be elected.†*

The President shall, at stated Times, receive for his Services a Compensation, which shall neither be increased nor diminished during the Period for which he shall have been elected, and he shall not receive within that Period any other Emolument from the United States, or any of them.

Before he enter on the Execution of his Office, he shall take the following Oath or Affirmation: — "I do solemnly swear (or affirm) that I will faithfully execute the Office of President of the United States, and will to the best of my Ability, preserve, protect and defend the Constitution of the United States."

Section 2. The President shall be Commander in Chief of the Army and Navy of the United States, and of the Militia of the several States, when called into the actual Service of the United States; he may require the Opinion, in writing, of the principal Officer in each of the executive Departments, upon any Subject relating to the Duties of their respective Offices, and he shall have Power to Grant Reprieves and Pardons for Offences against the United States, except in Cases of Impeachment.

He shall have Power, by and with the Advice and Consent of the Senate, to make Treaties, provided two thirds of the Senators present concur; and he shall nominate, and by and with the Advice and Consent of the Senate, shall appoint Ambassadors, other public Ministers and Consuls, Judges of the supreme Court, and all other Officers of the United States, whose Appointments are not herein otherwise provided for, and which shall be established by Law: but the Congress may by Law vest the Appointment

---

*Superseded by the Twelfth Amendment.
†Modified by the Twenty-fifth Amendment.

of such inferior Officers, as they think proper, in the President alone, in the Courts of Law, or in the Heads of Departments.

The President shall have Power to fill up all Vacancies that may happen during the Recess of the Senate, by granting Commissions which shall expire at the End of their next Session.

Section 3. He shall from time to time give to the Congress Information of the State of the Union, and recommend to their Consideration such Measures as he shall judge necessary and expedient; he may, on extraordinary Occasions, convene both Houses, or either of them, and in Case of Disagreement between them, with Respect to the Time of Adjournment, he may adjourn them to such Time as he shall think proper; he shall receive Ambassadors and other public Ministers; he shall take Care that the Laws be faithfully executed, and shall Commission all the Officers of the United States.

Section 4. The President, Vice President and all civil Officers of the United States, shall be removed from Office on Impeachment for, and Conviction of, Treason, Bribery, or other high Crimes and Misdemeanors.

Article III

Section 1. The judicial Power of the United States, shall be vested in one supreme Court, and in such inferior Courts as the Congress may from time to time ordain and establish. The Judges, both of the supreme and inferior Courts, shall hold their Offices during good Behaviour, and shall, at stated Times, receive for their Services a Compensation, which shall not be diminished during their Continuance in Office.

Section 2. The judicial Power shall extend to all Cases, in Law and Equity, arising under this Constitution, the Laws of the United States, and Treaties made, or which shall be made, under their Authority; — to all Cases affecting Ambassadors, other public Ministers and Consuls; — to all Cases of admiralty and maritime Jurisdiction; — to Controversies to which the United States shall be a Party; — to Controversies between two or more States; — *between a State and Citizens of another State*;* — between Citizens of different States; — between Citizens of the same State claiming Lands under Grants of different States, and between a State, or the Citizens thereof, and foreign States, Citizens or Subjects.

In all Cases affecting Ambassadors, other public Ministers and Consuls, and those in which a State shall be Party, the supreme Court shall have original Jurisdiction. In all the other Cases before mentioned, the supreme Court shall have appellate Jurisdiction, both as to Law and Fact, with such Exceptions, and under such Regulations as the Congress shall make.

The trial of all Crimes, except in Cases of Impeachment, shall be by Jury; and such Trial shall be held in the State where said Crimes shall have been committed; but when

---

*Restricted by the Eleventh Amendment.

not committed within any State, the Trial shall be at such Place or Places as the Congress may by Law have directed.

Section 3. Treason against the United States, shall consist only in levying War against them, or in adhering to their Enemies, giving them Aid and Comfort. No Person shall be convicted of Treason unless on the Testimony of two Witnesses to the same overt Act, or on Confession in open Court.

The Congress shall have Power to declare the Punishment of Treason, but no Attainder of Treason shall work Corruption of Blood, or Forefeiture except during the Life of the Person attainted.

Article IV

Section 1. Full Faith and Credit shall be given in each State to the public Acts, Records, and judicial Proceedings of every other State. And the Congress may by general Laws prescribe the Manner in which such Acts, Records, and Proceedings shall be proved, and the Effect thereof.

Section 2. The Citizens of each State shall be entitled to all Privileges and Immunities of Citizens in the several States.

A Person charged in any State with Treason, Felony, or other Crime, who shall flee from Justice, and be found in another State, shall on demand of the executive Authority of the State from which he fled, be delivered up, to be removed to the State having Jurisdiction of the Crime.

*No Person held to Service or Labour in one State, under the Laws thereof, escaping into another, shall, in Consequence of any Law or Regulation therein, be discharged from such Service or Labour, but shall be delivered up on Claim of the Party to whom such Service or Labour may be due.**

Section 3. New States may be admitted by the Congress into this Union; but no new State shall be formed or erected within the Jurisdiction of any other State; nor any State be formed by the Junction of two or more States, or parts of States, without the Consent of the Legislatures of the States concerned as well as of the Congress.

The Congress shall have Power to dispose of and make all needful Rules and Regulations respecting the Territory or other Property belonging to the United States; and nothing in this Constitution shall be so construed as to Prejudice any Claims of the United States, or of any particular State.

Section 4. The United States shall guarantee to every State in this Union a Republican Form of Government, and shall protect each of them against Invasion; and on Application of the Legislature, or of the Executive (when the Legislature cannot be convened) against domestic Violence.

---

*Superseded by the Thirteenth Amendment.

Article V

The Congress, whenever two-thirds of both Houses shall deem it necessary, shall propose Amendments to this Constitution, or, on the Application of the Legislatures of two-thirds of the several States, shall call a Convention for proposing Amendments, which, in either Case, shall be valid to all Intents and Purposes, as Part of this Constitution, when ratified by the Legislatures of three-fourths of the several States, or by Conventions in three-fourths thereof, as the one or the other Mode of Ratification may be proposed by the Congress; *Provided that no Amendment which may be made prior to the Year One thousand eight hundred and eight shall in any Manner affect the first and fourth Clauses in the Ninth Section of the first Article*; and that no State, without its Consent, shall be deprived of its equal Suffrage in the Senate.

Article VI

All Debts contracted and Engagements entered into, before the Adoption of this Constitution, shall be as valid against the United States under this Constitution, as under the Confederation.

This Constitution, and the Laws of the United States which shall be made in Pursuance thereof; and all Treaties made, or which shall be made, under the Authority of the United States, shall be the supreme Law of the Land; and the Judges in every State shall be bound thereby, any Thing in the Constitution or Laws of any State to the Contrary notwithstanding.

The Senators and Representatives before mentioned, and the Members of the several State Legislatures, and all executive and judicial Officers, both of the United States and of the several States, shall be bound by Oath or Affirmation, to support this Constitution; but no religious Test shall ever be required as a Qualification to any Office or public Trust under the United States.

Article VII

The Ratification of the Conventions of nine States shall be sufficient for the Establishment of this Constitution between the States so ratifying the Same.

Done in Convention by the Unanimous Consent of the States present the Seventeenth Day of September in the Year of our Lord one thousand seven hundred and Eighty seven and of the Independence of the United States of America the Twelfth. In Witness whereof We have hereunto subscribed our Names.

Go. Washington
President and deputy from Virginia

New Hampshire	*Connecticut*	*New Jersey*
John Langdon	Wm. Saml. Johnson	Wil. Livingston
Nicholas Gilman	Roger Sherman	David Brearley
		Wm. Paterson
Massachusetts	*New York*	Jona. Dayton
Nathaniel Gorham	Alexander Hamilton	
Rufus King		

Pennsylvania
B. Franklin
Thomas Mifflin
Robt.Morris
Geo. Clymer
Thos. FitzSimons
Jared Ingersoll
James Wilson
Gouv.Morris

Delaware
Geo. Read
Gunning Bedford jun
John Dickinson

Richard Bassett
Jaco. Broom

Maryland
James McHenry
Dan. of St. Thos. Jenifer
Danl. Carroll

Virginia
John Blair
James Madison, Jr.

North Carolina
Wm. Blount
Richd. Dobbs Spaight
Hu Williamson

South Carolina
J. Rutledge
Charles Cotesworth Pinckney
Pierce Butler

Georgia
William Few
Abr. Baldwin

Amendments to the Constitution (Including the Six Unratified Amendments)

Amendment I [1791]*

Congress shall make no law respecting an establishment of religion, or prohibiting the free exercise thereof; or abridging the freedom of speech, or of the press; or the right of the people peaceably to assemble, and to petition the Government for a redress of grievances.

Amendment II [1791]

A well regulated Militia, being necessary to the security of a free State, the right of the people to keep and bear Arms shall not be infringed.

Amendment III [1791]

No Soldier shall, in time of peace, be quartered in any house, without the consent of the Owner, nor in time of war, but in a manner to be prescribed by law.

Amendment IV [1791]

The right of the people to be secure in their persons, houses, papers, and effects, against unreasonable searches and seizures, shall not be violated, and no Warrants shall issue, but upon probable cause, supported by Oath or affirmation, and particularly describing the place to be searched, and the persons or things to be seized.

Amendment V [1791]

No person shall be held to answer for a capital or otherwise infamous crime, unless on a presentment or indictment of a Grand Jury, except in cases arising in the land or naval forces, or in the Militia, when in actual service in time of War or public danger; nor shall any person be subject for the same offence to be twice put in jeopardy of life or limb; nor shall be compelled in any criminal case to be a witness against himself, nor be deprived of life, liberty, or property, without due process of law; nor shall private property be taken for public use, without just compensation.

Amendment VI [1791]

In all criminal prosecutions, the accused shall enjoy the right to a speedy and public trial, by an impartial jury of the State and district wherein the crime shall have been committed, which district shall have been previously ascertained by law, and to be informed of the nature and cause of the accusation; to be confronted with the witnesses against him; to have compulsory process for obtaining witnesses in his favor, and to have the Assistance of Counsel for his defence.

---

*The dates in brackets indicate when the amendment was ratified.

Amendment VII [1791]

In suits at common law, where the value in controversy shall exceed twenty dollars, the right of trial by jury shall be preserved, and no fact tried by a jury, shall be otherwise reexamined in any Court of the United States, than according to the Rules of the common law.

Amendment VIII [1791]

Excessive bail shall not be required, nor excessive fines imposed, nor cruel and unusual punishments inflicted.

Amendment IX [1791]

The enumeration in the Constitution, of certain rights, shall not be construed to deny or disparage others retained by the people.

Amendment X [1791]

The powers not delegated to the United States by the Constitution, nor prohibited by it to the States, are reserved to the States respectively, or to the people.

Unratified Amendment

Reapportionment Amendment (proposed by Congress September 25, 1789, along with the Bill of Rights)

After the first enumeration required by the first article of the Constitution, there shall be one Representative for every thirty thousand, until the number shall amount to one hundred, after which the proportion shall be so regulated by Congress, that there shall be not less than one hundred Representatives, nor less than one Representative for every forty thousand persons, until the number of Representatives shall amount to two hundred; after which the proportion shall be so regulated by Congress, that there shall not be less than two hundred Representatives, nor more than one Representative for every fifty thousand persons.

Amendment XI [1798]

The Judicial power of the United States shall not be construed to extend to any suit in law or equity, commenced or prosecuted against one of the United States by Citizens of another State, or by Citizens or subjects of any foreign state.

Amendment XII [1804]

The Electors shall meet in their respective States and vote by ballot for President and Vice-President, one of whom, at least, shall not be an inhabitant of the same State with themselves; they shall name in their ballots the person voted for as President, and in distinct ballots the person voted for as Vice-President, and they shall make distinct lists of all persons voted for as President, and of all persons voted for as Vice-President, and of the number of votes for each, which lists they shall sign and certify, and transmit sealed to the seat of government of the United States, directed to the President of the

Senate; — the President of the Senate shall, in the presence of the Senate and House of Representatives, open all the certificates and the votes shall then be counted; — The person having the greatest number of votes for President, shall be the President, if such number be a majority of the whole number of Electors appointed; and if no person have such majority, then from the persons having the highest numbers not exceeding three on the list of those voted for as President, the House of Representatives shall choose immediately, by ballot, the President. But in choosing the President, the votes shall be taken by States, the representation from each State having one vote; a quorum for this purpose shall consist of a member or members from two-thirds of the States, and a majority of all the States shall be necessary to a choice. And if the House of Representatives shall not choose a President whenever the right of choice shall devolve upon them, before *the fourth day of March* next following, then the Vice-President shall act as President, as in the case of the death or other constitutional disability of the President.* — The person having the greatest number of votes as Vice-President, shall be the Vice-President, if such number be a majority of the whole number of Electors appointed; and if no person have a majority, then from the two highest numbers on the list, the Senate shall choose the Vice-President; a quorum for the purpose shall consist of two-thirds of the whole number of Senators, and a majority of the whole number shall be necessary to a choice. But no person constitutionally ineligible to the office of President shall be eligible to that of Vice-President of the United States.

Unratified Amendment

Titles of Nobility Amendment (proposed by Congress May 1, 1810)

If any citizen of the United States shall accept, claim, receive or retain any title of nobility or honor or shall, without the consent of Congress, accept and retain any present, pension, office or emolument of any kind whatever, from any emperor, king, prince or foreign power, such person shall cease to be a citizen of the United States, and shall be incapable of holding any office of trust or profit under them, or either of them.

Unratified Amendment

Corwin Amendment (proposed by Congress March 2, 1861)

No amendment shall be made to the Constitution which will authorize or give to Congress the power to abolish or interfere, within any State, with the domestic institutions thereof, including that of persons held to labor or service by the laws of said State.

Amendment XIII [1865]

Section 1. Neither slavery nor involuntary servitude, except as a punishment for crime whereof the party shall have been duly convicted, shall exist within the United States, or any place subject to their jurisdiction.

Section 2. Congress shall have power to enforce this article by appropriate legislation.

---

*Superseded by Section 3 of the Twentieth Amendment.

Amendment XIV [1868]

Section 1. All persons born or naturalized in the United States, and subject to the jurisdiction thereof, are citizens of the United States and of the State wherein they reside. No State shall make or enforce any law which shall abridge the privileges or immunities of citizens of the United States; nor shall any State deprive any person of life, liberty, or property, without due process of law; nor deny to any person within its jurisdiction the equal protection of the laws.

Section 2. Representatives shall be apportioned among the several States according to their respective numbers, counting the whole number of persons in each State, excluding Indians not taxed. But when the right to vote at any election for the choice of electors for President and Vice-President of the United States, Representatives in Congress, the Executive and Judicial officers of a State, or the members of the Legislature thereof, is denied to any of the *male* inhabitants of such State, being *twenty-one* years of age and citizens of the United States, or in any way abridged, except for participation in rebellion, or other crime, the basis of representation therein shall be reduced in the proportion which the number of such *male* citizens shall bear to the whole number of *male* citizens *twenty-one* years of age in such State.

Section 3. No person shall be a Senator or Representative in Congress, or Elector of President and Vice-President, or hold any office, civil or military, under the United States, or under any State, who, having previously taken an oath, as a member of Congress, or as an officer of the United States, or as a member of any State legislature, or as an executive or judicial officer of any State, to support the Constitution of the United States, shall have engaged in insurrection or rebellion against the same, or given aid or comfort to the enemies thereof. Congress may, by a vote of two-thirds of each house, remove such disability.

Section 4. The validity of the public debt of the United States, authorized by law, including debts incurred for payment of pensions and bounties for services in suppressing insurrection or rebellion, shall not be questioned. But neither the United States nor any State shall assume or pay any debt or obligation incurred in aid of insurrection or rebellion against the United States, or any claim for the loss or emancipation of any slave; but all such debts, obligations, and claims shall be held illegal and void.

Section 5. The Congress shall have power to enforce, by appropriate legislation, the provisions of this article.

Amendment XV [1870]

Section 1. The right of citizens of the United States to vote shall not be denied or abridged by the United States or by any State on account of race, color, or previous condition of servitude —

Section 2. The Congress shall have power to enforce this article by appropriate legislation.

Amendment XVI [1913]

The Congress shall have power to lay and collect taxes on incomes, from whatever source derived, without apportionment among the several States, and without regard to any census or enumeration.

Amendment XVII [1913]

Section 1. The Senate of the United States shall be composed of two Senators from each State, elected by the people thereof, for six years; and each Senator shall have one vote. The electors in each State shall have the qualifications requisite for electors of [voters for] the most numerous branch of the State legislatures.

Section 2. When vacancies happen in the representation of any State in the Senate, the executive authority of such State shall issue writs of election to fill such vacancies: Provided, that the Legislature of any State may empower the executive thereof to make temporary appointments until the people fill the vacancies by election as the Legislature may direct.

Section 3. *This amendment shall not be so construed as to affect the election or term of any Senator chosen before it becomes valid as part of the Constitution.*

Amendment XVIII [1919; repealed 1933 by Amendment XXI]

Section 1. *After one year from the ratification of this article the manufacture, sale, or transportation of intoxicating liquors within, the importation thereof into, or the exportation thereof from the United States and all territory subject to the jurisdiction thereof, for beverage purposes, is hereby prohibited.*

Section 2. *The Congress and the several States shall have concurrent power to enforce this article by appropriate legislation.*

Section 3. *This article shall be inoperative unless it shall have been ratified as an amendment to the Constitution by the legislatures of the several States, as provided by the Constitution, within seven years from the date of the submission thereof to the States by the Congress.*

Amendment XIX [1920]

Section 1. The right of citizens of the United States to vote shall not be denied or abridged by the United States or by any State on account of sex.

Section 2. Congress shall have the power to enforce this article by appropriate legislation.

Unratified Amendment

Child Labor Amendment (proposed by Congress June 2, 1924)

Section 1. *The Congress shall have power to limit, regulate, and prohibit the labor of persons under eighteen years of age.*

Section 2. *The power of the several States is unimpaired by this article except that the operation of State laws shall be suspended to the extent necessary to give effect to legislation enacted by Congress.*

Amendment XX [1933]

Section 1. The terms of the President and Vice-President shall end at noon on the 20th day of January, and the terms of Senators and Representatives at noon on the 3rd day of January, of the years in which such terms would have ended if this article had not been ratified; and the terms of their successors shall then begin.

Section 2. The Congress shall assemble at least once in every year, and such meeting shall begin at noon on the 3rd day of January, unless they shall by law appoint a different day.

Section 3. If, at the time fixed for the beginning of the term of the President, the President-elect shall have died, the Vice-President-elect shall become President. If a President shall not have been chosen before the time fixed for the beginning of his term, or if the President-elect shall have failed to qualify, then the Vice-President-elect shall act as President until a President shall have qualified; and the Congress may by law provide for the case wherein neither a President-elect nor a Vice-President-elect shall have qualified, declaring who shall then act as President, or the manner in which one who is to act shall be selected, and such person shall act accordingly until a President or Vice-President shall have qualified.

Section 4. The Congress may by law provide for the case of the death of any of the persons from whom the House of Representatives may choose a President whenever the right of choice shall have devolved upon them, and for the case of the death of any of the persons from whom the Senate may choose a Vice-President whenever the right of choice shall have devolved upon them.

Section 5. Sections 1 and 2 shall take effect on the 15th day of October following the ratification of this article.

Section 6. This article shall be inoperative unless it shall have been ratified as an amendment to the Constitution by the Legislatures of three-fourths of the several States within seven years from the date of its submission.

Amendment XXI [1933]

Section 1. The eighteenth article of amendment to the Constitution of the United States is hereby repealed.

Section 2. The transportation or importation into any State, Territory, or Possession of the United States for delivery or use therein of intoxicating liquors, in violation of the laws thereof, is hereby prohibited.

Section 3. This article shall be inoperative unless it shall have been ratified as an amendment to the Constitution by conventions in the several States, as provided in the Constitution, within seven years from the date of the submission thereof to the States by the Congress.

Amendment XXII [1951]

Section 1. No person shall be elected to the office of the President more than twice, and no person who has held the office of President, or acted as President, for more than two years of a term to which some other person was elected President shall be elected to the office of President more than once. But this article shall not apply to any person holding the office of President when this Article was proposed by the Congress, and shall not prevent any person who may be holding the office of President, or acting as President, during the term within which this Article becomes operative from holding the office of President or acting as President during the remainder of such term.

Section 2. This article shall be inoperative unless it shall have been ratified as an amendment to the Constitution by the legislatures of three-fourths of the several States within seven years from the date of its submission to the States by the Congress.

Amendment XXIII [1961]

Section 1. The District constituting the seat of Government of the United States shall appoint in such manner as the Congress may direct: A number of electors of President and Vice-President equal to the whole number of Senators and Representatives in Congress to which the District would be entitled if it were a State, but in no event more than the least populous State; they shall be in addition to those appointed by the States, but they shall be considered for the purposes of the election of President and Vice-President, to be electors appointed by a State; and they shall meet in the District and perform such duties as provided by the twelfth article of amendment.

Section 2. The Congress shall have the power to enforce this article by appropriate legislation.

Amendment XXIV [1964]

Section 1. The right of citizens of the United States to vote in any primary or other election for President or Vice-President, for electors for President or Vice-President, or for Senator or Representative in Congress, shall not be denied or abridged by the United States or any State by reason of failure to pay any poll tax or other tax.

Section 2. The Congress shall have the power to enforce this article by appropriate legislation.

Amendment XXV [1967]

Section 1. In case of the removal of the President from office or of his death or resignation, the Vice-President shall become President.

Section 2. Whenever there is a vacancy in the office of the Vice-President, the President shall nominate a Vice-President who shall take office upon confirmation by a majority vote of both Houses of Congress.

Section 3. Whenever the President transmits to the President pro tempore of the Senate and the Speaker of the House of Representatives his written declaration that he is unable to discharge the powers and duties of his office, and until he transmits to them a written declaration to the contrary, such powers and duties shall be discharged by the Vice-President as Acting President.

Section 4. Whenever the Vice-President and a majority of either the principal officers of the executive departments or of such other body as Congress may by law provide, transmit to the President pro tempore of the Senate and the Speaker of the House of Representatives their written declaration that the President is unable to discharge the powers and duties of his office, the Vice-President shall immediately assume the powers and duties of the office as Acting President.

Thereafter, when the President transmits to the President pro tempore of the Senate and the Speaker of the House of Representatives his written declaration that no inability exists, he shall resume the powers and duties of his office unless the Vice-President and a majority of either the principal officers of the executive department[s] or of such other body as Congress may by law provide, transmit within four days to the President pro tempore of the Senate and the Speaker of the House of Representatives their written declaration that the President is unable to discharge the powers and duties of his office. Thereupon Congress shall decide the issue, assembling within forty-eight hours for that purpose if not in session. If the Congress, within twenty-one days after receipt of the latter written declaration, or, if Congress is not in session, within twenty-one days after Congress is required to assemble, determines by two-thirds vote of both Houses that the President is unable to discharge the powers and duties of his office, the Vice-President shall continue to discharge the same as Acting President; otherwise, the President shall resume the powers and duties of his office.

Amendment XXVI [1971]

Section 1. The right of citizens of the United States, who are eighteen years of age or older, to vote shall not be denied or abridged by the United States or by any State on account of age.

Section 2. The Congress shall have power to enforce this article by appropriate legislation.

Unratified Amendment

Equal Rights Amendment (proposed by Congress March 22, 1972; seven-year deadline for ratification extended to June 30, 1982)

Section 1. *Equality of rights under the law shall not be denied or abridged by the United States or by any State on account of sex.*

Section 2. *The Congress shall have the power to enforce, by appropriate legislation, the provisions of this article.*

Section 3. *This amendment shall take effect two years after the date of ratification.*

Unratified Amendment
District of Columbia Statehood Amendment
(proposed by Congress August 22, 1978)

Section 1. *For purposes of representation in the Congress, election of the President and Vice President, and article V of this Constitution, the District constituting the seat of government of the United States shall be treated as though it were a State.*

Section 2. *The exercise of the rights and powers conferred under this article shall be by the people of the District constituting the seat of government, and as shall be provided by Congress.*

Section 3. *The twenty-third article of amendment to the Constitution of the United States is hereby repealed.*

Section 4. *This article shall be inoperative, unless it shall have been ratified as an amendment to the Constitution by the legislatures of three-fourths of the several states within seven years from the date of its submission.*

Amendment XXVII [1992]
No law varying the compensation for the services of the Senators and Representatives, shall take effect, until an election of Representatives shall have intervened.

Appendix

TABLE 1	Territorial Expansion		
Territory	**Date Acquired**	**Square Miles**	**How Acquired**
Original states and territories	1783	888,685	Treaty of Paris
Louisiana Purchase	1803	827,192	Purchased from France
Florida	1819	72,003	Adams-Onís Treaty
Texas	1845	390,143	Annexation of independent country
Oregon	1846	285,580	Oregon Boundary Treaty
Mexican cession	1848	529,017	Treaty of Guadalupe Hidalgo
Gadsden Purchase	1853	29,640	Purchased from Mexico
Midway Islands	1867	2	Annexation of uninhabited islands
Alaska	1867	589,757	Purchased from Russia
Hawaii	1898	6,450	Annexation of independent country
Wake Island	1898	3	Annexation of uninhabited island
Puerto Rico	1899	3,435	Treaty of Paris
Guam	1899	212	Treaty of Paris
The Philippines	1899–1946	115,600	Treaty of Paris; granted independence
American Samoa	1900	76	Treaty with Germany and Great Britain
Panama Canal Zone	1904–1978	553	Hay–Bunau-Varilla Treaty
U.S. Virgin Islands	1917	133	Purchased from Denmark
Trust Territory of the Pacific Islands*	1947–1986	717	United Nations Trusteeship

*A number of these islands have been granted independence: Federated States of Micronesia, 1990; Republic of the Marshall Islands, 1991; Republic of Palau, 1994. The Northern Mariana Islands is a commonwealth of the United States.

TABLE 2	The Labor Force (Thousands of Workers)						
Year	Agriculture	Mining	Manufacturing	Construction	Trade	Other	Total
1810	1,950	11	75	—	—	294	2,330
1840	3,570	32	500	290	350	918	5,660
1850	4,520	102	1,200	410	530	1,488	8,250
1860	5,880	176	1,530	520	890	2,114	11,110
1870	6,790	180	2,470	780	1,310	1,400	12,930
1880	8,920	280	3,290	900	1,930	2,070	17,390
1890	9,960	440	4,390	1,510	2,960	4,060	23,320
1900	11,680	637	5,895	1,665	3,970	5,223	29,070
1910	11,770	1,068	8,332	1,949	5,320	9,041	37,480
1920	10,790	1,180	11,190	1,233	5,845	11,372	41,610
1930	10,560	1,009	9,884	1,988	8,122	17,267	48,830
1940	9,575	925	11,309	1,876	9,328	23,277	56,290
1950	7,870	901	15,648	3,029	12,152	25,870	65,470
1960	5,970	709	17,145	3,640	14,051	32,545	74,060
1970	3,463	516	20,746	4,818	15,008	34,127	78,678
1980	3,364	979	21,942	6,215	20,191	46,612	99,303
1990	3,223	724	21,346	7,764	24,622	60,849	118,793
2000	2,464	475	19,644	9,931	15,763	88,260	136,891
2008	2,168	819	15,904	10,974	16,533	98,964	145,362

SOURCES: U.S. Bureau of the Census, *Historical Statistics of the United States, Colonial Times to 1970* (1975), 139; *Statistical Abstract of the United States, 1998*, table 675; *Statistical Abstract of the United States, 2010.*

Changing Labor Patterns

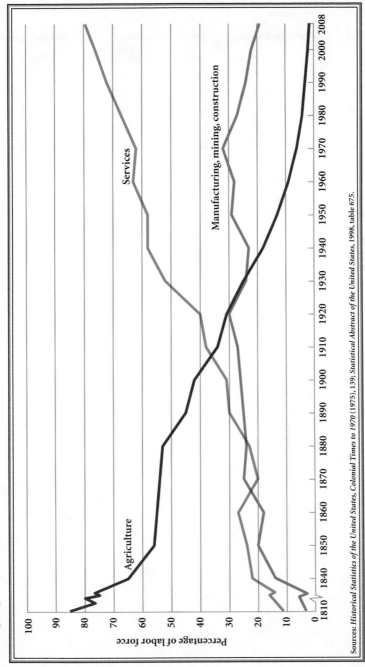

Sources: Historical Statistics of the United States, Colonial Times to 1970 (1975), 139; Statistical Abstract of the United States, 1998, table 675.

TABLE 3 Enumerated Population*

Year	Population	Percentage Increase	Year	Population	Percentage Increase
1610	350	—	1820	9,638,453	33.1
1620	2,300	557.1	1830	12,866,020	33.5
1630	4,600	100.0	1840	17,069,453	32.7
1640	26,600	478.3	1850	23,191,876	35.9
1650	50,400	90.8	1860	31,443,321	35.6
1660	75,100	49.0	1870	39,818,449	26.6
1670	111,900	49.0	1880	50,155,783	26.0
1680	151,500	35.4	1890	62,947,714	25.5
1690	210,400	38.9	1900	75,994,575	20.7
1700	250,900	19.2	1910	91,972,266	21.0
1710	331,700	32.2	1920	105,710,620	14.9
1720	466,200	40.5	1930	122,775,046	16.1
1730	629,400	35.0	1940	131,669,275	7.2
1740	905,600	43.9	1950	150,697,361	14.5
1750	1,170,800	29.3	1960	179,323,175	19.0
1760	1,593,600	36.1	1970	203,235,298	13.3
1770	2,148,100	34.8	1980	226,545,805	11.5
1780	2,780,400	29.4	1990	248,709,873	9.8
1790	3,929,214	41.3	2000	281,421,906	13.2
1800	5,308,483	35.1	2010	308,745,538	9.7
1810	7,239,881	36.4			

*Note: These figures largely ignore the Native American population. Until 1890, census takers never made any effort to count the Native American people who lived outside their reserved political areas and compiled only casual and incomplete enumerations of those living within their jurisdictions. In 1890, the federal government attempted a full count of the Indian population: The Census found 125,719 Indians in 1890, compared with only 12,543 in 1870 and 33,985 in 1880.

SOURCES: U.S. Bureau of the Census, *Historical Statistics of the United States, Colonial Times to 1970* (1975); *Statistical Abstract of the United States, 2012*; U.S. Bureau of the Census, Population Finder, http://factfinder.census.gov.

| TABLE 4 | Presidential Elections | | | | |

Year	Candidates	Parties	Percentage of Popular Vote*	Electoral Vote	Percentage of Voter Participation
1789	**George Washington**	No party designations		69	
	John Adams†			34	
	Other candidates			35	
1792	**George Washington**	No party designations		132	
	John Adams			77	
	George Clinton			50	
	Other candidates			5	
1796	**John Adams**	Federalist		71	
	Thomas Jefferson	Democratic-Republican		68	
	Thomas Pinckney	Federalist		59	
	Aaron Burr	Democratic-Republican		30	
	Other candidates			48	
1800	**Thomas Jefferson**	Democratic-Republican		73	
	Aaron Burr	Democratic-Republican		73	
	John Adams	Federalist		65	
	Charles C. Pinckney	Federalist		64	
	John Jay	Federalist		1	
1804	**Thomas Jefferson**	Democratic-Republican		162	
	Charles C. Pinckney	Federalist		14	
1808	**James Madison**	Democratic-Republican		122	
	Charles C. Pinckney	Federalist		47	
	George Clinton	Democratic-Republican		6	
1812	**James Madison**	Democratic-Republican		128	
	DeWitt Clinton	Federalist		89	
1816	**James Monroe**	Democratic-Republican		183	
	Rufus King	Federalist		34	
1820	**James Monroe**	Democratic-Republican		231	
	John Quincy Adams	Independent Republican		1	
1824	**John Quincy Adams**	Democratic-Republican	30.5	84	26.9
	Andrew Jackson	Democratic-Republican	43.1	99	
	Henry Clay	Democratic-Republican	13.2	37	
	William H. Crawford	Democratic-Republican	13.1	41	
1828	**Andrew Jackson**	Democratic	56.0	178	57.6
	John Quincy Adams	National Republican	44.0	83	

*Prior to 1824, most presidential electors were chosen by state legislators rather than by popular vote. For elections after 1824, candidates receiving less than 1.0 percent of the popular vote have been omitted from this chart. Hence the popular vote does not total 100 percent for all elections.

†Before the Twelfth Amendment was passed in 1804, the Electoral College voted for two presidential candidates; the runner-up became vice president.

Year	Candidates	Parties	Percentage of Popular Vote*	Electoral Vote	Percentage of Voter Participation
1832	**Andrew Jackson**	Democratic	54.5	219	55.4
	Henry Clay	National Republican	37.5	49	
	William Wirt	Anti-Masonic	8.0	7	
	John Floyd	Democratic	‡	11	
1836	**Martin Van Buren**	Democratic	50.9	170	57.8
	William H. Harrison	Whig		73	
	Hugh L. White	Whig		26	
	Daniel Webster	Whig	49.1	14	
	W. P. Mangum	Whig		11	
1840	**William H. Harrison**	Whig	53.1	234	80.2
	Martin Van Buren	Democratic	46.9	60	
1844	**James K. Polk**	Democratic	49.6	170	78.9
	Henry Clay	Whig	48.1	105	
	James G. Birney	Liberty	2.3		
1848	**Zachary Taylor**	Whig	47.4	163	72.7
	Lewis Cass	Democratic	42.5	127	
	Martin Van Buren	Free Soil	10.1		
1852	**Franklin Pierce**	Democratic	50.9	254	69.6
	Winfield Scott	Whig	44.1	42	
	John P. Hale	Free Soil	5.0		
1856	**James Buchanan**	Democratic	45.3	174	78.9
	John C. Frémont	Republican	33.1	114	
	Millard Fillmore	American	21.6	8	
1860	**Abraham Lincoln**	Republican	39.8	180	81.2
	Stephen A. Douglas	Democratic	29.5	12	
	John C. Breckinridge	Democratic	18.1	72	
	John Bell	Constitutional Union	12.6	39	
1864	**Abraham Lincoln**	Republican	55.0	212	73.8
	George B. McClellan	Democratic	45.0	21	
1868	**Ulysses S. Grant**	Republican	52.7	214	78.1
	Horatio Seymour	Democratic	47.3	80	
1872	**Ulysses S. Grant**	Republican	55.6	286	71.3
	Horace Greeley	Democratic	43.9		
1876	**Rutherford B. Hayes**	Republican	48.0	185	81.8
	Samuel J. Tilden	Democratic	51.0	184	
1880	**James A. Garfield**	Republican	48.5	214	79.4
	Winfield S. Hancock	Democratic	48.1	155	
	James B. Weaver	Greenback-Labor	3.4		

‡Independent Democrat John Floyd received the 11 electoral votes of South Carolina; that state's presidential electors were still chosen by its legislature, not by popular vote.

Year	Candidates	Parties	Percentage of Popular Vote*	Electoral Vote	Percentage of Voter Participation
1884	**Grover Cleveland**	Democratic	48.5	219	77.5
	James G. Blaine	Republican	48.2	182	
	Benjamin F. Butler	Greenback-Labor	1.8		
	John P. St. John	Prohibition	1.5		
1888	**Benjamin Harrison**	Republican	47.9	233	79.3
	Grover Cleveland	Democratic	48.6	168	
	Clinton P. Fisk	Prohibition	2.2		
	Anson J. Streeter	Union Labor	1.3		
1892	**Grover Cleveland**	Democratic	46.1	277	74.7
	Benjamin Harrison	Republican	43.0	145	
	James B. Weaver	People's	8.5	22	
	John Bidwell	Prohibition	2.2		
1896	**William McKinley**	Republican	51.1	271	79.3
	William J. Bryan	Democratic	47.7	176	
1900	**William McKinley**	Republican	51.7	292	73.2
	William J. Bryan	Democratic; Populist	45.5	155	
	John C. Wooley	Prohibition	1.5		
1904	**Theodore Roosevelt**	Republican	57.4	336	65.2
	Alton B. Parker	Democratic	37.6	140	
	Eugene V. Debs	Socialist	3.0		
	Silas C. Swallow	Prohibition	1.9		
1908	**William H. Taft**	Republican	51.6	321	65.4
	William J. Bryan	Democratic	43.1	162	
	Eugene V. Debs	Socialist	2.8		
	Eugene W. Chafin	Prohibition	1.7		
1912	**Woodrow Wilson**	Democratic	41.9	435	58.8
	Theodore Roosevelt	Progressive	27.4	88	
	William H. Taft	Republican	23.2	8	
	Eugene V. Debs	Socialist	6.0		
	Eugene W. Chafin	Prohibition	1.4		
1916	**Woodrow Wilson**	Democratic	49.4	277	61.6
	Charles E. Hughes	Republican	46.2	254	
	A. L. Benson	Socialist	3.2		
	J. Frank Hanly	Prohibition	1.2		
1920	**Warren G. Harding**	Republican	60.4	404	49.2
	James M. Cox	Democratic	34.2	127	
	Eugene V. Debs	Socialist	3.4		
	P. P. Christensen	Farmer-Labor	1.0		
1924	**Calvin Coolidge**	Republican	54.0	382	48.9
	John W. Davis	Democratic	28.8	136	
	Robert M. La Follette	Progressive	16.6	13	

Year	Candidates	Parties	Percentage of Popular Vote*	Electoral Vote	Percentage of Voter Participation
1928	**Herbert C. Hoover**	Republican	58.2	444	56.9
	Alfred E. Smith	Democratic	40.9	87	
1932	**Franklin D. Roosevelt**	Democratic	57.4	472	56.9
	Herbert C. Hoover	Republican	39.7	59	
	Norman Thomas	Socialist	2.2		
1936	**Franklin D. Roosevelt**	Democratic	60.8	523	61.0
	Alfred M. Landon	Republican	36.5	8	
	William Lemke	Union	1.9		
1940	**Franklin D. Roosevelt**	Democratic	54.8	449	62.5
	Wendell L. Willkie	Republican	44.8	82	
1944	**Franklin D. Roosevelt**	Democratic	53.5	432	55.9
	Thomas E. Dewey	Republican	46.0	99	
1948	**Harry S Truman**	Democratic	49.6	303	53.0
	Thomas E. Dewey	Republican	45.1	189	
	J. Strom Thurmond	States' Rights	2.4		
	Henry Wallace	Progressive	2.4		
1952	**Dwight D. Eisenhower**	Republican	55.1	442	63.3
	Adlai E. Stevenson	Democratic	44.4	89	
1956	**Dwight D. Eisenhower**	Republican	57.6	457	60.6
	Adlai E. Stevenson	Democratic	42.1	73	
1960	**John F. Kennedy**	Democratic	49.7	303	62.8
	Richard M. Nixon	Republican	49.5	219	
1964	**Lyndon B. Johnson**	Democratic	61.1	486	61.9
	Barry M. Goldwater	Republican	38.5	52	
1968	**Richard M. Nixon**	Republican	43.4	301	60.8
	Hubert H. Humphrey	Democratic	42.7	191	
	George C. Wallace	American Independent	13.5	46	
1972	**Richard M. Nixon**	Republican	60.7	520	55.2
	George S. McGovern	Democratic	37.5	17	
	John G. Schmitz	American	1.4		
1976	**Jimmy Carter**	Democratic	50.1	297	53.6
	Gerald R. Ford	Republican	48.0	240	
1980	**Ronald W. Reagan**	Republican	50.7	489	52.6
	Jimmy Carter	Democratic	41.0	49	
	John B. Anderson	Independent	6.6	0	
	Ed Clark	Libertarian	1.1		
1984	**Ronald W. Reagan**	Republican	58.4	525	53.1
	Walter F. Mondale	Democratic	41.6	13	
1988	**George H. W. Bush**	Republican	53.4	426	50.2
	Michael Dukakis	Democratic	45.6	111**	

**One Dukakis elector cast a vote for Lloyd Bentsen.

Year	Candidates	Parties	Percentage of Popular Vote*	Electoral Vote	Percentage of Voter Participation
1992	**Bill Clinton**	Democratic	43.7	370	55.2
	George H. W. Bush	Republican	38.0	168	
	H. Ross Perot	Independent	19.0	0	
1996	**Bill Clinton**	Democratic	49	379	49.1
	Robert J. Dole	Republican	41	159	
	H. Ross Perot	Reform	8	0	
2000	**George W. Bush**	Republican	47.8	271	51.3
	Albert Gore	Democratic	48.4	267	
	Ralph Nader	Green	2.7	0	
2004	**George W. Bush**	Republican	50.7	286	55.3
	John Kerry	Democratic	48.3	252	
2008	**Barack Obama**	Democratic	52.9	365	56.8
	John McCain	Republican	45.7	173	

TABLE 5 — A Demographic Profile of the American People

Year	Life Expectancy at Birth — White	Life Expectancy at Birth — Black	Median Age at First Marriage — Men	Median Age at First Marriage — Women	Number of Children under 5 (per 1,000 Women Aged 20–44)	Percentage of persons (age 16+) in Paid Workforce — Men	Percentage of persons (age 16+) in Paid Workforce — Women	Percentage of Paid Workers Who Are Women
1820					1,295		6.2	7.3
1830					1,145		6.4	7.4
1840					1,085		8.4	9.6
1850					923		10.1	10.8
1860					929		9.7	10.2
1870					839		13.7	14.8
1880					822		14.7	15.2
1890			26.1	22.0	716	84.3	18.2	17.0
1900	47.6	33.0	25.9	21.9	688	85.7	20.0	18.1
1910	50.3	35.6	25.1	21.6	643	85.1	24.8	20.0
1920	54.9	45.3	24.6	21.2	604	84.6	22.7	20.4
1930	61.4	48.1	24.3	21.3	511	82.1	23.6	21.9
1940	64.2	53.1	24.3	21.5	429	79.1	25.8	24.6
1950	69.1	60.8	22.8	20.3	589	81.6	29.9	27.8
1960	70.6	63.6	22.8	20.3	737	80.4	35.7	32.3
1970	71.7	65.3	22.5	20.6	530	79.7	41.4	38.0
1980	74.4	68.1	24.7	22.0	440	77.4	51.5	42.6
1990	76.1	69.1	26.1	23.9	377	76.4	57.4	45.2
2000	77.6	71.7	26.7	25.1	365	74.8	58.9	46.3
2010*	78.9	73.8	27.7	26.0		73.0	59.5	46.5

SOURCE: U.S. Bureau of the Census, *Historical Statistics of the United States, Colonial Times to 1970* (1975); *Statistical Abstract of the United States, 2001*; *Statistical Abstract of the United States, 2010*.

*Or latest available data.

Real Gross Domestic Product per Capita, 1790–2010

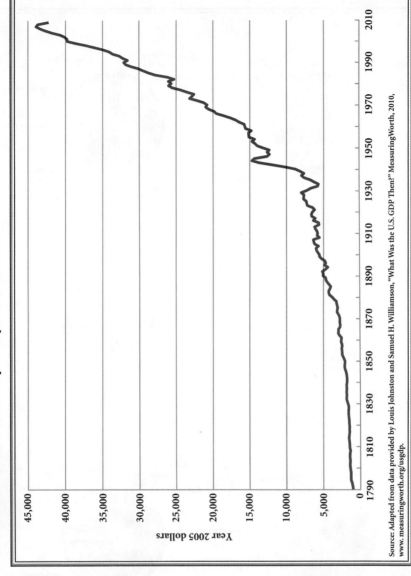

Source: Adapted from data provided by Louis Johnston and Samuel H. Williamson, "What Was the U.S. GDP Then?" MeasuringWorth, 2010, www.measuringworth.org/usgdp.

Main Sectors of the U.S. Economy: 1849, 1899, 1950, 1990, 2001, and 2008

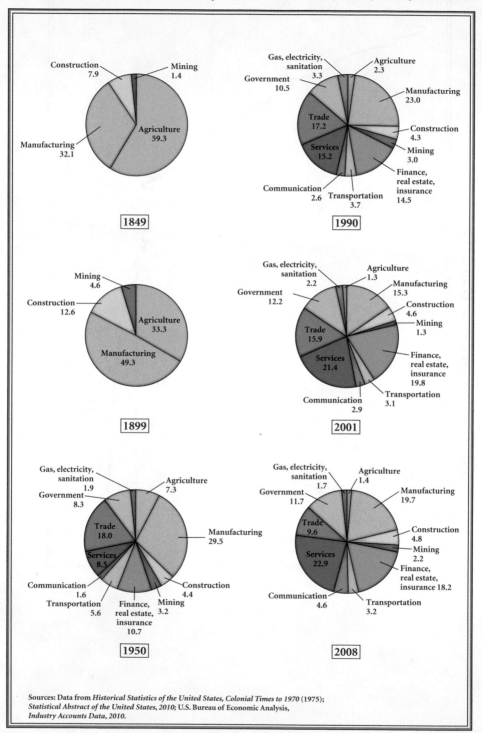

Sources: Data from *Historical Statistics of the United States, Colonial Times to 1970* (1975);
Statistical Abstract of the United States, 2010; U.S. Bureau of Economic Analysis,
Industry Accounts Data, 2010.

Glossary

American exceptionalism The belief that the United States, as the first modern republic, has a mission and destiny distinct from that of all other nations. This belief has often served as the basis for arguments that the United States should influence foreign affairs, in order to encourage other nations and peoples to adopt American institutions and practices. Proponents of American exceptionalism have argued that the United States is uniquely free of class conflict, imperial ambition, and other "Old World" problems. (p. 631)

anarchism The advocacy of a stateless society achieved by revolutionary means. Feared for their views, anarchists became the scapegoats for the 1886 bombing in Chicago's Haymarket Square. (p. 532)

assimilation Efforts by U.S. government agents and Christian missionaries to persuade people of color to adopt white ways. Through assimilation policies, Native Americans, for example, were pressured to abandon their traditional religion, dress, and customs, and adopt Christianity, speak only English, accept U.S. laws concerning private property, and adapt their work and family life to white expectations. (p. 497)

Black Codes Laws passed by southern states after the Civil War that denied ex-slaves the civil rights enjoyed by whites, intending to force blacks back to the plantations. (p. 448)

blacklist A list of people to be excluded from an activity or organization. In the nineteenth century, employers compiled lists of workers affiliated with unions and either fired them or refused to hire them. In the 1950s, governments and private businesses blacklisted alleged communists, denying them positions in government, motion pictures, and many industries and unions. (p. 529)

blue-collar workers Skilled tradesmen who work with their hands, such as carpenters, railroad workers, and industrial factory workers; the nickname came from the blue work shirts that many such men wore on the job. (p. 517)

business cycle The periodic rise and fall of business activity characteristic of market-driven capitalist economies. To increase profits, producers increase output and eventually create a surplus (oversupply); the surplus then prompts a cutback in output, which produces an economic recession. The major periods of pre–World War II economic expansion — 1802–1818, 1824–1836, 1846–1856, 1865–1873, 1896–1914, 1922–1928 — were followed either by short financial panics or extended depressions (1837–1843, 1873–1896, and 1929–1939). In the postwar period, several short recessions — in 1945, 1949, 1953, 1958, 1961, and 1969 — were relatively minor exceptions to steady economic growth. After the steep downturns of 1974–1975 and 1980–1981, there was relatively sustained growth through the 1990s. In 2008, however, the United States experienced its deepest recession since the 1930s. (p. 685)

capitalism A system of economic production based on the private ownership of property and the contractual exchange for profit of goods, labor, and money (capital). Although some elements of capitalism existed in the United States before 1820, a full-scale capitalist economy — and society — emerged only with the Market Revolution (1820–1850). After the Civil War, American capitalism changed in character, as large corporations came to dominate sectors of the economy and state and federal governments increasingly sought to regulate business activity. (p. 535)

carpetbaggers A derisive name given by southerners to northerners who moved to the South during Reconstruction. (The word derived from the cheap suitcases, known as carpetbags, that held their belongings.) Former Confederates despised these northerners as transient exploiters. Carpetbaggers actually were a varied group that included Union veterans who had served in the South, reformers eager to help former slaves, and others looking for business opportunities. (p. 463)

classical liberalism The political ideology, dominant in England and the United States during the nineteenth century, that celebrated individual liberty, private property, a competitive market economy, free trade, and limited government. In the late twentieth century, many economic conservatives embraced the principles of classical liberalism and opposed the principles of social-welfare liberalism. (p. 468)

closed shop A workplace in which a job seeker had to be a union member to gain employment. Nineteenth-century craft unions favored closed shops to keep out incompetent and lower-wage workers and to enhance their bargaining position with employers. For that reason, employers strongly opposed closed shops and sought laws to prohibit them. (p. 534)

containment The U.S. policy of the late 1940s which sought to contain communism within its existing geographic boundaries, namely the Soviet Union, Eastern Europe, and North Korea (and after 1949, China). Rather than seek to defeat communist governments through military confrontation, the United States would instead "contain" the influence of the communist powers. (p. 761)

cooperatives (co-ops) Organizations through which a group of customers, working together out of common interest, sought to purchase products at wholesale rates, passing on the savings to their members. In the 1880s, rural organizations like the Farmers' Alliance created cooperatives to obtain loans and to purchase farm equipment and an array of consumer products, from cloth and shoes to insurance policies. (p. 532)

deficit spending High government spending in excess of tax revenues; the practice is based on the ideas of British economist John Maynard Keynes, who proposed in the 1930s that governments should be prepared to go into debt to stimulate a stagnant economy. (p. 711)

deindustrialization The dismantling of manufacturing — especially in the automobile, steel, and consumer-goods industries — in the decades after World War II, representing a reversal of the process of industrialization that had dominated the

American economy from the 1870s through the 1940s. Struck hardest by this were the nation's "Rust Belt" of manufacturing states, which stretched from the Northeast through the Great Lakes region and the Upper Midwest. This long-term process began in the 1950s, but only drew national attention in the 1970s and 1980s. (p. 888)

desegregation The legal requirement that people of all races have equal access to public facilities and services, including public schools, parks, water fountains, railroads, hotels, and restaurants. According to desegregation laws, African Americans in the South, for example, could not be forced to use separate facilities from whites. (p. 465)

détente From the French word for "a relaxation of tension," this term was used to signify the Cold War policy of President Richard Nixon, who sought a reduction of tension and hostility between the United States and the Soviet Union and China in the early 1970s. (p. 912)

direct primary The selection of party candidates by a popular vote rather than by the party convention. The progressive reform that led to the direct primary was especially pressed by Robert La Follette, who viewed it as an instrument for breaking the grip of political machines on the parties. In the South, where it was limited to whites, the direct primary was a means of disenfranchising blacks. (p. 611)

dollar diplomacy Policy adopted by President Taft connecting U.S. economic and political interests overseas. The benefits of this policy would flow in both directions, as business would gain from diplomatic efforts on its behalf, while the strengthened American economic presence overseas would give added leverage to American diplomacy. (p. 668)

domesticity An ideology of marriage and family life, which called for men to practice self-discipline, temperance, and deference to female moral authority, while women refrained from paid labor in the workplace and devoted themselves to motherhood and family. Though domesticity stressed women's primary role in the home, it also sanctioned women's participation in religious missions and charitable efforts. Grounded in the ideals of republican motherhood and "separate spheres," domesticity was championed particularly by the elite and middle classes. (p. 459)

economies of scale The reduction of per-unit production and transportation costs (and increased profits) achieved through large-scale production. By developing mass-production techniques, a manufacturer reduces its cost on individual items (for example, from five cents per item to two cents), and can sell more of the product — and for a lower price — than its competitors. (p. 491)

eugenics The "science" of human breeding, grounded in the Social Darwinist idea that the progress of human evolution is hampered when "unfit" people are permitted to reproduce. Eugenicists lobbied for the forced sterilization of "mental defectives," including the mentally retarded. Influenced by contemporary racial and ethnic prejudices, they worked particularly to sterilize "unfit" people of color and to restrict immigration from Asia and Eastern and Southern Europe, arguing that new immigrants would dilute the racial purity of Americans descended from Western Europeans. (p. 560)

Exodusters African Americans who left the Deep South in the late 1870s, in the wake of Reconstruction's collapse and the depression of 1873, and sought homesteads on the western frontier. The Exodusters sought better opportunities in states such as Kansas, but like many farmers, they confronted falling crop prices and a harsh Plains environment, which was difficult to farm. (p. 490)

feminism Advocates of women's rights adopted this term in the 1910s to describe their belief that women should be equal to men in all areas of life. Earlier women activists and suffragists had accepted the notion of separate spheres for men and women, but feminists sought to overcome all barriers to equality and personal development. (p. 555)

fundamentalism An evangelical Protestant religious movement based upon rejection of some tenets of modern science and defense of the literal truth of the Bible. Fundamentalists opposed modernist Protestants, who tried to reconcile Christianity with Darwin's theory of natural selection and other scientific discoveries. Fundamentalists' promotion of anti-evolution laws for public schools led to the famous Scopes trial of 1925. In recent decades, fundamentalists have organized to support laws that would ban abortions and gay marriages. (p. 565)

gang-labor system A system of work discipline used on southern cotton plantations in the mid-nineteenth century. White overseers or black drivers constantly supervised gangs of enslaved laborers to enforce work norms and secure greater productivity. (p. 458)

general strike A strike that draws in all the workers in a society, with the intention of shutting the entire system down. Radical groups like the Industrial Workers of the World (IWW), in the early twentieth century, saw the general strike as the means for initiating a social revolution. (p. 619)

gold standard Monetary system by which a country links the amount of money circulating, at any given time, to the amount of gold held in its Treasury. Deliberate increases in the money supply, to encourage borrowing and stimulate economic activity, therefore depended not on federal policy decisions (as is the case today, through the Federal Reserve) but on increases in the national and global supply of gold. (p. 481)

grandfather clause A law permitting citizens to register as voters only if their grandfathers had been eligible to vote. Such laws were passed in southern states such as Louisiana, in an attempt to enfranchise all native-born white men and exclude African Americans from the polls, on the grounds that their grandfathers, during slavery times, had not been voters. (p. 607)

Great American Desert The name given to the drought-stricken Great Plains by Euro-Americans in the early nineteenth century. Believing the region unfit for cultivation or agriculture, Congress designated the Great Plains as permanent Indian country in 1834. (p. 487)

greenbacks Paper money issued by the U.S. Treasury during the Civil War to finance the war effort. Greenbacks were legal tender in all public and private transactions. Because it was issued in large amounts and was not backed by gold or silver, the greenback dollar's value fell during the war from $1 to 40 cents. In the 1870s and 1880s, economic reformers called for continued use of greenbacks, rather than a reduction of the money supply and placement of the United States on the gold standard. The Greenback-Labor Party, for example, argued that a larger money supply would aid workers, farmers, and borrowers. Their proposals were not implemented, however. See *gold standard*. (p. 481)

home rule Self-government by a state within the federal system. After the Civil War, southern Democrats advocated for home rule by painting Reconstruction governments as illegitimate impositions. By 1876, northern Republicans, too, were inclined to accept this claim. (p. 471)

horizontal integration A method employed by companies to raise market share and gain control over prices, by absorbing rival firms. Horizontal integration could be a cooperative process, in which several companies banded together out of common interest. It could also be accomplished through hostile takeovers, when a powerful company pressured or forced competitors to surrender their independence and be absorbed into the structure of the dominant firm. (p. 514)

ideology A systematic philosophy or political theory that purports to explain the character of the social world or to prescribe a set of values or beliefs. (p. 664)

impeachment The first step in the constitutional process for removing the president from office, in which charges of wrongdoing (articles of impeachment) are voted on by the House of Representatives. If the articles pass in the House, the Senate then conducts a trial to determine whether the impeached president is guilty of the charges. (p. 453)

imperial presidency The far-reaching use (and sometimes abuse) of executive authority during the second half of the twentieth century, especially the centralization of war-making powers, domestic surveillance and overseas espionage, and foreign policy functions in the office of the president. (p. 732)

imperialism Imposition of military, political, and economic control over another nation or people. In general, the term *expansion* is used for the imposition of such control over adjacent territories (such as the United States in the American West) while *imperialism* is used for territories overseas (such as the Philippines); in part because the former processes included the expectation of settlement by newcomers, and eventually statehood, while Filipinos did not win representation. Through both expansion and imperialism, however, the United States asserted its control without reference to the wishes of those who already occupied the land, and both processes met the nation's need for new resources, raw materials, and expanded markets. (p. 629)

Jim Crow A term — drawn from a satirical character named "Jim Crow," who appeared in antebellum minstrel shows — used in the age of segregation to describe facilities designated for blacks, such as Jim Crow railway cars. (p. 612)

Keynesian economics The theory, developed by British economist John Maynard Keynes in the 1930s, that purposeful government intervention in the economy (through lowering or raising taxes, interest rates, and government spending) can affect the level of overall economic activity and thereby prevent severe depressions and runaway inflation. (p. 711)

laissez-faire French for "let do" or "leave alone." The principle that the less government does, the better, particularly in reference to the economy. This has been an influential philosophy in the United States. In the nineteenth century, Democrats tended to advocate laissez-faire against state-building Whigs and Republicans. In the twentieth century — especially from the New Deal onward — Republicans have become the main champions of laissez-faire. (p. 785)

lien (crop lien) A legal device enabling a creditor to take possession of the property of a borrower, including the right to have it sold in payment of the debt. During Reconstruction, furnishing merchants took such liens on cotton crops as collateral for supplies advanced to sharecroppers during the growing season. This system trapped farmers in a cycle of debt and made them vulnerable to exploitation by the furnishing merchant. (p. 459)

literacy test The requirement that an ability to read be demonstrated as a qualification for the right to vote. This was a device easily used by registrars to prevent blacks from voting, whether they could read or not, and was widely adopted across the South, beginning with Mississippi in 1890. On the prejudicial assumption that illiterate voters were ignorant and could not inform themselves on political questions, and therefore cast illegitimate ballots, literacy tests were adopted in many parts of the United States around 1900. (p. 607)

mass production A system of factory production that often combines sophisticated machinery, a disciplined labor force, and assembly lines to turn out vast quantities of identical goods at low cost. Most important, perhaps, mass production deskills labor in order to reduce costs: Rather than a single skilled craftsman producing a product, many lower-paid, less-skilled workers carry out small, distinct tasks in the production process. (p. 520)

maternalism A justification for women's activism in politics and public life, based on the argument that women, as mothers or potential mothers, have special talents and sympathies. In the late nineteenth and early twentieth centuries, when few Americans believed in women's full equality, maternalism was a particularly effective way for women to defend their political activism. (p. 550)

military-industrial complex A term used by President Dwight D. Eisenhower in his 1961 farewell address to refer to the interlinked government, military, and industrial interests that emerged with the arms buildup of the Cold War. Eisenhower particularly warned against the "unwarranted influence" that the military-industrial complex might exert on public policy. (p. 759)

modern Of or pertaining to very recent events, rather than the distant past. Though historians describe aspects of many historical periods as "modern," in general they describe modern life as characterized by rapid change, particularly in response to industrialization. Under these circumstances, people found it difficult or undesirable to live as their parents and grandparents did and to maintain traditional assumptions and beliefs. Willingly or not, they responded to radically new conditions by changing their ways of life. (p. 539)

modernism A broad set of literary and artistic movements, extending through the first half of the twentieth century, in which writers and artists rejected traditional rules and conventions and sought new ways to represent reality. The earliest use of the term, by Cuban writer Rubén Dario, appears to date from the 1890s. Modernists often sought to turn nineteenth-century cultural conventions upside down, for example, by critiquing the idea of European and American "civilization" and "progress," and by celebrating artistic forms that had earlier been scorned as "primitive." (p. 562)

muckrakers Journalists in the early twentieth century whose stock-in-trade was exposure of the corruption of big business and government. Theodore Roosevelt gave them the name as a term of reproach. The term comes from *Pilgrim's Progress* (1678), a religious allegory by John Bunyan. (p. 583)

national debt The financial obligations of the U.S. government for money borrowed from its citizens and foreign investors. Alexander Hamilton wanted wealthy Americans to invest in the national debt so that they would support the national government. In recent decades, similar thinking has led the United States to encourage individuals and institutions in crucial foreign nations — for example, Saudi Arabia, Japan, and China — to invest billions of dollars in the American national debt. (p. 923)

nativism Antiforeign sentiment in the United States that fueled anti-immigrant and immigration-restriction policies against the Irish and Germans in the 1840s and 1850s, the Chinese and Japanese in the 1880s and 1890s, migrants from Eastern and Southern Europe in the 1910s and 1920s, and Mexicans in the 1990s and 2000s. Nativism prompted the Chinese Exclusion Act of 1882, the Immigration Restriction Act of 1924, and the internment of Japanese Americans during World War II. (p. 669)

natural selection The idea, proposed by Charles Darwin, that random genetic mutations occur in animal and plant species, some of which are adaptive and can therefore result in higher survival rates, thus causing species to change (or evolve) over time. For example, in a period of plant scarcity, a longer-necked giraffe has an advantage because it can browse higher branches, and would be more likely to survive and reproduce; over many generations of the same conditions, a longer-necked giraffe species would result. In the late nineteenth and early twentieth centuries, many Americans accepted Darwin's theory of evolution but rejected natural selection as its mechanism, seeing the process as cruel and incompatible with the idea of a benevolent Creator. (p. 558)

naturalism A literary movement that arose around 1900 in the United States, influenced by scientific and sociological arguments that described humans' "struggle with nature" and the "survival of the fittest." American naturalist fiction writers such as Theodore Dreiser and Stephen Crane depicted their characters as driven by powerful unconscious desires, as well as by economic and environmental forces beyond their control. Naturalist writers sought to depict their characters' inner psychological states, and some defied prevailing conventions by writing frankly about sexual desire. Naturalism helped give rise to *modernism* in literature and is itself sometimes viewed as a modernist form. (p. 560)

oligopoly In economics, the situation in which a given industry (e.g., steel making, automobile manufacturing) is dominated by a small number of large-scale companies. (p. 678)

pan-Africanism The political argument that people of African descent, in all parts of the world, face related problems — particularly racial discrimination — and share common goals. In the United States, pan-African leaders have urged African Americans to unite with other people of African descent to create movements for self-help and racial justice. (p. 677)

patronage The power of elected officials to grant government jobs and favors to their supporters; also the jobs and favors themselves. Beginning around 1820, politicians systematically used — and abused — patronage to create and maintain strong party loyalties. After 1870, political reformers gradually introduced merit-based civil service systems in state and federal governments to reduce patronage. (p. 602)

peonage (debt peonage) Forced labor, under a pretext of debt. As cotton prices declined during the 1870s, and many sharecroppers fell into permanent debt, merchants often conspired with landowners to make this debt a pretext for the sharecropper's forced labor. (p. 460)

piecework Unskilled labor, in sewing or other assembly work, for which workers were paid by the piece rather than with an hourly wage. A pieceworker might, for example, sew buttons on men's coats and receive a small payment for each coat she completed. Piecework has frequently been done by women, for very low pay, and often at home. (p. 519)

pocket veto A method by which the U.S. president can kill a piece of legislation without issuing a formal veto: The president "pockets" the bill by simply choosing not to sign it, and letting it expire after Congress adjourns. When congressional Republicans passed the Wade-Davis Bill in 1864, a harsher alternative to President Lincoln's restoration plan, Lincoln used a pocket veto to prevent the bill from being enacted. (p. 447)

political machine Nineteenth-century term for highly organized groups operating within and intending to control political parties. Political reformers believed the machines were antidemocratic, and Robert La Follette and other Progressive-era leaders targeted them. In municipal government, urban machines such as New York's Tammany Hall were often run by ethnic politicians; they won support from immigrant voters, who had few sources of aid in navigating the dangers of city life. Reformers instituted a merit-based civil service and primary elections to limit the power of political machines. (p. 584)

poll tax A tax paid for the privilege of voting, used in the South beginning during Reconstruction to disenfranchise freed blacks. Nationally, the northern states used poll taxes to keep immigrants and others deemed unworthy from voting. (p. 453)

polygamy The practice of marriage to multiple partners, most often, of one husband to multiple wives. Polygamy was customary among some Native American and African peoples; it was also practiced by many Mormons in the United States, particularly between 1840 and 1890. (p. 490)

predatory pricing Temporarily setting the price of a product below the cost of producing it, and accepting the resulting loss of profit, in order to undercut competitors and drive them out of business. Large corporations, which sold their goods all over the United States and sometimes abroad, could afford to use predatory pricing in local markets, against smaller rivals. After driving competitors out of business in a particular market, the corporation could then raise prices to a profitable level. (p. 512)

producerism The argument that real economic wealth is created by people who make their living by physical labor, and that merchants, lawyers, bankers, and other middlemen unfairly gain their wealth from such "producers." In the late nineteenth century, producerism was a popular ideology among farmers, skilled tradesmen, and factory workers. (p. 530)

progressives A loose term for political reformers, used especially during the Progressive Era (1880s–1910s) to describe those working to improve the political system, fight poverty, and increase government involvement in the economy. The term *progressive* was most often applied to urban and middle-class or elite reformers. The work of such reformers, however, was frequently prompted by protests from rural and working-class activists, who tended to propose more radical measures to combat the ills of industrialization. (p. 598)

protective tariff An import duty designed to protect domestic products from cheaper foreign goods. A hot political issue throughout much of U.S. history, protective tariffs became particularly controversial in the 1830s and again between 1880 and 1914, when Whigs and Republicans (for protectionism) and Democrats (for free trade) centered their political campaigns on the issue. (p. 478)

realism A literary and artistic movement, lasting roughly from the 1860s through the 1890s, in which writers and artists strove to offer accurate portrayals of everyday life. American realist writers such as William Dean Howells drew on the ideas of Europeans, particularly French writers Gustave Flaubert and Honoré de Balzac, and also used investigative journalism and nonfiction as models. Rather than giving stories the "right" endings, to prove an appropriate moral point, realists tried to show what might actually happen. In the visual arts, photography's prevalence played a key role in the rise of realism, but the movement also extended to painting: Artists such as John Sloan called for the depiction of everyday scenes — such as a boxing match or life in a city alley — rather than objects of conventional beauty. Realists helped point the way toward the later movements of *naturalism* and *modernism*. (p. 560)

recall A law that permits voters to remove an elected official from his post and elect a replacement, if they are dissatisfied with his or her performance, before the official has completed the full term for which he or she was elected. (p. 619)

referendum A direct vote on whether or not to adopt a particular law or government policy. The referendum allows citizens to make policy decisions directly, rather than (or in addition to) choosing elected officials who pledge to carry out specific policies. (p. 619)

scalawags A pejorative term (in fact, an ancient Scots-Irish word for worthless animals) applied to southern whites who joined the Republicans during Reconstruction. Ex-Confederates used this term for ex-Whigs and yeomen farmers who had not supported the Confederacy and who believed that an alliance with the Republicans was the best way to attract northern capital and rebuild the South. (p. 463)

scientific management A system of organizing work, developed by Frederick W. Taylor in the late nineteenth century, designed to both get the maximum productivity from the individual worker and reduce production costs, using methods such as the time-and-motion study. The system was never applied in its totality in any industry, but it contributed to the rise of the "efficiency expert" as well as the field of industrial psychology. (p. 520)

severalty Individual ownership of land. The Dawes Severalty Act of 1887 sought to end tribal ownership of land, and grant Indians deeds to individual property holdings; that is, severalty. Policymakers believed that individual landholdings, especially by male household heads, would contribute to Indian assimilation. (p. 499)

sharecropping The labor system by which freedmen agreed to exchange a portion of their harvested crops with the landowner for use of the land, a house, and tools. A compromise between freedmen and white landowners, this system developed in the cash-strapped South because the freedmen wanted to work their own land but lacked the money to buy it, while white landowners needed agricultural laborers but did not have money to pay wages. (p. 459)

Social Darwinism The application of Charles Darwin's biological theory of natural selection to the development of society, this late-nineteenth-century principle encouraged the notion that societies progress as a result of competition and the "survival of the fittest." Intervention by the state in this process was counterproductive because it impeded healthy progress. Social Darwinists justified the increasing inequality of late-nineteenth-century, industrial American society as natural. (p. 558)

Social Gospel A religious movement that called for people of religious faith to engage actively in reform work and public activism. A response to the problems caused by industrialization, the Social Gospel placed particular emphasis on anti-poverty work and urban reform. While the most famous Social Gospel leaders were Protestants such as Congregationalist minister Washington Gladden, the movement attracted considerable support among reform-minded Catholics and Reform Jews. Generally liberal in theology, Social Gospel advocates encouraged cooperation among people of different faiths. (p. 564)

social settlement Also sometimes referred to as a "settlement house," the social settlement was an urban institution invented in the late nineteenth century. In a social settlement, well-educated, elite, or middle-class reformers (often women) moved to a poverty-stricken urban neighborhood and established a community center to serve the needs of their own neighbors. Chicago's Hull House, founded by Jane Addams, was America's most famous social settlement. Addams emphasized that the settlement was not a charity organization, but an institution that addressed city problems in a systemic way, while enabling young college graduates to broaden their perspectives and live with a sense of purpose. (p. 590)

social-welfare liberalism The liberal ideology implemented in the United States during the New Deal of the 1930s and the Great Society of the 1960s. It uses the financial and bureaucratic resources of the state and federal governments to provide economic and social security to individual citizens, interest groups, and corporate enterprises. Social welfare programs include old-age pensions, unemployment compensation, subsidies to farmers, mortgage guarantees, and tax breaks for corporations. (p. 694)

soft power In diplomacy, the influence of U.S. cultural institutions, particularly those with broad popular appeal. The eager reception of Hollywood movies and

American popular music, for example, may influence public opinion in other countries favorably toward the United States. (p. 685)

spoils system The widespread award of public jobs to political supporters after an electoral victory. In 1829, Andrew Jackson instituted the system on the national level, arguing that the rotation of officeholders was preferable to a permanent group of bureaucrats. The spoils system became a central, and corrupting, element in American political life. (p. 602)

states' rights An interpretation of the Constitution that exalts the sovereignty of the states and circumscribes the authority of the national government. Expressed first by Antifederalists in the debate over the Constitution, and then in the Virginia and Kentucky resolutions of 1798, the ideology of states' rights became especially important in the South. It informed white southerners' resistance to the high tariffs of the 1820s and 1830s, to legislation to limit the spread of slavery, and to attempts by the national government in the mid-twentieth century to end Jim Crow practices and, more generally, to extend its authority. (p. 610)

suburbs Residential communities adjacent to urban areas that were originally connected to city centers by streetcar or subway lines and later by highways. Early suburbs appealed to the upper and middle classes in particular. By 1910, 25 percent of the population lived in these new communities. The 1990 census revealed that the majority of Americans lived in the suburbs. (p. 570)

suffrage The right to vote. In the early national period suffrage was limited by property restrictions. However, between 1810 and 1860, state constitutions extended the vote to virtually all adult white men and some free black men; subsequently, the Fifteenth (1870) and Nineteenth (1920) amendments to the U.S. Constitution granted the franchise respectively to black men and to women, making adult suffrage nearly universal. In the late nineteenth and early twentieth centuries, women activists working to gain woman suffrage were known as suffragists. (p. 452)

syndicalists Members of a revolutionary movement that, like socialists, believed in the Marxist principle of class struggle and advocated the organization of society on the basis of industrial unionism. The syndicalist approach was advocated by the Industrial Workers of the World (IWW) at the start of the twentieth century. (p. 619)

tariff A tax on imports. *Tariffs for revenue* raise money to pay government expenses; *protective tariffs* also shield domestic products from foreign competition. See *protective tariff*. (p. 610)

temperance, temperance movement A long-term reform movement that encouraged individuals and governments to limit the consumption of alcoholic beverages. Leading temperance groups include the American Temperance Society of the 1830s; the Washingtonian Association of the 1840s; the Women's Christian Temperance Union of the late nineteenth century; and Alcoholics Anonymous, which was founded in the 1930s. (p. 551)

Third World A term that came into use in the post–World War II era to describe developing or ex-colonial nations in Asia, Africa, Latin America, and the Middle East that were not aligned with either the Western capitalist countries led by the United States (the First World) or the socialist states of Eastern Europe led by the Soviet Union (the Second World). (p. 778)

trade unions Organizations of skilled workers, usually limited to men in a specialized field of employment (such as bricklayers, carpenters, or electricians). Trade unions tended to exclude women, and to emphasize direct negotiation with employers, rather than broad-based political action. (p. 528)

trust A legal entity, invented in the 1880s, which enabled a group of companies to combine and operate as a single unit. By doing so, they avoided competing with one another for customers, and were also able to raise market prices and gain near-monopoly power over a given market. To form a trust, each company agreed (some-times under extreme pressure from a powerful competitor) to deposit stock with a central trustee and submit to the management of a central board of directors. In popular usage, *trust* came to mean any giant corporation that dominated a sector of the economy and wielded monopoly power. (p. 480)

vaudeville A theater that offered audiences a succession of brief singing, dancing, and comedy routines. Vaudeville changed live entertainment from its seedier prede-cessors like minstrel shows to family entertainment for the urban masses. Vaudeville became popular in the 1880s and 1890s, just before the introduction of movies. (p. 577)

vertical integration A method employed by companies to control the cost of pro-duction, by gaining ownership of all parts of the manufacturing process, from raw materials through transportation and marketing. A steel company might, for example, seek to purchase coal and iron mines, and railroad lines that ran between these mines and its factories. A beer manufacturer might seek to own or license a nationwide network of saloons or pubs that sold its beer exclusively. (p. 512)

voluntarism The view that citizens should themselves improve their lives, rather than rely on the efforts of government. Especially favored by Samuel Gompers, voluntarism was a key idea within the labor movement, but one gradually aban-doned over the course of the twentieth century. (p. 619)

war of attrition A military strategy of small-scale attacks used, usually by the weaker side, to sap the resources and morale of the stronger side. Examples include the attacks carried out by Patriot militias in the South during the War of Independence, and the guerrilla tactics of the Vietcong and North Vietnamese during the Viet-nam War. (p. 643)

welfare capitalism A system of labor relations that stresses management's responsi-bility for employees' well-being. Originating in the 1920s, welfare capitalism offered such benefits as stock plans, health care, and old-age pensions and was designed to maintain a stable workforce and undercut the growth of trade unions. (p. 663)

white-collar workers Middle-class professionals who are salaried workers, as opposed to business owners or wage laborers; they first appeared in large numbers during the industrial expansion of the late nineteenth century. White-collar workers include lawyers, engineers, chemists, salespeople, accountants, and advertising managers. (p. 517)

Credits

Chapter 15
Voices from Abroad: The Devastated South. Allan Nevins, ed. Excerpts from *America Through British Eyes.* Copyright © 1968 Peter Smith Publishers. Reprinted by permission.

Chapter 16
American Voices: Becoming White. From *U.S. History as Women's History: New Feminist Essays.* edited by Linda K. Kerber, Alice Kessler-Harris, and Kathryn Kish Sklar. Copyright © 1995 by the University of North Carolina Press. Used by permission of the publisher.

Voices from Abroad: A Western Boom Town. Oscar Handlin, ed. *This Was America* (Cambridge, MA: Harvard University Press) Copyright © 1949. Reprinted by permission of the author.

Chapter 17
American Voices: Sold into Sexual Slavery. Judy Yung, *Unbound Voices: A Documentary History of Chinese Women in San Francisco* © 1999 by Judy Yung, published by the University of California Press.

Voices from Abroad: Pittsburgh Inferno. Oscar Handlin, ed. *This Was America* (Cambridge, MA: Harvard University Press) Copyright © 1949. Reprinted by permission of the author.

Chapter 19
Voices from Abroad: Coney Island, 1881. Excerpts from "Coney Island, December 1881" from *The America of José Martí* translated by Juan de Onis. Translation copyright © 1954, renewed 1982 by Farrar, Straus and Giroux, Inc. Reprinted by permission of Farrar, Straus and Giroux, LLC.

Chapter 21
American Voices: Making the Philippines Safe for Democracy. Henry F. Graff, ed. *American Imperialism and the Philippine Insurrection* (Little, Brown, 1969) pp. 137–39, 144–50. Copyright © 1969. Reprinted with permission of the author.

Voices from Abroad: Charles H. Williams, *Sidelights on Negro Soldiers* (Boston: B. J. Brimmer Co., 1923), 70–71; Tracey Lovette Spencer and James E. Spencer, Jr., eds. "World War I as I Saw It" *Massachusetts Review* 9 (2007) 141, 144, 156–58.

Chapter 22
Voices from Abroad: Europeans Encounter American Jazz. Chris Goddard, *Jazz Away From Home*, New York: Paddington Press, 1979, pp. 262, 274.

Chapter 23

American Voices: Ordinary People Respond to the New Deal. Letters from R. A. and M. A.: Michael P. Johnson, ed. *Reading the American Past*, Fourth Edition, 2 vols. Copyright © 2009 Bedford/St. Martin's. Reprinted with permission. Letter from Mrs. M. H. A.: Robert D. Marcus and David Burner, eds. *America Firsthand*, Seventh Edition Copyright © 2007 Bedford/St. Martin's. Reprinted with permission.

Voices from Abroad: A British Historian Looks at the Great Depression. Franz M. Joseph, *As Others See Us* © 1959 Princeton University Press, 1987 renewed PUP Reprinted by permission of Princeton University Press.

Chapter 24

American Voices: Women in the Wartime Workplace. Sarah Killingsworth: Studs Terkel, *The Good War: An Oral History of World War Two*, pp. 113–15. Copyright 1984 Studs Terkel. Reprinted by permission of Donadio & Olson, Inc. Peggy Terry: Studs Terkel, *The Good War: An Oral History of World War Two*, pp. 108–10. Copyright 1984 Studs Terkel. Reprinted by permission of Donadio & Olson, Inc.

Voices from Abroad: Japanese Relocation. From *Nisei Daughter*, pp. 176–178, by Monica Sone (Boston, MA: Little, Brown & Company, 1953). Copyright © 1953 by Monica Sone. Copyright © renewed 1981 by Monica Sone. Print rights by permission of Little, Brown & Company. Electronic rights by permission of the author.

Chapter 25

American Voices: Mark Goodson, "Red Hunting on the Quiz Shows," from *Red Scare: Memories of the American Inquisition: An Oral History* by Griffin Fariello. Copyright © 1995 by Griffin Fariello. Used by permission of W.W. Norton & Company, Inc.

Voices from Abroad: Truman's Generous Proposal. Jean Monnet, *Memoirs*, trans. Richard Mayne (New York: Doubleday, 1978).

Chapter 26

American Voices: Coming of Age in the Postwar Years. Elizabeth Pope, "Is a Working Mother a Threat to the Home?" *McCall's* (July 1955, quoted in Sonya Michel and Robyn Muncy, eds. *Engendering America: A Documentary History, 1865 to the Present* (New York: McGraw-Hill, 1999), 231–34. Susan Allen Toth, *Blooming: A Small-Town Girlhood* (Boston: Little, Brown & Co., 1978) 202–03.

Voices from Abroad: Everyone Has a Car. Oscar Handlin, ed. *This Was America* (Cambridge, MA: Harvard University Press) Copyright © 1949. Reprinted by permission of the author.

Chapter 27

American Voices: Desegregating Lunch Counters. "Franklin McCain," from *My Soul Is Rested* by Howell Raines, copyright © 1977 Howell Raines. Print rights by permission of G.P. Putnam's Sons, a division of Penguin Group (USA) Inc. Electronic rights by permission of Russell & Volkening as agents for the author.

Voices from Abroad: African Encounters with U.S. Racism. *Transition* by W. E. B. Du Bois Institute for Afro-American Research. Copyright © 1964. Reprinted with permission of Indiana University Press in the formats Textbook and Other Book via Copyright Clearance Center.

Chapter 28

American Voices: Letters to Dr. Spock. Excerpts from *Dear Dr. Spock: Letters about the Vietnam War to America's Favorite Baby Doctor*, edited by Michael S. Foley. Copyright © 2005 NYU Press. Reprinted with permission.

Voices from Abroad: Vietnam and the World Freedom Struggle. Ernesto Guevara, excerpts from *Che Guevara Speaks* pp. 144–59 Copyright © 1967, 2000 by Pathfinder Press. Reprinted by permission.

Chapter 29

American Voices: Debating the ERA. Phyllis Schlafly: *The Phyllis Schafly Report*, November 1972, 1–4. Reprinted with permission. Elizabeth Duncan Koontz: William A. Link and Marjorie Spruill Wheeler, eds. *The South in the History of the Nation* (Boston: Bedford/St. Martin's, 1999) 295–96.

Voices from Abroad: America's Crisis of Faith. David R. Arkush and Leo O. Lee (eds.) *Land Without Ghosts: Chinese Impressions of America from the Mid-Nineteenth Century to the Present* © 1999 by the Regents of the University of California. Published by the University of California Press.

Chapter 30

American Voices: Christianity and Public Life. Ronald Reagan, "Remarks made at the annual National Association of Evangelicals, Orlando, Florida, March 8, 1983" Reprinted with the permission of Simon & Schuster, Inc. from *Speaking My Mind* by Ronald Reagan. Copyright © 1989 Ronald W. Reagan.

Voices from Abroad: Japan and America: Global Partners. Yoichi Funabashi, "Japan and America: Global Partners" *Foreign Policy* 86 (Spring, 1992): 24–29 Copyright © 1992 by Foreign Policy. Reproduced with permission of Foreign Policy in the formats Textbook and Other Book via Copyright Clearance Center.

Chapter 31

American Voices: Cheap Labor: Immigration and Globalization. Christine Ahn, *Shafted: Free Trade and America's Working Poor*, pp. 32–38 Copyright © 2003 Reprinted by permission of Food First Books.

Voices from Abroad: A Strategy for the Iraq Insurgency. Reprinted by permission of J. R. Cole.

Index

A note about the index: Names of individuals appear in boldface; biographical dates are included for major historical figures. Letters in parentheses following pages refer to: *(f)* figures, including charts and graphs; *(i)* illustrations, including photographs and artifacts; *(m)* maps; and *(t)* tables.

Calgary

Regina

Vancouver

Seattle

125°W

Olympia

Spokane

WASHINGTON

Great
Falls

Missouri R.

NORTH DAKOT

45°N

Portland

Columbia R.

Salem

Helena

MONTANA

Yellowstone R.

Bismarck

Billings

OREGON

IDAHO

ROCKY

SOUTH DAKOT

Boise

Snake R.

WYOMING

Pierre

40°N

Great
Salt Lake

NEVADA

Reno

Salt
Lake
City

North Platte R.

NEBRASKA

Carson City

UTAH

Cheyenne

M
O
U
N
T
A
I
N
S

South Platte R.

Plat

Sacramento

San
Francisco

Oakland

SIERRA NEVADA

San Joaquin R.

San Jose

Green R.

Denver

COLORADO

Colorado
Springs

KANSA

Arkansas R.

Fresno

35°N

CALIFORNIA

Las Vegas

Colorado R.

Los Angeles

120°W

ARIZONA

Santa Fe

Canadian R.

Amarillo

Albuquerque

San Diego

Tijuana

Mexicali

Phoenix

NEW MEXICO

TEXAS

PACIFIC
OCEAN

Tucson

Colorada R.

Nogáles

Ciudad
Juárez

El Paso

Pecos R.

ARCTIC OCEAN

170°W   160°W   150°W   140°W   130°W

Hermosillo

Rio Grande

Sa
Antoni

RUSSIA

Arctic Circle

70°N

BROOKS RANGE

Chihuahua

Nueces R.

ALASKA

Yukon River

CANADA

Piedras
Negras

ALASKA RANGE

MEXICO

Nuevo
Laredo

60°N

Anchorage

Bering
Sea

Gulf of Alaska

Juneau

160°W   155°W

Saltillo

Monterre

22°N

Honolulu

ALEUTIAN
ISLANDS

0   250   500 miles

0   250   500 kilometers

PACIFIC OCEAN

HAWAI'I

20°N

0   50   100 miles

0   50   100 kilometers

Ciudad
Victoria

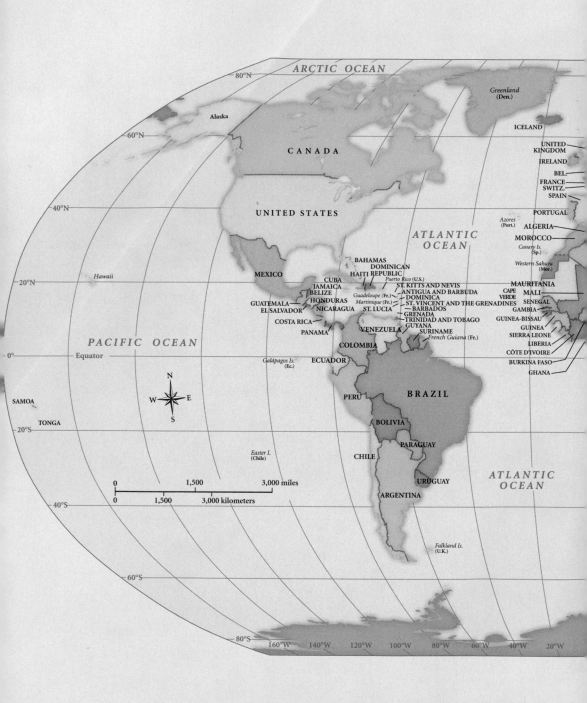

ARCTIC OCEAN

80°N

Greenland
(Den.)

60°N

Alaska

ICELAND

UNITED
KINGDOM

CANADA

IRELAND

BEL.
FRANCE
SWITZ.
SPAIN

40°N

UNITED STATES

PORTUGAL

Azores
(Port.)

ATLANTIC
OCEAN

ALGERIA

MOROCCO

Canary Is.
(Sp.)

BAHAMAS

Western Sahara
(Mor.)

DOMINICAN

20°N

Hawaii

MEXICO

CUBA

HAITI REPUBLIC

Puerto Rico (U.S.)

MAURITANIA

JAMAICA

ST. KITTS AND NEVIS

CAPE

MALI

BELIZE

Guadeloupe (Fr.)

ANTIGUA AND BARBUDA

VERDE

SENEGAL

GUATEMALA

HONDURAS

Martinique (Fr.)

DOMINICA

ST. VINCENT AND THE GRENADINES

GAMBIA

EL SALVADOR

NICARAGUA

ST. LUCIA

BARBADOS

GRENADA

GUINEA-BISSAU

COSTA RICA

TRINIDAD AND TOBAGO

GUINEA

PANAMA

VENEZUELA

GUYANA

SIERRA LEONE

SURINAME

LIBERIA

COLOMBIA

French Guiana (Fr.)

CÔTE D'IVOIRE

BURKINA FASO

Galápagos Is.
(Ec.)

ECUADOR

GHANA

0°

Equator

PACIFIC OCEAN

PERU

BRAZIL

SAMOA

Easter I.
(Chile)

BOLIVIA

TONGA

20°S

PARAGUAY

ATLANTIC
OCEAN

0   1,500   3,000 miles

CHILE

0   1,500   3,000 kilometers

URUGUAY

ARGENTINA

N
W   E
S

40°S

Falkland Is.
(U.K.)

60°S

80°S

160°W 140°W 120°W 100°W 80°W 60°W 40°W 20°W

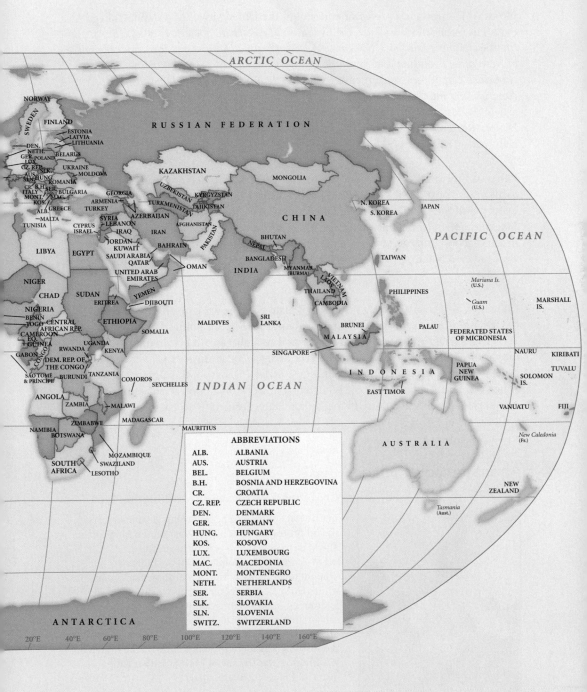

ARCTIC OCEAN

NORWAY
SWEDEN
FINLAND
ESTONIA
LATVIA
LITHUANIA
DEN.
NETH.
GER. POLAND BELARUS
LUX.
CZ. REP.
SLK. HUNG. UKRAINE
AUS. ROMANIA MOLDOVA
ITALY SER. BULGARIA
MONT. MAC.
KOS. GREECE GEORGIA
ALB. TURKEY ARMENIA
MALTA CYPRUS SYRIA AZERBAIJAN
TUNISIA ISRAEL LEBANON
IRAQ
JORDAN IRAN
KUWAIT
SAUDI ARABIA BAHRAIN
QATAR
UNITED ARAB OMAN
EMIRATES
YEMEN
DJIBOUTI

RUSSIAN FEDERATION

KAZAKHSTAN

MONGOLIA

UZBEKISTAN KYRGYZSTAN
TURKMENISTAN TAJIKISTAN

CHINA

N. KOREA
S. KOREA
JAPAN

AFGHANISTAN
PAKISTAN
BHUTAN
NEPAL
BANGLADESH
MYANMAR
(BURMA)
VIETNAM
LAOS
THAILAND
CAMBODIA

TAIWAN

PACIFIC OCEAN

Mariana Is.
(U.S.)
Guam
(U.S.)

MARSHALL
IS.

LIBYA
EGYPT

INDIA

PHILIPPINES

NIGER
CHAD
SUDAN
NIGERIA
BENIN
TOGO CENTRAL
CAMEROON AFRICAN REP.
EQ.
GUINEA
GABON CONGO
SÃO TOMÉ
& PRINCIPE
ERITREA

ETHIOPIA

SOMALIA

UGANDA
RWANDA
DEM. REP. OF
THE CONGO KENYA
BURUNDI TANZANIA

MALDIVES

SRI
LANKA

SINGAPORE

BRUNEI

MALAYSIA

PALAU

FEDERATED STATES
OF MICRONESIA

NAURU

KIRIBATI

TUVALU

ANGOLA
ZAMBIA
NAMIBIA
BOTSWANA
ZIMBABWE
MALAWI

COMOROS
SEYCHELLES

INDIAN OCEAN

INDONESIA

EAST TIMOR

PAPUA
NEW
GUINEA

SOLOMON
IS.

VANUATU

FIJI

MOZAMBIQUE
SWAZILAND
SOUTH
AFRICA LESOTHO

MADAGASCAR

MAURITIUS

AUSTRALIA

New Caledonia
(Fr.)

NEW
ZEALAND

Tasmania
(Aust.)

ANTARCTICA

ABBREVIATIONS	
ALB.	ALBANIA
AUS.	AUSTRIA
BEL.	BELGIUM
B.H.	BOSNIA AND HERZEGOVINA
CR.	CROATIA
CZ. REP.	CZECH REPUBLIC
DEN.	DENMARK
GER.	GERMANY
HUNG.	HUNGARY
KOS.	KOSOVO
LUX.	LUXEMBOURG
MAC.	MACEDONIA
MONT.	MONTENEGRO
NETH.	NETHERLANDS
SER.	SERBIA
SLK.	SLOVAKIA
SLN.	SLOVENIA
SWITZ.	SWITZERLAND

20°E 40°E 60°E 80°E 100°E 120°E 140°E 160°E

About the authors

James A. Henretta is a professor emeritus at the University of Maryland, College Park. His publications include *The Evolution of American Society, 1700–1815: An Interdisciplinary Analysis; "Salutary Neglect": Colonial Administration under the Duke of Newcastle; Evolution and Revolution: American Society, 1600–1820; The Origins of American Capitalism;* and an edited volume, *Republicanism and Liberalism in America and the German States, 1750–1850.* His most recent publication is a long article, "Charles Evans Hughes and the Strange Death of Liberal America" (*Law and History Review*), derived from his ongoing research on the liberal state in America: New York, 1820–1975.

Rebecca Edwards is a professor of history at Vassar College. Her research interests focus on the post–Civil War era and include electoral politics, environmental history, and the history of women and gender roles. She is the author of *Angels in the Machinery: Gender in American Party Politics from the Civil War to the Progressive Era* and *New Spirits: Americans in the "Gilded Age," 1865–1905.* She is currently working on a biography of women's rights advocate and People's Party orator Mary E. Lease.

Robert O. Self is an associate professor of history at Brown University. His research focuses on urban history, the history of race and American political culture, post–1945 U.S. society and culture, and gender and sexuality in American politics. His first book, *American Babylon: Race and the Struggle for Postwar Oakland,* won four professional prizes, including the James A. Rawley Prize from the Organization of American Historians (OAH). He is currently at work on a book about gender, sexuality, and political culture in the United States from 1964 to 2004.

About the cover image

Civil Rights Advocates in Washington, 1963

In this 1963 photograph, civil rights demonstrators sing in protest in front of the Washington Monument. The March on Washington for Jobs and Freedom, led by A. Philip Randolph and Bayard Rustin, brought together a quarter of a million blacks and whites from all corners of the country. In addition to drawing national attention to civil rights and galvanizing public opinion, demonstrators hoped to marshal Congressional support for a civil rights bill proposed by President John F. Kennedy. The March on Washington was the site of Martin Luther King Jr.'s historic "I Have a Dream" speech.